ENVIRONMENT AND MAN

W · W · NORTON & COMPANY · INC · NEW YORK

RICHARD H. WAGNER

ENVIRONMENT AND MAN

THIRD EDITION

" . . . To the wide world and all
her fading sweets . . ."

[Shakespeare, Sonnet 19]

Copyright © 1978, 1974, 1971 by W. W. Norton & Company, Inc. Published simultaneously in
Canada by George J. McLeod Limited, Toronto. Printed in the United States of America.

Library of Congress Cataloging in Publication Data

Wagner, Richard H., 1934–
Environment and man.

Includes bibliographies and index.
1. Human ecology   2. Pollution.   3. Population.
4. Environmental policy.   I. Title.
GF41.W33 1978   301.31   77–28214
ISBN 0–393–09066–3

2 3 4 5 6 7 8 9 0

CONTENTS

PREFACE   xiii

PART ONE : THE EARTH'S ENVIRONMENTS   1

CHAPTER ONE : THE PHYSICAL ENVIRONMENT   3

The Atmosphere . . 4   The Lithosphere . . 10
The Hydrosphere . . 7   Biogeochemical Cycles . . 15

CHAPTER TWO : THE BIOSPHERE   20

The Community . . 28   The Species . . 33
The Population . . 31

PART TWO : THE RESHAPING OF OUR ENVIRONMENT   39

CHAPTER THREE : MOVING EARTH   41

Grazing . . 42   The Forest Environment . . 59
Agriculture . . 47   Strip Mining . . 63
The Mountain Environment . . 56

v

CONTENTS

CHAPTER FOUR : THE TRANSPORT OF WATER   67

The Dam Nations . . 75   Connecting the Waters . . 83
Channeling the Streams . . 80

CHAPTER FIVE : BIOCIDES   88

Pandora's Panacea . . 89   Nonselectivity . . 108
Persistence . . 104

CHAPTER SIX : ORGANICS IN THE ENVIRONMENT   116

The Federal Food and Drug Administra-   Contaminants . . 121
    tion (FDA) . . 116   Preservatives . . 127
The Additive Array . . 117

CHAPTER SEVEN : INORGANIC POLLUTANTS   136

Mercury . . 136   Beryllium . . 149
Lead . . 142   Asbestos . . 151
Cadmium . . 148   Solutions . . 154

PART THREE : BUNGLING THE BIOTA   157

CHAPTER EIGHT : INTRODUCTION OF EXOTICS   159

The Columbian Exchange . . 162   Control of Introductions . . 174
Types of Introductions . . 165

CHAPTER NINE : EXTINCTION   184

Extinction by Direct Assault . . 186   Susceptibility to Extinction . . 205
Novel Uses Lead to Extinction . . 193   The Cost of Extinction . . 207
Habitat Destruction; Extinction by Sub-   The Road Back . . 209
    version . . 198

CHAPTER TEN : NATURE IN CAPTIVITY   215

Forestry and Fire . . 218   The Disappearing Coastline . . 226
Problems in the Parks . . 221   The Hierarchy of Natural Areas . . 232

PART FOUR : THE RISE OF THE CITY   239

CHAPTER ELEVEN : THE HOUSE   241

Diversity of Environment; Diversity of House . . 241

The Outer Environment . . 248
The Internal Environment . . 251

CHAPTER TWELVE : THE URBAN-SUBURBAN ENVIRONMENT   259

The Location and Form of Cities . . 259
The Microclimate of Cities . . 261
Urban Space . . 264

The Rise of Suburbia . . 273
New Towns . . 276

CHAPTER THIRTEEN : TRANSPORT: LIFELINE AND NOOSE   281

Environment and the Evolution of Transportation . . 281
Highways and the Landscape . . 284
Expressways in the City . . 293

ORVs and Amenity . . 296
We Take to the Air . . 298
Future Forms of Transport . . 299
Rights of Way . . 300

PART FIVE : THE THIRST FOR POWER   309

CHAPTER FOURTEEN : RADIATION: USE AND ABUSE   311

Microwaves . . 311
The Nature of Ionizing Radiation . . 314
Atomic Fission . . 316

Radioactive Fallout . . 319
Radiation Sickness . . 320
Nuclear Power and Radioactive Wastes . . 325

CHAPTER FIFTEEN : THE QUEST FOR ENERGY   336

Coal . . 338
Oil . . 342
Natural Gas . . 345
The Rise of Nuclear Power . . 347
Nuclear Fusion . . 352
Water Power . . 354

Geothermal Power . . 356
Solar Energy . . 358
Wind Power . . 360
The Conservation of Energy . . 361
Economics . . 367

CONTENTS

PART SIX : THE WASTE EXPLOSION   371

CHAPTER SIXTEEN : WATER POLLUTION : DILUTION IS NO SOLUTION   373

Catagories of Water Pollutants . . 374
Eutrophication . . 388
Some Solutions . . 391
Death of a Great Lake? . . 393

Thermal Loading . . 397
Simplifying the Ecosystem . . 400
Cooling the Coolant . . 402

CHAPTER SEVENTEEN : THE SUMP IN THE SEA   408

Using Estuarine Productivity . . 409
Abuse of a Bay . . 410

Oil on the Water . . 418
Nobody's Ocean . . 425

CHAPTER EIGHTEEN : THE AIR AROUND AND IN US   427

Sulfur Oxide Smog . . 428
Photochemical Smog . . 434
The Automobile as a Pollution
    Source . . 438
Effects of Photochemical Smog . . 439
Control of Photochemical Smog . . 442

Air Pollution and the Forest
    Ecosystem . . 446
Carbon Dioxide and Climate . . 448
Noise . . 450
Light Pollution . . 453

CHAPTER NINETEEN : SOLID WASTES: MIDDENHEAP INTO MOUNTAIN   455

Today's Waste . . 456
Yesterday's Disposal Techniques . . 466

New Approaches . . 470

PART SEVEN : WE THE PEOPLE: PROBLEM AND SOLUTION   475

CHAPTER TWENTY : LAND USE PLANNING   477

Zoning . . 484

Land Use Control Laws . . 488

CHAPTER TWENTY-ONE : ENVIRONMENTAL RESTORATION   494

The Historical Roots . . 497

The American Experience . . 507

CHAPTER TWENTY-TWO : SUPPORTING EARTH'S POPULATION   517

Food Resources and People . . 517   Future Technology . . 526
Present Technology . . 519

CHAPTER TWENTY-THREE : POPULATION CONTROL   538

Human Population Growth . . 539   Birth Control Methods . . 547
Motivation and Population   The Abortion Question . . 551
  Control . . 543   Future Population . . 553

CHAPTER TWENTY-FOUR : ALTERNATIVES   556

The Case for Economic Growth . . 557   Alternatives . . 567
The Rationale for No-Growth . . 559   Reorienting Our Priorities . . 570
The Dilemma . . 565

APPENDIX ONE   573

APPENDIX TWO   576

INDEX   579

PREFACE

TRADITIONALLY, many colleges and universities have advised their students to take at least one course in general biology, on the premise that their graduates ought to have some idea of their fundamental structure and of the physiological processes that govern their lives. Such courses on biological form and function can be lively, vital, and relevant if the instructor relates his material to the needs and interests of his students. All too frequently, however, they give short shrift to, or beg altogether, the critical question of human interaction with the lives and activities of other organisms and with the environment itself.

Because of our sudden awareness of the magnitude of environmental problems, efforts have been made on many campuses to fill this curricular gap with courses that recognize our tremendous impact on the natural world and analyze it from various points of view. Although there were scores of books covering the many individual aspects of the environmental field, as well as symposia, anthologies, and exposés, there were no balanced texts that pulled all the threads together. The first edition of this book was written to fill that need.

Since the first edition of *Environment and Man* went to press, there have been enormous changes both in the scope of environmental problems and in our reactions to them. Although the great furor of public concern has subsided as anticipated, governmental agencies—federal, state, and local—have finally been stirred into action. As a result, many problems that seemed intractable or unavoidable in 1970 are being dealt with and reduced to manageable proportions. To keep abreast of these sometimes dramatic changes, a second and now a third edition became necessary.

In this third edition there are four new chapters, the sequencing of some other chapters have been altered, and many parts of chapters have been extensively reworked to incorporate new information. Further Reading lists have been updated where appropriate, and the Appendices retained to provide a guide to the reader who wishes to take an active role in what is increasingly being recognized as a continuing and long-term struggle of heroic proportions.

As with the first two editions, it was not my intention to write another basic ecology text, for many fine ones already exist, but to provide an introduction to environmental problems that presupposes no background in the sciences, one that any college student or other interested reader could read with understanding and profit.

However, since the second edition of *Environment and Man* appeared in 1974, the ecological sophistication of students and the general public has continued to increase. Consequently, the third edition has been expanded to include a concise review of earth's physical and biotic environments as they pertain to some of the ecological principles that are illustrated in the book.

The central theme of this book is that our relationship to our environment has passed through several phases. In the beginning, we were shaped by an environment which acted as a selecting agent and controlled the evolution of our present features. Throughout this period we, like the other animals, remained in equilibrium with our environment. But then something happened that changed the face of the world, completely and irreversibly: we developed culture and thereby shattered this equilibrium. From that time on we have exerted an ever-increasing influence upon our environment.

The rise of agriculture, which many now believe to be the result of a population growth which hunting and gathering could no longer support, led to manipulations of earth, water, and our fellow organisms. Then the growth of cities increased our collective environmental impact by several orders of magnitude, involving transport, energy, wastes, and pollution of the air and water.

Although we are responsible for our environmental problems we also are capable of dealing creatively with them. The book concludes with several chapters which consider how we are beginning to grope for solutions to some of our most basic and thorny problems.

While the order of the chapters reflects my own approach to the subject material, worked out over several years' experience teaching a course in this area, others may prefer a different sequence. The comprehensive scope of the book should allow the sections or even individual chapters to be read and used in any order. To provide this flexibility, a full index is included. As with the first two editions, this book is printed on recycled paper. The preparation of this edition was facilitated by the editorial assistance of Mary Pell and Mary Shuford, and by Michael Capizzi who provided the index. The design and layout were done by Antonina Krass and Ben Gamit, and the jacket design by Ruth Bergman.

RICHARD H. WAGNER

San Francisco, California
June 1977

PART ONE

THE EARTH'S ENVIRONMENTS

Somewhere at some time in the past our antecedents slowly evolved in an environment which generously provided for their needs. Perhaps this period gave rise to our garden of Eden myth. While our contemporary environment is much too complex and intricate to summarize in a few chapters, we can examine some of the most salient aspects of it that have a particularly strong influence on our present welfare.

To gain some perspective on this environment let's step back to a place in time where earth's vast array of plants and animals existed in some kind of balance with the physical and biotic environment.

CHAPTER ONE

THE PHYSICAL
ENVIRONMENT

PERHAPS THE MOST memorable results of the billions spent exploring the moon in the last decade were those haunting pictures of earth seen from space. Of course we all knew that the earth was round (despite the protestations of the Flat Earth Society), that over two thirds of its surface was covered with water, and that great swirls of clouds slowly circled in its atmosphere. But never before were these characteristics so clearly delineated (Figure 1.1). For the first time we could appreciate our planet as a whole functioning system, and the term "Spaceship Earth" was one immediate response.

But even more striking to some observers was the feeling of vulnerability. Standing on terra firma we feel very impotent in the face of natural phenomena—thunderstorms, blizzards, or even rising tides. But when, far out in space, we stare at an earth shrunk to the size of a ripe peach, the potential impact of 4 billion of us on that peach suddenly becomes very real.

Because many of our effects on the environment are ubiquitous, long lasting, and subtle, it might be helpful to begin by considering earth and its environment without the complications of *Homo sapiens*. Then with some basic concepts and principles clearly in mind we will be better able to examine the environmental impact of our species.

The earth can be conveniently subdivided into four great interlocking systems; the atmosphere, a thin fragile envelope; the hydrosphere, the world ocean, lakes, and rivers; the lithosphere, the earth itself; and the biosphere, a veneer of life that has resulted from the interactions of the other spheres.

Fig. 1.1 Low pressure areas and their associated cold fronts circle endlessly around the Southern Hemisphere ameliorating the temperature extremes between the Saharan Desert, to the top, and Antarctica, the snow covered area to the bottom. (NASA)

THE ATMOSPHERE

Although dry air is a mixture of several gases it behaves like a single pure gas. When subjected to changes in temperature and pressure it responds like any one of its constituent gases. However, air's component gases behave quite differently when exposed to the various wavelengths of energy; upon these differences all life depends.

Nitrogen, which constitutes 78.08 percent of air, is the most abundant gas, followed by oxygen, 20.15 percent; argon, 0.94 percent; and carbon dioxide, 0.03 percent. Water vapor, which may occupy as much as 4 percent of the air volume under certain conditions, averages about 1 percent. The air also contains several other materials in trace amounts—methane, krypton, xenon, sulfur dioxide, dust, aerosols, and others. But most of the major energy processes that define the earth's environment involve nitrogen, oxygen, carbon dioxide, and water vapor.

The atmosphere can be divided into several zones based on temperature (Figure 1.2). For the first 16 kilometers (km) outward from the earth's surface the temperature of the atmosphere declines with increasing altitude. This inverse relationship of temperature to altitude is called the lapse rate. At about 16 km (lower at the poles and higher at the equator) the air temperature stabilizes, marking the outer edge of the troposphere. Because most of the water vapor responsible for weather is confined to the troposphere, this layer is quite turbulent. Since the molecular weight of water vapor is less than that of dry air, it should drift to the top of the atmosphere. However, the lapse rate keeps the water vapor from rising: as air cools it can hold less and less water vapor, thus the lapse rate serves to trap the bulk of the water vapor in the lower, warmer levels of the troposphere.

After a few kilometers of relatively constant temperature the lapse rate becomes negative; the temperature begins to increase with altitude. At this point the stratosphere begins. Because this layer is much calmer than the turbulent troposphere, contaminants in it tend to concentrate or stratify rather than be mixed or dispersed. The density of air becomes rather low at this altitude and the incoming radiation from the sun grows more intense. One result of this increased exposure to solar energy is the dis-

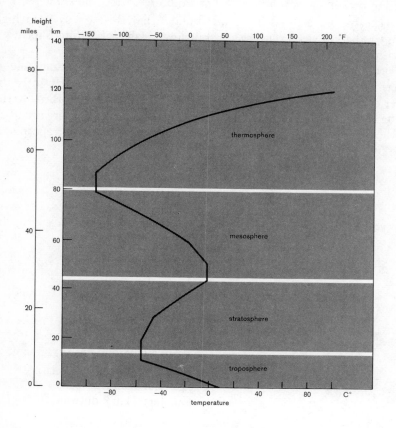

Fig. 1.2 Thermal structure of the atmosphere: most of the cyclical disturbances we call weather are restricted to the lowermost layer, the troposphere. (After H. Riehl, © 1972. Introduction to the atmosphere. 2nd ed. McGraw-Hill, New York, figure 16. Used with permission of McGraw-Hill Book Company)

sociation of molecular oxygen (O_2) into atomic oxygen, which re-forms as ozone (O_3). Ozone has a great affinity for ultraviolet radiation from the sun, and since it absorbs a very large proportion of this intense short-wave radiation, its presence shields the earth's surface and heats the stratosphere.

Above the stratosphere the temperature falls again, reaching its lowest point, –90°C, at about 80 km from the earth. At this point the composition of air is no longer constant, for no mixing is taking place and the atoms or molecules separate, the heavier ones at lower altitudes, the lighter ones higher up. The temperature begins to rise again at the upper edge of this layer, the mesosphere, but after 320 km or so the density of air becomes so low that temperature as we experience it on the earth's surface no longer has any meaning. As molecules absorb more energy they vibrate more rapidly. We perceive this vibration as heat—the more rapid the vibration and the greater the number of molecules, the greater our sensation of heat. So when the density of air is virtually zero, as it is in the outer reaches of the atmosphere, there is no longer a way to communicate temperature. At that altitude we would become thermometers ourselves, freezing or boiling depending on our exposure to the sun's energy. Perhaps because we evolved in an atmosphere that shielded us from high energy radiation we never developed organs capable of sensing shortwave radiation directly.

Together, the layers of the atmosphere act as an enormous energy filter/converter (Figure 1.3). In every 100 units of energy that enter the outer edge of the atmosphere from the sun, 3 units are absorbed by the ozone layer in the stratosphere and released as heat; 19 units are absorbed by the water vapor, dust, clouds, and carbon dioxide of the troposphere,

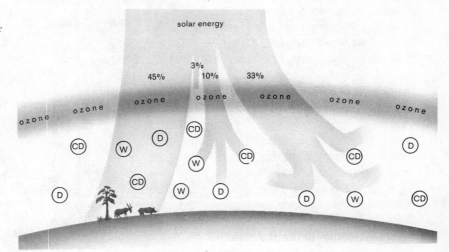

Fig. 1.3 *The atmosphere effectively intercepts over half the energy that strikes its outermost edge. One third is reflected or scattered by carbon dioxide (CD), water (W), and dust (D); almost one fifth is absorbed by the atmosphere's various components, and about 3 percent is absorbed by the ozone layer.*

and at least some of this energy is converted into longwave radiation or heat; 33 units are reflected or scattered from dust and clouds. Scattering is a selective process: because the shorter (blue) wavelengths of incoming visible light are scattered almost fifteen times as much as the longer (red) wavelengths, the sky looks blue. At the upper edge of the atmosphere where the density of scattering particles and molecules decreases, scattering also decreases and the sky looks black. Conversely, when the sun is rising or setting and its light passes through the densest part of the atmosphere, scattering is at a maximum and the sky appears yellowish-red. Absorption is also selective. As we have seen, ozone selectively absorbs ultraviolet; water vapor and carbon dioxide absorb heavily in the infrared portion of the spectrum. Despite their abundance in the atmosphere, oxygen and nitrogen absorb relatively little radiation. So, of the 100 units of shortwave energy that strike the upper limit of the atmosphere, only 45 actually penetrate to the earth's surface. The rest are ether reflected back into space, or converted into atmosphere-warming longwave radiation.

THE HYDROSPHERE

If water were not one of the most abundant compounds on the earth's surface, it surely would be prominently displayed in museums as an anomaly of nature. Some of its peculiarities and their environmental significance are:

1. Specific heat. All substances absorb heat at different rates; a block of aluminum heats more rapidly than a similar block of iron. To compare different substances' capacity to absorb heat we measure the amount of heat required to raise one gram of a substance 1°C at room temperature at standard pressure. This quantity of heat is called the specific heat of the substance. For water the specific heat is 1; that is, it takes one calorie to raise one gram of water 1°C. The specific heat of oxygen, in contrast, is 0.0156. Therefore it takes a great deal of heat to raise the temperature of water; of course to cool water this heat must be removed. Consequently water is notoriously slow either to boil or to freeze, as every cook realizes. In the global environment, water acts as an effective thermal buffer.
2. Heat of vaporization. Logically, you might expect that if 100 calories will raise the temperature of water from 0°C to 100°C in a linear fashion, the addition of one more calorie will begin converting water from the liquid to the gaseous phase. However, the unique hydrogen bonds that hold water molecules together in the liquid phase require 539 calories per gram to be broken. In contrast, this heat of vaporization is

7

204 for alcohol and only 67 for kerosene. For this reason water becomes the agent for the transport of huge quantities of heat around the surface of the globe. Of course when this water vapor condenses, 539 calories per gram are released to the air as heat.

3. Heat of fusion. It takes 80 calories per gram to melt ice. Until the last bit of ice is melted temperature will not change. This means that ice can absorb large quantities of heat without itself changing temperature.

4. Maximum density. As water cools it becomes increasingly dense, reaching its maximum density at 4°C, while it is still a liquid. Only three other materials in nature—antimony, bismuth, and gallium—are more dense as liquids than as solids. Below 4°C the density of water decreases again. Hence ice floats and bodies of water freeze from the top down. If the maximum density of water were reached at 0°C, ice would sink and bodies of water would freeze from the bottom up, making their melting and the survival of aquatic life most unlikely. The decrease in density also causes ice to expand, cracking radiators in automobiles and granite in the environment with equal ease.

5. High dielectric constant. Because the water molecule is polar (positively charged at one end and negatively charged at the other), the attractive force between ions of opposite charge (for example, Na+ and Cl−) is lessened when they are added to water. This makes water an excellent solvent.

6. High viscosity. Water's relatively high viscosity gives it a surface tension second only to that of mercury, and though it increases drag on any object trying to move through it, it also provides more buoyancy than most other liquids.

7. Gas solubility. The solubility of metabolically important gases in water is inversely proportional to their concentration in the atmosphere: 100 ml of water can dissolve 0.34 gm of carbon dioxide, but only 0.007 gm of oxygen and 0.003 gm of nitrogen.

DISTRIBUTION OF WATER IN THE ENVIRONMENT

Over 97 percent of earth's water supply lies in the world ocean; 2 percent is bound up in polar ice; and 1 percent is divided between flowing systems (rivers and streams) and standing systems (lakes and ponds). Anyone who has watched surf, tides, or currents can appreciate the dynamic energy of the ocean (Figure 1.4). But these are only the obvious kinetic manifestations of the ocean's energy. Less obvious is the potential energy of the ocean's heat. The most important source of this heat is the sun. Because of its enormous size, the world ocean intercepts over two thirds of all the energy that reaches the earth's surface. Almost 55 percent of this energy is involved in the evaporation of water from the sea. This

latent energy in the form of water vapor enters the air and is often carried by the winds to places far from the sea; when it condenses back into water, heat is released, warming the air. In this way, heat that enters the ocean in the Gulf of Mexico, for example, may be released to warm the air over Kansas. The 45 percent of incoming energy that does not evaporate sea water heats the upper layers of the sea, which expand. Since the most consistent heating of the ocean takes place in the tropics, lighter warm water slides north and south into the higher latitudes. This movement, deflected by Coriolis' force (the force generated by the earth's revolution) and pushed by prevailing winds, forms the major currents, which circulate in huge eddies, returning cold water from the polar regions to the tropics.

Often, for reasons that are not clearly understood, large patches of ocean perhaps a million square kilometers in area and up to 100 meters deep are heated or cooled as much as 2°C above or below the temperature of surrounding areas. This anomaly may persist for an entire season and recur in subsequent seasons in the same general location. The locations and temperature of these anomalies seem to affect the weather in adjacent continental land areas. Cold patches in the mid-Pacific and warm areas off California seem to be reflected in colder winters in the Eastern United States and warmer winters in the West. Conversely, warm anomalies in the Pacific appear to be related to mild winters in the East. However, the data are still too limited to be more than suggestive.

Fig. 1.4 Although many ingenious schemes have been devised to harvest the energy of ocean waves, surfing remains the most popular and certainly the most aesthetic.

9

THE HYDROLOGIC CYCLE

When warm, moist maritime air masses conflict with cool, dry air over large land areas, some of the water vapor precipitates out. The reason temperate latitudes (despite their name) produce frequent storms is that warm and cool air masses mix between the high and low latitudes. When we are caught in a convectional thunderstorm triggered by this meeting of air masses, it may seem that *all* the water vapor is being dumped on our heads, but no more than 20 percent of the water held by maritime air masses is lost over land.

Once scientists felt that most of the rainfall over land was the result of evapotranspiration, a term that describes the combination of evaporation from the land surface and transpiration from vegetation. If this were true, land use might profoundly affect both the quantity and distribution of precipitation. So some hoped and others feared that manipulating evapotranspiration would control precipitation. It was later determined that almost 90 percent of the precipitation falling over land areas is oceanic in origin, with perhaps 10 percent derived from land sources. This does not mean that moisture released by a magnolia tree in Louisiana into a moist air mass from the Gulf of Mexico will not fall on a basswood tree in Ohio, but that the amount will be insignificant. The principal effect of ocean-generated precipitation is to mix warm tropical air with cool temperate air, maintaining a relatively constant thermal environment on earth.

THE LITHOSPHERE

We now divide the surface of the earth into eight major plates of relatively rigid but light rock floating on denser, more fluid rock below (Figure 1.5). Because this lower material tends to circulate very slowly in large vertical cells, the surface plates gradually change position with respect to one another. The boundaries of these plates are marked by earthquakes and major faults, and most if not all mountain building has been traced to the collision of present or former plates. This concept of plate tectonics, or continental drift, is the most exciting development in the earth sciences since the discovery of glaciation over a hundred years ago. Like the earlier discovery, it provides a key to the interpretation of the landforms that characterize earth's landscape. But it is not the movement of continents or the building of mountains that concerns us here as much as the erosion of the exposed surfaces of these continental plates into the life-supporting layer that we call soil.

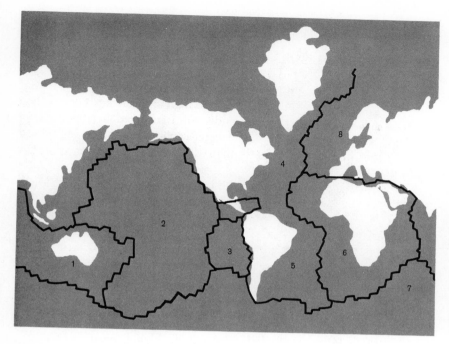

Fig. 1.5 Once the conti-
nents and ocean basins were
regarded as immovable en-
tities. But now we view them
as parts of large plates constantly in motion: (1) Australian Plate; (2) Pacific
Plate; (3) Nazca Plate; (4)
North American Plate; (5)
South American Plate; (6)
African Plate; (7) Antarctic
Plate; (8) Eurasian Plate.
(After U.S. Geodynamics
Committee, National Acad-
emy of Sciences)

SOIL FORMATION

Soil has its own history and is in some respects as alive as the plants that
live in it. It contains not only organic components, but so many interde-
pendent organisms that the resulting complex behaves like one large organism. Long ago, farmers noticed the association between parent rock
and soil type and it was assumed that this simple relationship existed
everywhere. Chalky soils were found on chalk, sandy soils on sandstone,
and clay soils on limestone. Later, however, when Asia, Africa, South
and North America were explored, it was discovered that rather uniform
soils were found in regions with varying types of parent rock, suggesting a
more subtle relationship between bedrock and soil.

Solid rock is continuously being broken down into small particles; this
process is known as weathering and may involve either physical or chemical factors. Alternate heating and cooling of the rock or freezing and thaw-
ing of water in its cracks can, in time, fracture the hardest rock, as we see
from the pile of rock fragments or talus found at the foot of most cliffs
(Figure 1.6). This is physical weathering. Other agents of physical weathering, running water and ice, can grind stone, pebbles, and sand into silt
and clay, the finest components of soil.

Physical weathering greatly facilitates chemical weathering. A piece of
granite, for example, may be broken down into its component minerals

11

Fig. 1.6   As this cliff face is
fractured by weathering, the
fragments pile up at the foot
in the talus slope which, because of its instability, is very
slowly colonized by plants.

up to ten times faster by the combined action of physical and chemical
forces than it would be by chemical weathering alone. Since rocks are made
of mineral crystals or older rock fragments cemented together, the minerals and the cementing substances are all soluble to a degree, and so can
be dissolved by rainwater. Pure rainwater would not make much headway
on an outcropping of rather dense and hard granite or basalt, but rainwater
is rarely pure. Carbon dioxide dissolves in rainwater as it falls through the
atmosphere, forming carbonic acid; although it is weaker than vinegar, it
still attacks rocks more vigorously than pure water does.

A parent rock can contribute to soil formation only the minerals it
contains. Once the minerals are released, however, their proportions in the
soil may be greatly affected by climate and the type of vegetational cover.
A simple granite, for example, might contain three minerals: feldspar,
mica, and quartz. Feldspar, a complex of potassium, aluminum, and silicon
dioxide, breaks down in the weathering process into soluble potassium
carbonate and kaolinite, a clay. Mica, containing magnesium as well as
the oxides found in feldspar, decomposes into soluble carbonates, the sesquioxides of iron and aluminum (sesqui- means 1.5 times, referring to the
3:2 ratio of oxygen to metal), and more clay. Quartz (silicon dioxide)
simply weathers from large pieces into smaller pieces.

A soil weathered from granite, then, would be expected to contain carbonates (the source of many plant nutrients), sand, clays, and sesquioxides. But the climate greatly affects the rate at which these soil components are either retained or washed away, leached by water percolating

through the soil. In a cool, moist climate, the sesquioxides and clays tend to be leached away, leaving behind a porous, sandy soil called podzol (from the Russian word meaning ash). Many of the light, grayish or brownish sandy soils of the temperate zones of the world are podzols. In the tropics and areas with a warm, moist climate, the silica or sand is leached out and the sesquioxides and clays remain. Because of the quantities of iron and aluminum in sesquioxide form, the soil is brightly colored in shades of red, orange, and yellow, and because of the clay content it is heavy and plastic in consistency. These plinthite soils or soils resembling them are found in the piedmont of the southern United States from Virginia to Texas, and in many other regions with warm, moist climates.

SOIL STRUCTURE

If rock weathered into tiny cubes like salt crystals, they would pack tightly together, leaving little room for either water or air. However, weathering produces rounded particles, and when these are packed together the interstices are filled with either air or water. In addition, the activities of plants and animals make large channels and holes that allow even more air and water to enter the soil.

Immediately after rain, most of the spaces between the soil particles are filled with water, much of which is lost to the water table by the action of gravity, or to the atmosphere by evaporation. The remaining moisture is gradually absorbed by plant roots and returned to the air through the plant's leaves. This transpirational loss of water from the plant is an integral part of the cycling of water in the environment.

Obviously, plants cannot grow without water, but it is less obvious that the air content of soil is important too. Plant roots contain living tissues as vital to the plant as its leaves, stems, and flowers. While water can move into the plant root by simple diffusion, minerals dissolved in the water may require an output of energy by the root to be absorbed. The source of this energy is photosynthesis. Plant leaves can use sunlight to split water molecules into hydrogen and oxygen ions (charged particles). The oxygen ions combine to form gaseous oxygen, but the hydrogen ions are fed into a complex series of reactions along with carbon dioxide and ultimately yield a sugar. Sugars can be burned at once in an energy yielding process called respiration, or transported to the roots, where they supply the energy needed to absorb certain minerals from the soil. But oxygen must also be available in the soil. In waterlogged soil all the spaces between particles are filled with water and there is very little oxygen. Plant roots, unable to respire properly, die and because of their critical function in supplying water and minerals, the plant also dies.

13

THE ORGANIC COMPONENT

The inorganic components—sand, air, and water—do not in themselves make soil. The organic material also necessary for fertile soil is called humus and is made up of partially decomposed vegetable material, leaves, rotting wood, and animal remains—their excrement as they live, their bodies when they die. Humus is the rich brownish-black crumbly top layer of leaf mold that you see when you brush away the dry leaves on a forest floor in the temperate zone. Large animals, such as elephants, deer, or rabbits, make some contribution to humus; mice, insects, and worms contribute even more. But, because of their numbers, bacteria, algae, fungi, and other microorganisms contribute more humus to the soil than all the big trees and animals combined. These organisms are also of critical importance in decomposing organic material and cycling nutrients.

Humus, which gets mixed with the mineral components of the soil by the burrowing of animals and the dying and rotting of plant roots, forms a fairly stable association with the clay in the soil, a clay-humus complex (Figure 1.7). This complex then forms aggregations, or clumps, of various sizes. The size determines the soil structure, which in turn helps to determine the kinds of plants that will grow.

As organic compounds and minerals in the soil gradually decompose, they dissociate into simpler and simpler compounds, and finally form ions that percolate through the soil and are attracted and held by the clay-humus particles. These ions comprise a reservoir that determines soil fertility. If there are plenty of clay-humus particles well saturated with minerals, the soil is said to be quite fertile.

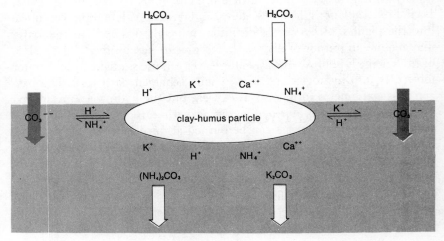

Fig. 1.7 A schematic drawing of a clay-humus particle shows the relationship between mineral nutrients and soil fertility. Carbonic acid combines chemically with the mineral nutrient ions in the particle, leaving hydrogen ions behind.

Carbonate ions from rainfall can extract minerals from the reservoir, leaving hydrogen ions in their place. If positively charged ions continue to be added to the soil from leaf fall, their loss to the carbonate ions that pass through is balanced, and the soil remains fertile. But if the replenishment of ions is interrupted or diminished, the existing ions will be leached away as carbonates and the soil will be less fertile.

SOIL ACIDITY

If the mineral nutrients are replaced with hydrogen ions, however, the soil becomes more acidic as well. Acidity is defined as the concentration of hydrogen ions, and is usually expressed by the symbol pH. A pH of 1 means that one in 10,000 parts by weight of the soil is composed of hydrogen ions. A pH of 2 means 1 in 100,000 parts; 3, 1 in 1,000,000 parts, and so forth. The lower the pH, the greater the acidity. The pH scale runs from 0 to 14. A pH that decreases from 7 is becoming increasingly acid; a pH that increases from 7 is becoming increasingly alkaline. A pH of 7 is neutral.

If hydrogen ions replace most of the minerals normally held by the clay-humus particles, the pH drops to about 4. On the other hand, if the clay-humus particles are saturated with minerals, the pH rises to about 7. If the soil is supplied with organic acids or lime, the pH may be lower than 4 or higher than 7. The pH of most soils is between 5 and 7. A low pH may affect the solubility of various minerals and hence impede the activities of vital microorganisms.

We cannot, however, infer the fertility of the soil from its pH alone. If we had a soil with a large quantity of clay-humus particles but they were only half saturated with minerals, the pH would probably be below 7. Another soil with a much smaller quantity of clay-humus particles that were fully saturated with minerals would probably have a pH close to 7. It would be a mistake to assume because of pH that the latter is more fertile than the former. A more accurate way to measure soil fertility is to assess the number of clay-humus particles present, determine from this number the nutrient exchange capacity of the soil, and from that its fertility.

BIOGEOCHEMICAL CYCLES

As we saw in our look at the hydrosphere, water cycles through the environment. Other major components of the atmosphere, hydrosphere, and lithosphere also cycle, this explains why their proportions in the environment are relatively fixed. These huge global cycles are called biogeochemical cycles because of the intricate involvement of plants, animals, and geological/chemical processes.

THE CARBON CYCLE

Carbon circulates in the environment through two cycles, one within the other in time. The outer or geological cycle involves much of the earth's 10^{15} [1] metric tons [2] of carbon locked up in sedimentary deposits as carbonates (from the shells and casts of marine organisms) and organic fossils such as oil, oil shale, and coal. The carbon in these deposits circulates only very slowly—in hundreds of millions of years—as these deposits are exposed and weathered away by erosion.

The inner or biologic cycle moves much more quickly (Figure 1.8). The residence time of carbon dioxide in the atmosphere, for example, is

Fig. 1.8 Three cycles, oxygen, carbon dioxide, and water, are intimately interlocked through the action of biological, chemical, and geological processes.

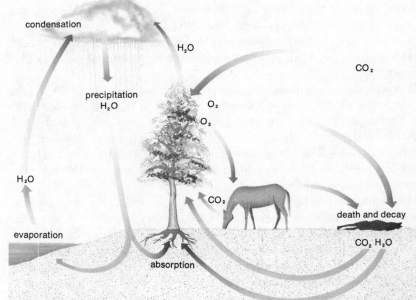

only three hundred years. That is, any given molecule of carbon dioxide stays only that long in the atmospheric pool before it is taken up by some aspect of the cycle. The reserve of stored carbon, 400 to 500 billion tonnes, is tied into the biomass of forests at the rate of 1–2 kilograms per square meter per year. This is the maximum rate, found only in tropical rainforests with optimum growing conditions. Temperate zone forests and cropland fix 0.2–$0.4 \ kg/m^2/yr$, while deserts and tundra fix as little as

[1] Exponentials are a handy way to express very large numbers. 10^{15} means 1 plus 15 zeros or 1,000,000,000,000,000. You name it!

[2] A metric ton (1000 kilograms), henceforth will be referred to as a *tonne. Ton* (2000 pounds) will refer to the old English system still used in the United States.

0.01 kg/m²/yr. Altogether land vegetation fixes about 40 billion tonnes per year, about the same as the plankton and seaweeds of the ocean. The carbon locked into the biomass of trees stays there throughout the life of the tree, as little as thirty years for a birch and as much as three thousand years for a Sierran giant sequoia.

Once again the sea plays an important role in the biogeochemical cycling of an important component of the biosphere; it acts as a sink for atmospheric carbon. At least 100 billion tonnes of carbon dioxide dissolve into the sea every year, and a nearly equal amount is returned by the sea to the atmosphere. Thus the sea serves as a buffer, keeping the amount of carbon dioxide in the atmosphere relatively constant. This has not always been true, for in the past tremendous quantities of carbon have been released into the atmosphere during periods of extensive volcanic activity. Despite the sea's ability to absorb carbon dioxide, it can do so only at a certain rate commensurate with the withdrawal of carbon by marine organisms. A lag in marine extraction together with an elevated level of atmospheric carbon dioxide might very well have greatly stimulated plant growth, producing the enormous deposits of coal and oil that characterize the Mississippian and Pennsylvanian periods of geologic history.

THE OXYGEN CYCLE

Of the total supply of oxygen on earth, 93 percent is locked up, like the carbon reserve, in carbonate rock and fossil organics, the sulfates in rock, and the ferric oxides of red sedimentary rock so conspicuous in the deserts of the Southwest. The remaining 7 percent is found in the atmosphere and in oceanic sulfates. There is increasing evidence that oxygen was not a component of the earth's original atmosphere or lithosphere, for the earliest rocks have few or no compounds containing oxygen. The first evidence of the appearance of oxygen seems to be the presence of banded iron rock almost three billion years old. The bands of iron are in the ferric or oxidized state, which is possible only with readily available sources of oxygen. The most likely source for this oxygen was the development of photosynthesis by very primitive predecessors of today's blue-green algae. Because of the high levels of ultraviolet radiation striking the earth's surface at this time, such early photosynthesizers could only exist in rather sheltered places. But over the succeeding billion years or so enough gaseous oxygen accumulated in the atmosphere to begin generation of the ozone shield. Once protected from ultraviolet radiation, photosynthesizing life became possible over a much greater area of the planet and the atmospheric concentration of oxygen grew steadily, allowing more complex forms of life to evolve. Today, life is so ubiquitous on earth that it has been estimated that the 1.5 billion cubic kilometers of water on earth is split into oxygen by photosynthetic plants and reconstituted back into

17

water by respiring plants and animals every two million years. Indeed, any given molecule of oxygen has been floating about the atmosphere for only two thousand years before we gulp it down to accept hydrogen atoms from the food our bodies burn.

THE NITROGEN CYCLE

Despite the abundance of nitrogen in the atmosphere, it is the plant nutrient most often in short supply. Relatively stable and inert, nitrogen must be converted or fixed into compounds that can be utilized by plants (Figure 1.9). Its importance to both plants and animals lies in the incorporation of nitrogen in the amino groups (NH_2) that form amino acids and proteins. Fixation of nitrogen requires energy, some of which is supplied by cosmic radiation, lightning, meteor trails, and other such exotica, which react nitrogen with oxygen or water to form nitrite or ammonia. But this source is relatively minor; it probably fixes no more than 7 million tonnes per year. The most important source seems to be biological fixation.

The nitrogen cycle is the most complex of the various biogeochemical cycles because of the great variety of oxidation states of nitrogen. It can be found in the highly oxidized form of nitrate (NO_3^-), the highly reduced form of ammonium (NH_4^+), or several states in between (NO_2^-, NH_2, NH_3). Since movement from one form to another can generate

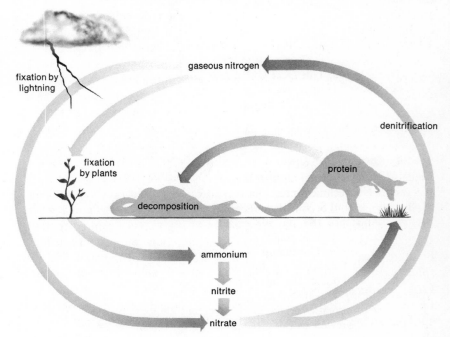

Fig. 1.9 The nitrogen cycle is of critical importance to the growth of plants that supply the amino acids necessary to build animal proteins.

18

energy, there are microorganisms in water, the soil, and in nodules on the roots of plants that facilitate these conversions. The cycle starts with the splitting of molecular nitrogen by atmospheric phenomena, a bacterium in a root nodule, or a blue-green alga. The end product is ammonia, which is either absorbed by plant roots or nitrified by the bacterium *Nitrosomonas* into nitrite. The bacterium *Nitrobacter* oxidizes nitrite into nitrate, which is either utilized by plants or denitrified by the bacterium *Pseudomonas* back to N_2O or N_2. When plants and animals die their proteins break down into amino groups, which are converted by still other microorganisms into ammonia.

Eighty-two percent of the total nitrogen on earth is in the earth's crust and sediments and 17 percent is in the atmosphere. Most of the tiny fraction remaining is dissolved in sea water and incorporated into the world's plants and animals. Although only a minuscule portion of the earth's supply of nitrogen circulates, that portion has provided life with a protein for its continuing evolution.

Thus the complementary biological processes of respiration, photosynthesis, growth, and decay join together the great interconnecting geochemical cycles of oxygen, carbon, and nitrogen into a delicately balanced system. Despite their global scale and the prodigious quantities of materials involved, our influences on the cycles are beginning to be observed. Unfortunately our knowledge of their detailed workings and interactions is so incomplete that we are unable to predict the results of either our conscious or unconscious tampering.

FURTHER READING

Coker, R. E., 1962. *This great and wide sea, an introduction to ocean and marine biology.* Harper, New York. An old standby, out of date in some particulars but still one of the most readable and synoptic accounts of the ocean.

Piel, G. et al. (eds.), 1970. *The biosphere.* W. H. Freeman, San Francisco. A good collection of articles from *Scientific American* that deal with various biogeochemical cycles.

Riehl, H., 1972. *Introduction to the atmosphere.* 2nd ed. McGraw-Hill, New York. Nontechnical presentation of a very complex environment.

Sanchez, P. A., and S. W. Buol, 1975. "Soils of the tropics and the world food crisis." *Science* **188,** pp. 598–603. Lays to rest some myths about the destruction of tropical soils.

Sullivan, W., 1974. *Continents in motion, the new earth debate.* McGraw-Hill, New York. A fine pulling together of the threads of the continental drift story—one of the most exciting of the century.

Williams, J., J. J. Higginson, and J. D. Rohrbough, 1973. *Sea and air, the marine environment.* 2nd ed. Naval Institute Press, Annapolis. A fairly comprehensive review of the mechanisms of the marine environment.

CHAPTER TWO

THE BIOSPHERE

THE NEXT TIME you cross the street on a rainy day, look closely at the puddle under your feet. That delicate iridescent sheen floating on its surface is a film of oil probably no more than one molecule thick. For all its diversity and vigor, the biosphere is no more than a comparably thin film covering the earth's surface. Wherever we study this "skin," we find the same components: plants and animals in some kind of environment, with some form of energy flowing through it. Any such system is called an ecosystem—it may be a drop of pond water, the pond, the watershed in which the pond is located, or the entire region. In fact, the whole earth is a huge ecosystem. It is this range of size that makes the ecosystem such a useful concept in sorting out the relationships among the abundant organisms in the biosphere.

ENERGY

Since energy is so crucial to the functioning of ecosystems, we should look more closely at some of its essential characteristics. We must always keep in mind the two basic laws of thermodynamics that govern the energetics of any ecosystem.

1. Energy can be transferred from one form to another but cannot be created or destroyed. We can store energy in a battery or a candy bar, but we haven't really created it; we have just transferred the energy stored in coal, falling water, or food into a more immediately useful or compact form. The ultimate source of all these energy forms is, of

course, the sun. It provided the energy to grow the plants that have become coal; the energy to evaporate the water which, having fallen onto the land, turns turbines on its way back to the sea; and the energy to produce peanuts, chocolate, and sugar from plants.

2. Once it enters a system, energy begins to dissipate, moving from more concentrated to less concentrated forms. Although energy is relatively easy to transform, with every transformation some energy is lost as heat. Therefore energy cannot cycle in a system like a gas or nutrient; it simply flows through. Without a relatively constant external source of energy, the earth would have run down like an unwound clock a couple of billion years ago. Of course the earth has its own internal source of energy, but this is diffused and well insulated from the biosphere by the earth's mantle of rock except in volcanic or geothermal areas.

PRODUCTIVITY

When we inventory an ecosystem, even a small one, the sheer numbers of species or individuals of a species can obscure the role each plant or animal is playing. Therefore it is often convenient to group organisms according to their use of energy.

Green plants are producers. Through photosynthesis they can store the sun's energy in the form of high energy phosphate bonds (ATP), which can then provide the energy to produce protein, starch, or fat. The rate at which plants fix solar energy is called their productivity, usually measured as calories of energy fixed per unit area per unit time. Keep in mind that productivity is a *rate*; the amount that can be harvested at any particular time is the standing crop.

An ecosystem's productivity depends on the availability of nutrients. Rich soil is an obvious source of nutrients, but environments such as estuaries and tidal marshes can be highly productive too. This productivity results from their ability to trap the nutrients found in shallow water. The clay sediments kaolinite and montmorillonite, which are quite abundant in most estuaries, are highly adsorbent—because of their large surface area the clay particles pick up and hold loosely a variety of ions. As plankton remove nutrients from the water, new supplies are released from the clay sediments that act as a nutrient buffer.

A good measure of this productivity is a comparison of the dry organic matter produced in a terrestrial system and an estuarine system. A typical wheat field produces 1.5 tons per acre per year (including straw and roots); a coastal marsh near Sapelo Island, Georgia produces 10 tons per acre per year. Little of this production is actually used, however. Broadly speaking, the great productivity of salt marshes and the estuaries, bays, mud flats, and tidal creeks with which they form an inseparable unit, is

THE BIOSPHERE

Fig. 2.1 A healthy stand of cordgrass in one of the few remaining salt marshes in Connecticut.

based on three communities of plants: cord grass (*Spartina*) in the marshes (Figure 2.1), mud algae on the creek banks, and microscopic plants called phytoplankton in the water.

FOOD WEBS

Although food chains are rarely very long (the second law of thermodynamics prohibits that), they can be very complex. In this case they are called food webs (Figure 2.2). The producer that supports a food web may not be intimately involved in an ecosystem, however. Sometimes the·standing crop is exported in the form of detritus or organic fragments. A shaded woodland stream ecosystem may derive most of its energy from the leaves that fall into it every year rather than from the fixing of solar energy by algae or other plants in the stream itself. In a salt marsh, the cord grass is the basis of the food web. Yet less than 5 percent of the cord grass is eaten in place, since few insects can survive both salinity and tidal flooding. Even the few hardy grasshoppers sometimes seen in the salt marshes excrete, undigested, two thirds of the material they eat. As the grass is crushed and fragmented by fall and winter storms, microorganisms break it down into fine organic particles containing large amounts of protein, carbohydrates, and vitamins. This detritus is distributed by tides, but various organisms retain and cycle it in the ecosystem. For example, phosphate is more abundant in estuarine ecosystems than in rivers or the ocean itself. The Altamaha River in Georgia contains 0.1 micrograms (μg) per liter, while coastal tidal creeks contain between 2–4 μg/1. This abundance is explained by the ecology of one of the most common animals in the southern estuaries, the ribbed mussel. As the mussel filters the water for food, the fine organic particles, which it does not eat, are stuck together with mucus into little particles called pseudofeces ("pseudo" because they do not pass through the mussel's digestive system but are eliminated before entering the mouth). These particles, rich in phosphate, remain in the area and are fed upon first by fiddler crabs, then by animals we ultimately eat, such as blue crabs and striped bass. The ribbed mussel is a classic case of an economically worthless organism playing an extremely valuable role—in this instance, cycling phosphate, a most important mineral nutrient. Trout lilies play a similar role in the eastern deciduous forest (see Chapter 9).

The mud algae of the estuaries include dinoflagellates—microscopic algae enclosed in sculptured jackets with whiplike tails or flagella—and diatoms. These organisms are usually so abundant that they give the muddy creek banks a characteristic brown or yellowish color. They adapt to the changing seasons and so can photosynthesize either at high tide in the summer when cooled by the tidal water, or at low tide in the winter

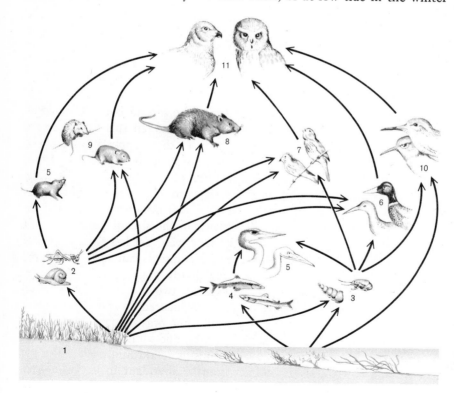

Fig. 2.2 This simplified food web is characteristic of midwinter in the glasswort salt marshes of the central California coast. The primary producers (1) in the marshes are eaten by snails and grasshoppers (2). Marine plants are fed upon by various invertebrate herbivores (3). Smelt and anchovy (4) feed on the marine and marsh plants. The first carnivores are the vagrant shrew, which eats invertebrates, and the great blue heron and common egret (5) which eat fish. Next is a large class of omnivores including mallard duck and clapper rail (6), song and savanna sparrows (7), Norway rat (8), salt marsh harvest mouse and California vole (9), and western and least sandpipers (10). Top carnivores, the short-eared owl and marsh hawk (11), they feed on most of the system's omnivores. (After fig. 3.6 (p. 42) in Ecology and Field Biology, 2nd ed., by Robert L. Smith. Copyright © 1966, 1974 by Robert Leo Smith. Used by permission of Harper & Row Publishers, Inc.

when warmed by the sun. By reproducing rapidly and washing off into the water, the diatoms and dinoflagellates provide a year-round food source both for filter feeders such as oysters, clams, and mussels, and for the tiny larvae and small crustaceans that are the basic food of most fish. We cannot overestimate the importance of the reproductive rate of these mudbank algae; those we see sticking to the mudbanks are only a very small fraction of the total yearly algal production. Although the population on the mudbank remains constant, huge numbers of algae are sloughed off. Much of the productivity of the estuarine ecosystem depends upon this process, which clearly shows why the standing crop (the algae on the mudbank) is often a poor measure of productivity.

Because the differing salinity of water determines its level in the estuarine water column, mineral nutrients tend to be trapped in wedges allowing more time for their uptake by organisms. Also, daily tides continuously provide food and oxygen while removing waste products. These factors result in good production of phytoplankton, which supplement the mudbank algae as a primary food source for the various consumers in the estuarine food web.

Another important plant-based food web exists in the mangrove marshes along parts of the Florida coast. Like the cord grass of the estuaries, the leaves of the red mangrove (Figure 2.3) provide the base for

Fig. 2.3 By extending their aerial roots into the soft bottom sediments, red mangroves gradually colonize extensive areas of mudflats along tropical coasts: here, near Parguera on the south coast of Puerto Rico.

this web. Three tons of leaves are shed per acre per year. The litter is initially attacked by crabs and amphipods, a group of small crustaceans, and quickly broken down. After nine months, the fallen leaves have been reduced to fragments about one millimeter wide. As this breakdown progresses, bacteria and fungi gradually cover the pieces, thereby raising both the protein and vitamin content of the fragments. While fresh leaves have a protein and vitamin content of 6 percent, after twelve months of decomposition the protein content of the leaf fragments has risen to 22 percent. This enriched supply of leaf pieces or detritus provides an important source of food for many species of worms, crabs, shrimp, insect larvae, small forage fish, and copepods, another group of small crustaceans. Over sixty species of young fish, prized as gamefish when adult, also feed on the mangrove detritus: these include tarpon, snook, and ladyfish. Other valuable species—menhaden, spotted sea trout, red drum, striped mullet, and blue crab—eat the small forage fish and invertebrates that feed on the detritus.

In a food chain or web, the producers must be rather more abundant than the primary consumers, or the chain quickly breaks down. The same relationship holds between the various consumer levels. Therefore the eating pattern or trophic structure of an ecosystem is a pyramid with a carnivore on the apex. To feed a top carnivore (a growing boy, let's say) high grade protein for one year requires 4.5 calves, who in turn require 10 acres of alfalfa or about 20 million plants. Similar pyramids can be constructed on the basis of standing crop, energy flow, or whatever criteria seem most appropriate to the ecosystem.

LIMITING FACTORS

Over 130 years ago a German agricultural chemist observed that the "growth of a plant is dependent on the amount of foodstuff which is presented to it in minimum quantity." This has become known in ecology as Liebig's Law of the Minimum. More prosaically, no matter how much butter and sugar you have, you cannot bake a cake without flour. Thus for any plant or animal to exist in an ecosystem, all the material it needs must be present in the right amounts. Plants, for example, require two groups of nutrients: macronutrients, which are needed in relatively large quantities because they are part of the plant's cell wall or protoplasm; and micronutrients, which although used in very small quantities in enzymes, are equally important to the plant. Even though all the macronutrients are available, a plant may be unable to grow if a micronutrient is not present, and vice versa.

In the life cycle of every organism there are points where too much or too little of some factor can be limiting. But these limiting factors may be quite different at different stages in the life cycle. A dogwood seed may not germinate unless the soil is fairly sweet; the seedling may be killed if the soil gets too hot; the mature tree may not flower if the winters are too cold or not cold enough; seeds may not be produced if the right pollinators are unavailable. Any one of these factors might limit the occurrence or spread of dogwood.

Limiting factors are often more obvious in aquatic than terrestrial environments. Every natural body of water contains life. Those with relatively small populations of plants and animals are called oligotrophic; their low level of fauna and flora results in very clear blue water. Bodies of water with high populations of aquatic life are termed eutrophic; because of the density of organisms the water is turbid and green. Eutrophication has many different causes, but generally it can be traced to the abundance of three nutrients: phosphorus, nitrogen, and carbon.

The concentration of phosphorus in water environments is normally low, about 0.02 parts per million (ppm), because most phosphates are insoluble in water. If much more phosphorus than this amount is added to an aquatic system, it is either incorporated into organisms and ultimately deposited in sediments, or precipitated directly in the form of inorganic compounds. Excess phosphorus always ends up incorporated into sediments, but the pathway it takes is of critical importance.

When a nutrient normally in short supply is added to a system it may trigger a rapid growth of organisms in that system (Figure 2.4). Phosphorus is just such a trigger factor in most aquatic systems. Microorganisms are often held in check by a lack of phosphorus. When it becomes available, however, they use it immediately, and with their rapid reproductive rates they can very quickly become extremely abundant. This population explosion, usually of one or more species of algae, is called a bloom, generally defined as 500 individuals of a species per milliliter of water.

If a given amount of phosphorus caused a bloom of a certain intensity, we could easily set up maximum allowable concentrations of phosphorus and control the bloom. Unfortunately, the information available on phosphorus and algal blooms indicates that there is no one-to-one relationship between the two. In some Wisconsin lakes, algal blooms have been recorded with a phosphorus concentration of 0.01 ppm. In other lakes, blooms have been observed where the phosphorus concentration was 0.001 ppm. Yet other lakes have not had blooms with a phosphorus level of 0.05 ppm, fifty times as great.

This inconstant relationship of phosphorus to algal blooms has led to the assertion that organic matter is really the key in environments where eutrophication is a problem, and that carbon is more often limiting than phosphorus. Adding large amounts of organic matter to aquatic systems stimulates a bloom of bacteria, which produce large quantities of free carbon dioxide, as much as 20 mg per liter. This in turn stimulates the

Fig. 2.4   A mass of filamentous algae in the nutrient-rich water of a trout hatchery in Pennsylvania.

rapid reproduction of algae, which contribute to the overall eutrophication of the system. Those who believe that phosphorus is the limiting factor respond that blooms occur in water with very low levels of phosphorus because the phosphorus is in the algae and not the water. So you pay your money and take your choice until more definitive evidence is available. Unquestioning acceptance of dogma is just as much a millstone in ecology as in religion or politics.

For example, it was once believed that lakes age gradually, progressing step by step from oligotrophic beginnings through slowly increasing eutrophy to become a marsh and finally a forest. But things are not quite so simple. Studies in the Lake District of England suggest that this picture of lake development should be re-examined. Apparently the thickness of bottom deposits in some lakes bears little relationship to the internal productivity; the watershed is the major source of sediments. When erosion in the watershed of a lake is severe, minerals are trapped in lake bottoms before the nutrients locked in these minerals can be leached away in the process of soil formation. When erosion is less intense and more leaching of soil takes place, the nutrients pass into the lake and stimulate biological productivity. When the watershed lacks vegetation, erosion is rapid; when it is covered with trees, erosion is much slower. The history of a lake and its watershed can often be read by

27

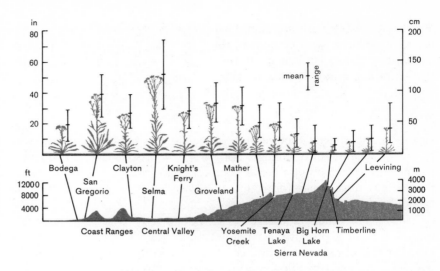

Fig. 2.5 Yarrow plants collected in various locations from the coast to the Sierran crest in California retain their characteristic heights when grown in a common garden at Stanford. This suggests that they are ecotypes, or locally adapted populations. (Redrawn from Carnegie Institution of Washington, 1948. "Environmental responses of climatic races of *Achillea*." Experimental studies on the nature of species III, no. 581)

analyzing the bottom mud and tracing the abundance of various nutrients layer by layer. When this was done at Esthwaite Water in England, sodium and potassium levels were found to be quite low soon after the lake was formed. As the watershed became covered with vegetation and erosion was checked, the levels of sodium and potassium rose. At the time of forest decline associated with human activities about five thousand years ago, these nutrients decreased again; they have continued to decline up to the present. A similar picture has been constructed for Linsley Pond in Connecticut, one of the most studied bodies of water in the world.

These studies imply that lakes may be eutrophic or oligotrophic from the very beginning and may remain in their initial state for thousands of years. They may change rather suddenly or they may even cycle from oligotrophy to eutrophy and back again. It now seems unlikely that all lakes are inexorably moving from oligotrophy to eutrophy.

Some species of plants or animals may have a wide tolerance range for one factor and a narrow tolerance range for another. While it is difficult to explain why some species are rare or narrowly distributed, we can safely say that broadly distributed species have a wide tolerance range for all the factors affecting their distribution. Another possibility is that these species may be composed of a series of locally adapted populations called ecotypes. Reciprocal planting or relocation can often reveal the existence of ecotypes in a population of plants or animals (Figure 2.5).

THE COMMUNITY

The ecosystem is an extremely useful concept in understanding the functional relationships among plants, animals, and the environment; but qualitative relationships are important too. This is especially true for the biotic component of an ecosystem, the community. Like an ecosystem, a community can be large or small; the organisms living in a rotten log, or the plants and animals of an old field or lake.

SUCCESSION

Since we usually study communities at a given moment, it is very easy to overlook community change. Sometimes change is rapid, even catastrophic: construction of a beaver dam across a stream, a landslide, windthrow from storms in a forest, fire. What then takes place is a process called succession. In some instances the original community may be reconstituted; in others, a different community may develop. Succession following from a preexisting community is called secondary succession (Figure 2.6a). But community change may also be very slow, particularly if there is no soil available—on a rock outcrop, for example. In this case subsequent colonization by plants and animals is called primary succession (Figure 2.6b). The result of either type of succession is a self-reproducing community that remains relatively stable in species composition until disturbed again. Once scientists thought that in any given

Fig. 2.6 (a) The joints in this granite outcrop are widened by weathering, a process aided by lichens. When enough soil has accumulated in the cleft to hold moisture, grasses are able to survive. They increase the amount of organic material, ensuring the survival of shrubs and tree seedlings whose roots further fragment the bedrock. (b) Originally this oak grove was kept open by recurring ground fires. Incorporation of the area into a national park limited fire, and now the fire-sensitive incense cedar is invading. Unless cleared out, it will shade out the oaks in a few decades.

29

region both primary and secondary succession headed inevitably toward a predictable climax community (the heavy hand of dogma again). But the availability of seeds, sprouts, and root suckers may decisively determine what type of self-reproducing vegetation results from any successional pattern, primary or secondary.

SPECIES DIVERSITY

The diversity of life can be something of a surprise, for most people notice their fellow organisms only when they are about to eat or be eaten. Even a weedy lot in the middle of a large city can teem with plants and insects. If you were to make a list of the plants and animals in any established self-reproducing community you would find a small number of species with many individuals and a large number of species with few individuals. To be sure, most of the energy flows through the dominant producer species, which represents most of the system's productivity; but it is the number of less common species that determine the species diversity of the community. Where the limiting factors of an environment tend to be physical or chemical, as in the tundra, species diversity is low and the community is unstable, or at least easily disturbed and slow to recover. In the eastern deciduous forest, where the limiting factors tend to be biologically oriented, species diversity is high and the community is stable. High species diversity tends to stabilize the community because all those "extra" species provide a much larger genetic pool to adapt to any environmental change that may occur.

ECOTONES

Species diversity is often highest in border areas between different communities—between prairie and forest, or hardwoods and conifers. The boundary may be very sharply defined (Figure 2.7); more often it is a

Fig. 2.7 Many ecotones, between forest and tundra for example, may extend over many miles. This ecotone between Jeffrey pine and sagebrush is relatively sharply defined. Ecotones are lines of tension: in good years of greater than usual rainfall the equilibrium may favor the pine, in bad years, the sage.

transitional area where the different communities mingle. This transition zone is called an ecotone and contains not only the species found in the adjacent communities but often species peculiar to the ecotone and found in neither adjoining community. A good example is the American robin, which feeds in grassy areas but nests in trees; an ecotone of mixed trees and grassland provides an ideal habitat for robins, while a dense forest or treeless prairie does not. Ecotones may be stable, or in a changing environment may lead the change, as when forest invades grassland or vice versa.

THE POPULATION

Communities are composed of populations of their constituent species. A population is like its individual members in that it grows, differentiates, and sometimes even dies. But it also has group attributes that do not apply to the individual, such as birth and death rate and age ratio. Most populations in a stable system have a relatively balanced birth and death rates. But when a population is colonizing new territory or recovering from some setback, its growth follows an S-shaped curve: first a period of apparently slow growth (slow because the initial population density may be quite low and it may take time for the population to increase its density even if breeding occurs at an optimal rate); more rapid growth as the pouulation density begins to rise; then a leveling off as the capacity of the environment is reached. The leveling usually involves population density rather than reproductive rate since most organisms breed as rapidly as possible except in times of severe stress or when population density outstrips available breeding sites. Since no environment has infinite resources, population density sooner or later reaches a limit. This limit is known as the carrying capacity. If it is exceeded, the quality of the environment drops and with it the excess population. Some populations stabilize after reaching the carrying capacity of their environment; others overrun the carrying capacity and either starve, cease to reproduce, or disperse, whereupon another cycle begins. Since all organisms are part of some kind of food web, population growth of some species is often closely tied to that of other species, particularly those involved in a predator-prey relationship.

Cyclic oscillation of a population with prey-predator linkage is well illustrated by the case of the snowshoe hare and the lynx or wildcat. The hare population increases to a maximum every nine to ten years. Predator species such as the lynx, which depend on hare for much of their food, increase in response to the more abundant food supply. The hare population crashes, and the lynx disperse or starve and become rather scarce until the hare population builds up again. However, the cause and

31

effect relationship here is not reciprocal. Although the lynx population growth and crash is linked to the hare's, the reverse is not true. Hare populations crash every nine to ten years, lynx or no lynx.

Population may be limited by density-independent factors such as climate or density-dependent factors such as predation, parasites, disease, and direct competition. Occasional hurricanes in the Florida Everglades have periodically demolished populations of great white heron regardless of their density at the time. This is density-independent control. The population crash of the snowshoe hare exemplifies density-dependent control of the lynx population.

POPULATION INTERACTIONS

When populations of different species share a common environment, their effect on each other may be antagonistic, beneficial, or neutral. Predator-prey and analogous parasite-host relationships are the two major antagonistic effects, and of course they are antagonistic only from the point of view of the prey or host. We as predators certainly don't feel antagonistic toward our prey. A cow approaching its moment of truth in an abattoir might feel differently. But it isn't convenient to ascribe feelings to prey lest we all end up as vegetarians. Food for thought?

Very occasionally, populations of predators or parasites may destroy their prey or hosts. But in the long run any tendency in this direction is damped out so that both species participating in the relationship survive. Exceptions usually involve introduction of new species without a matrix of associated control species (see Chapter 8).

Some beneficial forms of population interaction include commensalism and mutualism. Commensalism often occurs between fixed plants or animals and mobile ones. Many forms of marine life live in the burrows or shells of other species. Occasionally the relationship goes so far that each member of the pair benefits from the association. At its most extreme, the coupling becomes obligatory and the relationship is known as mutualism. Cows can no more digest cellulose than humans can, since both lack the required enzyme, cellulase. However, cows house microorganisms that do have this enzyme, which breaks down enough cellulose into digestible sugars to supply both the microorganisms and the cow. Many species of tree have root-fungi associations (mycorrhizae) that help feed the tree by making available normally insoluble minerals. One of the most extreme forms of obligate mutualism is the union of some algae and fungi to form lichens (Figure 2.8), a strange group of plants that are among the first colonizers of harsh environments, beginning what is often a long stage of primary succession.

Fig. 2.8   One form of lichen was seen in Fig. 2.6a. This is another branched form which covers the bark of many conifers on the western slope of the Sierra Nevada.

THE SPECIES

The ultimate biological unit in the ecosystem is the species or individual. Every species has a habitat, the place where it can be found within a community, and a niche. Habitat can be pretty well described geographically; moist woods, dry hillside, freshwater marsh and so forth. The niche is more complicated because it involves an individual's habits as well as its location, its relationship to other species, its trophic, or food-related relationships, how it modifies or is modified by its environment, and a hundred other issues even more difficult to pin down. The easiest way to differentiate habitat and niche is to think of the habitat as the address of an organism and the niche as its occupation. Presumably, no two species can occupy the same niche. If they appear to, the niches are probably subtly different.

A good example of finely tuned niche differentiation can be seen in the savanna of East Africa in Kenya and Tanzania. Several dozen grazing

33

animals exist on what appears to be a moderate amount and variety of forage, certainly no more lush or diverse than similar areas in the United States that support only three or four native grazers. The difference lies in the large number of closely related niches occupied by species whose habits, needs, and life cycles complement rather than compete. Take for example the relationship between the wildebeest and Thompson's gazelle in Serengeti National Park. At the end of the rainy season, large herds of wildebeest migrate, feeding as they travel on stands of *Themeda-Pennisetum* grassland. Trampling and heavy feeding apparently devastate the grass, leaving little food for any other grazers. But the grasses respond within thirty days after the passage of the wildebeest by sending out a dense growth of tillers (leafy runners), which are more easily digested and have a higher nutrient content than the mature foliage of the grass. The gazelles then move in and feed extensively on those areas most disturbed by the migrating wildebeest a month before. So although two grazers use the same grass, they occupy different niches and therefore coexist quite well in the same habitat. In this fashion an extraordinarily high species diversity has evolved, making maximum use of the energy provided by the ecosystem producers. As the complexity of the habitat increases, the number of niches increases, and with this the number of species filling those niches. In an undisturbed habitat in a reasonable state of equilibrium, most, if not all, niches are occupied. As habitats change, the niches also change. If an animal cannot adapt to the changes and so evolve along with its niche, it becomes extinct and its place is taken by a species that has evolved to fit that particular niche.

ADAPTATION

This tuning in to the habitat's opportunities comes about through natural selection. Plants and animals cannot intentionally change their physical equipment, yet changes do take place that adapt some organisms extremely well to their niches. How does this happen? Every living cell of an organism contains information in its nucleus that governs the cell's activities, either singly or in concert with other cells. But the reproductive cells are especially important because they produce the egg and sperm which, in higher organisms, are the only link between generations. The potential for change or evolution is greatly enhanced when the information containing material (DNA) of the egg or sperm is altered. Such alterations of DNA are called mutations and the environmental factors that cause them are called mutagens. Some of the more important mutagens are radiation (see Chapter 14), chemicals (see Chapter 6), temperature extremes, and ultraviolet light.

About 20 percent of the individuals in any generation carry recessive or concealed mutations. Since all organisms have some redundancy in their anatomy, mutations affecting major organs needn't be disastrous. But biochemical pathways are so complex even in "simple" organisms that spontaneous changes do not usually improve the organism's chances for survival.

Occasionally a mutation helps an organism to interact with its environment more efficiently; hence the mutant organism proliferates. Far more often, however, mutations lessen an organism's ability to cope with its environment. Suppose you felt your hi-fi could stand some improvement. One approach would be to expose the complicated circuitry and splash solder around at random. There is a remote possibility that you could somehow improve the quality of the sound, but the chances are overwhelmingly greater that you would make such a mess of things that the set would not work at all. If you had an infinite number of hi-fis and millions of years to experiment, sooner or later you would probably make an improvement. Such are the odds against a successful mutation.

Since mutations move from an individual to future generations only by way of the egg and the sperm, a mutation that impairs the offspring's ability to cope with its environment may cost the organism its chance to reproduce. As a result, unfavorable mutations are lost. Changes that are neither favorable nor unfavorable can be carried indefinitely, simply because there is no selection pressure to get rid of them. Finally, any mutation that increases even slightly the organism's ability to survive or to produce more offspring will be transmitted throughout the species population.

To see how mutation is related to evolution, consider the length of a giraffe's neck. Primitive giraffes had normal necks, but neck length varies in each generation, as do all body dimensions and characteristics. Giraffes with longer necks could reach slightly higher up a shrub for leaves. In times of drought, such giraffes had an advantage over shorter-necked giraffes with whom they were competing for food and survived to reproduce. In this way the longer-necked giraffes in each generation survived, passing this valuable adaptation on to succeeding generations. In time, giraffes were characterized by long necks (Figure 2.9).

In the long span of evolutionary time all organisms are subject to random mutational change. While the environment does the selecting, it selects differently for each species; a mutation that is useful to one animal could be a disaster for another. A spider monkey without a tail, for example, would be as inconvenienced as a human with one. While mutations producing monkeys without tails rarely occur, when they do the aberrant individual does not proliferate; hence, monkeys have tails and we do not.

35

Fig. 2.9 In the wild, this reticulated giraffe would be eating the leaves of the tree in its mouth. But since this is a zoo, trees wrapped in chicken wire are as close as it can come to nature.

So: we have looked briefly at earth as a system of systems—a set of Chinese boxes, one within the other, each a functioning group of organisms in an environment, subject to the same ecological principles whether a teaspoon of soil or a whole continent. Now we are ready to add the final ingredient—us. Much too often the responsibility for all that has happened to planet earth is laid about the head of a conveniently anonymous "man" as though that nasty creature were another species. But *we* are "man" and *we* must take credit for past, present, and future modifications that our culture and technology have allowed us to make. In the chapters to come we will be looking at these modifications—some on a modest scale, some of global significance, but all affecting both our future and that of the "fading sweets" of our world.

FURTHER READING

Colinvaux, P. A., 1973. *Introduction to ecology.* John Wiley, New York.
Odum, E. P., 1971. *Fundamentals of ecology.* 3rd ed. W. B. Saunders, Phila-
delphia.
Ricklefs, R. E., 1973. *Ecology.* Chiron Press, Portland, Oregon.

A representative selection of current basic ecology texts. Odum stresses ecosystem dynamics; Ricklefs strikes a good balance between theory and example;
Colinvaux takes an historical approach with attention to the development of
ideas.

PART TWO

THE RESHAPING OF OUR ENVIRONMENT

Once we plucked the apple of culture, the garden of Eden became a field, our food a crop, we the tillers, and the environment a hostile set of forces to be overcome. In this section we begin to trace the environmental disorders that have sprung up wherever we have gone, involving whatever we have touched. Our first meager efforts and tools led to an agricultural revolution that required permanent settlement and resulted in a sustained assault on the environment by steadily growing local populations. Sooner or later the growth of agriculture requires manipulation of water to nourish crops and reduce flooding, or to move products; and then it requires an expedient chemical means of combating the hordes of insects and fungi drawn to *their* gardens of Eden—the huge tracts devoted to a single species. But the wonders of chemistry do not stop with fields and orchards, factories and urban streets. Our chemical ingenuity marches right along with the food into our markets, our kitchens, and our mouths.

CHAPTER THREE

MOVING EARTH

Of ALL THE tools we picked up in the last couple of million years of our evolutionary history, fire stands out as the most basic and in some ways the most critical. An arrowhead or scraper blade might enable more protein to be added to the diet, but without fire far less of this protein could have been assimilated. Steak tartare made from the filet mignon of corn-fed beef is one thing; the raw drumstick of an ostrich or the shoulder of a wooly mammoth is quite another. But accelerated killing of animals for food, though it probably led to extinctions and emptied niches (see Chapter 9), had a relatively minor impact on the landscape compared to the unleashing of fire.

Fire is hard to come by without matches, as any cold, wet backpacker can testify. Once fire was obtained from lightning-struck trees, a flint and steel, or rubbed sticks it was kept going as long as possible. Only very recently have we begun to worry about putting campfires *out*. In simpler times, if abandoned fires escaped to burn forest or grassland, so much the better. Indeed, in many areas burning was practiced regularly to make game more visible; to encourage the growth of secondary succession vegetation, which often supported more game; to reduce the population of some bothersome animal such as poisonous snakes or ticks; and perhaps just for the hell of it. Even today a burning house in the city or barn in the country always draws a crowd.

The impact of intentional fires was great, particularly in arid or seasonally dry regions. The ecotone between forest and grassland is basically determined by moisture. In wet periods the forest advances; in dry years the grassland advances. Recurring fire gives a strong selective advantage to

41

grasses, since their buds are protected by the soil. Woody vegetation with its exposed buds and bark cannot compete after a fire, and grassland expands. Since fire has been used well back into our cultural past, its influence is extensive. Most of the large grasslands of the world—the North American Great Plains, the steppe of the Ukraine, the pampas of Argentina—have been greatly enlarged and their biota given a much larger theater for evolution by fires of human origin. When grassland is protected from fire or so overgrazed that there is little dried grass to carry a fire, trees or shrubs are usually quick to invade.

GRAZING

At some distant time in our past, we ceased following herds of grazing animals and began to direct the movement of animals and then to domesticate them to obtain more products—such as milk, cheese, and wool—than hunting alone provides. But grazing animals must be constantly on the move to obtain food (Figure 3.1), particularly in the arid regions where herding began. So permanent settlements were not possible at first. The environmental impact of grazing was relatively light at the beginning, but mountainous ecosystems already weakened by heavy cutting of timber were disturbed still more by uncontrolled grazing. The four major forms of domesticated livestock—cattle, pigs, sheep, and goats—collectively can destroy a forest very efficiently. Cattle are rather

Fig. 3.1 The coast ranges of Northern California are typified by grassy areas on exposed ridges. In recent years some of these have been heavily overgrazed by sheep, leading to erosion.

selective, eating the better grasses and flowering plants or forbs; because of their size and weight they compact light humusy soil into an easily eroded water-shedding surface. Pigs scavenge, eating acorns, nuts, and mushrooms; they also disturb the soil structure and tree seedlings by digging and rooting in the ground. Sheep crop plants very closely, which damages or destroys the plants if they have no opportunity to recover. Goats, which have been much maligned as four-legged locusts, merely apply the coup de grâce. They can reach high into trees and shrubs by standing on their hind legs and can even climb low trees to reach leaves and tender buds. By the time goats are allowed to graze on forested lands the preceding cattle, pigs, and sheep have left little enough for them to destroy.

THE SAHEL

The effects of livestock on forest reproduction are obvious enough. A more subtle effect has recently been discovered in that drought-devastated subsaharan belt, the Sahel (Figure 3.2). The transition from rather barren desert in the Sahara to littoral rain forest in West Africa involves three distinct belts based on the response of vegetation to increasing amounts of rainfall: the Sahel, the Sudan, and the Guinea. Savanna, grassland with an occasional tree, characterizes the Sahel. For almost two thousand years nomads herded their cattle south in the dry season to the edge of the more heavily vegetated Sudan zone. There was

Fig. 3.2 West Africa is divided into several vegetational zones along a moisture gradient from the dry Sahara to the wet coastal rainforest. (From W. E. Ormerod, 1976. "Ecological effect of control of African trypanosomiasis." Science 191: 815-821, figure 2. Copyright 1976 by the American Association for the Advancement of Science. Adapted from Keay, 1953. An outline of Nigerian vegetation. 2nd ed. Government Printer of Lagos.)

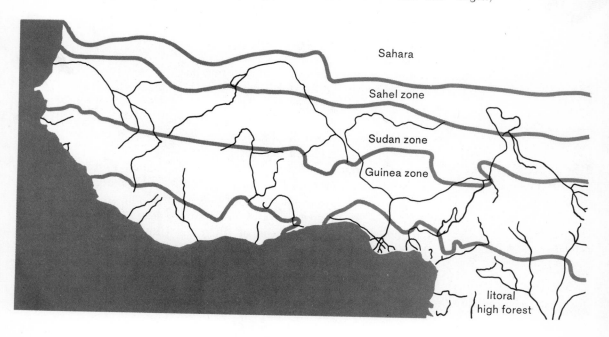

Sahara

Sahel zone

Sudan zone

Guinea zone

litoral
high forest

usually enough rainfall in the southern Sahel to support subsistence farming of drought-resistant millet and sorghum. By the time the cattle arrived each year, the fields had been harvested and the farmers were so eager to have their fields fertilized by the migrant livestock that they not only allowed the cattle to graze the crop stubble but traded millet to the herders for the welcomed manure. As soon as rain began to fall the herders headed north, following the grass, until they reached their home grounds, which by then had a mature stand of grass. As this was eaten and the dry season returned, the move south was repeated. Over many generations the routes, rate of movement, and time spent at watering places were regulated by tribal chiefs and enforced by tradition so that occasional droughts were taken in stride. The whole system represented a reasonable adjustment of herding to a severe environment and seemed to be the most productive use to which that environment could be put.

Then during the nineteenth century, when most western European countries set about acquiring empires, France took over much of northwestern Africa. The French carved up the Sahel into arbitrary administrative units that hindered the free north-south movements of the herders. Further, since nomads are notoriously difficult to tax, every effort was made to settle them and confine their grazing activities. Nor did the farmers fare better. To increase foreign exchange and make the colonies less demanding of the home country, cash crops of peanuts and cotton were planted on the best land; the more marginal land was left for food production. As a result, the fallow or resting period for these food-producing lands was reduced from fifteen to twenty years to one to five years, sharply decreasing the already limited productivity of these lands. Public health measures instituted by the French allowed the human population of the Sahel to increase by one third to 24 million. Then a series of wet years following the withdrawal of the French in 1960 led to the doubling of the livestock population, also to about 24 million, well over the carrying capacity of 15 million. In 1968 a drought began that lasted almost seven years. By the time it broke in 1975, 100,000 people had died, over seven million were made dependent on outside aid, and millions of cattle had perished.

On the surface, the story, though tragic, seemed routine enough—drought-induced famine. But then one of NASA's indefatigable shutterbug satellites took a photo of a typical burned-out area of the Sahel with a polygon of green vegetation in the middle of it (Figure 3.3a). Agronomist Norman MacLeod of American University in Washington, who discovered the apparent anomaly, found that the green pasture was separated from the parched desert by a barbed wire fence enclosing a 250,000-acre ranch established the year the drought began (Figure 3.3 b, c). The ranch was divided into five parts, one part grazed each year. Similar examples in Tunisia and the Sinai-Negev desert reinforce the

Fig. 3.3 *(a) Routine inspection of Landsat satellite photos of the Sahel region of Africa discovered this anomalous polygon of green in an otherwise barren desert.* (NASA) *(b) The polygon turned out to be the Ekrafane Ranch where controlled grazing allows a grass cover to exist even in times of drought. The grasses are the darker tones of gray to the left.* (Norman H. MacLeod) *(c) On the ground the sharp line in (b) can be seen to be the fence separating the ranch (right) from the heavily overgrazed countryside to the left.* (Norman H. MacLeod)

point that overgrazing, not drought, was responsible for the Sahelian famine. But the mechanism is more ominous than just that. Overgrazed land has a greater reflectivity or albedo than vegetated land. Thus it produces a cooler air layer above the desert than would have formed over vegetation. Cool air sinks, becoming warmer and dryer in the process, and thus squelching any possibility of the convectional rainfall that is the region's major form of precipitation. The less rainfall, the less vegetation, the higher the albedo, the less rainfall, and a circle is formed. Thus overgrazing can cause drought just as much as drought can cause overgrazing.

One response to the Sahelian famine was to drill deep wells into the large pool of water or aquifer beneath this region. Cattle were so attracted to the water that any vegetation that had survived the drought was overgrazed and trampled to death. Thus the animals died merely of starvation rather than of starvation *and* thirst. In addition, the area around each borehole became a mini-desert.

Another response has been to recommend eradication of the tsetse fly from the Sudan and Guinea zones, where a denser growth of trees and shrubs shelters the trypanosome-carrying tsetse fly, which makes cattle-raising difficult in this area. (Trypanosomes are protozoans which cause a debilitating disease, nagana, in cattle, and sleeping sickness in humans.) This would allow cattle from the Sahel to graze safely in a larger area. But if this takes place and cattle populations rise again in the Sahel, a future drought would not only devastate the Sahel again but extend the desertification into two more zones that now act as buffers between the Sahara and the rain forest to the south.

THE PRAIRIE DOG

Another unusual example of the result of overgrazing took place a little closer to home. Prairie dogs, rodents between a squirrel and a woodchuck in size, were formerly found on the high plains between Montana and North Dakota, south to Texas and New Mexico. Although they ate the native bunch grasses they much preferred forbs, either native species or introduced weeds and crops. Prairie dogs lived in large colonies or towns with a density as high as 25 animals per acre (Figure 3.4). From the time of settlement to around 1900, prairie dog populations increased explosively until in some areas, colonies were measured by the mile. One town in Texas covered 25,000 square miles and contained 400 million dogs. A combination of predator control, overgrazing, and introduction of crops seems to have triggered this dramatic increase. When bunch grass prairie was overgrazed, all over the West after the Civil War, forbs, the preferred food of prairie dogs, became much more abundant. At the same time, alfalfa and other broad-leaved crops were planted widely in the eastern high plains. When an already large population is suddenly given much more food just as its predators are being eliminated, uncontrolled population growth is inevitable. Subsequently the prairie dogs ruined large areas of the high plains for cattle and farming alike. Then it was discovered that 32 dogs ate the equivalent of one sheep and 256 dogs equaled one cow. Thus if that large town in Texas could support 400 million prairie dogs, it could also support 1,562,500 head of cattle. This discovery doomed the prairie dog. After several years of intensive poisoning the pendulum swung in the other direction, and today prairie dog towns are curiosities in the few places where they still exist.

AGRICULTURE

Perhaps as recently as ten thousand years ago the hunting and gathering of edible plants evolved into the purposeful planting and harvesting of grains and other crops. Compared with the amount of labor it took to gather wild plants, farming allowed a few people to raise enough food for themselves and others as well. Thus the rise of agriculture had two

Fig. 3.4 Prairie dogs have long been despised by farmers and ranchers because of their appetites (notice the bare soil or close-cropped vegetation surround the burrows) and their hole-digging proclivities (the burrow is 4 inches wide and often drops 12 feet vertically) which make the landscape treacherous for livestock. (Department of the Interior, National Park Service)

major impacts. Permanent settlements became not only possible for the first time, but mandatory. It also became possible to store a surplus of food, allowing a social stratification into the farmers, who were the producers, and priests, soldiers, and bureaucrats, who became the consumers. Earth was never the same again!

The whole point of agriculture is to channel the energy nature disperses into many producers and consumers into a few producers that can be easily planted, harvested, and stored. So the first impact of agriculture is to reduce species diversity, resulting in instability. Clearing and preparing the land take some energy, but far more is required over time to control competing producers (weeds) and competing consumers (fungi, insects, and rodents). Then harvesting the crop removes nutrients from the soil. Unless they are replaced, any soil, however fertile, will eventually become infertile. If the land slopes at all, erosion may be an important concomitant of agriculture; generally the greater the slope the greater the potential for erosion, but the intensity and seasonal distribution of rainfall also influence the amount of erosion. Even if competition from weeds and pests is controlled, fertility is maintained, and erosion is insignificant, the productivity of cropland may be affected by an increase in the frequency and severity of root diseases. Recent research indicates that this may be related to a previously unrecognized ethylene cycle in the soil. Ethylene, a common respiration inhibitor, is produced by a bacterium, *Clostridium*, which thrives in oxygenless (anaerobic) pockets in the soil. These pockets form near bits of organic matter when the oxygen-using (aerobic) bacteria feeding on this organic material deplete the local oxygen supply. Ethylene diffuses from the anaerobic pockets into the surrounding soil and inhibits the activities of the humus-consuming aerobic bacteria, harmful root fungi, and nematodes, roundworms that feed on plant roots. Sooner or later oxygen filters back into the anaerobic pockets and the cycle is joined. This balanced ethylene cycle allows organic matter and nutrients to be recycled slowly within the soil and controls root diseases. When soil is aerated by plowing, however, the cycle is broken, aerobic bacteria increase greatly, organic material is more quickly broken down, more nitrogen escapes into the atmosphere as a gas, and root disease proliferates. However, this problem is more characteristic of modern-day cultivation than of the crude methods used in ancient times.

If your tools are crude and your experience limited, farming is easiest in level, fertile, easily cleared soil with a dependable source of water and a long growing season. The subtropical river systems of the Middle and Far East satisfied these criteria, and so these environments spawned the civilizations that have since spread to the far ends of the earth. River-based civilizations in arid zones involve two types of irrigation: basin irrigation, the natural annual flooding of a river; and channel irrigation, the distribution of flood water over the land by manmade canals.

Egypt is an example of the first type, and Mesopotamia of the second. Both are worth a detailed look because one has continued to be highly productive almost to the present, while the other fell to pieces well over a thousand years ago.

EGYPT

The Nile River rises in the nutrient-rich volcanic highlands of Uganda and Ethiopia (Figure 3.5). In the late summer heavy rains falling in these highlands dissolved nutrients and carried them into the Nile. As the flood waters passed through the swamps of the lower Sudan, organic material was added to the nutrients and silt. By the time the river entered Egypt it overflowed its banks and saturated the dry floodplain soil. When the flood passed and the water drained away, a thin layer of silt and organic material was left behind. While the earth was still damp, crops were planted and harvested before the soil finally dried out again. Since the headwaters were heavily forested and underpopulated until very recently, the level of silt and organic matter remained relatively constant—high enough to replace naturally the nutrients removed in cropping, low enough so that siltation was not a severe problem. This extraordinary set of circumstances continued until 1902, when the first Aswan dam was closed and the cycle broken.

When a basin-irrigated valley like that of the Nile is intensively cultivated there is little space for grazing, so herding of livestock is confined to the hinterland. Little wealth accumulates among the nomadic herders while the settled valley farmers prosper, and a classic have/have-not tension develops between the valley culture and the herding-hunting culture. Such a conflict is the basis of the Bible story of Cain and Abel. At some point, political weakness in the valley or the pressure of overpopulation and famine among the herders leads to overthrow of the valley culture and the former herders become the ruling class. They soon dissipate their energy, the valley culture returns, flowers, decays, and falls once again. Though cultures bloom and fade, civilization goes on because the basic productivity of the system remains intact. Because the Nile Valley was basin irrigated, wars, revolutions, and anarchy had relatively little effect—the river flooded every year, and the soil was renewed.

Fig. 3.5 Because the headwaters of the Nile lie in the highlands of Uganda and Ethiopia, the annual floods used to carry dissolved nutrients and rich silt into the lower Nile Valley. These materials now accumulate on the bottom of Lake Nasser.

MESOPOTAMIA

The situation was quite different in Mesopotamia. The Tigris and Euphrates Rivers originate in the Armenian highlands of present-day Turkey (Figure 3.6). The Armenian highlands were less heavily vegetated and more heavily populated than the Nile headwaters when the valley was first settled. Consequently, the silt load of the Tigris-Euphrates

49

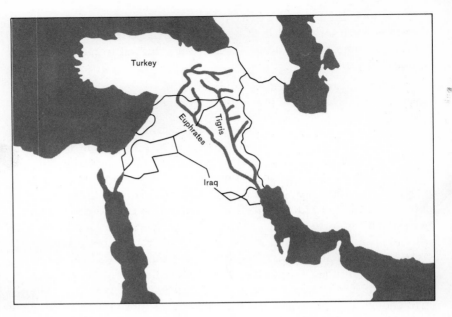

Fig. 3.6 Since the head-waters of the Tigris-Eu-phrates system were de-forested and eroded over a thousand years ago, the silt load of the rivers came to destroy the irrigated lands of Mesopotamia (now Iraq).

system was initially higher than that of the Nile and increased in proportion to the amount of deforestation and grazing-induced erosion in the uplands. This led to the elevation of the Euphrates above the level of the plains. To prevent the river from breaking through its high banks and flooding the land at the wrong time, permanent canals were necessary. They often leaked and the water table rose in the soil, carrying salts that were left on the surface as the water evaporated. This salinization process began about 750 A.D. Then the increasing load of silt had to be dug out of the canals, eventually raising levees along the banks and increasing the elevation of the canals. Periodic invasions from outside the system were more difficult to assimilate because in the chaos of warfare the canals were neglected. The accumulation of silt in many places required enormous amounts of labor to repair when the war was over. Throughout the first couple of thousand years of intensive irrigation in Mesopotamia the effort was made to maintain the canals. But rapidly increasing rates of erosion in the headwater region finally generated so much silt that irrigated districts began to be abandoned after each disruption and productivity gradually declined. The final blow was the sacking of Baghdad in 1258 A.D. At its height, around 750 A.D., Mesopotamia supported 30 million people. Today the population of Iraq, the present incarnation of the Mesopotamian civilization, is around 5 million, and the nation's productivity is based on oil rather than the fertility of its soil.

Although the rainfall in the eastern Mediterranean countries of Syria, Lebanon, and Israel has been seasonal throughout historic time, for thousands of years it was enough to sustain productive agriculture. Winter rains falling on wooded mountains percolated into the soil and supported year-round streams. In the lower areas, terraces retained and stored the seasonal rains in deep soil. But demands for timber deforested the highlands, heavy grazing exposed the soil, and the winter rains washed it away. Streams became clogged with erosional debris; they flooded in the winter and dried up in the summer, making irrigation impossible. Terraces were breached or neglected, particularly after the invasion of the Turks around 1200 A.D., and the soil lost. Today most of this area is a vast desert that supports few people—the highlands stark and stony, the lowlands bone dry most of the year. The only signs of previous productivity are the ruins of dams in the wadis or erosion gullies and the remains of terraces on the rocky slopes. Much the same pattern is seen throughout the Mediterranean world.

GREECE

A surprising amount of land in Greece originally supported thin, open forests with a good growth of grass on the mountain slopes and shrubs and grass on the plains. Homer, writing around 900 B.C., mentioned wooded Samothrace and the tall pines and oaks of Sicily. Five hundred years later, Plato remarked in the *Critias* that

> The parts, therefore, that are left at present are but as small islands, if compared with those that existed at that time; and may be said to resemble the bones of a diseased body; such of the earth as was soft and fat being washed away, and a thin body of the country alone remaining. But at that time the land, being unmingled, contained mountains and lofty hills; and the plains, which are now denominated Phellei, were then full of fat earth; and the mountains abounded with woods, of which there are evident tokens even at present. For there are mountains which now only afford nutriment for bees, but formerly, and at no very distant period, the largest trees were cut down from those mountains, as being adapted for buildings; and of these edifices, the coverings still remain. There were likewise many other lofty domestic trees; and most fertile pastures for cattle. This region, too, every year enjoyed prolific rain, which did not then, as now, run from naked earth into the sea, but, being collected in great abundance from lofty places, and preserved for use in certain cavities of the earth, diffused copious streams of fountains and rivers to every part of

51

Fig. 3.7 (a) Normally multichannel or braided rivers are found in the Artcic where large quantities of silt are released from melting snow fields or glaciers. This stream, the River Peneios in Greece has a braided channel from centuries of severe soil erosion in its watershed. (J. Donald Hughes) (b) Mt. Athos is one of the few places in Greece where some semblance of the original woodland still blankets the mountain slopes. The area belongs to a monastery which for 2000 years has held to a vow of chastity so strict that even female animals are forbidden. Without the presence of growing flocks of sheep and goats, grazing has been light, allowing the forest to survive. (J. Donald Hughes)

the country; the truth of which is confirmed by certain sacred remains which are still to be seen in the ancient fountains.[1]

What happened? Incessant grazing by growing herds of sheep and goats finished off the forests by destroying the seedlings that would have replaced old trees. As the older trees died out, a parklike forest developed with widely spaced trees and grass (the origin, perhaps, of the western concept of the park). Finally no trees remained at all. As grazing pressure increased, even the grass disappeared. Without trees or grass to keep the soil in place on steep slopes, extensive erosion occurred. Today much of the soil that once covered the mountain slopes, enabling trees and grass to grow, lies in deep layers on the plains or in the heavily silted rivers and their deltas (Figure 3.7). Many of the seaports of the ancient Mediterranean world are now miles from the sea because of this greatly accelerated silting process, which converted fertile coastal plains into marshes (malaria was first reported in Greece in 400 B.C.). The steep mountain slopes are stripped to bedrock in many parts of Turkey, Greece, Yugoslavia, Italy, Spain, and North Africa. Although the lower slopes are often densely covered with a growth of evergreen shrubs, called chaparral, garrigue, or maquis, this vegetation is of little economic value compared with the grass and forest that have been lost.

FROM FOREST TO FIELD IN EUROPE

The forests of central Europe were far more resilient than the Mediterranean forests. With more plentiful rainfall distributed evenly over the year, central Europe was covered with a luxuriant forest of beech and oak, so dense and forbidding that permanent settlement was delayed until farmers developed techniques to clear trees and plant crops. This was apparently done by chopping down or girdling trees, burning the brush, and then planting grain in the ashes—a practice that produced a good crop. As the forest began to grow back, stock could be pastured on the grasses and weeds that persisted under the thickening cover of trees and shrubs. Then the farmers moved on and the forest returned.

These intermittent agricultural disturbances, while relatively minor, did create conditions that stimulated the evolution of weeds. Plants found new environments in the campsites adjacent to the clearings. Hard-packed soil eliminated competition from plants indigenous to the forest, while trash heaps, enriched with organic remains, gave those plants able to tolerate the bright sun an excellent place to grow and reproduce. To this day most garden plants and weeds depend on us to provide direct

[1] Plato, 1944. *Critias*. Trans. Thomas Taylor. Bollingen Series III, Pantheon Books, New York, p. 235–236.

sunlight for their best growth, and quickly disappear when we allow the regrowth of forest trees or shrubs, which shade them. Moreover, we have encouraged the development of weed species by intentionally moving plants or seeds from one place to another, thus bringing together plants from widely separated areas as crop seed contaminants, and allowing them to hybridize and evolve into weeds. Then, by regular agricultural practices, the life cycles of weeds became closely synchronized with that of crop plants, assuring the contamination of our crops with certain weed seeds.

Clearing the forest affected agriculture in still another way. When the forest vegetation and its animal population were disturbed or reduced, insects, such as the Colorado potato beetle, that lived on natural vegetation transferred their attention to crops. Also, some of the parasites of the vanishing animals—for instance, the malaria-carrying mosquito—were able to make the transference to humans. As farming replaced hunting as the principal means of getting food, human populations grew much larger and more stable, creating centers for maintaining and spreading parasites and disease. Indeed, the larger the population of a village, town, or city, the greater became the danger of epidemic or plague. Therefore, many diseases, pests, and weeds date only from the beginning of agriculture, which allowed permanent settlements.

ROME

Forest clearance in Europe reached an early peak during the Pax Romana, (or Pox Romana as the barbarians probably regarded the period). The Romans were pragmatic, highly organized, and superb technicians; they dominated much of the known world, leaving an imprint we can see today in buildings, aqueducts (Figure 3.8), roads, and the division of arable land into equal units of 100. This pattern is still visible from the air; long abandoned fields appear as clearly as do the mounds constructed by Indians in the Ohio Valley. As the productivity of agriculture began to decline in Italy for many complicated reasons, including those that ultimately devastated the Near East, North Africa became Rome's major food supplier. The amazing productivity of this region, based less on a favorable climate than on careful use of what water existed, lasted well after the fall of Rome. Not until marauding bands of Berbers with no interest in farming swept in from the south did North Africa degenerate into desert.

After the Roman Empire fell to pieces and during the period of civil and religious wars, plagues, and other misfortunes which followed, the forest once again advanced over Western Europe, bringing about what was literally a "dark age." With the Renaissance and the rise of nation-states, clearing for farmland was resumed and the great European forest

Fig. 3.8 The Pont-du-Gard was constructed by Roman engineers to bring water to what is now the city of Nîmes, France. (French Government Tourist Office)

was again reduced to isolated patches. Because of the tradition of long-term ownership of land by one family, often for hundreds of years, the farmland was generally well cared for and today remains reasonably fertile and productive.

NORTH AMERICA

The European forests made this transition from forest to field over a period of at least a thousand years, but the North American deciduous forest fell in a far shorter time. To describe how dense and extensive this forest once was, it has been suggested that in 1620 a squirrel with an inclination for travel could have journeyed tree to tree from the Hudson to the Mississippi without once touching ground. Forgotten in the romance of this claim are the woodland Indians, who, unlike the buffalo hunters of the plains, burned clearings in the forest and raised pumpkins, squash, and corn. Indeed, the crops grown in those Indian clearings kept the Pilgrims alive that first winter in Massachusetts. Soon, however, the new colonists were clearing their own fields, and by 1820 much of New England was crop or pasture land. It took but a short time to discover that upland New England farms often produced more stones than pumpkins, and so farmers began moving west to New York State, then to Ohio, Indiana, and Illinois, abandoning the poor farmlands back East to the forest that covers much of New England today. Over two thirds of Connecticut —a very small state, approximately 50 to 100 miles, with a population of

Fig. 3.9 At one time this stone wall separated fields or pastures in the rolling countryside of Westchester County, New York.

2.5 million—is covered by forest, much of it second or third growth. Worthless from a forester's point of view, this suburban forest is of incalculable value as an aesthetic and recreational resource. Some idea of the extent of former clearance can be gained from the number of stone walls running through forests over a hundred years old (Figure 3.9). Hardly a woodlot in New England lacks its crumbling stone wall covered with poison ivy and inhabited by blacksnakes, skunks, and chipmunks.

Abandonment of poor or worn-out soil became a common pattern in the settlement of North America, especially in the South, as the boyhood wanderings of Abraham Lincoln attest. But today people no longer move from poor farms to better farms; they usually move from the farm, poor or rich, to the city. Hence, a second wave of land abandonment is now returning land that should never have been farmed back to forest.

THE MOUNTAIN ENVIRONMENT

Unfortunately, the fragile mountain ecosystems that were so battered in the Mediterranean region are under siege today in many of the underdeveloped countries of the Third World. We have not learned from two thousand years of history, for the same cycle recurs inexorably. But these mountain systems are our last.

Highlands occupy about 25 percent of the earth's surface and harbor about one tenth of its population. But over 1.6 billion people live in low-lands adjacent to and directly influenced by such highlands as the Himalayas, the Ethiopian plateau, and the Andes.

NEPAL

The Himalayas, which rise sharply from the plains of northern India, form the headwaters of the great rivers of Pakistan, India, and Bangladesh, the Indus, Ganges, and Brahmaputra (Figure 3.10). Much of the escarpment is controlled by three small states, Bhutan, Sikkim, and Nepal. The largest of these states, Nepal, has a population of 12 million and a rather traditional agrarian technology whose productivity cannot keep pace with population growth. Consequently farmers are being squeezed into farming steeper slopes. Erosion makes these slopes unstable; they often slide, burying villages and covering the farmland below with debris. Nearly 38 percent of the populous eastern hills consists of abandoned fields.

Once cattle provided manure to maintain the fertility of these fields. But as more marginal grazing land was farmed, the number of cattle decreased. Concurrently, firewood has become increasingly scarce and manure is more needed as a fuel than as a fertilizer. This lack further lowers the productivity of the fields and another circle is formed.

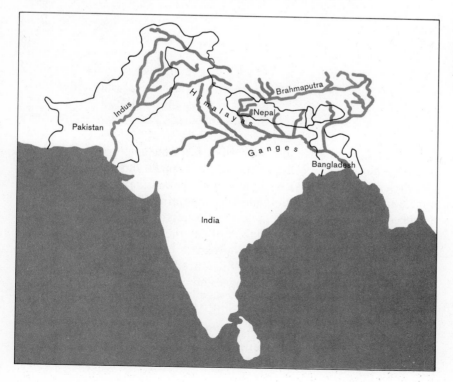

Fig. 3.10 The Indian sub-continent is drained by the Indus, Ganges, and Brahmaputra Rivers, which rise in the Himalayas.

ETHIOPIA

Much the same cycle has occurred in Ethiopia (Figure 3.11), except that Ethiopia is the third largest country in Africa, with a population of 28 million. The northern provinces of Tegre and Eritrea, which were settled first, suffered most from the degradation cycle; today bedrock is everywhere apparent, streams are either dry or in flood, and productivity is low. Addis Ababa, founded in 1883, is in the middle of the cycle. Charcoal gathering has destroyed forests for 100 miles around, although some planting of exotics such as *Eucalyptus* had helped check erosion. The Gamu highlands to the south are just beginning the cycle. As recently as

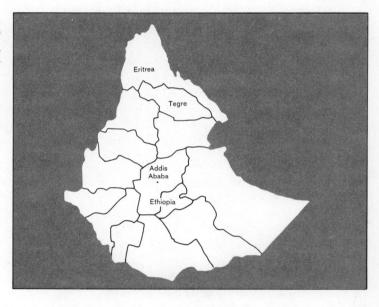

Fig. 3.11 Ethiopia, much of which remained heavily forested and undeveloped until a few decades ago, is undergoing the classic cycle of population growth, land clearance, overgrazing, erosion, and migration to the cities that has characterized virtually every culture associated with forested mountains. The provinces of Eritrea and Tegre have suffered the most from this cycle.

1968 the land was relatively well cared for. Steeper slopes were grazed; terraces stabilized the hillsides that were cropped; drainage channels on the slopes reduced erosion to manageable rates; the fields were manured, and crop rotation and fallowing were carefully practiced. All in all it looked as though a fairly stable and productive system could continue indefinitely. And so it could have but for the inevitable population increase. To provide food, grazing land had to be plowed, leading to fewer cattle, less manure, lower crop yields, a need for more cropland, further plowing of grazing land—the cycle goes on and on, always winding down.

THE ANDES

The pattern in the South American Cordillera is perhaps more like the Middle Eastern examples than the situation in the Himalayas and Ethiopia. For Andean valleys have supported water-based civilizations for almost a thousand years, in the latter phases under the domination of the Inca Empire. At the time of the Spanish conquest in 1532, the empire controlled 15 million people between present-day Colombia and Chile. Within a few years depopulation caused by disease and forced labor had reduced the native population to about 4 million. Land the Incas had farmed intensively passed into large ranches and estates on which the surviving Incas worked as serfs. The intricate irrigation facilities—canals, tunnels, and terraces—as well as the expertise and conservation ethic that held it all together fell apart. Today, population is booming in the Andean states, with 26 million in Colombia and 15 million in Peru alone. The highlands can no longer absorb the population growth, and in desperation the Andean governments are attempting to resettle highlanders in the upper Amazon Basin, which these countries share with Brazil. But most of the immigrants are ill prepared physiologically or technologically for the totally different environment of Amazonia. The land cannot be handled like the Andean highlands or dry coastal valleys. All too often, after a year or two of frustration cleared lands in the Amazon Basin are abandoned. It is not enough merely to have space for excess population, although many developing countries lack even this. The problem calls for very careful planning including intensive training of the immigrants, interim funding or credits to carry them until the land can support them, and innovative use of the unique Amazon environment itself. Otherwise the developed world's sugar-coated remedy—increased production through modern technology, pest control, and fertilizers—will only make more people the victims of the ultimate disaster.

But for all these highland areas the long-term solutions are broad, basic, and political rather than environmental. Population must be stabilized as humanely as possible while a viable environment still exists. The alternative is starvation, which will also control population but will leave the survivors with a ruined environment that may be beyond rehabilitation.

THE FOREST ENVIRONMENT

We have seen several depressing examples of the effects of deforestation or forest manipulation on the land. However these were basically gross effects, involving various aspects of hydrology—erosion, siltation, drought, and water supply. More subtle interactions exist between forests and the land, and we are also capable of damaging interference with these. Gases are by no means the only materials recycled in forest ecosystems. The roots of many hardwoods readily absorb minerals from deep in the soil. Some species are selective, absorbing greater quantities of certain mineral ions than others. Dogwood, for example, selectively absorbs calcium, much of which goes into the developing dogwood leaves in the spring. When the leaves fall at the end of the summer, calcium is added to the nutrient pool held by the clay-humus particles, making it available to plants with shallower root systems. Dogwood thus acts as a pump, bringing calcium from deep in the soil to the surface.

When the leaves of mineral-rich deciduous plants decay after their fall, they decompose and release minerals to the clay-humus particles, resulting in a rich soil with a pH around 7. Let us suppose that becuse white pine is considered to be more valuable than most hardwoods, we decide to cut down a grove of hardwoods and plant pine. Pine roots are less efficient than hardwood roots at absorbing minerals, so pine needles have a lower mineral content. In a few years the supply of rich hardwood leaves will be replaced with pine needles. More minerals will be lost from the clay-humus particles than will be replaced from the decaying pine needles. As a result, the fertility will decline, the hydrogen ions will accumulate, and the soil will become acidic; that is, the pH will drop. The fall of both fertility and pH will be accelerated by the resin content of the pine needles, since resin forms organic acids in the soil which lower pH and retard decomposition, further decreasing the availability of minerals. Thus, our manipulation of vegetation affects the nature of the soil.

MINERAL CYCLING IN TROPICAL FORESTS

In a temperate forest, most of the minerals made available by decomposition of organic litter or disintegration of the parent rock are quickly absorbed by plant roots and incorporated into the vegetation. If you were to stand in an oak-hickory forest in midsummer you would find several inches of slowly rotting leaves covering the rich topsoil, itself black with incorporated humus. Conversely, a tropical rain forest has such a continuing high rate of organic litter decomposition that no mineral pool has time to accumulate. Directly beneath the most recently fallen debris is a heavy, clay-containing, mineral soil. As a result of this tie-up of all available minerals in the standing vegetation, the cycling of minerals is rapid and direct. As soon as a leaf falls, it is decomposed and its minerals are absorbed by plant roots and channeled into the growth of another leaf. So tight is this cycling process that those few ions not absorbed by plant roots but leached through the soil into the water table, and then out of the system, are replaced by ions picked up by the tree roots from the slowly disintegrating bedrock below or from rainwater.

When a tropical forest is cut, minerals are suddenly released faster than crop plants or the remaining trees can use them. They leach out of the system and fertility drops sharply. If the disturbance covers only a few acres, weeds and short-lived successional species quickly invade the area, shield the soil, and begin to restore the balanced mineral cycle. But when very large areas are cleared, this kind of recovery may be impossible, for when the heavily leached sesquioxides are exposed to high temperatures, they bake into pavement-hard laterite. Once formed, laterite is almost impossible to break up, and areas that once supported lush forest quickly become scrubland at best.

Ignorance of this aspect of· forest ecology has had disastrous consequences in some tropical forests. A few years ago a large tract of rain forest in the Amazon Basin was cleared and cultivated. In five years the fields were virtually paved with hard-packed laterite. The ancient Mayan and Khmer civilizations of Mexico and Cambodia probably fell into decay in part because of the destruction of their soil by laterite formation following rain forest clearance.

A fascinating experiment set up by F. H. Bormann and G. E. Likens on a series of watersheds in a New Hampshire forest carefully monitored the minerals being added to the systems by rain and snow and those being removed via stream flow. This allowed a balance sheet to be drawn up. After a few years of undisturbed operation one watershed was logged with as little disturbance as possible. The trees were cut and delimbed but left on the forest floor, and a herbicide was used to prevent sprouts and weeds from growing. After two years the nitrate ions increased dramatically from 0.9 to 53 ppm. An unexpected result of this experiment was that the overfertilization of a sparkling brook produced a dense growth of algae (see Chapter 16).

Normally nitrate is highest in winter when plants are dormant, lowest in summer when plants are actively growing and using nitrate. As we see in the experiment just described, clear cutting, or felling all the trees in a given area, increases runoff by as much as 40 percent over the year (418 percent in normally low-water months when the vegetation loses much water from its surface by transpiration). Increased runoff increases the rate of leaching, but the reduced root absorption decreases the removal of minerals from the material leached out, and results in the loss of nitrate from the system. If watersheds are to be properly managed for high-quality water, logging must be recognized as a potential source of excess minerals as well as of silt from erosion; if watersheds are managed for a sustained yield of timber, then the loss of nutrients inherent in clear cutting must be considered. Obviously we need to know more about the impact of logging on the forest environment.

TROPICAL FORESTRY

Once the great hardwood forests of Europe and North America were gone, attention began to turn to the last source of hardwood, the tropical forests of southeast Asia, central Africa, and the Amazon Basin. None of these tropical forests were pristine wildernesses, of course. All had experienced shifting slash and burn cultivation: a small group or tribe of people cuts a few acres of forest, the fallen trees are burned and crops planted. The fertilizing effect of the ashes assures a good crop for a year or two. But ashes quickly leach away and the aggressive tropical weeds become difficult to control. The croppers then move on to another patch of forest and repeat the pattern. In 75 to 100 years the abandoned forest returns to self-reproducing rain forest via some type of secondary succession. If the forest is large enough and the human population small enough, most of the forest remains intact as a mature, stable ecosystem. But as the population increases, the fallow period is gradually reduced so that more and more successional vegetation rather than mature forest is found and the yield of the system declines. This is beginning to happen in the more isolated tracts of rain forest. However, a more important force is the expanding international market for tropical hardwoods. Japan has obtained cutting rights to 1.5 million acres in Borneo alone, and American companies are joining the movement with large concessions in the Philippines and Malaysia.

But timber exploitation in a tropical rain forest is a very different enterprise than in a temperate forest. A typical temperate zone hardwood forest may have only half a dozen exploitable species to contend with, and these are usually in stands or at least adjacent; thus selecting and removing trees is relatively convenient. In a tropical forest, however, species diversity is far higher—there may be a hundred species of trees, but only ten widely spaced individuals per acre may have commercial value. In addition the trees often require different sawing and drying techniques if their value is to be realized. Because of lianas and the branches of adjoining trees, 75 percent of the forest on an acre may have to be cut to get those ten trees out. Needless to say, the waste is tremendous. The concessionaire operates with few restrictions. The developing countries in which most of the tracts are located desperately need the foreign exchange and employment that the cutting of these forest will generate even though after they are gone in thirty years or so, nothing may be left.

If cutting is done in relatively small blocks, rainfall is adequate, and agriculture does not follow, regeneration of the forest is possible. But it is more likely that agriculture *will* follow, taking advantage of the openings in the forest. Or some form of exotic plantation—conifer, rubber, or oil palm—is established. Or perhaps the area is seeded to tropical grasses with the hope of establishing a cattle industry. Or cogon grass may invade and be exceptionally difficult to eliminate. This has already happened on 18 percent of the forest land cleared in the Philippines and certainly is an important factor in war ravaged Vietnam. At present only the more accessible lowland forests are being exploited, but as these are used up exploitation will move up the slopes in a familiar pattern of impact on the landscape.

The problem boils down to this: if we harvest the forest we remove the nutrients with it and make other productive uses of the land difficult or wasteful of energy; if we don't harvest the forest the productivity goes unused, which an underdeveloped country feels it cannot afford. The answer so far seems to be short term profit now, worry later, but there are other choices.

1. Strict control over cutting practices and rates to encourage regeneration of the forest for a sustained yield on the best sites;
2. More highly developed and encouraged salvage of slash and waste such as sawdust and fiberboard products or generation of sugar/methanol from waste cellulose (see Chapter 19);
3. Development of international markets for byproducts from species not of value as saw timber. (Considering what George Washington Carver did with the peanut there must be something of value in the biochemistry of a couple of hundred species!)

Given today's technology, there is no reason to repeat the incredibly exploitative and wasteful destruction of the white pine forests of New England and the Great Lakes states just a hundred years ago. If detailed planning takes time, so much the better. In their eagerness to make money from their forests, underdeveloped countries are practically giving the timber away. In ten years the world lumber/paper industry will be so desperate for wood that it will do anything to get it, perhaps even follow difficult sustained-yield–multi-use practices. At this point the host country will make a much better profit than at present. The spectacle of the oil-producing countries forming a cartel to control the international price of oil in the early 1970s suggests other ways to get a fair shake from multinational corporations.

STRIP MINING

All the general environmental manipulations we have discussed—farming, grazing, and logging—are associated with erosion not because they cause erosion but because the manipulations are too careless or too extreme for sensitive ecosystems. One basic manipulation is by nature intimately involved with erosional cycles—strip mining. Coal is the usual object, especially with today's spiraling demand for energy (see Chapter 11). The coal seams often lie below layers of soil and rock, the overburden, which must be removed. Traditionally in the United States, the overburden was stripped off to expose the coal and then the land was abandoned. The result was desolation: steep piles of discarded earth alternated with the trenches from which the coal had been removed. Because minerals leached from the piles of overburden often turned the soil acidic, very few plants could grow, and the area became a wasteland.

Today most eastern states have strict laws requiring backfilling of the trenches, recontouring of the ground surface to some semblance of its original state, and the planting of trees. Red pine or hybrid poplars can usually survive and even do well if the acidity of the soil is not too great. Such reclaimed areas, called spoil banks, may be used for recreation, particularly when they have collected water to form ponds for swimming or boating. Two problem areas remain in the East, however: those areas strip-mined before reclamation laws came into effect, and certain parts of Kentucky where coal seams occur in horizontal strata near the ridge tops. When roads are built to mine these veins or mountain tops are removed to expose them, the refuse is dumped down the sides of the mountain to collect in the valleys. When wet, these unstable slopes constantly slip and cannot be planted with vegetation. Once the coal is gone, mountainsides, entire valleys, and streams are so disrupted that any economic or recreational use is impossible for many years (Figure 3.12).

The problem in Kentucky continues to intensify, in part for economic reasons. Strip mining is, without question, profitable—return on investment can exceed 100 percent in some instances. Because of the speed of strip mining, significantly lower labor costs ($.50 per ton versus $2.75 per

Fig. 3.12 Contour strip mining for coal in West Virginia has destroyed the natural environment of the area. The ridge tops have been denuded and tailings slide into the river valleys below. (USDA)

ton for shaft-mined coal), and close to 100 percent recovery (only 50 percent in shaft mines where columns of coal must be left to support the shaft ceiling), stripped coal undersells mined coal by about $1.00 per ton. Small wonder that the proportion of coal obtained by stripping has almost doubled since 1973. Fully 75 percent of the strip-mined coal produced in 1970 was burned to produce 34 percent of the electricity generated by steam plants. But despite much concern about an energy crisis in this country, a fair amount of stripped coal is exported to Japan and the coal-hungry nations in Europe.

Because of the rising demand for cheap coal, especially if it is low in sulfur, the huge reserves of low-sslfur coal in the western states are just beginning to be stripped. Several enormous power plants are in operation or under construction in the Four Corners area of the Southwest where Arizona, New Mexico, Utah, and Colorado meet. Plans are under consideration for another strip mine—power plant complex in eastern Montana. The aridity of the western coal lands makes water important in their exploitation and rehabilitation. If the rainfall is over 10 inches per year, which applies to about 60 percent of the coal lands, the potential for rehabilitation is high if the best management available is used. However, it is unlikely that areas with less than 10 inches of rain per year can be revegetated even with a continuing energy input. The least restorable lands are in the Four Corners area; here the choice seems to be either not to develop or to settle for total devastation wherever coal is removed. Restoration of stripped landscapes is unlikely anywhere (see Chapter 21); a more achievable goal is rehabilitation—returning mined land to a stable ecological state that relates to the aesthetic values of the surrounding region.

In addition to disturbing the aesthetics and productivity of the surface environment, strip mining in the West would destroy surface drainage features, the dry washes that flood after thunderstorms. We can expect that the new channels that would be carved after stripping would add a heavy silt burden to the alluvial valleys that currently produce crops in this arid land. Furthermore, aquifers associated with the coal seams would be destroyed, interfering with the water supply of distant wells and lowering the water table. Death of the already scanty natural vegetation would increase erosion on land not otherwise disturbed by the mining and severely reduce the grazing available in both upland and alluvial valley ecosystems.

Although there is enough water to mine the coal and rehabilitate the landscape, the huge plants planned for converting coal into energy—coal fired generating, gasification, and liquefaction plants (see Chapter 11)—may demand more water than the region can supply or so monopolize the water supply that other forms of development or land use in the region may be repressed.

For economic reasons, it is unlikely that all the 128 million acres of western coal and lignite will be stripped. Of the 1.5 million most suitable acres, probably no more than 200,000 acres (300 square miles) will be stripped for power generation by 1999. If the energy conversion plants are constructed, however, the area mined will be very much larger. In any case, transmission lines might very well occupy more land than that disturbed by mining.

All this interest in strippable coal of course results from its cheapness. But strip-mined coal is cheap only if the true costs of its removal are ignored or borne by the public at large. When the production costs are calculated in terms of water pollution abatement programs, the social welfare of people whose lives have been disrupted, watershed damage through siltation, tax losses from debased real estate, and loss of recreational values, the inflated profits shrink dramatically. The Corps of Engineers has estimated that the cost of restoring the Coal River watershed in West Virginia would exceed $26 million, approximately the value of the coal removed. The cost of environmental rehabilitation is high now and is likely to become higher in the future. But the price is willingly being paid in West Germany. Rich deposits of lignite in the state of North-Rhine Westphalia are being efficiently mined and the land restored to productive use at a cost of $3000–4000 per acre. However the state, through a land planning commission, exercises far more control over the mining process than does any American state at present.

But as land use planning becomes more widely accepted in the United States (see Chapter 19) some of the more blatant abuses may be avoided.

FURTHER READING

Andrews, N., 1973. "Tropical forestry: the timber industry finds a new last stand." *Sierra Club Bull.* **58**(4), pp. 5–9. Brief account of the beginning of the end for tropical hardwoods.

Carter, V. G., and T. Dale, 1974. *Topsoil and civilization.* Rev. ed. University of Oklahoma Press, Norman. Intensive survey of the impact of soil misuse on civilization.

Eckholm, E. P., 1975. "The deterioration of mountain environments." *Science* **189**, pp. 764–770.

Hughes, J. D., 1975. *Ecology in ancient civilizations.* University of New Mexico Press, Albuquerque. Detailed examination of the environmental problems of ancient Greece and Rome.

Marsh, G. P., 1885. *The earth as modified by human action.* Scribner's, New York. The first synoptic recognition of our impact on our environment. Contains a fascinating wealth of detail.

Russell, W. M. S., 1969. *Man, nature, and history.* The Natural History Press, Garden City, N.Y. A broad historical review of past misuse of the land and its consequences.

CHAPTER FOUR

THE TRANSPORT
OF WATER

Water, water, everywhere,
And all the boards did shrink;
Water, water, everywhere,
Nor any drop to drink.

SOONER OR LATER we all find ourselves, like the Ancient Mariner, bemoaning earth's greatest paradox. For thousands of years our quest for water has been restricted only by our technological limitations.

The earth contains, in free form, a prodigious quantity of water—3.59×10^{20} gallons. Yet little is directly available to us. If we were to pile the various types of water found on earth into a column we would start with 2700 meters of sea water, then 50 meters of ice, 15 meters of fresh underground water, 0.4 meters of fresh surface water, and .03 meters of water vapor. Of all the fresh water available, only 71 centimeters per year falls on land. Unfortunately it does not fall uniformly.

Compared with other parts of the world, the United States' share of earth's water is generous, about fifty times our yearly demand of 112 billion gallons. Surely this ought to be an ample margin. But as population increases the supply slowly becomes critical—not because it is used up, but because we tend to use abundant water sources (rivers or lakes) for waste disposal and insist unrealistically on absolutely pure water for *every* human use. The problem is not short supply, but thoughtless contamination of that supply coupled with irrational demands for purity.

METABOLIC NEED

Most terrestrial animals need a limited amount of water; many satisfy this need from their food with a very small supplement of water. Some desert animals, such as the gerbil, fulfill all their water needs from their food supply and are able to exist without an independent supply of water. Our needs are quite modest. Although we are about 65 percent water, we require only a few quarts a day for maintenance, and, since much of this is supplied by food, often a pint or two is adequate. This innate ability to conserve water evolved over a very long time and probably had certain survival value where water was scarce, as in desert areas inhabited by primitive humans.

CULTURAL USE

Culture changed this irrevocably, however, and although today we *need* little more water than our ancestors of 20,000 years ago, we *use* incredible quantities in our daily activities. Flushing a toilet requires three gallons, while a single shower uses thirty gallons. Food preparation, laundering, and house maintenance add further to a total of about 180 gallons per typical residence per day.

PUBLIC WATER SUPPLY

Supplying this quantity of water to huge urban areas has required long-range planning by all communities. For eighty years after its foundation in 1781, Los Angeles managed to supply a small population with water derived from the annual precipitation of about fifteen inches. But a drought in 1862–1864 put an end to the huge cattle ranches that surrounded the town and the inevitable subdivision process began. Further population growth accompanied the arrival of the Southern Pacific Railroad in 1877 and the Santa Fe in 1885. By 1900 it was clear that future growth of the Los Angeles basin would require a large, dependable water source; the most convenient and economically feasible was the Owens Valley in the Sierras, 200 miles away. But Owens Valley was already occupied by ranches and small settlements that were naturally unwilling to become ghost towns for the benefit of distant Los Angeles. The ensuing struggle ended with the construction in the 1920s of a 200-mile-long aqueduct which assured Los Angeles' continued growth and the abortion of similar hopes for Owens Valley. The Colorado River was tapped in the 1930s after a long, contentious struggle by the watershed states over water rights to the Colorado's flow. By the 1960s even the combined water resources of the Colorado River and Owens Valley seemed limited, so the water supplies of underpopulated northern California were eyed.

This area is relatively well, although seasonally, watered from three major supplies: the Sacramento Delta, the Eel, and the Klamath Rivers. The first of these has been tapped by the federal Central Valley Project, which supplies 4.7 million acre-feet [1] of irrigation water to 1.5 million acres of land in the Central Valley. Another 4.2 million acre-feet are transferred by the State Water Project to southern California, where about half is pumped up 2000 feet over the Tehachapi Mountains to the cities of the Los Angeles basin, supplementing the area's supplies from the Sierras and the Colorado River. However, the take from the Sacramento Delta pool must be limited if the irrigation needs of the delta itself are to be met and enough Sacramento River water is to flow into San Francisco Bay to keep flushing sediment and pollution into the Pacific. The state (since southern California includes two thirds of the state's population) must then divert water from the last free-flowing streams in California, the Eel and Klamath River systems, to the delta. The result of such manipulation would ruin the rugged wilderness character of northern California and complete the subdivisional destruction of southern California by making air pollution rather than water a limiting factor in growth.

Interbasin transfer of water is most often advocated by two influential groups which have until very recently been the most unaware or uninterested in the environmental implications of their plans. Technologists have for too long been concerned only with the most technologically efficient way to gather water from areas of surplus and deliver it to areas of efficiency. Economists ponder how to make water that flows "wasted" into the sea into a commodity with value (that is, one that can yield dollars). This single-mindedness reached its most logical if grandiose culmination in a continental-wide plan called the North American Water and Power Alliance (NAWAPA), which was prepared by an engineering firm to "utilize the excess water of the northwestern part of the North American continent and distribute it to the water deficient areas of Canada, the United States, and Mexico." Making use of the unusual geographical, geological, climatological, and hydrological features of North America, this plan would take water now being poured into the Arctic Ocean and store it in an interconnected system of reservoirs at high elevation (Figure 4.1). This water could then be redistributed throughout the continent by means of a reservoir-canal-river system, not only producing a network of navigable waterways but generating power as the water flows to the sea. The cost has been estimated at $200 billion and the system would require twenty years to construct.

Such mammoth projects involving interbasin transfer of water are now being scrutinized more closely than in the past, particularly by the western states, which have always assumed that only water limited their growth, and that it must be supplied regardless of cost. But both assumptions—inevitable growth and the role of water in that growth—are finally

---

[1] An acre-foot is one acre flooded to the depth of one foot.

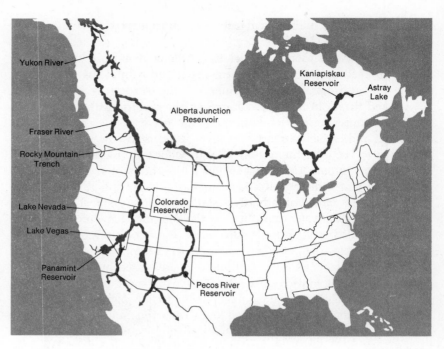

Fig. 4.1 The projected North American Water and Power Alliance (NAWAPA): the implications of technology on the environment are enormous in this scheme; the ecological implications are unknown. (Courtesy Ralph M. Parsons Co.)

being challenged. At least two states, Colorado and Oregon, have withdrawn support from some of the mindless boosterism that can be so destructive of environmental values—a small step, perhaps, but the beginning of an important change in attitude. It suggests that people have begun to recognize that every ecological system has a carrying capacity, and that when this is exceeded, the total economic and environmental costs soar well beyond the immediate return provided by increased growth.

Another factor that must be scrutinized much more closely in the future is cost. Most municipalities condone excessive waste of water: directly, by poorly constructed and maintained mains that leak up to 50 percent of the water they were designed to carry; and indirectly, by unrealistically low charges for water consumed by the public. Federal agencies, the Army Corps of Engineers, the Bureau of Reclamation, and the Soil Conservation Service persist in carrying out water-oriented projects—damming, irrigation, channelization, draining—whose utility is becoming increasingly marginal and which often work at cross purposes. Irrigation in many western states is so heavily subsidized that if the beneficiary of the projects were required to pay the costs, such agricultural development schemes would cease. Arizona uses 90 percent of its water supply for agriculture, which contributes only 10 percent of the state's income.

Yet to support that 10 percent the billion-dollar Central Arizona Project has been ballyhooed for years.

In view of such expensive struggles for water it is more than a little surprising to realize, as we have seen, that *there is no shortage of water in the United States, nor is there likely to be in the future,* no matter how many people live in the country and make demands on its water supply. Except for irrigation, no major water use consumes more than a fraction of the total water used.

All the water now "in captivity" is to be found in reservoirs, water supply systems, and industrial and municipal waste systems. If all this water were efficiently recycled, the annual increase in demand for new water would be exceedingly small. Loss to the atmosphere through evaporation from soil, rivers, reservoirs, plants, and animals, as well as metabolic demands by population increases, would easily be replaced by annual precipitation.

A DOMESTIC RECYCLING SCHEME

To be sure, a society that completely recycles its water will be a long time in coming. But such a plan is not as visionary as it might seem. At present, all water piped into our homes is grade A drinking water no matter how we use it. It makes little sense to throw away three gallons of grade A water just to dispose of a small volume of wastes in a toilet, or thirty gallons to get rid of a little detergent with its dirt and lint from clothes. A priority system of water use could easily be established, reserving grade A water for drinking, cooking, washing, and bathing. Grade B water reprocessed from grade A uses would be quite adequate for outdoor uses: car washing, lawn watering, filling swimming pools (these would still be cleaner than most public beaches), and flushing toilets.

Grade A water would be supplied from a well or reservoir direct to the faucet. After grade A uses, the waste water would be filtered and stored in a basement tank for grade B uses (Figure 4.2). In a recent pilot experiment, water from filtered laundry and bath use was simply stored in a basement tank and subsequently pumped into toilets for flushing, reducing water consumption by 39 percent in a typical suburban home. Even under prototype conditions, which are far more expensive than mass produced versions, the capital cost was only $500 and the savings in water and sewer rental amounted to $20 a year, which over the lifetime of the house (twenty-five years) would pay for the cost of installation. Such a simple recycling device could cut domestic water consumption by almost 50 percent if widely adopted.

A more comprehensive system could recycle carefully treated and purified sewage effluent into the water supply, drastically curtailing the need

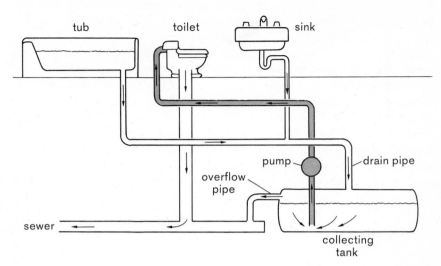

tub   toilet   sink

pump — drain pipe

overflow pipe

sewer

collecting tank

Fig. 4.2 With a few relatively simple and inexpensive modifications in the plumbing of a typical house, a considerable amount of water can be saved. Drainwater from the bathtub and sink flows by gravity to a collecting tank in the basement and then is pumped back upstairs to provide flush water for the toilet. (After Mark Bigatel)

for new water. Doubtless this strikes a repugnant note to most of us, who feel that the water from our tap is or should be as pure as distilled water. On the other hand, communities that draw their water supplies from rivers are already simply recycling the effluent from the town above, particularly during droughts, when many rivers continue to flow only because of the effluent contributed by towns along the banks.

DRINKING OUR EFFLUENT

A classic case of intentional, but desperate, reuse of effluent for water supply took place in Chanute, Kansas in 1956–1957. The drought of 1952–1957 was the most severe in Kansas history. By the fall of 1956 the Neosho River, which was Chanute's water supply, simply stopped flowing. Shutting off the water supply to industry was considered but rejected, because so many people would lose their jobs. Wells were then suggested, but well water was too saline to use. Hauling was too expensive and logistically complex. Finally recycling was adopted as the best solution. As luck would have it, a new sewage disposal plant constructed in 1953 produced an effluent with a lower bacterial count than the Neosho itself. The effluent was pumped into a holding pond for a number of days, then prechlorinated and recycled. The resulting water, carefully monitored by the state board of health, met minimum standards, although it had a musky taste and odor, a pale yellow color, and foamed when agitated. Some people were concerned about the effectiveness of chlorination in eliminating viruses, particularly the polio virus (this was before the various vaccines) and infectious hepatitis. And their concern seemed justified, since 20,000 to 40,000 cases of hepatitis were suspected to have resulted from similarly treated water distributed by the city of New Delhi, India a few years before.

After a few months the drought was broken by rains, the river flowed again, and Chanute returned to its previous water source. A doctors' survey conducted after resumption of normal water supply showed no illnesses that could be related directly to the use of recycled water. Apparently the major problem was the higher levels of various salts. If recycled water is to be used in the future, it will be necessary to have rigorous filtration systems to remove odor, taste, and color, and precipitation processes to remove salts. The virus problem will be more difficult to solve (see Chapter 16).

DESALINIZATION

Many articles have been published about the coming wonders of desalinization, complete with glowing promises about severing our dependence upon natural precipitation, making deserts bloom, changing climate, and other age-old fantasies. Any desalinization process, and there are many, requires energy; but only one process, electrodialysis, removes the salt directly. While desalinization is usually thought of as a sea-edge process, any brackish water is potentially desalinizable; the lower the concentration of salt, the more efficient and less expensive the separation. However, the need is often most critical in dry climates near an ocean, which provides the nearest source of water.

There are many methods of desalinization, some rather complex and all ingenious. The older processes, stills, use heat energy; the more recent processes use electrical energy. With the development of nuclear power plants it has been suggested that the two be combined, producing both electric power and fresh water. Such a plant projected for an artificial island off the coast of southern California was planned to produce 150 million gallons of water a day. But although everyone wanted cheap, abundant water, nobody wanted a nuclear reactor off *his* coast. Then too, nuclear power is having quite enough environmental, technical, and economic problems (see Chapter 15) without taking on the new problems of offshore siting *and* desalinization.

Perhaps one of the most ingenious schemes for augmenting fresh water supplies was suggested by Gerard and Worzel several years ago (Figure 4.3). Many small coastal islands in the tropics have grossly inadequate fresh water supplies because of their tiny catchment area, but by exploiting their exposure to constant prevailing trade winds of high moisture content and their proximity to cold, deep, nutrient-rich water, a variety of benefits could be obtained. Cold sea water pumped through

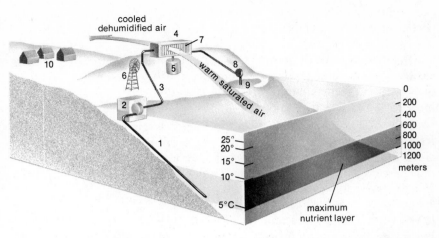

Fig. 4.3 *Proposed water recovery plant. (1) Large-diameter pipe to deep water. (2) Pump. (3) Connecting pipe. (4) Condenser. (5) Freshwater reservoir. (6) Windmill electric generator. (7) Baffles to direct wind. (8) Small turbine to recover water power. (9) Lagoon receiving nutrient-rich water for agriculture. (10) Community enjoying cooled dehumidified air. (Modified from R. D. Gerard and J. L. Worzel. 1967. Science 157. Copyright 1967 by the American Association for the Advancement of Science)*

an insulated pipe to a baffle would provide the cool condensing surface for condensation of moisture from the warm, moist trade wind. The condensed water could be stored in a cistern below, and the cool, dehumidified air could be used to air condition nearby buildings. The sea water coolant, rich in nutrients, could be released into a lagoon whose productivity would be increased, thereby supplementing the protein resources of the island. At least a part of the power needed to pump the water from offshore depths could be provided by a windmill powered by the same trade winds.

The biggest problem with desalinization is the cost. Although costs are being reduced constantly by building larger and more efficient plants, desalinization still compares unfavorably with competing sources of fresh water. Even if desalinization costs were reduced to those comparable with other water sources, there remains the problem of transport from the coast to the inland valleys and deserts. Moving anything against gravity is extremely expensive (all of the existing far-flung water supply systems work mainly *with* gravity flow). It has been said that if the quantity of water needed is large enough, it is cheaper to bring water from Baffin Bay to Baja California than to desalinate and transport sea water to the place where it is needed. The very existence of the California water scheme or the projected NAWAPA lends credence to that statement.

Desalinization will surely come to play a much larger role in the water supplies of major coastal communities in the future, but unless we develop some low-cost energy source to push water uphill, desalinized water will not quickly transform the arid regions of the earth into lush, tropical gardens. Indeed, to do so might have major climatological implications. Perhaps by the time this is feasible we will have developed the ecological insight to predict the consequences of such drastic changes.

THE DAM NATIONS

An intrinsic feature of most water projects, whether irrigation, hydro-electric power, water supply, or interbasin transfer, is the construction of dams. In arid regions large dams may completely alter the basic characteristics of the river they impound. A classic example is the Glen Canyon Dam on the Colorado River in Arizona.

GLEN CANYON DAM

Completed in 1963, this dam (Figure 4.4) changed the Colorado from a free river to one whose flow depends almost entirely upon water released from Lake Powell and run through turbines whenever there is a hot day in Phoenix and air conditioners demand power. Before 1963 the Colorado was a typical southwestern river—roiling and thick with brown sediments in late spring and late summer, when snow melt or thunderstorms sometimes pushed the flow from 3000 to as much as 300,000 cubic feet per second. Water temperature over the year varied as much as 22°C.

Now clear icy water around 10°C enters the river from the bottom of Lake Powell and is hardly warmed by the 450 km journey into Lake

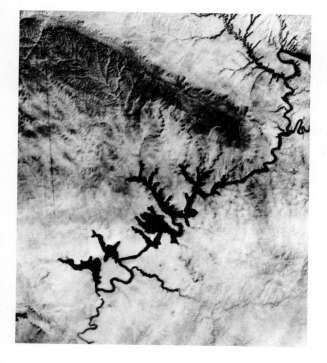

Fig. 4.4 The Glen Canyon Dam can just be seen as a white mark across the river in the lower left-hand corner. The whitish smudge running across the lower third of the photo is either a diffused contrail or a smoke plume from one of the power plants in the general vicinity. (NASA)

75

Mead. Sediments borne by the river have fallen from 1500 to 350 ppm and water levels have been stabilized between 20,000 and 4600 cfs. Because of the year-round cold water, the fish population has been radically altered, profound vegetational changes involving many introduced species are taking place along the banks, and the sandy beaches and bars are still being eroded and reworked as they come into equilibrium with the practically sediment-free water. The Little Colorado and other tributary streams may augment the flow of the Colorado and add some sediments when they are in flood, but the Colorado is a wild river no more.

The major use of the section of the river that passes through Grand Canyon National Park is recreational. Up to the early 1950s no more than two hundred people had followed John Wesley Powell's pioneering exploration of the Colorado in boats or rubber rafts. But since then over 100,000 people have floated down the river. The attraction of rafting over 161 rapids (the river falls almost 645 meters between the Glen Canyon Dam and Lake Mead) has made it necessary to limit the number of people allowed on raft trips to 10,000 per year. Some boatmen fear two results of the river's lower yearly flow and decreased sediment load: eroded beaches, primarily used for overnight camping; and increasingly dangerous rapids as tributary streams dump into a main channel debris which the lower flow cannot carry downstream.

These changes on 450 km of the Colorado have been profound but mainly aesthetic. One stupendous dam project, however, has had some unique effects extending far beyond the dam site or its lake.

ASWAN HIGH DAM

Constructed on the Nile in the United Arab Republic, the Aswan High Dam contains seventeen times the volume of the pyramid of Cheops at Giza and creates behind it Lake Nasser (Figure 4.5), nine km wide, one hundred fifty km long, and seventy-six m deep. One unusual aspect of this project is its effect on the Nile River. Historically, the Nile has flooded every year (see Chapter 3). As the fertile Nile flood water spread out into the Mediterranean, it dramatically increased the productivity of the coastal water from the Nile delta northeastward to Lebanon. This fertilizing effect was measured by a count of the primary producers, tiny algae cells that form the basic unit of the food chain in the sea. Before the Nile reached flood stage, there were 35,000 cells per liter; after flood stage, 2,400,000 cells per liter. One of the major harvesters of this primary food source has been the sardine; over 18,000 tons of sardines per year were caught in the UAR before the Aswan Dam was built.

Since the dam was closed in 1971, the Nile silt has been sedimented out on the bottom of Lake Nasser. Without the annual floods and silt deposition, the Nile valley and delta will have to be fertilized artificially.

Fig. 4.5 Lake Nasser is unusually long and narrow because of the configuration of the Nile floodplain that has been flooded. The Red Sea lies toward the top of the photo with the Arabian Peninsula beyond. (NASA)

Fortunately, the UAR is in a good position to do this: there are abundant deposits of phosphate available, and power from the Aswan Dam is already being used to produce nitrate. However, it would cost over $100 million per year to manufacture enough fertilizer just to replace the nutrients in the silt now lost annually to the bottom of Lake Nasser.

The effect on the sardine industry has been more serious. After closure, the annual catch fell from 18,000 tons to 500 tons, cutting the overall production of Egyptian fisheries by almost 50 percent. However, much of this loss may be recouped by fish harvested from Lake Nasser. But there now seems to be some doubt that the lake will ever fill completely because of the porous rock in the lake basin, which allows water to seep away into underground aquifers. Of course with the river running clear below the dam, the delta of the Nile has ceased to grow. In fact it has begun to erode, and it is feared that the brackish Lakes Idku, Burul-

77

Fig. 4.6   A view of the Nile Delta and the Suez Canal from Gemini 4 shows the Suez Canal running from the Mediterranean (left) to the Red Sea (right). The Great Bitter Lake is the small body of water between them, and the delta lakes Manzala, Burullus, and Idku are labeled A, B, and C respectively. (NASA)

lus, and Manzala (Figure 4.6), which now buffer much of the intensively cultivated delta from the Mediterranean, will become saline extensions of the sea and that cultivation will be adversely affected for several miles inland.

The creation of Lake Nasser has had another far-reaching effect, greatly increasing the breeding sites of the snail that carries a parasitic blood fluke causing schistosomiasis, malaria-carrying mosquitoes, and the black fly that carries trachoma, an eye disease.

The blood fluke enters the body in the free-swimming forms called cercariae (Figure 4.7). These make their way to the blood vessels of the bladder or intestine and mate there. Their eggs leave the body with the urine or feces and hatch into miracidia, which infect water snails. Inside the snail they reproduce asexually; one miracidium may produce as many as 100,000 cercariae. In this way large populations of infested snails may saturate the water with cercariae, which then infect humans, completing the cycle. In 1937 there was a 5 percent incidence of urinary schistosomiasis between Aswan and Cairo. Today 35 percent of the people in this stretch of the river are infected. As aquatic vegetation spreads in Lake Nasser, providing a habitat for the fluke-carrying snails, schistosomiasis can be expected to increase rapidly above the dam as well. The only sure ways to eliminate the infection are to increase sanitation facilities and to improve education; neither of these is widely available to the fellahin of Egypt.

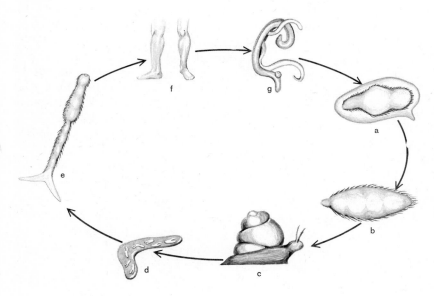

Fig. 4.7 The eggs (a) of the blood fluke Schistosoma masoni are laid in the small veins of the intestinal wall, which rupture and release them into the intestine. Here they mix with feces and are voided into water. The miracidia (b) emerge from the egg and burrow into the soft parts of a snail (c). There they form two generations of sporocysts (d). The second generation of sporocyst produces cercariae (e), which pass from the snail into the water and there come in contact with their mammalian host (f). After entering the body, the cercariae develop into adult male and female worms, which make their way to the intestines where they mate and produce eggs, completing the cycle. The easiest way to break the cycle is to prevent human feces from reaching standing bodies of water. (After E. C. Faust. 1949. Human helminthology. 3rd ed. Lea and Febiger, Philadelphia, figures 32, 34, 35, 37)

THE KARIBA DAM

The Zambesi River between Zambia and Rhodesia was dammed in 1959 to provide hydroelectric power for the copper producing area of Rhodesia. Irrigation and fishing were to be secondary benefits, but irrigation has not yet been realized and the fishery is of limited production. This was to be expected because of the oligotrophic nature of the river at this point—total dissolved solids were only 55 ppm—an unproductive river when dammed becomes an unproductive lake. After flooding there was an encouraging bloom of native fish that resulted from the release of nutrients on the new lake bottom. Once these were exhausted, fish production fell to a point no higher than the productivity of the valley before flooding.

CHANNELING THE STREAMS

The U.S. Army Corps of Engineers, charged with maintaining navigation on major rivers, began tampering with the Mississippi in 1837. Under the direction of one Robert E. Lee, the Engineers built confinement dikes to remove sandbars from St. Louis' harbor. Since then a number of massive works including levees, dams, revetments, and channels have narrowed, deepened, raised, lowered, and otherwise changed the cross-section of the river. Under normal conditions the Mississippi, like any alluvial river, erodes its banks and bottom during floods to make room for some of the flood water. The rest pours over the banks into the floodplain. However, since 1837 the Mississippi has lost one third of its channel volume in the long-term effort to keep it navigable. The result is that today's flood stages are higher than ever before. In general the navigational improvements have tended to make severe floods out of minor ones. In this sense, the 1973 flood between Burlington, Iowa, and Cape Girardeau, Missouri, which produced a 200-year flood level from a 30-year flow rate, was manmade. That is, a flow rate expected once every thirty years produced a flood expected only once every two hundred years.

Channelization of smaller streams did not begin seriously until 1954, when Congress passed Public Law 566 (the Watershed Protection and Flood Prevention Act). Under this law the Soil Conservation Service was charged with stream channelization to aid in the drainage of potentially farmable wetlands and to reduce flood damage. Thus we witness the spectacle of the Department of the Interior trying to save wetlands while the Department of Agriculture tries to reclaim them.

Like the sorcerer's apprentice, a good bureaucracy strives greatly to carry out its tasks until directed not to. Unfortunately, until environmental awareness penetrates to the decision makers, environmental degradation will continue. Some 8000 miles of streams in the United States have been "improved" in the past twenty years and another 13,000 miles of work is planned. Whatever the economic benefits, the environmental liabilities are many: destruction of waterfowl and game habitats, pollution of downstream lakes and reservoirs, increased upstream erosion and downstream flooding, interference with ground water recharge, and encouragement of floodplain development.

A case in point is the Blackwater River in northwestern Missouri near Kansas City (Figure 4.8). In 1910 a portion of the river was dredged, shortening it from 33.5 miles to 18 miles and sharpening the gradient from 8.8 feet per mile to 16.4 feet per mile. The faster moving water has consequently caused both the main stem and its tributaries to greatly increase their cross-sectional area, by 1173 percent for the former and

Fig. 4.8 *The Blackwater River in Missouri is typical of the many streams that have been transformed from productive aquatic systems to mere drainage ditches.*

2000 percent for the latter. Because of this erosion most bridges crossing the river have been either replaced or lengthened, some several times. Beyond the terminus of the dredged section flooding has become more frequent, with floodplain deposits of almost six feet over the last fifty years. In addition, fish production in the dredged segment has been estimated as less than one fifth that of the undredged portion of the Blackwater.

Channelization is not the only problem associated with rivers. In the Atchafalaya Basin of Louisiana a levee system was constructed to protect surrounding areas from flooding by the Mississippi. Unexpectedly, the levees empounded rainwater that normally drained into the river and caused new flooding in parts of the Louisiana parishes of Aroyelles, Evangeline, Rapides, and St. Landry.

Since 1936 the federal government alone has spent $9 billion in flood control projects, not to mention state and local expenditures. In spite of these enormous sums, flood damage has continued to increase to the present $2 billion per year. Clearly, floods are not acts of God but the acts of people building on flood plains.

WATERSHED PROBLEMS

Imagine a narrow rural valley with a stream flowing through it year round. The slopes are covered with trees and perhaps an occasional house built to take advantage of the rustic qualities of the environment. One day a bulldozer appears on the hillside above the valley and intensive development begins. During the construction period many tons of soil wash into the stream, followed by runoff from roofs and paved streets of the completed development. The rainwater no longer seeps into the ground and recharges the water table; instead it pours from storm sewers into the stream. Deprived of its source of recharging, the water table is lowered, requiring deeper and deeper wells for local water supply. The excess water in the stream causes flooding downstream where basements, previously dry, must be periodically drained or water-proofed. During periods of high water, septic tanks are flooded, the stream is polluted, and sewers become necessary to avoid public health problems. Because of previous silting the stream is dredged to handle the recurring flood waters, but this seems to make matters worse. Then the Corps of Engineers is asked to build an expensive dam upstream, which permanently floods much valuable bottom land behind the dam. Wells are running dry now, so a municipal water system must be installed. What is left of the stream alternates between feast and famine, flooding one season, dry the next. Finally it is agreed to confine it to a culvert to avoid future problems. This chain of consequences is not at all unlikely, but is it inevitable? By no means.

If the area including the wooded valley had been served by a planning commission or an ecologist trained to recognize potentially troublesome sites, the whole destructive process might have been avoided. Quite clearly there are some places where houses *should not* be built, or at least built only with extreme care and foreknowledge of the dangers involved. The function of a planning commission is to remove the trial and error approach and to suggest on a rational basis which land is most suitable for development and which land is better left undisturbed (see Chapter 20). The developer sees a swamp as reclaimable land that can be filled in and covered with houses: an environmentally informed planning commission might view that swamp as a sponge capable of absorbing 300,000 gallons of water per acre for every foot of rainfall added to it and wonder where all that water will go if the sponge is destroyed.

FLOODPLAINS

The usual alternative to a floodplain as a sponge is the construction of flood control dams upstream. But such structures are effective only if the storm falls in the fixed catchment basin and the storage capacity of the reservoirs is adequate to contain the runoff.

In June 1972, Hurricane Agnes produced severe flooding on the lower Susquehanna in Pennsylvania, resulting in property damage of more than $3 billion. Since there are twenty-three dams and many miles of dikes north of Harrisburg, many people asked why the flooding was so severe. The reason was the uneven distribution and extraordinary amount of the precipitation involved; as a result the smallest amount of rain fell in the vicinity of the largest dams. To contain another flood with the volume of Agnes in Pennsylvania would take the equivalent of 522 new dams in the Susquehanna River basin, 202 new dams in the Delaware River basin, and 10 new dams in the Allegheny River basin. This would require 129,000 acres of floodplain, much of which is already occupied by towns and cities, for the impoundments, and would cost more than the losses from Agnes.

A rational alternative is to return the floodplains to their natural function—the temporary storage of excess stream flow. This confines the destructive force of the flood to the main channel, gradually releases the excess water to the channel after the flood crest has passed, and deposits rich sediments on the floodplain soils. How can floodplains be returned to their original function? To do this all at once would be economically impossible. But suppose that after each flood, the most damaged roads, houses, and factories were relocated on higher ground rather than irrationally rebuilt on the same spot. In a few decades recurring flood losses could be dramatically reduced and the floodplain used for the recreational benefit of all.

The inherent logic in this approach to floodplain utilization seems finally to have penetrated the bureaucratic consciousness. Prairie du Chien, a small Wisconsin town of 6000 on the east bank of the Mississippi, was troubled by annual spring flooding. The solution proposed by the Corps of Engineers (not the local Sierra Club!) was to relocate 157 buildings out of the floodplain, demolish 40 buildings after their purchase by the federal government, raise 33 homes above the flood level, and floodproof 7 other buildings. The cleared floodplain was to become a greenbelt protected by local and state regulations.

CONNECTING THE WATERS

More than one hundred years ago, the Welland Canal was opened, allowing ships moving from Lake Ontario to Lake Erie to bypass Niagara Falls. Then in 1932 the canal was deepened to thirty-six feet. With this deepening, lampreys began to move from Lake Ontario, where they

Fig. 4.9 The conical structures of the oral disk of the lamprey are rasps which rub a hole in the side of the fish, causing bleeding. The lamprey feeds on the blood and the fish eventually dies. (U.S. Department of Commerce, National Marine Fisheries Service, National Oceanic and Atmospheric Administration)

were part of the natural fauna, into the western Great Lakes, where they had never been before (Figure 4.9). Within a few years the valuable catch of whitefish and trout in the western Great Lakes was sharply reduced, with severe economic repercussions in the fishing towns around the lakes.

The lamprey feeds on the blood of large fish by secreting a chemical to prevent the blood from coagulating. In this fashion the lamprey slowly kills the fish. The lamprey spawns in small streams that empty into the lakes; the larvae live in the streams for a few years, then move back into the lakes to complete their development, feeding on the valuable lake fish.

At first it seemed that the lamprey was here to stay. But in the late 1950s a chemical was found that would selectively kill the lamprey larvae without affecting other organisms. By the immensely laborious and expensive method of treating all tributary streams, some measure of lamprey control has been attained. Without question, it was the deepening of the Welland Canal that allowed the lamprey to enter new territory with such disastrous results. Fuller knowledge of the lamprey's ecological adaptability might have forewarned us of the possible introduction of the lamprey into the western Great Lakes, and precautions could then have been taken to avoid this in the construction of the Welland Canal.

The construction of inland canals or river-to-river waterways has continued, in part because government agencies once in motion tend to stay in motion, and in part because of the time-honored congressional tradition of the pork barrel. Some of the juggernaut's efforts have been prevented: the Florida Barge Canal, the deepening of the Apalachicola and Chattahoochee Rivers to make Atlanta into a seaport, and the Big Ditch Project to connect the Ohio River to Lake Erie. The latest in this series is the linking of the Tennessee and Tombigbee Rivers to connect the Tennessee Valley with Mobile, Alabama—two hundred miles of channel "improvement" with fifty miles of dams, locks, and canals. The cost is presently estimated at $1.5 billion, but this is only a beginning estimate; costs for such big projects usually inflate by one third per year. By 1980, if completed, the waterway will allow barges to haul chemicals, ore, and oil from Mobile to Knoxville and return with coal, steel, grain, and lumber, making Mobile, on the Gulf Coast, one of the South's major cities. When the cost-benefit ration of this project is scrutinized, only about $1.10 is returned for every tax dollar invested. This is another interbasin transfer of water with little consideration for environmental impacts or any negative economic ones. Barges use the waterway free of charge, but the competing rail systems, ailing though they are, must invest heavily to maintain their rights of way.

The two most famous canals, the Suez and Panama, although they join widely different bodies of water, had until recently features that effectively prevented faunal exchange between the two water masses. The Suez Canal connects the Mediterranean Sea with the Red Sea. Before the last glaciation in Europe, the two seas were connected naturally and shared a rich tropical flora and fauna. Then a fall in sea level, through the removal of water to form glacial ice, separated them, and the subsequent chilling of the Mediterranean eliminated many of its tropical species. Today there are many open niches in the Mediterranean, while the Red Sea has most of its biological niches filled. When the canal was dug across the Isthmus of Suez, it intersected a small lake that was highly saline because its bottom was covered with a thick layer of salt. Any organisms passing through the canal had to be able to tolerate a change of salinity from 45 parts per thousand in the Red Sea to 80 to 100 parts per thousand in the Great Bitter Lake section of the canal (see Figure 4.6). Since few organisms could tolerate such a change, this built-in salt barrier prevented more Red Sea organisms from passing into the Mediterranean.

In 1956 the canal was deepened to thirty-six feet; the greater flow so diluted the hypersaline water of the Great Bitter Lake that today the salinity of the entire canal is approximately that of the Red Sea. In the years since dredging, over 100 species of invertebrates have entered the Mediterranean from the Red Sea. Significantly, one of the twenty-four species of fish that have made the transit, the lizard-fish, has become an important element in the fishing industry of Israel, a rather ironic sidelight to Egypt's deepening of the canal.

Because of available niches in the Mediterranean, introduction of new fauna from the Red Sea may very well increase the productivity of the eastern Mediterranean without grossly upsetting the ecological balance. Some native Mediterranean species may be lost, but in this instance the genetic and economic potential of the new species may be worth the risk.

Such is not the case with the Panama Canal. At the time of its construction, the spine of mountains running through the isthmus made the digging of a sea-level canal like the Suez impractical. The center of the Panama Canal is by contrast a freshwater lake; ships passing between the Atlantic and the Pacific ascend and descend by means of locks. This lake makes an effective barrier to the passage of most forms of marine life, but there is a possibility that because of the outmoded size of the Panama Canal locks, a new sea-level canal may be constructed or the present canal may be extensively rebuilt. A sea-level canal seems economically feasible only with the use of nuclear explosives to dig the ditch and expel the debris. When the costs of liability for property damage, relocation of nearby populations, and secondary excavation of rubble slipping back into the canal are added, the total expense may preclude the building of a sea-level canal.

But if, despite the exorbitant cost, the canal is constructed, we must make use of previous experience from the Welland and Suez canals to project what might happen if animals from the Atlantic and Pacific can move freely from ocean to ocean. The oceans are quite different in many respects. The Pacific is colder, water temperature fluctuates more during the year, and the tidal range is greater—almost twenty feet, compared with one and a half feet in the Atlantic.

The two oceans have been separated by Central America for only three to four million years, so the fauna are certainly similar. Yet in this time there has been some divergence. According to Ira Rubinoff, a marine biologist at the Smithsonian Institution, there are several possible results of species mixing in one or the other ocean:

1. If two populations were able to interbreed, the hybrids might eliminate either or both parent forms.
2. If the populations were farther apart genetically, the imperfect hybrids might eliminate the parents, but be incapable of long-term survival themselves.
3. If the populations did not interbreed but occupied similar niches, one might outcompete and replace the other.

Before a sea-level canal is constructed, we should investigate these possibilities in a series of controlled experiments, looking at those species most likely to make the move from one ocean to another. Few would argue that a sea-level canal should not be built simply because a few species of fish might become extinct, but the implications are broader than this. The fisheries and sea life of both coasts of Central America are of great importance to the economy of the region. Until we can predict with some assurance which species will dramatically increase their populations, or, conversely, which will become extinct, we cannot afford still another economically engineered, ecologically blind experiment.

Our economic and material needs will continue to demand the development and completion of projects such as canals, dams, and stream channelization. We can continue to build on a purely economic and technological basis, picking up the ecological pieces as we go along; or we can become emotional and bemoan every lost earthworm or crushed ant, while turning a deaf ear to the crying of a hungry child. The only rational approach is to anticipate the massive technology-oriented development projects of the future and weigh the prospects very carefully. In this way we may preserve some semblance of the natural world. On the basis of what we have learned from past projects, we should have some idea of the potential ecological problems previously unthought of by engineers or economists. In the interval between a project's conception and realization—often several decades—much descriptive and experimental environmental information can be obtained. Mathematical models might be developed to make it possible to predict potential problems years in advance; at the very least, this would give sufficient research and development time to meet these problems.

We need to broaden the current approach to cost analysis, now largely based on what is economically and technologically feasible, to include other values, especially the recognition that projects affect the environment. Our first obligation is to other people, but we cannot ignore the plants, animals, and soil of the world as we scheme and dream, earthmovers and nuclear explosives ready. Our continued existence depends on the continued well-being of *all* plants and animals, not just corn and cows. Our disregard for the other organisms on earth is not just a manifestation of myopia; it is based on our abysmal ignorance of the relationships between plants, animals, and their environments.

FURTHER READING

Balon, E. K., and A. G. Coche (eds.), 1974. "Lake Kariba: a manmade tropical ecosystem in central Africa." *Monogr. Biol.* **24.** Junk, The Hague. A collection of papers monitoring changes in Lake Kariba since the closure of its dam.

Belt, C. B., Jr., 1975. "The 1973 flood and man's constriction of the Mississippi River." *Science* **189,** pp. 681–684. A discussion of the role of river manipulation in flooding.

Dolan, A. H., and A. Gallenson, 1974. "Man's impact on the Colorado River in the Grand Canyon." *American Scientist* **62,** pp. 392–401. The impact of the Glen Canyon Dam on the "free-flowing" Colorado River below.

Seckler, D. (ed.), 1971. *California water: a study in resource management.* University of California Press, Berkeley. A group of papers that examine some of the many interbasin transfer projects in California.

Van der Schalie, H., 1974. "Aswan Dam revisited." *Env.* **16**(9), pp. 18–20, 25–26. A second look at the ramifications of the Aswan High Dam several years after the project was completed.

CHAPTER FIVE

BIOCIDES

IF IT WERE possible to spray a cotton field with some miraculous compound and kill all the boll weevils without harming any other organism in the community, we would have a pesticide, a material capable of selectively killing a pest. Unfortunately, no such compound is known; if the boll weevils are killed, so are many other animal species, both destructive and beneficial—spiders, mites, and occasionally fish, amphibians, birds, and even mammals. So the term pesticide is somewhat general, even misleading; insecticide, while more accurate, gives no hint of potential victims other than insects. The most general term that avoids these overlapping difficulties is biocide. If this has a grim ring to it, like genocide, perhaps it is fitting. For many people still feel that the earth would be better off without insects, mites, ticks, spiders, and all manner of "creepy-crawly" things.

Although odious when overused, biocides *do* serve a purpose and there is no intention here of denying it. We should, however, have some idea of the role these materials play in the systems into which we introduce them; we should have a rational basis for determining at what point biocides become too expensive in economic and environmental terms. Since most of what we know about the environmental effects of biocides has come from thirty years of experience with DDT, many examples will deal with this biocide. Even though it is no longer in common use in this country, DDT produces many environmental effects that are potentially possible with *any* biologically active compound thoughtlessly introduced into the environment.

More than a hundred years ago, in 1874, a German Ph.D. candidate, Othmar Zeidlar, synthesized an organic compound for his dissertation, as generations of students have since done. Young Zeidlar published his work as a short note in a professional journal, took his degree, and dropped from sight.

The compound Zeidlar synthesized was not unusual, even for 1874; a series of substitutions had transformed the original ethane (C_2H_6) into a dichloro-diphenyl-trichloro-ethane (Figure 5.1). So dichlorodiphenyltrichloroethane (DDT) sat on the shelf with a thousand other organic

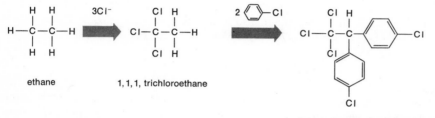

ethane   1, 1, 1, trichloroethane

dichlorodiphenyltrichloroethane

Fig. 5.1 In a series of reactions substituting three atoms of chlorine for three of hydrogen, then two chlorinated rings for two more hydrogens, dichlorodiphenyltrichloroethane (DDT) can be synthesized from the simple compound ethane.

chemicals synthesized over the years until the late 1930s, when Paul Müller, a Swiss entomologist looking at the insect-killing properties of various compounds, found that Zeidlar's material was an extremely effective insect killer. DDT was "discovered" and for his contribution Müller was awarded a Nobel Prize in 1944.

In 1942, some DDT was brought to the United States, where the military quickly appreciated its potential usefulness. As a result of DDT, World War II was the first war in which more men died of battle wounds than of typhus and other communicable diseases spread by insects. After the war, DDT was used most effectively to combat a number of insects that carried thirty diseases, including malaria, yellow fever, and plague; within ten years of its first widespread use, DDT had saved at least 5 million lives. Millions of houses and tens of millions of people were sprayed with DDT in campaigns against fleas, houseflies, and mosquitoes and the diseases these carriers transmit.

Clearly a new age of chemical pest control was underway. DDT was not the first chemical used against insects, of course. Paris green (copper acetoarsenite), first used in 1867 against the potato beetle, holds that distinction. But with DDT we see the first time a totally new synthetic material was introduced into the environment on a large scale.

BIOCIDE SPECTRUM

Spurred by the success of DDT, the chemical industry explored the bio-cide possibilities of other chemicals.

Today there are seven main groups of biocides available to control a broad variety of plants and animals: arsenicals, botanicals, organophos-phates, carbamates, organochlorines, rodenticides, and herbicides. The three most important and dangerous from the point of view of environ-mental contamination are the organophosphates, organochlorines, and herbicides.

ORGANOPHOSPHATES

Among the first organophosphates to be marketed were parathion and malathion, which are still in use although their days are probably num-bered. Their mode of action on terrestrial organisms is quite specific.

Nerve impulses are conducted across the gap between adjoining nerve fibers by a compound called acetylcholine. As soon as the impulse has bridged the gap an enzyme, cholinesterase, destroys the acetylcholine present, preventing further impulse transmission. Organophosphates deactivate the cholinesterase, allowing a stream of impulses to flow uninterrupted along the nervous system, resulting in spastic uncoordina-tion, convulsions, paralysis, and death in short order. While quite toxic, organophosphates are not persistent and have much less effect on aquatic than on terrestrial organisms.

ORGANOCHLORINES

Also called chlorinated hydrocarbons, organochlorines include the best known of all the synthetic poisons: endrin, heptachlor, aldrin, toxaphene, dieldrin, lindane, DDT, chlordane, and methoxychlor. Unfortunately, we do not understand clearly just how the organochlorines work. Apparently the central nervous system is affected, for typical symptoms of acute poisoning are tremors and convulsions. Chronic levels have various effects. In aquatic organisms, which are especially sensitive to this class of com-pounds, the uptake of oxygen through the gills is disrupted and death is associated with suffocation rather than nervous disorder. Another group of chlorinated hydrocarbons closely related to DDT, the polychlorinated biphenyls (PCBs), have recently emerged as an environmental threat (see Chapter 6).

HERBICIDES

Plant killers are not new. Indeed, some arsenicals have been used for 50 years; but shortly after World War II scientists developed a new group of herbicides that involve plant hormones or auxins. Normally auxins are produced by the leaves of a plant; in the proper concentration they keep the leaves attached to the stalk or stem. In the fall, auxin levels normally drop and a layer of large, thin-walled cells forms where the leaf connects to the plant. When these cells rupture, the leaf falls. By applying a compound that lowers the auxin content of a leaf it is possible to defoliate a plant prematurely. This is commonly done before harvesting cotton to avoid plugging the mechanical cotton harvester with leaves.

Conversely, by adding auxin at the right concentration, leaf fall and fruit drop can be inhibited, thereby decreasing loss from preharvest drop of fruit. If excess auxin is applied, however, plants respond by increasing their respiratory activities considerably beyond their ability to produce food, literally growing themselves to death. Strangely, the commonly used herbicides with high auxin activity, 2,4-D, and 2,4,5-T, affect only broad-leaved plants. This made them useful in Vietnam to clear vegetation and thereby prevent ambushes along roadsides and the edges of waterways, infiltration of men and supplies across the demilitarized zone and the Laotian border into South Vietnam, and troop buildups in remote areas. Three major herbicides were used: Agent Orange, a mixture of 2,4-D and 2,4,5-T, which persists for several months; Agent White, a combination of 2,4-D and picloram, which remains active in the soil for as long as several years; and Agent Blue, cacodylic acid, whose major ingredient is sodium dimethyl arsenate, another compound that accumulates in the soil. The first two herbicides were sprayed primarily on forest vegetation, the third primarily on food crops, particularly in the mountains. About 58 percent of the total amount of herbicides used was Orange, 31 percent was White, and 11 percent Blue. Starting in 1962, the herbicide program peaked in 1969; in 1967 it consumed virtually the entire United States production of 2,4-D and 2,4,5-T.

Although an eighth of the total land area of South Vietnam was sprayed, the impact of herbicides on Vietnam's vegetation has been varied. Mangroves, for example, are extremely susceptible to herbicides (Figure 5.2); one spraying causes a complete kill with essentially no evidence of regeneration after many years. As a result, perhaps half of Vietnam's mangrove vegetation, 744 square miles, has been totally destroyed. Other hardwoods, however, are generally more resistant to herbicides. Usually, only 10 percent of the trees die with one spraying and the seedlings and saplings, which are the crucial stage of tree life, are not particularly affected. A second spraying within a year, however, heavily damages these young trees and may kill 50 percent or more of the mature timber. At least 4 percent of the forests of South Vietnam have been sprayed more than once (and another 15 percent once). Some estimates suggest that as much as 5 percent of the mature hardwoods has been destroyed. This wood, worth $500 million, would have supplied South Vietnam with timber for over thirty years.

Fig. 5.2 Mangrove is particularly sensitive to defoliants, often being killed with one spraying. Regeneration is very slow. (Arthur H Westing)

The impact of defoliation goes beyond the simple economic loss of timber. Destruction of the normal vegetal cover can stimulate the growth of cogon grass and bamboo (Figure 5.3), weedy species of little (if any) value but of vigorous growth. Once these are well established, reproduction of trees is impeded, and elimination of these two species is difficult. Consequently the recovery of sprayed forests may be long delayed or even prevented in some places. Recovery of forests may also be delayed by loss of nutrients. Most tropical forest ecosystems contain most of their nutrients in their tissues or biomass rather than in the soil (see Chapter 1). When the forest is destroyed, either by cutting and burning

Fig. 5.3 This rubber plantation in Long Khanh Province, Vietnam, was sprayed with herbicides in 1967. By 1970 cogon grass, a weedy species that is very difficult to control, had invaded and become well established. (Arthur H. Westing)

or by herbicides, the nutrients quickly leach away and are only very slowly replaced from long-term weathering of the subsoil.

The destruction of vegetation affects animal life too, particularly in the mangrove swamps, where the annual production of leaves is of critical importance to the detritus food web on which many estuarine organisms depend (see Chapter 2). Although reliable data are lacking on the populations of fish, molluscs, and crabs in the delta areas affected by spraying, work on similar vegetation in Florida suggests that animal populations, including commercially important species, are adversely affected. Radical shifts in the kinds of birds might be anticipated too. Lack of cover would tend to reduce the abundance of all species, but populations of species that eat insects that in turn feed on leaves would be depressed, while species feeding on wood-eating insects would become more abundant. Since many widely scattered tropical tree species are pollinated by birds, bats, or insects, decreased populations of the pollinators might in turn affect rates of reproduction of the trees and reduce the food supply of fruit, nuts, and seeds which many species in a tropical forest need to survive. But perhaps the most devastating effect of defoliation in a tropical forest is the loss of cover on which so many species of both animals and plants depend.

Despite its effects on plants and animals, the most disturbing consequence of the use of herbicides in Indochina has been the reports of increased rates of stillbirths and the birth of deformed babies in some of the most heavily sprayed provinces of South Vietnam. The herbicides were sprayed at ten or more times the normal dose rate used in the United States, and whole tankfuls were sometimes dumped if the spray plane ran into any sort of difficulty. This tragic effect on human fetuses stemmed from the presence of trace amounts of a teratogenic or fetus-deforming compound, dioxin, in the Agent Orange used. Although the level of dioxin in the Agent Orange has been estimated at 10–15 ppm, since 93 million pounds of Agent Orange have been splashed about the Vietnamese countryside, roughly 1000 pounds of dioxin have found their way into the environment. Subsequently, dioxin has been found in a few parts per trillion (pptr) in South Vietnamese river fish, shellfish, and human milk. In some fish the dioxin concentration was over 500 pptr (half of a lab population of guinea pigs is killed by 500 pptr). Other evidence suggests that dioxin may form when vegetation sprayed with Agent Orange is burned.

In response to increasing public concern about the effect of herbicides on the people and environment of Vietnam, and the apparent conclusion by the Department of Defense that herbicides had only limited strategic usefulness, they were phased out of use in the later stages of the war, in 1970–1971.

As a result of its experiments in Vietnam, the U.S. Air Force has 2.3 million gallons of Agent Orange herbicide, which contain about 79 pounds of dioxin, stored in 55-gallon drums—one third in Gulfport, Mississippi, and the rest on Johnston Island, eight hundred miles southwest of Honolulu. Stymied in its efforts to sell the herbicide, the Air Force now plans to incinerate it in the Pacific on a specially constructed ship.

DEVELOPMENT OF BIOCIDES

To develop a commercial biocide, chemical companies must invest a great deal of time, research, and money. First, a large variety of materials must be screened for biological activity; toxicity is not always obvious from a formula. Then tests in the laboratory on a wide spectrum of pests determine toxicity levels of likely compounds. Those that are strongly toxic to one or more pests are tested for the effect of multiple doses and long-term effects, up to a month (a considerable part of the life cycle of many insects). Small plot studies by cooperating state agricultural research stations then work out problems of formulation and field dosage. Next the cooperation of farmers is enlisted for large-scale trials on a number of crop plants in different soils, climates, and regions. All the data from these preliminary steps are then presented to the proper government regulatory agency. If approved, the compound is registered for use and marketed. Long-term toxicity tests continue as the product is used commercially. Ultimately, under this system, the consumer does the final testing. Since the cost of marketing a biocide may run to several million dollars, none of which is returned until the product is sold, chemical companies are understandably anxious to recover their investment after years of development by promoting the use of their product. Fortunately, biocides are usually a small part of the total business of most large chemical companies; this lessens somewhat the pressure to rush a product onto the market prematurely. However in 1973 1.2 billion pounds of biocides were used in the United States.

Despite testing by industry and regulation by government, biocides have caused problems, some resulting from the very characteristics that made them useful pest killers. These problems can be grouped into four categories: resistance of the target organism; accumulation in food chains; persistence in the environment; and nonselectivity. Let's look at each of these problem areas in some detail.

RESISTANCE

For a short while, biocides seemed about to push the mosquito and housefly into extinction. But by 1947, trouble developed. Italian researchers reported that the housefly was becoming resistant to DDT; corroboration soon followed from California. Soon other insects became resistant too: the malaria-carrying mosquito, then lice, fleas, and a number of other disease vectors that had formerly been controlled by DDT. Twelve insects were found to be resistant by 1948, 25 in 1954, 76 in 1957, 137 in 1960, and 165 in 1967.

Ironically, resistant pests have appeared everywhere man has sprayed, simply because the development of resistance depends upon killing as many pests as can be exposed to the selected poison. Until recently, this has been the goal of pest control.

When an insect population is exposed to a new biocide, up to 99 percent of the population is eliminated. The remaining 1 percent is by random coincidence immune or resistant to the chemical. A 99 percent wipe-out sounds almost as good as extinction. But the few resistant individuals can now reproduce almost without competition, a result of the elimination of both their peers and their predators. Breeding at a rate of ten generations a season, a resistant housefly population could become the most abundant strain in about five years.

Simple resistance to biocides is bad enough for the farmer, but in some instances even more serious problems occurred. After several years' exposure to cyclodiene, cabbage maggot strains were selected that were not only resistant to the biocide, but lived twice as long and produced twice as many eggs as nonresistant forms.

A classic example of unanticipated selection for pest resistance is the lygus bug on California cotton (Figure 5.4). The lygus bug sucks plant juices from buds, blossoms, and young cotton bolls. Each of these stages that fails to develop means one less cotton boll. In 1967, a large chemical company marketed azodrin, a new organophosphate; after much advertising, over a million acres were sprayed in California alone. While the new biocide was not persistent, it was toxic to a broad spectrum of insects and eliminated almost all insects in the sprayed fields. Its lack of persistence allowed migration of lygus bugs into the sprayed fields where their natural enemies had been eliminated (predators are always much less numerous than their prey, and therefore recover much more slowly from biocide applications). Then the lygus bug population increased and another spraying was required—then another and another. After several seasons, it can be expected that the lygus bug will be resistant to azodrin.

The killing of beneficial insects along with the lygus bug increased the population of, and damage from, the boll worm, with the result that application of azodrin may well have decreased the yield of cotton through the increased activities of the boll worm. In addition, studies on the cotton plants showed that many buds do not form bolls and all bolls do not necessarily ripen even under the best of conditions. In fact, many buds and bolls that were attacked by lygus bugs would not have

Fig. 5.4 The lygus bug found on cotton in California may not be the pest it has been assumed to be. (USDA)

95

ripened anyway. In an experiment set up by University of California entomologists, the yield of cotton was not significantly different between sprayed and unsprayed plots. Hence it was quite probable that the lygus bug was not even a pest!

This type of situation can easily be repeated because the grower, often an absentee landholder or corporation, wants someone to sample his fields occasionally, advise on the presence of potentially dangerous pests, and suggest some control. Very often the "someone" is a field salesman for a chemical company. In the cotton-growing areas of California, there are a handful of extension entomologists and over 200 salesmen representing 100 companies. Should anyone be surprised that fields are sprayed unnecessarily?

ACCUMULATION

Many biocides that are only slightly soluble in water are quite soluble in fat. Therefore algae accumulate these biocides in their cellular fat bodies on the order of parts per million. This uptake from water is called bio-accumulation. An organism that eats algae may accumulate a biocide in tens of parts per million. This increasing concentration of biocides in a food chain is called bio-magnification. By means of these processes, an extremely small quantity of a persistent biocide in water, in equilibrium with a much larger amount in the bottom mud, has unexpected effects in an ecosystem—far beyond the original intent of those who first introduced these materials into the environment. For example, bottom mud in Green Bay, Wisconsin contained 0.014 ppm DDT. But small crustaceans in the same environment had accumulated 0.41 ppm, fish 3 to 6 ppm, and herring gulls at the top of the food chain, 99 ppm—enough to interfere with their reproduction (Figure 5.5).

Of course, biological magnification is not limited to aquatic organisms. One early example of this process developed from the attempt to control Dutch elm disease with DDT. The Dutch elm disease is caused by a fungus that plugs the water-conducting vessels of the elm, killing the tree (Figure 5.6). Since the fungus is spread by two species of bark beetles, attempts to control the disease have focused, quite naturally, on the insects. The program of spraying elms with DDT began in 1947. While DDT effectively killed the bark beetles and slowed the spread of the disease, it seemed in some instances to kill birds too, especially robins. The robin population on the campus of Michigan State University in East Lansing, Michigan, was reported to have dropped from 370 to 4 birds in four years, and almost no nests produced young during these years. In another instance, the robin population of Hanover, New Hampshire, a town that regularly sprayed its elms with DDT, fell considerably below that of a nearby town that did not spray. In both Michigan and New Hampshire, large numbers of dead birds were found to

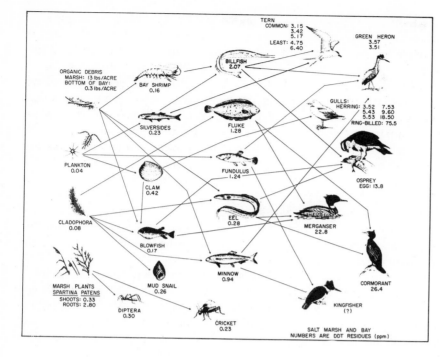

Fig. 5.5 Estuarine food chains have been contaminated with DDT. The primary producers—phytoplankton, algae, and marsh plants—absorb DDT from mud or the water and store it in their cellular fat bodies. By passing this DDT on to the consumer, the level may gradually accumulate to large doses. (Brookhaven National Laboratory)

contain DDT in excess of the 30 ppm that has been observed to be lethal in robins.

In both instances, spraying seems to have been rather exuberantly carried out; DDT was applied in doses much heavier than necessary,

Fig. 5.6 (a) At one time the streets of most northeastern cities and towns were lined with these airy and graceful American elms; (b) but the Dutch elm disease slowly began to kill American elms. (c) Today elms are no longer found in most towns and the stark remains haunt hedgerows and country lanes.

97

thus killing more robins than usual. If DDT is applied to trees either in leaf or during dormancy, it drips to the ground beneath the trees and is accumulated by earthworms. The soil beneath a sprayed elm tree may contain 5 to 10 ppm DDT; an earthworm that ingests this soil for its organic content may contain 30 to 160 ppm. A robin feeding almost exclusively on earthworms during the early spring, when elms are usually sprayed, might easily receive a lethal dose of DDT through this chain. Many apparently have. In this way a food chain can be poisoned and increasing levels of a noxious substance passed upward through the links.

BIRDS OF PREY AND DDT

The most serious and best documented example of bio-magnification can be seen in the reproductive failure of certain birds of prey, especially the peregrine falcon, bald eagle, and osprey, which have undergone disastrous population decreases since 1945.

The peregrine falcon has completely disappeared from the eastern United States, the bald eagle has become rare, and the osprey uncommon. Charles Broley, who studied the bald eagle in Florida for a number of years, watched the population of eagles in one area fall from 125 nests producing about 150 birds a year in 1940 to 43 nests producing 8 young in 1957. In 1958 only 10 nests and 1 young bird were found. Similar decreases have been reported in osprey populations in Maine and Connecticut. In all three species eggs fail to hatch or are easily broken and eaten by the brooding bird. DDT concentrations in both the eggs and adult birds were found to be high. Falcons from an area as remote as the Northwest Territories of Canada were reported to contain 369 ppm of DDT in their fat.

How is DDT implicated in the decline of these birds? The high levels of DDT found in the fat of many birds of prey results from the same concentration process seen in the earthworm-robin chain. Birds of prey are carnivores; they eat other birds and animals whose fat may contain substantial quantities of DDT picked up from their habitats. DDT seems to affect calcium metabolism; it is, of course, the calcium deposited around the egg that produces a strong shell. This metabolic disturbance results in eggs with much thinner and weaker shells than normal, eggs that are easily broken (Figure 5.7). This was suggested by a study comparing the weight of bird eggs in museum collections before and after the introduction of DDT in 1947. Birds with declining populations had substantially lighter (hence, thinner) shells after 1947 than birds with stable populations (Table 5.1). It should be pointed out that the declining species tend to feed on species which themselves are several steps removed from the primary consumer. The birds of prey with stable populations usually

Fig. 5.7 (a) DDT interferes with calcium metabolism in many birds, resulting in delicate eggshells which break easily, as in this pelican egg. (W. Gordon Menzie) (b) Here are two cross sections of Japanese quail eggshells magnified 400 times. The bird producing the egg on the left was fed a diet containing DDT; the diet of the bird that produced the normal egg on the right did not contain DDT. The structural weaknesses make the former egg quite fragile. (Wide World Photos)

Table 5.1
Relationship of Eggshell Thickness to
Population Decline of Certain Birds of Prey*

POPULATIONS	WEIGHT OF EGGSHELL (% CHANGE)
DECLINING	
Bald eagle	−18
Osprey	−25.1
Peregrine falcon	−18.8
STABLE	
Red tailed hawk	+ 2.7
Golden eagle	+ 2.9
Great horned owl	+ 2.4

* Hickey, J. J. and D. W. Anderson, 1968. "Chlorinated hydrocarbons and eggshell changes in raptorial and fish-eating birds." *Science* **162,** pp. 271–273.

feed on the primary consumer directly. Hence they are exposed to much lower amounts of DDT.

Further evidence pointing to a DDT interference in eggshell characteristics was shown in a study where sparrow hawks, which were fed a mixture of 3 ppm dieldrin and 15 ppm DDT, laid eggs 8 to 10 percent thinner than those of control birds. The offspring of these birds laid eggs 15 to 17 percent thinner than the control eggs. Clearly DDT interferes with calcium metabolism.

Birds tend to accumulate biocides because they cannot excrete liquids as rapidly as mammals. Scavengers feeding on dead animals are even more likely to pick up large amounts of a biocide. But predators, especially, tend to accumulate biocides because they often prey on weak or abnormal animals whose disability may reflect a high body burden of a biocide. A study of mice and shrews in a spruce-fir forest in Maine after one pound of DDT per acre was applied to control an outbreak of spruce budworm showed that shrews had 10 to 40 times the amount of DDT residue of mice. This was because of the carnivorous diet of shrews and led to a maximum of 41 ppm the year the forest was sprayed. After nine years, while the DDT residues of mice seemed to be approaching normal, the level in shrews remained unusually high, 2 to 6 ppm. Even though the level probably had little effect on the shrews themselves, what about the predators feeding on shrews? Reproductive failure has been noted in ospreys feeding on organisms with an amount of DDT residue equivalent to that found in the shrews. One can only wonder what DDT load foxes and bobcats are carrying around, years after the initial introduction of DDT in their forest environment.

The Mexican free-tailed bat winters in Mexico, where it feeds on insects contaminated with organochlorines, but returns to the southwestern United States to breed. Until 1960 populations were large (Figure 5.8), but since then they have declined dramatically, 97 percent in some areas. Research indicates that young bats acquire from their mothers' milk DDT which is deposited in their body fat. During migration, when this fat is metabolized, the DDT and its derivatives are deposited in the brain, where lethal quantities, several hundred ppm, have been recorded.

CONTAMINATION OF THE OCEAN

It is not surprising that local ecosystems that have been sprayed with various persistent biocides pass these materials on in ever higher concentration through food chains. It was something of a shock, however, to learn that Adelie penguins on the Ross Ice Shelf of Antarctica had traces of organchlorines in their body fat. Although the amounts were small, 13 to 115 parts per billion (ppb) in liver tissue and 24 to 152 ppb in fat, the fact that there was *any* organochlorine at all, thousands of miles from the nearest possible point of contamination, was alarming. At first it was thought that the presence of several thousand scientific and support personnel nearby might be contaminating the environment in some way through discarded material, clothing, garbage, or fecal wastes, for organochlorines were not used for any purpose in Antarctica. But subsequent investigation in still more remote areas of Antarctica indicated that local penguins and cormorants contained 0.001 to 0.48 ppm DDE (a degradation product of DDT) and 0.011 to 0.140 ppm DDE respectively. The wide-ranging skua (a gull-like sea bird) contained 0.89 to 26.0 ppm DDE. Furthermore, pelagic or open ocean birds like the albatross, which touch land only to breed, were found to contain traces of various biocides.

Even more alarming than food chain contamination has been the report that concentrations of organochlorines as low as a few parts per billion have reduced the rate of photosynthesis in four species of marine algae grown under laboratory conditions. While the present level of organochlorines in the world ocean is in the parts per trillion range, should it ever increase to parts per billion, photosynthesis by the oceanic algae might be curtailed. Considering that a sizable percentage of the

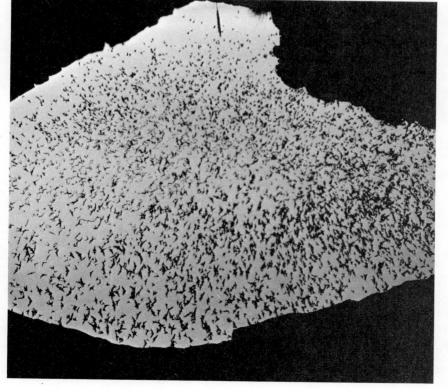

Fig. 5.8 At one time the sight of huge flights of bats leaving Carlsbad Caverns at dusk was one of the major attractions at the park. But today there are few bats left; apparently DDT picked up from their wintering grounds in Mexico has dramatically reduced their numbers. (Department of the Interior, National Park Service)

earth's photosynthetic organisms which produce oxygen are found in the ocean, the world's oxygen cycle could conceivably be affected with both predictable and unpredictable results.

Tidal systems have for many years been used as a convenient disposal area for human wastes. The daily tides remove enough wastes to prevent the eutrophication that would destroy a lake. At the same time, predatory microbes attack many potentially dangerous bacteria such as *Escherichia coli* and *Salmonella*. These predators locate their prey by chemotaxis, homing in on the chemical "fingerprint" of the prey species. Chlorinated hydrocarbons inhibit this chemotaxis and so may not only affect the producers, but also the tidal system's ability to cleanse itself.

The conclusion from all these diverse threads is unmistakably clear: contamination of food chains is no longer a local affair in direct relation to biocide application at some specific point; the oceanic food chain, remote from land-based biocide usage, is capable of being contaminated. How could the enormous world ocean, stretching thousands of miles around the earth, become contaminated, whatever the scale of our activities? Some hint might be taken from the Bravo series of H-bomb explosions in the Pacific (see Chapter 14), which resulted in the catching of radioactive tuna in Japanese waters thousands of miles from the blast site. Tuna, the last link (before us) in their particular food chain, accumulated fallout to a dangerous degree. Likewise, organochlorines have collected in atmospheric dust hundreds and thousands of miles from dusting or spraying activities. One study showed that only 26 percent of a biocide spray intended to reach corn plants at tassel height actually made it; the rest was wafted away by wind currents. When washed out of the air by rain, biocides can enter any ecosystem anywhere in the world. Since oceans occupy 75 percent of the earth's surface, contamination was just a matter of time. The pathway of contamination seems to be land to air to ocean and perhaps finally burial in the ocean depths.

This seems to be borne out by work in the Santa Barbara Basin off the California coast. Because of the winter rain cycle in Southern California and the anaerobic conditions in the bottom sediments, a series of clear cut layers or varves has built up on the bottom of the basin like the rings of a tree. By measuring the organochlorine content of these varves, scientists determined that these sediments provide a major sump for the biocides that until recently entered the ocean directly from the waste stream of a Los Angeles manufacturing plant.

BIOCIDES IN HUMANS

If animals can accumulate and concentrate biocides from their food, one wonders how much DDT we have accumulated from our food chain and if there is any evidence of potential harm. Like just about every other organism, we have accumulated DDT in our body fat. At the height of DDT use we all averaged 8 to 10 ppm DDT in our body fat. Whether this was or will be harmful is the subject of a sharp and continuing debate. Until 1965 no medically documented cases of sickness or death in humans could be traced to proper use of biocides. Of course any number of children and agricultural workers have died through careless handling of biocides, for often people do not read labels or follow instructions. Careless handling of virtually any substance, biocides not excepted, can be disastrous at times. In 1962, for example, seven infants in a hospital nursery died when salt was accidentally added to their formula instead of sugar. If, then, there is no evidence that disease or death in humans has resulted *directly* from the proper use of biocides, what are the long-term prospects?

DELAYED EFFECTS?

Apparently no one need fear inordinate residues of biocides on fruits and vegetables, for the Food and Drug Administration has set up maximum allowable levels of biocides on food products and keeps careful watch on food shipped through interstate channels. The fear of dying from one poisoned apple is as unreal as the Snow White fairy tale. But, the fact that we are all carrying a supply of various biocides, regularly replenished from our environment, leads us to wonder about long-term problems caused by a body burden of any biocide. There are three logical categories of biocide effects: no effects; effects that are too subtle to be correlated with biocide levels; and effects that will appear in the future. One recalls with some uneasiness the case involving a group of women who worked in a watch factory in the 1920s painting the dials with a luminescent paste containing radium. At the time, radium was regarded as harmless, so the women habitually pointed the tips of their brushes by wetting them with their tongues. Thirty years later, many of these women began dying of mouth and tongue cancer. Today we can be appalled at the naïveté of allowing people to "eat" radium, but at the time there were no known adverse effects.

In tests where men were fed 3.5 and 35 mg of DDT a day for a period of time, no ill effects were seen. DDT accumulated in proportion to the amount consumed, then reached an equilibrium point between storage and excretion. When the dose was discontinued the .body burden began to fall. Apparently the body stores DDT in response to intake rather than independent accumulation, so a person in a high DDT environment will store more DDT than a person in an environment with lower DDT levels. Although no one has died directly because of DDT properly used, many claims have been made and are being made that associate high DDT body burdens with various organ failures and mal-functions. But whether DDT caused these problems directly or indirectly or was just an innocent bystander has not been clearly demonstrated.

However, there are some interesting associations. A group of Canadian children living in a forest that was sprayed with a fenitrothion/DDT mixture suffered some central nervous system disability and liver prob-lems (Reyes syndrome) after exposure to a virus that usually does not elicit such effects. Reyes syndrome has also been associated with outbreaks of influenza B and the Coxsackie and herpes simplex viruses. Research with mice found that the solvent and emulsifier used in applying most biocides, particularly those insoluble in water, caused more mortality than either the controls or pure biocides. Considering the widespread use of aerosol biocides (20 million gallons per year of oil-based products are used in the United States as biocide emulsifiers and dispersal agents), any tendency of these supposedly inert materials to increase the harm-fulness of viruses can only be viewed with alarm.

The lethality or side effects of biocides can also be affected by the body's condition. In underdeveloped countries chronic protein short-ages together with mineral and vitamin deficiencies may lower the re-sistance to certain biocides, especially endrin, parathion, and captan. This is particularly true as the "green revolution" (see Chapter 22) puts so-phisticated biocides into the hands of unsophisticated users who may not take the necessary precautions.

PERSISTENCE

We tend to regard the soil as some kind of biological incinerator; what-ever we dump is supposed to be decomposed. But some of the organic biocides are unknown in a natural environment and enzymes that can de-grade them are simply not available. The half-life (the time required for half the original quantity of a substance in the environment to decom-pose) of DDT is around 15 years, toxaphene 11, aldrin 9, dieldrin 7, chlordane 6, heptachlor 2 to 4, and lindane 2. These are maximum values; in some environments biocides decompose much more quickly, but the figures give some idea of the time it can take for the environ-ment to cope with these materials. Decomposition, fortunately, does not depend solely on microbial attack, or we might never get rid of some persistent organochlorines. Volatilization into the air, photodecomposi-tion by various wavelengths of solar energy, mechanical removal in crops, and leaching are also involved in reducing levels of persistent biocides; but volatilization and microbial degradation are the most important.

The danger of persistence is best seen in the organic biocide with the longest half-life, DDT. Though only slightly soluble in water (ppb),

DDT is readily absorbed by the bottom mud of aquatic systems. As DDT in the water is degraded or removed by organisms, fresh supplies from the bottom mud are released. Because of its relatively long half-life, DDT can be released continuously into an aquatic system for years.

RESIDUES

Biocides also persist in terrestrial environments. When spray schedules are maintained over a long period of time, residue levels build up. The soil beneath some orchards in Oregon was estimated to have retained over 40 percent of the DDT applied over a seventeen-year period. Some well-sprayed orchards accumulated 30 to 40 pounds of DDT per acre per year; others have totaled, despite degradation processes, as much as 113 pounds per acre after six years of spraying. Persistence is not limited to the newer organochlorines, though; arsenic trioxide has accumulated in some parts of the Pacific Northwest up to 1400 pounds per acre—a concentration that often poisons the crops themselves.

Some years ago the watershed around Lake George, New York was sprayed with 10,000 pounds of DDT per year for several years to control a gypsy moth outbreak. A decline in the population of lake trout followed. Although DDT residues ranged from 8 to 835 ppm in the adult trout and 3 to 355 ppm in the eggs, the adult fish were unaffected and the eggs hatched normally. Further research showed that the young fry were very sensitive to DDT, just when they were about to begin feeding. At DDT levels over 5 ppm there was 100 percent mortality.

Herbicide residues have also had some unanticipated effects. Coccinellids, the ladybird beetles which are voracious eaters of aphids (Figure 5.9), may become sluggish and far less effective predators and their larvae may grow 60 percent more slowly when affected by low levels of 2,4-D. This plant killer has also been observed to cause rice stem borers to grow 45 percent larger in treated rice plants and it may reduce the natural resistance of fish to parasitic microorganisms.

In the sublethal dosage, 2,4-D has increased the potassium nitrate content of sugar beets, which are frequently used for cattle food, from 0.22 to 4.5 percent dry weight, a nitrate level that is quite toxic to cattle. In another instance a low exposure to 2,4-D increased the sugar content of ragwort, a plant toxic to cattle but usually unpalatable to them. With an increased sugar content the cattle's avoidance was overcome and they were attracted to a still poisonous plant.

Another unsuspected effect of 2,4-D may be to increase the incidence of pests on crops. Corn plants sprayed with 2,4-D had significantly larger populations of corn leaf aphid, European corn borer, and southern corn leaf blight than control plants, apparently as a result of a herbicide-induced increase in the protein content of the sprayed plants.

Fig. 5.9 This adult ladybird beetle is polishing off an aphid. The larvae of these beetles are also effective in controlling plant aphid populations. (USDA)

While 2,4-D is quickly metabolized and 2,4,5-T lingers only a few weeks, picloram is quite persistent. Coupled with its biological activity (100 times 2,4-D) and solubility, the persistence of picloram means that its percolation into the water table and transfer to unsprayed areas is quite likely. Its persistence and potency were strikingly demonstrated in a tobacco field with an unusual distribution of stunted plants. With much effort, this pattern was traced to droppings left by mules used to plow the field. The mules had been pastured in a field treated with picloram, which had passed unchanged through the mules' guts and leached out of the droppings, affecting the tobacco.

Herbicides also have the potential to be transformed by soil microorganisms into a variety of other compounds, some harmless, some dangerous. Propanil (3,4-dichloroproprionanilide) is commonly applied to the soil for postemergence control of weeds. Propanil is particularly useful in controlling barnyard grass in rice fields, so it is widely used. In the soil propanil breaks down to proprionic acid, which is quickly metabolized by soil microorganisms, and DCA (3,4-dichloroaniline). Logically the DCA molecule should be split in two and metabolized; instead it is polymerized or stuck together with other DCA molecules to form TCAB, which is stable, persistent, and closely related to carcinogenic azo compounds. Although TCAB does not seem dangerous, its mere presence indicates that we don't really know and cannot always predict what happens to biocides when they enter the soil and are transformed by microorganisms.

While the general population has most of its contact with biocide residues in food, farm workers may be exposed chronically to relatively high levels of organophosphate biocides left on crops they are harvesting. This is especially important since these biocides can be absorbed through the skin. Because of the general nature of organophosphorus poisoning—headaches, sweating, diarrhea, nausea, vomiting, and abdominal pains—many cases go unreported or are diagnosed as flu, especially if migrant workers with a language barrier are involved.

Perhaps the most difficult aspect of persistent biocides is that they cannot be contained. About 50 percent of cultivated land in the United States receives biocides; 3 percent of grasslands and less than 0.3 percent of forests are treated each year. Altogether, 50 percent of the total United States land area remains untreated, and yet virtually all animals, ourselves included, carry traces of DDT and other persistent biocides.

AN END TO A PROBLEM?

In response to this and other evidence, the United States joined other western nations in banning DDT in 1972. Action was taken over the protests of the manufacturers and certain agricultural interests who found the evidence against DDT insufficient and continue to cling to simple solutions to complex problems. Such solutions are immediately satisfying, to be sure, but ultimately unproductive. In 1974 aldrin and dieldrin were banned and in 1975 heptachlor and chlordane usage was sharply limited. In the next few years the remainder of our most persistent and virulent chlorinated hydrocarbons and organophosphorus biocides will probably be subjected to similar limitations.

Since the ban on DDT in 1972 some interesting results for various species supposedly affected by DDT in the environment have been reported. The brown pelican seems to be making a comeback on the West Coast, from 4 young fledged in 1969 to 1185 fledged in 1974. Part of the increase (on Anacapa Island and Isla Coronada Norte) was the result of increased nesting in response to an increase in the northern anchovy population. However, the average number of young per nest has risen to 0.9, an encouraging sign even if it is 30 percent below the 1.2 to 1.5 per nest that maintains a stable population. Eggshell thickness has also increased. This response seems linked to the elimination of DDT wastes from local sources and the subsequent reduction of DDT residues in anchovies by 97 percent, from 4.3 ppm to 0.15 ppm.

Migratory songbirds analyzed since 1969 have lost a considerable amount of their DDT body burden, from 17.8 ppm in 1969 to 2.06 ppm in 1973. Osprey on Long Island which in 1966 produced 0.07 young per nest and laid eggs with a DDT/DDE content of 15 ppm were found in 1974 to be producing 1 fledgling per nest and laying eggs with a DDT/DDE residue of only 1.37 ppm. Bald eagles in the Chesapeake Bay area once seemed doomed; now they are making a comeback and there are even plans to reintroduce the peregrine falcon to the eastern United States from a population being bred in captivity. Best of all, our intake of DDT has declined from 13.8 mg per day in 1970 to 1.88 mg per day in 1973 and our average residue in body fat has fallen from 8 ppm to 5.9 ppm.

Despite these indications of the impact of DDT dispersal into the environment, pressure to resume use continues unabated, as does the export of millions of pounds per year, mainly to underdeveloped countries. In 1974 special permission was granted by the Environmental Protection Agency to the U.S. Forest Service to spray large areas of Douglas fir forest in the Blue Mountains of Oregon with DDT to control the Douglas fir tussock moth (*Orgyia pseudotsugata*) (Figure 5.10). This species, a native like the spruce budworm in the East, erupts occasionally according to a widely recognized pattern: year one, noticeable larvae; year two, outbreaks with severe defoliation; year three, population collapse from natural controls. Despite familarity with this pattern, the Forest Service used DDT the year the population would have collapsed anyway. Since the outbreak was mostly on National Forest land and sal-

Fig. 5.10 Sexual dimorphism is particularly striking in the Douglas fir tussock moth. The female (below) is wingless and must depend upon a pheromone to attract the winged male (above). (USDA)

vage rights are usually rather profitable to logging companies, who are constantly pressuring the federal government to increase logging in the National Forests, it is difficult to appreciate the hysteria that forced the EPA to make this exception. If this is a one-shot deal it won't matter much, but if it has set a precedent, we have learned nothing since DDT was first unleashed in 1945.

NONSELECTIVITY

Not all of the problems caused by biocides in the environment derive from resistance, biological magnification, or persistence. Killing the wrong organism at the wrong time can be just as great a problem. One example of these unexpected effects occurred several years ago in the Near East. Jackals had been a problem for years in the settlements along the Mediterranean coast of Israel. Attracted by garbage, they stayed on to eat crops and increased greatly in number. In 1965 the government set out bait poisoned with "1080" (sodium fluoroacetate). The bait was widely distributed and no attempt was made to avoid poisoning other animals. As a result of this program, the jackals were eliminated but so were the mongoose, the wild cat, and the fox. With their predators eliminated, hares increased enormously, causing greater damage to crops than the jackals had before. Moreover, Palestine vipers, usually controlled by the mongoose, appeared in large numbers around settlements, to the consternation of the inhabitants.

Even more unpredictable were the results of spraying thatched-roofed huts in Borneo with DDT to control a malaria-carrying mosquito. The cockroaches and lizards that are normally quite common in these rather simple structures were injured or killed by the biocide and eaten by cats, many of which died as a result. Without cats to keep their population in check, rats increased greatly, giving rise to the fear of plague and other rat-transmitted diseases. As if this weren't enough to bear, the houses themselves began to collapse: the population of moth larvae, which normally feed on the thatch roofs, increased considerably, for while the larvae avoided DDT-sprayed materials and survived, their predators and parasites were killed. Although the British Royal Air Force came to the rescue with a massive cat replacement effort called Operation Cat Drop, which alleviated the rat problem, the villagers, not surprisingly, were reluctant to endure another round of house spraying, whatever the benefits.

Intensively cultivated land is highly sensitive to the disruptive effects of nonselective biocides. Rice fields which are flooded during the growing season in Louisiana also produce red crayfish, a local delicacy that nets the rice farmer an addition to his income beyond what he makes from

Fig. 5.11 The flowers on this McIntosh apple tree are normally pollinated by bees. The more bees, the heavier the resulting crop of apples. When natural populations of bees have been reduced or eliminated by biocides, farmers are often forced to rent hives, which are trucked into the orchards at flowering time, to save their crop. (USDA)

the rice crop. However, to control the rice stinkbug, toxaphene often mixed with DDT or dieldrin was used. Because of an extreme sensitivity to toxaphene, fish were sometimes killed in large numbers. Gallinules and tree ducks were also killed by eating sprayed rice. When the switch was made to malathion and parathion to avoid damage to fish and wildlife, it was found that crayfish were quite sensitive to parathion and substantial crayfish kills took place before a combination of chemicals could be worked out that endangered neither fish, birds, nor crayfish and still protected the rice.

Much more portentous has been the gradual decline of the world's domestic bee population. The number of tended hives is down 11 percent, a loss of 200 billion bees. Part of this is indirectly attributed to biocides; the use of herbicides in West Germany has reduced the cornflower population of wheat fields, which formerly served as an important food source for hive bees after the flowering season in orchards had passed (Figure 5.11). In Guatemala and Nicaragua, spraying the cotton crop with a biocide reportedly killed one third of the domestic bee population. Since bees are quite sensitive to a number of biocides, indiscriminate spraying can adversely affect the setting of fruit and other bee-pollinated crops. In some areas, hives have to be imported by the thousands from bee growers to assure pollination of fruit trees.

Natural ecosystems can also be strongly affected by the application of broad-spectrum biocides, which kill insects indiscriminately. The red spider mite normally is kept under good control by a variety of organisms, especially a predatory mite. When spruce forests along the Yellow-

109

stone River in Montana were sprayed to control the Englemann spruce beetle, the spider mites, which lived in web-like structures on the undersides of the needles, were protected from the spray, but the predatory mites were killed. The following year, although the Englemann spruce beetle was controlled, there was a huge wave of spider mite damage that was worse than that of the spruce beetle.

A similar example was reported from South Lake Tahoe, California. After five years of fogging with malathion to control mosquitoes, lodgepole pine scale populations increased dramatically in the sprayed areas. This was apparently caused by the malathion-induced depression of parasites that normally control the scale. A year after spraying was terminated in 1971 the scale infestation collapsed.

One of the most unfortunate examples of misdirected use of biocides is in the control of cosmetic pests such as the citrus thrip, which attacks the stem end of oranges. Since growers are paid anywhere from seven to twenty times as much for fresh fruit as for juice oranges, they naturally try to assure that their fruit is as highly rated as possible. But thrip burrows in the skin of an orange have no effect whatever on the sugar content, flavor, or texture of the part of the fruit we eat. Consequently the grower pays for sprays that are not only unnecessary but may lead to insect outbreaks far more damaging to the groves than the citrus thrip: all this is for the sake of a "perfect" orange, which the public has been brainwashed into demanding as the only orange worth eating.

Finally, the recent past has seen cases where whole regions, not just fields or forests, were sprayed unnecessarily and indiscriminately. During the early enthusiasm over the innate superiority of chemicals to all other approaches, the concept of mass control arose. By means of various biocides the fire ant was to be eliminated and the Japanese beetle contained.

The fire ant is a minor pest introduced from Argentina into the southeastern United States. It builds mounds one to two feet high, inflicts painful stings, and occasionally damages crops and livestock. The USDA with its technological muscle came rushing to the rescue and began spraying large areas of the Southeast with dieldrin or heptachlor at the rate of two pounds per acre. While this was reduced in later years, over 2.5 million acres of land were treated by air in this program. Although the fire ant did not destroy livestock, wildlife, or crops to any important extent, the biocides in some instances did. After $15 million was spent on mass control, the Southeast still had to live with the fire ant—plus heptachlor residues in the environment. The failure of this operation was witnessed by the continued life of the pest. Unfortunately the USDA has continued pressuring the states to spray aerially, now with mirex, a persistent, broad-spectrum, chlorinated hydrocarbon. Even more unfortunate is the insistence that the fire ant could, much less should, be eradicated. Perhaps the USDA's concern is real, but its purview is narrow since it deals only with crop plants and their problems. Mirex in the environment shows no such discrimination and kills native ants of great ecological importance in their environments as well as the introduced fire ant.

It was recently discovered that 2 to 5 percent of mirex decomposes into kepone. This biocide, carcinogenic, neurotoxic, and environmentally stable, was withdrawn from use after employees of the Life Science Products plant in Hopewell, Virginia developed severe nervous system disorders. Mirex is now being phased out and will not be in use after 1978.

Another example of overenthusiastic mass control was the Japanese beetle eradication program. In the first few decades after its introduction in the United States from Japan, this pest was widely distributed in the Northeast and ate everything in its path. But with the introduction of biological controls (see Chapter 8), particularly a bacterium (milky disease) that attacks the beetle grub, populations have stabilized so that the dense clusters that covered grape vines, rose bushes, and most garden plants during the 1940s are no longer a severe problem. Beetles are occasionally seen during the summer (Figure 5.12) but are nowhere as abundant as they once were.

Fig. 5.12 The Japanese beetle, once the scourge of the eastern United States, seems to have been brought under control by widespread distribution of a bacterium that kills the beetle grubs.

At first, however, the response by government agencies to the continual westward spread of the Japanese beetle was a compulsive drive to eradicate the beetle in the new areas colonized. Consequently, close to 100,000 acres in Missouri, Kentucky, Illinois, Indiana, Iowa, and Michigan were broadly treated with two to three pounds of aldrin, dieldrin, or heptachlor per acre. As might be expected, chlorinated hydrocarbons at this dose rate endangered vertebrates as well as beetles, not only in initial contact but through stable, persistent residues. A recent attempt in Michigan by an environmentally oriented pressure group to prevent mass control techniques from being used against a small Japanese beetle population was not successful, but the area to be sprayed and the dose rate were decreased.

The aim in both instances, to eliminate or control potentially damaging pests, was certainly in the public interest, but the technique of mass indiscriminate aerial spraying was not the best solution. Instead of thinking, "If one aspirin relieves a headache in thirty minutes, thirty aspirin should relieve it in one minute," we should be thinking, "If aspirin cures the headache but causes an upset stomach, maybe we ought to try another remedy."

But the most ominous of all the problems generated by biocides has been the degree to which farmers have become overdependent on them, perhaps seen at its most extreme in orchards across the country.

SPRAY SCHEDULES

A hundred years ago orchards were small, containing perhaps a few dozen or at most a few hundred trees. There were enough adjoining fields and forest to allow a considerable amount of natural control. But as the orchards became larger, introduced pests could easily move from orchard to orchard, and because of the huge concentrations of trees they could inflict considerable damage. With the advent of organic sprays of low selectivity, whatever natural controls existed were reduced or eliminated, letting more pests survive and requiring more sprays. Today a typical commercial apple orchard requires a minimum of nine sprays of various biocides:

1. In early spring when the trees are still dormant a spray is applied to eliminate aphid eggs that have overwintered.
2. When the fruit buds begin to show green, trees are sprayed to control mildew, scab, mites, and red bug.
3. As flower buds begin to turn pink, a spray is needed every seven days to attack apple scab. There is no spraying during full flower to allow for the pollinating activities of bees, without which there would be no apples.
4. After petals fall, a spray is applied for codling moth, curculio, red-banded leaf roller, cankerworms, mites, mildew, and scab.
5. A cover spray is added a week after petal fall to get codling moth, leaf rollers, cankerworms, curculio, and scale.
6. After ten more days a second cover spray is added to combat curculio, codling moth, leaf roller, fruit spot, and scab.
7. In ten to twelve days a third cover spray is added.
8. A fourth cover spray is added twelve to fourteen days later, to catch codling moth, sooty blotch, scab, and fruit spot.
9. Two weeks later, a fifth cover spray is added to kill apple maggot, leaf roller, fruit spot, sooty blotch, scab, and codling moth.

By mid-July, a second batch of codling moths is likely; then, of course, there are black rot, white rot, fire blight, and so on endlessly.

The farmer is caught squarely in the middle. If he stops spraying he is left with either no crop at all or gnarled, wormy crabapples that no one will buy. If he continues to spray, new pests will appear, old ones will become resistant, and he will sooner or later be forced out of business, unable to afford spraying twenty-four hours a day.

A similar dilemma was faced by farmers in the Cañete Valley in Peru. Modern organic-synthetic biocides were introduced between 1949 and 1956 to control seven major pests on the chief crop, cotton. At first the yield of cotton increased, from 406 pounds per acre to 649 pounds per acre. But by 1965 the yield had dropped to 296 pounds per acre and major pests had increased from seven to thirteen, several of them highly resistant to the biocides. Worst of all, the lowered yield of cotton plus the increasing frequency and expense of biocide application was driving the farmers into bankruptcy.

INTEGRATED CONTROL

The solution in Peru was a break with total dependence upon organic, synthetic biocides and adaptation of a more sensible blend of control measures called integrated control. The heart of this program is decreased use of biocides and the toleration of a few pests in return for freedom from biocide-resistant hordes. There are alternatives to the exclusive use of biocides: development of resistant crops; biological control (see Chapter 7); and cultural methods like destruction of crop refuse, deep plowing, timed planting, and rotation of crops, which collectively can eliminate overwintering stages or upset the often delicate timing that synchronizes pest and crop.

Knowing the problem and trying to work with it can be more successful in the long run than a blind attack with a broad-spectrum biocide. The California spotted alfalfa aphid becomes a problem when large tracts of alfalfa are cut. By harvesting the fields in strips, refuges are left in the un-mown strips for the natural enemies of the aphid—fifty-six predators and parasites per square foot in the specially mown fields, versus fourteen per square foot in fields harvested normally.

The California grape leafhopper developed resistance to the organo-phosphates ordinarily used for control. Workers noted that the wasp *Anagrus* actively attacked the leafhopper but only during the latter part of the growing season, which left the young grape leaves open to leaf-hopper attack early in the season. When wasps were absent from the vine-yards they were attacking another leafhopper on blackberry bushes some distance away. Blackberry bushes had grown in the vineyards, but were regarded as weeds and killed with herbicides. When blackberries were reintroduced to vineyards, the predatory wasp had an alternate prey within easy reach, which helped to maintain the wasp population at a high enough level to control the grape leafhopper effectively.

Integrated control, however, means not just alternatives to organic chemicals but moderate use of all controls, including chemicals. A ra-tional, balanced approach that considers ecological factors rather than ignoring them might use the guidelines that follow.

Before any control is attempted it must be determined that the supposed pest is actually causing the damage attributed to it. Millions of dollars' worth of spray chemicals have been wasted on false assumptions. Then a survey should be made of the natural control agents that normally work to limit the population of the pest. If the pest is introduced and has no apparent enemies, locate the predators, parasites, and pathogens from its place of origin (no organism is without these associates!), screen them carefully to avoid making the situation worse by adding more pests, and attempt controlled introduction. Make every effort to preserve and increase the number of natural control organisms, native or introduced. Such biological controls have been much more effective than chemicals in many instances, for the pest cannot possibly develop resistance. Do not panic at the first appearance of a pest. Give the natural controls some time to operate. If chemicals prove necessary to achieve control, use the smallest amount that will be effective, instead of trying to kill every pest in the field. Then spray only when necessary, avoiding routine spray schedules. Remember that overkill and routine spraying quickly lead to pest resistance and elimination of natural controls, requiring still more sprays, which is what we are trying to avoid. Wherever possible, avoid broad-spectrum biocides, particularly if they are persistent. Persistence tends over the long period to eliminate more beneficial organisms than pests.

If these guidelines are followed, most of the disadvantages of biocides can be avoided. In fact, many of these materials can take their place as useful tools in the continuing war against the great variety of potential pests that man has inadvertently been nurturing through his ecosystem disruption and simplification. If mass indiscriminate spraying continues, the problems seen by the late Rachel Carson will seem like bedtime stories compared with the grim realities ahead.

FURTHER READING

Anderson, D. W. et al., 1975. "Brown pelican: improved reproduction off the southern California coast." *Science* **190,** pp. 806–808. Hope for the recovery of a threatened species.

Brown, M., 1975. "An orange is an orange." *Env.* **17**(5), pp. 6–11. A discussion of the environmental costs of cosmetic produce.

Crocker, J. F. S. et al., 1976. "Lethal interaction of ubiquitous insecticide carriers with virus." *Science* **192,** pp. 1351–1353.

Geluso, K. N., J. S. Altenbach, and D. E. Wilson, 1976. "Bat mortality: pesticide poisoning and migratory stress." *Science* **194,** pp. 184–186. Birds are not the only vertebrates to suffer from bio-accumulation of biocides.

Liang, T. T., and E. P. Lichtenstein, 1974. "Synergism of insecticides by herbicides: effect of environmental factors." *Science* **186,** pp. 1128–1130.

Luck, R. F., and D. L. Dahlsten, 1975. "Natural decline of a pine needle scale (*Chionaspis pinifoliae* [Fitch]) outbreak at South Lake Tahoe, California following cessation of adult mosquito control with malathion." *Ecology* **56,** pp. 893–904. A classic example of the misuse of a broad-spectrum biocide.

Oka, I. N., and D. Pimentel, 1976. "Herbicide (2,4-D) increases insect and pathogen pests on corn." *Science* **193,** pp. 239–240. This paper, like Crocker's and Liang's, examines interactions and synergisms of materials that weren't supposed to react.

Spear, R. C., D. L. Jenkins, and T. H. Milby, 1975. "Pesticide residues and field workers." *Env. Sci. & Tech.* **9**(4), pp. 308–313. A look at the problem of biocides from the point of view of the field worker rather than the consumer.

CHAPTER
SIX

ORGANICS IN THE
ENVIRONMENT

AMERICAN SUPERMARKETS TODAY are filled with the greatest abundance and variety of food ever available. But the list that sweeps from proletarian potato to gourmet truffle includes more and more foods that have been affected by contaminants or additives in growth or processing. Contaminants are substances, organic or inorganic, retained accidentally in marketed foods; they include biocide residues on plants and antibiotics and hormones in meat. Additives, on the other hand, are purposely added to foods during their preparation or processing to assure longer shelf life or greater attractiveness, consistency, flavor, and ease of preparation.

THE FEDERAL FOOD AND
DRUG ADMINISTRATION (FDA)

Historically, the concern of the public and hence of government regulating agencies has been with adulterants—the "chalk in milk" or "water in beer" kind of thing that was common until the turn of the century. Public indignation reached a·peak in 1906 with the publication of Upton Sinclair's muckraking novel *The Jungle*, exposing conditions in the meatpacking industry. As a result of the widespread demand for standards, the administration of Theodore Roosevelt set up a Food and Drug Administration to control the practices of the food and drug industry and to protect the public. Its first director, Harvey W. Wiley, interpreted the Food and Drug Act quite broadly and within six years had incurred the

116

wrath of his sponsor by attacking Coca-Cola for its caffeine content and questioning the safety of saccharin. Wiley resigned under pressure in 1912 and the Food and Drug Administration has since interpreted its mandate to protect the public somewhat more conservatively. However, the scope of the FDA's activities has of necessity broadened as the food industry adapted increasingly modern technology to the preparation and processing of food for the expanding market and Congress passed the Delaney Amendment which forbade any additive which caused cancer in animals. Because of the incredible complexity of pest control (see Chapter 5), one of the chief functions of the FDA today is to license the use of biocides, set standards for residues, and monitor food products for their residue content. But of equal importance to the FDA and the public is the increasing flood of additives used by the food industry in processing food for public consumption.

THE ADDITIVE ARRAY

In the "good old days" products were simple, the variety limited, and the quality, by today's standards, poor; but processing and packaging were relatively direct. Today few foods escape some treatment between farm and market. On your next trip to the supermarket, read some of the labels which, by law, must indicate at least in general terms the contents of all food items (Figure 6.1). A surprising number of labels fairly bristle with such words as acid, alkali, anticaking agent, antioxidant, bleach, buffer, disinfectant, drying agent, emulsifier, extender, artificial flavor, fortifier, moistener, neutralizer, preservative, sweetener, thickener—to mention just a few. Table salt, for example, may contain sodium silico aluminate, dextrose, tricalcium phosphate, potassium iodide, and polysorbate, in addition to sodium chloride. Some food additives are common inorganic salts, but many are compounds whose effect may extend well beyond their intended sphere of activity. This larger sphere of unintended action is the human body.

1. *Tang Instant Breakfast Drink*
2. *Special Morning Vanilla Instant Breakfast*
3. *Betty Crocker Ready-to-Spread Frosting*
4. *Cremora Instant Non-Dairy Creamer*
5. *Royal Instant Butterscotch Flavor Pudding and Pie Filling*
6. *Weight Watchers Dietary Frozen Dessert*
7. *Lucky Whip Dessert Topping*
8. *Pillsbury Creamy Vanilla Frosting Mix*

117

A. sugar, shortening (with freshness preserver), water, cocoa processed with alkali, corn syrup, wheat and corn starch, mono and diglycerides, nonfat dry milk, salt, polysorbate 60, artificial and natural flavors, potassium sorbate, soy lecithin, sodium phosphate, citric acid, pectin, dextrose, sodium citrate

B. pasteurized blend of water, hydrogenated vegetable oil, sugar, starch, sodium phosphate derivatives of mono and diglycerides, sodium caseinate, polyoxyethylene (20) sorbitan tristearate, mono and diglycerides, salt, cellulose gum, calcium chloride, vanilla and artificial flavor and color, charged with nitrous oxide and carbon dioxide

C. nonfat dry milk, corn syrup solids, sodium caseinate, lactose, vanilla extract, dibasic calcium phosphate, magnesium hydroxide, sodium ascorbate, lecithin, artificial flavors, ammonium carrageenan, tetrasodium pyrophosphate, ferric ortho-phosphate, vitamin A, vitamin E acetate, niacinamide, calcium phantothenate, manganese sulphate, basic copper carbonate, pyridoxine hydrochloride, cyanaco-balamin, thiamine mononitrate, potassium iodide

D. corn syrup solids, vegetable fat, sodium caseinate, dipotassium phosphate, mono-glycerides, sodium silico aluminate, calcium gluconate, beta carotene, and ribo-flavin (artificial colors)

E. sugar, citric acid, calcium phosphates, gum arabic, natural flavor, potassium citrate, vitamin C, cellulose gum, hydrogenated coconut oil, artificial flavor, artificial color, vitamin A, BHA

F. sugar and dextrose, modified food starch, sodium and calcium phosphates, salt, vegetable shortening, algin, artificial flavor and color, BHA and citric acid in corn oil

G. sugar, corn syrup, vegetable shortening, wheat starch, nonfat dry milk, modified food starch, salt, mono and diglycerides, polysorbate 80, artificial flavoring, artificial coloring

H. concentrated skim milk, water, sugar, polyglycerol esters of fatty acids (emulsifier), micro-crystalline cellulose, fructose, cellulose gum, artificial flavor, dibasic potassium phosphate, guar gum, carrageenan, ascorbic acid, ferrous sulfate, artificial color, vitamin A palmitate, niacinamide, calcium pantothenate, pyridoxine hydrochloride, thiamin hydrochloride, riboflavin, and calciferol

Tang is a trademark of General Foods Corp.; Special Morning, of Carnation Corp.; Betty Crocker, of General Mills, Inc.; Cremora, of Borden, Inc.; Royal, of Standard Brands, Inc.; Weight Watchers, of Weight Watchers International, Inc.; and Lucky Whip, of Lever Brothers Co.

Fig. 6.1 Here is a scrambled list of common foods found in most supermarkets. Above are the products, below are the contents listed on the labels. Can you match them?

From the very beginning, the use of additives by the food industry has polarized the consuming public. The larger group accepts whatever the industry wishes to include in its processing, assuming that the industry knows best and that if the ultimate product is "bettered" somehow, then it is worth the cost. A smaller but much more vociferous group equates the word chemical with poison and assumes that *any* chemical, organic or inorganic, added to food is poisonous. Unfortunately many faddists have joined the cause, so that the issue is no longer whether certain additives are harmful or not; the desire for wholesomeness and the yearning for the natural blend into a great crusade against all food additives.

The food-additive protest, however multifarious its background and nature, is by no means as irrational as its critics suggest. Some additives *are* poisonous when taken in large enough doses (Figure 6.2), although few people have been literally "poisoned" by an additive. Most problems have arisen from the implication through animal testing that large quantities of certain organic compounds may cause cancer in a great variety of body sites and organs. Since the threat of cancer is often brandished as a side effect of many additives, we should take a closer look at the disease and its relationship to chemical additives.

The nature and cause of cancer is one of the great medical puzzles. Something apparently goes wrong in a cell, causing it to divide without differentiation. That "something" might be a virus, a particle of beryllium oxide, an asbestos body, or some organic compound, perhaps innocuous in itself, that is metabolized by the body into a form that interferes with cell metabolism and causes cancer to develop. The proliferation of cancerous cells ultimately becomes so demanding of the body's resources that organ failure and death ensue. We cannot examine the structure of a prospective additive and predict if, where, and when it may cause cancer. We cannot predict how such a compound will be metabolized by the body, whether the metabolite will be rendered harmless or whether it will be far more destructive than the original material ingested. Today we can only infer from animal testing on a purely trial and error basis that if a compound causes cancer in a rat or monkey then it might do likewise in humans. When cancer has been indisputably demonstrated in animals, the offending material is assumed to be a carcinogen in our bodies and is either not put into use or withdrawn from use.

It would be extremely convenient if all we had to do to assure our complete safety in using additives was to demonstrate that they did not cause cancer or other debilities in a variety of test animals. But it is not that simple. Some compounds do not cause cancer in all test animals; a

ORGANICS IN THE ENVIRONMENT

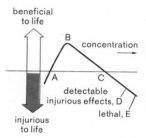

Fig. 6.2 *For many substances the difference between being beneficial or poisonous is merely a matter of concentration. At point A there may be no demonstrable effect; at point B the effect may be beneficial; at point C a substance may again be neither beneficial nor harmful; at point D harmful effects can be demonstrated; and at point E death may occur.* (From a letter to the editor by R. A. Horne. *Science* 177: 1152. Copyright 1972 by the American Association for the Advancement of Science)

119

dye, 2-naphthylamine, for example, causes cancer in dogs and humans, but not in rats, rabbits, or cats, while sodium arsenite causes cancer in humans but not in experimental animals. In addition there are the problems of deciding on the number of experimental animals that will assure a fair test, the diet on which to place them during testing, the stage in the life cycle to test (young, adult, pregnant, old), the duration of the experiment (some cancers develop in the offspring of the adults exposed to the test material), and whether administration should be oral, by injection, or by application to the skin surface. While many of these problems can be handled by standard experimental procedures, the testing of new drugs or additives has been both time-consuming and extremely expensive.

Further uncertainties arise from the latent period between the time of incipient damage and its expression in the form of a detectable cancer. It is not the youth of twenty-one smoking five packs of cigarettes a day, inhaling asbestos fibers, or ingesting a coal tar food dye who develops lung cancer, but the prematurely aging adult of fifty or sixty. Who can remember what was eaten or breathed twenty or thirty years ago that could explain a present stomach, kidney, or lung cancer? Human metabolism varies widely; even in the best of health, no two people are likely to metabolize a given compound in exactly the same way. During illness or organ malfunction a compound may be metabolized differently than during a normal state. Finally, additives may interact; an additive that normally is not absorbed in the intestine may be readily absorbed with ill effect if an emulsifier is present. So the whole subject of the impact of food additives on human health is far more complex than the "purists" and "adulterers" would have us believe.

The position of the food-processing industry is concisely stated by R. Blackwell Smith, Jr. of the Medical College of Virginia:

> Substantially every substance, including pure water and table salt, may be harmful if a sufficient quantity is swallowed or otherwise introduced into the body; and conversely, it is a generally accepted fact that there is no substance sure to kill or harm if swallowed or taken otherwise, provided the amount taken be sufficiently small . . . an additive or other chemical is not and cannot be of itself either poisonous or non-poisonous, hazardous or non-hazardous, harmful or safe; but every additive or other chemical may be safe at some level or mode of intake and hazardous at another level or mode of intake. The question, then, is not one of *whether* but essentially one of *how much*.[1]

[1] *Science and food: today and tomorrow.* 1961, NAS-NRS Publ., 887. Washington, D.C.

This argument is typically rebutted by William Longgood:

> Poison is harmful to the human organism. . . . When it is ingested by a human being there is damage. The more poison, the more damage. . . . The fact that the dose may be reduced until damage no longer can be seen or measured by man's instruments does not mean that the damage no longer exists; it merely means that it no longer can be seen.
>
> The vested interests that profit from the sale and use of chemicals in foods are scornful of this attitude. They say it is not scientific. As "scientific" proof of the alleged harmlessness of eating small amounts of poisons in foods, they solemnly point out that it is possible for a person to cram enough salt or water down his throat to kill himself. This is supposed to prove that everything is harmful and even fatal if taken in large enough jolts.
>
> What this strange logic claims is that because a little salt is innocent and a lot is harmful it follows that all other substances that are harmful in large amounts are safe in small amounts.
>
> Of course salt or water and the hundreds of poisons used in food cannot be equated in this way. Salt and water are necessary to life, while virtually none of the food chemicals is necessary or even useful to life; with only rare exceptions, these chemicals are antagonistic to living tissue. The question is not whether they harm those who consume them, but the extent of the harm.[2]

Realizing that we may be faced with a value judgment, perhaps the question to ask is not whether additives harm or how much, but why use them at all. Suppose, because of an atypical quirk of metabolism, one person in a million developed cancer from benzoate of soda, used to prevent spoilage of cider. The additive allows this delicious and healthful beverage to be available and enjoyed year round by the 999,999 unaffected people. Would the death of this person be justified by the pleasure or nutrition of the survivors? How about 1 in 100,000, or 1 in 1000? At what point is the cost balanced by the benefit?

CONTAMINANTS

Biocides as contaminants were discussed in Chapter 5. But there are other groups of contaminants that can and have caused problems by not being metabolized as was supposed and so being carried to the consumer's table.

[2] Longgood, W. F., 1960. *The poisons in your food.* Simon & Schuster, New York.

ANTIBIOTICS

The discovery of "wonder drugs" led to their widespread application and use for everything from a minor infection to a major disease. This tendency to over-prescribe led to extreme sensitivity of some people to certain antibiotics, penicillin especially. There was also an increasing resistance of disease organisms to antibiotics, a situation quite parallel to the resistance of insects to biocides.

When applied to animals, antibiotics effectively controlled, often for the first time, various poultry and stock diseases. But like the overanxious farmers with biocides, stock raisers began to treat their animals frequently, first as a preventive, then as a growth inducer. For it was found that when antibiotics were routinely given to chickens, gut bacteria, which normally slow the rate of growth, were sufficiently inhibited to allow the chicken to be marketed sooner at a greater weight and profit, though perhaps contaminated with the antibiotics. Mastitis, an udder disease in cows, can be treated with penicillin, but the penicillin is passed into the milk. In this instance, milk should be discarded for three days following treatment and antibiotic use should be halted for several days before marketing either the animal or the product to prevent contamination. *But this not always done.*

The danger is twofold. People who are highly sensitive to penicillin or other antibiotics may be exposed without their knowledge or control. In addition, if the population at large is constantly and unknowingly exposed to antibiotics, resistant forms of organisms may develop, making the drugs useless in a time of real need. Furthermore, recent evidence indicates that drug resistance is a genetic factor that can be transferred from one organism to another, even one species to another. Thus, gastrointestinal bacteria such as *Escherichia coli*, found in the large intestine of humans *and* animals, could acquire and pass on the resistance factor to any of several pathogenic bacteria normally responsive to the effects of antibiotic drugs. Routine feeding of almost 3 million pounds of antibiotics to livestock each year enhances the real possibility of the development and spread of drug resistance not only in livestock and humans, but in pathogens as well. Antibiotics are also used to inhibit bacterial growth on dressed chickens in stores. Although most of the antibiotic is destroyed in the cooking process, the danger lies in the false confidence that *all* disease organisms are thereby inhibited. *Salmonella*, a food-poisoning organism, is not inhibited and may increase to a dangerous state in a few days. Also, the illusion is created for the consumer that the food is fresher than it is. The consumer can only purchase by appearance, depending on the honesty of the producer or distributor for quality. Often one suspects that this dependence is abused.

Antibiotics, if they are to live up to their name, should never be used routinely, for the short-term profit is never worth the long-term risk to the livestock or the consumer, either during the life of the stock or upon its processing. In their enthusiasm for progressive techniques, food handlers do not always follow precautions, like the English butcher who sprayed his beef with DDT, and proudly announced that he spent eighteen shillings a week on "modern sprays." One can safely assume that antibiotics are occasionally misused with similar exuberance. In response to these problems, the FDA is slowly moving toward making antibiotic-containing feeds prescription drugs, a step taken by other nations many years ago.

HORMONES

With increased interest in and research on the development of hormonal contraceptives, a compound called diethylstilbestrol (DES) was synthesized that had biological effects similar to those of the female sex hormone, estrogen. It was found that when a pellet of DES was inserted under the skin of a chicken's neck, the animal rapidly gained weight and became plump and fat; a further useful effect was its ability to emasculate cocks into capons chemically, without castration. Poultry raisers could produce more chickens at lower cost and, of course, higher profit. The pellets, however, did not always dissolve before marketing, which must have led at times to a biologically effective dose of sex hormones for the unlucky consumer of a soup made with chicken necks.

The balance between male and female is a fine one and a very small amount of estrogen-simulating hormone (hormones are unaffected by cooking) can prove disastrous. Then too, some chickens were marketed containing as many as twelve pellets, some of which had migrated to other parts of the chicken. Furthermore, it was discovered after a few years of use that although a DES-treated chicken did indeed look better and weigh more than a normal chicken, it was because of increased fat and water content, not increased protein. Even the fat proved worthless, forming a gooey mess when fried.

In 1960 the FDA declared DES off-limits for chickens. DES was used in beef and lamb production, however, until 1973. While sixteen cents' worth of DES implanted behind a heifer's ear supposedly produced $12 of extra beef, or 15 percent faster growth on 12 percent less feed, no such dramatic response was found in pigs, which thus remain untreated. While the amount of synthetic hormone ingested by eating beef treated according to directions is well below the level necessary to affect the delicate physiology of sex hormones, there are suggestions that synthetic estrogens may cause cancer in men under certain conditions. Certainly, im-

123

properly applied amounts with an insufficient period allowed for full absorption and metabolic breakdown present a danger to the beef-eating public. With growing evidence of side effects from synthetic hormones used as contraceptives (see Chapter 23), the risk of contaminating virtually all beef produced in the United States with synthetic hormones for the short-term gain of $12 a head seemed to outweigh the benefits. Then in 1971 vaginal cancer was found in some women whose mothers had taken DES to prevent miscarriages during their pregnancies. In response to increasing concern about the potential carcinogenic effect of residual amounts of DES in meat, the FDA banned DES in cattle food in 1972. In 1973, when small amounts of DES continued to turn up in liver, the last remaining use of implanted pellets of DES was also discontinued. Producers threatened higher beef prices, even though no one ever claimed that the consumer got more protein for his money; only the grower benefited by selling a heavier steer sooner. However, a United States Court of Appeals decision closely following the FDA ban in 1973 overrode the ban on a technicality. As of this writing DES is still being used to fatten beef for market.

PCBS

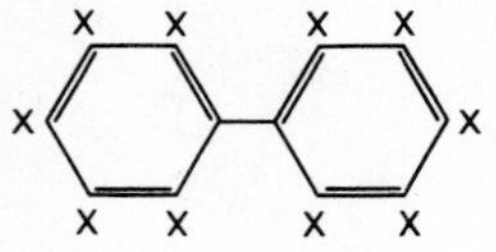

While many of the organic compounds that threaten us are associated with processed foods, increasing numbers have been and are being introduced to the environment unintentionally or in the belief that they are harmless. Polychlorinated biphenols (PCBs) are among the most worrisome of these. By no means a recent development, PCBs have become increasingly widespread in industry over the last forty years; they are used in the manufacture of electrical capacitors, insulating fluids, carbonless copy paper, plasticizers, and a multitude of other products. Between 1930 and 1971 over a billion pounds of PCBs were produced; almost three fourths of this amount probably entered the environment, where PCBs were first discovered in the flesh of Baltic fish in 1966. Since its chromatographic "signature" closely resembles that of DDT (Figure 6.3), part of the impact of DDT in some situations can probably be ascribed to PCBs. Like DDT, PCBs are insoluble in water, very soluble in fat and oil, thermally stable up to 862°C, and resist biological and chemical decomposition. Unlike DDT, which is a single compound, PCBs are a group of over sixty different but related compounds. In 1968, just after they were discovered in the environment, a number of people in Japan were poisoned with rice oil that had become contaminated with 2500 ppm of PCBs. The illness, called yushi disease, included swelling of the upper eyelids, visual problems, acne-like skin eruptions, heightened skin pigmentation, hearing loss, and neurological disorders. In addition, these effects were transmitted across the placental membrane, affecting fetuses

Fig. 6.3 *The PCB molecule is made up of two benzene rings joined together. Chlorine atoms may become attached at any of the points marked by Xs. Because of the large number of possible chlorine substitutions, there is no one formula for PCB, but rather a mixture of several of the possibilities.*

and newborns. Because of the long residence time of PCBs in the body, recovery time is rather slow.

At least 84 million of us in the United States have as much as 1 ppm of PCBs in our body fat. Recent work, however, suggests that like the dioxin impurity found in 2,4,5-T, the acute effects of PCBs are due to the highly poisonous chlorinated dibenzofurans. American produced PCBs seem to be free of this dangerous contaminant and are supposed to be less toxic than DDT, for example. Our worry is the long-term sublethal effects, which are harder to document but more threatening to the environment.

After the lamprey had been controlled in the Great Lakes (see Chapter 4), the federal government spent $175 million to restock the lakes with salmon and lake trout, hoping to restore the fishing industry. But the effort has been wasted. Fish with 10–15 ppm of PCBs (the accepted limit is 5 ppm) have been found in Lake Michigan, forcing cancellation of salmon fishing in some Great Lakes states. If the maximum permissible body burden of PCBs were 1 ppm, few fish from the Great Lakes would be harvestable. The Hudson River was recently closed to striped bass fishing because the fish contained high levels of PCBs, 11 to 89 ppm. Researchers found that the major source of the PCBs was a General Electric plant in Hudson Falls, which had been releasing thirty pounds of PCBs per day into the river for some time. PCBs have turned up in a number of unexpected places—shredded wheat and noodles (apparently carbonless copy paper containing PCBs was used in making the packages), animal feed, plastic food wrapping, and polystyrene coffee cups.

Faced with the increasing distribution and concentration of PCBs in the environment, Monsanto Chemical, the sole United States producer, voluntarily agreed to sell PCBs only for use in closed systems. In addition the FDA restricted the use of PCBs in the production of food and feeds, and set tolerance limits for a wide range of foods found to contain PCBs (milk, 2.5 ppm; poultry and fish, 5 ppm; eggs, 0.5 ppm). However, PCBs have continued to accumulate in the environment despite these controls. At least ten tons per year entered the Pacific from the sewer outfall of Los Angeles alone. The lag between the quantities of PCBs already in the environment and the concentrations presently recorded in various organisms probably means that large quantities of PCBs are now in landfills or shallow estuarine sediments. Since PCBs are stable, much of this material can be expected to contaminate the adjoining environment sooner or later.

Perhaps as a result of the kepone incident (see Chapter 5) and rising concern about the ubiquity of PCBs in the environment, in 1976 Congress finally passed a Toxic Substances Control Act, which phased out all uses of PCBs and required notification of the EPA ninety days before a chemical can be produced commercially or put to a significant new use. If the EPA feels that the compound may be dangerous in the environment it may delay production and require testing. However the EPA was given only $10 million per year to evaluate 30,000 chemicals already at large and the 500 to 1500 new ones produced each year.

VINYL CHLORIDE

Phonograph records and floor tiles represent two major uses of vinyl chloride in our everyday lives, but countless products and foods are packaged in this plastic, which more and more evidence seems to be indicting as a carcinogen. Twenty cases of angiosarcoma, a rare liver cancer, have been reported in workers who were exposed to vinyl chloride. Over 700,000 workers in the United States alone come into contact with this ubiquitous compound. Even more ominous are reports of more frequent stillbirths and miscarriages among the wives of vinyl chloride workers. As of 1975 vinyl chloride exposure standards for workers were set at 1 ppm. It had been assumed that the harmful effects of vinyl chloride were limited to people who inhaled vinyl chloride dust. But more recent research indicates that vinyl chloride fed to rats produces liver and other cancers. Considering the number of vinyl chloride bottles, containers, and packages currently in use, millions of people could be exposed to potentially dangerous compounds leached from vinyl chloride containers.

In support of this concern, vinyl chloride concentrations as high as 1.9 ppm have been found in the air above landfills in Edison, New Jersey and Los Angeles. While the gas was traced to buried polyvinyl chloride sludge from local chemical plants rather than to plastic items, 57 plants in the United States make polyvinyl chloride gas, pellets, or resins, and 7500 plants use the substance in manufacturing. So this source of contamination is widespread.

BCME

Another unexpected contaminant, the product of the reaction of formaldehyde and hydrochloric acid (bis-chloromethyl ether), has been reported to cause lung cancer in animals exposed to 0.1 ppm. Since formaldehyde-HCl solutions are widely used in the textile, chemical, and paper/wood products industries, and in standard analytical chemical, pathology, and histology tests and procedures, lab technicians and organic chemists may be exposed to yet another carcinogen.

CHLORINATED HYDROCARBONS

A final example of manmade environmental hazard from unexpected organic sources is the contamination of public water supplies with chlorinated hydrocarbons, some of which may be carcinogenic. These chlorinated hydrocarbons were not produced as biocides or dumped as waste products, at least not directly. In the early 1970s epidemiologists discovered that 15 percent more white males were dying of cancer in New Orleans, which obtains its drinking water from the Mississippi, than in nearby localities drawing their water from other sources. Recently developed analytical techniques applied to the New Orleans water supply discovered 66 chemicals in the water. Most were present in very small amounts, less than 1 μg per liter; but chloroform, a suspected carcinogen, was as concentrated as 100 μg per liter. Ironically, the source of the chlorine in many chlorinated hydrocarbons on the list was the chlorine used to "purify" New Orleans' drinking water. The Mississippi's vast drainage and the numerous petrochemical plants on its banks provide it with a goodly variety of hydrocarbon compounds. But the chlorination process forms chlorinated derivatives that are more carcinogenic than the precursors in the river water. Most of these compounds can be removed by activated charcoal filtering or by replacing the chlorine in the water purification process with ozone (see Chapter 16).

PRESERVATIVES

One of the chief problems with food is its relatively short storage life. Since earliest times man has tried to preserve his perishable foods by drying or adding salt, sugar, or spices. Today, benzoic acid or sodium benzoate is often used to preserve liquids which might otherwise ferment, sulfur dioxide is generally used to preserve dried fruit, and sorbic acid is used for various other products.

While many of these preservatives allow broad distribution and reasonable shelf life of processed foods, preservatives are also used to embalm food that is too far gone to be acceptable as fresh. Such a practice leads to the adding of artificial colors, then flavors—compounds that might be more dangerous to health than the original preservatives.

One of the most commonly used preservatives is sodium nitrite. Since 1925, sodium nitrite has been added to meat products at a level of about 200 ppm to inhibit botulism, which produces a deadly toxin, and to impart a pleasant pinkish hue to a product that otherwise would be an unappetizing gray. All was apparently well with bacon and the hot dog, the two nitrite-preserved foods we eat most frequently, until a few years ago. Then nitrosamines, a group of carcinogens, began to be found in air, soil, water, and sewage wastes. This fitted into a problem that had long puzzled epidemiologists—the connection between the high levels of some forms of cancer in urban areas and the high levels of nitrogen dioxide in cities. Nitrogen dioxide itself has never been shown to cause cancer. But combined with water, nitrogen dioxide can form nitrous acid, which combines with amines to form nitrosamines.

Nitrosamines can be made from the nitrite in hot dogs or bacon when these foods enter the acid stomach. The nitrite may react with creatinine in the meat fibers of the food to form creatinine-5-oxime. This carcinogen has been found in rat stomachs in proportion to the amount of nitrites the animal has eaten. When bacon is fried the nitrite reacts with amines, also found in bacon, to form a nitrosamine called nitrosopyrrolidine, which occurs in fried bacon at the concentration of 10 to 20 ppb. This is a very small quantity, comparable to one kernel of corn in 800 bushels; certainly no one is going to die from one fatal slice of bacon. But what about a lifetime of three or four slices every morning? Normally we would be protected from the deleterious effects of nitrite by the Delaney Amendment. But additives in use before the Delaney Amendment was enacted in 1958 were exempted and placed in a category labeled Generally Regarded As Safe (GRAS). Moves to remove nitrites from the GRAS list have been opposed by the food industry, which fears that botulism cannot be controlled as effectively with other preservatives and that the public will not accept the taste or appearance of hot dogs and bacon without nitrites.

ANTIOXIDANTS

An adjunct to the preserving process is the inhibition of the natural tendency of fatty acids, especially those which are unsaturated, to oxidize or become rancid (Figure 6.4). Most prepared foods with unsaturated fatty

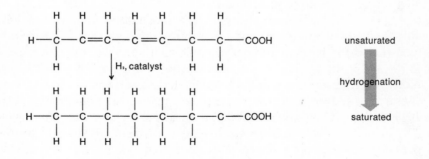

Fig. 6.4 An unsaturated fatty acid has many double bonds between carbon atoms. When these double bonds are replaced by hydrogen atoms the fatty acid is said to be "saturated." "Polyunsaturated" simply means that there are many double bonds present. These double bonds must be protected from oxidation by additives called antioxidants.

acids contain an antioxidant to preserve the original fresh flavor of the food and extend shelf or storage life. Some commonly used antioxidants are butylated hydroxyanisole (BHA), propyl gallate, and butylated hydroxytoluene (BHT). The antioxidant properties of these compounds are often enhanced by ascorbic, citric, and phosphoric acid. Once again, as with certain emulsifiers and detergents, the effect of some antioxidants, especially BHT, may extend beyond the food in which it is ingested to the body itself, inhibiting the uptake of oxygen by hemoglobin in the red blood cells.

On the other hand, this same antioxidant effect may benefit the body as well. The incidence of stomach cancer has been decreasing for the past fifty years, in part because more and more foods are refrigerated. Refrigeration suppresses the conversion of nitrate in food to nitrite. BHT/BHA as well as vitamins C and E may inhibit the conversion of nitrate to nitrite in the body. This would be a pleasant switch from our usual expectations from additives, but it also reminds us of how little we know about how our food is metabolized, with or without additives.

ACIDS

Most acid additives are perfectly safe and have been used for many years without problems. Baking powder or cream of tartar (tartaric acid) reacts with baking soda and produces carbon dioxide, a leavening agent that makes bread and cake light. Phosphoric, citric, and malic acids are used extensively to counteract the otherwise excessive sweetness of most soft drinks. It is not the acids that are a problem to health, but the overindulgence in pastry and soda to the exclusion of more nutritious food.

EMULSIFIERS

In general, an emulsifier breaks up fats and oils into tiny particles; when used in bread it acts as a softening agent. Homemade bread hardens quickly as it grows stale; commercial bread with emulsifiers stays soft much longer. This gives the shopper the illusion of freshness and reinforces the now erroneous conclusion that soft bread is fresh bread. Emulsifiers also allow the water content of bread to be increased, resulting in the characteristic soft spongy texture of commercial white bread. Pound for pound there is likely to be more air and water in commercial loaves than in homemade bread—air and water the consumer pays for in lieu of flour. One emulsifier, polyoxyethylene, no longer used in the United States, was found to increase greatly the rate of iron absorption in some animals. Excessive deposition in the liver can lead to cirrhosis and cancer.

Other emulsifiers such as glycerides, lecithin, sorbatin, and alginate are used in baked goods, ice cream, and confections. In baked goods, emulsifiers improve the fineness, uniformity of texture, and softness. Smooth consistency in ice cream depends upon the uniform size of ice crystals, which is controlled by alginate or emulsifiers and stabilizers.

129

ARTIFICIAL SWEETENERS

Saccharin, discovered in 1879, has been used for many years as a sugar substitute, especially by diabetics, who must control their sugar intake. In 1950 a second group of nonnutritive sweeteners, the cyclamates, was introduced. While saccharin has over 300 times the sweetening power of sucrose (cane sugar), cyclamates are only thirty times as sweet.

Since saccharin was not thought to be metabolized by the body, it was considered safe within recommended dose limits (1 g per day). But recent research seems to indicate that saccharin, like cyclamates, may be carcinogenic, and the drug may be restricted in its use. However, many countries restrict or prohibit its use, not because of ill effects but to avoid misleading people into substituting a nonfood for a food of high caloric value. Cyclamates were apparently metabolized, at least by some people; some 20 percent of cyclamate users generated a breakdown product that, when applied to rat cells, caused chromosomes to break up. Further possible danger was suggested by the linking of cyclamates to birth defects in chickens. For this reason cyclamates were banned from foods in 1970.

While saccharin might be excused as a useful sugar substitute for diabetics, cyclamates were totally unnecessary. They entered the market in response to the recent fetish for losing weight by every possible means except reduction of food intake. Rather than give up soft drinks or even cut down consumption, the weight-conscious public was only too happy to have its soft drinks without their calories. But deprived of energy-yielding sugar, a soft drink becomes a nonfood, an expensive way to restore body fluids compared with water.

FOOD DYES

Of all the food additives, nonvegetable or coal tar dyes are at once the most hazardous, based on past experience, and the most unnecessary. No brief can be made for their nutritional or preservative value, only the rather weak rationale that the consumer demands vivid colors in his food —oranges must be orange, butter yellow, and cherries scarlet. Many dyes have been demonstrated to be carcinogenic; therefore, many closely related compounds are suspect. But which to suspect is an apparent source of confusion. England allows thirty dyes, the United States fifteen; but the English ban nine of our dyes and we ban most of their thirty. This reinforces real doubt about the wisdom of ingesting *any* coal tar dyes.

Further uneasiness about food dyes arose when the FDA banned Red Number 2 in 1976 on the basis of cancer formation in rats. This dye, which had been tested and found acceptable, had been used for many years. Suddenly we were told that further use of Red Number 2 would be dangerous and that it would be replaced by another dye, Red Number 40, whose carcinogenic properties are little better known. Unfortunately, even as we play this game of musical dyes the chance of products without dyes decreases steadily. The economics are simple: processing foods is more profitable than simply marketing them. Why should a company sell you potatoes at 20 cents a pound if it can dehydrate them and make you pay $1.00 a pound?

A rather bizarre effect that has been attributed to food dyes and flavors is hyperactivity in children. Supposedly, the artificial flavoring and dyes in one soft drink can affect a sensitive child for two to three days. Only further research can tell whether this is a valid conclusion or merely pinning the tail of a frustrating condition on a convenient and conspicuous donkey. But we are rapidly learning to expect the unusual from the innocuous.

One solution to the problem of food dyes, currently under research and development, is to use long polymers (molecules whose subunits repeat) that are too large to cross the lining of the alimentary canal into the body.

Many of the additives we have discussed are, of course, combined in certain products; indeed, a few of these products contain little but additives. Maraschino cherries, for example, are preserved with sodium benzoate, firmed with calcium hydroxide, bleached with sulfur dioxide, artificially flavored, then given their bright green or red color with a coal tar dye.

Several years ago two firms marketed blueberry pancake mix depicting luscious blueberries prominently on the packages. The "blueberries" in one mix, according to the FDA, were made chiefly of sugars, nonfat dry milk, starch, coconut pulp, artificial coal tar coloring, artificial flavoring, and a very small amount of blueberry pulp. The second firm's "blueberries" were of an equally startling composition: sugar, gum acacia, citric acid, starch, artificial coloring and flavoring, and some blueberry pulp. Since these purple pellets were hardly blueberries, the FDA forced the manufacturers to change the labels.

OUR DAILY BREAD

While doctored cherries and fake blueberries can easily be eliminated from the diet, other more basic foods have a depressingly long list of additives on their labels. Assuming that the ideal food is transported from the field to the dinner table with the minimum amount of tampering and maximum retention of plain good taste and food value, bread has fallen rather far from the ideal.

131

The wheat grain as harvested is mostly endosperm, a storage tissue of starch and protein attached to the small embryo or wheat germ. Surrounding the grain are the seed coats. They contain vitamins E and B, certain minerals, and amino acids, while the wheat germ contains unsaturated fatty acids.

At one time in flour processing, the grain was ground into flour including both the germ and the seed coats or bran. Thus all of the vitamins and minerals were preserved and passed on through the baked bread to the consumer. But to many the bread was coarse and heavy, and the flour was quickly spoiled by the activities of insects attracted to the rich grain and by the fatty acids in the wheat germ becoming rancid. In the late nineteenth century a new process was developed to roll the grain instead of grinding it. In this process, the starchy endosperm powdered while the oily germ rolled flat. When shaken through sieves, the germ could be separated from the flour. This allowed the flour to be kept longer without spoiling.

But flour must be matured or aged to reach its maximum workability; during this period of storage there is an opportunity for insects to attack the flour. Then it was discovered that nitrogen trichloride or agene (today dyox or chlorine dioxide is used because of potential danger from agene) could mature the flour instantly. But at the same time it bleached the flour white, decoloring the pale yellow fragments of the seed coats and endosperm left from the milling process. While this produced a flour of indefinite keeping power, it was practically devoid of its vitamins and minerals—vitamins A, B, and E, calcium, and iron. What was left was mostly starch and 7 to 11 percent protein.

In previous years, when bread was an integral part of every meal and fresh fruit and vegetables were not available year round, many people depended upon bread for vitamins. During World War II, white bread was finally enriched by adding vitamins. Bread producers continue to advertise the fantastic energy and vitamin values of their ultrasoft and moist bread, which must often be toasted to attain sufficient substance to retain the contents of a sandwich. Few appreciate the irony of a situation where the flour processor mills out some twenty vitamins and minerals, puts four back, then touts his product's enrichment!

Of course this need not be, for flour can be milled to preserve much of the nutrition without sacrificing its storage life, and matured without resorting to vitamin-destroying bleaches. But the public seems more concerned with the aesthetics of the product than its nutritional value. This faulty sense of priorities is unfortunately characteristic of the consuming public—an overconcern with appearance coupled with a lack of awareness or concern for the real purpose of food. If bread is merely a convenient way to sop up gravy, then we might as well use our spoons. If it is a source of vitamins and minerals necessary for maintaining good health, then it is senseless to mill out these vitamins for whatever reason and replace a few at the consumer's additional expense in the name of good nutrition. The alternative is not a whole wheat bread, which some faddists tout as a cure-all, but a flour milled to retain most or all of its native nutrients, obviating the expense of adding them in the baking process.

Perhaps as a result of the recent furor over rats dying of malnutrition on a diet of white bread or the "empty" calories of many breakfast cereals, a wide range of speciality breads, breakfast cereals, and unbleached flour has become available. So the public at last has a choice.

Faced with public apathy about nutrition, nutritionists are beginning to favor adding vitamins and minerals to the trash/snack foods people consume in preference to old-fashioned square meals. So in the near future we may be able to exist, literally as well as figuratively, on potato chips, cookies, pizza, cake mix, ketchup, and instant coffee (Figure 6.5).

Fig. 6.5 *This shopping cart contains many of the staples of contemporary American cuisine.* Bon appétit!

OVERBREEDING

Unfortunately the old stand-bys, fruits and vegetables, are not the source of vitamins and nutrients they once were. Hundreds of years of breeding for yield, resistance to pests, ease of harvest and processing, color, texture, and flavor have ignored nutrient content and possible increases in the content of toxic substances. The irradiation of potato seed tubers increased yield; it also increased the toxic alkaloid solanin by 60 percent. In response to this problem, the FDA is preparing to regulate changes in nutrient value or the amount of toxic substances in food crops. A 20 percent decrease in nutrient content and a 10 percent increase in toxic substances will probably be regarded as a threshold for FDA intervention.

With all the potential combinations and recombinations of the organic molecules we already discard into the environment, why do we continue to invent new ones to make the mess worse, especially when epidemiologists tell us that much cancer in humans has environmental causes? The reason is economic. Screening a chemical by traditional techniques costs at least $100,000 and takes two to three years. Since thousands of new compounds are unleashed every year, few have been screened. The recent Toxic Substances Control Act should help plug this loophole.

For some time we have needed a single, inexpensive, quick test that would give some clue about the potential impact of a new chemical on the biosphere. One promising technique has been worked out by Bruce Ames, a biochemist at Berkeley. It uses a strain of the bacterium *Salmonella typhimurium* which has lost its ability to make histidine, an amino acid. When a culture of this bacterium is exposed to a mutagenic chemical it mutates back to producing histidine, grows, and makes an observable colony in a petri dish. The more colonies per dish, the stronger the mutagenic properties of the chemical being tested. The test costs around $200 per chemical and takes three days to carry out. Other tests have been devised that utilize yeast, fruit flies, and special cultures of mammalian cells. According to Ames, 90 percent of 174 known carcinogens cause mutations in his strain of *Salmonella*. Unfortunately, the test does not predict the probability that a mutagen is carcinogenic. Still, such techniques open the door to possible mass screening of most if not all the chemicals being released in new products and processes. At a time when *everything* seems potentially harmful, such tests would go a long way toward making our external and internal environments less dangerous than they have recently come to be.

FURTHER READING

Ahmed, A. K., 1976. "PCB's in the environment." *Env.* **18**(2), pp. 6–11. Good review of the PCB problem.

Cleave, T. L., 1975. *The saccharine disease: conditions caused by the taking of refined carbohydrates such as sugar and white flour.* Keats Publishing Co., New Canaan, Connecticut.

Holden, C., 1974. "Food and nutrition: is America due for a national policy?" *Science* **184**, pp. 548–550. A critique of the food most of us eat.

Kolata, G. B., 1976. "Chemical carcinogens: industry adopts controversial 'quick' tests." *Science* **192,** pp. 1215–1217. Better a quick test than no test?

Layne, E. N., 1972. "The ABCs of PCBs." *Audubon,* **74**(1), pp. 116–118. More on the ubiquitous PCBs.

Marx, J. L., 1974. "Drinking water: another source of carcinogens?" *Science* **186,** pp. 809–811. Carcinogens are where you find them.

Shapley, D., 1976. "Nitrosamines: scientists on the trail of prime suspect in urban cancer." *Science* **192,** pp. 268–270. Some background on the carcinogen linked to the nitrates used to preserve cold cuts.

Yudkin, J., 1972. *Sweet and dangerous.* Bantam Books, New York. Dr. Yudkin's book, like Cleave's, looks at some of the negative effects of our favorite source of calories.

CHAPTER
SEVEN

INORGANIC
POLLUTANTS

BECAUSE OUR BODIES are made of organic matter, we are especially conscious of the effects of organic chemicals on the complex biochemistry of life. But inorganic chemicals often escape the attention they deserve; it is usually long after they have been adopted that their danger to our health is recognized.

Of the many inorganic substances that interact harmfully with physiological systems, mercury, lead, cadmium, beryllium, and asbestos are potentially the most dangerous because they are stored in the body and have a cumulative effect.

MERCURY

The Hatter was the first to break the silence. "What day of the month is it?" he said, turning to Alice: he had taken his watch out of his pocket, and was looking at it uneasily, shaking it every now and then, and holding it to his ear.

Alice considered a little, and then said "The fourth."

"Two days wrong!" sighed the Hatter. "I told you butter wouldn't suit the works!" he added, looking angrily at the March Hare.

"It was the *best* butter," the March Hare meekly replied.

"Yes, but some crumbs must have got in as well," the Hatter grumbled "you shouldn't have put it in with the breadknife." [1]

[1] Carroll, L., 1939. *The complete works of Lewis Carroll*. The Nonesuch Press, London.

In Lewis Carroll's day, hatters *were* often mad. Their condition was noticeable enough to be enshrined in a popular expression, but not until recently was the madness recognized as an occupational hazard of hatters or people who worked with animal skins. At one time fur pelts were processed with mercuric chloride and anyone who worked with the treated skins ran the risk of mercury poisoning. Hatters, who fashioned men's hats from beaver skins, were especially vulnerable to mercury fumes. Today, mercury compounds are no longer used in processing furs, nor are beaver hats wildly popular, so the phrase "mad as a hatter" has passed from common speech and even understanding. Mercury poisoning, however, remains a hazard.

Because of its vague initial symptoms—fatigue, headache, and irritability—mercury poisoning often goes unrecognized at first. Later, arm and leg numbness develops, followed by disruption of balance, blurring of vision, deterioration of muscular coordination, emotional disturbances, and finally wasting away of muscles.

Mercury in naturally occurring stable compounds causes no problems, but its liberation in the form of soluble salts from a group of mercury compounds with industrial or agricultural uses is beginning to raise some concern.

INORGANIC MERCURY COMPOUNDS

Inorganic mercury compounds are used by over eighty industries including plastics, industrial chlorine, and electronics. Until recently most cases of mercury poisoning resulted from occupational exposure: accumulation of inorganic mercury in the kidneys affected readsorption and secretion of sugar, protein, and salts; and accumulation in the brain caused loss of coordination. But in 1953 a number of people living in the vicinity of Minamata Bay, Japan, became ill with a strange series of disorders. Ultimately over a hundred cases were reported, many ending in death or permanent disability. Investigations finally linked the disorders with seafood taken from Minamata Bay; hence the ailment was known as Minamata disease. One case history gives some idea of its nature:

A 14-year-old boy who had been agile and bright before his illness is said to have eaten a large number of crabs and small fish from a posted area of Minamata Bay during a ten-day period in July, 1958. A few weeks later he noted numbness around his mouth and in his hands and feet. He did not have fever, headache, or a stiff neck. He . . . became clumsy in buttoning his clothes and handling his chopsticks; his family observed that he staggered slightly when walking. His auditory acuity and attention span diminished, and he developed the mannerisms and behavior of a younger child. . . . His memory for most recent events was adequate, but he was unable to perform calculations beyond the eight- or nine-year old level. When observed in 1960, he was still hospitalized in the Minamata City Hospital. . . . His physical disability was considered mild, but his inability to calculate and remember complex Japanese written characters made it impossible for him to continue in school.[2]

Of fifty-two cases originally studied, seventeen died and twenty-three were permanently disabled.

Other circumstantial evidence linking the disease to the eating of seafood from Minamata Bay was the death of large numbers of cats belonging to afflicted families. Judging from the symptoms, the illness was a form of mercury poisoning. In Minamata City, at the head of the bay, a chemical plant had greatly increased its production of vinyl chloride; simultaneously the number of cases of Minamata disease increased.

Mercuric chloride is used as a catalyst in the production of vinyl chloride. Since sixty grams of mercuric chloride are "lost" per ton of vinyl chloride manufactured, it has been calculated that in one year nearly 2000 kilograms of waste mercury were generated: 1000 kilograms were washed from the vinyl chloride produced and another 1000 kilograms of spent catalyst was discarded. Although the source of the mercury was inorganic and insoluble, when it settled in the bottom mud of aquatic systems it was converted into water-soluble methylmercury, which accumulates in organisms. Although the Minamata plant had settling basins and improved waste treatment facilities, enough inorganic mercury was transformed into organic forms to enter the bay's food chain and poison the bottom mud, shellfish, fish, and finally people. The methylmercury content of mud from the bay had a range of 12 to 2010 ppm, shellfish had 38 to 102 ppm, the people who died from Minamata disease, 13 to 144 ppm in kidney tissues.

These instances of the conversion of inorganic mercury to poisonous organic mercury are dramatic, but they are limited to the vicinity of plants that use inorganic mercury compounds in their processing. Of still greater concern to the general public is the entry of mercury into the environment directly through organic mercury compounds.

ORGANIC MERCURY COMPOUNDS

There are two types of organic mercury: aryl salts of mercury (those with carbon rings attached), which break down into inorganic mercury in the body, and alkyl (straight chain hydrocarbon) salts of mercury, particularly methylmercury, which are able to diffuse easily through membranes and

[2] Kurland, L. T. *et al.*, 1960. "Minamata disease." *World Neurology*, 1, pp. 370–395.

spread throughout the body. Methylmercury also produces somewhat different symptoms than inorganic compounds of mercury.

MERCURY IN THE ENVIRONMENT

In 1970 a number of reports of mercury accumulation above 0.5 ppm in marine fish, especially swordfish and tuna, caused much concern. The concern was followed by much confusion when 90-year-old and 2000-year-old oceanic fish tissue was found to have mercury levels as high or even higher. These puzzling results can be interpreted in several ways: that since there has always been mercuric contamination of fish we needn't worry about the small additional amount we add through our activities (less than 1 percent of the present mercury concentration in the sea); or that because oceanic fish already have naturally high levels of mercury in their tissues and the difference between tolerably high natural levels and harmful levels is very small, we can ill afford to increase that body burden by carelessly adding more mercury to aquatic systems (Figure 7.1).

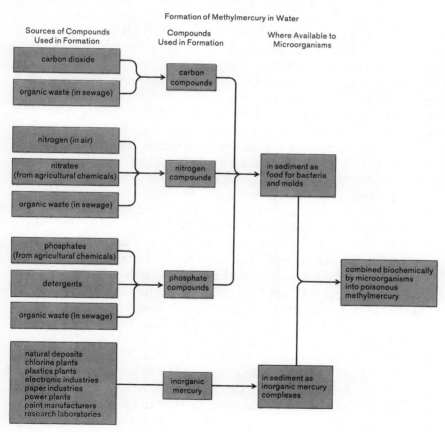

Fig. 7.1 The occurrence of the biologically active methylmercury in water depends on many factors besides the manufacture and release of methylmercury itself. (Adapted from an illustration that appeared in "A progress report on mercury." John M. Wood. *Environment* 14(1): 36-37. Copyright © 1972 Scientists' Institute for Public Information)

Mercury most commonly enters ecological systems through the widespread use of fungicides, for mercury compounds are potent killers of fungi. Organic compounds of mercury, especially methylmercury, have been widely used by pulp mills to keep fungi, bacteria, and algae, which thrive on wood pulp, from clogging up the machinery. By 1970 methylmercury released into the environment from this source had accumulated in freshwater fish to such an extent (more than 0.5 ppm) that people were advised not to eat fish caught from the St. Lawrence, Oswego, and Niagara Rivers as well as Lakes Erie, Ontario, Champlain, and Onondaga. In response to this problem most pulp mills have either eliminated or drastically curtailed use of fungicides containing mercury, and chloralkali plants which produce mercuric chloride are being phased out. As a result, the mercury content of fish in northern Ontario dropped 40 percent between 1970 and 1974 but it is still often much higher than 0.5 ppm. One reason is that bacteria and fungi in aerobic as well as anaerobic aquatic environments can apparently convert mercury from inorganic to organic forms, which can then be accumulated in food chains.

Another use of mercury-containing fungicides has been the treatment of seeds to prevent or inhibit the growth of molds during storage and after the planting of seed in the spring. In 1970 the tragic poisoning of an entire family who ate pork fed on methylmercury-treated grains illustrated the danger of such a practice.

Swedish farmers, until recently, regularly dusted up to 80 percent of all grains sown with a fungicide containing methylmercury. The poisoning of birds who ate treated seed led to investigations that showed that eggs produced in Sweden contained four times the mercury of eggs from other European countries, 0.026 ppm contrasted with 0.007 ppm. Although these levels are not considered dangerous, the World Health Organization (WHO) warns against more than 0.05 ppm.

When hens were fed treated seeds, the methylmercury content of their eggs rose to 4 ppm. The question then arose whether grain grown from treated seeds would retain any of the methylmercury and pass it along in a food chain. Experiments in Sweden indicated that seeds of plants grown from methylmercury-treated seeds contained 0.030 ppm mercury, while the plants from untreated seeds produced seeds with only 0.014 ppm mercury. When hens were fed treated seed their eggs contained 0.29 ppm mercury; the eggs of hens fed untreated seed contained 0.010 ppm mercury. As a result of such data, changes in the formulation of the fungicide and in its application rate were recommended to Swedish farmers. A less toxic form of organic mercury, methoxyethylmercury, replaced the highly toxic methylmercury, and only seeds containing mold were treated before planting. This reduced the percentage of treated seeds from 80 percent to 12 percent. The yield of grain was not reduced by these practices, and the mercury level in eggs decreased from 0.029

ppm in March 1964 to 0.010 ppm in September 1967.

In the United States, methylmercury fungicides are widely used in agriculture, especially in wheat-growing areas. Although preliminary testing by the United States Department of Agriculture has not corroborated the Swedish finding of appreciable amounts of mercury in seeds of plants grown from treated seeds, further testing might well demonstrate this.

Treated seed is routinely eaten by game; as a result, pheasants in Montana in 1969 contained between 0.05 ppm and 0.45 ppm of mercury. In California that same year, pheasants with a mercury level of 1.4 to 4.7 ppm were found, and a general level of at least 1 ppm in the pheasant population of Alberta, Canada made it necessary to cancel the pheasant-hunting season in that province.

Although the Food and Drug Administration allowed *no* mercury residue in or on foods until 1970 (in compliance with the much-debated zero tolerance rule or Delaney Amendment), currently the fungicide manufacturer has only to demonstrate that residues are harmless.

At present levels of fungicide use, with or without zero tolerance, the question is not *whether* foods contain mercury (apples often contain 0.1 ppm, tomatoes 0.1 ppm, potatoes 0.05 ppm, eggs and meat 0.1 ppm), but whether these levels are harmful or may be a cumulative threat in the future.

It should be noted that current tests analyze for total elemental mercury, not the more biologically reactive methylmercury. Also, two different types of analysis are commonly used. The flameless atomic absorption spectrometer method is cheap but less accurate than the neutron activation analysis method, which though quite accurate is expensive. The mercury levels reported are therefore not always accurate, nor do the findings of different research teams using the different methods always agree.

Most European countries have varying tolerance standards for mercury in foodstuffs. Despite the formal zero tolerance level for mercury residues in the United States, few crops are presently being routinely monitored for methylmercury residues by the United States Department of Agriculture. It might be prudent, in view of uncertainty about the toxicity of the methylmercury in food, to substitute less toxic forms of mercury in widely used fungicides. This would probably reduce, in grain directly and in the food chain indirectly, the mercury residue resulting from the accidental ingestion of treated grain by livestock or birds. The time thus bought might permit us to develop fungicides of more selective toxicity, affecting just the target fungus and not all other life a well.

While methylmercury from fungicides has had some spectacular effects on seed-eating birds, the amounts used are too small to explain widespread contamination in other animal species. Analysis of the mercury content of a number of coal sources suggests that at least 3000 tons of mercury are released per year by the burning of coal all over the world; this is close to the amount released by industrial processes. However, containing mercury from the combustion process would be far more difficult than controlling industrial mercury.

LEAD

Between 1954 and 1964, 128 children died of lead poisoning in the United States, but the lead source was neither air pollution nor careless use or storage of a biocide. Until 1958 most interior paints contained lead pigments; since that time lead has been replaced by titanium. However, some old houses were painted countless times with lead paint; as a result, thick chips of leaded paint fall off as the walls and ceilings

Fig. 7.2 Peeling paint has great fascination for children, who are tempted to break off the pieces and eat them, thus ingesting the lead they may contain.

peel (Figure 7.2). Putty also contains lead and is even more likely to be found in substandard dwellings. A third source of domestic lead is the ink used in the glossy color pages of magazines: yellow ink may contain as much as 2900 ppm of lead; red, 4100 ppm; blue, 445 ppm; and black, 275 ppm. A child who eats 4 square inches of such paper per day can ingest enough lead for a toxic dose. Simply burning a typical Sunday supplement magazine can put 5 mg of lead into the air.

The reason children, regardless of social or economic status, are victimized by environmental lead from common household sources is due to a behavior syndrome called pica (the ingestion of nonfood particles). Although the reason for the syndrome is not completely clear, it seems to be related to a deficiency of iron in the body. Pica is not limited to children; some adults, particularly pregnant women, eat clay or cornstarch in excessive amounts. One out of fifteen children in ghetto areas suffers from lead poisoning resulting from the ingestion of lead in old paint or putty. Since one chip the size of a fingernail can contain 50 to 100 mg of lead, a few chips could easily amount to 100 times the total adult intake per day.

Lead-based paint need not be ingested to cause problems, however. In the past few years several cases of lead poisoning have been reported in houses undergoing remodeling. The sanding and burning of lead-based paint fills the air with fine dust and fumes, which are incorporated into the body when inhaled. Children with no previous history of eating paint chips have been hospitalized, along with their parents, in the Capitol Hill area of Washington, D.C., a neighborhood undergoing renewal. If you are planning to remodel an old house or apartment by removing paint applied previous to 1940, use a face mask and arrange for alternative living space until the dust settles and can be vacuumed up.

Although acute lead poisoning has easily recognizable symptoms, chronic or asymptomatic poisoning may have no symptoms or symptoms so vague that they could be ascribed to any of a dozen causes. Decreased appetite, clumsiness, irritability, headache, vomiting, and fatigue are the usual nonspecific symptoms of chronic lead poisoning. Consequently, the condition may never be diagnosed at all, or it may be recognized only after irreversible damage has been done.

Lead ions are absorbed from paint chips in the stomach and distributed initially throughout the soft tissues of the body. While in this soluble ion form, lead is both mobile and toxic. Damage, of course, depends upon the concentration of lead in the body. Because the soluble lead in the soft tissues is in equilibrium with the blood, blood analysis usually gives a fair indication of the amount of soluble lead in the body at any given time. Most of this soluble lead is excreted in the urine, which also indicates the level of body lead. Some lead is deposited as insoluble salts in bone tissue. If it remained there, treatment for lead poisoning would be simple, but under certain conditions, in children especially, the bone lead can be returned to the bloodstream in a soluble form.

In its most toxic state, lead interferes with the biosynthesis of heme, a component of the hemoglobin of red blood cells and of the cytochrome enzymes that are important in energy metabolism. In the central nervous system lead causes the brain capillaries to leak blood serum. Because of the rigidity of the skull, the resultant pressure injures brain cells and causes permanent brain damage. Most of these symptoms, reflecting damage from large doses of lead, are quickly recognizable and it is possible to administer treatment in time to prevent permanent damage. The most frequently used treatment is to bind the soluble lead in the system to special compounds called chelators, which carry the lead out of the body in the urine. But chelators must be used with great care, for if there is a large lead residue in the stomach, chelators may encourage such rapid absorption of lead as to cause death. Chelators may also release lead already stored in the bones, causing further complications. So it is important that the digestive tract of a child with acute lead poisoning be free of all leaded materials before treatment begins. Unfortunately, many children saved from one episode of lead poisoning return to the same dangerous environment only to succumb to the same syndrome again.

ASYMPTOMATIC LEAD POISONING

It is the asymptomatic aspect of chronic lead poisoning that can be the most dangerous in children. Often several tests are required before lead poisoning can be diagnosed and, unless it is looked for, it may go unnoticed. A sample of 1000 children in Chicago ghettos found seventy victims of lead poisoning without symptoms and three with obvious symptoms; and a study of 79,199 New York City children found three times the frequency of excessive lead levels in the blood of black two-year-olds as in Puerto Rican or white children. It has been calculated that as many as 50,000 children in the United States suffer from the asymptomatic form of lead poisoning. Even though physical recovery is possible, brain damage often ensues, for the ages one to five are critical years in the growth and development of the brain. In another study of 425 Chicago children suffering from lead poisoning, 39 percent developed various neural injuries leading to mental retardation.

The solution to this problem is in part a medical one. Ghetto children subject to possible lead poisoning should be examined much more frequently to uncover and treat as promptly as possible any cases of lead poisoning that show up. Leaded paints must be removed from substandard housing in a rehabilitation program designed to upgrade this type of housing wherever possible. Where rehabilitation is impossible, urban redevelopment projects should replace substandard housing. This is the only sure way to eliminate thousands of cases, recognized and unsuspected, of lead poisoning. It is bad enough for ghetto dwellers to endure the death of lead-poisoned children, but the insidious effect of sublethal doses in causing mental deterioration or retardation is a totally unnecessary result for which the entire community must share the blame and ultimate cost.

While dramatic and most certainly tragic, poisoning of children from doses of leaded paint does not represent our sole exposure to lead in the environment. Lead, like most other elements, exists in the natural environment, although in very low concentrations. The Industrial Revolution, however, followed by the proliferation of the automobile, particularly in the Northern Hemisphere, has gradually increased the background of lead in the environment. Dated samples of snow and ice from the Greenland ice cap near Thule indicate that up to 1750 there were about 20 μg of lead per ton of ice; by 1860 this had increased to 50 μg per ton; in 1940, 80 μg; in 1950, 120 μg; and in 1965, 210 μg. This represents an increase of 400 percent between 1750 and 1940, and a 300 percent increase in background levels since 1940. The highest samples from Antarctica equal the lowest from the Arctic. This reflects the great preponderance of land area in the Northern Hemisphere, the presence there of most of the sources of environmental lead, and the general lack of air circulation between the Northern and Southern Hemispheres, the same phenomenon encountered in the concentration of fallout (see Chapter 14). Although some of this lead comes from industrial sources, the striking correlation of atmospheric lead with other automobile emissions suggests that the internal combustion engine has been the major source of lead in the atmosphere. This has been confirmed by Chow and Card, of the Scripps Institute of Oceanography, who report that it is possible to distinguish between the lead from coal and gasoline by comparing their isotopic composition.

Lead has been added to most gasolines in the form of tetraethyl lead mixed with ethylene dibromide and ethylene dichloride plus a marker dye, since 1923. The lead is added to increase the effective octane rating of the gasoline without increasing its octane number; that is, without increasing the proportion of the more expensive, more volatile components of gasoline, its performance is improved. Lead also protects the engine exhaust valves from rust accumulation.

In 1923, the use of leaded gasoline was inconsequential; but in the intervening years, 2.6×10^{12} grams of lead have been combusted and distributed over the entire Northern Hemisphere. Much of this lead has run off into the oceans, leading to an increase in the lead content of the surface waters. Runoff from roads following a dry spell can contain lead concentrations of 1 to 14 ppm.

On a typical day the "autopolis" of Los Angeles generates 30,000 pounds of lead from the 7 million gallons of gasoline that are burned, which helps to explain why the atmospheric lead concentration of Los Angeles is 2.5 μg per cubic meter compared with 1.4 μg in Cincinnati or 1.6 μg in Philadelphia. This urban concentration is about fifty times the concentration of lead in rural air, and 5000 times the natural concentration. At peak traffic periods at congested points, the lead concentration may rise as high as 45 μg per cubic meter. Inhaling city air with a lead concentration of 1 μg per cubic meter, one could absorb 20 μg of lead in a day. In addition to the lead we breathe in from the air, we ingest an average of 300 μg of lead a day in foods and liquids.

One curious source of lead in our diet is the lead chromate that until recently was used in the cheerful yellow paint on most pencils. One maker used 12 percent lead, although 1 percent was considered the maximum safe level. More important was the total amount of lead per pencil, about 0.2 mg—dangerously close to the 0.3 mg per day maximum allowed for children. While the Pencil Maker's Association has voluntarily stopped using leaded paints or uses no more than 1 percent lead, there are untold millions of leaded pencils at large. Pencil chewers beware!

A final demonstration of the ubiquity of lead: near-empty toothpaste tubes have been found to contain enough lead to deliver a dose of 1800 ppm of lead to a child who brushes his teeth twice a day. Since the normal childhood dose of lead is 130 ppm per day, a child who enjoyed eating toothpaste because of its candy-like taste could be in trouble. In response to this and related research, most toothpaste manufacturers are shifting to plastic or plastic-aluminum tubes. Since a choice now exists, it would be wise to avoid leaded toothpaste tubes whenever possible.

Since our oral intake of lead every day is fifteen times the amount of lead we breathe, some people think airborne lead is not a significant hazard. On the other hand, only 5 percent of the lead that passes through the alimentary canal is absorbed, while close to 40 percent of the lead inhaled by the lungs is absorbed. Cigarette smokers, for example, have a slight but consistently higher concentration of lead in their blood than nonsmokers since lead is concentrated in tobacco leaves by lead arsenate residues in the soil from previous spraying or lead aerosols from vehicular traffic.

In either case, the body permanently retains little lead, but lead is toxic in its temporary soluble state. When the lead content of the air rises from 1μg per cubic meter to 15 μg, as it frequently does in large cities, the intake of lead rises from 20 μg to 300 μg a day. This is no longer one fifteenth of orally consumed lead, but its equal, effectively doubling the intake of lead to 600 μg per day. No city has an *average* of 15 μg per cubic meter of lead in its air today. Nor would this be likely in the future, if the automobile and oil companies agreed to eliminate tetraethyl lead from gasoline. If lead is eliminated it will probably be because leaded gasoline fouls antipollution devices required by federal and state governments.

FUTURE EFFECTS

To assess the effect of lead from industrial and automotive sources, we must consider whether the rate of environmental accumulation of lead has increased over the last few years, whether such an increase is mirrored by an increase in our body lead, and whether there is a threshold below which atmospheric lead causes no physiological damage.

Observations from the Arctic, Antarctic, and the world ocean indicate that lead is increasing in the environment. Reports of increasing body burden, however, are conflicting. One survey indicates a significantly higher lead content in American lungs (51 ppm) than in African lungs (26 ppm). But another report analyzing the lead content in the blood of various populations found as much lead in remote tribes in New Guinea as in people living in some large American cities. Unfortunately we have no base line with which to compare contemporary populations. Because of the ubiquity of lead in the environment for hundreds of years, *all* human populations have probably been exposed and contaminated. Since the sea surface has an abnormally high lead content compared with its depths, a result of atmospheric fallout, there is no reason to suspect that any human population, however remote from civilization, can be used as a control. However, a report by workers in California concludes that "further increases in atmospheric lead will result in higher blood lead levels in the population in a predictable relationship." [3]

We know that normal levels of lead in the blood range between 0.05 and 0.4 ppm. The range between 0.4 and 0.6 represents occupational exposure and 0.6 to 0.8 is abnormally high. Above 0.8 ppm recognizable lead poisoning usually results. The average level of lead in the American population is 0.25 ppm. The question is whether this average is "normal" or whether it already represents a serious increase from past levels, thereby reflecting the documented increase in environmental lead. If that is so, then any further increase might well be dangerous. The past has given us an example of chronic lead poisoning in Rome. The use of lead water pipes and, more seriously, lead cooking vessels by the upper class in ancient Rome probably caused the virtual disappearance of this class by increasing the rate of stillbirth. All this quite probably contributed to the ultimate fall of the Roman Empire.

Whereas we know that 0.8 ppm in the blood can cause lead poisoning, we cannot be sure that 0.7, 0.6, and 0.5 ppm are innocuous. Indeed, recent research with animals indicated that body burdens of lead compa-

---

[3] Goldsmith, J. R. and A. C. Hexter, 1967. "Respiratory exposure to lead: epidemiological and experimental dose-response relationships." *Science* **158**, pp. 132–134.

rable to those in humans reduced the animals' resistance to infectious diseases. While this relationship has not been established for us it is a possibility. But perhaps our perception of correlations between environmental stress factors and abnormal physiology or psychology is not yet sensitive enough to recognize low-level effects when we see them.

CADMIUM

Closely related to zinc and mercury, cadmium is a soft, silvery-white metal used in large quantities in electroplating and in nickel-cadmium batteries, but found as a contaminant in a host of other materials—motor oil, rubber tires, plastics, scrap metal, metal ores, coal and oil, and fungicides, to name just a few. When these products are heated, burned, or used, cadmium is released to the atmosphere as an oxide; almost 5 million pounds of cadmium entered the atmosphere in 1968.

Cadmium, which is used in twice the quantity of mercury, made its debut as a potential threat to man's health at about the same time and place—the 1950s, in Japan. Since then over fifty people in mining areas in northern Japan have died of a degenerative bone disease called itai-itai (literally "ouch-ouch" in Japanese). Many other Japanese are severely crippled as a result of excessive exposure to cadmium. Apparently, low levels of calcium and vitamin D in the diet sensitized the Japanese to the excess cadmium in their environment.

Although no one in the United States has yet died of exposure to cadmium, there is a growing suspicion that airborne cadmium is related to hypertension and associated heart diseases. Unlike mercury, cadmium's toxicity does not depend on its chemical form; any cadmium ion will bind to the sulfhydryl groups in enzymes, halting oxidative phosphorylation in the respiratory cycle. Since cadmium is concentrated in some blue-green algae, which can be poisonous, many cases of cadmium poisoning may go undetected. A strange association between hypertension and soft water may relate to cadmium in the following fashion: soft water, low in magnesium and calcium, is more acidic than hard water. It may be acidic enough to leach cadmium from water pipes that in hard-water regions are insulated by layers of precipitated salts or scale.

Like lead and mercury, cadmium accumulates in the body. The average ingestion of 70 to 80 μg per day in the United States is mostly excreted in the urine, but the 2 μg that are retained lead to a body burden of 30 mg by middle age. Smoking a pack of cigarettes a day can increase uptake of cadmium by 4 μg per day. Since cadmium binds to blood protein as well as to enzymes, 75 percent of the body burden is found in the liver and kidneys. Fortunately the placenta seems to form an effective barrier to cadmium movement during pregnancy.

The cadmium content of food is generally quite low, less than 0.05 ppm. But rice and wheat may contain as much as 1 ppm, oysters 3 ppm, and animal organs 12 ppm. The relatively high level of cadmium in oysters, which selectively accumulate the metal, has delayed the setting of a federal guideline on permissible levels of cadmium. A level that has been suggested by some, 2 ppm, would rule out consumption of most oysters harvested in the United States.

BERYLLIUM

Because of its familiarity and long use, the toxicity of lead was recognized quite early. The toxicity of beryllium was much less obvious.

In 1933 some German workers employed in a factory extracting beryllium metal from its ore became ill with severe respiratory symptoms including bronchitis. At the time it was thought that fluorides associated with beryllium were the cause. But in the mid-1940s, with the growth of the fluorescent lamp industry, a number of similar cases were reported. In 1946, seventeen workers in a fluorescent lamp factory in Salem, Massachusetts became seriously ill and some died. Although the evidence seemed to point to beryllium compounds used to make the lamp phosphor (beryllium carbonate and zinc beryllium nitrate), the United States Public Health Service concluded that beryllium was not toxic. The toxicity of beryllium was finally established a few years later, when similar symptoms were observed in foundry, lamp, and neon sign workers, all of whom worked with beryllium metal or its oxide.

Beryllium evokes a variety of symptoms, which makes diagnosis difficult at times; victims usually complain of shortness of breath, aches and pains, and a dry cough. This is often followed by severe weight loss and kidney damage. Cortisone or other steroid hormones are sometimes useful in alleviating symptoms, but because beryllium is difficult to remove from the body, there is no known cure for beryllium disease. Often irreversible damage has taken place by the time of diagnosis.

BERYLLIUM POISONING

Beryllium is indeed quite toxic; whereas 150 μg of lead per cubic meter of air is considered a safe exposure, as little as 5 μg of beryllium per cubic meter of air can cause chronic beryllium poisoning. Further, beryllium behaves in a most peculiar manner. First, there is the neighborhood effect. Despite large amounts of toxic arsenic, mercury, and lead released into the atmosphere by industry, no case of poisoning from these metals has been recorded in the neighborhood of the polluting factory. Beryllium poisoning, however, has been recognized in people living as far as three quarters of a mile from a beryllium processing plant. One such community experienced sixteen cases, including five fatalities. Then there is the oddity that in the neighborhood of the plant, while people living closest to the beryllium source had a greater tendency to develop beryllium disease than those living farther away, within the plant itself this dose relationship did not apply. The beryllium concentration in the air of the neighborhood reporting the beryllium poisoning ranged from 0.01 to 0.1 μg per cubic meter, while that in the plant was 1000 times higher. Yet of 1700 workers only nine developed beryllium disease (0.5 percent) whereas neighborhood people had a beryllium disease rate twice as high. Stranger still, the nine plant workers who became ill were not those who had been exposed longest to the largest amount of beryllium, but people who had been exposed for only a few months or had worked only a short time at the factory. In some instances fifteen years elapsed between exposure and illness. Finally, postmortems on victims showed no relationship between the amount of beryllium concentrated in the lungs and the severity of the disease. Facts like these give many sleepless nights to epidemiologists. The best conclusion that can be drawn from these observations is that people vary in their sensitivity to beryllium: some are almost immune and others extremely sensitive to very small amounts.

As a result of these demonstrations of beryllium toxicity, the use of beryllium-containing phosphors in fluorescent lamps was discontinued in mid-1949. Although cases of beryllium poisoning from broken lamps were described for several years thereafter, once the old tubes had been replaced there were no further complications either in manufacture or use of fluorescent lamps. Another type of lighting still poses problems, however. The delicate mantle used in camp lanterns is fortified with beryllium to strengthen the ash that remains after the initial burning. In the first fifteen minutes of burning a new mantle, 400 μg of beryllium is released. Since 17 million mantles are sold and presumably burned every year, this represents a great deal of beryllium release, particularly if the mantle is burned in the confines of a tent or camper. As long as beryllium is used in the manufacture of mantles, it would be wise to break them in only in well ventilated places.

Most industries that use or process beryllium today take elaborate precautions involving high-speed ventilators and shields to eliminate or sharply reduce the amount of beryllium particles or oxide in the air. Standards have been established, although on rather flimsy experimental evidence, that recommend not more than 2μg per cubic meter of beryllium over an eight-hour day in the atmosphere of a factory. Further, no one should be exposed to more than 25 μg per cubic meter at any time.

Finally, neighborhood effects may be eliminated if the atmospheric concentration of beryllium is less than 0.01 μg per cubic meter.

Today the incidence of beryllium poisoning in large plants maintaining responsible programs of industrial hygiene is quite low, certainly comparable with other types of job hazards. No fatalities from beryllium have been recorded since 1950.

But as beryllium finds new uses, the probability of its release into the environment increases. Beryllium was about to enter the space age with the discovery that suspensions of beryllium fibers provide a magnificent source of power when burned in a rocket engine. When research had progressed to the test firing stage, it was calculated that so much beryllium would be released in the firing of a rocket that someone eighteen miles from the launching site would be exposed to the same dose as a beryllium worker on the job twenty-four hours a day for thirty consecutive days. Fortunately, little has been heard since about beryllium-fueled rockets.

ASBESTOS

A few years ago researchers made a study of the Insulation Workers Union of New York starting with the 632 members enrolled on December 31, 1942. Ten years later the causes of death of union members compared with a statistical sample of men in comparable circumstances except for their exposure to asbestos. It was found that 255 union men had died compared with 203 men in the comparison group; forty-five workers died of lung cancer or lung disease, compared with six or seven in the comparison group; twenty-nine died of stomach cancer, compared with nine or ten in the comparison group; and twelve died of asbestos disease, while there were no deaths from this cause in the comparison group.

Some 100,000 to 125,00 people work directly with asbestos, and up to 3.5 million or 5 percent of the total work force of the United States works with asbestos at some time in some capacity in the construction and shipbuilding industries. With the widespread use of asbestos has come a distinct increase in the number of mesotheliomas. A diffuse cancer that develops on the mesothelium or lining of the chest or abdominal cavity, mesothelioma was extremely rare until fairly recently. Fourteen of the 120 asbestos workers who died most recently in New York died of mesothelioma. This was to be expected since mesothelioma has been linked to high concentrations of asbestos fibers in the air.

Somewhat less expected was the report of forty-seven cases of mesothelioma from a sample in Cape Province in South Africa. Although this area is rich in asbestos deposits, very few of the victims had worked with asbestos directly. Still more surprising was a report in 1960 that of 6312 people X-rayed in a Finnish county that had asbestos mines, 499 had a condition previously associated only with asbestos workers. None of these 499 had ever worked in an asbestos mine, but most lived near one. A survey in a nearby county without asbestos mines found no diseased condition in a population of 7101.

Even more remotely circumstantial but still suggestive is the case of

> a fourteen-year-old boy with mesothelioma, [who] had no occupational contact with asbestos nor did any of his family. On questioning, the boy's father told the authors that his boy . . . had helped him while he had replaced most of the plaster board during extensive remodeling of his house.[4]

While plasterboard itself does not contain any asbestos (even the gypsum used is covered with recycled paper), the compound used to seal the joints between wallboard sheets contains asbestos fibers, which can be released to the air if the joints are sanded before painting. A wide variety of joint fillers such as spackle may also contain asbestos fibers. Even baby powder, and presumably other cosmetic preparations containing talc, may contain asbestos fibers; ten out of nineteen baby powders recently tested did.

Apparently, when asbestos fibers are inhaled they become coated with a material containing iron and an asbestos body is formed (Figure 7.3).

[4] Lieben, J. and H. Pistawka, 1967. "Mesothelioma and asbestos exposure." *Arch. Env. Health* **14**, pp. 559–563.

Fig. 7.3 The rod-shaped particles in these photomicrographs are asbestos bodies in lung tissue. (Professor I. J. Selikoff, Mt. Sinai School of Medicine, New York)

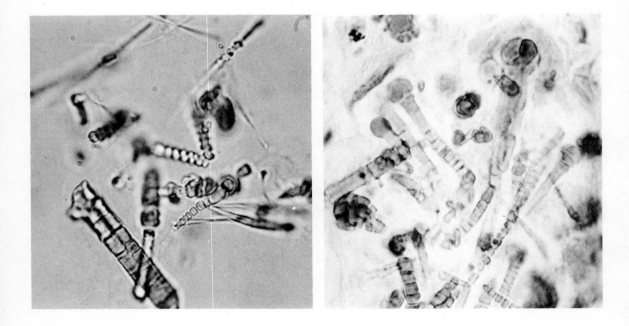

While large amounts of asbestos bodies were found in the lungs of asbestos workers, careful autopsies of people supposedly remote from asbestos exposure showed a surprising incidence of asbestos bodies: 26 percent of 500 consecutive autopsies in Capetown, South Africa; 50 percent of 1975 autopsies in New York; 30 percent of housewives; 40 percent of white collar workers; 50 percent of blue collar workers; and 70 percent of construction or shipyard workers. Of forty-two cases of mesothelioma investigated in Pennsylvania, twenty represented people who worked with asbestos, eight lived in the vicinity of an asbestos plant, and three had a family contact with someone who worked with asbestos. These patterns of neighborhood and familial exposure resemble those of beryllium and suggest that asbestos, like beryllium, may affect people differentially rather than on a linear dose scale.

FIBER INHALATION

The major concern about asbestos is not the safety of today's asbestos workers, for once the danger of asbestos fiber inhalation was recognized several years ago, it became the task of responsible industry to provide, and responsible unions to demand, a margin of safety by proper ventilation, respirators, and shielding. The chief concern is that asbestos can be extremely damaging to the health of many individuals who are remote from direct contact with the stimulus. Unfortunately, the potential toxicity of asbestos is not at all widely recognized and it is handled quite casually by people who assume it is as harmless as cement or plaster. There are many case histories of people who died some years after such a casual exposure.

If this is true of asbestos, what about fiber glass? First introduced in 1940, fiber glass today is used in over 33,000 products—filters, cloth, insulation, to name just a few. Initially the fibers were relatively coarse and apparently innocuous. But to increase the uses of the fibers, thinner and longer fibers were developed; these often fell in the toxic range of less than 3 μm in diameter and more than 20 μm in length. Particles in this size class seem to be strongly associated with various carcinomas, though it is still not known whether the chemical nature of the fibers or merely their form makes them so dangerous. In the last decade more and more ductwork for heating and cooling systems has been constructed of fiber glass instead of sheet metal. Some concern has been expressed about the release of fiber glass, especially in hospitals and schools equipped with such ductwork. However, preliminary tests seem to indicate that more fibers enter such systems than emerge from them and that fiber-laden dust dating from the construction of a building may persist for years. Ultimately, however, both fiber glass and asbestos fibers find their way to landfills where they enter the air as the debris is crushed and manipulated by bulldozers before burial.

FIBER INGESTION

As the fiber glass case suggests, inorganics in fiber form pose special dangers. For some time it was considered a medical curiosity that Japanese men had an incidence of stomach cancer seven times that of United States males. Examination of the talc-coated rice favored in the Japanese diet indicated the presence of several million asbestos-form fibers per gram. In Japan the incidence of stomach cancer is lower in areas where rice is less frequently eaten; it is also less among overseas Japanese whose diet is more westernized. The evidence implicating asbestos fibers is circumstantial but suggestive. Since asbestos fibers are used in filtering beer and have been isolated from the finished product in numbers well over a million per liter, public water supplies have been investigated and found contaminated with asbestos fibers as well. A taconite plant on the shore of Lake Superior, for example regularly dumps thousands of tons of tailings containing asbestos fibers into the lake, contaminating the water supplies of nearby cities. Although litigation attempting to halt this practice crawls on, the dumping continues. Not just drinking water but beverages such as sherry, port wine, vermouth, and soft drinks, have been found to contain substantial numbers of asbestos fibers. The hazard of orally ingested asbestos fibers is not fully known, but studies are under way.

SOLUTIONS

The basic problem with all five inorganics mentioned in this chapter has been the almost total lack of knowledge about either the threshold at which human health is adversely affected or the cumulative effect of low levels of inorganics already present in the body and likely to increase as atmospheric pollution worsens. Mercury, lead, and cadmium seem to follow a linear curve of dose-effect; the more lead, cadmium, or mercury, the greater the likelihood that certain symptoms will develop in the exposed population. But beryllium and asbestos follow no rules, making them by far the most dangerous to handle and be exposed to. Although you can assign maximum permissible doses of mercury, lead, and cadmium (subject to revision as more information becomes available about low-level effects), the apparent random effect of beryllium and asbestos vitiates the permissible dose approach.

Perhaps inorganic materials are best treated like poison ivy. This is a plant to which people are differentially sensitive. Some people break out with a rash from head to toe after simply walking downwind from an ivy patch, while others can roll in it without ill effect. The only advice about poison ivy botanists or physicians can give to the general public at our present crude level of understanding is to avoid it wherever possible. Maybe this is the best advice for the general public to follow with beryllium or asbestos for the present. But, of course, the public cannot always avoid certain potentially dangerous inorganic materials. It then becomes the responsibility of the industry producing these materials and finally the government or agencies controlling the environmental relations of the industries to protect the general public. This can be done either by strictly controlling the emissions of dangerous by-products, dusts, aerosols, fibers, or whatever, to a point well below that demonstrated to have deleterious effects on nonworkers, or by eliminating such emissions altogether.

It is possible that a small amount of these inorganic materials is indeed harmless and that our concern over a few isolated cases represents an alarmist position. But until much more experimental data is available to provide rational scientific guidelines about the quantities of various inorganic materials that can be tolerated by the environment and ourselves, discretion had better play a greater role in our value system than it has until now.

FURTHER READING

Chisolm, J. J., Jr., 1971. "Lead poisoning." *Scientific American* **224**(2), pp. 15–23. An excellent review of the effect of lead on human physiology.
D'Itri, F. M., 1972. *The environmental mercury problem.* CRC Press, Cleveland. Good background material.
Friberg, L., 1971. *Cadmium in the environment.* CRC Press, Cleveland. A systematic overview of what is known about the distribution and effect of cadmium.
Gilfillian, S. C., 1965. "Lead poisoning and the fall of Rome." *Jour. Occup. Med.* **7**, pp. 54–60. Intriguing account of the effect of lead upon history.
Montague, K., and P. Montague, 1974. "Fiberglass." *Env.* **16**(7), pp. 6–9. Glass fibers may be carcinogenic too.
Schroeder, H. A., 1974. *The poison around us: toxic metals in food, air, and water.* Indiana University Press, Bloomington. A brief survey by a toxicologist.
Selikoff, I. J., 1969. "Asbestos." *Env.* **11**(2), pp. 2–7. An excellent review of the asbestos problem by the world's foremost authority on the medical aspects of asbestos.

PART THREE

BUNGLING
THE BIOTA

Of course the biotic environment does not remain uninvolved in the increasingly intense environmental manipulations we have been discussing. Species are introduced, exterminated, and imprisoned in preserves. Our activities have gone so far that a wilderness area is no longer one that we haven't changed but rather one that we agree to try not to alter further in the future.

CHAPTER EIGHT

INTRODUCTION

OF EXOTICS

ABOUT 100 MILLION years ago, a massive continent called Pangaea, which included present-day South America, Africa, Australia, Antarctica, Europe and North America, began to be pulled apart by the forces of continental drift (see Chapter 1). Continuous land masses were fractured by rift valleys, then broken by straits that became channels, seas, and finally oceans. Land areas that had been long quiescent underwent mountain building episodes that began to separate the inhabiting species and limit their distribution. Climatic alteration, related both to mountain building and to other global phenomena, ultimately led to continental glaciation that ended the Tertiary period (Figure 8.1) and further limited the distribution of organisms. The stresses produced by these changes led to the extinction of some groups and reduction in range of others. But the same stresses also stimulated rapid evolution among the plants and animals that were genetically able to adapt to changing conditions.

NATURAL INTRODUCTIONS

By the middle of the Tertiary, the continents had been isolated for some time. Then formation of a land connection between North and South America (the Isthmus of Panama) and between Siberia and Alaska (the Bering land bridge) allowed animals and plants to move from their isolated centers of specialization and speciation. These movements are still taking place today. Glaciation further mixed the once-isolated stocks of plants and animals.

159

Fig. 8.1 *Geologic time is divided into eras and periods of varying duration and remoteness from the present. The Tertiary period is particularly important to our study of man-environment interactions because of the development at that time of the broad-leaved forests. (After Holmes)*

PERIODS AND EPOCHS	DURA- TION	TIME PRIOR TO PRESENT DAY	DISTINCTIVE LIFE
	(MILLIONS OF YEARS)		
PHANEROZOIC			
CENOZOIC ERA			
Quaternary	1 or 2	1 or 2	Modern man
Recent			
Pleistocene	1 or 2	1 or 2	Stone Age man
Tertiary			
Pliocene	9 or 10	12	Great variety of mammals Elephants widespread
Miocene	13	25	Flowering plants in full development Ancestral dogs and bears
Oligocene	15	40	Ancestral pigs and apes
Eocene	20	60⎱	Ancestral horses, cattle, elephants, and
Paleocene	10	70⎰	primates
MESOZOIC ERA			
Cretaceous	65	135	Extinction of dinosaurs. Mammals and flowering plants slowly appear
Jurassic	45	180	Dinosaurs abundant Birds and mammals appear
Triassic	45	225	Flying reptiles and dinosaurs appear First corals of modern types
PALEOZOIC ERA			
Permian	45	270	Rise of reptiles and amphibians Conifers and beetles appear
Carboniferous			
Pennsylvanian	35	305⎱	Coal forests
Mississippian	45	350⎰	First reptiles and winged insects
Devonian	50	400	First amphibians Earliest trees and spiders Rise of fishes
Silurian	40	440	First spore-bearing land plants Earliest known coral reefs
Ordovician	60	500	First fish-like vertebrates
Cambrian	100	600	Abundant fossils first appear
PRECAMBRIAN			
Late Precambrian	1000	2000	Scanty remains of primitive invertebrates: sponges, worms, algae, bacteria
Earlier Precambrian	1500	3500	Rare algae and bacteria back to at least 3000 million years for oldest known traces of life

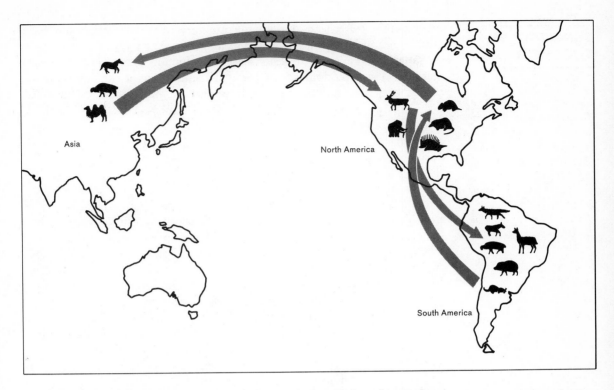

South America was invaded by tapirs, llamas, peccaries, foxes, dogs, cats, otter, and deer from North America; these drove many of the primitive marsupials into extinction or migration. One marsupial, the opossum, invaded North America from South America and is still extending its range northward. The porcupine and armadillo are also fairly recent invaders of North America. The Bering land bridge allowed elephants and deer to move into North America from Asia, while it also allowed horses, camels, and tapirs to move from North America to Asia (Figure 8.2).

Usually this process of range extension is extremely slow, but it may be quite rapid. Both the cardinal and mockingbird, formerly limited to the South, were considered rare visitors in Pennsylvania or Connecticut thirty years ago. Today, both birds breed in these northern states and seem to be extending their range farther north. Shortly after World War II, cattle egrets moved, with the help of storm winds, to South America from Africa. They then worked their way to Florida and now breed regularly along the southern coast from North Carolina to Texas.

By and large, the post-Tertiary plant and animal redistribution had stabilized by the time we arrived on the scene. But once again these relative isolations are being disturbed, not by continental drift, climate,

Fig. 8.2 During the late Tertiary and early Pleistocene, land bridges came and went between Asia, North America, and South America. They brought about a large-scale migration of animals among these continents: deer and mammoth entered North America from Asia, and the horse, tapir, and camel colonized Asia from North America; the porcupine, opossum, and armadillo came north from South America; and the fox, horse, tapir, peccary, shrew, and llama moved from North America to South America.

161

or land bridges, but by our unique mobility. For our wanderings have encouraged the introduction of plants and animals on a scale never before possible. For thousands of years these introductions were limited to crop plants and weeds, domesticated animals and their pests; but more recently, a greater and more varied number of plants and animals has been shifted about, accidentally or purposefully—sometimes with catastrophic results.

THE COLUMBIAN EXCHANGE

Perhaps the most dramatic introductions resulted from the discovery of the Western Hemisphere by Western Europeans. Columbus and subsequent explorers, conquerors, and colonists found an extraordinary new world populated with strange plants, animals, and people that boggled the minds of Europeans accustomed to the limited flora and fauna of Europe and already intolerant of each other, let alone heathen savages. Ignoring the variety of new plants, many quite edible, Spanish settlers deplored the lack of wheat, wine, and meat in the diet of the natives and soon introduced their familiar crops and livestock. Grazing quickly eliminated many of the endemics (species with limited distributions) in the West Indies and in combination with aggressive European weeds modified what native flora remained (see Chapter 21). But the two most important introductions had an unprecedented and unexpected effect on the native Indian populations. Within a few years after colonists had begun to arrive regularly, Indians began dying by family, by village, and then by tribe. As soon as the native Americans made contact with the Europeans, smallpox, measles, typhus, pneumonia, and pleurisy swept through the native population. Resentful Indians in Peru apparently tried to infect the colonists by dumping diseased corpses into wells and contaminating food. They failed, for the Europeans had immunity from long contact with the diseases and the Indians did not. No one can estimate accurately how many native Americans perished; a conservative guess is probably several million in both North and South America. Some tribes like the Carib and Mandan were exterminated; others were so reduced that their culture was lost. The holocaust was variously viewed by most contemporary observers: as a convenience by those who wanted to settle land occupied by Indians, and an inconvenience by those who needed plentiful labor. The term "genocide" would not be coined for another four hundred years.

The second fateful introduction was the horse. Although the horse evolved in North America, it became extinct there sometime after becoming established in Eurasia. By 1500 North American Indians had forgotten the horse their ancestors may have exterminated (see Chapter 9).

Consequently they were astonished to see Spaniards mounted on horses. A very considerable part of the success of Pizarro and other conquistadores against larger numbers of warlike Incas and Aztecs was related to the Indians' initial awe and fear of the horse. Such feelings quickly turned to admiration and envy for the animal's utility. Within a few decades many Indian tribes in both South and North America had horses.

But it was in the Great Plains of North America that the horse made its greatest impact. Lack of convenient transportation kept the Plains Indians tied to part-time farming in the river valleys. They ventured onto the plains after buffalo only as long as the meat they obtained could be dragged back to the village by dogs harnessed to a pair of poles called a travois. The horse enabled the Indians to transport far heavier loads for much greater distances, and hunting buffalo on horseback instead of on foot provided a generous food surplus for the first time (Figure 8.3). Having broken their ties to past cultural necessities, many tribes of Plains Indians entered a glorious two-hundred year period of rapid cultural evolution. The impact on surrounding tribes was profound, and just beginning to sort itself out when Lewis and Clark began their journey west in 1804. Within seventy years this short-lived flower was plucked —the Indians sequestered on reservations, the buffalo hunted almost to

Fig. 8.3 *The Plains Indians quickly adapted to the horse after its reintroduction into the Americas by the Spaniards. On ceremonial occasions the costume of both horse and rider could become quite elaborate.* (Courtesy of the American Museum of Natural History)

extinction, and the descendents of the Indian ponies ultimately rounded up.

But the Indians of the New World had revenge for their suffering. In 1493 a sailor in Barcelona fell ill with a strange disease resembling smallpox in some ways yet quite distinct in others. Later that year Charles VIII of France pulled together a typical army of 50,000 allies and mercenaries, crossed the Alps, and raped and pillaged his way south to Naples. Circumstances not being conducive to a long stay, he and his army then raped and sacked their way back to Lyon. In 1495 the army was disbanded and the ex-soldiers carried syphilis to the far corners of Europe. Not everyone agrees that Columbus introduced syphilis to Europe, but circumstances make it seem highly probable—reason enough for American Indians to celebrate Columbus Day with some fervor.

More easily identified elements of the Columbian Exchange were the amazing fruits and vegetables of the New World—corn, peanuts, potato, tomato, sweet potato, manioc, squash, pumpkin, chile pepper, lima, butter, kidney, navy, and string beans, papaya, guava, pineapple, avocado, and the very best dope of the day, cacao and tobacco. All soon made their way onto the European dining table. Some were quickly and easily accepted; others, like the potato and tomato, were for many years regarded as unworthy of the European palate or even poisonous. Today it is difficult to think of German cuisine without the potato, or Italian food without the tomato, yet both are exotics introduced within the last five hundred years.

Wherever Europeans settled they carried their fauna and flora with them. Red deer were introduced early in the settlement of New Zealand. With no serious grazing competition and no predators, there were soon many more deer than could be controlled by hunting. The deer began to compete with sheep, destroy crops, inhibit forest regeneration, and finally, by overgrazing, to cause serious soil erosion. Today there is no limit or closed season on red deer in New Zealand; in fact, the government offers free ammunition to anyone who will kill them. But the red deer are still flourishing.

A similar incident occurred in Australia. Unlike New Zealand, Australia had many vertebrates, but because of its long isolation its vertebrates were mostly the primitive marsupials—possum, kangaroos, wallabies, and the like—which were generally outcompeted by the more advanced mammalian stock the settlers introduced. Like the New Zealanders, new Australians missed the familiar animals of home and soon introduced the rabbit. To their credit, they introduced the fox as well, as a predator. But in Australia foxes and rabbits seemed to go their own ways; the fox never amounted to much as a rabbit predator while the rabbit became one of the greatest pests of all time, as will be discussed later in this chapter.

What went wrong in these two cases? Why did perfectly well-behaved European animals suddenly become pests? No animal or plant exists in a world limited solely by physical and chemical factors. With few exceptions, for every plant or animal there is a potential consumer or predator that checks its population growth. There are also parasites, and parasites of parasites. A few years ago, John Tilden took a long, careful look at a plant that grows on the sand dunes of California and Oregon. "Associated with it he found, by two years of systematic observation, 257 species of arthropods of which 221 were insects. Of the latter 65 were parasites and that was not complete. There were 53 species of primary herbivores—leaf-nibblers, leaf miners, stem-borers, leaf-suckers, root feeders, gall-makers; 23 species of predators; 55 species of primary parasites, 9 of secondary parasites; and even one tertiary parasite." [1] All of these organisms interact so that there are rarely too many or too few objects of their predation. This is why a stable ecosystem usually contains relatively constant numbers of plants and animals from year to year. But when you pluck a plant or animal from its ecological context and fling it into another environment it will either disappear almost immediately or proliferate with unbelievable fecundity. This is a direct measure of the importance of ecological associations in maintaining stable populations.

Even today, we know far too little about the ecological relationships of plants or animals to be able to predict which course the introduced plants or animals will take in a new environment. Obviously elephants would be short-lived in Labrador, but what about zebras in New Mexico or bamboo in Louisiana? Of course not all introductions have been disastrous, nor have they all been intentional; let us examine the record.

TYPES OF INTRODUCTIONS

INSECTS

Few insects have been intentionally introduced except in a desperate attempt to combat proven pests biologically, but accidental introductions have been rife. The Japanese beetle has already been discussed in Chapter 5. Of even greater impact has been the gypsy moth. Leopold Trouvelot, a French astronomer employed by the Harvard Observatory, tried to crossbreed several silk-producing moths with the aim of finding a strain resistant to a disease threatening the French silk industry. One of his sub-

[1] Elton, C. S., 1958. *The ecology of invasions by animals and plants.* Methuen, London.

165

jects was the gypsy moth (Figure 8.4), notorious in Europe for its destructive effect on the leaves of shade trees. In 1869 Trouvelot accidentally allowed some gypsy moths in his collection to escape near his home in Medford, Massachusetts. Seemingly, they disappeared into the blue. But twenty years later, in 1889, Medford was overwhelmed by an incredible swarm of caterpillars.

> The numbers were so enormous that the trees were completely stripped of their leaves, the crawling caterpillars covered the sidewalks, the trunks of the shade trees, the fences and the sides of the houses, entering the houses and getting into the food and into the beds. . . . The numbers were so great that in the still, summer nights the sound of their feeding could plainly be heard, while the pattering of their excremental pellets on the ground sounded like rain. Valuable fruit and shade trees were killed in numbers by their work, and the value of real estate was very considerably reduced. . . . To read the testimony of the older inhabitants of the town, which was collected and published by a committee, reminds one vividly of one of the plagues of Egypt as described in the Bible.[2]

Fig. 8.4 Female gypsy moths in the process of laying their eggs. Surrounded by a tough layer of fibers, the eggs overwinter on the trunks of trees, rocks, or fenceposts, and hatch into hungry larvae just as the leaves emerge in spring. (California Department of Food and Agriculture)

In response to this scourge, the state government was persuaded to employ some control measures, which were moderately successful until 1910, when Massachusetts decided enough money had been spent killing caterpillars and canceled the appropriation. By 1905 the gypsy moth infestation was not only out of control again but beyond the resources of state action; the federal government had to step in. Throughout the 1930s and 1940s the gypsy moth was not a serious problem, although there were occasional outbreaks and a gradual spread to New Jersey and Connecticut. When DDT became available after World War II, it seemed that the gypsy moth could be eliminated once and for all. But it didn't work out that way. A series of hurricanes in the 1950s spread the larvae and adults all over the Northeast and the increasing use of recreational vehicles spread the egg masses all over the country. What had happened?

Populations of gypsy moths built up to peak levels, which were then sprayed with DDT or sevin. While the moth population was thinned, its natural predators were wiped out. Unfortunately, the moth was able to build up its population before the predators did and another population cycle occurred, calling for another aerial spraying. The net effect of spraying, despite the gratification of seeing larvae die, seems to be setting up population outbreak after outbreak. The result is tailor-made for biocide manufacturers but disastrous for the environment.

Suppose we changed our approach and let the gypsies eat. What would

[2] Howard, L. O., 1930. *A history of applied entomology (somewhat anecdotal)*. Smithson. Misc. Coll., 84.

happen to the defoliated forests? Just such an option was followed in the Jockey Hollow Area of the Morristown National Historical Park in New Jersey, which for three years running, 1967 to 1969, was severely defoliated by gypsy moths. The National Park Service held fast against considerable pressure to spray. In 1970, the population collapsed; by 1972 egg masses were infrequent. Almost 10,000 trees died and an equal number were weakened. But 75 percent of the forest remained intact and in better condition than before because of lessened competition for nutrients and water. The gypsy moth had simply thinned the forest.

A similar role is played by the other dramatic defoliators of North America, the Douglas fir tussock moth, the eastern spruce budworm, the southern pine bark beetle, and the oak leaf roller. These species are all native, but their impact on the forests they attack is the same. Normal insect grazing, which generally consumes between 5 and 30 percent of the annual foliage crop, seems not to impair annual production in forests. In fact, growth may be accelerated. Outbreaks of these problem defoliators are not at all random. They seem to occur in stands that are overaged, overstocked, or under stress from water or nutrient deficiencies. When overmature timber is removed and competition is reduced, growth and production in the survivors increases measurably, even though there may be a lag of ten to fifteen years before it can be seen. Consequently it seems probable that insects are not the dreaded scourges of our forests, but regulators of primary productivity and nutrient cycling with a vital cyclic function to perform in the long-term dynamics of forest ecosystems. The message seems clear: if we don't harvest mature timber and thin overstocked forests, insects will.

INSECT EXPORTS

Practically every crop in the United States has at least one introduced pest of economic importance. Introductions have not been one-way, however. Two examples of a North American native causing problems abroad are the Colorado potato beetle (Figure 8.5) and the grape phylloxera. The potato beetle, when originally discovered, was feeding quite contentedly on a wild relative of the potato in the Rocky Mountains. In 1859 potato cultivation came to Colorado. Sometime that year the beetle discovered the domestic potato. By 1874 the beetle had reached the Atlantic coast and a short time later it was inadvertently carried to Europe. By 1930 most of western, central, and southern Europe had become infested.

During the Korean War, North Korea and China accused the United States of dumping canisters of potato beetles on their potato fields. But in view of the expansion of its range in the hundred years since its discovery, the Colorado potato beetle hardly needed the assistance of the CIA to manage its dispersal!

Fig. 8.5 The infamous Colorado potato beetles with their eggs. (Courtesy of the American Museum of Natural History)

The phylloxera is an insect that sucks juices from the rootstock of grape vines. Native to the grapes of eastern North America, the phylloxera usually does no particular damage. When it was introduced into France on the rootstocks of American grapes just before the Franco-Prussian War in 1870, the result was catastrophic. At a time when France could least afford further calamity, vines began dying throughout her world famous wine districts. For a few years grape juice for wine production was limited to that wrung from dried grapes shipped in from uninfected areas abroad, surely a low point for the French spirit. Within ten years the insect was killing vines in Germany and Italy as well. But the wild American grape came to the rescue by providing resistant rootstocks to which the superior European grapes could be grafted. In another few years, production was back to normal, with the curious result that today all French grapes have "American" roots.

A few years ago the popular press and TV made much of an imminent invasion of killer bees from South America: serious threat or science fiction? African bees are noted for both their ferocity and their productivity. In the 1950s Brazilian researchers imported African bees with the idea of crossing them with the more docile but less productive Italian honeybee, which doesn't survive in the tropics. Before the work could be carried out, the African bees escaped and hybridized with the European bees on their own. The resulting hybrid produced one third to one half more honey but retained some rather aggressive traits. Hence the killer bee myth. Although the "killer bees" are slowly moving through the tropics toward North America, their tropical African heritage keeps them from forming the winter clusters that enable European bees to survive the temperate zone winter.

Fish introduction *seems* to have caused few problems, but this is only because the displacement and even extinction of anything but the most popular game fish have until quite recently gone unnoticed by most people. Fish are introduced for a variety of reasons: the support of sport and commercial fisheries; the release of bait fish; the control of insects or aquatic weeds; and the release of pet fish. Often the introduced fish compete directly with some native fish for food or habitat, causing the native to decline. Some introduced bass and trout are aggressive predators; bass and trout predation has eliminated the Owens pupfish and Modoc sucker in many California waters. The introduced green sunfish has replaced the native California roach, and many streams are now barren in the summer because the sunfish cannot tolerate the characteristic high temperature/low oxygen summer conditions to which the roach is adapted. In some places introduced species genetically swamp closely related native species. In this fashion the introduced rainbow trout threatens the Lahontan cutthroat, golden, and red trout of California.

In 1967, *Cichla ocellaris*, the peacock bass, was introduced accidentally into Gatun Lake in the Panama Canal Zone. While *Cichla* is excellent eating and a good sport fish, it has greatly simplified and perhaps destabilized the normal food web in Gatun Lake (Figure 8.6). A similar

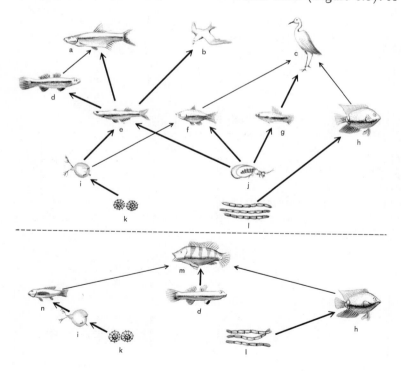

Fig. 8.6 (Top) Generalized food web in Gatun Lake before introduction of the peacock bass or where this species is absent; (bottom) the bass-simplified food web. The thicker the arrow, the more important the food source to the consumer. Key to organisms: (a) tarpon; (b) tern; (c) herons and kingfishers; (d) to (h) various species of small fish; (i) zooplankton; (j) terrestrial insects; (k) very tiny phytoplankton; (l) filamentous green algae; (m) adult peacock bass; (n) young bass. (After T. M. Zaret and R. T. Paine, 1973. "Species introduction in a tropical lake." Science 182: 449–455, figure 3, by A. Spight. Copyright 1973 by the American Association for the Advancement of Science)

169

simplification took place in Lake Atitlán in Guatemala. Until 1958 the local Indians obtained needed protein from small native fish which they smoked and from a species of crab which they could also sell for a small extra cash income. In 1958 the government introduced largemouth bass in hopes of starting a commercial or sport fishery. After fifteen years the bass are few and far between; the crabs and small fish have succumbed to the predation of the introduced bass; and the local Indians have been left with nothing but a good intention.

While fears of released piranha fish tearing Florida swimmers to ribbons have not yet been realized, despite their occasional release, a catfish introduced from Asia has caused some concern in southern Florida. Able to breathe out of water for up to twelve hours and wriggle cross-country, these catfish can live under conditions lethal to other species. Naturally the Florida Fish Commission is concerned that with its voracious appetite the "walking" catfish will outcompete more desirable freshwater fish.

Another widely and thoughtlessly introduced fish is the goldfish. Most people have compunctions about flushing unwanted goldfish down the toilet, so they release them in nearby ponds or streams, where they often reproduce vigorously to the exclusion of more desirable fish—goldfish may be pretty, but tasty they are not.

BIRDS

For centuries, birds as pets have been moved about the earth at our whim. During the Victorian age this effort reached an almost frenzied peak. In city after city acclimatization societies were formed to introduce the avian glories of Europe and the East to the urban areas of the northeastern United States. Birds such as the nightingale, skylark, and English robin were introduced again and again, but without success; even the English sparrow (house sparrow), which had long been regarded as a pest in Europe, was repeatedly introduced. Some measure of the extent to which this craze gripped otherwise conservative institutions can be seen in the purchase and release of 1000 sparrows by the city government of Philadelphia in 1869.

Unfortunately, the sparrow succeeded where the nightingale and skylark did not. Soon the noisy, dirty little birds were everywhere, chasing away native birds, nesting in great piles of trash and under eaves, and eating large quantities of grain. By 1883, Philadelphia thought better of its humanitarian action and passed a law making it lawful to kill or destroy in any way possible the bird it had so enthusiastically introduced.

Before long, however, the house sparrow had extended its range all over the United States and Canada. But like the housefly, the Norway rat, and the common pigeon or rock dove, the sparrow was never able to sever its connection with civilization. It was unwilling or unable to wander too far from the largesse provided by our disturbance of the environment—the true measure of a pest or weed. In a few decades, house sparrow populations gradually declined, perhaps because of the decline of the horse when the automobile came into widespread use. Horse droppings undoubtedly provided a nutritional margin that helped carry sparrow populations through severe winters. Today house sparrows remain common and seem to have made a secure niche for themselves as an accompaniment of human civilization, but they are nowhere overly abundant. The starling has had a similar history except that its numbers have not yet stabilized.

Another bird associated with man and his cities is the rock dove or city pigeon (Figure 8.7). Surviving almost exclusively on what they can

Fig. 8.7 *As messy as they are, rock doves do provide animation in some otherwise dreary cityscapes.*

glean from abundant city garbage or crumbs generously scattered by well-meaning urbanites eager for the sight of any bird, pigeons have increased into enormous flocks in many cities. Ledges, windowsills, and the exuberant architectural ornaments on older buildings are used as nest sites and the pigeon's copious excrement has become one of the vicissitudes of life in most cities. Pigeons have persisted despite occasional efforts to reduce their numbers. It has become clear, however, that pigeons are capable of infecting us with several diseases—parrot fever (psittacosis or ornithosis), cryptococcal meningitis, histoplasmosis, and encephalitis. Today urban pigeon populations are regarded as more than a mere nuisance, and serious efforts are being made to control their numbers. By

BUNGLING
THE BIOTA

Fig. 8.8 The monk parakeet, a recent accidental introduction to the avifauna of the eastern United States, may very well reoccupy the niche vacated by the native but now extinct Carolina parakeet. This monk parakeet is attacking figs, but a wide variety of less exotic fruit is also attractive to this species. (O. S. Pettingill, Jr., from National Audubon Society)

generously spreading pigeon feed treated with a contraceptive drug in suitable gathering places, large numbers of pigeons are rendered infertile, allowing the ravages of age, alley cats, and taxicabs gradually to reduce the pigeon population to manageable terms. There are still pigeons in New York City, but not the huge flocks that there once were.

In the late 1960s the monk parakeet (Figure 8.8) became one of the most recent additions to the fauna of the United States. These birds were imported by the thousands for the caged bird market. Dozens were released or escaped in the New York area and soon were building nests and laying eggs. At first these efforts were unsuccessful because the monk parakeet's native habitat is Argentina and Bolivia, south of the equator; hence the birds began nesting activities in their spring, which is our fall. This should have limited their spread, but after a year the birds became acclimated to the Northern Hemisphere and began rearing young. By the early 1970s monk parakeets were being spotted in twenty-five states, from Maine to Alabama and west to North Dakota. In view of the large size of the bird, ironically about the same as the extinct Carolina parakeet (see Chapter 9), and its voracious appetite for fruit, many people are concerned that another starling or house sparrow has been unleashed. Consequently, attempts are being made to locate and eradicate monk parakeet colonies before the situation gets out of hand.

MAMMALS

In 1859 Thomas Austin imported a dozen pairs of European rabbits to Australia and released them on his ranch. Six years later, after killing 20,000 of them, Austin still had 10,000 left. This fecundity is quickly explained: a female rabbit can breed at four months, then average six litters of six young (called kittens) a year thereafter. Theoretically, one pair of rabbits can generate about 13.7 million offspring in three years! Fortunately, mortality is around 80 percent and adults rarely live more than one year. Nonetheless, in a few short years Australia was faced with a national problem because five rabbits ate as much grass as one sheep. Trying to capitalize on the grave mistake of introducing the rabbit, Australia soon became the world's major supplier of rabbit meat and rabbit fur. But the loss of sheep range more than balanced any economic gain from the rabbit. Besides direct grazing competition, the rabbit burrows extensively undermined buildings, initiating soil erosion and further ruining range land.

All means of control were attempted—trapping, shooting, netting, poisoning, fumigation of burrows, even erecting a 1500-mile fence designed to keep the rabbits from moving into western Australia—but these measures were of little avail. By 1953 the ideal habitat and minimal natural

predation allowed the rabbit population to increase, despite control measures, to an estimated *one billion rabbits* over an area of a million square miles (Figure 8.9). Some of the economic burden this rabbit population placed on the Australian economy can be seen by the calculation that if there were no rabbits in Australia the land could support another 100 million sheep. Recently the rabbit population was reduced considerably by biological control, a method that will be discussed later in this chapter.

Australia's experience with the rabbit is perhaps an exception, for although there have been problem introductions of muskrat into Europe and nutria into the United States, the most severe problems have usually arisen when mammals have been introduced to small islands. Occasionally chains of errors have followed an initial introduction. Many years ago rabbits were introduced as a supplemental food source on some rather barren windswept islands southeast of Australia. When the rabbits began to compete with the sheep, the economic mainstay of the islands, cats were brought in to reduce the rabbit population. But the cats preferred the eggs of sea birds nesting on the islands and used by the natives as food. In desperation, the islanders brought in dogs to control the cats; however, while the dogs merely chased the cats, they attacked and ate seals on beaches, depriving the islanders of still another food source. In view of the wide range of problems stemming from introduced animals it is heartening that most introductions are unsuccessful.

Fig. 8.9 Rabbits gathering at a water hole in Australia during a drought. At the time the photo was taken there were one billion rabbits in Australia. (Australian Information Service)

PLANTS

One of the most important forest trees in eastern North America until about 1900 was the chestnut. A singularly useful tree, the chestnut grew tall and straight, providing good saw timber; the bark and wood had a high tannin content, which was used in the curing of hides and which preserved the wood from rapid decay in contact with soil, making the chestnut especially useful for fence posts and rails; the nuts were of excellent quality for roasting and provided much food for game and livestock; and finally, it was a fine shade tree, widely planted and as widely admired:

> Under a spreading chestnut-tree
> The village smithy stands; [3]

The village smithy went out with the horse and buggy; unfortunately so did the chestnut. A wealthy New York gentleman imported a number of foreign chestnut trees to plant on his Long Island estate just before the turn of the century. A few years later he noticed that his American chestnuts were dying. In a few more years, chestnuts were dying all over Long Island, then New York, Connecticut, and New Jersey. By 1940 the chestnut no longer existed as a forest tree in North America. The cause of its demise was a fungus introduced on trees brought from China. The Chinese species of chestnut apparently evolved with the fungus and developed a tolerance to it, but the American chestnut had no such immunity; in fact it proved extremely susceptible. The fungus slowly girdles the trunk of the tree, filling the water-conducting vessels of the wood with its growth, and the crown of the tree, deprived of water, slowly dies. Because the roots remain viable the chestnut continues to sprout, but just enough fungus spores remain in the environment to kill the sprouts after a dozen years or so, preventing the regrowth of any sizable tree. Some chestnuts have been vainly sprouting in this manner for over fifty years. Although the loss of such an important tree was staggering, because of the resistance of the wood to decay, dead trees are still being cut in the southern Appalachians, where they remain a declining source of the split-rail fencing once so popular in suburbia.

CONTROL OF INTRODUCTIONS

As the list of disastrous introductions lengthened, we slowly became aware that although we had the unquestioned ability to transport or-

[3] Longfellow, H. W., 1903. *The complete poetic works of Henry Wadsworth Longfellow*, Houghton Mifflin, Boston.

ganisms—moose, mice, or measles—wherever we pleased, we could not pull the strings that would make these organisms behave as we wished.

QUARANTINE

The most obvious solution to the problem of introductions is to avoid them in the first place. Most countries have strict regulations prohibiting random importation of any plant or animal stock which might cause problems or carry potentially harmful pests or diseases. The United States requires that all plants entering the country from abroad be fumigated or carefully inspected to eliminate plant diseases or insect pests. Imported wild animals must spend a quarantine period in Clifton, New Jersey, to be sure the animals are disease free. Even then federal law forbids their release in this country without a permit from the Secretary of Agriculture. Such strictures in force in the United States have sharply decreased the number of new introductions since 1900. But despite these measures, unwanted plants and animals still occasionally get through.

ERADICATION

If the infestation is discovered quickly enough, eradication is usually attempted. Hoof and mouth disease in cattle or the Mediterranean fruit fly on oranges in Florida are examples where the unwanted organism was eliminated by quick action before it was well-established or too widespread. Eradication is far more easily envisioned than accomplished. Too often eradication is initiated when the chance for success does not justify the potential damage to other species; this was the case in the campaigns against the fire ant in the Southeast, and the Japanese beetle in the Midwest.

BIOLOGICAL CONTROL

Should an organism evade both border quarantine and eradication attempts and become established, there is a third line of defense that does not necessitate an endless series of biocide sprays. Every organism, as we have seen, is surrounded in its natural habitat by a plethora of other organisms with which it has evolved and to which it is related through producer-consumer, predator-prey, or parasite-host bonds. If the new habitat of an introduced species is a reasonable facsimile of the old and if the web of associates is left behind, as it almost always is, there are few checks and the population may explode.

Why are organisms new to a habitat not immediately eaten and eliminated or at least assimilated? The bonds mentioned develop over long periods of time and are quite conservative. Interlopers have no place. A bird is as loath to sample a beetle it has never seen before as a shopper is to buy rattlesnake meat at the supermarket. After many years, however, predator-prey relationships slowly form and the species is gradually absorbed by the environment as the house sparrow and Japanese beetle have been. But the period of absorption may take hundreds of years.

Biological control can speed up this process of natural absorption by introducing whatever consumers, predators, or parasites are available from the old habitat to bring an introduced species under control in the shortest possible time. Biological control is not a new approach, but since it is neither quick, easy, nor always successful, biocides were for a time considered the best solution—that is, until their drawbacks became too glaring to ignore. Today there is renewed interest in the possibilities of biological control.

The first step in applying biological pest control is to study the pest's life cycle intimately to see where the weak points are and where controls might be successfully applied. Then the original habitat is carefully studied so that the interrelationships between the control species and the target species are fully understood. Before any introduction of control agents is attempted, careful screening must be carried out to be sure that a second pest is not introduced. A convenient rule is that an introduced control species should prefer starvation to attacking some species other than the pest to be controlled. The new habitat must also be generally suitable to the intended control species. The control species must be reared or cultivated in large enough numbers so that there is a fair chance of success when it is introduced. Finally cultural practices should be modified wherever possible to encourage survival and reproduction of the control species. When these steps are carefully carried out with one or more control species, the target species *may* be effectively controlled.

Despite the time, expense, and uncertainties, many pests have been quite effectively controlled, some spectacularly, using biological methods. Just about any organism from virus to sea cow can be used as a biological control.

STERILIZATION

The object of sterilization is to interfere as unobtrusively as possible with the reproductive cycle of a pest organism so that everything progresses normally except that eggs will not be fertilized and the reproductive cycle will be broken. This has proven quite successful with pigeons, as we have seen, and has been used with insects such as linden bugs as well. A chemical sterilant is currently being developed to halt sperm reproduction in rats permanently. One dose is calculated to do this effectively without adverse effect on the rat's sex drive or general health. A female mated with a sterile male displays pregnancy symptoms but does not mate again for eleven days, twice the usual nonreceptive period. This measure reduces the number of possible litters by half and promises to be quite effective in lowering the rat population.

Know your organism thoroughly, then focus on a weak point in its life cycle. This rule was followed successfully by E. F. Knipling, using radiation on the screwworm fly. The adult is a metallic blue fly about three times the size of a housefly that lays eggs in wounds or even in the navels of newborn warm-blooded animals. The feeding maggots cause a sore whose discharge attracts more flies until hundreds or even thousands of maggots may infect the animal. After five days the maggots drop to the ground, pupate, then emerge as adults. In a few days the adults mate and the female lays her eggs, completing the life cycle. In warm regions ten to twelve generations a year are possible. The screwworm is limited in the United States to southern Florida and the southern parts of Texas, New Mexico, Arizona, and California.

Knipling's idea was to expose the screwworm pupae to a dose of radiation that would sterilize the males without other side effects; 2500 roentgens (a unit of radiation) was found to do this nicely. Since the females mate but once, mating with a sterilized male would result in sterile eggs. It was found that a ratio of 9:1 sterile to fertile males would result in 83 percent sterile matings. After some preliminary tests, an eradication program was begun to eliminate the screwworm fly from Florida. Using assembly line methods in an airplane hangar, 50 million screwworm pupae per week, both male and female, were irradiated then released. Over a period of eighteen months 2 billion flies were released over 70,000 square miles of Florida, southern Georgia, and Alabama. The program was begun in January 1958. One year later the screwworm fly was eradicated from the southeastern states. Reinfestation is prevented by the colder Gulf Coast between Florida and Texas, which eliminates the possibility of reinfection from overwintering flies and by animal inspection stations which check all livestock crossing the Mississippi. The technique is now being used in Mexico, where it is hoped that the screwworm fly can be eliminated north of the Isthmus of Tehuantepec.

After this outstanding success, follow-up studies are investigating the possibility of using the method against other large-scale pests such as the gypsy moth, codling moth, boll weevil, and others. But the most valuable lesson demonstrated by this type of biological control is that introduction of sterile but otherwise normal species into a population has far greater impact in reducing the population than simply removing or killing an equal number of individuals. If it succeeds with other major pest species, this technique of sexual sterilization may make biocides unnecessary.

VIRUSES

The European spruce sawfly was introduced into eastern Canada in the 1920s, and before long it had destroyed 3000 square miles of timber. When a virus important to its control in Europe was accidentally introduced, the insect was practically eliminated in three years. Even more impressively, the Australian rabbit problem was finally but quickly brought under control by a virus disease, myxomatosis. Indigenous to rabbits in Brazil, where it causes a minor skin disease, myxomatosis was incredibly virulent when introduced to captive Australian rabbits. After determining that the virus affected only the rabbits, infected rabbits were released, and before the end of a year the virus, spread by mosquitoes, was killing rabbits by the hundreds of thousands. After a couple of years the virulence began to decline, eliminating the possibility of extermination, but the measure still provided better control than could have been achieved by any other method.

This appeal of viruses as a biological control lies in their specificity in contrast to biocides. Of the 280 viruses isolated from various insects, the most promising belong to a group called the nuclear polyhedrosis group. Normally, these rod-shaped viruses are encapsulated in a proteinaceous sheath that insulates them from the environment. This coat is dissolved in the insect gut, and the activated virus penetrates the insect cells, ultimately killing them. When properly diluted, evenly distributed, and applied at the right stage of insect development, viruses can be extremely effective.

After many years of work, viruses have finally been registered for use against the cotton bollworm and the tobacco budworm. As additional viruses are tested and found safe as well as successful they may begin to supplement if not replace some of the biocides in use today.

BACTERIA

For a number of years one bacterium (*Bacillus thuringiensis*) has been commercially produced to control the cabbage worm and alfalfa caterpillar. The bacterium is extremely virulent and spreads rapidly.

Another related bacterium, discovered in New Jersey in 1933, attacks the grubs of Japanese beetles. Because the infected grubs turn white, the infection is called the milky disease. The spores, which are resistant to extremes of temperature and moisture, are easily applied to the soil as a dust. Since the spores pass unharmed through the digestive tract of any animal eating the infected grubs, they remain viable and slowly spread throughout the environment. When large areas are treated, very effective, long-lasting control of Japanese beetles can be obtained without the de-structural side effects of mass aerial spraying. Between 1939 and 1953 the USDA in cooperation with various state and federal agencies distributed 230,000 pounds of spore dust at 160,000 sites in fourteen eastern states. Much of the reduction in the Japanese beetle population over this period may well be due to the slow but effective spread of this bacterial infection.

INSECTS

The most widespread and certainly the oldest form of biological control involves insects. Successful control of both plant and insect pests by insects has been obtained many times. Two examples illustrate the possibilities.

The prickly pear cactus was introduced into Australia as early as 1788. It was used then, as it still is in Mexico and the southwestern United States, as a defensive or sheltering hedge around ranch houses. But by 1870 it began to get out of control. In 1900, 10 million acres were covered with the cactus; by 1920, 60 million acres were infested. Both mechanical and chemical controls were too costly because of the huge areas affected. As early as 1912 research was begun to survey the natural enemies of the prickly pear. Of the several possibilities, a plain brown moth called *Cactoblastis* was selected and reared in the laboratory. Over a ten-year period nearly 3 billion eggs were distributed. The eggs hatch into caterpillars which tunnel inside the flat cactus segments, the stems, and even the roots. When this is followed by bacterial rots, the plants are quickly destroyed. By 1933, prickly pear was under effective control in Australia. Although the cactus was not eradicated, there is a large enough resident population of *Cactoblastis* to prevent any widespread regrowth of the prickly pear.

Not long after oranges had been introduced in California as a major crop in the late nineteenth century, the cottony-cushion scale, a sucking insect that weakens the tree and reduces the orange crop, was introduced from Australia. A search in Australia by C. V. Riley, an early pioneer in biological control, turned up a ladybug called the vedalia beetle, which when introduced to California proved extraordinarily successful in reducing damage (Figure 8.10). So successfully did the vedalia beetle control the scale that it began to be taken for granted. When broad-spectrum biocides were first used on orange groves in California seventy years later and the vedalia population declined, cottony-cushion scale again became a serious pest almost overnight.

Fig. 8.10 These vedalia beetles are feeding on the large white cottony-cushion scale. The populations of this pest are effectively reduced by introducing the vedalia beetle. (University of California, Department of Entomology, Division of Biological Control, Riverside)

BIORATIONAL AGENTS

Springing from the research of Carroll Williams at Harvard in the 1950s, insect control through hormones has great promise. Later work by Karel

Slama at Prague in the late 1960s seems to confirm this. Slama learned that less than a millionth of a gram of the juvenile hormone analog DMF[4] applied to the female linden bug sterilized the insect for the rest of its life; yet doses of 10,000 times the sterilizing dose did not kill it. Further, if males were treated with 100 μg of DMF not only were the females with which they mated sterilized, but when these females mated with untreated males, enough DMF was passed on to sterilize the next females with which the untreated males mated. None of the eggs resulting from these matings hatched.

Another juvenile hormone analog, Methoprene, made by Zoecon Corporation, has been registered by the EPA for use against one type of mosquito. As little as three to four ounces spread over one acre of breeding ground prevents mosquito larvae from maturing. While it lasts the seven to ten days of the mosquito life cycle, the hormone breaks down within two weeks.

Only after years of work with juvenile hormones isolated from insects was it discovered that plants produce juvenile hormone analogs called precocenes. Such agents isolated from the common garden plant *Ageratum* cause milkweed bug nymphs to metamorphose prematurely into imperfect adults with shortened life spans, and Colorado potato beetles to burrow into the ground, where they pass into diapause, a dormant stage.

If these hormones are specific and can be developed for, say, the twenty most damaging insects, the technique could be a valuable substitute for the synthetic chemicals on which agriculture has become dependent. But if they are broad-spectrum, capable of affecting predators as well as prey, hormones will be no improvement over present techniques and only postpone facing the inevitable—that there is no ideal solution to any problem.

PHEROMONES AND PHYTODEXINS

The female gypsy moth is such a weak flier that males must seek the female out over a great distance. To guide the male to his destiny, the female exudes a powerful scent or pheromone which can be smelled by a male several miles away. By grinding up female moths, a pheromone was developed that could attract males from miles around to a trap or poison target where they could be killed. Today this scent, disparlure, identified and synthesized, has been successful in helping to control the gypsy moth. Another pheromone, gossyplure, has been synthesized from the pink cotton bollworm and used successfully in field tests. Con-

[4] A juvenile hormone analog is an artificially produced compound similar in structure and biological activity to the naturally occurring hormone.

trol of the pink bollworm using the pheromone was comparable in effectiveness and cost to the use of traditional biocides. The possibilities of finding and using other sex attractants suggest another useful approach to the selective control of pest insects. The insect cannot develop resistance to its own sex attractant without destroying its normal reproductive behavior, so the attractant should retain its effectiveness indefinitely.

Even more complex are the compounds called phytodexins, which have been known since 1940. Toxic to fungi and bacteria, they are produced by plants in response to pest attack much as interferons or antibodies are produced in the human body after attack by a disease organism. Apparently elicitors from the attacking fungi stimulate the production of phytodexins. Research on this class of compounds is beginning to unravel the nature and structure of the elicitors. If synthesized, these could provide a totally new group of fungicides.

OBSTACLES

As exciting as many of these recent developments are, they may never get out of the research lab, let alone have a chance to compete with standard chemical control methods. Most of the biocides in use today were developed and marketed by large corporations with no other aim than a return on investment. Since the largest profit is made by the pesticide with the widest spectrum of use, most of the rather ingenious control possibilities mentioned above would be unprofitable to most of the large corporations with the facilities and capital for extensive development of new techniques. Another roadblock is the elaborate testing now required by the EPA and FDA before the new techniques can be registered even though these techniques are specific, non-persistent, and non-toxic in the general environment. Ironically, the complex of tests set up to protect the public from indiscriminate introduction of broad-spectrum, toxic, and persistent chemicals works against replacing such control agents with more ecologically sound ones.

One possible way to facilitate the research and development of new agents would be for the developer to prepare a research impact statement that would determine the effect of regulation on proposed research before it is undertaken. This overview would expose the way regulation inhibits research; then modifications might be made by the regulatory agency. Lengthy and expensive toxicological tests are presently required before the field testing that determines whether a given approach is even feasible. This is putting the cart before the horse and makes it difficult for small, flexible companies to compete with the larger corporations, which have large stakes in status quo technology.

181

While replacement of broad-spectrum, persistent biocides is highly desirable, the inherent instability of monoculture (large acreages devoted to one crop) demands that they be replaced by some alternate forms of pest control. If biological and integrated control techniques are unduly delayed by overzealous application of rules and testing procedures just when biocides are being removed from use, we are caught between a stone and a hard place at a very awkward time.

If plants and animals were introduced with care to include the complex consumer-predator-prey-parasite organisms associated with the introduced species, populations would stay under control. But introductions have always been random, a species here and a species there, which precludes any short-term stabilization. Population regulation requires an enormous input of energy. Too often we have panicked and caused more problems in our clumsy efforts to exterminate what cannot be exterminated.

The wisest policy is to avoid introduction until enough is known about a species both in its home and in its new habitat to evaluate the possible environmental repercussions of the introduction. Once a species is introduced we should learn to live with it, but at the same time we should exploit every means of natural control at our disposal, for long-term control by biocides is not only ineffective but self-defeating.

Every species has in its life cycle some point where natural control can be exerted effectively. By seeking out these weak points and exploiting them, we can work *with* natural processes rather than expend large amounts of energy on trying to overwhelm them. Someday we may come to realize that much of our so-called struggle for existence is unnecessary.

FURTHER READING

Bull, J., and E. R. Ricciuti, 1974. "Polly want an apple?" *Audubon* **76**(3), pp. 48–54. Parakeets, the latest in avian introductions.

Crosby, A. W., Jr., 1974. *The Columbian exchange: biological and cultural consequences of 1492.* Greenwood Publications, Westport, Connecticut. A fine documentation and summary of the impact of the discovery of the New World on the Old, and vice versa.

Djerassi, C., 1974. "Insect control of the future: operational and policy aspects." *Science* **186,** pp. 596–606. A very sound discussion of the difficulties inherent in developing alternatives to standard chemical biocides.

Elton, C. S., 1958. *The ecology of invasions by animals and plants.* Methuen, London. Beautifully written classic account by one of the most respected ecologists of the twentieth century.

Graham, F., Jr., 1972. "The war against the dreaded gypsies." *Audubon*

74(3), pp. 44–51. Some common sense finally applied to the emotional gypsy moth problem.

Mallson, W. J., and N. D. Addy, 1975. "Phytophagous insects as regulators of forest primary production." *Science* **190,** pp. 515–522. Presents the interesting view that long-term insect cycles regulate the nutrient cycles and primary production of forests.

Maugh, T. H., Jr., 1976. "Plant biochemistry: two new ways to fight pests." *Science* **192,** pp. 874–876. More alternatives to biocides.

Moyle, D. B., 1976. "Fish introductions in California: history and impact on native fishes." *Biol. Conserv.* **9**(2), pp. 101–118. A detailed look at the consequences of years of uncontrolled introductions of fish in the natural (and unnatural) waters of California.

Zaret, T. M., and R. J. Paine, 1973. "Species introduction in a tropical lake." *Science* **182,** pp. 449–455. Some data presented here should give pause to planners of faunal improvement schemes.

CHAPTER NINE

EXTINCTION

In the last 20,000 years, dozens of mammal and bird species have disappeared from their niches without replacement. Something unusual must have happened, for the spacing of the extinctions over several thousand years makes it difficult to ascribe them to climatological or geological events alone. Furthermore, most of the extinct animals were large—the mammals over 100 pounds and the birds fairly large and conspicuous too.

The large North American mammals were hardest hit—70 percent became extinct during the last 10,000 to 15,000 years of the Pleistocene epoch. Horses and camels, which had evolved in the New World, became extinct on this continent, as did mammoths and mastodons, which had migrated into the New World over the once dry land of the Bering Strait. The ground sloth, the saber-toothed tiger, the tapir, the dire wolf, the giant buffalo, an antelope, and the giant beaver also disappeared, and yet there was no concomitant loss of small mammals, plants, or aquatic organisms.

A surprising number of the fossilized bones of these animals and birds were discovered in association with charcoal and stone tools, such as arrowheads or spear points, some still embedded in the bones. Was it possble that Paleo-Indians had hunted these animals to extinction? At first this idea was denounced as ridiculous. Who could imagine a Paleo-Indian with his crude weapons exterminating the mighty mastodon or the swift horse?

We are not certain what really happened, but in a time of severe environmental stress caused by glacially induced climatological and vegetational changes, certain animal populations may have been pushed beyond the point of survival by our predecessors. To envision the Paleo-Indians' possible role as exterminator, we have to look beyond the image of a spear-carrying savage killing one mastodon or horse. As the Plains Indians of historic times demonstrated again and again, herds of animals could be driven by fire off cliffs or bluffs to their destruction. Especially if the animals' numbers had already been reduced by unusual natural stresses, this practice could have led to their extinction.

If Paleo-Indians were instrumental in exterminating so many large mammals, how did any escape? Possibly some, like mountain sheep and goats, were saved by occupying rough country; others, like moose, bear, and deer, found refuge in woodlands. Those escaping extinction on the open prairie may have been both abundant and fecund enough to keep pace with the effort to kill them for food.

Even in Africa, whose broad plains teemed with the greatest variety of grazing animals in the world, at least 30 percent of this fauna was lost during the late Pleistocene. More African animals have survived to the present day because human evolution was also underway in Africa at this time. Thus some animals had time to develop defenses against our special predatory activities. In North America, however, we suddenly appeared upon the scene from Asia, occupied the continent, and began hunting animals that had never had a chance to adapt to our special type of predation.

Fig. 9.1. *As improbable as it may seem, the dodo did exist on Mauritius in the Indian Ocean until the seventeenth century. Its flightlessness, however, sealed its doom.* (Courtesy of the American Museum of Natural History)

Our role as exterminator can be inferred from the wave of extinctions that followed our occupation of new continents or islands around the world: the disappearance of the giant kangaroo and other large animals when the Bushmen came to Australia; the loss of twenty-seven species of moa (a large ostrich-like bird) when the Maori reached New Zealand; and the elimination of the dodo from Mauritius (an island in the Indian Ocean) by Dutch and Portuguese sailors in the sixteenth and seventeenth centuries (Figure 9.1). Most of the niches left by these extinctions remain unfilled.

An interesting exception, as we saw in Chapter 8, is the niche occupied by the horse in North America. Ten thousand years after its extinction in North America, the horse was reintroduced by the Spaniards and successfully reoccupied its old niche. For some years the Spanish horse or mustang was quite common in the Southwest. But with the arrival of American settlement and American-type horses, Spanish-descended mustangs were slowly replaced by the more prosaic wild horse. These animals were slaughtered for years to make dog food (see Arthur Miller's moving film *The Misfits*). Finally an aroused public pressured the Bureau of Land Management, on whose lands most of the wild horses are found, to set aside a wild horse range in the Pryor Mountains of Montana.

At times it seems that we are bent on reducing the thousands of

Table 9.1
Some Endangered Animals in the United States *

ANIMAL	NUMBER IN COTERMINOUS UNITED STATES
Timber wolf˙	1300 (12,000 with Alaska)
Grizzly bear	1000 (12,000 with Alaska)
Black-footed ferret	Unknown, but rare
Southern sea otter †	1200
Florida panther	50–100
Guadalupe fur seal ‡	1000
Florida manatee or sea cow	1,000
Key deer	600
California condor	40
Florida Everglades kite	120
Southern bald eagle	700
American peregrine falcon	150 (500 with Alaska and Canada)
Attwater's greater prairie chicken	2200
Masked bobwhite	0 (some reintroduction now being tried in Arizona)
Whooping crane	80 (in the wild)
Eskimo curlew	Extremely rare
Puerto Rican parrot	20
Ivory-billed woodpecker	Unknown, but rare
Kirtland's warbler	400
Ipswich sparrow ‡	4000
Pine barrens tree frog	500

* Source: *Threatened wildlife of the United States*, 1973. Bureau of Sport Fisheries and Wildlife, Resource Publication No. 114.
† threatened status
‡ not on official list

species of birds and mammals to a few dozen we consider desirable; the rest are viewed as expendable (Table 9.1). Our attacks on the organisms of the world have varied from outright assault to insidious nibblings, with the same destructive result. In this chapter we will look in greater detail at the negative impact we have had on our fellow organisms.

EXTINCTION BY DIRECT ASSAULT

Many animals have disappeared simply because they were edible. Others have become extinct because they became fashionable in our eyes. A few examples of more recent extinctions are discussed here.

THE PASSENGER PIGEON

Half as large again as the mourning dove and at least as savory, the passenger pigeon was probably the most abundant bird we have ever en-

Fig. 9.2 *A popular sport in the early nineteenth century was shooting wild pigeons, here the passenger pigeon.* (The Bettmann Archive)

countered (Figure 9.2), yet in a few decades it was hunted to extinction. In 1810 the ornithologist Alexander Wilson saw a flock of pigeons in Kentucky which he calculated to be 240 miles long and a mile wide. Wilson estimated the flock to contain 2.23 billion birds! Unlike geese or ducks, which flock only during migration and never in such numbers, passenger pigeons were gregarious throughout the year. Nesting was erratic, depending upon the availability of food. Usually, when beechnuts were plentiful, the birds nested in Michigan and Pennsylvania; when acorns were abundant, Wisconsin and Minnesota were favored. In 1871 one of the largest nestings ever observed took place in Wisconsin. The pigeons nested in almost every available tree over a strip seventy-five by fifteen miles covering over 850 square miles. Anywhere from five to a hundred nests were built in each tree. Such a nesting naturally attracted hunters from all over the country. One conservative estimate placed the number of pigeons in that nesting area at about 136 million.

The males and females sat on the nest alternately. The males left at daybreak, returning at midmorning to relieve the females, who fed until early afternoon, returning to allow the males a final afternoon feeding. This traffic to and from the nesting area presented a unique opportunity for hunters. One eyewitness gives this account of the proceedings:

And now arose a roar, compared with which all previous noises ever heard, are but lullabys, and which caused more than one of the expectant and excited party to drop their guns, and seek shelter behind and beneath the nearest trees. . . . Imagine a thousand threshing machines running under full headway, accompanied by as many steamboats groaning off steam, with an equal quota of R.R. trains passing through covered bridges— imagine these massed into a single flock, and you possibly have a faint conception of the terrific roar following the monstrous black cloud of pigeons as they passed in rapid flight in the gray light of morning, a few feet before our faces. . . . The unearthly roar continued, and as flock after flock, in almost endless line, succeeded each other, nearly on a level with muzzle of our guns, the contents of a score of double barrels was poured into their dense midst. Hundreds, yes thousands, dropped into the open fields below. Not infrequently a hunter would discharge his piece and load and fire the third and fourth time into the same flock. The slaughter was terrible beyond any description. Our guns became so hot by rapid discharges, we were afraid to load them. Then while waiting for them to cool, lying on the damp leaves, we used, those of us who had [them], pistols, while others threw clubs, seldom if ever, failing to bring down some of the passing flock.[1]

Hunting was not limited to pigeons on the wing; birds were attacked on the nest with sticks, woods were set afire, and trees were chopped down. After a few more years of this kind of hunting, people began to wonder where the pigeons had gone; some said Canada, others, Australia. But the passenger pigeon could not escape from the unremitting pressure of the hunter. Why was the passenger pigeon not saved from extinction? Surely a few thousand birds of all those billions could have been preserved.

Here the birds' social habits worked against them. When the large flocks were broken up into hundreds or even thousands, the breeding instinct was somehow inhibited and nesting was sporadic or not even attempted. With continued hunting and cutting of the hardwood forests that supplied most of their food, nesting, and roosting sites, the pigeons faded into oblivion. Once extinction was apparent and perhaps unavoidable, a great wave of remorse swept the land, but to no avail; the last passenger pigeon, an aged female called Martha, died on September 1, 1914, in the Cincinnati Zoo. We must conclude that the passenger pigeon could not be saved: when reduced to numbers congruent with the space we were willing to share with it, reproduction was apparently impossible and extinction inevitable.

[1] Schorger, A. W., 1937. "The great Wisconsin passenger pigeon nesting of 1871." *Proc. Linn. Soc. N.Y.*, 48, pp. 1–26.

Similar sentiment bathed the last pitiful remnants of the buffalo that once blackened the American prairie (Figure 9.3). Approximately 25,000 buffalo still remain in zoos, reservations, and private collections. However, we are forced to admit that the buffalo and the passenger pigeon would not be compatible with present day use of either the Great Plains or the eastern deciduous forest. Picture today a herd of even one million, much less the original 60 million buffalo, wandering from Texas to Montana and back every year, or a flock of a million passenger pigeons settling on an Ohio county to feed!

Fig. 9.3 Only a few thousand bison are left in the United States. These four happen to be grazing in Golden Gate Park, rather far from their native habitat on the Great Plains. But the living is easy and their reproductive potential is high.

THE GREAT AUK

However, we cannot evade our responsibility by assuming that extinction is inevitable for *all* wild animals, or that an essential incompatibility exists between humans and beasts. Unlike the passenger pigeon, the great auk was never overly abundant. A flightless sea bird resembling the penguin, the great auk once nested on rocky islets around the periphery of the North Atlantic from Maine to Spain. Although a superb swimmer and diver, the great auk was extremely clumsy on land and was easily killed when ashore. Fishermen from northern Europe on extended fishing voyages found the auk a welcome source of otherwise unobtainable fresh meat. By the time Jacques Cartier visited the coast of Newfoundland in 1534, the great auk was already becoming much less widely dis-

189

BUNGLING THE BIOTA

tributed and growing locally rare in northern Europe. On Funk Island off Newfoundland, Cartier found large colonies of auks and soon the slaughter began in the New World as well as the Old. As the Grand Banks off Newfoundland became known to fishermen, the North American population of auks was drastically reduced by expeditions that herded whole flocks into stone compounds where they were methodically clubbed to death and rendered for their oil or salted for their meat.

By the early 1800s, the North American great auks were gone. A few lingered on rocky islets off the coast of Iceland, but with the butchering of two birds in 1844, the species was clubbed into extinction. Had today's concept of renewable resource been in existence in the nineteenth century the great auk could well have been saved, for even at that time a brief study could have determined how many birds could be taken for their flesh, oil, or feathers without seriously reducing the population. Unfortunately, animals were not then viewed as a valuable resource. We assumed that when one was gone there was always another. But we have seen our last great auk.

Fig. 9.4 In 1840, at the height of the golden age of whaling, when this water color was done by a New Bedford whaler, the odds were fairly even between whale and man. (The Whaling Museum, New Bedford, Mass.)

WHALES

While it would be reassuring to think that times have changed and that nations now want to maintain their animal populations as a valuable resource, the recent dramatic decrease in the population of several species of whales indicates that this is not yet the case.

The great and romantic age of whaling flowered between 1825 and 1860 (Figure 9.4), then withered as prosaic but easily available kerosene

replaced whale oil. While several species of whale produced good oil, only the sperm whale provided ambergris, a wax-like substance still used as a perfume base, and spermaceti, a fine oil of great value. Unlike the toothed sperm whale, the right, bowhead, and gray whales have a mouth full of horny plates through which they strain sea water containing their shrimplike food. These plates are the whalebone used for years in corset stays and buggy whips.

Although whalers worked energetically in the nineteenth century, whaling was inefficient and limited to the most easily caught whales. In the twentieth century, as new uses were found for whale oil and whale meat, interest in whaling revived, and with modern techniques whaling again became a serious business enterprise. Now, however, huge factory ships are capable of locating, killing, and processing *all* useful species of whale with great efficiency (Figure 9.5).

After World War II, the International Whaling Commission attempted to establish some rules for whaling, but the nations that signed were only obliged to set their own catch limits and regulations. The commission offered scientific advice but signatory nations were not bound to follow it. As each nation continued to take what it pleased, whales soon became few and far between. Today only the U.S.S.R. and Japan continue high-pressure whaling operations, and the focus of whaling efforts has shifted from the Antarctic to the northern Pacific.

In 1900 the world population of large whales was approximately 4.4 million; today it is around 1.1 million and includes 600,000 sperm,

Fig. 9.5   Today the big ones no longer get away. This factory ship is about to process a fin whale (shown belly up). (Popperfoto)

300,000 minke, 100,000 fin, and 85,000 sei whales. Eight severely over-harvested species make up the balance of the population.

Some species like the gray, bowhead, and right whales have been protected, and the humpback whale has been partially protected for several years. But protection isn't worth much on the high seas. In 1962 off Tristan da Cunha in the south Atlantic the largest known herd of the supposedly protected southern right whale was "harvested" to the last pound by a whaling fleet that happened by.

The whale in greatest danger of extinction is the blue whale, the largest animal ever to live: it is often more than 100 feet long and weighs up to 130 tons. The blue whale population has been reduced to around 6000, a level so low that even with complete protection, which it has had since 1967, this whale may slowly slip into oblivion. Apparently the nations that continue to exploit whales have decided that it is economically advantageous to use the full capacity of their whaling fleets until whaling is no longer profitable and then dispose of the whole fleet rather than cut back operations to the level of indefinite sustained yield at a smaller profit.

Japan, one of the last two major whaling nations, has been singled out, somewhat unfairly, by conservation organizations in the United States and Europe for a boycott of manufactured goods in retaliation for Japan's refusal to accept stringent limitations on the size of its whale catch. While it is easy to take the whale's side in the controversy, the matter is more involved than a struggle between good and evil. Because of an acute shortage of protein in their diet, the Japanese generally eat far more fish and seafood than Americans. Most beef is imported and quite expensive. Hence, whale meat provides a valuable and inexpensive source of protein, about 9 percent of the total meat diet. In lieu of abundant meat, much vegetable protein is consumed in the form of soybeans, which Japan imports mostly from the United States (3.5 million tonnes in 1973). In 1973–1974 a drought caused a 19 percent drop in soybean production. Further demands on the soybean crop were made by a shortage of fishmeal resulting from over-fishing of the anchovy in Peru. So in 1973 the United States suspended soybean exports. Previous to this the Japanese whaling catch dropped by 40 percent from 203,000 tonnes in 1965 to 122,700 tonnes in 1973. Since at the same time the American tuna fleet was killing and wasting per year over 100,000 porpoise inadvertently caught in its nets without governmental intervention, it is not surprising that the Japanese refused to abandon large capital investment in their whaling industry because a few conservationists were unhappy. However as the whale harvest continues to decline, whaling fleets become obsolescent, and world pressure to cease whaling operations continues to mount, both Japan and the U.S.S.R. will probably abandon whaling before the last barrel of oil is extracted from the last whale. Whether whale stocks will recuperate is another matter since krill, the shrimplike food of many of the large whales is just beginning to be exploited in the Antarctic.

FASHIONABLE EXTINCTIONS

Numbers of other animals have been reduced to the extinction point because of their attractive fur or feathers. The sea otter was very nearly exterminated before it was completely protected. Although still limited to only a few points in its former range from northern Japan across the north Pacific to California, the sea otter seems to be increasing slowly in numbers and distribution, allowing the Russians to harvest a small number from their otter population.

Until banned by international agreements, a vigorous trade in millinery-feathers at the turn of the century threatened the African ostrich, several species of egret, and the birds of paradise found in New Guinea. Today the African leopard, Indian tiger, and Florida alligator are threatened because of the demand for their fashionable skins. Even though changes in fashion have spared species from extinction in the past, time is short and pressure on these species great. Most reputable furriers refuse to handle skins from animals officially listed by the International Union for the Conservation of Nature and Natural Resources, which maintains a Red Book of endangered species of the world. Although the alligator is protected in every state over its range but Texas, it was widely poached in Florida, even in the Everglades National Park. A national ban on interstate shipment of hides has done much to assure the survival of alligators in the South; and a recently negotiated international treaty expected to be ratified by over eighty nations offers some hope that the endangered species of the earth may survive for a few more decades.

NOVEL USES LEAD TO EXTINCTION

Killing wild animals for food or for their skins can perhaps be rationalized, but killing a gnu to make a flyswatter out of its tail, an elephant to convert its feet into waste paper baskets, or a buffalo to make a tobacco pouch with zipper out of its scrotum, is perverse (Figure 9.6). In the United States, mummified baby alligators or baskets made of armadillo "shells" are as tasteless as a cookie jar made out of a human skull.

While no one claims the imminent extinction of elephants to satisfy the waste paper basket trade, the walrus is definitely threatened by the souvenir market. Although there are perhaps 30,000 Pacific walruses left, as many as 7000 are killed each year in Siberia and Alaska for their ivory tusks, which are worth $2 a pound. Since the tusks of a large male may weigh twenty pounds each and the ivory carved into ornaments or figures

Fig. 9.6 *Tasteless curios such as these elephant foot wastebaskets can exist only when a thoughtless public provides a market.* (Tierbilder/Okapia, Frankfurt/Main)

may be worth up to $100 a pound, walruses are actively hunted. Both the U.S.S.R. and the United States regulate the hunting of walruses within their territory, but walruses are citizens of neither country; without an international treaty to guarantee protection, this species may also be doomed.

SUPERSTITION

The wild mountain goat or ibex was exterminated in the Swiss Alps in the seventeenth century because of its supposed beneficent powers:

> Almost every part of its body was considered to have some healing virtue or other beneficial property, be it aphrodisiac, talisman, or poison detector. A particularly wide range of medicinal effects was attributed to the hair balls occasionally found in the ibex's fourth stomach compartment. These "bezoar balls" were reputed effective against fainting, melancholy, jaundice, hemorrhoids, hemorrhagic diarrhea, pestilence, cancer, and other ills. The ibex's blood was considered a cure for bladder stones; the heel bone helped combat spleen diseases; the heart yielded a strength-giving tonic; and even the droppings were utilized as medicine against anemia and consumption as well as a rejuvenating agent. The many reputed pharmaceutical properties brought the ibex no benefit; on the contrary, its body was so highly sought after that by the seventeenth century it was already extinct in the Swiss Alps.[2]

[2] Ziswiler, V., 1967. *Extinct and vanishing animals.* Springer-Verlag, New York.

Of course today's Swiss are somewhat more sophisticated, but many Chinese still believe that rhinoceros horn in powdered form is a powerful aphrodisiac. The result of this superstition has been the reduction of the three Asian species of rhinoceros to the point of extinction; in 1964 there were 600 Indian rhinos, 150 Sumatran rhinos, and only twenty-one Javan rhinos. Even the African species of rhino has been affected by this "magic." Although both the black and white African rhinos are protected, over 1000 are poached each year, which has reduced the black rhino to around 13,000 and the white to 3900 individuals.

TROPHY HUNTING

The Arabian oryx is a graceful gazelle-like animal with long tapering horns. In recent years its extinction in Arabia was assured by oil-rich Arab notables who took to running down the last fragmented herds in jeeps or airplanes and machine-gunning them to the last individual. In view of the inevitable results of such "sport," an expedition was mounted several years ago to capture breeding stock of these animals while they still existed. These were shipped to Phoenix, Arizona, where successful efforts were made to establish a breeding herd to preserve the species and ultimately allow reintroduction to Arabia when the safety of the oryx could be assured (Figure 9.7).

It is only fair to note, however, that trophy hunting is much more regulated than this example would suggest and few other animals are in immediate danger from this sport.

Fig. 9.7 *The Arabian oryx, threatened with extinction in its native home, has been given a new lease on life by a breeding program in progress at the Phoenix Zoo. After several years of breeding there may be enough oryxes to provide stock for reintroduction in suitable parts of Arabia and the Middle East.* (Phoenix Zoo)

195

COMPETITION WITH MAN

In the early years of their settlement of South Africa, Boer settlers, eking out a living by running stock or farming, viewed any competition from natural sources as expendable and felt justified in leveling their guns on any wild animal in range. In a few years the Cape lion, blue buck, and two species of zebra, the quagga and subspecies of Burchell's zebra, were extinct, and the Cape mountain zebra, bontebok, and white-tailed gnu were reduced to specimens in game reserves.

Similarly, the only parrot native to the United States, the Carolina parakeet, was eliminated because of its fondness for man's crops. It was easy prey because of its habit of circling in flocks again and again around fallen members until all were destroyed. The last of these green and yellow birds, a lone specimen in a zoo, died in 1914.

Occasionally the numbers of desirable species are reduced in vain. As a result of the presence of the tsetse fly, large areas of Rhodesia have been closed to settlement and livestock raising has been curtailed. When it was believed that large mammals were the only reservoir for the trypanosome that caused sleeping sickness, control was sought by killing large numbers of zebra, gazelle, and antelope—500,000 during the control attempt. Later researchers found that small mammals and birds also acted as hosts for the trypanosome. This huge loss of large mammals was needless, for the tsetse fly remained unchecked.

Control of predators has long been a controversial subject in regions with a large livestock industry. To be sure, mountain lions and coyotes do take livestock occasionally; a few individuals may kill consistently. But massive predator control programs have the same destructive environmental impact as broad-spectrum biocides—the poisons are not confined to the target species, and wildlife in general suffers. Some effects of predator control are more subtle. Constant predator control pressure disrupts the normal territoriality of coyotes and the survivors develop different habits that may include dependence on livestock. Also, the removal of coyotes lowers competition among survivors stimulating larger litters than normal, thus negating some of the effect of the control program. Widespread indiscriminate poisoning may also kill the normal food species, thus driving the predator to the only food left, the livestock the poison was distributed to protect. In view of the vast sums of money that have been spent annually to control predators, it might be cheaper for the government to pay a rancher for stock that can be proved to the government's satisfaction to have been killed by predators. In 1972 a sheepman (not a wild-eyed conservationist) estimated that 1500 of Arizona's 350,000 sheep were lost to coyotes the preceding year. This is 0.43 percent, rather less than the claims of 10 or 20 percent or more that are commonly tossed about. At a value of $25 a head, the coyote damage was only $37,500. In the same year state and federal agencies spent over $250,000 to control predators in Arizona. Responding finally to public pressure, the federal government in 1972 stopped using poisons to kill predators on public lands. In 1973, as a result of pressure from sheepmen, the law was amended to allow certain uses of sodium cyanide. Ironically, for all the years of control efforts and millions of coyotes killed, the coyote population is increasing nationally and the sheep are declining. Although the decline is a result of economics rather than coyotes, it seems quite likely that coyotes will long outlast sheep on the great American range.

LIVE ANIMAL TRADE

Our desire to see a variety of animals with minimum discomfort and danger has led to the establishment of zoological gardens or zoos. Some, like the zoos at San Diego, the Bronx, or Lincoln Park, are quite extensive; others are quite small. Altogether there are perhaps 100 large zoos in the world, creating a steady demand for wild animals, particularly the rarer ones. A platypus or giant panda will always draw a larger crowd than a lion or zebra and since many public zoos depend on admission fees or attendance figures to maintain or increase their appropriations, there is constant pressure to exhibit the rare and the unusual. This pressure is transmitted to collectors and ultimately to animal populations throughout the world. A good case in point is the orangutan.

Native to Borneo and Sumatra, this large ape is a favorite exhibit in zoos. But as the orangutan became rarer, the demand increased sharply and irresponsible animal collectors redoubled their efforts. The situation was aggravated by placing a premium on the young apes, usually collected only by killing the mother. In an effort to save the orangutan in its native habitat, most zoos, to their credit, no longer purchase this or other animals in danger of extinction. In some cases where extinction seems imminent, however, a special effort is made to establish a breeding stock in the safety of a zoo, as was done with the Arabian oryx.

Another potential danger to wild animal populations, especially monkeys, is the rising demand for animals for experimental purposes, especially in medical and testing laboratories. It is perhaps ironic that as we generate more and more products of potential danger to ourselves such as drugs, additives, and pollutants, we need more and more *animals* in testing programs. Many of these animals—rabbits, hamsters, guinea pigs, and rats—are bred especially for this purpose, but the monkey possesses the best analog of man's metabolism and thus is eagerly hunted in Central and South America. Although some effort is being made today to set

197

up breeding colonies of the most desirable species, thus increasing supply and assuring greater uniformity and higher-quality animals, it will be several years before the demand can be satisfied.

Both zoos and medical research, however, have used a small number of animals compared with the pet market. Until 1967, parrots were banned from this country by the Public Health Service, for they were known to carry parrot fever (psittacosis), which could be passed on to humans. Recently a wide array of other birds has been found to carry this virus, which has accordingly been renamed ornithosis. Since human contact is much more likely with pet birds than wild ones, parrots remained on the banned list. Then it was found that by holding the birds in an isolation center, treating them for several weeks, and observing them for another period, the disease could be controlled. The ban was lifted and a different kind of "parrot fever" swept the country. The five-and-dime stores, which handle most of the parrots sold in the United States, are unable to supply the demand.

The parrots are collected by Indians in the rain forests of the Amazon Basin, mostly in Colombia. Considering the amount of handling they undergo from tree to household cage, it has been estimated that only one in fifty birds survives the transition. This means that in 1968, 500,000 parrots died to supply the 10,000 that were sold. Yearly removal of half a million parrots may be well within the reproductive potential of the species, or it may seriously threaten their survival. The problem is that no one knows what effect the soaring market for pet parrots is having in the source country. The Amazon Basin, although rapidly changing (see Chapter 13), is still in many ways *terra incognita*, and none but the broadest ecological generalizations can be made. One effect has been noted, though: the Indian collectors, attracted to the easy money offered by traders, neglect their traditional livelihood to pursue the parrots. After the local supply is exhausted, the trader moves on, leaving the Indian collectors economically high and dry.

Until the impact of this increased rate of parrot removal can be ascertained, harvesting of these birds should not be left in the hands of irresponsible entrepreneurs, for just this type of unregulated exploitation has led to extinction of species in the past.

HABITAT DESTRUCTION; EXTINCTION BY SUBVERSION

Our direct attack on a species is an obvious form of extermination or extinction, but more subtle processes often have the same fatal results for the organisms involved. Short of destroying the organism itself, destroying its habitat is perhaps the most effective indirect avenue to extinction.

Fig. 9.8 Few birds can equal the seven-foot wing-spread of the whooping crane. These four birds are on their wintering range at the Aransas National Wildlife Refuge in Texas. (U.S. Department of the Interior, Fish and Wildlife Service)

At one time, the island of Madagascar was completely clothed in a rich forest. Its long isolation from the rest of Africa resulted in the preservation of an unusual group of primitive primates, most of which were tree dwellers. In recent years, development has destroyed over 80 percent of Madagascar's forest, leaving this unique collection of primates clinging, literally and figuratively, to the scattered remnants. Already one form is extinct, four more are quite rare, and twenty-three are threatened. Unless steps are taken to preserve some tracts of undisturbed forest as refuges, this entire group of primates will disappear.

Probably the most publicized species courting extinction is the whooping crane. This five-foot-tall wading bird is completely white except for a bright red crown, black moustache, and black wing tips, which make it a spectacular sight on the ground or in the air (Figure 9.8). The whooping crane originally nested in marshes in the prairie states and wintered on the Gulf Coast. Never especially abundant, the crane was initially reduced by hunting as it made its long migrations from its breeding grounds in Canada and the United States to its wintering ground. The bird was not especially edible, but it presented a striking target to the hunter. Later, as the prairie states came under cultivation, marsh after marsh was drained. A combination of habitat destruction and hunting reduced the whooping crane to a low of fifteen birds in 1942 despite the establishment in 1937 of the 47,000-acre Aransas Wildlife Refuge to protect the species' wintering range.

Since then the wild whooping crane population has increased to around sixty birds. In addition, some birds are in captivity in an effort to increase their numbers artificially.

A promising new technique is cross-fostering. Eggs from the wild population are removed (new ones are laid) and flown to nesting sandhill cranes, a closely related species, in a wildlife refuge in Idaho. The whoopers are reared by their foster parents and led to and from wintering grounds in New Mexico. Conservationists hope that in five to seven years they will breed with each other rather than with the sandhill cranes and establish a new population in the wild, providing a hedge against a disaster in the original population.

Certainly it is easier to empathize with endangered species of animals, but some 2000 species of plants across the world are also endangered. Many of these are endemic species, plants whose very limited ranges or specialized habitats make them very sensitive to environmental manipulations. Trees and shrubs are conspicuous enough to elicit some protection—for example, California long ago set aside the last grove of Torrey pine near San Diego as a state park to preserve the species, and the big tree has received state and federal protection in the Sierras (Figure 9.9). But for every protected tree or shrub there are dozens of rare herbs, grasses, sedges, and ferns whose passing as a species goes virtually un-

Fig. 9.9   While not the tallest living organisms, big trees are certainly among the most massive. Note the figure leaning against the base of the tree to the left.

200

noticed. Much of the problem is due to our incomplete knowledge of plant distributions; an isolated colony of a grass or fern could well be destroyed by highway construction before anyone knew it was there. But despite these problems steps are being taken to compile lists of endangered plants. The Smithsonian Institution has published such a list that includes almost 10 percent of the United States flora. In Hawaii, which had many endemics, 266 plants are extinct and 1267 more are threatened with extinction.

Perhaps because of the recognition recently given to endangered species, there is a growing awareness that habitats of these species can be endangered too. How can a rare bog plant be preserved without saving the bog where it must grow; how can we save an orangutan, if its rain forest environment has been reduced to a scrubby savanna or manioc field? At this point we need a list of endangered environments as well as plants and animals. Mere listing does not of course save either a species or an environment, but it does focus public attention on those entities that are rapidly being lost and provide some motivation for setting aside not only adequate habitats for rare species, but habitats that in themselves are rare.

But preservation of a habitat does not necessarily assure protection of its species. Careless introduction of foreign plants and animals can have very harmful effects on natural ecosystems too.

ANIMAL AND PLANT INTRODUCTION

Despite unusual examples like the dodo, the great auk, and the passenger pigeon, we have directly caused the extinction of relatively few animals, particularly in comparison with the destruction wrought by animals we have introduced in certain areas. Most striking among these introduced animals are rats, goats, pigs, cats, and dogs in that order. Rats attack all ground-breeding animals of appropriate size and have caused the extinction of nine species of rails (a small marsh bird, often flightless on isolated islands). Goats were widely introduced on many islands by ships that left them as a kind of living larder to provide a supply of fresh meat for the next visitor. "Desert islands" are as much the result of goat overpopulation and overgrazing as of any accident of nature. With the destruction or gross alteration of vegetation, indigenous species lose breeding sites and shelter; hence the fauna of many of these goat-inhabited islands has suffered impoverishment and extinction.

Another calamitous example of the impact of animal introduction occurred in the sugar cane fields of the West Indies, which were plagued with rats whose depredations destroyed much of the crop. The mongoose, a fierce, weasel-like native of Asia, was introduced to reduce the rat population. The mongoose *did* attack rats for a while, but soon began to attack

Fig. 9.10 (a) Originally much of the foothill and Great Valley grasslands in California looked something like this—dispersed clumps of perennial bunch grass with native annual grasses and flowers scattered in between. (b) After many years of grazing first by cattle, then by sheep, the bunch grasses have disappeared and even the introduced annuals have been reduced to a slight fuzz among the stones.

every other ground dweller. Amphibians, reptiles, and birds were preyed upon until several species became extremely rare.

Foreign species are not always introduced intentionally. The original grasslands of the Great Valley of California were composed of perennial bunch grasses (Figure 9.10a, b). Centuries of overgrazing opened the way for the invasion of and ultimate takeover by annual grasses whose seeds were brought in from the Mediterranean countries in the wool of sheep and with the seeds of crop plants.

Once introduction has taken place, elimination is very difficult, particularly if the plant is annual or the animal small. Even if eradication of the introduced species can be achieved, it may not be possible or desirable to restock the native organisms (see Chapter 8).

Damage to endangered species may result, paradoxically, from efforts to protect their habitat by the elimination or control of supposedly destructive factors such as fire.

The California condor (Figure 9.11), one of the largest vultures in the Western Hemisphere, has been restricted by development to a horseshoe-shaped range in the coastal mountains of California from Coalinga south to near Ventura and north again to east of Bakersfield. The center of this range has been protected by its inclusion in the Sespe Wild Area of the Los Padres National Forest. Despite its name, Los Padres National Forest, set up to protect part of the Los Angeles watershed, contains more chaparral than trees. Large areas of easily burned chaparral, before fire protection, presented a mosaic of burned and open patches surrounded by a dense growth of shrubs. When fire protection was begun with the formation of the national forest, large tracts were solidly covered with dense chaparral. Unfortunately the condor population is slowly ebbing. Its forty individuals, though protected by law, make conspicuous targets, supporting their twenty pounds in flight with a ten-foot wingspread.

Although condors may live up to forty years, they do not begin to breed until they are five years old, and then produce only one young every other year thereafter. The birds are restricted to their present small range mainly by urbanization, since the condors feed upon carrion, which has become scarce as a result of small, well-cared-for cattle ranches and the trend toward grain farming.

Because of its enormous wingspread, the condor needs room to approach its food supply, and, more important, to take off after heavy feeding. Thus, open space is vital to the condor's survival. Since fire elimination tends to close chaparral stands, controlled burning helps the condor in some respects. However, care must be taken to avoid over-burning, since the heavy brush helps keep people out of nesting areas.

When, after several years of habitat manipulation, the number of con-

Fig. 9.11 One of the sixty California condors left, soaring in search of food in its home range. (U.S. Department of the Interior, Fish and Wildlife Service)

Fig. 9.12 A female Kirt-land's warbler feeding her young. Notice the protection provided by the jack pine whose branches can be seen at the top and bottom of the picture. (G. Ronald Ausking from National Audubon Society)

dors continued to decline, the Audubon Society recommended a program of captive breeding. If the program is adopted, juvenile condors will be captured with the hope that they will mate and rear young in a special breeding and research facility near the species' traditional habitat. Ultimately young condors will be released to the wild to build up local breeding stocks.

A much less conspicuous bird is the Kirtland's warbler, which breeds only in an 85- by 100-mile area in the north central region of the lower peninsula of Michigan (Figure 9.12). The nesting area is limited to dry, porous, sandy barrens covered with patches of jack pine, a scrubby pine of minor commercial value. After the white pine forests originally covering this area were cut or burned, jack pine was one of the few plants able not only to survive but to thrive in the frequently burned barrens. This is in part because the pine cones of the jack pine remain tightly closed and attached to the tree, protecting the seeds, often for years. When seared by fire or dried by the death of the tree the cones pop open, scattering several years' supply of seeds over the ground. These quickly germinate in the fire-cleared mineral soil and a stand of young trees results. Although Kirtland's warbler nests on the ground, it requires the protection of living pine boughs in thickets near the ground, which allow the birds to enter and leave the nest unobserved. This arrangement of branches occurs only when the trees are about six feet tall and disappears when the trees get much over fifteen feet tall. Trees shorter than six feet are too far apart and lack the necessary thick lower branches. In older trees the lower branches are shaded out and die, reducing cover.

With the extensive fires following logging in the 1870's, the number of trees with the proper characteristics increased enormously and the population of Kirtland's warbler was probably at its greatest. When fire was eliminated or restricted in this part of Michigan after the turn of the century, and large areas of jack pine began to grow taller than the warbler required, the warbler population started to fall. In 1975 it was estimated that fewer than 400 birds remained. A program of rotational controlled burning of patches of jack pine forest at least forty acres in extent (the minimum breeding territory for a pair of Kirtland's warblers) has recently begun. Conservationists hope this will ensure a stable warbler population and reduce the chance of extinction.

Before settlement, the Kenai Peninsula in Alaska was primarily a forest of spruce with lichen-covered open patches of ground. Large herds of caribou depended on lichens for their winter food supply. When we appeared in the late nineteenth century much of the forested area was burned and the lichens destroyed. In a few years, deprived of their winter food, the caribou were gone.

The spruce killed by fire was succeeded by willow, alder, and aspen. Since moose require the buds and bark of these successional species as thir winter browse, just as the caribou need lichens, the large fire-generated stands of these hardwoods allowed a significant increase in moose survival. In fact, so spectacular was the increase in the moose population that the government reserved a very large portion of the Kenai Peninsula as a National Moose Range. Then as the short-lived alder, willow, and aspen were replaced by spruce in the natural sequence of events, the moose population declined again, raising the prospect of a mooseless Moose Range.

But when unauthorized fires swept through the Moose Range, restoring successional browse, the moose population quickly recovered. Now that the lesson has been demonstrated, the size of the moose population in the Kenai is being controlled by planned fires to maintain a certain proportion of the forest in a fire recovery stage, thereby providing moose with the winter food supply they need.

SUSCEPTIBILITY TO EXTINCTION

Although no species is immune to extinction, some are extinction-prone. Any species that has a naturally low population level or is subject to violent fluctuations in its numbers is in danger. The population of the California condor, like that of the whooping crane, hovers between forty and sixty, for as we have seen a condor pair produces only one egg every two years. With such a low reproduction rate, population growth is unlikely and susceptibility to catastrophe is greatly enhanced. Inbreeding has sharply limited the gene pool. This reduces the genetic variability, which in turn reduces the species' flexibility in the face of environ-

205

mental change. But reduction to low numbers need not in itself doom a species to extinction. A species with a high rate of reproduction, when there are no pressures against it, may be able to bounce back from the edge of extinction. For example, the great white heron suffered a 40 percent reduction in the Florida Everglades as a result of Hurricane Donna in 1960, but by 1963 the population had returned to its former level of about 1500 individuals. Similarly, the northern elephant seal was reduced to twenty individuals in 1884. Under protection it has increased to 30,000 and has begun reoccupying its former range. However, the genetic variability of the population is severely limited, making the seal especially vulnerable to future environmental modifications.

Some species feed on only one or a few other species, which automatically limits their distribution and makes them prone to extinction. The Everglades kite, for example, feeds on one species of snail. As land is drained for cultivation or development, the snail is being exterminated and its overspecialized predator with it.

The Australian koala feeds mostly on eucalyptus leaves. If the eucalyptus forests disappear, the koala will too. The ivory-billed woodpecker (Figure 9.13) is another species with a limited food source—beetle larvae in *recently* dead trees. Most other woodpeckers, including the closely re-

Fig. 9.13 *There is a very slim chance that a few ivory-billed woodpeckers may hang on in South Carolina, Louisiana, or East Texas. But unless large tracts of old-growth bottomland forest are preserved in these areas, their extinction is assured.* (Courtesy of the American Museum of Natural History)

lated pileated woodpecker, accept a broad variety of larvae that successively inhabit dead trees for years after the death of the tree. This need of the ivory-billed woodpecker for recently dead trees requires large tracts of mature timber, which have become rare in the South. This need may doom the ivory-billed woodpecker to extinction.

SPECIALIZED BREEDING SITES

The wood duck at one time became quite rare. Unlike most ducks, it requires a nesting cavity, and as old hollow trees disappeared, so did the duck. When this need was recognized and suitable nesting boxes were erected in marshes, the wood duck population sprang back.

Kirtland's warbler, as we have just seen, is even more specialized in its nesting requirements, which limit it to a small area in Michigan's pine barrens. Some fish have equally specialized nesting sites. Salmon must have streams with gravel bottoms to receive their eggs. Silted streams are unsuitable because the eggs become buried in the silt and suffocate.

ISLAND DISTRIBUTION

Many of the world's birds and mammals, now extinct, were restricted to islands. This limited both their numbers and their ability to survive the introduction of predators. Because many small islands originally had few predators, birds sometimes lost their ability to fly. When we introduced predators they eliminated these flightless birds.

Both lakes and isolated mountain ranges form ecological analogs of islands, limiting the range of a species and often imposing special environmental conditions which lead to the evolution of unique forms distinct from related populations. A subspecies of bighorn sheep became extinct because its limited range in the Black Hills allowed it to be hunted without respite. The freshwater shark and porpoise of Lake Nicaragua, and the seal of Lake Ladoga in the U.S.S.R., are all species that, although still extant, may in the future become extinct for the same reason.

THE COST OF EXTINCTION

During human history, more than 150 birds and mammals have become extinct. At least half of these have been full-fledged species; the rest have been subspecies, races, or geographical variants of still existing forms. The question we must ask is: what are the implications of this loss? With millions of species of animals and plants still remaining, some as yet undescribed, why should 150 animals be missed?

We, of all these hosts of organisms, are the only animal species capable of completely exterminating any other form of life. All other species are bound in predator-prey relationships that exercise checks and balances upon excessive increase or decrease in population levels. Although these levels may cycle with time, they do so within certain limits.

Sometime in the last few million years, we became dissociated from these checks and balances and became a superpredator. But with this ability to drive any species into extinction at will comes first a need, then a responsibility for restraint. The need develops from the growing awareness that no species exists in an environmental vacuum. Organisms and their environments are inextricably interrelated. Scores, perhaps hundreds, of species may depend upon a key plant or animal such as a redwood, buffalo, or sand dune shrub (see Chapter 8). But why are all these associates so important that we should guard against the loss of any one of them? The answer lies in our relationship to this species diversity.

We have traditionally tried to concentrate the energy from sunlight into a few easily harvested species. While the practice of monoculture accomplishes its aim reasonably well, the price paid in crop protection is high: biocides to control weeds, insects, fungi; hormones to control fruit set, preharvest drop and so on. Despite this tremendous input of energy, things still go wrong. Insects and fungi develop resistance and new pests are encouraged by the destruction of their predators. At times, as we saw in the spray schedule for an apple orchard (see Chapter 5), we seem to have a tiger by the tail in our attempt to maintain simplified ecosystems.

When species diversity in natural ecosystems is reduced, either willfully or inadvertently, the same kinds of problems seen in monoculture begin to arise. But a natural ecosystem cannot be treated like a cornfield and routinely sprayed to control some beetle or caterpillar. A biocide that might be tolerated in a cornfield could so scramble the food web in a woodlot that the original problem would be lost in the ensuing chaos. Moreover, while we can afford the energy input to maintain a field of corn because of the value of its yield, we cannot possibly afford the economic burden of maintaining natural ecosystems that maintained themselves until disturbed by our activities.

The trout lily (*Erythronium americanum*) (Figure 9.14), widely distributed in the eastern deciduous forest, is a rather small perennial plant that blooms in early spring before the overstory trees leaf out, quickly ripens its seed, then disappears. Most of the year there is little evidence of its existence. But recent work at the Hubbard Brook Experimental Forest in New Hampshire suggests that the ephemeral trout lily conserves potassium and nitrogen by incorporating them into its leaves at a time when leaching of nutrients from the soil is at its annual maximum. In early summer, when the above-ground parts of the trout lily decay, the nutrients are returned to the soil just when other species are

Fig. 9.14. *Although the trout lily is visible for only a brief time in the spring, its role in the cycling of potassium and nitrogen in the forest ecosystem is important.* (Charles C. Johnson)

at the height of their annual growth cycle. As this example suggests, until we know exactly the role of every organism in an ecosystem, we cannot abandon any species as superfluous, not even that pitiful flock of sixty whooping cranes. If we do, we run the risk of future population explosions of fungi, insects, rodents, or the breaking of nutrient cycles that might well dwarf any of our problems to date.

However logical our need for all extant species may be, to place the case for continued survival of endangered species solely upon our present or future need begs the issue of responsibility. If we were passive bystanders we could rationalize extinction as a purely natural phenomenon. But it is certainly fair to say that since our emergence *no* extinction has been a purely natural one. Just as we bear a certain responsibility toward domesticated species which have become dependent upon us, we have an obligation toward wild species which through no fault of their own have become dependent upon human activity for their continued existence. Each of these species, gnat or gnu, represents a pool of genetic information that uniquely adapts it to its environment. When this information is lost through extinction, a valuable key to survival with all of its potential economic, scientific, and aesthetic worth is irretrievably lost as well. It is time for us, as self-aware members of most of the earth's ecosystems, to develop the ecological sensitivity to refrain from invoking the enormous power of extinction we have inherited from our ancestors. We must do this in enlightened self-interest, to be sure, but also because we have come to feel that all other organisms on earth have a right to exist equal to our own and that our traditional dominion over beast and fowl is not a mandate for mindless exploitation but a charge of responsibility.

THE ROAD BACK

Most extinctions need not have happened. With the exception of a very few species like the passenger pigeon, which seemed unable to adjust its life style to accommodate our pattern of land use, most species presently extinct might be living now had there been a little care and foresight at the right time. Controlled harvesting, for example, might have saved the great auk, the dodo, Steller's sea cow, and the Black Hills bighorn sheep. Thus it is imperative that we profit from the mistakes of the past and accept the fact that there is no inherent reason why man should hurry any organism into extinction. Large-scale efforts have already saved some organisms from imminent extinction, and for a few others the future seems hopeful. Techniques of wildlife management, breeding, reintroduction, and even resynthesis are being more widley used and offer hope for saving threatened species.

MANAGEMENT

Perhaps the greatest challenge is to institute proper management of a wildlife resource before its numbers become so low that emergency measures are necessary. The concept of management is not new, but many mistakes were made before it came to be properly applied. In the early 1900s the mule deer herd on the Kaibab Plateau of Arizona was reduced in numbers; sportsmen blamed the traditional enemy, the predator. The government responded with a predator control campaign, which practically exterminated mountain lions from the plateau. The deer quickly responded, but without natural control they increased so greatly that their browse could no longer support them, and thousands starved to death. The survivors so severely overgrazed what remained of the vegetation that the effects were noticeable for decades afterward. Although the mountain lion population was allowed to recover somewhat after this fiasco, the damage had been done.

Management is now viewed as going beyond mere protection of the "good guys" from the "bad guys." Important management tools are removal of surplus stock by controlled shooting, manipulation of vegetation, and control over multiple use of summer *and* winter range of wildlife. Habitat management using controlled burning is employed to create nesting sites for Kirtland's warbler in Michigan, and to retain a mosaic of open spaces for the use of the California condor in Los Padres National Forest in California.

However, efforts to increase the population of bighorn sheep in the Sierra Nevada between California and Nevada have foundered because of inadequate control of the winter range. The sheep have adequate summer grazing in the meadows of Sequoia and King's Canyon National Parks, but when they move down into the national forests below to graze during the winter much of the range is already occupied by domestic sheep or mule deer. Few national parks or game refuges are large enough to be self-regulating. The same problem has occurred in the Serengeti Game Reserve in Tanzania: animals migrate out of the protected area during part of the year for some favored graze that is not included in the reserve. In such situations arrangements must be made to accommodate the year-round needs and activities of the animals, if they are to be maintained in a truly wild state.

NATURAL BREEDING

A few species have survived only in captivity. Both the gingko and dawn redwood (*Metasequoia*) trees (Figure 9.15) were rediscovered growing in temple gardens in China. Both had been thought extinct, but

Fig. 9.15   This metasequoia in Golden Gate Park grew from seed brought back from China in 1948.

today they are planted throughout the world. Another Chinese species, Père David's deer, was discovered in Peking's Imperial Garden in 1861, long after all wild individuals had become extinct. Today there are several hundred in zoos and private collections in Europe.

The peregrine falcon, which was especially sensitive to DDT, has disappeared from much of its former range in North America. Fortunately two subspecies are still fairly common in their range: Peale's falcon in the Queen Charlotte Islands and eastern Aleutians, and the tundra falcon in the Arctic from Alaska to Greenland. Professor Thomas Cade at Cornell has been working for several years on a breeding project aimed at recreating a peregrine population in the eastern United States from captive stock. Initially tundra falcons are being used but since they migrate every winter to South America, where they pick up DDT, other possibilities are being examined. These include Peale's falcon and the Spanish falcon, which has adapted to life close to inhabited areas and feeds mostly on pigeons. The goal is to produce and release 250 peregrines a year from 1980 to 1995 with the hope that these 4000 individuals will form a wild population of at least 150 actively breeding pairs, about the number that once nested in the eastern United States.

A successful breeding program has been carried out with the Hawaiian goose or nene, which had been reduced to less than fifty birds when a few pairs were bred in captivity in England. In a few years there were enough nene to restock their original habitat in Hawaii. Today there are over 1000 nene, captive and wild.

STACKING THE DECK

Often there isn't time to breed stock, patiently accumulating a population surplus that can be used for reintroduction. Developments in experimental embryology over the past several years have suggested improving on nature by utilizing the techniques of superovulation and artificial insemination. Certain drugs can induce superovulation—release of many eggs at once instead of the sequence characteristic of the species. Artificial insemination techniques involve sperm that can be frozen for several years and used to fertilize the eggs in the womb of the female. Since all the fertilized eggs cannot be carried to term by the original female, the fertilized eggs can be flushed out and implanted in the womb of closely related, less endangered species, which ultimately give birth to the young of the desired species. Suppose as an example that a female European bison (an endangered species) were superovulated and artificially inseminated with European bison sperm. Suppose 25 fertilized eggs resulted; these could be flushed out and implanted in 25 American bison cows, a closely related but more abundant species. In a few months the world would possess 25 more European bison. Although this process has not yet been performed on an endangered species, there is every reason to expect it to be a valuable, if last-ditch, tool for saving species close to extinction.

REINTRODUCTION

By 1900 the Russian antelope or saiga was almost exterminated. A careful research program by Soviet scientists managed to increase the breeding stock to about 1000 individuals. When more information about its habits, food, and nutrition had been gathered, the saiga was reintroduced to its former range. With over 2.5 million saiga in 1960, a controlled harvest was allowed for the first time. Each year since, over a quarter of a million saiga have been harvested, producing 6600 tons of meat, 240,000 square yards of hides, and large amounts of industrial fat. Thus a species in danger of extinction was restored as a resource and sustained productivity was achieved on land unsuitable for cattle grazing.

Similarly, the trumpeter swan of North America was reduced to a few dozen birds in Yellowstone National Park and an adjacent hot spring area at Red Rock Lakes, Montana. This latter area was designated as a wildlife refuge in 1935, and by 1958 enough swans had bred to allow introduction of breeding pairs into refuges in Oregon, Washington, Nevada, Wyoming, and South Dakota, where they nested successfully. In 1968 the total population of trumpeter swans was around 5000, with over 800 in the United States.

Perhaps of greater interest to hunters was the revival of the wild turkey. This large game animal, which Benjamin Franklin preferred to the bald eagle as the national bird to be represented on the Great Seal, was so abundant in colonial days that it was sold for a penny a pound. But by 1920 overhunting, deforestation, and loss of the chestnut, its prime food source, had eliminated the turkey from three fourths of its natural range. A program initiated by the state game department of Pennsylvania reintroduced wild turkey stock in appropriate gamelands in the state, thereby increasing the number of turkeys in Pennsylvania to nearly 50,000. From this stock, turkeys have been reintroduced to New York, Connecticut, and Massachusetts. As the number of wild turkeys increases, these states may offer hunters an open season, as has become possible in Pennsylvania.

Fortunately there seems to be enough public concern to continue federal support for programs of the Department of the Interior that are making strenuous efforts to prevent further extinctions of native American species. Though welcome, this support comes somewhat belatedly, considering that the National Audubon Society has been protecting populations of rare birds since the early 1900s. The Boone and Crockett Club and the Izaak Walton League have also been concerned with wildlife values for many years. Internationally the World Wildlife Fund has supplied money for protection of endangered species all over the world (see Appendix 2 for a more complete list of organizations concerned with the preservation of wildlife and its environment). With the concerted efforts of all interested parties there is no reason for further unnatural extinctions to occur.

FURTHER READING

Bonnell, M. L., and R. K. Selander, 1974. "Elephant seals: genetic variation and near extinction." *Science* **184**, pp. 908–909. Explores the impact of near extinction on the genetic pool.

Branch, E. D., 1962. *The hunting of the buffalo.* University of Nebraska Press, Lincoln. Fascinating retelling of a tragic saga.

Caras, R., 1970. *Source of the thunder, the biography of a California condor.* Little, Brown, Boston. Fictionalized but intriguing account of the life of a California condor.

Kroeber, T., 1962. *Ishi in two worlds.* University of California Press, Berkeley. A poignant example of our treatment of the native Americans.

**BUNGLING
THE BIOTA**

Mayfield, H., 1960. "The Kirtland's warbler." *Cranbrook Institute Sci. Bull.* **40,** Bloomfield Hills, Michigan. The relationship between this rare warbler and fire is carefully discussed.

Myers, N., 1975. "The whaling controversy." *American Scientist* **63,** pp. 448–455. Well-balanced discussion of the whole whaling problem.

Schorger, A. W., 1955. *The passenger pigeon, its natural history and extinction.* University of Wisconsin Press, Madison. A fine account of the extinction of the passenger pigeon.

Trefethen, J. B., 1970. "The return of the white-tailed deer." *American Heritage*, February, pp. 97–103. Interesting history of the white-tailed deer since white settlement.

Zimmerman, D. R., 1976. "Endangered bird species: habitat manipulation methods." *Science* **192,** pp. 876–878. The latest techniques being used to build up populations of endangered birds.

NATURE
IN CAPTIVITY

ALTHOUGH FOR THOUSANDS of years we have struggled against what we considered a hostile environment, the environment also has to struggle to defend itself not only against those who would overmanipulate or destroy it, but against those who would literally love it to death. Population growth and renewed interest in outdoor activities are beginning to have a devastating impact on nature, from traditionally battered urban parks to formerly pristine wilderness areas. With this pressure likely to increase in the future, it becomes all the more important to preserve and restore present natural and recreational areas; and to acquire, soon, a broad spectrum of new ones.

PARKS

While much wilderness has been destroyed, some has been transformed into parks. This transformation is most clearly seen in densely populated England. The thick oak forest that once covered England was methodically cut for ship timbers and lumber and replaced by cultivated land. By the seventeenth century, forests were limited to those selected as crown lands to be reserved for royal hunting parties and the forests that frequently surrounded the country manor houses of the aristocracy. By the eighteenth century, these woodlands, managed for both timber and game, had lost much of their wildness. Often too, they were grazed, which tended to open the forest by curbing tree reproduction. Over the years these hunting parks became fixed in the public mind as representing natural vegetation (see Chapter 21). When the wealthy members of

215

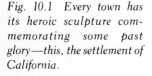

BUNGLING
THE BIOTA

Fig. 10.1 Every town has its heroic sculpture commemorating some past glory—this, the settlement of California.

the rising middle class began to construct country estates, landscaping often reflected the influence of the hunting parks of the older estates.

In *Pride and Prejudice,* Jane Austen describes a walk in such a park:

> They entered the woods, and bidding adieu to the river for a while, ascended some of the higher grounds; whence, in spots where the opening of the trees gave the eye power to wander, were many charming views of the valley, the opposite hills, with the long range of woods overspreading many, and occasionally part of the stream. Mr. Gardiner expressed a wish of going round the whole Park, but feared it might be beyond a walk. With a triumphant smile, they were told, that it was ten miles round.

In the American colonies, New England towns and villages had their green or common, but these were obviously intended as places of public ownership where sheep and cattle could be conveniently pastured. The idea that parks were for public pleasure grew slowly. And no wonder, for pleasure in an outdoor setting, or in any setting for that matter, was anathema to the established church of the late eighteenth and early nineteenth century in New England. This attitude began to change when orthodoxy gave way to the more liberal Congregational and Unitarian Churches in the nineteenth century. Indeed, moral fiber became so relaxed that one liberal man of some wealth donated a large tract of land to the city of Worcester, Massachusetts, as a public park for the *enjoyment* of the people of that city. Shortly thereafter, New York City became the second American city to establish a public park. Elaborately landscaped by Frederick Law Olmsted, Central Park set the tone for the creation of public parks from coast to coast, until few towns were without some patch of green with statue, fountain, or flagpole (Figure 10.1).

216

The first explorers of the West, hardy trappers and Indian traders, brought back tales of fantastic mountains and valleys, geysers of steam, gleaming caves, and huge trees. Subsequent expeditions corroborated even the wildest of these tales. Because of the Victorian glorification of the romantic, there developed a demand that some of these natural marvels be preserved for the wonderment and enjoyment of future generations (Figure 10.2). Surprisingly, many such monuments of nature *were* preserved; and this at the height of an era of westward expansion when nature was

Fig. 10.2 Thomas Cole and William Cullen Bryant view the sublimities of nature in a painting by Asher B. Durand. (Collection of the New York Public Library, Astor, Lenox, and Tilden Foundations)

217

considered by railroad, mining, lumbering, and cattle interests to have been created for our exploitation. Between 1870 and 1900, four of the nation's best-known national parks were established: Yellowstone (1872), Yosemite (1890), Sequoia (1890), and Mount Rainier (1899). The National Park Service, which inherited these natural wonders when it was founded in 1916, had as its prime duty their protection and preservation. Similarly, the Forest Service inherited huge tracts of land formerly in the public domain to protect and manage for a sustained yield of forest products.

FORESTRY AND FIRE

Attempts have been made many times and in many cultures to manage and regulate forests for water supply, grazing, and the cutting of timber. However, formal education in forestry did not develop until 1825, when schools were established in Germany and France. The concept of forest management came late to North America's seemingly inexhaustible forests. Not until the superb white pine forests of New England and then the Great Lakes area were gone did people begin to consider the possibility of managing the remnants and second growth for sustained yield. Since there were no schools in the United States, professional training had to be obtained abroad in the highly respected schools of Europe, particularly in Germany.

The major emphasis of European forestry in the nineteenth century was protection of the forest. Considering the population density of Europe even then, the demands made on forests for kindling were great, and although gleaning rights to this forest by-product were often passed from father to son for generations, forests had to be protected from poaching. But European forests also had to be protected from fire. Fire was considered an enemy in the carefully tended conifer forest plantations, and any role that it might have played in the ecology of natural vegetation was thereby blurred.

However, what was useful in the forest plantations of Europe was not necessarily useful in the incredibly large and ecologically diversified forests of North America. Because fire was considered intolerable in European forests, it was not surprising that this view was extended by European-trained foresters to *all* forest types in North America. Fire exclusion came to be regarded as a basic article of forest management, first by private foresters, and later by the government's Forest Service.

LONGLEAF PINE AND FIRE

After much of the best white pine had been cut in the Northeast and the Great Lakes area, attention passed to the hitherto neglected longleaf pine forests distributed in a band along the coastal plain from Virginia to Texas. The trees were well spaced, with a light cover of grasses on the forest floor. After the initial logging of longleaf stands, it was noticed that reproduction was poor, leading to replacement by much less valuable hardwoods or other species of pines. It was supposed that ground fires, quite prevalent in the region, and the foraging of hogs destroyed the seedlings, and that if both of these factors were controlled and enough seed trees were left to provide a seed source, the forest would soon regenerate itself.

A young forester by the name of Chapman took a close look at the ecology of longleaf pine and realized that the species, far from being eliminated by ground fires, actually seemed to have many features suggesting long association with fire as a part of its environment. He noticed that the young seedling at the ground surface develops a fat bud, surrounded by a tuft of needles. Then, for the next three to seven years, the seedling puts most of its energy into developing a deep taproot. Because of its close resemblance to a clump of grass, this phase of longleaf pine development is called the grass stage. After seven years the seedling suddenly begins active vertical growth, and in a few years' time grows ten to fifteen feet. Thereafter the sapling grows at a more conventional rate but develops thick fire-resistant bark. Chapman concluded that periodic ground fires may singe the tuft of needles but leave the terminal bud and taproot intact. By using energy stored in the taproot over the three to seven years spent in the grass stage, the seedling is able to make exceptional growth in height over a period of two or three years, time enough to get the more sensitive new branches up and away from the danger of fire. Then development of thick fire-resistant bark protects the young tree from further ground fires.

Drawing on his observations as early as 1909, Chapman noted that "fire always has and always will be an element in longleaf forests, and the problem is not how fire can be eliminated, but how it can be controlled so as, first, to secure reproduction; second, to prevent the accumulation of litter and reduce the danger of a really disastrous blaze." [1] This sound appraisal of the situation was not taken seriously at first.

DATA VERSUS DOGMA

Because he was not affiliated with the Forest Service, Chapman was free to speak out. The Forest Service seemed already to have made up its mind about the role of fire in all forests, contending that southern forests were no different than any other in their need to be completely protected from fire. An experiment was set up in Louisiana in 1915 to

[1] Schiff, A. L., 1962. *Fire and water: scientific heresy in the Forest Service.* Harvard University Press, Cambridge.

demonstrate the effect, both combined and singly, of foraging pigs and ground fires in eliminating longleaf reproduction.

An acre of young seedlings was divided into quarter-acre plots and treated as follows: one plot was burned and grazed, a second was unburned and grazed, a third was burned and not grazed, and a fourth was neither burned nor grazed. By 1918 the two grazed plots were completely cleared of longleaf pine seedlings. By 1924 the Forest Service reported that in the third plot some seedlings were killed and others were not growing as well as the larger number of seedlings in the fourth plot. So fire was condemned for damaging longleaf reproduction and growth. Its fire policy thus affirmed experimentally, the Forest Service terminated the experiment and landowners were strongly urged to eliminate fire from their pine stands.

Chapman, however, continued to follow the now officially abandoned experiment and found that by the late 1920s the trees in the third or fire-thinned plot began making much faster growth than the unthinned trees in the fourth plot, where the crowded trees began to stunt each other's growth. The Forest Service, however, though informed of these results, never got around to publishing them and continued in its well-established dogma that fire must be eliminated from longleaf stands.

Too frequent burning in the Southeast reinforced the now rigid attitude of the Forest Service toward fire. Seeing no possible value in woods burning, the Forest Service in the late 1930s hired a young psychologist named Shea to explore the psychological reasons behind the stubborn tendency of the local people to burn the woods. As Shea put it, "it was hoped that here might be found a point of vaccination that with an improved educational serum would reach the germs of the woods-burning desires." [2] Reinforcing the dogma that no good could be found in a destructive practice, Shea concluded that:

> the sight and sound and odor of burning woods provide excitement for a people who dwell in an environment of low stimulation and who quite naturally crave excitement. Fire gives them distinct emotional satisfactions which they strive to explain away by pseudo-economic reasons that spring from defensive beliefs. Their explanations that woods fires kill off snakes, boll weevil and serve other economic ends are something more than ignorance. They are the defensive beliefs of a disadvantaged culture group.[3]

In a final effort to modify these inherited beliefs, the Forest Service invented a talking bear to symbolize the grave danger that fire held for all forests and their inhabitants. To this day a solemn, reproving, or im-

[2] Shea, J. P., 1940. "Our pappies burned the woods." *Amer. For.* **46**, p. 159.
[3] Ibid.

ploring Smokey the Bear asks the visitors to "please help prevent forest fires" in national parks and forests from coast to coast.

Then in the late 1930s a children's novel, *Bambi*, was made into a feature-length cartoon by Walt Disney. Who can forget the climactic scene where Bambi, Thumper, and all their friends flee from that worst of all evils, the forest fire. By now the man in the street was firmly convinced that there was no place for fire in the forest.

But by the early 1940s, clearly something was wrong in the great longleaf pine forests of the Southeast. Both private and public forests, which had been laboriously protected from fire, were afflicted. There was no reproduction. There was a very damaging brown spot fungus on the needles of the grass stage seedling. There was massive invasion of worthless hardwoods, which shaded out the longleaf seedlings. And worst of all, there were catastrophic fires fueled by twenty- to forty-year accumulations of combustible trash. In some forests more wood was lost from a single fire than was supposed to have accrued from all those years of fire protection. Beginning to doubt the advice of the Forest Service, private owners set up controlled burning to reduce the danger of wholesale conflagration in their forests. By the late 1940s the Forest Service was finally forced to admit that controlled burning, at the right time and under the right conditions, was not only effective in reducing dangerous litter accumulation, but was absolutely necessary to the survival of longleaf pine stands. Controlled burning would assure that the longleaf pine seeds had a mineral soil seedbed free of litter, that the brown spot disease would be reduced by occasional singeing of the grass stage leaves, and that hardwood invasion would be reduced (Figure 10.3).

Today the Forest Service and most foresters realize that fire in the forest environment is by no means *always* bad. No one suggests indiscriminate use of fire by anyone, anytime; but in the right time and place, with the proper conditions, for certain species, fire can be an essential management tool. Where evidence exists that fire has always been a regular part of the environment, as in the ponderosa pine forests of the Southwest, the longleaf pine forests of the Southeast, or the Douglas fir forests in the Northwest, it makes little sense to exclude fire because it is damaging to spruce forests in Bavaria or white pine forests in Wisconsin. But the Forest Service is still left with a dilemma. On the one hand it must ask people to follow the admonition of Smokey the Bear not to set forest fires; on the other hand, it must deliberately burn many of those same forests as a necessary management practice upon which the very existence of many western forests and national parks depends.

PROBLEMS IN THE PARKS

Preservation of major geologic features like Zion, Bryce, or Grand Canyon is relatively easy. They change so slowly that we have the illusion in

Fig. 10.3 (a) This Texas pine stand is crowded with hardwood invaders that shade out pine seedlings. (b) Periodic controlled burning removes the fire-sensitive hardwoods. (c) This pine forest in Mississippi is kept "clean" by periodic prescribed burning. (Photographs from U.S. Forest Service)

222

Fig. 10.4 This grove of pines was reopened by controlled burning after years of fire control had allowed weed trees to form a dense understory.

our short lifespans of no change at all. But lesser environmental features such as plants and animals are constantly and rapidly changing. One such feature common to our national parks was the stately groves of trees—Douglas fir, ponderosa pine, redwood—their massive trunks suggesting the columns of great cathedrals (Figure 10.4). Beneath, like a primordial garden, the ground was carpeted with grasses and flowers. The coincidental resemblance of these forests to the European concept of a well-tended park surely gave early impetus to their preservation as parks, but ironically, it very nearly brought about their ultimate destruction.

Park officials seemed to ignore the fact that trees grow old, die, and are replaced by other trees, all in dynamic balance with various environmental factors. Instead they excluded fire, removed diseased trees, and even tried to control natural predation to protect the "good" animals from the "bad." All efforts were made to stop time—to preserve the scene just as the early settlers saw it.

But in a few years things began to go awry. With the elimination of fire, twigs, needles, branches, and fallen trees began to pile up (Figure 10.5). Decomposition of these fallen materials proceeded slowly in the hot, dry western forests. Without fire to remove litter, seedlings of the desirable species were often unable either to germinate or, if they did, to survive the shade.

Under the regime of fire elimination, the desirable trees were unable to reproduce in national parks, and seedlings of shade-tolerant species, such as conifers, began to invade, forming a dense undergrowth that obscured the beautifully spaced trees the parks were set up to preserve (Figure 10.6). This not only impaired the view, but because of the deep layer of highly combustible litter and the equally combustible understory of conifers, parts of some national parks became veritable tinderboxes. No longer could a fire be localized near the ground in needles and dry grass. Once the litter was ignited the fire would quickly jump into

223

Fig. 10.5 The tinder-dry manzanita and pine branches will be ignited sooner or later and the resulting fire may possibly eliminate the canopy trees as well.

the understory and then into the crowns of the giant ponderosas, redwoods, or Douglas firs. A crown fire is the end of any forest, and if many of them occurred, the recreational, aesthetic, and scientific qualities of parks would disappear for many years.

That this is not altogether a recent problem can be seen in an 1887–88 report of the commission charged with the responsibility of maintaining Yosemite Valley. In part the report stated:

> Several times during the period of my labors on your behalf, it required suddenly almost the entire force of twenty or thirty men to divert the all consuming course of forest fires on the floor of the valley. Since the annual practice of the Indians in burning off the dried grasses and leaves has been discontinued, and even forbidden by law, the accumulation of vegetable matter beneath the trees has been practically undisturbed, until a growth of young pines has sprung up all over the valley, and destroyed much fine meadow land. A campfire carelessly left, or a match thrown among the leaves, has caused several fires within the past two or three years that could not be extinguished. They burned until the walls, the roadway, and streams defined and determined their course.[4]

[4] Gibbens, R. P. and H. F. Heady, 1964. "The influences of modern man on the vegetation of Yosemite Valley." *Calif. Agric. Exp. Sta. Manual* **36.**

This was true of Yosemite in the 1880s and it is now true of Lassen, Sequoia, and King's Canyon. The expense of hand-clearing trash species and removing forest floor litter from huge areas of rough country is enormous. To attempt this with bulldozers would severely injure tree roots, expose the forest floor to erosion, and be completely impossible in inaccessible areas. Fire is too long overdue to be used now without grave danger. What can the Park Service do? The only practical solution, regardless of expense, seems to be hand-clearing, acre by acre, and removal of combustibles, followed by controlled burning every few years to keep litter to a minimum and to eliminate trash trees when they are still small seedlings. But because this hand labor is so terribly expensive, the task will take many years—years filled with the risk that large tracts of forests will suddenly explode in a grand conflagration, should a fire ever get out of control some hot, windy day in late summer.

The preservation of forests that began ten, fifty, or one hundred years ago is clearly impossible if we try to extend their existence by merely erecting a protective "fence." A forest *can* be maintained just as a hedge can be kept at a desired height—with active management requiring constant care. If we are to manage effectively, we must use ecological research to devise management techniques and then apply them unrelentingly.

Fig. 10.6 Incense cedar often invades pine forests where fire control has been practiced for many years.

225

THE DISAPPEARING COASTLINE

Problems of a rather different sort have arisen in the National Seashore Areas which have been established in the last few decades along the Atlantic coast. The east cost of North America from Long Island south to Yucatán, Mexico is characterized by a chain of barrier islands (Figure 10.7) isolated from each other by inlets and from the mainland by lagoons or bays. Until recently these barrier islands retained a wild beauty characteristic of the interface between land and sea, just as the Great Plains embody the beauty of the land-sky interface. Because of this charm, these island beaches have been popular recreation areas for many years. Visitors first made day trips by excursion steamers, then built crude summer cottages, and finally plush, year-round homes.

Barrier islands and their beaches, formed largely of sand, are quite unstable, despite their characteristically heavy cover of grasses, shrubs, or even low trees. Both the barrier island and its beaches have an erosion cycle: that of the island is hundreds or perhaps thousands of years long, while that of the beach is annual. These cycles cause barrier islands to grow or shrink, unlike rocky islands, which usually just get smaller as they are eroded away.

The movement of longshore currents parallel to the mainland and the force of storm waves coming in at various angles to the beach line keep island barriers moving in two directions—along the coast and toward the land. Longshore currents move in a fairly constant direction and tend to remove sand from the up-current end of the islands and to deposit it

Fig. 10.7 Much of the East Coast of the United States is lined with barrier islands. Although many have become National Seashore Areas, more are open to development, "stabilization," and subsequent erosion.

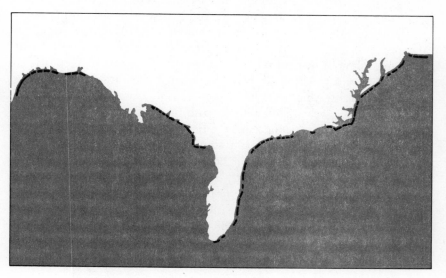

on the down-current end. Structures built on the eroding end eventually topple into the water; those on the growing end will soon be hundreds of yards from the water's edge.

In the winter, large storm waves stir up the sand on the beach face and pull it offshore, eroding the beach by as much as two or three yards. Anyone visiting the beach at this season might well wonder what has become of last summer's broad expanse of sand. During the succeeding spring and summer, gentle wave action pushes the sand back onto the beach from the offshore bars where it was deposited during the winter storms. By Memorial Day or the Fourth of July weekend, the beaches on the eastern coast of the United States are restored. This annual cycle is even more obvious along the California beaches. Although these beaches are not usually associated with barrier islands but are found at the foot of cliffs, they have the same rhythm of winter removal and summer replacement of sand. This is strikingly shown in the educational film, *Beach, A River of Sand*.

Barrier island beaches, then, are constantly on the move, and part of their charm as natural phenomena lies in this movement. But with discouraging frequency an eager summer resident has built a house in the dunes or on the beach only to find to his dismay that his house and property are moving into the sea.

The fact is that beaches, barrier islands, and sandbars are ephemeral features of the environment. They will persist if sea level, climate, sand supply, and offshore currents remain constant, but not in exactly the same position from year to year. Problems arise when we want to stabilize the unstable.

Cape Hatteras National Seashore Area in North Carolina provides a classical statement of some of these problems. The trouble began with the establishment of a permanent road in the 1930s. To protect the road from the sea it was decided to stabilize the low dunes running along the upper beach. Snow fencing was set up, grasses planted, and the dunes began to grow to impressive height, effectively shielding the road from storm waves. But as the dunes grew in height the width of the beach narrowed from 450 feet to less than 90 feet. In addition, the foreslope of the high dunes was attacked by every storm, which severely eroded and occasionally breached the dunes. The reason for this is straightforward: the profile of an unaltered natural barrier island is low, with few dunes of any size (Figure 10.8). The barrier island accommodates the energy of storm waves by presenting no serious obstacle to their attack. The sea simply washes over the barrier island, leaving a delta of sediments (Figure 10.9) in the lagoon. The delta is soon colonized by marsh plants and the inlet or channel silts up. When the dunes have been stabilized, preventing easy overwash, the wave energy is concentrated on the beach and foreslope of

Fig. 10.8 *Core Banks, part of Cape Lookout National Seashore in North Carolina, has been little influenced by man. Storms are free to wash over the barrier island, leaving deltas on the lagoon side that are soon vegetated by marsh plants. The dunes are low, so the wave energy is expended in overwash rather than beach erosion; thus the beach is quite wide compared with that in Fig. 10.10.* (Photo by Paul J. Godfrey, National Park Service)

Fig. 10.9 *The Moriches Inlet on Fire Island, New York just after it was opened by a storm. Sand washed into the bay by the storm waves will be vegetated by salt marsh species after the inlet silts up.* (U.S. Air Force)

the high dunes and these features erode (Figure 10.10). When the dunes are breached the road is either washed out or covered with sand. Further problems occur when inlets are kept open with jetties that inhibit the longshore movement of sediment, starving beaches down-current from the inlet.

Fig. 10.10 After the road was constructed, fencing was used to stabilize and increase the height of the dunes which run parallel to the beach. While the road was protected, the beach began to erode away. (Photo by Paul J. Godfrey, National Park Service)

WILDERNESS AREAS

The idea of preservation as stopping time dies hard. Many who have been disillusioned by the changes resulting from increasing use of national parks have pressed for wilderness areas—remote, inviolate, unspoiled. But the idea of a brooding, mysterious, and awesome wilderness is finished. We now view the wilderness in an entirely different light. In an age of crowded, dirty cities, the wilderness has come to symbolize a refuge, the last place where we can breathe clean air, drink freely from streams, and get away from other people. Unfortunately, wilderness has become a symbol viewed in romantic anthropocentric terms, its cycles of destruction and renewal ignored because they extend beyond our lifespan. This attitude will surely lead to the same difficulties encountered in the national parks. A true wilderness should be viewed biocentrically; its forests must be free to burn, free to be attacked by insects, free to be blown down by storms, and free to be carried away by floods, all because these are natural events to which the forest is adapted to respond. When left alone, forests

229

regenerate themselves. The new forests may be different from the old, but things change in a natural ecosystem.

The idealized wilderness is a myth. We must have the wilderness, but not for selfish gratification. At stake is the survival of ecosystems, free to change in accordance with natural variations in the environment, without our interference and notions of good and evil, a last refuge of absolute freedom in a world of increasing technological control.

How big should a wilderness be? It depends on what we are trying to preserve. Let's suppose we want grizzly bears. In Yellowstone, it takes 75 km² of good grizzly habitat to support each bear, or 300 km² for a family of four bears. To prevent serious inbreeding there should be at least two families. This would require 600 km². Similar areas would be needed for minimal populations of wolves and mountain lions. Now eight wolves or grizzly bears is a ridiculously small population to try to maintain. But of eighty-nine wilderness areas presently set up, only ten are larger than 1000 km² and twenty-six larger than 600 km². All of these are concentrated in eleven western states.

If one block of our minimum sized wilderness of 600 km² were set aside for each of the sixty-six major vegetation types in the United States the total area, 40,000 km², would still represent less than 1 percent of the total land area of this country.

How stable would these blocks be? We have to consider that wilderness areas are biological islands at least for some of the animals we try to preserve in them. When Gatun Lake was created as part of the Panama Canal project, a mountain became an island as the waters rose. In 1923, 209 species of birds lived on this island Barro Colorado. Since that time forty-five species have disappeared. Some losses resulted from changes in vegetation, but others can only be explained by the island effect. Other work in the Andes and on small mangrove islands suggests that the number of species present on such a site is directly proportional to its area and inversely proportional to the distance from the nearest source of recruitment. On the basis of these observations, models have been set up to predict how long a given animal population will survive on its "island."

PEOPLE, PARKS, AND WILDERNESSES

If people lived within national parks and wilderness areas by hunting and gathering, their populations limited by the availability of food, these areas, if not their wildlife, could last indefinitely. But they will not last, because people, sustained from outside sources, are pouring into these areas in increasing numbers, destroying by their very presence the natural landscape the parks were set up to preserve. On one holiday weekend in

*Fig. 10.11 Once upon a
time national parks were remote, so comfortable ac-
commodations were pro-
vided. Today many people
view such structures, even
when they are as charming as
this, as resort-type intrusions
better located somewhere
else.*

1970, the Yosemite Valley, seven miles long and two miles wide, contained over 50,000 people, packed bumper to bumper in their cars.

Another aspect of the people problem is found in many older parks,
which have rather extensive development centers. The Old Faithful-Lake-
Fishing Bridge area in Yellowstone, Grand Canyon Village, and the upper
Yosemite Valley each has a resident summer staff of 1000 plus lodging
for 2500 tourists, housed in facilities constructed in some of the most
scenic parts of the parks (Figure 10.11). The reasons are historical. Not
until 1920 was there any reasonable access to most western national parks.
Because the parks, then as now, were poorly funded, visitors were encouraged in an effort to capture some popular support that might counter
hostile political and economic interests. Certainly no one expected the
mass use that has ensued. Early visitors had the time and money to lin-
ger, and so they were catered to by convenient hotels, restaurants, and
other facilities close to the scenic marvels they had come so far to witness.

Another problem has been concessions. Because Congress provided no
funds for visitor facilities, private capital had to be solicited and rewarded
with a fair return on investment. Since 1966 four large corporations have
become park concessionnaires. In their eagerness to get a return on their
investment, some concessionnaires got carried away. For example, MCA
Inc., which holds the Yosemite concession, proposed converting Yosemite into Convention City by constructing a convention center, a new
winter sports complex at Tuolomne Meadows, a new hotel at Glacier
Point, and other accoutrements of a year-round luxury resort.

231

The most obvious way to control such excesses is to eliminate private profitmaking concessions from national parks and to move the development centers to the park gates. Such a move would have both positive and negative effects. Most of the land surrounding most western parks is federally owned, and the less stringent rules and regulations governing these lands would be more attractive to private capital. Some facilities already exist just outside some parks—Yellowstone, Glacier, and Rocky Mountain. Moreover, visitor impact on the park would be much diminished by increasing use of land outside the park. Unfortunately, perimeter facilities would probably not be very popular with many park users; the surrounding federal lands are mostly under the administration of the Forest Service, which traditionally has had less than cordial relations with the Park Service; local interests would probably be involved, complicating matters still further; and many of the existing park gate facilities are even tackier than the ones within the parks. But the greatest obstacle lies in the large capital investment already made in present facilities—$30 million in Grand Canyon City alone. Clearly no solutions are possible until the budget of the chronically starved National Park Service is at least doubled from its present piddling $250 million. Perhaps as much as $1 billion per year may be necessary for a few years to get the national parks back into a condition that will allow them to survive into the next century.

THE HIERARCHY OF NATURAL AREAS

Many types of natural ecosystems—indeed the most scenic ones—are found in national parks and wilderness areas. But various governmental agencies also hold immense portions of the West that are used for timber, watershed protection, grazing, and recreation and offer a fine variety of natural ecosystems. While the scenery is not usually as spectacular as that in the parks, there is far more opportunity to enjoy the outdoors free from crowds of people. In the future, as the population of the United States increases, more and more of this public land will probably have to be managed strictly for recreation. If this can be done, the pressure on existing parks may be reduced. Public lands of all types will also serve in future years as the last source of national parks, for most suitable private land will soon be either developed or priced beyond reach.

State parks fill an important role in making the natural world available to people who cannot travel to the great western national parks. Quite generously scattered across the country, state parks are within an hour's drive for most people. Finally, local parks provide contact with some semblance of nature, if only in the form of grass, trees, and squirrels.

Fig. 10.12 *Every park subjected to heavy pedestrian use has its example of erosion. The thickened bark on this eucalyptus tree in Golden Gate Park suggests that about two feet of soil have moved elsewhere since the tree was planted.*

As one descends the hierarchy of reserved natural environments from national park to city park, size and scenic qualities decrease, but *use* increases dramatically. Central Park, although huge by city park standards, is literally being worn to the bedrock by the enormous pressure exerted upon its facilities by New Yorkers (Figure 10.12). Unless alternate recreational facilities are provided in the form of smaller vest-pocket parks, or far more maintenance is provided for Central Park than is currently available, or both, the park will succumb like an isolated field of wheat to a swarm of locusts.

SCENIC EASEMENTS

We conventionally think of natural reserves as separate, specified areas. There are many other possibilities. One of the most useful of these is the device of scenic easement. Easement allows a property holder to retain ownership of land, yet sell or lease the right of way, air rights, or the right to develop. Thus land of great scenic value could remain in private hands, but the right to change the landscape by development might be sold or leased to a governmental body. The government, of course, would not exercise this right, but would leave the land in its natural state. The property owner would get some financial return for his sacrifice in not developing his land, and the public would gain by not having to buy the land outright to preserve its beauty.

A classic example of the use of scenic easement was the securing of easements on the development of land across the Potomac River from

Mount Vernon, thereby preserving a view that Washington himself must have seen. Without such an arrangement the opposite bank would doubtless have sprouted high-rise apartments, marinas, and shopping centers, destroying the illusion of stepping back into history that is so carefully and beautifully fostered at Mount Vernon. While we have preserved a view, we have also saved a stand of irreplaceable riverbank forest.

PARKWAYS

Easements are especially useful in the construction of parkways and the preservation of riverscapes. Their scenic value is a tremendously important aspect seldom considered in plans to acquire and reserve open space. Driving along the Blue Ridge Parkway in Virginia and North Carolina gives the feeling of intimate contact with nature. Although the Park Service bought most of the land bordering the parkway, much has been leased to local farmers to preserve the interplay of woods and fields. Thus the monotony that might otherwise have resulted from long tunnels through the trees has been relieved.

RIVERS

A combination of federal, state, and local parks together with scenic easements has been proposed to retain the relatively unspoiled beauty of the Connecticut River in New England, the Hudson in New York (Figure 10.13), and the Potomac in the mid-Atlantic states. Ironically, the pollution of these rivers has prevented the commercial development that has already spoiled many cleaner streams. But time is running out: as the pollution in these three rivers is reduced, steps must be taken to forestall the usual haphazard development projects with ecologically sound master plans that will assure the continued beauty of the rivers as well as recreational and economic uses.

TRAILS

In 1937 the Appalachian Trail was opened, running 2000 miles from Mount Katahdin in Maine to Springer Mountain, Georgia. Like the proposed scenic rivers, the trail is a composite of federal, state, local, and private ownership, which has worked well over the years, allowing public access to some superb natural areas. Other shorter foot trails have been established around the United States and many are now being developed. In the planning stage, for example, is a north-south trail through Florida.

But trails are as subject to overuse as parks or other recreational areas. A hiker, particularly in shoes with Vibram lugs, which have been estimated to be fifty to a hundred times harder on a trail than tennis shoes, can cause much damage to a trail, especially if he takes shortcuts around switchbacks. Horses are far worse, however—the combination of their heavy weight, small bearing surface, and sharp hooves can exert 1500 pounds of pressure per square inch. One pack train wandering across an alpine meadow can leave a track that may take several years to heal. Droppings along a trail are not the most pleasant trail companions either, particularly in wet weather. Compaction in soft meadow soils may lower a trail three to four feet below the general surface. Over a longer period, erosion may similarly carve harder surfaced trails.

Wherever possible, alternative trails should be blazed to allow a period of rehabilitation for overused trails in the most popular areas. This procedure has worked well for campsites in some parks.

NATURE PRESERVES

Among the smallest natural reserves are so-called nature preserves. Usually they are small-scale, under 1000 acres, often under 100 acres. They are composed of ponds, salt marshes, woods, prairies—features that are in danger of disappearing altogether. Mostly privately owned by schools, clubs, and conservation organizations, they serve a vital purpose in pre-

Fig. 10.13 A river valley does not have to be a virgin wilderness to be beautiful, as this view of the Hudson River Valley from Bear Mountain State Park in New York demonstrates. (Photo by Harry Thayer, New York State Department of Commerce)

serving natural areas too small to be considered for national or state parks. The Nature Conservancy, a private organization, has been instrumental in saving many of these small areas from bulldozers or sanitary landfill operations and holding them for future enjoyment and study.

Other areas capable of multiple use are golf courses, rights of way of various types, and even cemeteries. All preserve open space that can be used for alternative purposes.

NATURE IN AN URBAN SETTING

All these categories are destined for occasional use, at best. The nature many of us live with is in our backyards, or if we are apartment dwellers, the trees in the street, the ivy growing on the wall, or the geraniums on the windowsill. Our connection with nature, however tenuous, can be maintained in the dreariest apartment by a window full of house plants as carefully nurtured as the oldest tree in Sequoia National Park. To a confirmed urbanite, the sight of an ailanthus tree growing behind a tenement, or pushing its way through the rubble at the edge of a parking lot, is a treasured thing indeed (Figure 10.14).

Fig. 10.14 Nature in the city is often limited to a window full of house plants and scraggly ailanthus trees in unlikely places.

The greatest problem in the effort to save some fragments of a once-natural world has been the failure to recognize the hierarchy of natural systems from parking-lot ailanthus to redwood. Each community has its place in the world and each is equally important. We must have as broad a spectrum of natural environments as can be assembled, from entire forests, deserts, mountains, and lakes down to ponds, bogs, woodlots, and single trees. Our spectrum should also include a wide range of uses, from inviolate wilderness available only for scientific study, to open space so heavily used that its vegetation must be continually renewed. We are, of course, a part of the natural environment just as the natural world is part of us. While the opportunities still exist, land must be earmarked for *all* categories of natural areas. Once a salt marsh has been filled with waste, a sand dune leveled for houses, or a valley flooded by a reservoir, the options for preservation and continued renewal are forever lost, for there are limits to environment reconstruction. Failure to act now can only impoverish future generations, which will have problems enough to bear. Let us give them at least a glimpse of how planet earth once looked.

FURTHER READING

Abbey, E., 1968. *Desert solitaire: a season in the wilderness.* McGraw-Hill, New York. A beautifully written account of Abbey's experience as a park naturalist in Utah.

Fitzsimmons, A. K., 1976. "National parks: the dilemma of development." *Science* **191**, pp. 440–444. A good overview of the reasons why many national parks are more like national recreation areas.

Huth, H., 1957. *Nature and the American.* University of California Press, Berkeley. A leisurely look at our changing attitudes toward nature.

Johnson, W. A., 1972. *Public parks on private land in England and Wales.* Johns Hopkins Press, Baltimore. An interesting contrast to the problems faced in preserving natural areas in the United States.

Kozlolwski, T. T., and C. E. Ahlgren (eds.), 1974. *Fire and ecosystems.* Academic Press, New York. A series of papers dealing with the effects of fire on a wide variety of ecosystems.

McHarg, I. L., 1969. *Design with nature.* Natural History Press, Garden City, New York. A very personal view of the landscape by a landscape architect with exceptional ecological awareness.

Nash, R., 1967. *Wilderness and the American mind.* Yale University Press, New Haven. Traces the wilderness concept through American history.

Shepard, P., 1967. *Man in the landscape.* Random House, New York. A literary review of man's past and present relationship with nature.

Sullivan, A. L., and M. L. Shaffer, 1975. "Biogeography of the megazoo." *Science* **189**, pp. 13–17. A discussion of the problems of trying to assume maximum species diversity in parks of less than desirable size.

PART FOUR

THE RISE
OF THE CITY

All the manipulations of the environment described so far evolve naturally from the agricultural revolution and the settling down of wandering hunting/gatherers or herders. But there are other results of settlement: the environmental enclosure we call a house and the aggregation of these houses into the highly modified environment of the city. The rise of the city has in turn generated a number of problems. The larger the city, the larger the hinterland required to support it and the greater its reliance on transportation to keep raw materials flowing in and finished products flowing out. So cities have an impact on their environment quite out of proportion to their areal extent.

CHAPTER ELEVEN

THE HOUSE

ALTHOUGH OUR FIRST SHELTER WAS a ready-made tree or cave, migration into areas without convenient natural shelter together with a culture that provided new tools and materials both required and allowed us to build a variety of artificial structures. For the thousands of years that we have occupied earth, these structures have slowly evolved by trial and error into some starkly functional and often elegantly simple buildings. Once disdained by architects, this native architecture is being studied today as a superb marriage of form and function. A few examples from greatly contrasting environments will give some idea of the relationship between form, function, and environment.

DIVERSITY OF ENVIRONMENT;
DIVERSITY OF HOUSE

One of the best adaptations to an especially hostile environment was the development of the igloo by the Eskimo. Dome-shaped and constructed of blocks of hard-packed snow, the igloo offered minimal resistance to the sweep of the wind during the winter when the tents used in summer were unsuitable. Internally, the dome shape allowed the largest volume possible with the least supportive structure and made the most effective use of point sources of heat, a simple oil lamp and the people themselves. The igloo was made by layering snow blocks in an arching spiral (Figure 11.1). By carefully packing the chinks with snow and burning an oil lamp inside, the interior of the igloo was glazed into a shiny, smooth surface

Fig. 11.1 The igloo (Eskimo for "house"), once used as an overnight shelter for hunting parties, was a fine example of functional native architecture. Today, snowmobiles make it possible for hunters to return to their villages of more substantial structures each night. (Courtesy of the American Museum of Natural History)

that not only sealed the igloo but reflected light and heat, much as aluminum foil might. When the interior was covered with furs and skins, the igloo was quite comfortable, at least compared with the conditions outside: at midnight, air temperature inside an igloo was 2°C while outside air temperature was minus 34°C. During the day inside air temperature rose as high as 4°C compared with minus 23°C outside.

The other environmental extreme, the desert, has also had a profound effect on the shelters of native peoples. The desert, unlike the Arctic, poses problems of daily rather than seasonal extremes. The temperature ranges from 43°C to 15°C over a twenty-four-hour period, a range that puts an enormous strain on any cooling system. These extremes are modified, however, by the use of local materials, stone and clay (adobe), for houses with thick walls and roofs that insulate the interior of the building from the blistering heat outside (Figure 11.2). Temperature in

Fig. 11.2 These buildings at Taos Pueblo in New Mexico are built of soft clay bricks or adobe. Their thick walls and roofs effectively insulate the inhabitants from the sharp temperature extremes of the New Mexican desert. (Courtesy of the American Museum of Natural History)

a typical adobe dwelling at 2 P.M. was 29°C inside and 40°C outside, while at night the temperature was 27°C inside and 18°C outside. During the day the thick walls and roof acted as insulators, heating slowly as they absorbed the sun's rays. At night the process was reversed; the desert air cooled quickly, but the warm walls and roof radiated heat throughout the night, protecting the occupants from the outside chill.

In the tropics, the problem is not temperature variation, either daily or seasonal, but the need for adequate shade, proper ventilation, and protection from heavy downpours. The native peoples achieve these ends by reducing or eliminating side walls and erecting a steeply pitched roof, thickly thatched. Thin, coarsely woven side walls take advantage of every breeze, and the thick thatch both insulates the shelter beneath from the heat of the sun almost overhead, and sheds the daily rain shower quickly and almost silently (Figure 11.3). In contrast, the tin-roofed wooden shacks that often replace the thatched structures are cramped, stuffy, and noisy.

Fig. 11.3   The thatch roof of a house in Thailand allows rain to roll off quickly and quietly while the loosely woven sidewalls allow circulation of air. (Alice Mairs)

Until fairly recently, areas with similar climates exhibited similar architecture no matter where they were located. A townhouse in Thailand (Figure 11.4) strongly resembled a house in New Orleans; a stone-adobe house in hot, dry Afghanistan (Figure 11.5) looked very much like a New Mexico pueblo; and a fishing village in Singapore Harbor (Figure 11.6) might be located along the Amazon River in Brazil.

The widespread migration of people into a New World with climates different from those they had known required adaptation to the local environment even when this meant a change in traditional building methods. For example, people from Plymouth, England, where winters are mild and summers cool, were obliged to adapt the type of dwelling with which they were familiar to the much colder winters and hotter summers of Plymouth, Massachusetts. In consequence, the rooms and windows

Fig. 11.4 This rather substantial townhouse in Thailand has a tile roof with a broad overhang, wide porch, and louvered shutters to shield from the sun and allow maximum circulation of air. (Alice Mairs)

Fig. 11.5 Hot dry climates everywhere elicit the use of thick-walled structures that insulate well, as in these houses in Istalik, Afghanistan. (Alice Mairs)

Fig. 11.6 An ideal marriage of form and function in a kelong, a structure from which men fish with nets, built on stilts in Singapore Harbor. (Alice Mairs)

became smaller, the ceilings lower, and the fireplaces massive (Figure 11.7). In contrast, the summers in Virginia and the Deep South states necessitated large rooms with high ceilings and wide porches or verandas often sheltered by a portico or overhang—all of which allowed maximum insulation, shade, and circulation of air.

As people continued to move, following the frontier to Ohio, the plains states of Illinois and Iowa, then Oregon or California, their houses reflected the changing climate. Pioneers from New England recreated New England villages in northern Ohio, which has a climate similar to New England's. Today some small Ohio towns strongly resemble parts of New England, even in their names. Farther west this flavor is lost as the farm and ranch houses built from the 1840s to the 1860s were adapted to the influence of local climate.

The basic reason for the wedding of form and function in native architecture lies in the sensitivity to and acceptance of the environment by most native cultures. But times are changing in most countries. The new and old coexist for a time, then the old way disappears. Unfortunately

Fig. 11.7 The New England winters are long and cold. Consequently this house, the famous House of Seven Gables in Salem, Massachusetts, has small windows and huge fireplaces in every room. (Courtesy of Essex Institute, Salem, Mass.)

the new usually means a break with the past—the Eskimo gives up his igloo or tent for a wooden-frame house, the African his thatched hut for a tin-roofed shack (Figure 11.8). But much that is good may be discarded with the apparently outmoded materials, techniques, and life styles. With so much of the world in transition between traditional tribal culture and a modern industrialized society, technology and ecologically sensitive architecture could help enormously to bridge the gap between the past and the future.

The Eskimo and his igloo demonstrate this point quite well. No one would want to confine an Eskimo to an igloo and deny him more advanced housing. But the igloo is basically a dome, an architectural form that has been ingeniously developed by the American engineer-architect Buckminster Fuller. Using modern methods and materials the igloo could be transformed into a functional and comfortable house in sympathy with the local environment and preserving a traditional form that could help Eskimos bridge the gap between their cultural past and future. The same approach could be used in desert or tropical regions. Of course, architects have not been insensitive to these possibilities. Much has been learned from traditional dwellings and applied to regional design.

In the United States the gap between function and form widened gradually. With the rise of mass communication—first national magazines and mail order catalogs, then movies, radio, and television—cultural homogenization began to erode local and regional differences in house types. The growing affluence of farmers and middle-class tradesmen in the nineteenth-century United States allowed a shift from a functional type of dwelling to a dwelling preoccupied with form. The simple farmhouse assumed Greek revival characteristics, and later, at the height of the Victorian era, townhouses were swathed in elaborate wooden ornamentation (Figure 11.9).

Today you can drive around any town in the United States and see bungalows built in the 1920s side-by-side with Tudor, Spanish, and French provincial styles from the 1930s, Cape Cod houses from the 1940s, and apartment houses incorporating a variety of styles.

The gap between form and function thus opened has been bridged to some extent by technology, which made possible the thousands of square miles of tract housing in the world, struck from a common mold and planted in the ground like some monster crop. There is, certainly, some regional differentiation—shake roofs in California, glass walls in Florida, small windows and full basements in Wisconsin. But one could easily switch houses between Fullerton, California and Oshkosh, Wisconsin and make them work in their new environment. What, then, is the price of making a house work in an environment to which it is ill-adapted—a thousand dollars a year in heating or cooling expenses? Before we can examine the cost, literal or figurative, of housing that is out of equilibrium

Fig. 11.9   This San Francisco Victorian house had the good fortune to be snatched from the jaws of a redevelopment project, moved several blocks, then lovingly restored.

with its environment, we must look at what constitutes a suitable external environment for man's dwellings.

THE OUTER ENVIRONMENT

Two tendencies have been at work in the design of dwellings as packaged environments. One is toward the elimination of the connection between the inner and outer environments by building a windowless, possibly underground house. This would solve most of the environmental problems that bedevil architects: maintenance of external surfaces; control of flies or mosquitoes in summer and drafts in winter; expense of heating and cooling; glare and shadows, with illumination of the exact intensity and brightness desired. With outside dust eliminated and inside dust filtered out by the obligatory air conditioning system, such a house would be extremely easy to keep clean. Occupancy would, of course, depend on a never-failing power source to heat, cool, ventilate, and illuminate; but auxiliary generators are available. Such an underground house would allow total landscaping of the lot above, particularly desirable where lots are small and expensive. When you pay several thousand dollars for a lot it seems somehow wasteful to cover most of it with your house.

The other approach runs in the opposite direction. The contact between inside and outside environments is broadened to the point where it is difficult to separate the two. This approach is most successful in mild climates where houses may literally enclose a piece of the outside environment in the form of a garden, as was done in the atrium of a Roman villa. Large areas of glass wall can be used to remove the feeling of separation between inner and outer environments, or multiple stories and cantilevers can thrust the inner environment into the larger outer environment of treetops or sky.

This approach to environmental integration has been used in cold climates as well as warm climates, but more skillful design is required in the former, since the inner and outer environments are so disparate that their integration must remain illusory. Only in a mild climate, such as that in Florida, along the Mediterranean, in Southern California, or in the warm desert areas, can the two be physically integrated.

Since most dwellings are very much a part of the surface environment, the orientation on a lot is critically important to the distribution of natural light within the dwelling, the ease or difficulty of heat control, and maintenance of a dry cellar or garage. Far too often, the developer's placement of streets on a tract reflects the most mathematically efficient way of subdividing property into the maximum number of lots. Houses are built on these lots either parallel to or at some standard angle to the

street (Figure 11.10), giving the house buyer little choice about the exposure of his house to sunlight or to wind.

Fig. 11.10 Tract houses, whether free-standing or built in rows, are constructed as the streets run with no undue consideration of environmental or aesthetic values.

The house exists in two environments: in the seasonal environment the sun appears from different angles and for varying lengths of time throughout the year; in a daily environment there are constantly changing patterns of light and shadow. On September 21 and March 21 in the Northern Hemisphere the sun rises at 6 A.M. and sets at 6 P.M.; on June 21 the day runs from 4:30 A.M. to 7:30 P.M. and on December 21 from 7:30 A.M. to 4:30 P.M. Fortunately one needs neither a mathematician nor a computer to predict the results of any particular dwelling orientation if one knows the aspect of the site and the shape of the building. A machine called a heliograph, available to most architects, can reproduce the various seasonal changes in lighting as the earth circles the sun. Using such a device a small model of a house can be oriented, taking into consideration light, temperature, and exposure factors.

Although an eastward-facing wall receives the same radiation as one facing west, the westward-facing wall is irradiated during the hottest part of the day, making it the warmest wall of the dwelling. When this is anticipated, some care can be taken to avoid placing a kitchen behind that wall or to devise shielding to check heat absorption. Because of the low angle of the sun in winter, the south wall is heated more in winter than in summer; on the other hand, in the summertime the north wall receives most of its sunshine and the roof twice the radiation of any of the walls.

249

But this constantly changing heat load on a house can be predicted, and steps can be taken to cope with it by the basic orientation of the house, design features, and landscaping. Since zoning often confines both the architect and builder by allowing only a certain orientation a specified number of feet back from the street, the architect often finds it impossible to arrange the rooms to accommodate both summer shade and winter sun. Well-designed plantings may help. In brick or stone houses, the warm west wall can be shielded from the late afternoon sun by the strategic placement of trees or a deciduous vine such as Boston ivy. When the ivy sheds its leaves in the fall, the wall is warmed by the winter sun (Figure 11.11). In the summer the ivy leaves form an insulating layer of air that shields the masonry from the heat of the sun.

Fig. 11.11 Because it faces west, this brick house absorbs much radiant energy. The deciduous ivy that covers the wall welcomes the warmth of the winter sun and shelters the house from the summer sun.

The force of cold winter winds can be broken by planting hedges or belts of evergreens. Windbreaks have been planted with excellent results throughout much of the Midwest in the Dakotas, Iowa, Nebraska, and Kansas. Thirty-foot trees significantly reduce wind velocity 400 feet to the leeward. Dwelling design plus strategic placement of trees, shrubs, and vines can warm a house as much as 10°C in winter and cool it by 9°C in summer. This is equivalent to moving from New Jersey to upper New York State for the summer and down to Virginia for the winter. Al-

though these expedients incorporate neither new materials nor new techniques and indeed are only extensions of common sense, often they are not utilized. This is perhaps a result of ignorance but is more likely due to the wide availability of air conditioners and other products of technology.

Naturally, with modern heating systems and air conditioning, a standard tract house could probably be built atop Pike's Peak or in Death Valley and be made livable if not comfortable, but only at great expense. The whole point of adapting a dwelling to its setting by design, orientation, and planting is to gain maximum benefit from the natural heating and cooling the environment affords (Figure 11.12). But so far we have been complacently running roughshod over the natural landscape, using our technology to make every lot and every dwelling suit the builder's convenience.

Fig. 11.12 Twenty years ago these subdivisions were as barren as the one in Fig. 11.10. But the growth of trees and shrubs is beginning to soften the harsh outlines of the streets and afford some measure of climate amelioration to the occupants of these houses. (Thomas Airviews)

THE INTERNAL ENVIRONMENT

Whatever its relationship to the outside environment, a dwelling's function is to shelter from the elements. We are most comfortable at a temperature of about 22°C. This is determined by the rate of heat loss by the body. If it is too rapid we are cold; if too slow, we are too hot. At 22°C, apparently, the rate of heat loss is just about right. Since 22°C is a reasonably typical temperature in the tropics, we assume that we originated in those regions and developed a need for substantial shelters when we migrated from tropical climates and required artificial means of recapturing this optimum zone of comfort. The diversity of houses we have examined illustrates attempts to recreate this comfort level by whatever means available.

When we view a shelter or house as an enclosed environment, what factors are important to our health and comfort? Certainly temperature, but also light, humidity, ventilation, and perhaps that intangible aesthetic that transforms a house into a home.

TEMPERATURE

We can tolerate, with protection, the extreme natural range of –76° to 63°C. Since the outside air temperature is only occasionally within our ideal comfort range, 21° to 24°C, one prime environmental function of a house is to add or remove heat.

Heat is intentionally supplied to houses by a great variety of materials: wood, charcoal, coal, oil, natural gas, or electricity, directly or indirectly by heat pumps or heat exchangers. Since all these sources are derived ultimately from the combustion process, air pollution is a direct consequence of heating houses. Of all the heat sources, electricity provides the best opportunity to control pollution. Emissions from a few power plant stacks are easier to control than pollution from millions of combustions from individual heat sources (Chapter 18). While it would be nice to have individual power plants, nuclear or solar, to fill all our power needs for heat and electricity, it will be some time before such units are in widespread use.

Artificial heat is not, of course, the only heat supply in a house. As we saw in the previous section, conduction and radiation from roofs and walls heated by the sun are important sources of heat, which have been used to advantage in regions with a fair amount of winter sunshine without severe cold. Manipulating the size, shape, and orientation of the windows can keep a well-designed house comfortably warm during much of the winter with solar heat (see Chapter 15). This heat source needs reinforcement from conventional sources only during long periods of overcast weather or extreme cold.

Other sources of heat, of minor significance in private dwellings but of some magnitude in a crowded store, apartment, or office building, are body heat and lighting appliance heat. A 100-watt bulb gives off about 500 British thermal units (Btu) an hour and a human body about half again as much. When thousands of people and powerful lighting fixtures are involved, the resulting heat can be a substantial amount. Several buildings have already been constructed to make use of this source of heat: a large post office in Houston, a sixty-story tower in Chicago, and other buildings in Pittsburgh and Portland, Oregon. The system is basically simple. Air leaving the building and warmed by the activities inside is passed over a system of water-filled coils. Fresh air entering the building is warmed as it passes over the hot water coils. Some of the buildings have water tanks to store heat when the building is unoccupied. This heat recovery system works until the outside temperature falls to −12°C; then supplementary heating becomes necessary. This is a particularly obvious example of the economic and ecological good sense implicit using what would otherwise be wasted.

Heat removal is usually achieved by air conditioning, either central or room units. If both the roof and walls of a dwelling are well insulated, reasonable control over summer temperature can be achieved simply by opening doors and windows at night and closing them early in the morning. Since it is more important and difficult to prevent entrance of excess heat than to prevent its loss, the location and overall design of a house become essential in controlling internal temperature.

HUMIDITY

Another obvious function of a dwelling is as a shelter from rain, but almost any type of structure will afford this protection. More important is the control of moisture in the internal environment of a house. There are two ways to measure the moisture content of air: the vapor pressure or the relative humidity. Vapor pressure is a measure of the actual amount of moisture in the air at any given temperature; relative humidity is an expression of how much moisture the air is holding compared with how much it *could* hold at that temperature. A relative humidity of 80 percent at 27°C means that the air is 80 percent saturated with moisture. This is not equivalent to a relative humidity of 80 percent at 10°C because as the temperature of air falls its capacity to hold moisture decreases. Thus 80 percent relative humidity at 32°C may be unbearable, while 80 percent humidity at 15°C may be quite comfortable, because warm air can hold so much more moisture than cold air.

In the winter we may have the apparent paradox of a house at 15 percent relative humidity and 24°C losing moisture to an outside environment of 50 percent relative humidity at 13°C. Even at 15 percent relative humidity a house at 24°C contains more moisture than half-saturated air at 13°C, so moisture diffuses from a point of higher concentration inside to a point of lower concentration outside. Also, as the internal tem-

253

perature of a house increases during the winter heating season, the relative humidity is bound to drop since the warmer air is capable of holding far more moisture than is generated by household activities alone.

The chief problem in most American dwellings in summer is not the heat but the humidity, to coin a cliché. Hence, any air conditioning system must dehumidify as well as cool the air passing through it.

In the winter, the problem is just the opposite. The small amount of vapor released from our breath, washing, and bathing tends to diffuse out through the walls and roof of the house, thereby reducing the relative humidity of a heated dwelling to as low as 10 percent—comparable with many desert regions of the world. This combination of high temperature and low humidity has a destructive effect upon furniture, causing wood to shrink and glue to dry out. The effects on people are analogous; the nasal and throat membranes dry out, especially at night, creating conditions favorable to many respiratory viruses and bacteria. It is no coincidence that winter is the reason for colds. Vaporizers can often alleviate the dryness of a small room, but it is more effective and convenient to do this centrally with a humidifier on a furnace. This can be easily accommodated in a hot-air type of heating system but is more difficult to install with hot water, steam, or electric heat.

LIGHT

In earlier times, reliance on candles or lamps made the location, number, and size of windows or skylights to let in natural light critically important to household activities. Electric lighting assures plentiful artificial light, and the location of windows in a building is much less important today than it once was. Windowless buildings can and are being built and, if anything, seem to be more effectively illuminated than windowed structures with their glare and uneven lighting. More is involved, however, than good or bad illumination, for windows not only let in light but let people see out. It is psychologically satisfying to be able to relate yourself to time and place by glancing out of a window and, if the view is at all pleasant, it provides mental respite from the pressure or boredom of routine.

A controversy rages as to whether schools should have windows. There seems to be no good evidence that lack of windows produces student claustrophobia, and a windowless school does have more space. While one suspects that arguments for windows are based more on tradition and sentiment than on demonstrable undesirable effects of windowless buildings, students are already too isolated from the environment. Perhaps the constant awareness of the real environment outside the window might in a small, even insidious way, remind both student and teacher of life in a natural as well as a synthetic environment. Beyond the mere presence or absence of natural light, sunlight plays an important psychological role in determining mood. Sunlight pouring into a room on a cold winter day is relaxing and cheering and raises the spirits of those confined indoors.

Glass transmits 82 to 90 percent of the visible portion of sunlight but almost no ultraviolet rays, so it is impossible to get a winter tan by lying in sunlight under glass. However, special glass has been developed that allows up to 60 percent of the ultraviolet to be transmitted. If it were simply a case of getting a tan, a sunlamp would do as well, but ultra-violet light, besides its tanning effect and importance to vitamin D synthesis, is an important germicide; most germs are killed by exposure to the ultraviolet in sunlight for little over an hour. Exposing the interior of a house to the natural disinfecting power of unfiltered sunlight might be useful enough in maintaining normal sanitation and cleanliness to be considered in the design, orientation, and glass specifications of a modern house.

Windows also generate the greenhouse effect described in Chapter 18. The shortwave radiation of sunlight passes easily through the window glass, strikes an object or surface in the room, and is converted into long-wave radiation or heat that cannot pass back through the glass and so accumulates in the room. This effect is quite noticeable in a room with many windows admitting sunlight; for this reason houses with large areas of windows or glass walls must be carefully designed and situated so that this effect can be exploited in winter and controlled in summer.

VENTILATION

Beyond the perception of strong kitchen or bathroom odors or perhaps a vague notion of stuffiness, most people are unaware of the need for ventilation in their homes. Air already contains the usual mix of nitrogen, oxygen, carbon dioxide, water vapor, and dust. In addition, people give off twenty-three liters per person of carbon dioxide per day, plus variable amounts of water vapor, hydrogen sulfide, ammonia, propionic acid, and various organic compounds. Large quantities of grease aerosols are spread about by frying foods, carbon particles are added from burning foods and tobacco, and dust is constantly generated from bedding, rugs, and clothing. Occasionally malfunctioning furnaces or space heaters may release carbon monoxide in quantities large enough to cause death by asphyxiation. More common is the combustion of cigarettes in poorly ventilated rooms, where carbon monoxide buildup may lead to dizziness or impaired judgment.

Both burned grease and tobacco smoke may contain carcinogens. While there are no statistics on how many people have died of lung cancer by inhaling burned fat aerosols or someone else's tobacco smoke, there is no reason to believe that these materials are harmless simply because our relationship to them is passive. In general these manmade materials decrease our sensitivity to the stimuli that are integral to our functioning as alert and creative individuals.

Ventilation is, of course, particularly important in the winter, when doors and windows of most northern homes are covered with storm windows to conserve heat. But it is necessary all year round where tall apartment houses abut each other. Most cities require air shafts in such buildings to assure interior apartments of at least some ventilation, but these shafts are rarely effective. Air conditioners in city apartments often serve the multiple functions of cooling and circulating the air, as well as removing some of the pollutants. The filter of an air conditioner removes only particulate matter, however, so the urbanite is still exposed to sulfur dioxide and smog, air conditioner or no.

A recent report of the EPA comparing hydrocarbon levels inside buildings to levels in the street outside found that carbon monoxide levels exceeded federal health standards 23 to 47 percent of the time during the heating season. This is of particular concern to occupants of buildings situated in the air space over highways, a practice that is becoming increasingly popular where construction sites are at a premium (Figure 11.13).

Fig. 11.13 Air rights construction is becoming increasingly popular in densely populated cities where land values are high. But it is difficult to control the entrance of air pollutants and noise from the traffic flowing below. These four apartments and transportation terminal rise over the approach to the George Washington Bridge in New York. (The Port of New York Authority)

It is ironic that technology, with its potential for making our personal environment more comfortable, is so often misused. Instead of providing innovative solutions to basic human needs, technology replaces good design, and the basic environmental factors that define a house, within and without, are ignored. If a house is drafty, we push up the thermostat; if it is stuffy, we turn on the air conditioner; and if it is smelly, we squirt a perfumed aerosol about. Each of these problems could be solved through careful study of our basic life needs and application of the best in design and the most relevant technology to satisfying those needs. But this rational approach will be deferred indefinitely if we continue to settle for the mediocre in housing, for its very acceptance denies the possibility of anything better.

There is much we can do. In existing housing we can select a heating scheme that contributes the smallest amount of pollutants to the outside environment; we can insulate to control heat entrance and loss; we can humidify or dehumidify the air; and we can landscape to ameliorate temperature and wind velocity extremes. In planning or selecting a house we can be aware of the need to consider temperature control of the interior. We can plan for potential flooding or drainage problems in choosing a site. We can examine floor plans carefully to control summer and winter natural light values. Where large tracts are still in the planning and development stage, individuals can see whether local zoning regulations merely keep people or structures out, or whether they deny freedom to orient a house properly on its lot. The builders can determine what provisions are to be made for power supply (wires above or below ground), sewage disposal, water supply, potential air pollution, schools to accommodate more children. Special hearings are often required by planning commissions before a subdivision can be developed; these hearings give the public a chance to voice opinions on the desirability of the project and its impact on the outer environment of surrounding property owners.

In public housing in large cities the quality of the home environment can be improved and maintained by adoption of strictly enforced building codes requiring minimum standards in all dwelling units. Public official can be forced to consider the outer and inner environments of public housing much more carefully than they have in the past.

The key, then, to providing a comfortable and healthy home environment lies in recognizing our environmental needs, making sure they are included in our housing plans, then taking appropriate political action to assure that these plans are realized. When this is done, and we have the requisite knowledge and technology, no human need suffer the indignity of enduring a personal living space that would be regarded as unhealthy for a pet tropical fish, an orchid, or a computer (Figure 11.14).

Fig. 11.14 While this urban slum or favela *in Brazil seems built into the air, the houses are actually clinging to the face of a very steep hill.*

FURTHER READING

Aronin, J. W., 1953. *Climate and architecture.* Reinhold, New York. Views the relation of houses to the climate of their site.

Banham, R., 1969. *The architecture of the well-tempered environment.* Architectural Press, London.

Geiger, R., 1965. *The climate near the ground.* Harvard University Press, Cambridge. A fascinating text that looks at microclimates and our relationship to them.

Kira, A., 1966. *The bathroom, criteria for design.* Center for Housing and Environmental Studies, Cornell University, Ithaca, New York. Critique of the most neglected room in any house.

Olgyay, V. G., 1951. "The temperate house." *Arch. Forum* **94**(3), pp. 174–194. Many tables, charts, and graphs relating the house to the pattern of the changing seasons.

Ordish, G., 1960. *The living house.* Lippincott, Philadelphia. A charming study of the forms of life that have inhabited an old English cottage, reflecting changing life styles.

Rapoport, A., 1969. *House form and culture.* Prentice-Hall, Englewood Cliffs, New Jersey.

Rudofsky, B., 1964. *Architecture without architects.* Museum of Modern Art, New York. A fine survey of folk architecture.

CHAPTER TWELVE

THE URBAN-SUBURBAN
ENVIRONMENT

HOWEVER SUITABLE AN environment it provides, for most people the house is an extension of their personal space, enhancing personal satisfaction and well-being. Unfortunately, when houses are packed into dense concentrations or when apartments are stacked in huge impersonal towers, some personal space is sacrificed for common space. Hallways, lobbies, streets, and parks become the living room of the urbanite.

Because of this concentration, the city has changed the natural environment in which it was situated and created a new environment with unique demands. All environmental problems seem exacerbated by cities—air and water pollution, noise. Even the suburbs share an increasing burden of environmental problems. Yet well over half the population of the United States lives in cities or towns that occupy only 1 percent of the total land area. While many of these urbanites would prefer to live in the suburbs and more than a few suburbanites would like to move to the country, a surprising percentage of city and suburban dwellers live there by choice and are quite happy to limit their rural experiences to occasional vacations. Despite monumental problems, cities are exciting places to live, offering a quickened tempo for both cultural and intellectual opportunity. But these are subjective values. Viewed as the one manmade environment, urban areas are sharply differentiated from the countryside in many ways.

THE LOCATION AND FORM OF CITIES

Gertrude Stein once described a rather nondescript American city by saying, "When you get there, there's no there, there." Most cities with a sense of identity are strongly related to topographical forms. London and Paris are located on major rivers, Istanbul on a strategic strait, Rio de Janeiro and San Francisco on superb harbors. More recent cities—Denver, for example—have been shaped by railroads and major highway intersections. But transportation routes themselves are strongly influenced by the dictates of topography (see Chapter 13).

Although the location of a city is basically related to the surface features of the countryside, once located, a city is subtly affected by the less obvious subsurface features. Venice was built on the marshy Po River delta in Italy both for protection from attack by land and for easy access to the sea, reflecting the extensive mercantile interests of the city. For centuries Venice prospered, but in recent times the lowering water table beneath the city has begun to cause its buildings to sink slowly. As the piles on which the buildings rest are exposed to air, they decay; their erosion is quickened by the wakes of the motorboats that have largely replaced gondolas and rowboats. The city is now endangered.

Mexico City, though very differently situated, has a similar problem. Built on a dry lake bottom at an altitude of 8000 feet, Mexico City has experienced a gradual lowering of the water table that has caused many buildings to sink; the most spectacular example, the Palace of Fine Arts (Figure 12.1), has sunk many feet below street level. Removal of oil from an oil field under Long Beach, California caused parts of that city to

Fig. 12.1 The Palace of Fine Arts in Mexico City is a massive building whose great weight has caused it to settle into the soft subsoil that underlies the city. (Mexican National Tourist Council)

subside as much as twenty-nine feet, until water was pumped into the field to stabilize the ground level.

While subsurface features can alter the future of a city once it is already there, they can also determine the shape a city may take. Approaching New York City by car or plane, one can see the rather uneven distribution of tall buildings on Manhattan Island. Toward the southern end, skyscrapers are grouped in the Wall Street area, and a second group is clustered in the midtown area from 34th to 60th Streets. In between, skyscrapers are conspicuously absent. While historical and economic factors are partly responsible for this distribution, its principal cause is the accessibility of stable bedrock. The taller the building, the firmer must be its footing in bedrock. Manhattan is fortunate to have a stable platform of hard rock under much of the city, but at different depths. To the north this formation comes to the surface in the midtown area, and is easily seen in Inwood, Morningside, and Central Parks. But as one goes south the bedrock begins to dip below ground. South of 30th Street it is deeply buried, hundreds of feet below the surface. Further south again, in the Wall Street area, it comes up within forty feet of the surface, and then, with the exception of the outcrop of Governor's Island in New York Harbor, it plunges far below the surface again. The expense of excavating more than a hundred feet to reach bedrock has so far prevented the erection of very tall buildings in the section of Manhattan between 30th and Wall Streets.

THE MICROCLIMATE OF CITIES

As large cities grow, so does their impact on the environment. The overall climate of a city reflects the region where the city is located. But large cities can modify some of the climatological factors in their immediate vicinity, resulting in a relatively small-scale but important variation in climate called a microclimate. When you think of the ways that a city differs from an equal area of forest or farmland, the reasons for microclimates become apparent.

TEMPERATURE

With growth in area and three-dimensional complexity, the mean temperature in the city tends to rise, forming what has been called an urban heat island. It results from the loss of evaporative cooling normally provided by vegetation and exposed soil, the gain of reradiated heat from pavement and building surfaces, and heat produced directly by factories and buildings. Walk down a city street on a hot summer's night and feel the hot breath of air conditioners from apartments and the heat shim-

261

Fig. 12.2 If all the ice now present at the poles should melt, the sea would rise by about 500 feet, flooding much of the eastern United States and most of the population centers of the Pacific coast.

mering up from the pavement. In wintertime, notice the heat rising from subway grills in the sidewalk, or the clouds of steam pouring out of manholes or storm sewer gratings. These heat sources have a cumulative effect since the rough profile of the city deflects the wind, which might otherwise sweep some of this heat away.

The most striking temperature differences between the city and the country are seen in the daily high and low temperatures, which tend to be moderated in cities. A city weather report illustrates this pattern. Expected lows are always lower in the suburban areas than the city center and the rural areas beyond are lower still. Conversely, although the city center gets quite warm on a summer day, the highs for the area may be in the suburbs or even in the country. The difference lies in daytime shading and nighttime reradiation.

Despite the concrete mass of the city, shading by tall buildings or narrow streets prevents sunlight from striking many potential radiation surfaces, thus lowering maximum temperatures. On the other hand, the minimal shading in suburbs allows maximum heating of paved surfaces, roofs, and the walls of low buildings. On a summer's night, long after the country has become chilly and the suburbs comfortably cool, the city is still sweltering, perhaps only a few degrees cooler at midnight than at sundown. By sunrise, when the city is beginning to cool, the tall buildings are already being warmed. The mass of the city, then, acts as a buffer, damping the temperature extremes experienced in the suburbs or the countryside beyond.

While these microclimates do not produce dramatic changes in climate,

over the years statistically valid changes have been noted. The city of
Kyoto, Japan experienced an increase in mean temperature of 1.8°C between 1880 and 1935, a period of rapid industrialization and growth. Now
1.8°C may seem insignificant, but remember, this is a mean. You
should remember too that an elevation of just 5°C in the mean temperature of the earth would be sufficient to melt all remaining ice caps, and
to raise the ocean level by about 500 feet, flooding the world's coastal
cities (Figure 12.2).

PRECIPITATION

Particulate matter provides nuclei for the condensation of atmospheric
moisture into precipitable drops or rainfall. The city's effects on rainfall
are difficult to quantify, but some data suggest that as cities grow the
rainfall on the city proper increases. As the English city of Rochdale
became industrialized and grew, its rainfall measured over ten-year periods increased: 1898–1907, 42.81 inches; 1908–1917, 45.83 inches; and
1918–1927, 48.65 inches. Interestingly, there was a statistically significant
drop of 0.37 inches on Sundays during the period when measurements
were taken. Particulate matter in the atmosphere was lower on Sunday
than on the six working days of the week.

Particulate matter may affect surrounding towns as well as the urban
area. Gary, Indiana is covered much of the time by an enormous pall of
smoke from its steel mills. As the cloud drifts eastward, it apparently
triggers rain. LaPorte, Indiana, thirty miles southeast of the complex,
recorded 31 percent more precipitation, 38 percent more thunderstorms,
and 246 percent more hail days between 1951 and 1965 than comparable
towns to the north and south.

Cities may also produce an orographic effect; that is, their domes of
warmer air force the moisture-laden clouds upward into colder air, which
triggers rain further on. At times when the temperature of Buffalo, New
York is 10°C higher than its environs, precipitation plumes can be traced
many miles inland—a dramatic demonstration of the climatological impact of cities.

Although rainfall seems to be greater over cities than their surroundings, at least in the long run, there is distinctly less snowfall in cities
than in the surrounding countryside. In temperate areas, especially along
the coast, most heavy snow falls when the temperature is near the freezing mark. Often the city temperature is just high enough to change the
snow into rain as it falls through the warm air enveloping the urban area.
On such occasions the city may remain bare while the surrounding suburbs receive several inches of snow. When snow does fall on a city, the
city-generated heat may cause it to melt as fast as it falls; even when it
accumulates, it melts more rapidly than suburban snow.

While certain streets or areas of most cities can be quite windy because of local updrafts between buildings or the channel effect of towering buildings lining a narrow street, an equal number of places in a city are quite protected from wind. Because of the rough surfaces they present to the wind, cities tend to experience reduced *average* wind velocity in direct proportion to their size and density. Between 1909 and 1930 the mean wind velocity in Detroit, even when measured 259 feet above the street, decreased from 14.8 to 8.7 feet per second.

Regardless of its velocity, the air of cities, as we will see in Chapter 18, is especially rich in fly ash, dust, and particulate matter of all sorts. These materials have a climatological effect as well as an aesthetic and public health impact. Particulate matter can reduce a city's natural radiation by 15 percent; the reduction is uneven across the radiation spectrum and tends to be greatest in the ultraviolet range. This portion of the solar spectrum is extremely important in the production of vitamin D in the skin.

Pollutants produced by a city are not confined to the immediate vicinity, of course; they drift downwind. Much of the background pollution in the United States can be traced to the combined emissions of metropolitan areas upwind. In St. Louis, for example, a trailing pall of smog characterized by ozone levels twice that of the background can be identified 80 to 120 km from the city.

URBAN SPACE

To anyone who commutes regularly between a city and its suburbs, the microclimate of the city is obvious enough. Even more obvious as one enters a city from its suburbs is the almost complete loss of contact with natural vegetation. Except for a few scattered parks and occasional tree-lined streets, the urban scene is too often one of stark, dirty buildings (Figure 12.3). Unfortunately suburbs, which should be green wedges pushing into cities to relieve their starkness, instead tend to be gray fingers extending from the city and extinguishing the interplay of artificial and natural features that soften and humanize our environment. The problem is not purely the lack of open space—parking lots and plazas can provide that—but of space softened by trees, greenery, water, and different textured surfaces that mitigate harshness and muffle city noise.

A lack of these amenities might be expected to contribute to poor mental health in many urbanites. In fact, a study made in 1954, the famous Midtown Manhattan Study, found that 23 percent of the residents in an East Side New York neighborhood needed psychiatric help. Twenty years later however, a follow-up study seemed to indicate that urban mental health had improved to the point where people who lived in cities with a population greater than 50,000 had symptom scores nearly 20 percent lower than people in rural areas or in cities with less than 50,000 in population.

It should be kept in mind too, that while poverty, familial disorganization, and parental psychopathology are characteristic of urban and ghetto life, many of these social and psychological patterns were set up in the small towns and rural areas where numbers of present urbanites originated. The reason people have flocked to cities from the Deep South, the Ozarks, or Puerto Rico is not that cities, however falsely, offered so much, but that rural slums offered so very little. While urban slums are visible to millions, rural slums are usually hidden away in remote areas and known only to their inhabitants. For all its problems—jackhammers in the street; wailing police cars and fire trucks; subway trains that shriek, roar, and stall; grime and crime—the city provides a better chance for self-fulfillment and mobility than virtually any other environment.

Space is too important in ameliorating the city environment to remain an aesthetic afterthought of the developer. To appreciate the importance of properly designed or sensibly retained urban space, we must first look at the relation between cities and their suburbs and the natural environments that once surrounded them.

Fig. 12.3 The Schmitt Music Center in Minneapolis wanted to advertise its product and enliven an otherwise drab brick wall. This was the solution. Thank you, Mr. Schmitt! (The score is Ravel's "Gaspard de la nuit.")

Fig. 12.4 Once a chain of wind-blasted sand dunes, Golden Gate Park after a hundred years of careful tending looks as though it has always been there—cool, green, and welcoming.

OPEN SPACE IN OLDER CITIES

Older cities more than newer suburbs appreciate the value of open space. Many cities have tried to pace their growth with either internal park systems or peripheral greenbelts to insulate them from the surrounding suburbs. Cleveland and Washington, D.C. have attempted to preserve some open space by creating parks from the floodplains of many small streams that drain the region. These parks form necklace-like skeins running through the city, breaking up the monotony of heavily urbanized areas and providing open space for residents.

Both London and Vienna have pioneered in the attempt to separate the city from its suburbs by a broad belt of undeveloped land, called a greenbelt, that encircles the city. Other cities have been able to set aside large blocks of land that today are irreplaceable: New York's Central and Prospect Parks, Philadelphia's Fairmount Park, and San Francisco's Golden Gate Park, for example (Figure 12.4). Many more opportunities exist to utilize open space that now lies unused. Most waterfront cities on rivers, harbors, or lakes have turned away from their natural waterfront orientation and, by expressway development or redevelopment schemes, have isolated the public from the most obvious focus for their recreation. Landscape architect Ian McHarg estimates that, of the twenty-two miles of Delaware River frontage available to Philadelphia, eight would more than suffice for port facilities; the remainder could be reclaimed for parkland, refocusing Philadelphia on the river. Much the same can be said of New York or Boston, where miles of rotting piers testify to past use and present inactivity. In New York, after great pressure by citizen's groups, people were allowed to use a city-owned pier, the Morton Street Pier. This gave New Yorkers the only access to the Hudson River between 72nd Street and Battery Park, a distance of more than five miles. Yet dozens of other unused piers rotted into the Hudson. More recently the city government has attempted to rise to the challenge by recommending the use of five more strategically located old piers as unique recreational areas.

One sign that we are coming to appreciate the importance of recreational open space has been the development of vest-pocket parks and playgrounds in many large cities. Parks need not be large, with acres of grass and groves of trees. The simple juxtaposition of different textures of stone, small fountains or pools, or murals (Figure 12.5) can be just as rewarding aesthetically. Ideally every block should have such a respite from the trauma of city life.

Measurements of sulfur dioxide on a transect across New York City's midtown district dramatically show Central Park's impact on diluting

Fig. 12.5 A few years ago this minipark was a typical jumble of weeds and trash. There is still some trash, of course, but the park is heavily used by children, sunbathers, and dogs.

gaseous pollutants (Figure 12.6). An expanse of lawn or even a narrow strip is three to six times more effective in trapping dust than is a smooth flat surface of equal area. Trees are even more effective in helping to settle out particulate material. London's Hyde Park, though only one square mile in area, reduces the concentration of smoke passing through it by as much as 27 percent.

While ground surface areas are often unavailable for open space use, the rooftops of cities offer a vast reserve of "land" presently utilized only by nesting nighthawks. Although the cost of converting rooftops of present buildings into gardens would be prohibitive in most instances, since the buildings were designed neither to support the additional load nor to provide safe or convenient access, future buildings could be planned

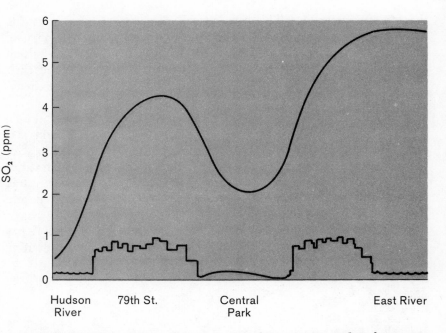

Fig. 12.6 The dip in this curve of SO$_2$ concentration in the air over Manhattan graphically shows the effect that open space can have in diluting the pollution being produced all around it. (From Joseph J. Shomon, 1971. Open land for urban America. Johns Hopkins Press, Baltimore, p. 30)

to include open space for public or semipublic use—a garden for apartment residents or an open-air cafeteria or restaurant for office workers.

The conflict of natural and manmade environments is not restricted to larger cities and their suburbs. Growth in small towns, starting with the building up of a few main streets, is accompanied by much protest as lawns are paved and old trees removed. The smaller the town, the more resistance is invoked by the destruction of these symbols of past provinciality. Trees and unbroken concrete are incompatible. For a tree to remain healthy it must have space for its feeder roots to obtain moisture and nutrients. As lawns disappear and the pavement encroaches, the feeder root system is progressively curtailed until the limbs, which exist in equilibrium with the feeder roots, begin to die (Figure 12.7). Old trees are doomed under these conditions and young trees planted hopefully as replacements are severely limited in the size they can attain by the minimal space available.

URBAN RENEWAL

While vest-pocket parks can be superb additions to the city, large-scale urban renewal projects often mar the city's fabric. The American genius for euphemism was evident when the term "slum clearance" was replaced by "urban renewal." Slum clearance suggests removal of slums without implying what will be put in their place or where the slum dwellers will go (Figure 12.8). Urban renewal, on the other hand, connotes a rekindling or recreation of the essence of urban living that has often been

Fig. 12.7 One way to keep trees in equilibrium with their environment is to prune their tops severely every year, an ancient practice called pollarding. The plane or sycamore trees next to the building have just been trimmed; the tree in the foreground sports its annual crop of twigs but will soon be shorn.

Fig. 12.8 Some open space is useful; some is useless. This portion of the Western Addition section of San Francisco once contained some of the finest Victorian buildings in town. But rather than rehabilitate them they were razed so that the area could be revitalized. Many years later the empty blocks are still waiting for their promised vitality.

regarded as snuffed out in slum areas. In practice, urban renewal has often meant the inept replacement of an old slum with a new one or the displacement of low-income families into another slum so that the cleared land can make a profitable return, perhaps in the form of luxury apartments, high-rise office space, or cultural centers and sports facilities.

269

Often slum development is accelerated by the practice of redlining. Large banks and savings and loan associations characteristically refuse to grant loans to whole neighborhoods regardless of the credit worthiness of individuals within the neighborhood. Without outside money to undertake repairs, remodeling, or refinancing of loans, houses fall into disrepair, responsible people move out, foreclosures become common, and vandalism increases.

People in the worst slums interact and relate to one another in the only space they have, the streets. Such streets, thronged with people almost around the clock, are often far safer than elegant tree-lined streets in well-to-do suburbs.

ANTISOCIAL ACTIVITY

When a slum is "renewed," buildings, streets, and whole blocks are swept away and frequently replaced by vertical towers separated by strips of green lawn. By day the renewed areas may be bright and cheerful, but at night they may be deserted and dangerous. Sometimes even the building interiors are not safe; blind corridors, elevators, and stairwells provide ample room for antisocial activity.

Why the antisocial activity? In a street-oriented slum the activity and interest on the street seem to pervade the hallways and corridors of the tenements lining the street. If you were to wander in off the street you would find many doors open, children playing in the halls, men and women chatting from their doorways or leaning out of windows. The street and its extensions into the houses form a social outlet for the people, all the more important when planned open spaces are unavailable.

In a typical renewal development, the commons of the street and halls is gone, lost in the impersonal bulk of buildings (Figure 12.9). Once the interaction and activity of the street have disappeared, the people turn inward. There is no reason to look out of the windows, there is no street activity, there is no fire escape to sit on, no front stoop, no sense of intimacy in the hallways. Wander into one of these buildings; doors are closed and halls are empty. Deprived of the opportunity to interact, people are withdrawn and resentful, often without knowing why. Antisocial acts become more frequent and less noticed. This phenomenon is by no means limited to low-income renewal housing. There have been repeated instances of violence in middle- and upper-class areas in New York, Chicago, and other large cities.

In all probability, social violence has many roots, and overcrowding may be just one. Another possibility suggested by James Prescott, a neuropsychologist, is that sensory pleasure and violence are reciprocally related. Societies that give their children much physical affection tend to have a low level of adult physical violence. Those few societies with high infant physical affection and high adult physical violence usually repress premarital sex. Hence it isn't at all strange that our society regards sex-with-violence films such as *The Straw Dogs* and *A Clockwork Orange* as entertainment and views sex-with-pleasure films like *Deep Throat* as filth. This suggests that violence is not limited to urban ghettos but is a societal disease.

City planners sometimes seem unaware of the social importance of streets as environmental space, for although renewal projects provide open space, most of it is apparently unsuitable for social activity. More often a city planner or architect *does* understand the spatial needs of people but is thwarted by archaic bureaucrats and hard-nosed bankers who will not fund imaginative solutions, myopic labor leaders imprisoned by rules no longer needed to protect their workers, and manufacturers with a vested interest in yesterday's technology.

Fig. 12.9 One answer to the redevelopment problem is the blockbuster. Painted an appropriately sick pink, this low-income housing unit is called the Pink Palace by its often mugged and burgled inhabitants.

Scale is also important, for the characteristic high-rise redevelopment project is constructed on an impersonal scale. Often much is made of its self-containment—entertainment areas, a supermarket, open space, and so on. But from the point of view of many tenants, the project is cut off from the city and remote from the quality of their old neighborhood and the rich life it supported.

This is not to say that slums are desirable. Far from it. Poorly heated in the winter, stifling in the summer, often overrun with cockroaches and rats, with trash in the hallways, the smell of urine on the stairs, peeling paint full of lead, cracking plaster, broken plumbing—a slum is a rotten place to try to live. But in their ardor to improve on slums, city planners and model-happy architects often throw out the baby with the bathwater.

271

Fig. 12.10 Rehabilitation has finally come of age. All over the country older houses are being freed of their misguided modernizations and restored to their original grace and charm. This multiple-flat Victorian building had been stripped of its plaster and redwood trim and stuccoed. Now the stucco is being stripped away and the ornaments replaced. When repainted, it will add a little luster to the dull end of San Francisco's Sutter Street.

REHABILITATION OF EXISTING HOUSING

One logical approach to renewal of a slum neighborhood is to rehabilitate as much housing as possible. Many slum areas are made up of solidly constructed houses that, if renovated, could be made more comfortable than most new construction and at lower cost. Some excellent examples of rehabilitation can be seen around the country—Wooster Square in New Haven, parts of the West Village and upper West Side in New York, Society Hill in Philadelphia, to name just a few (Figure 12.10). In most of these instances, however, the poor were simply shunted to another slum when the middle class discovered another "charming" neighborhood to "save." But the principle remains—housing can be rehabilitated.

A pilot experiment in New York pointed the way by cutting a hole in the roof of a sound but shabby tenement and lowering prefabricated bathrooms and kitchens into the replumbed and rewired building. The operation could be completed in a couple of days with minimum disruption of the occupants' lives by boarding them in a hotel until the work was done. Unfortunately, the experiment was abandoned when costs came to over $20,000 per family. But with application of the vaunted American know-how, a mass production approach should bring costs down to the level where whole blocks could be upgraded, preserving the open-space value of the streets without unduly disrupting the social life of the community and maybe even improving on things by knocking out a house here and there for intensive-use parklets.

If, however, the quality of housing is beyond rehabilitation the most logical approach for a city planner to take is to find a city neighborhood

272

that "works" like Boston's North End, the old French Quarter of New Orleans, parts of New York's Greenwich Village or Chelsea, and find out *why* it functions smoothly, has a low crime rate, safe streets, and relatively happy people who get along peacefully with each other. What environmental factors are at work and how do they affect the people? Then the planner-architects should do their utmost to build in the features that seem to make people happy. The world's cities have had enough of idealistic models that work for no one and in some ways are more demoralizing than the slums they replace.

THE RISE OF SUBURBIA

Throughout history, cities have been compact and densely populated; yet because of their relatively small population—10,000 to 100,000 until a few hundred years ago—they were able to coexist with the natural environment that surrounded them. Until the use of gunpowder became widespread in the thirteenth century and put an end to city walls, the medieval urbanite could walk through a gate into fields, forests, or onto the shore, which were all in intimate contact with the city (Figure 12.11).

Cities remained small because of the attrition of war and disease; the

Fig. 12.11 Mont St. Michel, both literally and figuratively an island, exemplifies the medieval walled city turned in upon itself but in intimate contact with its environment. (French Government Tourist Office)

notorious Black Death or bubonic plague reduced the population of some European cities by 80 percent. But the self-contained medieval cities were most effectively breached by changing times; people spilled into the countryside and the cities grew beyond their ancient walls. The Industrial Revolution drew many people to new jobs, and the resulting factories and housing pushed even further into the surrounding countryside. New cities and towns also sprawled over vast areas where raw materials needed for industry were available, as in the Ruhr Valley in Germany, or Detroit and Chicago in the United States. The final impetus to growth of cities in both the United States and Europe came from the striking advances in public health services and the advent of public transport systems, first the railroad, then the tram and trolley, finally the subway and automobile. This pattern of city growth is now being seen in other countries undergoing rapid industrialization, such as Japan and Korea.

We think of cities in the United States today as being densely packed with people, but urban density has been falling for many years while the suburbs have grown. In 1910 New York City contained 64,000 people per square mile; by 1960 the density had fallen to 13,000 people per square mile. Rapid transit systems have played an important role in this dispersion, as have changes in the standard of living. The average New York City household sheltered 4.5 people in 1910 but only 3.1 people in 1960. This means that one and a half times as much housing was required in 1960 as 1910 for a comparable number of people. This housing now surrounds the cities rather than constitutes them. Of course, such statistics apply only to those who have come to enjoy both a higher standard of living and the ensuing greater mobility. Those who have neither remain packed in tenements.

GROWTH OF A MEGALOPOLIS

The flight from the city began after World War I, continued through the 1920s and 1930s, and exploded after World War II. War-induced recovery from the Depression together with the return of millions of servicemen to civilian life caused a tremendous upsurge in the rate of home ownership. Veterans' Administration and Federal Housing Administration loans and mortgages as well as federal tax deductions on mortgage interest made it, for the first time, cheaper to buy than rent. Home ownership suddenly was within reach of greater numbers of people. Of course, some people moved from the country and small towns into suburbs, but the main impetus behind the growth of suburbs was the disenchantment and socioeconomic mobility of former urbanites.

By 1960, suburbs had coalesced into sprawling tracts, smothering the landscape and severing the cities' last link with open space (Figure 12.12). A city dweller could no longer take a bus or trolley to the end

of the line and find himself in the country. To get to the country from a city's downtown became a major expedition, involving hours of driving in very heavy traffic.

By 1961 the large cities of the Eastern Seaboard of the United States were beginning to bleed together into one large, increasingly urbanized mass that Jean Gottmann called a megalopolis. The largest megalopolis in the United States covers 500 miles from Portsmouth, Virginia to Portsmouth, New Hamphire, and includes Washington, Baltimore, Philadelphia, New York, and Boston; others are scattered over the rest of the United States and the world.

Will the United States soon be completely covered by merging megalopolises? By 1950 urbanization had occupied only 18 million of the 1904 million acres of the continental states. Even if urbanization continues at a rate of 1 million acres a year, and if we assume a half-acre per house and a proportion of 40 percent houses to 60 percent services, streets, factories, and other urban uses, by 2010 a population of 360 million would still occupy only 75 million acres of the land area of the United States. This might engulf 18 percent of current cropland, but with a doubling of productivity it might be possible to produce more food on less land, as is now done in some crowded European countries. But what is lost in this projection of possibilities is the location of urbanizing regions. Do we want coastlines, rivers, and lakes made inaccessible to the general public by uncontrolled growth? This question will be addressed more fully in Chapter 20.

Fig. 12.12 Like an amoeba, the city extends its psudopods to encompass the last remaining open space. Perhaps the view from these houses is pleasant, but the view of them certainly is not.

NEW TOWNS

As cities have grown beyond manageable size and often have become remote from any natural environment, some planners have attempted to
overcome the mistakes of old cities by starting new ones. The reasoning
usually runs: a near-perfect environment would be within our grasp if
we chose just the right site and carefully planned buildings and streets set
in parklike grounds. But this planner's utopia continues to elude us.

Much has been said about the impossibility of successfully governing a
city with over a million population. The ideal size submitted by planners
varies from 30,000 to a couple of hundred thousand. Clearly a city of 10
million has exceeded manageable proportions. However, if the existing
population of, let us say, France were evenly distributed into cities of a
few hundred thousand people scattered throughout that country, some
sixty new cities would have to be built, which would simply urbanize
large areas of presently rural France.

The English pioneered the establishment of new towns in an effort to
relieve pressure on London and other urban regions. Following the ideas
of Ebenezer Howard, who developed the concept of the garden city, several new towns were planned in every detail and then established, but reactions from their inhabitants have been mixed. One town constructed
with twelve houses to the acre provided gardens front and back, which the
designer included to please working class families from big city slums
who had never had more than a flowerpot. But young couples resettled
in these units felt isolated from old friends and family in the cities they
left behind; young wives felt that the gardens insulated them from mean-
ingful contact with neighbors and kept them from making new friends to
replace those left behind (apparently another example of the misunder-
stood role of space in the human environment); the husbands found
there was no neighborhood pub to get away to and no recreation comparable to that available in the city. Then daily commuting to work took
time and money, neither abundant for a working man. Many newcomers
to these new towns, like the young couples mentioned, leave after a
while, preferring the overcrowded cities. After a few years have passed,
the new turns mellow, as has the English new town of Letchworth. Yet
there is a cloying sameness that one must expect from something con-
ceived in its totality at one moment. Diversity of building styles is, after
all, a strong point of old towns. Letchworth is quite successful, however,
compared with Cumbernauld near Glasgow, Scotland. This new town is
built around a rambling building called the city center, which was
placed at the highest point of the city and apparently designed as a piece
of conspicuous architectural sculpture. Unfortunately, environmental considerations seem to have been overlooked and the center acts as a wind

tunnel, presenting little environmental improvement over conventional cities that just happened. In addition, this fixed center provides the only focus, indeed relief, from the rather drab housing units which effectively insulate the city from the lovely Scottish countryside. Still, these considerations are trivial when Cumbernauld is compared with the Glasgow slums it was intended to relieve.

Another type of new town is an intentional suburb, a satellite town built without the presumption that it need stand alone. Two new Swedish satellite towns, Vällingby and Farsta, have shopping and cultural areas of their own but are connected by a high-speed rapid transit system (see Chapter 13) to downtown Stockholm, which offsets possible shortcomings of the new town. Tapiola, near Helsinki, Finland, is another successful satellite town.

Some new towns constructed on a grand scale are two capital cities, Brasilia and Canberra. Brasilia has had a cold response from the public servants who are obliged to live there. After dark and on weekends the monuments, grand and imposing (Figure 12.13), are deserted, as are the recreational areas of many of the apartment blocks. The action is in the shanty town of temporary buildings constructed to house the workers who built and are still building Brasilia. Since the location is politically rather than environmentally determined and civic activities are sharply limited, the boredom of a new capital is not too surprising. Indeed officials are often given a hardship allowance to redress their isolation from the natural center of a country's culture.

Fig. 12.13 However brilliant the architectural conception, totally planned cities often lack human-scale amenity. Brasilia, in particular, seems to suffer from this preoccupation with monumentality. (Varig Brazilian Airline)

We might be better off if housing and, collectively, cities could be flexible enough for people to do their own thing, like children with building blocks. Somewhat short of this technological miracle but interesting nevertheless is modular housing, which is being tried in many cities. Attached to a superstructure, modular units can be flexibly and creatively arranged to fit the whole structure into any existing neighborhood. But it is as foolish for a planner to try to design a new town without knowledge of its intended occupants as it would be for an ecologist to try to recreate a salt marsh without any knowledge of the animals that he might expect to live there. Ebenezer Howard was quite probably on the right track with his notion of city units separated by greenbelts, for the largest and most densely populated city inevitably breaks up into blocks and neighborhoods, as thoroughly isolated from the city as a whole as suburbs miles away. If one could add the amenity of comfortable housing and convenient open space for a spectrum of recreational outlets, Howard's garden city might be considered a form of neighborhood. Perhaps the successful neighborhood can provide a prototype for the long sought utopia of planners.

Fig. 12.14   Reduction to the absurd: the formal lawn has come a long way from the English landscapist's ideal.

THE FUTURE OF THE CITY

Cities and their suburbs are likely to continue to sprawl across the United States. All people seem to have an insatiable need for some bit of territory over which they have absolute control (Figure 12.14). It thus becomes the responsibility of architects and planners to build this privacy and individual control into urban areas. But the chaotic, sprawling sub-

Fig. 12.15 Although this mural graces a Bay Area Rapid Transit station, it suggests that BART was not viewed as a gift from heaven by all the people of San Francisco.

ubs with which we are familiar need not be chaotic or sprawling. Preservation of some open space through parkland, agricultural reserves, scenic easements, and cluster zoning (see Chapter 20) can provide breathing space and some sense of relationship between manmade and natural forms. Long-range regional planning is imperative before any amelioration of the grimmer aspects of urban life can be hoped for. With some idea of which areas should grow, when, and how, transport problems can be anticipated and included in long-range plans.

The present environmental problems of urban areas are not insoluble, however. Indeed there is every reason to expect that there will be successful cities in our future if we take the long overdue step of infusing a few billion dollars into a full-scale study of the total environment of cities. We need to know how transportation systems can be designed to meet the needs of *people* (Figure 12.15); what makes one neighborhood exciting to live in and another boring; how we can make the best use of space in our urban designs; what environmental factors are involved in chronic mental problems and how they can be controlled; what human needs are not met in present housing, both old and new.

These are questions that can be approached logically and answered rationally; the solutions can then be considered in any future plans for redesigning old cities or building new ones. There will soon be too many of us to continue the cruel idiocy of trial-and-error experimentation with people's lives, especially at a time when more people are moving from the country to urban areas than ever before. By the year 2000, it is estimated that over three fourths of the American people will live in towns and cities with populations of over 5000. If we start now to solve the age-old environmental problems of cities there is a chance that these cities may be not only habitable but enjoyable.

FURTHER READING

Costonis, J. J., 1974. *Space adrift, landmark preservation and the marketplace.*
University of Illinois Press, Urbana. Some answers to the problem of rehabilitation versus urban renewal.

Detwyler, T. R., et al., 1971. *Urbanization and environment, the physical geography of the city.* Duxbury Press, Belmont, California. A good detailed
review of the reciprocal effects of city and environment.

Draper, P., 1973. "Crowding among hunter-gatherers: the !Kung bushmen."
Science **182,** pp. 301–303. Crowding per se may not be the whole explanation for urban violence.

Gill, D., and P. Bonnett, 1973. *Nature in the urban landscape: a study of city
ecosystems.* York Press, Baltimore, Maryland. Would you believe four
hundred coyotes in Los Angeles?

Hall, E. T., 1966. *The hidden dimension.* Doubleday, Garden City, New
York. Incisive examination of man's private and public use of space.

Jacobs, J., 1965. *The death and life of great American cities.* Random House,
New York. A common-sense point of view that cuts through much of the
persiflage surrounding city planning.

Mumford, L., 1961. *The city in history.* Harcourt, Brace & World, New York.
Leisurely and thorough, Mumford blends scholarship and style.

Prescott, J. W., 1975 "Body pleasure and the origins of violence." *Bull.
Atomic Scient.* Nov., pp. 10–20. Discusses the interrelationships of sensory pleasure and violence.

Rudofsky, B., 1969. *Streets for people; a primer for Americans.* Doubleday,
New York. Well illustrated book pointing out the use of streets as urban
space.

Tunnard, C. and B. Pushkarev, 1963. *Man-made America: chaos or control?*
Yale University Press, New Haven. If you read any book on this list, read
this one. Beautifully thought out and illustrated, it gives penetrating insight into our attack upon the environment in the guise of urbanization.

CHAPTER THIRTEEN

TRANSPORT: LIFELINE
AND NOOSE

CITIES HAVE BECOME so vast that any vestige of self-sufficiency they may once have claimed has long since disappeared. In order to function they rely completely on complex transport systems to move their managers, workers, raw materials, goods, and services. But these transport systems are also responsible for many of the urban ills that threaten the system they support. The dual nature of transport as a lifeline and a noose is a problem rooted in the past.

ENVIRONMENT AND THE EVOLUTION
OF TRANSPORTATION

Although each of the successive modes of transport has had its impact upon the environment, the environment in turn has had a definite role in shaping and directing both the type of transport and its lifespan. To see this in its historical perspective let us examine the interaction of transportation and environment in the United States since 1800.

WAGON ROADS

One of the most important early innovations in the United States was the development of a sturdy, commodious wagon by German settlers in the Conestoga Valley near Lancaster, Pennsylvania. Freely adapted from the crude wagon of their homeland, the Conestoga wagon quickly came into wide use in the early nineteenth century to transport freight between the rapidly growing cities of the Eastern Seaboard. Settlement followed the easy wagon routes, north along the Connecticut and Hudson Rivers, southwest following the Great Valley, and west along the James and Rappahannock Rivers into western Virginia and Maryland. This developing country was not trackless, however; buffalo, elk, and other large game had long followed the easiest grades over mountain passes and along river valleys. These trails were used by the Indians and finally by the white settlers with their wagons. Other trails were cut and developed into wagon roads by army campaigns—Braddock's and Forbes' roads to the forks of the Ohio and later Daniel Boone's wilderness road that led over the Cumberland Gap into the frontier country of Kentucky beyond.

POST ROADS

As the wilderness trails extended westward, the people remaining behind needed more than single-file tracks or crude wagon roads; all-weather roads able to handle heavy freight traffic all year round became imperative. Using a roadbuilding technique developed by a Scotsman named McAdam, a paved road was laid between Philadelphia and Lancaster in the late 1700s. It was soon followed by the National Post Road leading west from Washington roughly parallel to the present Interstate 70. Macadam pavement in the early nineteenth century did not mean asphalt or concrete, of course, just a graded layering of crushed stone. But anything that replaced mud, dust, and frozen ruts was a welcome improvement. Because the federal government was loath to subsidize this construction, such improved roads were opened as toll roads. In fact, around 1800 such a speculative fever took hold that nearly 6000 miles of toll roads were authorized in New York State alone. But the resulting high rates for transport of freight spurred the development of another transportation innovation of the early nineteenth century—canals.

CANALS AND RIVERBOATS

Greatly interested by the enthusiastic development of canals throughout Europe, especially in France and England, speculators were ready to compete with toll roads in the growing business of transportation. Politicians were also eager to open new areas to settlement. Their attitude came in part from the general enthusiasm for growth and progress, but also from the handsome profits to be made from speculation in land once its value was increased by improved access.

In 1825 the Erie Canal, which connected the Great Lakes to New York City, was constructed for $7.5 million. This was the first of many steps that ultimately made New York City the largest and most important city in the Western Hemisphere. In nine years tolls had paid off both construction cost and interest for the canal; travel time between New York and Buffalo was reduced from twenty to eight days, and freight rates cut from $100 to $10 per ton. Small wonder that the next two decades saw an unprecedented wave of canal construction; over 1700 miles of canal were built in Pennsylvania alone, while Baltimore eagerly invested $11 million in the B & O Canal.

In 1811, Robert Fulton, inventor of the steamboat, formed the Mississippi Steamboat Company to carry shipping between Pittsburgh and New Orleans. Soon steamboats were on the Ohio, Mississippi, and Missouri Rivers and shipping grew rapidly, greatly increasing the importance of New Orleans and the new towns of Memphis, St. Louis, Nebraska City, Council Bluffs, Leavenworth, and St. Joseph. But by 1860 the heyday of the steamboat and the canals as major forms of transportation in the United States had come and was about to pass, doomed by the rapidly expanding railroads.

THE RAILROAD

In 1825, the year the Erie Canal opened, Colonel John Stevens built a steam locomotive. Within four years the Baltimore and Ohio Railroad connecting the Atlantic Seaboard and the Ohio Valley opened for business. The options of post road, canal, riverboat, or rail that were successively offered to the East were for many years unavailable to the trans-Mississippi West. Until the railroads could span this almost unsettled vastness, animal power was the only practical form of transportation. The Conestoga wagons with their high sides, large size, and canvas-covered tops were still the first choice of settlers pushing west from the river towns of Independence, St. Joseph, and Leavenworth; later, similar wagons made by Murphy, Carson, and the Studebaker brothers joined in opening the West to trade and settlement. The Oregon, Bozeman, and Santa Fe Trails and the Central Overland Road, developed in part by Army surveyors to establish and service outlying forts, were the most heavily used.

Soon, however, the railroads had pushed west to the Missouri River, and having eclipsed all but the Erie Canal in the East, began to compete with the steamboat trade on the western rivers. New cities such as Chicago, St. Paul, and Omaha, with rail connections to the East and serving as jump-off points for travel farther west, rapidly began to outshine the older river towns of Nebraska City, St. Joseph, and Leavenworth. Steamboats were slow and, because they were obliged to follow the rivers, indirect. Like the earlier toll roads in the East, their rates were high enough to be easily undercut by the railroads.

The impact of the railroad on the West was immediate and longlasting. The destruction of the vast buffalo herds was quickly accomplished from the base provided by the railroads, which made possible and profitable the transportation of hides, meat, and bones to the East. Not only did railroads have the power of life and death over any town along their prospective routes in the more settled East, but they could and did found towns en route further west, using land granted by the government. By 1900 the railroads reigned supreme, but the next actor was waiting impatiently in the wings. Henry Adams once said that his generation of Americans was mortgaged to the railroad; ours is mortgaged to the automobile.

HIGHWAYS AND THE LANDSCAPE

As the railroads took over trade once carried by wagons and stages, less attention than ever was paid to roads. Then, around the turn of the century, the rise of bicycling as a sport of fad proportions focused attention on the pitiful state of road maintenance and construction. The point was heroically made by the epic journey of Thomas Stevens, who bicycled from San Francisco to the East Coast in 1884, 3700 miles in three months. Today high school boys make coast-to-coast trips on their bicycles every summer, but they have the benefit of roads Mr. Stevens lacked. The League of American Wheelmen lobbied actively for construction of roads, ostensibly for bicycling, but they were cognizant too of the importance to the local farm economy of farm-to-market roads connecting outlying farms to railroads. By the time the automobile made its debut, the public had been aroused to the need for improved roads, and with the added stimulus of the car, good roads were soon forthcoming.

THE GROWTH OF HIGHWAYS

Initially towns were connected center to center for maximum accessibility. As long as there were few cars, there were no problems; traffic and parking were easily accommodated by two-lane interurban highways. These town-to-town roads gradually expanded into a network. The influence of local topography and land usage on their pattern is obvious to the road map reader. Even today you can easily identify a section of the country by the pattern of its highways. For example, as you can see from a road map, the roads in central Pennsylvania tend to arc southwest to northeast following the curving ridges and valleys of the Appalachian Mountains (Figure 13.1a); in Kansas, although the land is flat and roads could theoretically go in any direction, the land is all farmed, and since no one wanted a road to cross his field, the roads follow section lines with many right-angled turns, giving the appearance of a giant checkerboard (Figure 13.1b); in West Virginia the roads twist and turn as they move across a plateau heavily marked by streams and rivers (Figure 13.1c).

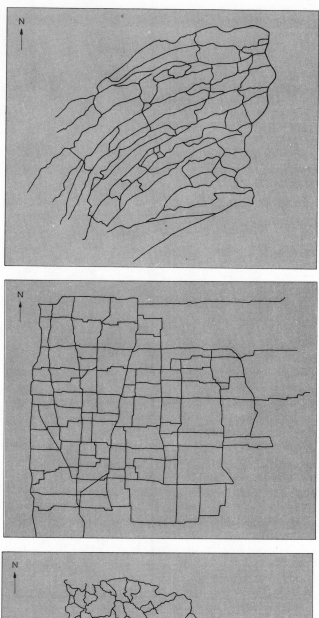

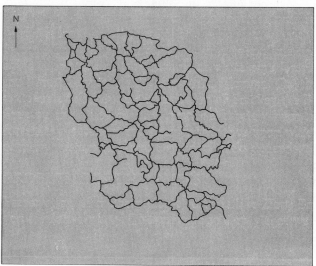

Fig. 13.1   (a) Roads extend over the landscape of least resistance, so their pattern on a map gives a graphic indication of the landforms of the area they traverse: in Pennsylvania, the roads follow the valleys between the ridges that curve from the southwest to the northeast. (b) In Kansas, where the land is relatively flat but intensively farmed, the roads follow section lines to avoid bisecting farmland, and so the pattern is a checkerboard. (c) In West Virginia, the landform is a deeply dissected plateau. Roads must descend steep slopes to cross rivers and narrow valleys and then climb back up to the plateau surface again, or else follow the winding routes of the watercourses. This results in a pattern of squiggly lines and explains why it takes so long to drive across West Virginia, a relatively small state compared to Kansas. Of course, interstate highways with their many bridges and minimal grades eliminate both the problem and the pattern.

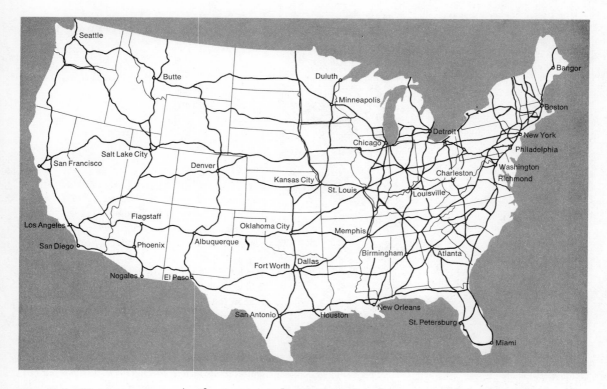

Fig. 13.2 The interstate highway system connects all major cities with over 41,000 miles of high-speed expressways.

As the towns and cities continued to grow, often along new or improved highways, and the congestion of their sprawl was added to the increasing number of cars, it became more difficult to get from one town to another. As more and more people became mobile, both through their possession of automobiles and their widening spheres of interest, they were no longer satisfied to drive from town A to town E through B, C, and D, but wished to go from town A directly to town E. As truck transport developed and began to give the same competition to the railroads that they had given to the rivers and canals, still more pressure developed for through traffic routes that bypassed the congested towns and cities. Their construction was begun in the 1930s in the more densely populated areas and continued after World War II.

But population growth and commercial development began to attack these bypasses almost as soon as the concrete was dry; clearly the country needed roads that separated opposing traffic, controlled access, and had separated intersections. Divided lanes were available long before the automobile; Commonwealth Avenue in Boston is an example. But the Bronx River Parkway in New York, the Merritt Parkway in Connecticut, and the Pennsylvania Turnpike in Pennsylvania were the first major roads in the United States to combine all three characteristics and become expressways. About the same time, Germany began her system of autobahns, planned by teams of engineers and architects who were sensitive enough to environmental considerations to include nesting places for birds in their bridges. When World War II broke out, road building came to a halt for six years. But afterwards, there was a rash of toll expressway or turnpike building, mostly in the northeastern United States. Then in 1956 the federal government began an enormous program of interstate expressways designed to connect virtually all cities with 50,000 or more population (Figure 13.2). Over 41,000 miles of these limited access divided highways were to be provided. The cost has grown to $60 billion, and the completion date of 1972 has been extended indefinitely. As a result of the interstate system, we have gone the full cycle in many cities, from roads built from city center to city center, to bypasses, and back to downtown expressways.

HIGHWAY DESIGN

Modern expressways are planned with great care and the roadways fitted to the landscape according to very specific rules. Unfortunately, until quite recently these rules had nothing to do with the particular aesthetic values of the countryside over which the expressways were rolling. The route was, and sadly still is in many places, determined by the expense of a particular route modified by its projected use. If this directed that an expressway should go through an historic site, a grove of redwoods, a state park, a marsh, or a pond, all were sacrificed to the supposed greater good of the transportation corridor that replaced them.

The National Environmental Policy Act (NEPA) now requires an environmental impact statement (EIS) for any project receiving federal funding. The EIS has been helpful in drawing attention to the environmentally destructive routings of many highway projects and its hearings provide an opportunity for some public contribution to the decision-making process.

Expressways and standard two-lane roads are blueprinted as carefully as a building; every drain, curve, grade, ramp, overpass, or underpass must be specified. This can result in a well-engineered route with no sharp curves or steep grades. The choice between an attractive road in harmony with the landscape and one that seems to have been carelessly laid down lies with the designing engineer. A properly designed road must be articulated horizontally, vertically, and laterally with the countryside it traverses.

Only rarely can roads be set arrow-straight onto a landscape; even when they can, as on a coastal plain or a plateau, this is usually undesirable because the monotony is dangerous to the driver. Most roads are designed on the basis of tangents (straightaways) and curves, much like the tracks of model trains, which come in straight and curved pieces. Engineers fit

287

Fig. 13.3 By fitting long straightaways and short curves together, a road appears to lurch drunkenly across the landscape.

these tangents to the curves to carry the road along the proper route, climbing or avoiding hills, approaching towns or rivers. When long tangents and short curves are used the road looks awkward and the curves appear too suddenly (Figure 13.3); the driver is alternately lulled and forced to react. One alternative is to shorten the tangents and lengthen the curves; this improves the driver's reaction, but it is as difficult to fit in short tangents as it is short curves.

Perhaps the best alternative, at least in hilly country, is a continuous curvilinear configuration in which the road constantly curves gently to make the best fit with the landscape (Figure 13.4). Such roads are no more difficult to build, although they may be slightly more expensive to design. But a road with long tangents and short curves may ultimately cost more because of a greater accident rate and because of the potentially greater expense of fitting the road to the landscape by cutting and filling —a process that can be exceedingly expensive. Aesthetically, in the proper topographical setting, a continuous curvilinear design creates a far more attractive harmony between manmade and natural environments than any alternative.

Interstate expressways by law, and most other federal and state routes in practice, have grades limited to 5 percent—that is, a five-foot rise in 100 running feet. This vertical fitting of road to landscape can also be achieved by tangents, curves, and curvilinear design. Often a road using the long tangent and short curve approach in its horizontal alignment does the same thing in the vertical plane. The result is a jumble

of awkward transitions: downhill runs that seem to bend sharply at the bottom, uphill segments that break into nowhere at the crest of a hill (Figure 13.5). With a curvilinear or at least a long curve and short tangent design, these awkward transitions can be avoided; once more the gain is both in aesthetic appearance and safety.

The first expressways followed natural contours and curved in harmony

Fig. 13.4 Continuous curvilinear roads present a much more graceful fitting of a highway into the landscape. (Thomas Airviews)

Fig. 13.5 Highways must be carefully aligned in the vertical as well as the horizontal plane. The grade transitions in this road are visually if not physically too abrupt.

Fig. 13.6 Winter rains constantly wash debris onto this road surface, closing it with nearly every storm.

with the landscape. But these roads, although their windings and curves might have been pleasing on foot or in a Model T, were exceedingly dangerous when packed with fast cars driven by people in a hurry. Relying on the power of earthmoving machines, road engineers replaced these parkways with beeline routes cutting through hills and rolling on filled beds over valleys, with no attempt to repair, much less avoid, the damage to the landscape. Steep cuts were not only ugly scars that defied revegetation (Figure 13.6) but, prone to erosion, they showered the roadway with rock and mud with every rain, and required constant maintenance. Today state and even local roads are constructed to avoid excessive cutting and filling, even if the road is longer as a result. Necessary cuts are beveled and planted, improving their appearance and stabilizing them against erosion.

ROADSIDE PLANTING

Most interstate expressways have plantings in suburban areas, at intersections, and occasionally along lengthy segments. These are well-intentioned and expensive, but sometimes very poorly executed. The whole point of expressway landscaping is to fit the road into the landscape with as little disturbance as possible to the natural environment and at the same time, by ensuring good visibility, to allow maximum speed and safety.

Two areas in which many roadside plantings fail are scale and appropriateness. While it is a fine gesture for a local garden club to help beautify our expressways by planting pansies in the median strip, the effect is utterly lost at fifty-five miles per hour. Many landscaped plantings also fall into this category. Trees or shrubs are strung out in lines or isolated groups that even when mature will look scattered and chaotic. Mass planting on a bold scale can overcome this problem. Ironically the most lavishly planted highways are found in the semidesert of California, where nothing would grow along the freeway without extensive irrigation. But mass planting of lush ivies, bayberry, oleander, iceplant, and other ornamentals makes some of the Los Angeles and San Francisco freeways among the most beautifully landscaped in the world (Figure 13.7).

This brings up the other planting problem—appropriateness. If the planting is in a dry region where native shrubs are few or lack the proper scale but where irrigation is available, exotic ornamentals might very well be appropriate. In a well-watered region with an abundance of native trees and shrubs, it makes little sense aesthetically, ecologically, or economically to plant expensive exotics. The Long Island Expressway, for example, runs for much of its length through an oak-pine scrub forest.

Fig. 13.7 Because of the equitable climate and the need for irrigation over half of the year, California freeways are among the most beautifully and lavishly landscaped roads in the world.

Instead of planting species native to this local forest, such as scarlet oak, bear oak, and pitch pine, to coordinate the highway with its environment, the "beautifiers" have planted little clumps of Austrian pine and tulip trees, which effectively divorce the road from its natural environment. So planted, the road could as well be in Maine or Georgia.

The great contemporary Brazilian landscape designer, Burle-Marx, trained in Europe like most of his countrymen, returned to Brazil and rebelled against the slavish use of European ornamentals in Brazilian parks and gardens whose landscaping ignored the incredible richness of the native Brazilian flora. Overcoming provincial prejudice, Burle-Marx used native materials with brilliant success. The same principle can be followed on American highways.

Another approach would be to allow natural revegetation to occur wherever possible. This would sharply reduce maintenance since plantings of ornamentals often require much tending. An example of this natural approach to highway planting can be seen on another Long Island highway, the William Floyd Parkway. Rather than removing the oak-pine woods evenly along the right of way, the designer made the grassy shoulder of variable width, sometimes stretching to the edge of the right of way, sometimes allowing trees to approach the road, giving a flexible, scalloped appearance that ties the road beautifully to the wooded land through which it passes.

An unplanned result of planting grass as a stabilizer along highway margins is that the lush pasture attracts deer, especially in heavily wooded country. The wild deer are easily frightened by headlights, and the casualties both of deer and motorists are high. Construction of fences has been helpful but is quite costly. An ecological solution to the problem would be to find an aesthetically pleasing roadside stabilizer or a planting that would be unpalatable or unattractive to large grazing animals.

THE ENVIRONMENTAL IMPACT OF HIGHWAYS

Because the development of highways in the United States has been gradual and roads have a historic lineage going back to cow tracks, game trails, or Indian paths, we tend to lose sight of the incredible impact road construction can have on undeveloped regions. A potentially dismal example is provided by the construction of the trans-Amazon highway. The 2000-mile highway is being built through one of the last and largest undeveloped forests in the world. Running 200 miles south of, but parallel to, the Amazon River, it will connect Recife and João Pessoa in Brazil with the borders of Peru and Bolivia. Another route, this one north-south, is being constructed to connect Santarém on the Amazon with Cuiabá. Motivated by the Brazilian government's long-standing and reasonable desire to develop the heart of Brazil, but precipitated by the plight of the impoverished population of drought-stricken northeastern Brazil, the road, much of it two-lane and unpaved, is mostly complete and will allow people from northeastern Brazil to resettle in Amazonia. Apparently, a magnificent opportunity to plan an orderly and ecologically sound development of the Amazon Basin is being lost in a boom syndrome reminiscent of the frontier days of the American West: hurried construction of a transportation route "opening" the frontier; wild speculation in lands bordering it; vague promises of riches for the lucky settlers; and potential environmental disaster likely for all. At present rates of clearance, the entire Amazon rain forest will be cut in thirty-five years and ill-fated attempts made to farm the plinthite soils (see Chapter 1). It needn't be this way, of course, and there is still time for the Brazilians to pull the fat from the fire. But considering the time it took the United States to begin to appreciate the impact of our highways and other manipulations on the environment, a change in attitude is unlikely, at least until the resource has been exploited and destroyed. Despite our accomplishments in environmental rehabilitation and restoration (see Chapter 21), the Amazonian rain forest, once destroyed, will not be restored in our lifetime.

EXPRESSWAYS IN THE CITY

Despite the formidability of building a road through the Amazon rain forest, building roads in rural areas is relatively uncomplicated compared with the problems that arise from planning the constructing expressways through urban areas. No one, rich or poor, wants to sacrifice his property, house, or business to highway construction. Road designers knew that city parks were the least vigorously defended parcels of land in most cities; consequently interstate expressways were invariably routed through them.

After park upon park had been compromised, if not ruined, people began to protest, first on their own, and then with the help of their lawyers. This led to a Supreme Court decision in 1971 ordering a review of a segment of I-40 through Overton Park in Memphis, Tennessee to determine whether approval to route the highway through the park was "arbitrary, capricious, an abuse of discretion, or otherwise not in accordance with law." Routine violation of parklands is now somewhat less likely.

THE HIGHWAY IN THE GHETTO

Another promising corridor for the routing of urban expressways has been slum districts. The poor, it was considered, could always find another slum or be relocated in some form of public housing. The land left over from expressway construction could be redeveloped with luxury apartment or high-rise office buildings and the whole package called urban renewal. But the poor are beginning to find their tongues too, and as a result urban expressway construction in ghettos is also being blocked.

Citizen protest over leveling of parks and slums has brought about some rethinking of the role of highways in the urban environment. Expressway construction is a big business backed by a formidable lobby of construction firms, labor unions, steel and concrete producers, car manufacturers, gasoline and tire dealers, and organizations of car owners. The more roads we build, the more workers are employed, the more profits are made. If cities are congested, the reasoning runs, we need more expressways to handle the traffic. When these are filled we add more lanes, then double decks, then parallel roads. Ignoring the limited capacity of city streets, more expressways bring more congestion.

CARS AND CITIES

Gradually the limited capacity of cities to absorb automobiles is being recognized and beltways are being constructed to divert cars away from the city's center rather than force them through the city's business district. Relieved of the burden of through traffic, a city can then have the flexibility to innovate. Some cities have separated cars from people, constructing underground plazas and shopping malls. Ironically it is usually the people who are put underground, leaving the vehicular traffic to enjoy the light and air of the surface. Another possibility followed by many cities across the country has been to ban all vehicular traffic from certain main shopping streets, converting them into pedestrian malls with sidewalk cafés, parks, paved areas, planters—an exciting inducement to shop in the adjoining stores (Figure 13.8). Adequate peripheral parking is, of course, essential to the success of any such plan.

Any alternative to expressways through cities must involve mass transit. Buses, subways, and suburban trains have long been belittled by the highway lobby for obvious reasons. One result has been the neglect of mass transit, which has discouraged its use to the point of reinforcing the opinion that mass transport is outmoded and inadequate, and that the automobile is the only transit of the future.

The key to the issue of more highways versus more mass transit seems to lie in the Highway Trust Fund. Set up by Congress and financed by a special gasoline tax, this fund grows by $5 billion a year and has been, until very recently, devoted solely to constructing more highways—attracting more cars to pay more gasoline taxes to build more highways. While many apparently feel that this large user's fund should be spent only on highways, others feel that at the very least cities should have the option of using their share to refurbish, rebuild, and construct mass transit systems in lieu of more highways.

Consequently changes in the act that established the Highway Trust Fund now allow a small portion of the fund to be used for mass transit programs in cities across the country. But considering the billions that have been poured into highway construction in the last twenty years, compared to the miniscule amounts used to support mass transit, it should hardly come as a surprise to learn that the use of mass transit systems has declined drastically. In 1929 the average American used public transport 115 times per year; in 1958, fifty-four times. The reason is simple—mass transportation has not kept pace with the automobile in its technology, convenience, or comfort. When an effort is made to provide convenient, clean, and comfortable *rapid* transit, including buses, trains, and subway cars, many commuters are happy to leave their cars at home.

The problem is deeper than simple merchandising, however: environmental considerations and their psychological ramifications enter the picture. Very often the only privacy a typical white-collar worker has is the daily commuting trip in his car. The road may be jammed bumper to bumper but the personal space of his car is *his*. It represents a glimmer of independence in an otherwise thoroughly routine life. For this reason there will always be those who drive their cars as close to their work area as possible. But even they can be accommodated at least in part by some form of mass transport. Large parking lots or garages on the edges of a city would allow suburbanites to drive part way, since mass transport is often ineffective in low density suburbs, and take a train, bus, or subway to the central business district. This approach is now being tried in Hartford, Connecticut. Comparing capacity in persons per lane per

Fig. 13.8 Once typically filled with traffic and noise, this street in the business district of Fresno, California has been transformed into a pedestrian mall. (Fresno County and City Chamber of Commerce)

hour, cars on a city street can carry 1400 people, buses 7500. On an expressway cars can handle 3500 people, buses 15,000, rapid transit trains 60,000.

ORVS AND AMENITY

Off-road vehicles (ORVs) are a logical product of America's fascination with gadgets, greatly increased leisure time, and swelling affluence. While the motorcycle is hardly new, snowmobiles, trail bikes, and all-terrain vehicles have been introduced in the last fifteen years and air-cushion devices hover offstage (Figure 13.9). These innovations came upon us suddenly, catching lawmakers unawares with the environmental and social problems caused by thoughtless use of these vehicles.

Perhaps the most obvious problem is noise. Like the pleasure a small boy gets from taping a piece of carboard to the wheel of his tricycle to make a noise, a considerable part of the pleasure in operating many types of ORVs is the sense of power communicated by noise. A snowmobile's whine sounds like a chain saw and can be heard for miles.

While the noise of an ORV is an aesthetic minus for the general public, it may be pathological for a consistent user. Partial hearing loss has been reported in 85 percent of the adult Eskimo population in the Baffin area of northern Canada. Finding the snowmobile more efficient than the traditional dogsled, Eskimo hunters in many parts of the Arctic have increased their mobility, spending ten to twelve hours per day on their vehicles. But the cost in physical disability is apparently going to be high.

Since the various kinds of ORVs can invade any environment, their widespread use allows little respite for people who prefer natural sounds in natural environments. The industry is quite capable of decreasing the noise level of ORV engines by at least 50 percent; perhaps it would do so if it were convinced that the public would buy a quiet ORV. Unfortunately, restrictive legislation will probably be necessary to force industry to act.

Erosion and destruction of vegetation are the next most important effects of ORVs. In some parts of California almost 60 percent of the vegetation has been destroyed by motorcycle use. Mountain meadows, grasslands, and deserts are particularly attractive to ORV users and particularly sensitive to their impact (Figure 13.10). Snowmobiles are especially hard on tree seedlings and golf greens. Littering is, of course, extended by ORV users far beyond the edges of major highways and settled areas.

Game harassment, while practiced by only a few, is likely to become a critical problem. Animals in the dead of winter or carrying young are likely to be weak, and harassment can cause death or abortion of young.

Fig. 13.9 With constant use by ORVs, grassy slopes become denuded, then begin to gully. A few more years of this treatment will destroy this hillside.

Streams and lakes with limited accessibility during summer can be quickly and methodically fished out in midwinter, and nesting birds can be encouraged to abandon their nests if frequently disturbed. Finally, destruction of vitally needed predators—foxes, coyotes, wolves, and mountain lions—particularly in remote areas, is becoming a problem.

Vandalism, whether cutting fences or breaking and entering of isolated cabins, is still another problem. From the point of view of the ORV operator, safety is of some concern. Anyone, young or infirm, can get very far from help in an ORV. Reckless driving resulted in 82 fatalities in the 1969–70 snowmobile season alone.

But perhaps the most difficult problem is how to meld the conflicting interests of a cross-country skier and a snowmobiler, or a backpacker and a trail biker.

There are several ways to lessen these problems: legislation setting up rules and regulations that can be enforced by required registration fees for all ORVs; vehicle use zoning for ecologically sensitive areas, seasonal prohibition of use where necessary, and channeling of use into established routes or trails; federal legislation requiring uniform standards for safety equipment, permissible noise, and pollution control devices. There is no reason why ORV enthusiasts and nonmobile outdoorsmen cannot both satisfy their inner needs, but quite obviously this cannot happen without regulations and standards, strictly enforced.

Fig. 13.10   This is becoming a common sight in many arid zone states where ORVs operate anywhere their drivers please without considering their environmental impact. When this slope becomes too rutted to use safely, there is always another somewhere else.

WE TAKE TO THE AIR

For many cities the epitome of growth and progress is the size of their airport, the number of planes landing and taking off, the number of people who funnel through their transportation centers to other parts of the nation or world. These activities *do* generate money, which accrues to the city, but the problems generated by airport complexes are seldom faced realistically or defined economically. Air and noise pollution will be discussed in Chapter 18. The problems that concern us here are the congestion caused by overuse of ground facilities and the huge space demands of expanding international airports.

No city in the world has more congested airports than New York. Kennedy, LaGuardia, and Newark airports, all bursting at the seams, must handle such dense air traffic that holding patterns often have dozens of jets endlessly circling the metropolitan area waiting to land. Something is clearly wrong when you can fly from Miami to New York in two hours, then be obliged to circle the airport for one hour before landing.

There is no reason why more people cannot fly direct to Europe or South America from any number of cities throughout the United States. Many cities have large airports capable of handling much of the traffic that passes through the ever-narrowing funnel of New York's Kennedy Airport. Why, if you live in Altoona, shouldn't you be able to fly from nearby Pittsburgh to London or Rome? Couldn't customs facilities be set up at these airports as well as at Kennedy, Boston, and Washington? If this feeder traffic were diverted, present overcrowded facilities would be adequate until more basic technological changes could be worked out.

But the standard answer to overcrowding at airports is to expand them or build new ones; consequently the search went on for a fourth huge jetport for the New York area for some years. No matter where a fourth jetport would be located in the New York metropolitan area, even if a preexisting military base were used, the environment of miles of surrounding countryside would degenerate through the resulting development, noise, and air pollution. But the sky can accommodate just so many planes in holding patterns before the whole system breaks down into chaos.

Since each new generation of jet planes is larger, requiring longer runways, and ever-larger terminals to accommodate increasing loads of passengers, economic alternatives to the present system must be found. But if huge airports are to remain the standard in air transport, efficient mass transit systems capable of moving goods and passengers quickly to and from the airport, whatever its distance from the city, become imperative. At present, only two American cities, Cleveland and Boston, have this kind of link with their airports. The time for developing solutions to the problems of congestion and space is growing short. While New York was casting about for a site for a huge new jetport, other cities were eying natural environments that could not be replaced: Chicago, Lake Michigan; San Francisco, its bay; and Miami, the Everglades. With truly *rapid* transit systems, regional airports could be constructed at some distance from congested cities, pooling the resources of a region and at the same time sparing those natural environs of large cities that still exist.

FUTURE FORMS OF TRANSPORT

The future promises more than refurbished trains or air-conditioned buses, for there is no reason why technology cannot be applied to the problem of moving people rapidly *on* the surface of the earth as well as above or beyond it. Popular science magazines are filled with fascinating schemes for magnetogasdynamic propulsion, gravity tubes, and various suspension systems—air cushion vehicles, magnetic suspension systems— all of which are based on perfectly plausible physical principles capable of working if technology is assisted with investment dollars. More immediately useful are highspeed trains capable of moving people from one end of megalopolis to the other at 150 miles an hour. The Tokaido Express, which runs between Tokyo and Osaka in Japan, is probably the best example of the application of present technology to a standard form of transport. The Express has also supplied some interesting statistics: passenger traffic is growing at the rate of 26 percent per year; at the same time air traffic between Tokyo and Osaka has fallen from 22 to 6 percent of the travel load. This certainly is a boost for supporters of highspeed rail connections between nodes in the megalopolises of the United States. Such connections, it seems, would also ease congestion at airports and perhaps reduce the pressure for more and larger airport facilities.

But to achieve even 150 miles an hour in a train requires complete rebuilding of the roadbed. With some modifications of the existing track the metroliner service between Washington and Boston has become not only possible but profitable, weaning commuters away from their cars if not their commuter planes. Speeds rivaling those in Japan must await further roadbed improvements, though.

A much more modest intracity program often called dial-a-ride involves small vehicles carrying ten to twenty-five passengers. Passengers phone in their request for service. A computer directs the driver over a flexible route that delivers the passengers to their destinations with the minimum of detours. Unlike mass transit systems, capital costs are low; most of the cost goes into operating expense and salaries. Thus, like mass transit, this doorstep transit cannot pay its own way. If we are to have some form of efficient mass transit, we must abandon the old notion that fares must support the operation and regard transit as a public service to be supported from general tax funds like fire, police, and hospital services and public schools. Because federal and state governments are unwilling to continue their subsidy of the capital costs of transit systems into the operation stage, most cities have opted for huge, expensive, heavy rail systems, which may not always be the best choice.

One thing is certain, however: there is no *single* answer to the transport problem in urban areas. To preserve the fabric of cities and restore some degree of amenity to their environment, the ultimate solution will probably involve mass transport systems designed to move people rather than vehicles within the city and from selected collecting points beyond the downtown area. It will require beltways that allow traffic to bypass the limited capacity grid of city streets. It must offer some system of pedestrian and vehicular separation, either by converting districts or neighborhoods into pedestrian islands, limiting the type of traffic or timing its access on other streets, or putting vehicular traffic underground, giving pedestrians their proper place in the sun.

It will certainly have to favor existing systems by giving priority to buses on streets and freeways, providing more express services, arranging better collection facilities to reduce walking distance and traveling time, increasing the frequency of service, augmenting crosstown routes, and increasing the expenses of automobile use by raising tolls and city parking charges.

But the most obvious answer to the transit problem has received the least attention: reduce the frequency of travel. At least 50 percent of white collar workers could work at home if given the right communication devices; 50 percent of all shopping trips could be eliminated by the same means. The telephone is after all a rather crude way to communicate. Cheaper and better conference calls, video display terminals, slow-scan video graphic systems, and videophones could help substitute moving information for moving people. The obstacles would be formidable, for polls indicate that most people want to live away from their jobs; but this is often the result of the negative attitude most people have about their work. Most work in today's society *is* boring. A four-day work week and staggered work hours might help. But it makes little sense to spend billions to construct a transit system and millions more to keep it running for four hours of intensive use per day.

RIGHTS OF WAY

The movement of goods and people requires corridors or rights of way, which traditionally have been devoted to a single use. No one would think of taking a casual stroll down an expressway or having a picnic on a railroad track. But there are other rights of way whose uses are not so clear-cut. The development of huge regional power plants has led to miles of power transmission lines. Pipelines, originally built to transport oil, now move natural gas, chemicals, and even coal, crushed and mixed with water.

THE ALASKA PIPELINE

In 1968 huge deposits of oil and natural gas were discovered in Triassic sediments some one to two miles below the tundra of Alaska's North Slope. Roughly 15 billion barrels of oil and 736 billion m^3 of natural gas are being tapped and transported to an increasingly energy-hungry market (see Chapter 11).

Since neither road, rail, nor convenient sea routes were available, a pipeline was built by the consortium of oil companies that is exploiting the field. The most direct route ran 125 miles over the North Slope, 90 miles over the Brooks Range, rising to 4800 feet at Dietrich Pass, then 350 miles over the interior plateau and across the Yukon River, 75 miles over the Alaska Range, crossing the Denali Fault, 100 miles across the Copper River basin, 40 miles over the Chugach Mountains, and finally 40 miles to Valdez, where tankers carry the crude to refineries in the Pacific Northwest, California, or to export markets. A staggering engineering feat considering the topography alone, the construction was complicated by permafrost (permanently frozen subsoil) over a portion of the route. Since the oil comes out of the ground at 82°C, there is the problem of melting the permafrost and rupturing the pipe. At least 83 million cubic yards of gravel were excavated for the route, and of course roads were constructed to allow the pipe to be transported and laid. Despite precautions in the crossing of known faults and rivers with highly variable flows, the prospects for future pipe rupture and contamination of a virgin wilderness with crude oil are great.

But what of the gas? Since Alaska will not allow it to be wasted by burning and demand for natural gas is growing, a pipeline will have to be built to carry gas as well as oil to markets. But there are no facilities for gas liquefaction in Valdez, nor are there special tankers available to carry liquefied gas to market; so the gas pipeline has been routed tentatively through Canada to the midwestern United States.

The ostensible point of the Alaska pipeline was to deliver its 1.2 million barrels a day to the West Coast, which was expected to need that extra volume by the time the pipeline and attendant facilities were completed. However a recession, increased oil prices, and lower projected demand suggest that no more than half the 1978 output can be effectively absorbed by this market. What to do with the surplus oil? It could of course be left in the ground to appreciate in value like money in the bank;

it could replace the foreign oil now being used, in part, in West Coast refineries; it could be shipped through the Panama Canal or around Cape Horn to eastern markets; it could be piped over the Rockies in new pipelines or unused natural gas lines; or it could be traded to Japan. Cynics suggest that despite the need for Presidential and Congressional approval of foreign sale, the last option was the original intent; domestic shortage or not, export provides the greatest profit. Oil is of course pumped out of the ground for no other reason.

MANAGEMENT OF RIGHTS OF WAY

Whatever commodity is being transported, rights of way must be managed so that the service they perform is not impeded by the environment. A basic reason for highway plantings, after all, is to stabilize the right of way by preventing rock falls or mud slides. Powerline and pipeline rights of way, which are often roadless, are usually covered with vegetation of some sort that must be managed to prevent damage to the facility. When land in well-watered areas is cleared, the disturbed ground is soon covered by weeds, then grasses, shrubs, and finally trees in succession. The goal of right of way management is to maintain vegetation at some particular stage in this succession, usually the grass or shrub stage.

According to Frank Egler, a distinguished plant ecologist who has studied plant succession and its manipulation for many years, the direction of the succession is greatly influenced by the types of plants already present at the time cultivation is ceased. If these can be manipulated, the end result can be both predicted and controlled.

The standard approach of power companies, pipeline operators, and highway departments has been to spray their rights of way with herbicides to kill trees and shrubs selectively, leaving only grass (Figure 13.11). This works well up to a point; shrubs and trees *are* temporarily eliminated. However, the sprayed trees and shrubs turn brown and become an unsightly fire hazard. Because the spray does not kill the roots of the unwanted woody plants they continue to sprout and spraying must be repeated every year or two. Even if these existing woody plants could be eliminated from the unnatural grasslands, seedlings would be a constant problem.

The blanket spraying operation presently favored by chemical companies and by many right of way operators has proven to be a mistake. Egler has demonstrated in trial plots and field observations that shrubs encouraged by the selective killing of competing trees form a much more stable ground cover than grass, and one that requires far less maintenance. In addition, shrubs provide a greater variety of browse and food for wildlife than grass. While highway rights of way are no place for grazing ani-

Fig. 13.11 When power lines follow line of sight routes over hills the resulting swath is an aesthetic disaster.

mals, other types of rights of way offer no such conflict of interest. Managed according to Egler's technique, a powerline or pipeline right of way would have a strip of low perennial plants—goldenrods and bracken fern —which can keep out tree seedlings with a little selective spraying. Beyond this there might be another strip of low shrubs—viburnum, shrub dogwoods, blueberries, and low junipers—and beyond these on the forest edge there might be alders, shrub willows, dogwood, and redbud. The particular species would, of course, vary from place to place as with highway shoulders and medians, but use of variety of plants from the natural flora would be the guiding principle everywhere.

Instead of the expense of spraying large amounts of herbicides over the entire area, shrubs could be maintained indefinitely by one man walking the right of way once every few years with a knapsack sprayer. Once the shrubs are established, maintenance may even be unnecessary, for seedlings of potentially competitive trees would be shaded out. One section of a powerline right of way in New York State covered with a shrub called sweet fern has had no maintenance for almost forty years. Since Egler estimates that close to 10 million acres in the eastern United States alone are being used as rights of way, any program that would increase their use by wildlife or even people would certainly be worth looking into in a progressively park-hungry world. In short, Egler's techniques would promote the highest conservation values for the lowest cost and meet the engineering needs for maintenance of the line. The delay in applying cological principles to rights of way management ultimately results from ignorance and apathy among the utility companies who, encouraged by chemical companies, view every shrub as a potential tree.

POWERLINE AESTHETICS

Power lines, unlike pipelines or roadsides, have one major aesthetic liability: their ugly towers, resembling overgrown erector sets, may completely dominate the countryside they traverse (Figure 13.12). In 1967, 7 million acres were taken up by powerline rights of way, and this figure is likely to triple in the near future unless alternatives are found.

But aesthetics are only part of the problem. The economics of high-voltage transmission lines is curious, to say the least. Since the conductors are not insulated, as the voltage on the line increases either the diameter of the wire or the number of wires must increase. If the wire dimensions are not increased the higher voltage leaks off in the form of corona discharge—the high-energy electrons that comprise the current leave the wire and charge the air. Since thick wire is expensive, heavy, and stiff, it is usually cheaper to use smaller towers and lines even if much electricity escapes as corona discharge. Most of the small diameter lines in use

Fig. 13.12 We do have a knack for ordering the chaos of nature. However, San Bruno Mountain will be around in some form or other long after these pylons have gone to meet their maker.

today were designed to operate at 50 to 60 percent of the critical voltage (the voltage at which corona discharge begins). But the high-voltage lines now being constructed or planned will operate at up to 83 percent of the critical voltage, resulting in more frequent, sometimes continual corona discharge. Today, 765 kilovolt lines are in operation and plans call for lines carrying 1500 kv.

Corona discharge causes a constant crackling and humming along the right of way and a blue glow at night. The high-energy electrons react with air pollutants as well as the gases characteristic of air to produce highly reactive atoms or molecules with unpaired electrons (free radicals) and ozone. The electromagnetic field interferes with TV and radio reception, which is a nuisance. More serious are possible effects on people who live under or within four hundred feet of a power line. So far reports on the effects of magnetic fields on humans are scattered and vague, for research has only begun. But in lieu of definitive answers, thousands of people who live in rural areas near high-voltage lines are being used as guinea pigs so that power companies can hustle their product to customers who have grown accustomed to electric carving knives, toothbrushes, and can openers.

The obvious solution would be to put the lines underground, like the utility lead-in wires of a house. But high-voltage lines are expensive to bury using present technology. If direct current transmission, which has much lower line loss, were used, it would have to be inverted back to alternating current for distribution, requiring expensive equipment. These problems are being researched; by the year 2000 gas dielectric, resistive cryogenic, and superconducting systems now under development will allow most power transmission lines to be placed underground.

If power needs continue to double every ten years, we shall have still more power lines. If they are constructed with some regard both to the appearance of their hardware and to the environment through which they pass, then many of the lines to be built in the next thirty years can at least be made as inconspicuous as possible until technology can give them a decent burial.

Although power lines, because of their high voltage, cannot be placed underground for the present, this is not true of the 220-volt lines that enter our houses or the lines strung up and down our streets (Figure 13.13). Fortunately large cities were forced at an early date to place their wires underground (Figure 13.14), simply because of the vast numbers of lines. Many new communities around the country are being constructed using underground utility lines from the start, as a selling point. The cost is either shared by contractor and utility or passed on to the buyer in the purchase price. One factor that prevents older neighborhoods from switching to underground lines is that the cost would have to be borne by the householder directly. Many would view this as unneces-

Fig. 13.13 Despite the passage of a hundred years and mind-boggling advances in technology, we still find it convenient and cheap to string our utility wires on poles everywhere but the downtown districts of our largest cities.

Fig. 13.14 Large cities were forced to eliminate overhead wires many years ago, as this 1881 cartoon suggests.

sary, particularly at a time when they must also replace septic tanks by expensive community sewage systems in a nationwide effort to combat water pollution.

Unfortunately, we have grown accustomed to seeing utility poles running along streets and highways, much as we have grown up with the sound of airplanes in the sky overhead. It is probable that if both were to disappear, most people would never know the difference, particularly when the landscape is ugly to begin with.

We have long accepted the idea that the ugliness and destruction that result from transportation are inevitable, the price we must pay for progress. This is part of the old struggle-against-nature syndrome, which seeks to overwhelm the environment by the brute force of technology and then to make that technology a convenient scapegoat for the environmental chaos that has resulted. Whenever the interaction of environmental factors is understood, technology can smooth the way and lead to a resolution of potential environmental conflicts. Each of the transportation modes we have discussed can be fitted into the natural environment with minimum adverse effects if we can develop an ecological sensitivity that allows the environment some basic rights. If these rights are protected and if we have help from technology, we can coexist with nature despite all our roads, airports, and transmission lines. But if we continue to ignore the modest demands the environment makes upon our use of it, then all the technology we can devise will not suffice to put right the endless problems we will generate.

FURTHER READING

Horowitz, J. C., 1974. "Transportation controls are really needed in the air cleanup fight." *Env. Sci. and Tech.* **8**(9), pp. 800–805. A critical analysis of present transit systems.

Newman, J., 1974. "A ride for everyone." *Env.* **16**(5), pp. 11–18. An innovative transit system.

Orski, K., 1973. "Fast trains." *Env.* **15**(3), pp. 6–10. A look at the possibilities of rail transport over the next twenty years.

Stratford, A. H., 1974. *Airports and the environment, a study of air transport development and its impact upon the social and economic well-being of the community*. St. Martin's Press, New York. A good summation.

Viets, J., 1975. "A space age comeback for the sailing cargo ship." *San Francisco Chronicle*, 24 November. A novel use of wind power.

Young, L. B., 1974. *Power over people*. Oxford University Press, New York. Long neglected, the side effects of overhead power lines are given a hard look here.

PART FIVE

THE THIRST FOR POWER

It takes energy to keep our increasingly complex civilization going. Traditionally we have divided energy sources into two categories: life-destroying and life-sustaining. Only recently have the two categories come together in two senses: the effort to harvest useful energy from potentially destructive nuclear fission/fusion and, ironically, the discovery that supposedly safe forms of energy may be dangerous. Perhaps we should remember that both the sword *and* the plowshare have a sharp edge.

CHAPTER FOURTEEN

RADIATION:

USE AND ABUSE

RADIATION IS THE emission and transmission through space of energy in the form of waves or particles. The radiation spectrum (Table 14.1) is a broad one, ranging from long radio waves to short and intense cosmic rays. While much of our concern is directed toward the more energetic gamma rays emitted by radioactive substances, there is increasing evidence that other portions of the electromagnetic spectrum may be hazardous as well.

MICROWAVES

Ever since the exciting discovery of radio waves early in this century, the tendency has been to explore and utilize the increasingly shorter waves in this portion of the electromagnetic spectrum, particularly the microwave region between 100 cm and 1 mm. During the 1940s it was found that the distance to a target could be determined by bombarding it with microwaves and timing the speed of their return. Radar has since been widely used not only by the military but at airports and harbors. Microwave technology has been applied to garage door openers, burglar alarms, diathermy machines, broadcasting satellites, ovens, and the microwave relay stations that transmit TV and telephone signals from coast to coast (Figure 14.1). In recent years the generation of microwaves from all these sources has proliferated to such an extent, particularly in urban areas, that some electrical engineers refer to the result as electronic smog.

Although we absorb microwave radiation, for many years scientists

311

Table 14.1
The Electromagnetic Spectrum *

TYPES OF RADIATION	APPROXIMATE WAVELENGTH (METERS)	ENERGY PHOTON (CALORIES)
Radio, TV	2×10^4	2.4×10^{-30}
	4×10^1	1.2×10^{-27}
Microwaves Radar		
	3.3×10^{-4}	1.4×10^{-22}
Infrared heat		
	7×10^{-7}	6.9×10^{-20}
Visible light		
	4×10^{-7}	1.2×10^{-19}
Ultraviolet		
	1.2×10^{-8}	3.8×10^{-19}
Short UV		
	5×10^{-9}	9.6×10^{-18}
X rays		
	1.2×10^{-11}	3.8×10^{-15}
Gamma rays		
	1×10^{-14}	4.6×10^{-12}
Cosmic rays		
	1×10^{-15}	4.6×10^{-11}

Visible			
	Red	6300–7600	
	Orange	5900–6300	
	Yellow	5600–5900	$\times 10^{-10}$ m
	Blue	4900–5600	
	Green	4500–4900	(10^{-10} m = 1 Ångstrom unit, Å)
	Violet	3800–4500	

* Source: Glenn H. Miller, 1972. *Principles of College Chemistry*. Canfield Press, San Francisco, p. 368.

Fig. 14.1 A postwar phenomenon, microwave relay towers have sprouted like mushrooms on hilltops all over the country.

thought that the energy involved was too slight to do any damage. One physicist described the probability of microwave damage in terms of getting a tan from moonlight. Consequently, in 1971, the United States government accepted as safe an exposure level of up to 10 milliwatts per square centimeter (one tenth of the exposure then considered the threshold of microwave damage). Much of the research on which this rather arbitrary standard was based involved exposing animals to microwaves with the energy of hundreds of milliwatts/cm². In contrast, research in the USSR followed up microwave worker complaints of headaches, dizziness, eyelid spasms, loss of hair and appetite, depression, and weariness. The pathology behind these rather vague and easily overlooked symptoms included endocrine changes, changes in blood pressure and blood protein, hallucinations, altered brain wave rhythm, slowing of heart rate, and cataracts. On the basis of this research, the maximum permissible dose of microwave radiation in the USSR and eastern Europe is .01 milliwatts/cm².

Subsequent research in the United States has claimed that cataracts on the posterior surface of the lens, normally an unusual site for cataracts, can be associated with relatively low levels of microwave radiation. One researcher has suggested that microwave radiation, by reducing the elasticity of tissues, may increase the incidence of certain forms of heart disease in areas where the background of microwave radiation is high.

Despite accumulating evidence of the potential harm of microwave radiation, government and industry, which may be concerned about expensive lawsuits should the maximum permissible dose be lowered, still insist that exposure to as much as 10 milliwatts/cm² is perfectly safe. Microwave ovens are allowed to leak up to 5 milliwatts/cm² even when properly operating and sealed (Figure 14.2). Apartments and offices in high-rise buildings near TV transmitters may receive as much as 2 milliwatts/cm². Although the safe dose level is not at all certain, it is plain that if the maximum allowed exposure of .01 milliwatts/cm² in the U.S.S.R. is too low, our standard of 10 milliwatts/cm² is definitely too high. Until the controversy is settled with hard data, a standard of 1 or even .1 milliwatts/cm² seems prudent.

Fig. 14.2 The microwave oven is becoming as common in homes as the TV, which it somewhat resembles, even to the leak of radiation.

THE NATURE OF IONIZING RADIATION

In 1895 Wilhelm Roentgen, working with an evacuated glass tube with metal electrodes at either end, found that an electric current applied to the electrode at one end of the tube emitted a mysterious ray through the electrode at the other end. The ray penetrated opaque substances, causing a zinc-sulfide screen to glow or emit light. Roentgen called his discovery the X-ray. Apparently the rays were given off by the metal of the tube plate when stimulated by an electric current. Not long after, Henri Becquerel placed some minerals containing uranium ore on a carefully covered photographic plate and found that they exposed the plate even in the dark by giving off rays similar to those noticed by Roentgen. Becquerel observed also that only minerals containing uranium showed this trait. Pierre and Marie Curie became interested in the phenomenon and found that in addition to uranium, thorium and radium were also radioactive or capable of giving off radiation.

Radium was of particular interest to physicists because it was found to

314

give off three kinds of radiation, called alpha, beta, and gamma. Alpha radiation was later identified as positively charged particles or protons, beta radiation was found to be negatively charged electrons, and gamma radiation was similar to the X-rays discovered by Roentgen.

When radium gives off alpha particles, a gas called radon is formed. The atomic weight (protons plus neutrons) of radium is 226. If an atom of radium loses an alpha particle with an atomic weight of 4, the remaining atom, radon, should have an atomic weight of 222. It does. Later it was found that when an atom of lithium is struck by a proton, it splits into two alpha particles accompanied by an energy release. The splitting of any atom into fragments is called fission. Although lithium yields little energy, other atoms like uranium yield tremendous amounts of energy when split.

ISOTOPES

Many elements were found to have stable forms called isotopes, slightly different in atomic weight but otherwise identical to the regular element. Heavy hydrogen or deuterium, which will someday be a source of fusion power (see Chapter 15), is one example. Irene Curie and her husband, Frédéric Joliot, found that when they bombarded aluminum with alpha particles, neutrons were given off and a strange species of phosphorus appeared. Normal phosphorus has no isotope, but the new species disappeared in fifteen minutes, leaving silicon! The Joliot-Curies had produced a new kind of isotope, an unstable one, called a radioisotope, which rapidly decayed into another element. Thus began a whole new era of artificially produced radioisotopes, an era that will continue as long as we manipulate atoms.

Today, radioisotopes have been produced for every known element, both intentionally for research and inadvertently in the fallout of atomic bombs. The variety of these radioisotopes is truly fantastic; not only do they vary in the kinds of radiation they emit, but in their longevity as well. Longevity of radioisotopes is described in terms of half-life, the length of time it takes for one half of their radioactivity to dissipate. Carbon-14 has a half-life of 5600 years: that is, after 5600 years one half of the radiation will be left, in 11,200 years one half of one half or one fourth is left, and so on. Other radioisotopes have much shorter half-lives than carbon-14: for example, strontium-90, 28 years; cesium-137, 27 years; iodine-131, 8 days. Because of their variety and inherent radioactivity, radioisotopes can be introduced into biological or geological systems and their movement followed by sensitive radiation counters, allowing a better understanding of many processes that involve the movement or cycling of atoms. This is possible because such radioisotope tracers, despite their radioactivity, behave chemically exactly like their normal analogs.

ATOMIC FISSION

The 1930s were heady times for nuclear physicists; discovery piled on discovery, providing new insights into the nucleus and its organization, and also suggesting further manipulations of atomic and subatomic particles. In 1939, Hahn and Strassman, German chemists, who had been looking at the chemistry of uranium when it was bombarded with slow neutrons, were surprised to find barium as one of the by-products. Uranium has an atomic number of 92, barium 56. Usually when uranium or any other element is bombarded with various particles, the atomic numbers of the by-products are rather close to the original. But barium is remote in every way from uranium.

Then Lise Meitner, an Austrian physicist, had the brilliant idea that when uranium absorbs a neutron it splits into two fragments. After all, lithium was known to split into two alpha particles. If so, what was the other fragment? The atomic number of krypton is 36 (92 – 56) and krypton turned out to be the other fragment. But the most exciting part of this disintegration of uranium lay in tallying the neutrons involved. Uranium has 146 neutrons in its nucleus. It absorbs one, making 147; but the two fragments, barium and krypton, have 82 and 47 respectively, totaling only 129. This leaves 18 neutrons, which are released when uranium undergoes fission. Suppose these neutrons were absorbed by other uranium atoms and more neutrons and energy were released as a result; we would have a chain reaction generating much energy and still more neutrons. The means of unlocking vast stores of atomic energy seemed at hand.

But there are three isotopes of uranium, U-238, U-235, and U-234. Did all three undergo fission, and if not, which one did? Pure uranium contains 99.3 percent U-238, 0.7 percent U-235, and 0.006 percent U-234; of these it was found that only U-235 underwent fission by capturing a slow neutron. Although U-238 captured fast neutrons, fission did not take place. This posed a problem in sustaining a chain reaction.

THE CHAIN REACTION

Slow neutrons cause U-235 to undergo fission but in the process it releases 18 fast neutrons per atom. These are captured by U-238 rather than U-235, stopping the reaction. What of the U-235 that absorbs neutrons? It is unstable and forms a new element, neptunium. This too is unstable and forms still another element, plutonium. Fortunately, plutonium fissions as well as U-235 and can be derived from the abundant

U-238 isotope, which is more easily obtained in quantity than U-235. A chain reaction once again seemed possible.

Why the excitement over this fission reaction? If one pound of U-235 or plutonium could be induced to undergo fission, it could release a sudden explosive force equivalent to 10,000 *tons* of TNT, or, if released gradually, power equal to 12 million kilowatt hours!

But *pounds* of U-235 or even plutonium are not easily obtained. Could neutrons somehow be slowed down, favoring their absorption by U-235 instead of U-238? By introducing such light elements as beryllium or carbon, which do not easily absorb neutrons, the velocity of a fast neutron can be slowed as it bounces off these light elements, thereby increasing the opportunity for its absorption by U-235.

Strangely enough, the capture of neutrons by a fissionable material is related to its volume, while the loss of neutrons is related to its surface area. But as a quantity of matter grows in size its volume increases faster than its surface area. Therefore, the larger the piece of fissionable material, the greater the number of neutrons retained for fissioning the U-235. This brings up the important concept of critical mass. The fissionable material must be large enough to retain sufficient neutrons to sustain a chain reaction. Since U-235 is so scarce, and we never use more than is necessary, what is the critical size for U-235? It depends in part on the purity, for impurities usually absorb neutrons as well as U-235 does. Early calculations indicated a critical mass of 2 to 200 pounds of U-235. This was like asking for a ton of hummingbird tongues! Several possibilities were open: first, processing tons of uranium ore to get pure uranium, then separating U-235 from U-238; second, bombarding U-238 with fast neutrons to get the fissionable plutonium; or, third, introducing purified moderators (beryllium or carbon) into a purified mixture of U-235 and U-238 to produce the desired quantity of slow neutrons.

While all these avenues were explored, the third produced the first sustained chain reaction. In a squash court at the University of Chicago an atomic pile (quite literally) was constructed of bricks of a purified form of carbon (graphite) between which pieces of uranium were placed. To prevent the possibility of too vigorous a reaction, control rods of cadmium, which absorbs neutrons, were inserted into the pile. The graphite blocks slowed the neutrons so that they could be absorbed by the U-235 and enough slow neutrons were available to sustain the reaction. On 2 December 1942 controlled atomic fission was achieved.

Once a sustained chain reaction was obtained, fabrication of an atomic bomb was relatively simple. Researchers only needed to prearrange several noncritical masses of fissionable material, each supplied with a neutron source, and fire them together into a critical configuration. In a fraction

Fig. 14.3   An atomic bomb test near Bikini Atoll, 1946. (Department of Energy)

of a second enough fission reactions could take place to cause an explosion of incredible dimensions (Figure 14.3).

THE HYDROGEN BOMB

Although a large atomic bomb is more than adequate to destroy any military target, a super or hydrogen bomb was developed, an example perhaps of the "bigger and better" fixation that seems to preoccupy modern society. The hydrogen bomb involved a fusion principle, just the opposite of the fission process in the atomic bomb. Instead of supplying neutrons to split atoms, heat was supplied to fuse atoms of hydrogen into helium, releasing huge amounts of energy. To do this required a seemingly impossible amount of heat—100 million °C! Since this level of heat was possible on earth only in an atomic explosion, it was necessary to trigger the fusion reaction by a fission reaction. So the H-bomb was created, concluding, we hope, the evolution of such grim devices.

Some years ago our attention was riveted to the destructive aspects of atomic energy by Hiroshima, Nagasaki, and a long series of tests in Nevada and the Marshall Islands. More recently, with the adoption of a test ban treaty by most nations, the peaceful uses of atomic energy have come to the fore, first with atomic fission power plants and then with the longer-term potential of power from hydrogen fusion (see Chapter 15).

RADIOACTIVE FALLOUT

We still have a legacy from that weapons-oriented past, however. Exploding nuclear devices created large quantities of radioisotopes, 15 percent of the total bomb energy. Because of the variety of material in the bombs and in the soil and water of the test sites, each explosion produced a broad spectrum of radioactive isotopes. Some of these are short-lived, lasting only fractions of seconds; others last minutes, hours, days. Still others last centuries, even millennia. But all emit radiation that is potentially harmful in a variety of ways.

Injected high into the stratosphere by the bomb explosions, the radioisotopes gradually sifted down, mostly over the Northern Hemisphere; a classic example of short-sighted experimentation without the least notion of the long-term effect on us or our environment.

FOOD CHAIN CONTAMINATION

Fallout from bomb testing programs in the 1960s was a particular problem in the arctic tundra, where the food chain is dramatically short. Caribou in the New World and reindeer in the Old World feed extensively on lichens in the winter. Because of the large amount of fallout in the Arctic (one fourth to one half of that in the temperate zone), and their slow rate of growth, lichens accumulate cesium-137 to a level well above that of other plants. When these radioactive lichens are eaten by caribou or reindeer the cesium-137 is concentrated still more in the meat of these animals. Should the caribou be eaten by a wolf or a hunter, the level increases again. The cesium-137 concentration doubles at each step in the food chain from lichen to caribou to us. This radiation concentration is especially clear in the arctic ecosystem because of the simplicity of the system and the limited socioeconomic development of the people —in the winter, caribou have only lichens to eat and the Eskimos have little to eat but caribou. Cesium-137 has a half-life of about thirty years; that is, one half of its radioactivity will dissipate every thirty years.

There are other examples of radioisotope concentration in ecosystems. Zinc-65 is readily absorbed by oysters, clams, and scallops in that order, not only by contact in their gill area but by ingestion of food as well, for diatoms absorb zinc-65 quite readily. In the late summer of 1956, after the spring H-bomb tests in the Pacific, some of the tuna caught by Japanese fishermen all over the Pacific were disturbingly radioactive. Radioactivity is measured by a device that counts the bursts of radiation from a radioisotope. One fish registered 4500 counts per minute (cpm) in its kidney, 1200 cpm in its stomach, 1800 cpm in its intestine, 2500 cpm in its liver, and 1200 cpm in its heart. Although there was little radioactivity in the edible flesh, there was concern about the sources of this radioactivity. An expedition sent into the Pacific by the Japanese government discovered that sea water over 1300 miles northwest of the bomb site used in the tests registered over 100 cpm. But that did not explain the excessive radioactivity in the tuna. The answer lay in food chain concentration, leading to potentially dangerous contamination of the top consumer in the chain, tuna. Over 457 tons of tuna with counts above 100 per minute were destroyed, causing panic in the fish-eating Japanese public and financial ruin to many in the tuna trade. Picture the consternation in the United States if beef were suddenly found to be radioactive!

Not all radioisotopes are produced so straightforwardly. In follow-up studies after bomb tests in the Marshall Islands, investigators were puzzled to find high levels of cobalt-60 in shellfish. But cobalt-60 was not one of the radioisotopes produced by the blast. Apparently some other blast-generated material, a neutron emitter, bombarded the natural isotope, cobalt-59, producing indirectly cobalt-60. The possibilities for harmful contamination are enormous.

Fortunately a test ban treaty has been signed by all nations testing atomic devices except China and France. Although 200 million tons of radioactive debris were thrown into the atmosphere to fall out over a period of several years, most of this material has finally come to rest since the virtual cessation of atmospheric testing. In 1970 the fallout of strontium-90 was only a twentieth of what fell in 1963. While massive fallout from testing is apparently in the past, the proliferation of nuclear and fossil fuel power plants threatens a continued source of airborne radioisotopes, although at a level far lower than that of the 1950s and 1960s.

RADIATION SICKNESS

All of us have come into contact with radiation through fallout from bomb tests. The levels, however, are very low and the effect is probably quite long-term, if it is measurable at all. What about the more spectacular exposure to radiation that leads quickly to sickness and often death?

IONIZATION

As we saw earlier, there are three major types of radiation, alpha, beta, and gamma. The first two are particles with relatively little energy; alpha particles are barely able to penetrate the skin and beta particles can penetrate only a millimeter or so. So under normal conditions these two types of radiation cause only skin burns, although when matter emitting either of these radiation types is inhaled or incorporated into the body significant damage may result. Gamma radiation, the third type, is the most energetic and potentially the most dangerous since it can penetrate most substances, certainly the human body, with ease.

Whether alpha, beta, or gamma, radiation usually affects living tissue by causing ionizations that, in turn, cause cellular damage. A cell is composed largely of water. When a water molecule is irradiated, an electron is knocked out of orbit. The ejected electron may then become attached to a normal water molecule, making it unstable. These unstable molecules split into hydrogen ions (H^+), hydroxide ions (OH^-), and the free radicals OH· and H·. Free radicals react with various molecules in the cell, which can then no longer function normally, and the cell dies.

MEASUREMENT OF RADIATION AND DOSE

Although many units are used to describe radiation in its various aspects, we need be concerned only with two types: disintegrations in a radioactive substance producing radiation and ionizations in air or tissue caused by these radiations. To measure the first type, we use the curie, defined as 3.7×10^{10} disintegrations per second and roughly equal to the radioactivity of one gram of radium together with its decay products. The radioactivity of materials is usually described in curies, millicuries (10^{-3}Ci),[1] microcuries (10^{-6}Ci), or picocuries (10^{-12}Ci), sometimes called micromicrocuries. But this gives us no information about dose. The roentgen (r), named for the discoverer of X-rays, measures the number of ionizations caused by radiation in air and is defined as the amount of radiation causing 1.6×10^{12} ionizations in one cubic centimeter of air. Since we are more concerned with dose rate in tissues than in air, two other units have been devised: the rad, which is 100 ergs (a unit of energy) absorbed by one gram of tissue; and the rem, which is a unit of absorbed dose taking into account the relative biological effect of various types of radiation. For our purposes a rem or a rad is about one roentgen.

A dose of 1000 r is fatal to all humans. A liver cell receiving 1000 r would be exposed to 2 million ionizations. Since a liver cell has about 2 billion protein molecules, only one of every thousand protein molecules would be likely to be ionized. Yet this is enough to cause the death of the cell.

About 50 percent of people irradiated at 500 r die. This statistical

[1] This is a shorthand way of writing 1/1000 of a curie. A picocurie would be 1/1,000,000,000,000 of a curie.

point is called the LD-50 (lethal dose for 50 percent of the population). At levels of 100 to 300 r, radiation sickness develops. The first symptoms, nausea, vomiting, diarrhea, and nervous disorders, are followed by a period of relative well-being. Then the secondary symptoms begin: fall-off in red and white blood cell numbers, hemorrhages just below the skin, loss of hair, and ulcerations in the mouth and gut. These symptoms may also disappear, permitting slow recovery. Perhaps the most dangerous phase is the period of low white blood cell level. Since the white cells defend the body against disease organisms, a person may survive the radiation only to die of a disease like pneumonia or influenza.

The tissues most sensitive to radiation are those that reproduce rapidly under normal conditions: the blood-forming tissues, bone marrow, lymph nodes, spleen, thymus in children, liver in fetuses, gonads which produce either sperm or eggs, epithelium which lines the intestinal tract, and all embryonic tissues which are in a state of flux. The symptoms of nausea, vomiting, and diarrhea are the result of disturbances or death of the cells lining the digestive tract; the hair loss is caused by injury to the hair follicles. The lens of the eye, which is covered with epithelial cells, is also quite sensitive to radiation and may develop a cataract or opacity.

Survivors of acute radiation in the 100 to 300 r range often suffer some permanent hair loss, cataracts, low fertility, and an increased tendency toward leukemia. Beyond this dose range, 600 r leads to irreversible destruction of bone marrow, 1000 r to irreversible intestinal damage, and greater than 3000 r causes death of the central nervous system. Of three men involved in nuclear accidents, one received 800 r and died in 26 days, a second exposed to 1000 r died in 9 days, and a third received 12,000 r and died in 36 hours. Between 25 and 100 r there are no visible symptoms, just a decrease in the number of white blood cells. Below 25 r there are no measurable changes.

RADIATION AND HEREDITY

Radiation has a greater potential and demonstrated effect on reproductive cells than on asexual or somatic cells. Damaging or even slightly altering the chromosomes in the egg or sperm can cause mutations that lead to abortions, deformed births, or less obvious genetic defects. Though only 10 percent of mutations have been calculated to be radiation produced, the mutational rate is proportional to the total amount of radiation absorbed by the sex cells. It makes little difference whether they receive 10 r in one year or 1 r a year for ten years. Most measurements show a linear relationship between dose and damage. So in a sense there is no such thing as a harmless or "safe" dose of radiation. This is why there is such concern in many scientific circles about seemingly insignificant amounts of radiation, in fallout or in more mundane exposures

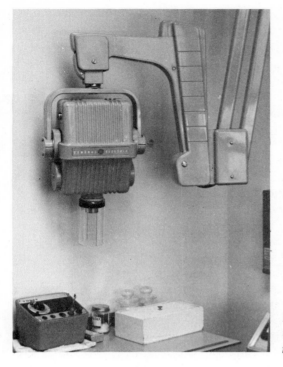

Fig. 14.4 *Although the dentist's X-ray machine delivers a rather small dose of radiation per shot, it probably irradiates more people than any other human-generated radiation source.*

such as X-ray examinations. James Crow, an eminent human geneticist, stated that even if the maximum fallout of the late 1950s were continued over a thirty-year period and amounted to a total of only 0.1 r in that time, 8000 children in the world's population of the next generation could be born with gross physical or mental defects as a result of that radiation.

Of all the radiation beyond the natural background, X-ray examinations far surpass that received from fallout. The United States population is probably the most X-rayed in the world (Figure 14.4), yet there is no overt evidence of any increase in mutations, higher incidence of birth defects, or shorter lifespans that can be directly attributed to radiation. Indeed, another human geneticist, Hermann Muller, regards more frequent reproduction by people with genetic defects as a far greater danger to our genetic wellbeing than any level of radioactivity currently encountered.

Although we have recently heard more about fallout and artificially produced radioisotopes, radiation has always been with us. At sea level we all pick up at least 0.1 r a year and up to 50 percent more radiation at altitudes over one mile (a result of greater cosmic ray intensity). A quarter of this background level comes from cosmic rays zooming in from outer space, another quarter from various radioactive elements in

323

the body, the rest from soil and rocks. Fallout amounts to 0.001 to 0.005 r per year for most people, less than 5 percent of the natural background. In some parts of India and Brazil, radioactive sands emit as much as 17.5 r per year and houses built on these deposits receive 2 r per year, compared with 0.69 r per year in New York City. Long-term studies have been initiated to determine whether this higher than normal background radiation has had any measurable effect on the local population.

RADIATION AND PLANTS

The role of radiation as an environmental variable is somewhat more obvious in plants. A reasonable picture of radiation effects in a natural ecosystem is given by an experiment done at Brookhaven National Laboratory by G. M. Woodwell. A piece of relatively homogeneous scrub oak-pitch pine forest was irradiated with a powerful source of gamma rays. The intense radiation killed plants, but differentially. Pine trees were more sensitive than oaks, oaks more sensitive than blueberry, and blueberry more sensitive than a particular sedge (a grass-like plant growing on the forest floor). The radiation was emitted from a point source about fifteen feet above the ground; hence the dieback was circular around the source (Figure 14.5). The trees and shrubs were generally more sensitive to radiation than the sedge, because the sedge buds were at ground level and somewhat protected; the buds of trees and shrubs were fully exposed

Fig. 14.5 A radioactive source is located in the mast at the center of the circle of dead and dying trees in an experimental forest. This experiment determines the effect of radiation on a forest area over a defined period of time. (Brookhaven National Laboratory)

to the radiation. Variations in radiosensitivity among the trees and shrubs were partly caused by differences in the number and size of the respective plants' chromosomes. One theory, pioneered by A. H. Sparrow, suggests that cells with a small number of large chromosomes are more likely to be damaged by radiation than cells with a large number of small chromosomes, simply because the former offer a larger target. Moreover, the many small chromosomes of the latter possess more duplicate genetic information, so that when one or two are damaged a number of others can take over their function.

NUCLEAR POWER AND RADIOACTIVE WASTES

Despite this long recital of environmental and health problems caused by a greatly increased flow of various kinds of radiation into the environment, there has been a silver lining in the radioactive cloud. Some radioisotopes, cobalt-60 and gold-198 for example, have been extremely useful in cancer therapy. Phosphorus-32, carbon-14, and oxygen-18 are used for tracer work in physiology, ecology, and geology. But the most spectacular beating of sword into plowshare has been the use of atomic energy to produce power (see Chapter 15).

A pessimist might with some justification claim that technology, while seeking to solve old problems, always manages to create new ones. The new problems we face when radiation is used in power plants are not insoluble, but as more nuclear power plants are built, they become increasingly important.

In 1957 the Atomic Energy Commission (AEC) released a document dealing with the theoretical possibility and consequences of a major accident in a large nuclear plant. "Large" in 1957 meant 200,000 kilowatts (kw). This theoretical plant was near water, thirty miles from a city of 1 million, and at the end of a 180-day fuel cycle—and thus invested with 400 million curies of radiation. Assuming general release of this radiation through massive failure of containment structures and procedures, 3400 people would die, 43,000 would be injured, $7 billion of property would be damaged, and over 150,000 square miles of agricultural land would be affected. Today's reactors are larger by a factor of ten, but though the 1957 report was updated the new figures were never released to the public. The core density of a 1000-megawatt (mw) reactor is 40 percent higher than the 1957 theoretical model and the fuel cycle is longer, allowing a far greater buildup of fission products.

To reassure the public about the safety of nuclear power plants, the AEC commissioned a study called *An Assessment of Accident Risks in United States Commercial Nuclear Power Plants*, which was prepared by a private research team headed by Dr. Norman Rasmussen, a nuclear

Fig. 14.6 The dome that shields this reactor is a characteristic feature of nuclear-fueled power plants, this one at Lower Alloways Creek Township, Salem, N. J. (Public Service Electric and Gas Company)

engineer at MIT. Subsequently the AEC was split into a regulatory agency, the Nuclear Regulatory Commission (NRC), and a research agency, the Energy Research and Development Agency (ERDA). The report the NRC received is usually called the reactor safety study or Rasmussen report. In general it was quite reassuring, concluding that an American had as much chance of being killed by a nuclear power plant disaster as of being struck by a meteor. Critics of the report felt that statistics were carefully selected to present nuclear power in the most favorable light. Also, sabotage—not unlikely in a time of rising terrorist activity—was ignored because no mathematical modes could be devised to deal with it; the reliability of untested safety systems was assumed; and the report did not compare the risks of nuclear power with those of competing technology.

Are present reactors safe? Well, there is no chance of a thermonuclear explosion. But there is a chance that high-level fission products may escape into the environment. The precautions are great: a typical reactor is constructed on a nine-foot-thick slab of concrete and is protected by a dome (Figure 14.6) of vapor-proof steel covered with three feet of concrete. Considering all the high-pressure plumbing in a pressurized water reactor (PWR) and the critical importance of the coolant water, there is a chance, however small, that the coolant system could rupture and fail and the fuel rods heat up to the melting point. Just such an accident happened, against all odds, in the Enrico Fermi fast breeder reactor near Detroit in 1966. While no radioactivity escaped from the plant, experts considered the incident a near miss.

The Fermi reactor accident was caused by sloppy workmanship in construction. Unfortunately we have seen too many examples of poor design in reactors and components, loose supervision and quality control during construction, faulty construction materials, and inept handling of fission products. Most of these criticisms could be leveled at the construction of any building or factory in the United States today, but in the design and construction of nuclear reactors the awesome power of radioactivity is being risked.

Present-day reactors (see Chapter 15) are not necessarily unsafe; but they can be made far safer, starting with more careful site selection. A few years ago a nuclear plant was almost constructed on the San Andreas Fault near Bodega Head in northern California (Figure 14.7). Recent estimates of underground siting suggest an added cost factor of only 10 percent, which raises the possibility of reactors being constructed underground, perhaps far closer to cities than now seems prudent. A general tightening up of standards for design, materials, and construction would certainly help, but a major improvement in reactor safety cannot be expected until today's water-cooled reactors are replaced with more advanced designs.

If that is the best protection we can expect against accidental release of radioactivity, what about routine discharge of radioactive substances?

Fig. 14.7   The water-filled hole is the site of the now abandoned Bodega Head atomic power plant. The San Andreas Fault occupies the trough to the right. Ironically the quite potable water in the diggings is being hotly contested by the town of Bodega Bay and the State Park Commission, which now owns the property.

RADIOACTIVE POLLUTANTS

There are three kinds of radioactive pollutants from nuclear power plants: solid, liquid, and gaseous. Solid wastes may consist of such items as tools, reactor parts, and clothing, which may be quite radioactive depending upon their use and are usually buried in cement drums in trenches on land or at sea.

Liquid wastes come in part from leaky seals and valves in the extensive plumbing of PWRs. These low-level wastes are stored and their radioactivity measured. Depending on their accumulated activity, the wastes are released in batches. Other liquid wastes result from isotopes formed when impurities in the coolant water and corrosion products from the coolant pipes are bombarded with neutrons escaping from the core area. This can be controlled somewhat by demineralizing the coolant water before it enters the heat exchange area, but some radioisotopes will always be generated from this source. A reactor in the 150 to 300 megawatt range would generate 1 to 10 curies per year in the form of cobalt-58, chromium-51, manganese-54, iron-59, and molybdenum-99. Because of the low radiation level of these wastes, they are usually discharged into the environment.

The fuel elements themselves are an even more dangerous source of both liquid and gaseous radioactive wastes. Although they are clad in either stainless steel or zirconium alloy, carefully fabricated to minimize leakage, it is apparently impossible to attain or to sustain complete sealing. Minute cracks allow radioactive fission products to escape into the primary coolant. In some instances, the high radiation level causes the cladding to flake or weaken, allowing still more leakage. When the steam is condensed for return to the pile of a PWR, the gaseous fission products are separated and held in storage for thirty days or more. This allows time for many of the short half-life isotopes to decay. The remaining wastes are then vented through the reactor stack. A boiling water reactor (BWR) generates a greater volume of radioactive gases that are held for only thirty minutes before being vented through the stack. Consequently BWRs release much larger quantities of gaseous radioisotopes than PWRs. Gaseous releases from both types of reactors would be substantially reduced with new systems developed by GE and Westinghouse that cost less than 1 percent of the capital cost of the plant.

One of these gases, you will remember, is krypton-85. Because krypton-85, though radioactive, is chemically inert it was thought to be relatively harmless compared to other fission products like iodine-131. But its relatively long half-life, 10.76 years, and the lack of any removal agent allows krypton-85 to accumulate in the atmosphere. As a beta-emitter, krypton-85 can create ions in the atmosphere, and these ions can potentially affect thunderstorm electrification, enhance the coalescence of cloud droplets into raindrops, and contribute to the formation of sulfate aerosol particles. Should the world trend toward nuclear power continue, much more consideration must be given to such subtle effects.

DISPOSAL OF RADIOACTIVE WASTES

The biggest problem lies in disposing of the fission products. Sooner or later, usually in one to three years, fission products accumulate to the point where the chain reaction stops or is poisoned, that is, the neutrons are being absorbed at greater rates by the fission products, leaving fewer to sustain the chain reaction. At this point the fuel elements, now extremely radioactive, are removed and shipped in specially cooled and shielded containers to a fuel reprocessing plant. Here they are chopped up and placed in concentrated nitric acid. The fission products and unreacted fuel are dissolved and separated. The unreacted fuel can be used again but the fission products, concentrated somewhat by evaporation, are stored as a liquid in stainless steel underground tanks. With a radioactivity that is usually between 100 and 1000 curies per gallon, enough heat accumulates to keep the tanks boiling like teakettles.

At one time the federal government contracted for all fuel reprocessing, but now private enterprise has been allowed to enter the field. A plant planned for South Carolina would have released from its stack 12 million curies per year of krypton-85 and 500,000 curies per year of tritium since reprocessing plants are not required to follow the strict standards required of nuclear power plants.

Assuming the present level of efficiency (25 percent), almost one and a half tons of fission products are produced per 1000 megawatts of power. Already hundreds of millions of gallons of high-level wastes are in storage. Since these wastes will remain highly radioactive for hundreds of years while the life of the tank is measured in decades, underground storage tanks represent at best a temporary solution to the waste disposal problem (Figure 14.8).

Though high-level wastes are considered too hazardous to be dumped into the ocean, intermediate- or low-level wastes are disposed of there, often without a clear idea of the dangers involved. One obvious risk would be containers breaking and releasing their radioactive contents, which might be washed up on crowded beaches. Contamination of food chains, as we have already seen in Pacific tuna, could easily occur also. Concentration of wastes on continental shelves might make the future exploitation of oil, gas, or metal nodules awkward. All too often, wastes are not dumped at either the required distance from shore or the proper depth. At too great a depth the containers may be crushed by sea water pressure, releasing their contents immediately. Nor is it known how long the containers last on the sea bottom, and how far and in what direction they are moved by underwater currents.

In the future, before the quantity of wastes from increasing numbers

of reactors overwhelms the possibilities of storage in liquid form, reduction to a solid state and incorporation into ceramics or glass, both environmentally resistant, may be possible. These stabilized solids could be permanently stored in dry, stable salt mines of which there are large numbers in New York, Kansas, and along the Gulf Coast. By the year 2000, twelve acres a year of such salt mine storage space will be needed to dispose of high-level reactor wastes.

Present disposal of radioactive wastes can best be summed up by citing the three basic approaches: dilute and disperse, used for high-volume, low-activity wastes; delay and decay, used for medium-activity wastes where slow movement through soil allows time for radioactive decay; concentrate and contain, reserved for high-activity wastes, now stored underground in tanks.

MINE TAILINGS

Radioactive wastes involve more than the reactor and its by-products: uranium must be mined, purified, and processed into fuel elements, and as we have seen, when the elements are exhausted they must be reprocessed. Each of these steps produces radioactive wastes. Two examples will suffice. Scattered around the Colorado River Basin are huge piles of uranium tailings (Figure 14.9). Ground to a sandlike consistency to remove the uranium, these tailings contain radium-226 with a half-life of eighty thousand years. Radium, like strontium-90, is absorbed by the bones. As radioactive dust from the piles blows into rivers and ultimately into Lake Powell and Lake Mead, the radium-226 level has increased

in places to twice the maximum permissible level suggested for human consumption. Near Durango, Colorado, a million tons of tailings containing radium-226 sits near the Animas River. As it erodes, this material will certainly increase the radium-226 content of the river. Crops grown on irrigation water from the Animas River already contain twice as much radium-226 as crops grown above the tailings. Since radium is concentrated in hay and alfalfa that is eaten by cattle and in turn by us, it is possible that yet another food chain is being contaminated by radioactivity. Of course, the tailings should be stabilized by grading and planting, which would greatly reduce erosion into surface drainage. This approach has been followed to some extent by state and federal agencies, but apparently not at a rate that has kept up with continuing production.

Further problems have arisen from the use of tailing sand for children's sandboxes and by contractors as a base for concrete slabs or in the backfilling of basements. As the radium-226 decays, radon, a radioactive gas, is given off (Figure 14.10). Although radon has a short half-life, it has been established as the prime cause of lung cancer in uranium mine workers. As a result of the use of uranium tailings in construction, many people have been exposed in their homes to levels of radiation many times higher than the maximum dose allowed miners in a uranium mine, the equivalent of nearly 553 chest X-rays in one year. In some instances houses have had to be abandoned.

Once again, as with strip mine spoil banks, no one seems interested in the tailings once plants cease operation. The million tons of tailings in the Colorado River Basin may contain as much as 8000 grams of radium-226. When it has been carried by the rivers of the basin and deposited in

Fig. 14.9 Abandoned uranium mine tailings are found throughout the western states, and have been used for construction in the form of fill, concrete, and mortar. Once thus fixed in a building, the tailings release radioactive gases that may accumulate to dangerous levels. (New York Times)

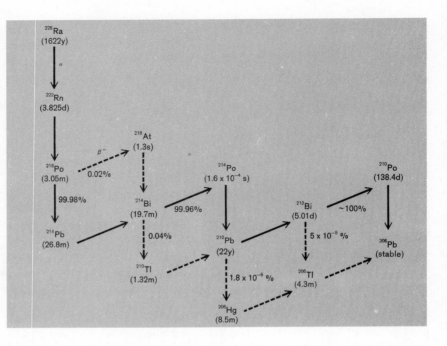

Fig. 14.10 The pattern of radioactive decay in ^{226}Ra. ^{222}Rn passes into the atmosphere from ^{226}Ra in soils and in superphosphate fertilizer added to the tobacco fields. The radon daughters— ^{218}Po, ^{214}Pb, ^{214}Bi, ^{214}Po, and ^{210}Pb—since they are airborne, fall out on the tobacco leaves. The figure in parenthesis represents the radioactive half-life of the radioisotope. The solid line suggests the amount of disintegration by primary path of decay; the dashed line, by secondary path of decay. (After E. A. Martell, 1975. "Tobacco radioactivity and cancer in smokers." American Scientist 63: 404-412, figure 1. Reprinted by permission, American Scientist, Journal of Sigma Xi; The Scientific Research Society of North America)

the bottom sediments of Lake Powell and Lake Mead, it may well be put out of circulation. But radium-226 may become a much larger problem than it is now as this arid region makes increasing use of river water.

While uranium mine tailings are an obvious source of radioactivity, phosphate slime ponds in Florida are not so obvious. However, phosphate-bearing rock contains radium-226. As the rock is processed, equal volumes of phosphate fertilizer and waste rock are produced. The slurry-like wastes are impounded behind earthen dikes where the wastes settle out slowly; the pond becomes dry in ten to twenty-five years. By 1973 over 40,000 acres of settling ponds had been constructed in south central Florida and more were being built at the rate of 2500 acres per year. The radioactivity of the rock waste is concentrated by processing to 45 pico-curies (pCi).

In 1971 a slime pond dam failed and sent 2 million gallons of slime into the Peace River in Polk County, carrying with it 16.5 Ci of radium-226. Almost two years later the river contained twice the permitted level of radium-226.

Not all the waste is abandoned as slime, however. Some is reclaimed as gypsum, which contains 25 pCi per gm of radium-226. Much research has been undertaken to recycle this radioactive gypsum into wallboard. Since this wallboard would contain 25 pCi per gram of radium-226, which decays into the radioactive gas radon-222, this means of recycling gypsum might not be such a good idea. In addition, an acid solution the industry calls "contaminated water" is used to transport the gypsum solids. This water contains 90–100 pCi per liter of radium-226, thirty times the maximum permissible concentration for radium and three times the NRC standard for unrestricted uses. Some of the "contaminated water" is disposed of in pits that are in contact with the water table. Consequently, radium values as high as 79 pCi per liter have been monitored in shallow ground water in the vicinity of phosphate mills.

But these are local problems. What of the acid phosphates widely distributed as fertilizer? Much is used to coax a tobacco crop out of the worked-out soils of the piedmont tobacco belt in the South. Phosphate dust may come in direct contact with the sticky leaves of the tobacco plants (Figure 14.11), introducing radium-226 and its decay products polonium-210 and lead-210 onto the leaves. Or the daughter product radon-222 may diffuse into the air, combine with other gas molecules, attach to tiny dust particles less than 0.1 μm in radius, and then stick to the trichomes or hairs on the tobacco leaf surface. These radionuclides quickly decay to lead-210, which has a half-life of twenty-two years. When the tobacco is burned in a cigarette, the radioactive lead is fused into very small spheres of insoluble calcium metaphosphate, a derivative of the acid or superphosphate applied to the fields. Soluble particles in smoke dissolve in lung fluid and are rapidly removed from the body. But insoluble smoke products are partly sequestered in

Fig. 14.11 The glassy looking structures magnified 125 times are trichomes on the surface of a tobacco leaf. The dark blobs at the tips are glands that exude a sticky substance that captures and retains phosphate dust and radon daughter ions. (Photo by M. B. Gardner from E. A. Martell, figure 2. Reprinted by permission, American Scientist, Journal of Sigma Xi, The Scientific Research Society of North America)

lung tissue and partly transported by white blood cells to lymph nodes, bone marrow, and the spleen. Some seems to penetrate into blood vessels and thence throughout the body. The residence time of these alpha-emitting insoluble particles in the lungs is around two years.

Natural alpha emitters are not uncommon in the air, water, and most food chains. When soluble in body fluids they are mostly eliminated, except for some uptake in bones, so that there is a balance between intake and elimination. The activity level of soluble alpha emitters is about 10 pCi per kilogram of lung tissue. Insoluble alpha emitters, in contrast, have an activity level almost 1000 times as high. It is not directed at an organ in general, but concentrated in the vicinity of each insoluble particle. This microdistribution of alpha activity and the dose-time distribution of irradiation determine tumor risk.

The upshot is that alpha emitters, rather than cosmic rays or other natural sources of radiation, may be the cause of radiation-induced cancer. There even seems to be some evidence that the atherosclerosis plaques associated with strokes and heart disease may be arterial tumors instigated by alpha radiation from insoluble particles that have ulcerated their way from lung tissue into the arteries. While still hypothetical, this possibility does give some pause for thought.

RADIATION LEVELS

Since radioactivity is so easy to measure and its effects are well-known compared with those of many biocides, standards were set up, somewhat arbitrarily, long before intensified radioactive waste production began. Three categories, each with its own permissible level, were established by the International Commission on Radiological Protection. This group recommended a limit to workers in radiation-oriented industries of four rems (roughly 5 r) a year for blood and sex organs, thirty rems a year for the eye, skin, thyroid, or whole body radiation, and fifteen rems a year for other organs. The individual should receive only one tenth of that permitted the occupational group and the general public one thirtieth of the occupational level. This assigning of permissible dose evidently assumes a threshold for various types of radiation and places the permissible dose somewhere below this level despite evidence that *any* amount of radiation can cause damage. To be sure, avoidance of all radiation is impossible since background alone provides 0.1 to 0.5 rems a year.

In the late 1960s two researchers at the Livermore Radiation Laboratory, John Gofman and Arthur Tamplin, caused a great stir when they announced that the maximum permissible dose of *manmade* radiation, 0.17 rems per year, was far too high and could result in 32,000 extra deaths from cancer per year if all Americans were exposed to that level of radiation. While that was unlikely to happen, the standard implied that the AEC was prepared to let it happen. In response to this claim the National Academy of Science appointed a panel, the Committee on the Biological Effects of Ionizing Radiation, to review the whole issue. While viewing Gofman and Tamplin's claim as somewhat exaggerated, the committee did state that perhaps 6000 extra deaths per year could result from the 0.17 rem maximum dose. The Nuclear Regulatory Commission, which now seems to have effective control over setting radiation standards, is reviewing the report and may well abandon blanket exposure limits for the general population. It might make more sense to impose strict limits for specific sources which would discourage the natural tendency to irradiate a population up to an authorized level, presuming no other source of radiation in a given area.

It is senseless for anyone to expose himself needlessly to radiation. It is even more senseless for whole populations to be unwittingly subjected to any increase in radiation levels that can be prevented; it is also unnecessary, because we have the technology to remove radioisotopes from effluent wastes, whatever their source. It has simply been cheaper and more expedient to disperse them into the environment. As earth's population continues to grow we can no longer allow the environment to slip from the desirable to the merely tolerable if life is to have any value beyond bare existence.

FURTHER READING

Boeck, W. L., 1976. "Meteorological consequences of atmospheric krypton-85." *Science* **193,** pp. 195–202. Apparently krypton-85 is not as inert as has been thought.

Brodeur, P., 1976. "Microwaves I and II." *The New Yorker* 13 December, pp. 50–110; 20 December, pp. 43–83.

Calder, R., 1962. *Living with the atom.* University of Chicago Press, Chicago. Easily read discussion of radioactivity in the environment.

Cohen, B. L., 1976. "Impacts of the nuclear energy industry on human health and safety.'" *American Scientist* **64,** pp. 550–559. Painstaking review.

Hecht, S., 1954. *Explaining the atom.* Rev. ed. Viking Press, New York. Beautifully written account of atoms, atomic energy, atom bombs; easily accessible to the layperson.

Lapp, R. E., 1971. "The four big fears about nuclear power." *New York Times Magazine,* 7 February. A concise analysis of some of the major points of popular anxiety about the use of nuclear reactors.

Martell, E. A., 1975. "Tobacco radioactivity and cancer in smokers." *American Scientist* **63,** pp. 404–412. Perhaps all the talk about tars and nicotine in cigarettes is beside the point.

CHAPTER
FIFTEEN

THE QUEST
FOR ENERGY

Energy is Eternal Delight.
WILLIAM BLAKE, 1793

LATE ONE NOVEMBER afternoon in 1965 for the first time in memory, the lights went out in New York City. Not just a block or two but all of Manhattan, Queens, and the Bronx were plunged into darkness. For thousands stranded in elevators and subways, the blackout meant suspended motion as well. Because of the unusually mild weather, the crazy novelty of the situations in which most people found themselves, and the restoration of power before the next nightfall, the city survived pretty much intact. The principal result seems to have been a minor population explosion nine months later, marking the night when hundreds of thousands of people, denied one form of entertainment, remembered another.

The cause of the blackout, which took much detective work to unscramble, was an extraordinary combination of human and mechanical failure; but in retrospect the incident seems to mark a turning point in the pattern of energy production and use. Until that November night, electricity was thought to be a commodity like water—inexhaustible and cheap. Since that night a combination of economic, political, and ecological events have made it clear that Blake's statement is only a poetic metaphor, especially since a repeat performance in July 1977 was accompanied by widespread looting.

Unlike materials, which can cycle or be recycled in the environment,

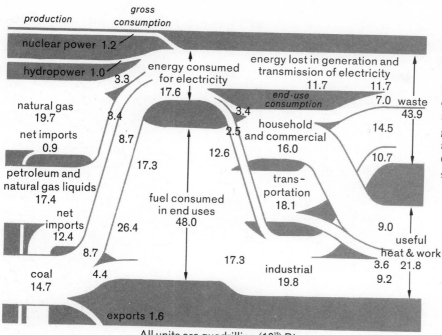

Fig. 15.1 The various sources of the power produced in the United States, and their proportions, are indicated along the left side of this diagram. The fate of this power can be followed by moving to the right. (Earl Cook, Texas A&M University)

energy flows in a one-way trip from source to sump (Figure 15.1). The source for most of our current uses is the sun, which through a complicated series of reactions throws immense quantities of energy out into space; the sump is the heat into which all energy is ultimately transformed. Although only a small fraction of the sun's energy is intercepted by the earth, it is enough to keep all the organic and inorganic cycles working (Chapter 2). Through the photosynthetic process, plants can store some of the solar energy food. Although the efficiency of photosynthesis is quite low, trapping only a small percentage of the sunlight striking the earth, the prodigious quantity of solar energy and the sheer numbers of plants have made possible the food webs of which we are a part today. So the internal energy we use to function as individual organisms flows from the sun through green plants to us. The external energy we use to function as a society follows a similar pathway, except for an enormous time lag. The fossilized remains of plants and animals alive hundreds of millions of years ago have come down to us as coal, oil, and natural gas in quantities we once throught were inexhaustible.

If only a modest function of the earth's share of solar energy could be transformed into useful power, then the eternal delight of energy could be shared by all of earth's people. For the present, the average American needs twenty times the energy available to an Asian to support himself in the style to which he has grown accustomed. Since we lack direct access to the virtually unlimited supply of solar energy, it takes 35 percent of the world's available energy, mostly the fossil fuels, to supply America's energy needs.

As the energy demands of other industrially advanced countries continue to increase, the most convenient fossil fuels, oil and natural gas, are bound to become limited, then limiting. The threat of vanishing supplies of energy has given rise to much concern about an "energy crisis."

But the United States has within its territory all the resources to continue to supply energy indefinitely. The difficulty seems to be marshaling the right technology at the right time. This requires foresight, planning, and perhaps a bit of luck, since research and development of new technology depends on the rate of investment, which in a nondirected economy like ours is always uncertain.

COAL

Of all the fossil fuels, coal has been used for the longest time. It made possible the Industrial Revolution and the urbanization on which that revolution depended. While the environmental price was high, it was paid, and the use of coal continued to increase until the close of World War II. With more fuel available for nonmilitary uses after the war, and with the discovery of huge new deposits of oil and natural gas in the Middle East and Venezuela at about that time, coal began to lose favor and millions of homeowners switched from the mess and labor of coal-fired furnaces to modern oil or gas burners. At the same time industries discovered the greater ease of handling oil and gas and also began abandoning coal. So as the emphasis switched to the glamour fuels, oil and gas, coal production languished. The postwar era also saw the beginning of the nuclear age, filled with hopes for the peaceful use of atomic energy. It was claimed that dirty fossil-fueled power plants would soon be replaced by clean nuclear plants; what this cheerful estimate ignored was that it took almost fifty years to switch from wood to coal or coal to oil.

But by the early 1970s nuclear-fueled plants had run into snags—engineering, environmental, social, and political—and weren't being built nearly fast enough to keep pace with the demand for power, much less to replace the older fossil-fueled plants. Many power companies, desperate for power, discarded plans for the "new age" reactors and built huge fossil-fueled plants, two or three times the size of the old ones and requiring enormous quantities of coal. The rush back to coal was further stimulated by a request from the federal government in late 1973 that oil-fired boilers be switched to coal wherever possible. To facilitate this

338

switch, clean air regulations were waived so that high-sulfur coal could be burned for the time being. With these developments, the market for coal picked up and a new phase of strip mining began, exploiting not only the older soft coal fields in Appalachia, but the large fields in the Great Plains states of North Dakota, Montana, and Wyoming (Figure 15.2).

The coal reserves of the United States are enormous—1.5 trillion tons, which at current or even accelerated rates of use should last for several hundred years, by which time more extensive and efficient energy sources should be ready. Although abundant, coal is not an ideal energy source. It is the least homogeneous of all fuels, varying not only from field to field but from seam to seam. The four major characteristics of coal that concern environmentalists are heat content, sulfur, ash, and toxic trace element content. Unfortunately, coal reserves are usually compared by weight, ignoring the often striking disparity in heat content. Anthracite coal has the highest fuel value but is very scarce. Bituminous coal is more

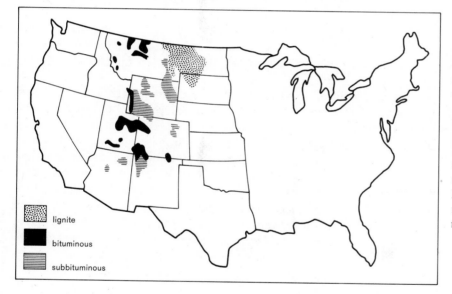

lignite

bituminous

subbituminous

Fig. 15.2 Large parts of the Rocky Mountain basins and the northern Great Plains are underlain with extensive deposits of lignite, bituminous, and sub-bituminous coal. Adapted from *Introduction to Geography,* 3rd ed. by Henry M. Kendall, Robert M. Glendinning, and Clifford H. MacFadden, copyright © 1962 by Harcourt Brace Jovanovich, Inc. and reproduced with their permission)

abundant in the eastern coal fields but has a lower fuel value and a rather high sulfur content. Sub-bituminous coal and lignite from the large western fields in North Dakota, Montana, and Wyoming have a low sulfur content, but the lowest fuel value as well.

The sulfur component of coal has two forms: inorganic or pyritic sulfur, which oxidizes when exposed to air or water and causes acid mine water pollution problems (see Chapter 16); and organic sulfur, which when burned forms sulfur dioxide, a major air pollutant (see Chapter 18). The sulfur content of coal ranges from 0.2 to 10 percent. In 1971 the Environmental Protection Agency set 0.6 pounds of sulfur per million Btu as the maximum allowable emission from new coal-fired power plants larger than 25 megawatts. Almost 65 percent of United States coal reserves contain less than 1 percent sulfur, which would make them ideal for power plants trying to restrict sulfur dioxide emissions. But these western reserves are far from eastern markets and the heat content is so low that nearly three times as much of this sub-bituminous coal and lignite must be burned to equal the heat output of the high-sulfur bituminous coal of the eastern fields. Obviously this generates an equivalent amount of sulfur dioxide. Therefore casual comparison of weight or sulfur content of coal reserves can be quite misleading. A more useful standard would be pounds of sulfur per Btu.

Besides sulfur, coal contains trace elements that are rapidly becoming recognized as toxic even in small quantities; mercury, beryllium, arsenic, lead, fluorine, and selenium. The heavy metals in particular accumulate on the smallest particles of ash, which are hard to remove from emissions and are most likely to penetrate deeply into our respiratory systems.

Ash also varies from one type of coal to another. Unfortunately western coal has a higher ash content than most eastern coal; when this coal is combusted, 65 to 85 percent of the ash goes up the chimney as particulate emissions.

Compared with oil, coal has serious disadvantages. It is dirty; it must be converted into oil or gas to fuel internal combustion engines; it is bulky and wastes storage space; and it is expensive to transport. Efforts to overcome many of these difficulties are just beginning and so for at least a decade coal use will be hampered by nineteenth century technology. Construction of power plants close to the source of the coal is of course one solution to some of these problems, but since the demand for natural gas at present exceeds the supply, more attention is being given to converting some of the low-grade coal into natural gas products. Although work has just begun, three processes are beginning to look promising: gasification, fluidized bed firing, and magnetohydrodynamics.

COAL GASIFICATION

By grinding coal into a granular powder, treating it with steam and oxygen or air, then purifying the resultant gas, high-energy methane, free of sulfur, carbon monoxide, or free hydrogen can be produced. While the process is relatively simple in outline, the details are more complex and the cost of the good-quality methane produced is high. To produce enough synthetic gas from coal to alleviate the natural gas shortage, the quantity of strip mined coal would have to be doubled, with the environmental costs that implies. Additional demands would be made on the environment for cooling water, about 20 percent of which would be consumed in the gasification process. However, since gasification is carried out in closed vessels, it does not pollute the air. Gasification research and development is just beginning, and it is not at all certain when gas from coal will reach the market in any quantity. Had the necessary research been undertaken during the 1950s and 1960s, we could easily be using coal now to help meet the need for natural gas. Hindsight, however, is always 20/20.

FLUIDIZED PROCESS

While coal gasification appears to be a practical method for reclaiming high-sulfur coal by conversion into natural gas, it is possible to combust coal directly in a way that does not release sulfur oxides to the atmosphere, thus making available large reserves of high-sulfur coal for power production and relieving some of the drain on oil and gas supplies in areas where air pollution is critical.

In most power plants coal is pulverized, then injected with air into a very large box whose walls contain tubes filled with boiling water. This allows for maximum transfer of heat from the burning coal dust to the boiling water. Traditionally the soot, fly ash, and sulfur oxides went up the chimney to be shared with the world. But modern air pollution control standards require that particles be trapped by electrostatic precipitators and that the release of sulfur oxides be lowered by various types of scrubbers. Both processes, however, are expensive to install and maintain. A much more satisfactory solution would be to devise new ways to burn coal.

One very promising process places granulated coal on a moving grate, then feeds air upward into the bed so that the particles of burning coal float freely on the grate. When heated to 1100°C the coal ash adheres to itself and forms aggregates that are carried by the moving grate to an ash pit instead of being released up the chimney as fly ash. The excess level of carbon necessary to maintain the temperature at which ash adheres causes incomplete combustion, which produces carbon monoxide and hydrogen sulfide; but they can be converted by secondary combustion above the bed into carbon dioxide and sulfur dioxide. If limestone is added to the coal on the grate, most of the sulfur dioxide can be absorbed and removed from the combustion chamber. If the lime is roasted in the auxiliary chamber, the sulfur dioxide can be released in a high enough concentration to make commercial-grade sulfuric acid. The limestone, once divested of the sulfur, can then be cycled back into the combustion chamber. Unfortunately, conventional pulverized-fuel firing methods are so widespread that it will probably be some time before this newer technique of fluidized-bed firing can be brought into wider use.

MAGNETOHYDRODYNAMICS

An even more advanced technique to use coal more efficiently for power generation is magnetohydrodynamics. In an ordinary steam power plant the steam drives a turbine that revolves metal armatures through a magnetic field, causing a flow of electrons, which constitutes captured current. An MHD generator is much simpler: a stream of very hot, partially ionized gases flows through an intense magnetic field, forming a current that is collected by electrodes in the sides of the chamber and bled off. Because of the direct generation process and the lack of moving parts, an MHD plant can be 10 to 20 percent more efficient than fossil-fueled steam plants or nuclear plants. Another advantage is that the seed particles of potassium sulfate or dioxide that are used to ionize the gases react with the sulfur in the gas, precipitating it out. Since the seed particles must be recovered and recycled for economic reasons, most of the sulfur is removed. This means that high-sulfur coal, which is abundant in the eastern United States, can be very conveniently used. Since the exhaust gases are quite hot (the MHD generator must run at around 2400°C) a steam turbine might be used in tandem to generate more power. The high operating temperature of an MHD generator will of course generate nitrogen oxides. But research suggests that these can be reduced to acceptable levels by controlling the composition and temperature of the combustion gases.

At this point in development (the U.S.S.R. has a 25-megawatt generator in operation, but the United States is just getting a research program together) the problems seem to be technological rather than environmental: the high corrosiveness of the 2400° gases, which affects electrodes and the generator walls; the expense of the large superconducting magnets; and instability of the ionized gas. A closed cycle approach supported by General Electric is beginning to look promising. A pilot device using coal is expected to produce 1.5 mw with an efficiency of 30 percent, a considerable improvement over the low efficiencies of earlier models.

OIL

Unlike coal, which occurs in well-defined strata whose geology has been relatively well worked out for years, oil deposits are confined by vagaries of bedding and pressure to portions of highly porous sedimentary rock layers, making the location of oil less predictable than the location of coal. Present reserves of oil in the United States are estimated to be about 100 billion barrels. If our current rate of consumption continues, we have about twenty years' supply of oil left if we depend exclusively on domestic resources. Oil imports, which constitute about 50 percent of the total amount we use, have come mostly from Venezuela, with smaller amounts from Canada and the Middle East. In the next ten years, oil imports are likely to continue to rise as the United States seeks to delay total depletion of its domestic reserves. The recent shift from South American to Middle Eastern sources reflected a growing preference for the low-sulfur oil of Libya over the high-sulfur Venezuelan oil until the oil embargo of 1973–1974.

However, the immediate problem seems to be not a shortage of crude oil but a lag in refining capability, particularly for the low-leaded gasolines required by automobiles with pollution control devices. The reduction in gas mileage because of the increased weight of cars, the greater frequency of air conditioning and automatic transmissions, and pollution controls also put greater strains on refining capacity. These factors will increase the demand for gasoline by at least 20 percent in the next few years. If past gasoline shortages should recur and prices of gasoline rise again as a result, the restriction on use of cars that might be necessary could help improve both the energy supply and the air pollution problem. Since a significant proportion of car usage involves trips of less than ten miles, doubling gasoline prices, coupled with lower gas mileage, might encourage a number of drivers to walk or explore other modes of transport.

SYNTHETIC FUELS

Extremely large deposits of oil sands in Alberta, Canada and oil shales in Wyoming, Colorado, and Utah hold some promise for supplementing the supply of crude oil. The oil sands are saturated with a petroleum so viscous that it does not flow and so cannot be pumped out of a well like normal crude oil. The Athabasca deposit in Alberta covers an area of 9000 square miles, and together with a couple of smaller deposits nearby is estimated to contain around 300 billion barrels of oil. While exploitation of the oil sands has begun, there has been little economic incentive to persevere because of the competition from regular crudes. However, the size of the deposit is tempting, and the similarity of the oil to crude oil means that it can be refined without major modification of existing oil refineries.

Oil shales are something else: rather than being in a liquid or viscous form the hydrocarbon content is in a solid form called kerogen. Although kerogen resembles crude it contains nitrogen as well as a great deal of sulfur; both must be removed in the refining process. The largest and richest deposits of oil shales in the United States are found in the Green River Formation that occupies the Piceance Basin of Colorado,

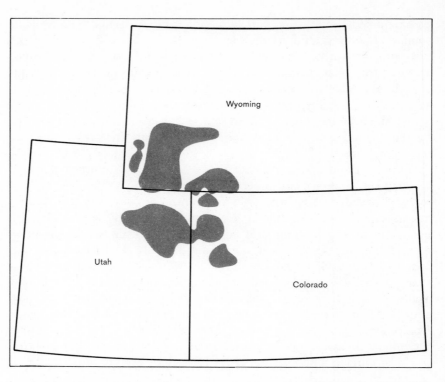

Fig. 15.3 Oil shale is found in many places in the United States, but the richest deposits are found in a series of geologic basins in Wyoming, Utah, and Colorado. (After Metz, 1974. "Oil shale: A huge resource of low-grade fuel." Science 184: 1271-1275, figure 1. Copyright 1974 by the American Association for the Advancement of Science)

the Uinta Basin of Utah, and the Green River Basin of Wyoming (Figure 15.3). The kerogen content of the shales is quite uneven, varying from zero to 1.5 barrels per ton. So although the total oil content of the Green River shales is estimated at 1.43 trillion barrels, perhaps only 80 billion barrels are likely to be recovered with contemporary techniques.

Suggestions that nuclear explosives be used to free the oil below ground are rather unrealistic. Project Gas-Buggy, designed by the AEC to free natural gas in rock strata 4000 feet below the surface, successfully released 8.5 million cubic meters of gas per year into a crushed-rock cavity formed by a 29-kiloton atomic bomb explosion. Assuming a constant flow of gas, 85 million m^3 of gas could be produced in ten years. To supply the annual gas consumption of 650 billion m^3, the yield of this one explosion would have to be multiplied 7000 times. Seven thousand atomic bomb explosions a year would have profound environmental implications and be very expensive as well. Since the same technology used in the Gas-Buggy experiment would probably be applied to below-ground extraction of oil from sands or shales, the peaceful atom may be of limited use as a cheap way to exploit the Green River shales.

The environmental impact of processing oil sands and oil shales is similar to the result of strip mining of coal, except that the waste from oil shale, because of its processing, occupies more volume than the origi-

344

nal shale. This presents a waste disposal problem of some magnitude if we intend to reclaim the sites.

Many oil companies have formed subsidiaries or consortia to explore the possibilities of obtaining oil from shale, but their interest is probably a hedge against future desperate need or, more likely, lower profits or higher cost of Middle Eastern crude. Recently, pilot plants in both oil sands and shale have been abandoned because the government has so far refused to agree to purchase production at an artificially maintained price. The companies are understandably reluctant to make a major commitment when oil prices are high only to be stuck with expensive shale oil if and when natural crude prices fall.

One attractive alternative to gasoline is based on methanol. In 1972 a billion gallons of methanol (1 percent of the gasoline refined that year) were produced in the United States at 18 cents a gallon. Methanol can be made from a variety of sources: natural gas, oil, oil shale, wood, and farm or municipal wastes. It is easily stored and transported in conventional carriers. Best of all, it can be mixed with gasoline in proportions up to 15 percent without major effect on gasoline's burning characteristics. Tests on older (pre-1970) automobiles indicated that a methanol-gasoline mix increases fuel economy by 5 to 13 percent and decreases CO emissions by 14 to 72 percent. But unless the methanol is kept water-free it may separate from the gasoline, and the higher volatility of methanol may cause vapor locks in hot weather or when the engine is running hot. These problems could be avoided by modifying automobile engines to run on pure methanol. Of course this could only be accomplished by giving gasoline producers a monopoly on methanol production comparable to the one they now hold on gasoline. Such a shift would, however, make the United States independent of foreign energy sources—for what that's worth.

Just such a shift is beginning to take place in Brazil, where the government has begun a program to substitute ethyl alcohol made from sugarcane for increasingly expensive imported oil. If successful, Brazil will become the first developing country to achieve self-sufficiency in energy without large reserves of native or foreign oil.

NATURAL GAS

Gas, together with salt brine, is an integral component of oil deposits; the gas-to-oil ratio is around 170 m³ per barrel. In the early years of oil drilling the natural gas was blown off or burned, for there was no market or means of transport for it. But during World War II several pipelines were constructed to transport vitally needed oil from the east Texas oil fields to the Northeast and Midwest without running the gauntlet of

German submarines, which made coastal transport risky. After the war some of the lines were converted and greatly expanded to bring natural gas to the urban centers of the eastern states. In a relatively short time a substantial market was made for gas; it has been increasing ever since. Gas is especially valuable as a source of heat because it has 1.6 times the energy value of oil. Present reserves of natural gas are estimated at 38 trillion m^3, but only a portion has been exploited, apparently for lack of economic incentives. This is clear from the strange price schedules for natural gas, which allowed 83 cents per hundred m^3 for gas from a well drilled before 1973, $1.80 per hundred m^3 after that date. But these rates applied only to interstate shipment; intrastate prices ranged from $3.50 to $7.00 per hundred m^3—whatever the market would bear. Small wonder producers of interstate gas sat on their supplies.

But natural gas reserves are not limited to those associated with oil fields. Other reserves are associated with coal, shale, oil sands, and geopressured beds. All coal beds contain methane adsorbed to the coal; quantities vary from 1 to 20 m^3 per tonne of coal with an average around 7 m^3 per tonne. Methane associated with known deposits of coal could yield 8.5 trillion m^3. Considered a nuisance in mining operations, much of this resource is now wasted. By drilling a well into a coal seam and increasing the permeability of the coal to methane by lateral shafts, some of this methane supply could be utilized.

Much of the Northeast and Midwest is underlain by Devonian shale, which contains 0.63 to 0.95 m^3 of methane per tonne—altogether 14 trillion m^3, some of which can be recovered by hydraulic fracturing. Similarly, the 17 trillion m^3 of gas associated with the oil sands in the Rocky Mountain Fort Union and Mesa Verde reserves can be made to yield gas by fracturing the gas-bearing layer of clay, chalk, or sandstone held within the shale formation. Finally, large aquifers 2500 to 8000 meters below the surface of the Gulf Coast, which have a temperature of 150°C and a pressure twice that normally found at this depth, contain 1.28 m^3 of methane per barrel of water. Estimates of the total gas resources available from these geopressured beds range from 85 to 1400 trillion m^3. To be profitable, a well must produce 100,000 barrels of methane-containing water a day, prodigious by today's standards. To generate 28 billion m^3 of gas per year would require 1000 producing wells that would cost $3 million each. Disposing of this much water might be a problem, especially if the dissolved solid content is high and the land subsides after the water is withdrawn. But water at 150°C might be used to generate electricity.

While these supplies are not easily recoverable, these sources may well be able to produce enough natural gas to bridge the gap between declining domestic sources of energy and the new technology of the twenty-first century. Unfortunately during the halcyon years of plentiful gas and oil supplies, when there was ample time for research, neither industry nor government committed itself to explore and develop interim sources of energy that would buy time while more remote sources were being explored. Research in alternate combustion techniques and gasification of coal, utilization of oil sands and shales, and liquefying gas for more economical transport should have been started immediately after World War II. Indeed in 1947 Congress authorized the Bureau of Mines to begin research in some of these areas, but appropriations were not approved by the Bureau of the Budget and not until almost fifteen years later was the Office of Coal Research founded and provided with a rather modest budget—a typical example of the penny-wise, pound-foolish policies that governments, regardless of political persuasion, seem to follow.

Because of the lead time necessary to develop new technology it will be at least 1980 or 1985 before any alternate source of gas or oil can be developed beyond the pilot stage and so make even a minor contribution to the energy deficit that is beginning to appear, at least in some sectors of the energy market.

THE RISE OF NUCLEAR POWER

Through the efforts of the AEC, exercising its mandate to explore the peaceful uses of atomic energy, and of industry eager to use new technology to reduce costs and increase profits, a new energy source for power production was developed—nuclear fuel. There is a popular misconception that nuclear-fueled plants are radically different in their mode of power generation. They are not. Of course, heat is generated from a radioactive source rather than a fossil fuel, but the rest of the power train is the same. The heat produces steam, which turns turbine blades, which run a generator, which produces electricity. The major improvement is the elimination of the combustion products of fossil fuels, which have contributed greatly to air pollution (see Chapter 18). The price of this boon is an increase of almost 50 percent in the already heavy demand for cooling water in the condensing system, and the various radioactive wastes—liquid, solid, and gas—that are released. Nuclear fuel requires lower steam pressure and the less efficient use of steam results in more waste heat. Also, 10 percent of the waste heat from fossil fuel plants goes up the smoke stack and is dissipated in the air, whereas in a nuclear plant all the waste heat must be transferred to the water coolant. Hence, nuclear plants produce 10,000 Btu per kilowatt-hour rather than the 6000 produced by fossil-fueled plants.

THE LIGHT WATER NUCLEAR REACTOR

The fuel source of a typical reactor is a mixture of U-235 and U-238 packed as uranium oxide pellets into stainless steel or zirconium alloy rods about one-half inch in diameter and several feet long (Figure 15.4). These are grouped together in subassemblies close enough to sustain a controlled chain reaction. Reactor fuel is not pure enough to form a critical mass, so there is no danger of a nuclear explosion. Altogether, a reactor core may contain hundreds of thousands of pounds of uranium

Fig. 15.4 This bundle of uranium oxide fuel elements is being readied for installation in a nuclear reactor. (General Electric)

oxide. The chain reaction is moderated by control rods of cadmium and the core is kept at a temperature of 551°C by a cooling system containing water. The light water reactor (LWR) is so called because plain water, rather than heavy water (which is enriched with heavy isotopes of hydrogen), is used as the coolant. Up to this point all reactors are the same. The variations involve the way the primary coolant is used. In the boiling water reactor (BWR) the primary coolant water is heated to boiling in the reactor vessel and the steam is tapped to drive a turbine (Figure 15.5). With a pressurized water reactor (PWR), the primary coolant is prevented from boiling by sufficiently high temperature and pressure. The pressurized, heated water passes into a heat exchanger, which converts the secondary coolant water into steam that drives the turbine. Light water reactors are very inefficient sources of power: less than 1 percent of the potential energy in the fuel is utilized, and because of the lower temperature of the steam produced, the efficiency of the thermodynamic steam cycle is low also—32 percent compared with 38 percent for the large fossil-fueled plants. But LWRs were never intended to be more than an interim source of energy. The LWRs, which took advantage of the technology developed for the nuclear submarine, were scheduled to be replaced by reactors which regenerate their fuel (breeders). However, because of technical problems with both the LWRs and the experimental breeders, it looks as though we will be stuck with the LWRs for several more decades. If dry cooling towers are used, their 12 percent greater cost could be returned by the far greater flexibility allowed in siting. The present generation of water-cooled plants is much too closely tied to large sources of cooling water, necessitating construction on lakes, rivers, and the seashore, all potential prime recreation areas. Efficiency could be significantly increased by using a high-temperature gas-cooled type of reactor. These reactors, by using a gas such as helium to drive the turbine directly, could avoid both the inefficient steam cycle and the water cooling problem.

Although fission power plants have been highly touted as pollution-free, at least in the lack of combustion products, the gas diffusion plants in Oak Ridge, Tennessee that concentrate and enrich the uranium necessary to fuel the nuclear plants produce effluents and consume huge

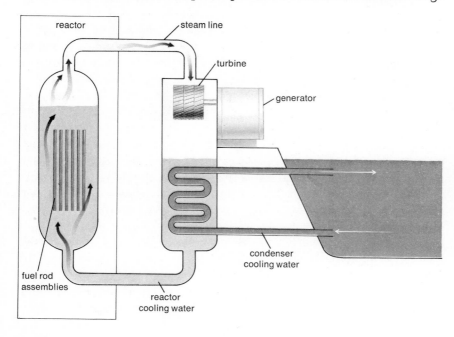

Fig. 15.5 The fuel elements in a nuclear reactor are usually cooled by a primary coolant in a closed system. To cool the primary coolant a secondary coolant is necessary. It is the dumping of this secondary coolant into the environment that causes thermal loading problems. (Modified from Environment 11, 1969)

349

Fig. 15.6 California's Folsom Dam impounds the Sacramento River. Should it fail, a wall of water would virtually destroy Sacramento. Nevertheless, an even larger dam is being considered upstream at Auburn at a site with greater seismic activity.

quantities of electric power produced by the Tennessee Valley Authority's huge coal-burning plants. These not only pollute the air but indirectly wreak havoc on the landscape of Kentucky, the source of their strip-mined coal. Despite these problems, 58 LWR plants are in operation and more are under construction or planned, but not nearly as many as were announced just a few years ago. Higher fuel costs, skyrocketing capital costs, and construction delays have caused many utilities to throw in the towel. The NRC attributes part of the problem to poor labor productivity, construction problems, and equipment failure. The industry in turn blames the NRC-mandated environmental impact statements, quality assurance program, and constant safety-related design changes. But behind these economic problems lie even greater political problems. More and more concern is being expressed about the desirability of nuclear reactors. Some of the problems have been resolved: the Calvert Cliffs decision has obliged new projects to prepare environmental impact statements, and the NRC has decreed a limit of 5 millirems per year at the plant fence compared with natural background levels of 100 millirems per year. Unsolved problems include reliability of emergency core cooling systems, reprocessing of spent fuel, and storage of high-level radioactive waste.

Despite the reassuring Rasmussen report (see Chapter 14), the public seems less impressed by the small chance of a reactor meltdown and disastrous release of radioactivity than by the number of casualties that single event would cause. There seems to be some psychological limit to the number of deaths the public will tolerate from one nuclear incident, and reactors approach that limit. But still another thread must be considered, a thread knotted and tangled by emotion, fear of change, and distrust of arcane technology. How else can you explain people's willingness to live below the Folsom Dam (Figure 15.6) on California's Sacramento River, knowing that its failure would cause at least 260,000 deaths in the heavily populated Sacramento Valley? And the LWRs that cause all these problems were only intended to fill the energy gap until breeder reactors, the *pièce de résistance* of nuclear engineers, could take their place.

BREEDER REACTORS

Breeder reactors differ from LWRs in several particulars. The most important is that they produce a greater neutron flux, which means that neutrons are left over from the chain reaction to convert isotopes conveniently placed in the reactor into fissionable fuels. In this way cheap and more abundant fuels can be produced; for example, the isotope thorium-232 or uranium-238 is converted into the fissionable U-233 or Pu-239. In the fast breeder reactor the excess neutrons are not moderated or slowed but are allowed to react directly with the breeder materials. Consequently, fissionable fuel is produced faster and the ultimate cost of the power produced is lowered. The fast breeder will double the fissionable fuel in ten years.

The breeder design under most intensive development in the United States is the liquid-metal-cooled fast breeder reactor (LMFBR) (Figure 15.7). The liquid is sodium, which is highly reactive in air and prone to

Fig. 15.7 One of the first breeder reactors, the Enrico Fermi Power Plant in Michigan. Plagued with problems, the reactor was permanently shut down in 1973. (Department of Energy)

form bubbles that can block the tubing and hinder the cooling of the core elements. If the core overheats, the containment vessel may rupture and leak radioactivity. While loss of the sodium coolant by accident is less likely than loss of the water coolant in an LWR, coolant loss in an LMFBR is far more dangerous. Since the LMFBR produces a much greater flux of neutrons, it operates much closer to the limits of an uncontrolled chain reaction than the LWR.

By rushing the LMFBR the AEC put all its eggs in one basket, for there are other promising breeder types, including gas-cooled and thermal breeders. The LMFBR is being counted on for significant power generation by about 1990, but since it is still unproven in scaled-up commercial power plants, there could be a serious power shortage if the LMFBR design gives us as much trouble as did the LWR.

The advantages of the breeder reactor are the 50 to 80 percent utilization of fuel, the elimination of the power-hungry gas diffusion plants, the greater thermodynamic steam efficiency (40 percent), and the ability to produce fissionable fuels from abundant and relatively inexpensive isotopes of thorium. Unfortunately plutonium-239, the fissionable fuel that is bred, is exceedingly toxic and has a half-life of 24,400 years. Coolant loss, which might lead to escape of radioactivity, is another omnipresent danger. Fears have also been expressed that as breeder plants begin to produce large amounts of plutonium, worth $10,000 per kilogram, a black market may develop and fissionable materials may get into the hands of saboteurs or terrorists. Simple designs for atomic bombs have been published in Europe, and with a few kilos of plutonium such devices can be put together in a basement or garage.

NUCLEAR FUSION

With the development of the hydrogen bomb came the realization that if the fusion reaction that characterized the bomb could be controlled, mankind's need for energy could be very well satisfied for an indefinite period. The fusion process takes place when a suitable material, usually a heavy isotope of hydrogen, either deuterium or tritium, is heated until the nuclei and electrons become dissociated from each other and form plasma. Dissociation of deuterium into plasma begins to take place at 5000°C; if the plasma is then heated to the incredible level of 100 million degrees centigrade, the nuclei, which normally repel each other, become so energized that they slam into one another and fuse, releasing enormous quantities of energy. The trick is to keep a relatively low-density plasma at a temperature high enough so that more energy is harvested than is invested in the process.

Since the fission chain reaction became a reality just three years after the theory was developed, it was at first thought that control of fusion might be equally rapid. But plasma technology was virtually unknown and had to be painstakingly worked out before much progress could be made with containment problems. If plasma must be heated, even for a very short time, to 100 million degrees centigrade to initiate fusion, then the plasma's container must be radically different from anything technology has produced in the past. Three approaches seem promising. The first is a magnetic "bottle" that suspends the fuel in its magnetic field, avoiding destructive contact with any container wall. Of the three types of magnetic field designs now being intensively worked on—the doughnut, pinch, and magnetic mirror—the doughnut or toroidal shape, particularly the Russian tokamak version, seems the most promising.

The second approach to a controlled-fusion reactor involves lasers. A laser is simply a machine that produces a pure stream of light concentrated in a single wavelength. Because of the lack of interference from other wavelengths, the beam is very intense and sharply focused. When a laser beam is focused on a small pellet of deuterium and tritium, the pellet heats up to the fusion point before it has a chance to explode. In other words, the inertia of the expanding pellet confines the fusion reaction. In another laser approach, the fuel pellet is hit from several sides, heating up the outside of the pellet. This layer ionizes and blows off at such a high velocity that the rest of the pellet reaches the fusion point from the resultant high pressure directed inward. This means that the laser power necessary for fusion can be reduced by 1000, to only one million joules.[1] But the most powerful laser available so far can only generate 600 joules. More powerful lasers are being developed. A major advantage of the laser approach to fusion control is that the scale can be small enough to power communities, ships, or factories, and there is a possibility of direct conversion of nuclear power into electricity. The magnetic field approaches, in contrast, are likely to be gargantuan, in both size and cost, and would produce power by pumping neutrons into a lithium shield that in turn would heat water to steam to drive that familiar turbine.

The third approach would produce a very high energy beam (gigaelectron volts) of heavy ions by means of an accelerator. If the resulting beam is split, the various components could strike the fuel pellet from a number of directions and initiate the desired fusion explosion. Ignition of one pellet per second, yielding the equivalent of one ton of TNT in a chamber with a 10-meter diameter, could generate 1000 mw of electrical power.

Whatever approach finally proves effective, it seems likely that a sus-

[1] One million joules is equivalent to about one quarter of a kilowatt hour.

tained reaction might make commercial power available, after extensive development time, between 1990 and 2000.

While fusion power is certainly a longer shot than the other devices and techniques already described, it does have two major advantages over fission reactors: the fuel resources are virtually unlimited, and the danger of a nonnuclear explosive accident is remote, at least with the laser approach. Deuterium, one component of the fuel, is extremely abundant in seawater and could be extracted very cheaply. Tritium would be produced in a fast breeder fission reactor. Like fission reactors, fusion reactors release no combustion products into the atmosphere. The efficiency of a fusion reactor has been estimated to be about 60 percent.

Of course there are environmental problems with fusion reactors—you can't get anything for nothing. Because of the nature of the fuel, the by-products of the reaction are very high-energy neutrons, which are quite damaging to the structural materials in the reactor, and tritium, the third isotope of hydrogen. Tritium is a volatile and highly reactive isotope with a half-life of twelve years. Although its radioactivity is confined to low-energy beta particles, tritium is a light gas that can easily replace hydrogen and must be regarded as a biological hazard. Tritium release might amount to sixty curies per day but could possibly be held to as little as one curie per day for a large reactor. This range is comparable with the tritium release during the reprocessing of fuel rods of a fission reactor. Despite these problems, the fusion reactor, if and when it becomes available, offers far more promise than the light water fission reactors now in use and the fast breeder reactors under development, from the point of view both of the availability of fuel and of environmental pollution.

Unfortunately if pure fusion proves economically unfeasible we are likely to be left with a hybrid fusion-fission reactor which, as you might suppose, will combine all the complexities of fusion technology with all the problems of fission.

WATER POWER

Although water is the oldest means of generating energy, its proportional contribution has declined steadily over the years despite some rather spectacular installations that generate up to 1000 megawatts. The maximum possible water power capacity for the United States is 161,000 megawatts, of which only 28 percent has been realized. This figure is unlikely to increase substantially in the future, for while water power is nonpolluting, the reservoirs that provide the head of water to turn the turbines must be regarded as temporary, since many may be filled by sediments in 100 years or less. Furthermore, there is growing resistance to damming virtually every free-flowing river for power (Figure 15.8).

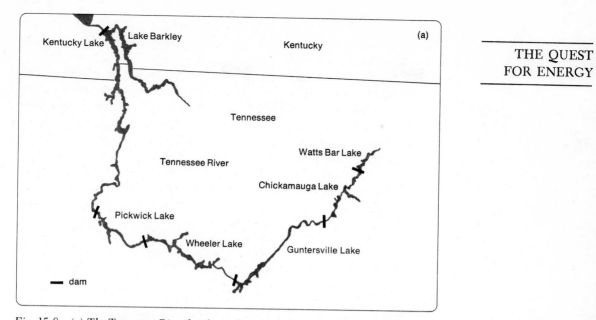

Fig. 15.8 (a) The Tennessee River has been almost totally converted from a river into a series of pools. (b) These huge reservoirs have caused the once-free Missouri River to become a series of lakes in the Dakotas.

The rivers most attractive to the engineer looking for an exploitable fall of water are also the wild rivers flowing through canyons, with falls or extensive areas of white water, that are most attractive to the recreationist (see Chapter 4). As with other environmental manipulations, there is a trade-off between environmental goods and economic goods; the problem is to be sure that we have an accurate balance sheet before a project is begun. Environmental impact statements required by the federal government for public projects and by some states for private projects certainly provide some more accurate means of evaluating environmental impact probabilities. But great care must be taken that these evaluations do not degenerate into a perfunctory check-off of phantom problems or just another bureaucratic hurdle whose purpose is to inhibit "progress."

TIDAL POWER

Hydroelectric power uses a unidirectional flow of water; tidal power, on the other hand, takes advantage of the two-way flow of the tide by channeling it into basins so constructed that the tidal amplitude is great. Although tidal power projects are locally attractive and may be able to compete in output with other types of power installations, the world potential for tidal power is a piddling 13,000 megawatts, compared with even the 2,900,000-megawatt possibilities of hydroelectric power.

For many years the governments of the United States and Canada have toyed with the idea of a tidal project in Passamaquoddy Bay, off the Bay of Fundy, which is well known for its extreme tidal range. With an area of 262 square kilometers and an average tidal range of 5.52 meters, the bay is capable of producing 1800 megawatts of power. But the best design submitted could capture only 11 percent of this potential power, so the project was never funded. The dam would work by means of gates to be closed at dead low tide, then opened at full high tide. When the tidal basin had filled the gates would be closed again. On the next low tide the gates would be reopened. Since the basin would continue to flood and drain the impact of the dam on the estuary would be less than with a unidirectional dam, which would create a permanent reservoir. But the transfer of nutrients important to the productivity of both the bay and the offshore water might be curtailed, and the delicate adjustments of intertidal organisms to tidal levels could be disrupted by sudden raising and lowering of the bay level.

GEOTHERMAL POWER

In general, there is an increase of 0.5°C for every 100-foot descent into the earth's crust, so that very deep mines are usually uncomfortably

warm not only because of poor ventilation but from the earth's inherent heat. In most areas of the crust this temperature gradient is much too gradual to permit efficient utilization. However, as there are deposits of ores in the earth's crust so there are deposits of heat, which cause ground water to boil to the surface as hot springs and geysers, particularly in areas of geologically recent volcanic activity and at the boundaries of the major crustal plates. The possibility of utilizing this natural heat has long been recognized and electric power from geothermal energy is being produced in several countries. At present in the United States geothermal power is being produced only in California (Figure 15.9), although geothermal deposits exist in several other western states. The steam from drilled wells is filtered to remove abrasive particles and then passed through special turbines designed to operate efficiently at the pressure and temperature of the steam, which is much lower than that produced by fossil-fueled plants. The exhaust steam is condensed into water, which is used in the cooling towers; but because of trace chemicals and salts about 20 percent of the condensed water is injected back into the ground. Although the lower temperature and pressure of geothermal steam make the power plants one third less efficient than fossil-fueled plants, the geothermal plants are cheaper to build and operate.

Despite their convenience and economic competitiveness with fossil fuel or nuclear power plants, geothermal steam plants are not without environmental problems. The salinity of the waste water is often six

Fig. 15.9 Geothermal steam is being used increasingly to generate electricity. These units were constructed by Pacific Gas and Electric near Geyserville, California.

357

times that of sea water, and the waste water may contain toxic trace elements and radionucleids as well. Not only is there a potential environmental problem, but the salts can precipitate out in pipes and valves, causing continuing maintenance problems. Also, large volumes of water would be removed to propel the turbines; but by injecting the saline or toxic wastes into the ground, subsidence might be avoided. This must be done with some care, however, to avoid producing earthquakes, which have plagued some deep well injection projects (see Chapter 16). Since the hydrogen sulfide associated with most geothermal sources is quite soluble in water, air pollution is still another problem. Sulfur oxide production in some proposed geothermal plants has been estimated as equal to or greater than that produced by a fossil-fueled plant of equivalent size.

SOLAR ENERGY

Efforts to tap solar energy have been made, fitfully, from time to time, but the attempts have been hopelessly inefficient or impractical. The real problem was probably lack of economic incentive to pursue a new energy source when others were more available. But the galloping demands for clean power are about to bring us to a rational exploitation of even this last froniter.

While the total radiation the earth receives is mind boggling, sunlight is notoriously intermittent in all but a few fortunate spots, and as air pollution continues to increase, sunlight is becoming more and more diffuse everywhere. Nonetheless, solar energy will surely come to play a much greater role in the total energy picture over the long run. This is likely to happen in two phases: first, the development of solar-powered systems for home heating and cooling; and later, the use of solar heat to produce electricity directly by photovoltaic cells or other means.

SOLAR HEATING AND COOLING SYSTEMS

Most solar heating systems are basically an application of the greenhouse effect (see Chapter 18): a black metal surface, shielded with glass to reduce heat loss, absorbs sunlight and transfers the heat to water, part of which is circulated during the day and part stored for release during cloudy weather or at night. Conversely, an air conditioner that uses an ammonia-water system has been devised at the University of Florida. Solar energy drives the ammonia from the water and the ammonia is collected and condensed; when cooling is desired the liquid ammonia, by evaporating and expanding, cools the system that contains it and, through convection, the air. The ammonia vapor dissolves back into the water to repeat the cycle. Because of rigid building codes and the initially high cost of such systems, public acceptance of modular solar heating and cooling devices is likely to be slow.

SOLAR POWER PLANTS

Sunlight, if focused with a Fresnel lens onto a pipe, can be concentrated up to ten times its normal intensity. By covering the pipe with special coatings that reradiate only 5 to 10 percent of the energy they absorb, and by placing the pipe in a vacuum chamber, heat can be conducted, either directly by conduction or indirectly by gas pumped through the pipe, to a central heat-storage medium of molten salts. Connecting a steam boiler and turbines to the heat-storage unit would allow continuous generation of power. A 1000-megawatt power output would require 13.5 square miles of collecting surface.

A third possibility would catch the sunlight falling on a square-mile surface and reflect it to a solar furnace on a 1500-foot tower placed in the center of the collecting array. The solar energy could heat the water to 1700°C and use this hot water to produce power by an MHD generator. Nine square miles of collecting surface would generate about 1000 megawatts. Power could be stored by using some of the electricity generated to split water into oxygen and hydrogen. By recombining these elements in a fuel cell, or by burning hydrogen directly as a fuel, electricity could be generated at night or during cloudy weather. Other possibilities for storage of solar energy are flywheels, magnetic fields, pumped storage, compressed air storage, and storage batteries.

While economic as well as technological problems are serious, the rising costs of traditional fuels and decreased costs of mass-produced solar power components could make such systems competitive. Most of the traditional environmental problems are avoided by solar power techniques, but of course subtle new ones are introduced. Earthbound solar power plants only utilize energy that has already entered the earth's atmosphere. Even though efficient energy absorbers collect more energy than would a comparable area of the earth's highly reflective surface, this loading factor is probably not critical. But a large array of solar energy receivers deployed over a large area could conceivably increase the earth's heat load, because heat that might otherwise be reflected from the earth's atmosphere or surface is being transported to earth in the form of electricity, which when consumed ends up as heat.

Perhaps the ideal answer to conversion of sunlight into electricity lies in photovoltaic cells. Developed to provide power for space vehicles and satellites, photovoltaic cells make it possible to bypass the efficiency-lowering thermodynamic cycle of steam and turbine. But their cost is far too high, their efficiency is low, their lifetimes are too short for cost to be amortized over a period of years as is usually done, and they cannot store energy.

In principle, photovoltaic cells absorb solar photons and generate positive and negative charges that diffuse across the cell and recombine to develop about a half a volt per cell. To obtain high voltages, large numbers of cells must be connected in series. The direct current output would then be converted to alternating current for consumer use. The three materials most used in photovoltaic cells are silicon, cadmium sulfide, and gallium arsenate. Silicon cells must be made out of single silicon crystals, which are expensive to make: the cost of the very high-grade silicon necessary for crystals free of impurities is $60,000 per ton. Cadmium sulfide cells can be made from very thin films instead of crystals, but the cell efficiency is only 6 percent and they break down rapidly in sunlight. Gallium arsenite cells are more efficient (18 percent), but gallium is too rare a metal to allow the production of huge panels with millions of cells.

WIND POWER

Theoretically only 59 percent of the kinetic energy of wind passing through an area swept by windmill blades can be harvested; of this energy, probably no more than 75 percent can be caught even with the best design. But if sufficiently large, a wind power generator could be built for $400 per installed kilowatt, a price competitive with nuclear plants or coal-fired plants with air pollution controls. Despite its modest efficiency, a wind power generator is more efficient than present-day solar power. A wind of 20 mph can generate nine times as much power as a 10 percent efficient solar thermal unit, for wind power increases as the cube of wind velocity. The obvious answers to calm air are a national grid in which some units would always be producing power at the maximum rate, the use of wind-generated power as a supplement to other power sources, and storage techniques.

While most wind power schemes think small, providing power to a house or small complex of buildings, more ambitious plans have been suggested. William Heronemus, a professor of civil engineering at the University of Massachusetts, proposed a battery of wind power stations off the coast of New England (a region which, because of its lack of energy resources, pays the highest electric rates in the country). Eighty-three units each with 164 stations of 13 windmills would generate 159 billion kilowatt hours per year at a cost of $22 billion, approximately the cost of comparable nuclear or fossil-fuel plants. The power would not be utilized directly but would produce hydrogen from sea water, which would be stored in tanks and burned to produce electricity.

Wind power is attractive because it is renewable, clean, relatively efficient, and involves present rather than future technology, always an asset in a time of massive cost overruns. But like any change from the status quo, both wind and solar power face an uphill fight against utilities that have long enjoyed power monopolies, and have become accustomed to thinking in terms of economies of scale, monster power plants, extra-high voltage transmission lines, and complicated business arrangements. Small wonder that on-site individual power plants do not appeal to big corporations or large utilities. Beyond the coolness of business lies the vast bureaucratic wasteland of property tax laws, building code standards, construction methods, labor practices, and mortgage criteria.

SEA THERMAL POWER

Even more esoteric than wind power is the derivation of power from the temperature differential between surface and deep tropical water. Since tropical seas never fall below 25°C, power can be generated twenty-four hours a day, obviating the need to store energy. The process is quite simple in principle. A working fluid in a heat exchanger vaporizes at the warm end of the temperature differential and turns a turbine, then deep cold water cools the fluid back to the liquid phase for another cycle. However, efficiency is low, about 2 percent, because of the low temperature differential of the sea water. Costs, though high ($1500 per kw), compare with those of nuclear plants at $1000 per kw. But the heat exchanger must handle 13 million gallons of water per minute in a 100 mw plant and corrosion and fouling would be difficult problems to overcome. If desalinization were part of the plant design, costs might be made more attractive.

THE CONSERVATION OF ENERGY

With a rising demand for energy and a stable or decreasing supply of at least some conventional fuels, it has finally become necessary to begin putting an end to the lavish waste of power that characterizes our culture. Without resorting to the threat of a change in life style that seems to traumatize our society, we should be able to reduce the demand for power. This will require some foresight and planning, to be sure, but if we postpone it too long, obligatory changes in our way of life might become necessary. This is a prospect most of us would find unpleasant. What, then, are the possibilities of conserving energy?

INDUSTRY

Collectively, industry uses about 42 percent of the nation's energy supply; the principal users are the manufacturers of primary metals, petrochemicals, food, paper, glass, and concrete. About 17 percent of the energy is used to produce steam for various processes, 11 percent produces direct heat, and 8 percent is used to drive machinery. Nearly 10 percent of this energy is supplied by gas, 26 percent by coal, 17 percent by oil, and only 11 percent by electricity. There has already been a significant rise in the efficiency of most industrial processes that is reflected in reduced consumption of energy. Between 1960 and 1966 the steel industry managed a 13 percent decrease in the energy necessary to produce a ton of steel. This wasn't done to decrease energy consumption per se, of course, but to cut manufacturing costs to meet the competition of cheap steel from Germany and Japan. But as energy costs begin to climb more sharply, further cuts, some probably rather sizable, are expected.

The aluminum industry is especially ripe for change. At present the electrolytic process consumes 10 percent of all industrial power. A new chemical process involves the step-by-step hot reaction between manganese and aluminum chloride. Not only is there a 95 percent saving in power consumption, but common clay as well as bauxite ore can be used in the process.

A significant increase in the rate of recycling would have an important effect both on industrial consumption of energy and on the solid waste problem (see Chapter 19). Since finished products have already been processed, their recycling often takes less than one fifth the energy required to manufacture them from virgin raw materials to begin with. Of course there are exceptions, such as cans, which because of their special coatings of tin and plastics are difficult to recycle.

AGRICULTURE

But industry is not the only conspicuous consumer of energy. The production of raw agricultural commodities ranks third in energy consumption after steel and petroleum refining. All crops do not require equal inputs of energy, however. Field crops such as oats, corn, wheat, and soybeans, and perennial fruits consume the least cultivational energy and occupy the largest acreage. Annual vegetables like cauliflower, celery, and broccoli are the most energy-intensive crops: it takes as much energy to grow one acre of cauliflower as it takes to build a six-passenger automobile. Fuel accounts for 4 to 6 percent of this energy cost. Consequently more and more farmers are beginning to practice minimum tillage—planting and fertilizing plants in untilled soil in one operation can save

2.5 gallons of gas per acre. However, more herbicides and biocides are required to obtain yields equivalent to those from conventionally cropped fields. When plants are grown under artificial conditions energy costs soar—greenhouse-grown plants require 70 times the energy of field-grown plants, and plants grown under lights need 300 times as much energy as normal. Agricultural energy demands can be reduced by greater use of natural manures, increased crop rotation, integrated pest control, changes in cosmetic standards, and a reduction in processing and packaging.

TRANSPORTATION

If the various transportation modes are examined as energy consumers, the most efficient—trains, barges, mass transport systems—are being replaced by the less efficient trucks, cars, and planes (Table 15.1). As this

Table 15.1
Energy and Price Data for Intercity Freight Transport, 1970 *

MODE	ENERGY (BTU/TON-MILE)	PRICE (CENTS/TON-MILE)
Pipeline	450	0.27
Railroad	670	1.4
Waterway	680	0.30
Truck	2,800	7.5
Airplane	42,000	21.9

* Data taken from Hirst, Eric, 1973. *Energy intensiveness of passenger and freight transport modes, 1950–1970.* Oak Ridge National Laboratory, Oak Ridge, Tennessee.

shift has taken place the energy consumption of transportation has increased significantly. Of the 3 billion barrels of oil required for transportation in 1970, 55 percent was used by cars, 21 percent by trucks, and 8 percent by planes. The remaining 16 percent was split among trains, buses, barges, pipelines, and so forth. Since the average American car gets only 12 miles to the gallon, half what the average European car gets, the automobile's demand on petroleum supplies seems likely to increase, at least over the short run. Removal of lead from gasoline would also increase the use of crude oil by a million barrels a day.

The car-buying public is perhaps ultimately responsible for the excessive consumption of fuel by cars, since it seems to prefer dinosaurs to lizards. But federal and state governments have consistently encouraged the use of cars, trucks, and planes by direct and indirect subsidies of expanded road and airport construction, while at the same time they have allowed outmoded rules and controls to stifle railroads and mass transport. As a result, railroad stations have become dismal symbols of urban decay and neglect. Reversal of government policy is always unlikely. But if billions of dollars were poured into mass transit systems, enabling them to compete with the automobile, and if railroads were rejuvenated so they could compete with the ubiquitous truck, the consumption of crude oil could be reduced significantly over a ten- to fifteen-year period (see Chapter 13). The creation and subsidy by the federal government of Amtrak, the agency that now operates rail passenger service, is a tentative step in the right direction. Reducing the weight and horsepower of cars and paying greater attention to fuel efficiency in developing engines to replace the notoriously wasteful internal combustion engine will help also. But the greatest impetus toward automobile fuel economy will come from the increased prices of gasoline. These high prices will probably be with us for good. The oil embargo did illustrate that energy demand is more sensitive to price and that economic growth is less dependent on energy growth than most economists had supposed.

BUILDINGS

Just as automobiles are rarely designed to run efficiently on low-grade fuel or to burn that fuel cleanly, so are buildings seldom designed to conserve energy. The major design requirement, at least for commercial buildings, is the maximum square footage for the minimum price. While the construction of these buildings and the manufacture of the materials requires only about 8 percent of the electricity produced in the United States, maintenance of the buildings already constructed takes a whopping 50 percent of the available power. This drain could be reduced by at least 25 percent if greater attention were given to energy conservation during the production of materials, assembly, maintenance and operation, and finally demolition. All these aspects are related to the design of the building, which in turn is the responsibility of the architect. But the architect must satisfy his client, who supposedly pleases his tenant, and so the buck passes back to the consumer.

Selection of materials is largely influenced by the practical experience of what best provides the greatest margin of safety in the completed structure. Rather than making a scientific analysis of how much should be used of what materials, builders have calculated safety margins rather generously. The generosity of the calculations has been climbing as the overall quality of construction declines. Masses of materials, especially concrete, have commonly replaced careful design and construction. Prefabricated buildings, which require less material and take less time and energy to put up or take down, are one solution—but their full acceptance would necessitate revising building codes that favor buildings constructed in the field. Since concrete requires much energy to produce, large reductions in the use of concrete could result in saving almost 20 billion kilowatt hours per year, enough electricity for 3 million families.

Synthetics, plastics, and aluminum as building materials require far more energy to produce than steel and wood. To produce the aluminum skin for a skyscraper, for example, requires almost three times the energy needed to produce and use stainless steel. Once such a building is constructed there are heavy continuing demands for power to light, heat, and cool the structure.

In the last decade the minimum lighting level recommended by the Illuminating Engineering Society, which is closely affiliated with light fixture manufacturers and utility companies, has risen steadily. Experiments that reduced the recommended 100 foot-candles in a general office environment to 35 f.c. indicated that tasks were more easily performed with *less* eyestrain, fatigue, and tension. Although the fluorescent lamps that are used almost exclusively in office buildings consume only one fourth as much power as the incandescent lamps still used in most homes, the excessive lighting of most new commercial buildings more than makes up for the economy. Again, cheap electricity appears to be the cause; suburban banks and shopping centers blaze all night long, wasting large amounts of power for no purpose except security or perhaps advertisement. Rising power rates will probably be effective in reducing this abuse.

Heating is another major source of excessive power consumption. Nearly 60 percent of the energy required by a house is used for heating, 12 percent for cooking and refrigeration, 15 percent for hot water, and 10 percent for lights and small appliances. Underinsulation and a trend toward electric heating have contributed to this excessive power consumption. Doubling the insulation presently considered adequate would in many instances halve the energy requirements of heating and cooling, and pay for itself over the lifetime of the building. While electric heating is a rather efficient way to heat a given unit of space, it is very inefficient to produce and transmit. The increasing popularity of electric heat is due in part to the cost-conscious builder, who finds it cheaper to install than a furnace, and in part to building managers, who find rentals much more profitable if the tenant foots the heating cost as part of his electric bill.

Insulation is an important aspect of energy conservation in any structure, but especially in suburban houses that, since they are free-standing, have a greater surface area over which heat may be lost or absorbed. This heat load can be effectively countered by air conditioning, but the energy cost is higher than it need be. The energy cost can be reduced if the house is adequately insulated during construction or remodeling, if the roofing material is highly reflective, and if attic fans are installed to prevent heat buildup beneath the roof.

When all of these details are planned into a new building, far more energy can be saved. Test housing erected in Little Rock, Arkansas with 2×6 studs on 24-inch centers, 6-inch fiber glass insulation, smaller double glazed windows, and overhanging eaves used half the heating/cooling energy of comparable houses. As a result the cost of heating the house by electricity amounted to $77 per year.

When air conditioners are used some attention must be paid to their efficiency, which can vary from 4.7 to 12.2 Btu per watt hour (the more Btu per watt hour the higher the efficiency). Customarily ignored by both manufacturers and consumers, inefficient air conditioners have inflated electric bills needlessly during the cooling season. Today, however, the more enlightened manufacturers list, and wise consumers request, the cooling capacity of their air conditioner in terms of Btu per watt hour.

Other small but potentially significant energy drains involve pilot lights on appliances, which can be replaced by electronic ignition systems; frost-free refrigerators, which use twice the energy of manual-defrost units; fireplace flues left open when the fireplace isn't being used; and incandescent lamps, which consume four times the energy of fluorescent lamps.

Life style of course can play a surprisingly important part in energy conservation. It has been estimated that if everyone set his thermostat 1°C higher in the summer and 1°C lower in the winter, 219 million barrels of oil could be saved per year. But this would be possible only in well-insulated houses. Those that are poorly insulated allow less flexibility in controlling energy loss. Mobile homes, which are increasing in popularity as permanent housing (one of every four new houses is a mobile home), are prefabricated, so there is an energy saving in their construction. And because of their small size, heating and cooling should be more efficient. But poor insulation makes many of them greater consumers of heat-control energy than they need be.

Perhaps the most logical way around the inefficiency of heating, cooling, lighting, and steam generation is to integrate these services into a total energy system. A centrally located, efficiently run power plant could supply heat, air conditioning, steam, hot water, and electricity to a compact group of buildings, a shopping center-apartment house complex, for example, or a subdivision with homes, schools, churches, shopping center, and recreation center. It would be even more logical to include solid waste disposal as a heat source. Such a project now underway in Boston involves a medical community of 35,000 people. It will be served by an oil-fired 52,000-kw plant supplemented by a steam turbine driven by the combustion of forty tons of garbage generated by the community. Gases from the garbage will be recycled back to the steam boiler for 100 percent combustion and the hot water will be used to heat the buildings. In industry, cogeneration, the generation of power from steam used in various processes, can significantly reduce power needs. European industries have made such use of their process steam for many years.

ECONOMICS

Although economics is closely related to all environmental problems, its clearest link is with the energy crisis, as we see in the current shortage of natural gas and the impending shortage of electric power and gasoline. Many people have doubtless wondered why a country with huge reserves of coal, oil, and gas, together with the technological base to develop more exotic alternatives at will, could possibly be faced with an energy shortage. Yes, fossil fuels are a nonrenewable energy source compared with fusion or solar power. But surely a government concerned with our welfare has an energy policy to plan the rate of development and exploration so that, as one energy source is depleted, others will be available to supply whatever energy is required. Unfortunately, until very recently such a national policy did not exist, and oil companies were allowed to increase profits through a depletion allowance while the natural gas industry had its profits reduced by being forced to maintain unrealistically low prices. The impact of such policies was the overproduction of domestic oil and underproduction of gas. The Federal Power Commission, which is charged with regulating the power industry, has no independent survey capability; it depends instead on figures obligingly supplied by the industry it is supposed to regulate. Small wonder that many feel that the natural gas shortage has been "arranged" by an industry sitting on an ample, if not abundant supply, whose value is not reflected in the present rate schedule. According to one scenario, when the pressure is sufficiently high the FPC will be forced to increase natural gas prices and the producers will "discover" they had more gas reserves than they supposed and the short-term shortage, at least, will be over.

A similar economic explanation has been suggested for the 1974 gasoline shortage. The large consortia that collectively exploit the oil resources of the Middle East are seeing their profit margin steadily whittled away by the increasingly aggressive producer countries, eager for control of their resources as well as increased profits. Faced with the specter of lower profits and potential loss of control, the oil companies would understandably like to minimize their dependence on Middle Eastern oil by rapid development of the continental shelf deposits of Alaska and the Atlantic coast. But environmentalists concerned over the Santa Barbara oil spill (see Chapter 17) have forced a government slowdown in the leasing of these offshore areas. A gasoline shortage could serve as a very effective lever: if it inconveniences the public sufficiently, it could pressure the government into overruling the environmentally concerned "obstructionists," allowing a more rapid development of oil deposits with less stringent environmental safeguards.

The upshot of such a situation would be to isolate people concerned with ecological as well as economic values and impose an artificial either/

or solution to the energy problem: either the power industry must be allowed to exploit oil or gas deposits wherever and whenever it pleases, and construct refineries and deepwater ports in the most convenient locations, or the country will suffer from shortages of electric power, natural gas, and gasoline. The tactic is widely used: for years the Corps of Engineers said either dams or floods; the biocide industry, biocides or starvation. But there are *always* alternatives, and they can be economically sound, if not universally popular. Perhaps the quickest way to solve the energy crisis would be to increase substantially the price of fuel of all kinds. Waste of energy is so great in the United States because the cost is so low compared with the cost of other goods and services.

Less than 5 percent of the typical American family budget is spent on energy; it represents only 1.5 percent of the total value of manufacturing goods. Indeed, until 1971 the cost of electricity declined in relation to the cost of virtually all other materials. Rate structures that favor the large user (and waster) of power with lower rates have supplied no incentive for more economical use of energy. The very structure of the electric utility is based on a rather strange kind of economics. Capital costs of power plant construction are exceptionally high, so the larger the plant, the greater the profit from ultimate sale of power. This results from a curious tax ruling that bases permissible profit on the percentage of capital investment. So it is often more profitable for a utility to build a new power plant than to purchase power from another company. The expansion is justified by promotion of the use of electricity. One way around this would be to create a national power grid, which could facilitate the distribution of power from power-rich to power-poor regions, and might reduce the need for new generating capacity by 20 percent. Naturally such a plan is strongly opposed by the electric power industry, because it would threaten its death hold on local power supply. Electric power has always been a sellers' market; this explains the enormous rate differential around the country. Allowing utilities to deduct the cost of advertising promotion of their product from taxes rather than profits has further inflated the growth of power demand, to the point where many urban power companies are barely able to meet the demand they have stimulated. While no one would suggest that a company discourage the public from using its product, it is unconscionable to stimulate the use of electrical gadgets merely to fill the valleys between the daily or seasonal peaks of energy consumption.

As the cost of power and fuel increases, people are likely to take greater interest in their rate of energy use. We could achieve perhaps as much as a 25 percent reduction in our total energy consumption by simply turning off unused lights and air conditioners, loading dishwashers and washing machines fully, or taking public transportation instead of using cars. The eased demand for power would allow time for more careful exploitation of fossil fuel deposits; for siting refineries, pipelines, and deepwater terminals as they become necessary; and for the development of new technologies that may have a lesser environmental impact than those in present use. The government must play a prime role as well as the consumer, for a major factor in the "energy crisis" has been lack of a coherent long-term plan for energy resource development. Only the government is in the position to chart such a course by its control over power and fuel rates, review of environmental impact statements, leasing of offshore oil and gas deposits, its role in supporting transportation modes, and support of research and development of energy sources that are more efficient, less environmentally damaging, and indefinitely renewable.

There is no reason whatever for the present "shortages" to be continued into the indefinite future when so much could be done by a concerned government with the active support of the people to increase supply as well as reduce demand.

FURTHER READING

Freeman, S. D., 1974. *Energy: the new era.* Walker, New York. Good summary.

Heichel, G. H., 1976. "Agricultural production and energy resources." *American Scientist* **64,** pp. 64–72. Explores the possibilities of conserving energy in agriculture.

Hirsch, R. L., and W. L. R. Rice, 1974. "Nuclear fusion power and the environment." *Env. Conserv.* **1**(4), pp. 251–262. Nuclear fusion power has its problems too.

Reed, T. B., and R. M. Lerner, 1973. "Methanol: a versatile fuel for immediate use." *Science* **182,** pp. 1299–1304. An alternative to gasoline.

Robson, G. R., 1974. "Geothermal electricity production." *Science* **184,** pp. 371–375. Survey of the state of the art.

Schipper, L., and A. J. Lichtenberg, 1972. "Efficient energy use and well-being: The Swedish example." *Science* **194,** pp. 1001–1013. Interesting comparisons.

Soucie, G., 1974. "Pulling power out of thin air." *Audubon* **76**(3), pp. 81–88. A look at the possibilities of large scale wind power plants.

Steadman, P., 1975. *Energy, environment, and building.* Cambridge University Press, Cambridge, England. The house as an energy sieve—what can be done about the problem.

Swann, M., 1976. "Power from the sea." *Env.* **18**(4), pp. 25–31. There is no shortage of ingenious ideas for generating power.

von Hippel, F., and R. H. Williams, 1975. "Solar technologies." *Bull. Atomic Scient.* November, pp. 25–31. Explores the practical realities of power from the sun.

369

PART SIX

THE WASTE EXPLOSION

As monumental as the problem of energy supply has become, the problem of handling wastes generated directly or indirectly by that energy is even greater, for waste exists in so many diverse forms. The solvent properties of water assure its use as a major waste collection/transport system, with the sea as the ultimate repository. The air is open to all volatiles and fine particles. At least water and air dilute and disperse. Solid wastes, however, cannot be hauled indefinite distances for burial and they do not always combust.

*Eutrophic — lots +
little oxygen*
of nutrients &

WATER POLLUTION:
DILUTION IS NO
SOLUTION

TRADITIONALLY pollution, like prostitution, is any departure from purity. But in the environment it has come to mean departure from a normal rather than a pure state; otherwise we would have to say that water is polluted with algae, fish, or fowl.

Pollution is, of course, a subjective and often emotionally charged term, one we have used to describe the environmental traumas of fire, overproductive or deoxygenated water, smoke- or dust-filled air, and background radiation that have always existed. Natural traumas become pollution when our activities overwhelm the ecosystem's capacity to handle them, thereby causing an imbalance in the system. This imbalance requires an enormous input of energy to correct. Further, because of our activities, environmental traumas are now regional instead of local, continuous rather than episodic. Water and, as we will see in Chapter 18, air, are the two most polluted parts of our environment.

Because of its unique bipolar properties (see Chapter 1), water readily dissolves a great variety of substances; substances that remain insoluble are at least dispersed. Where human populations are small and widely scattered, dilution *is* a reasonable solution to waste disposal. Rivers and streams can, in a few miles, carry out the work of breakdown, absorption, oxygenation, or consumption, and small amounts of pollutants are effectively dispersed.

In primitive times, once waste water from a village of a few hundred people had been carried a few miles downstream, the water was purified naturally—at least, enough to be drinkable in the next village. When villages became towns and towns cities, rivers could no longer break down the quantity of pollutants poured into them, and the effluents from each population center flowed into the water supply of the next. Running water almost everywhere became sewage water, seemingly ending the concept of dilution as a solution to pollution. But when the true costs of proper pollution control at the source became widely recognized, the idea of dilution was revived. One of its recent incarnations was in a proposal to build two dams on the New River in Virginia to generate electric power. The proposal provided that 400,000 acre-feet of the reservoir's total capacity of 3,261,000 acre-feet would be released periodically to flush chemical wastes from the Kanawha River at Charleston, West Virginia down into the Ohio, the Mississippi, and finally the Gulf of Mexico. Fortunately the permit issued by the FPC to construct these dams was revoked by Congress in 1976 and 26 miles of the New River (ironically one of the oldest rivers in the world) have been protected.

CATEGORIES OF WATER POLLUTANTS

SALINE WASTES

Occasionally, salt brines from mines or oil wells are released into normally fresh water. Although some organisms can tolerate a certain range of salt concentration, many disappear as fresh water becomes brackish. If the salt level remains constant, salt-tolerant species often appear and reproduce successfully. A marine species of the green seaweed *Enteromorpha* became quite abundant on the bottom of a New York stream that was badly polluted with salt brine. However, because of constantly fluctuating levels of most pollutants, organisms that might otherwise adjust to the new conditions rarely have the opportunity to become naturalized, so neither native nor newly introduced organisms can survive.

A far more serious type of salt pollution has developed as the use of sodium chloride-calcium chloride mixtures on snowy roads in winter has increased to over 6 million tons per year. Although limited to states with a winter snow problem, the quantities of salt used in these states is staggering: 20 tons per mile or 4 pounds per linear foot along each side of a two-lane road. The salt runoff changes the osmotic balance of the soil bordering the highway and makes plants much more susceptible to drought. Sugar maples seem especially vulnerable to salt in the soil, and ancient specimens are dying along rural roads all over New England. Massive intrusions of salt into the water table from carelessly placed and unprotected storage piles have contaminated many wells, and runoff from highways into storm sewers and natural watercourses is beginning to affect aquatic life in some places. Apparently because the chloride ion complexes strongly with mercury, contamination of fresh water with deicing salt can release mercury from polluted bottom sediments. The problems this excessive use of salt can cause seem a high price to pay for snow and ice removal. One cannot help but wonder how many accidents are caused by poor visibility through salt-smeared windshields, or by the slippery slush that quickly follows application of salt to highways. Perhaps salt is indispensable in maintaining safe highways in winter, but far more salt is being applied than the job requires. Faulty equipment, poor supervision, and bad judgment all contribute to the problem. But now that the environmental fate of highway salt is being traced (Figure 16.1), steps

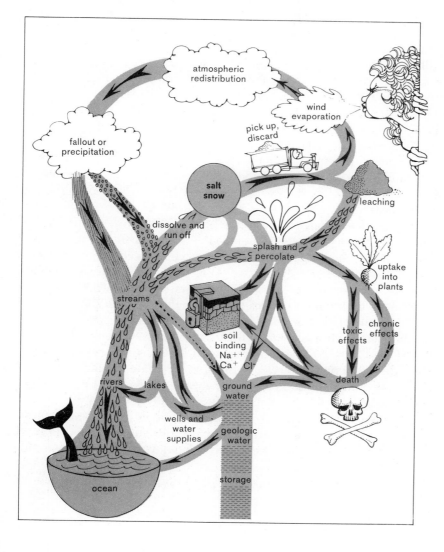

Fig. 16.1 *The environmental fate of salt applied to highways in winter is rather more involved than was supposed in the past. The possible effects go well beyond the death of plants along the roadside.* (From a drawing by Jim McClure in *Farm Economics,* February 1973)

can be taken to assure at least its proper use and at most its replacement by safer alternatives.

ACID WASTES

In 1803, T. M. Morris made one of the first references to acidic drainage in America when he noted, "The spring water issuing through fissures in the hills, which are only masses of coal, is so impregnated with bituminous and sulphurous particles as to be frequently nauseous to the taste and prejudicial to the health." [1] Morris was referring to natural seepage, which has apparently always been a minor problem. But since the opening of the nation's first coal mine in Pennsylvania in 1761 the problem has become far more widespread. Of course, acidic water from mines increases with production of coal, but it also continues long after mines are abandoned.

Joshua Gilpin visited a coal mine in 1809 and stated that "above the coal is several feet of a mixed kind of bad coal and iron abounding in sulphur and in vitriol efflorescing in white and yellow crystals." [2] The materials Gilpin was describing were iron pyrites, which enter streams following strip mining. Certain bacteria are able to obtain energy by changing iron from one oxidation state to another (ferrous to ferric). They use the energy to respire and reproduce. With an unlimited source of food they multiply greatly; the by-products are the orange-red precipitate of ferric hydroxide that stains riverbanks and channels, and the acidity caused by the release of sulfuric acid.

This set of reactions not only drastically lowers the pH of the stream and contributes huge quantities of iron and sulfates to the water, but it reduces the availability of oxygen in the stream as well. In the low-water season of summer and early fall, the pH may rise to 4.5, but with the high water of winter and spring, flushing of wastes from strip mines and mine shafts by tributary streams may lower the pH to 2.5. At pH levels below 4.0 all vertebrates, most invertebrates, and many microorganisms are eliminated. Most higher plants are absent, leaving only a few algae and bacteria to save the stream from total sterility. One species of higher plant, the needlerush (*Eleocharis acicularis*), is quite resistant to low pH and shows great promise as a possible means of rehabilitating acid-damaged streams.

Acid mine drainage is a serious problem wherever coal is mined. In the United States, the most severely affected areas are parts of Pennsylvania, Ohio, West Virginia, Kentucky, Illinois, Missouri, and Tennessee;

[1] Braley, S. A., 1954. "Acid mine drainage: I The problem." *Mechanization* **18**, pp. 87–89.
[2] Ibid.

in Europe, parts of the British midlands, France, Germany, and Poland. Most coal mining areas now have strict regulations which have greatly reduced pollution from contemporary sources. Regulations, however, do nothing for already abandoned shafts or stripped areas, which continue to discharge acid wastes into the nearest drainage. Control of these abandoned workings will have to come bit by bit, adding enormously to the ultimate cost of acid pollution control.

Although coal mining operations add the greatest amount of acid to streams, other industries produce wastes which affect pH too. Continuous casting and hot rolling mills use sulfuric acid (pickling liquor) to clean oxides and grease from the processed metal. When the pickling solution becomes diluted with iron salts and grease, it must be replaced with fresh solution. Since over 50 percent of all steel products are treated with pickling liquor at the rate of fifteen gallons of liquor per ton of steel, a considerable volume of spent liquor is disposed of every year. After pickling, the metal is rinsed to stop the pickling action; every ton of steel requires another eighty gallons of water, which picks up about 15 percent of the acid. Because of their acidity these spent pickling and rinse solutions are a most difficult waste water problem.

ORGANIC WASTES

The most common pollutants are organic. These materials are not poisonous to stream life, nor do they necessarily affect pH. Their effect is more subtle. Most organic materials are attacked by bacteria and broken down into simpler compounds. To do this, bacteria require oxygen. The greater the supply of organic food, the larger the population of bacteria that can be supported, and the greater the demand on the oxygen supply in the water. This demand for oxygen by the bacteria is called biological oxygen demand, BOD. The BOD is a useful index of pollution, especially that related to the organic load of the water. Because all stream animals depend upon the oxygen supply in water, the BOD is of particular importance in determining which forms of life a polluted stream can support. Fish have the highest oxygen need; usually cold-water fish require more oxygen than warm-water fish. Invertebrates can tolerate lower concentrations of oxygen, and bacteria still lower.

Two invertebrates are able to tolerate such a low oxygen level that they have become recognized as a kind of biological index of oxygen depletion. One is a small worm called *Tubifex*, and the other is a bright red larva of a tiny midge called *Chironomus*. Both live in the bottom mud in numbers that are inversely proportional to the oxygen content of the water. In badly polluted water *Tubifex* populations have been estimated at twenty thousand individuals per square foot. In unpolluted water *Tubifex* may be absent altogether.

Sometimes when the organic load is especially great and the water warm, oxygen is so depleted that the usual oxygen-requiring or aerobic decomposers are replaced by species that don't require oxygen (anaerobic), with a quite different group of end products (Table 16.1).

Table 16.1
Comparison of Decomposer End Products under Differing
Conditions *

AEROBIC CONDITIONS	ANAEROBIC CONDITIONS
$C \rightarrow CO_2$	$N \rightarrow NH_3 +$ amines
$N \rightarrow NH_3 + HNO_3$	$S \rightarrow H_2S$
$S \rightarrow H_2SO_4$	$P \rightarrow PH_3$ and phosphorus compounds
$P \rightarrow H_3PO_4$	$C \rightarrow CH_4$

* Based upon data in Klein, L., 1962. *River pollution Vol. II. Causes and effects.* Butterworth, London.

While methane, CH_4, is odorless, amines have a fishy smell, hydrogen sulfide, H_2S, smells like rotten eggs, and some phosphate compounds have a wormy smell. When these are added to the smell of decaying fish or algae, the shift to anaerobic conditions is not a pleasant one.

Now and then severe pollution from excess organic matter occurs in natural situations, as when heavy leaf fall temporarily overwhelms a small stream, creating a large BOD and possibly killing fish. But most organic wastes are related to our misuse of our environment by the release of untreated human and animal wastes as well as those from industrial processing—blood, milk solids, grease, pulp liquor, washings from fruit and vegetables.

Much progress has been made in redesigning food processing machinery and techniques to reduce both the volume of water required and the BOD of the wastes. Potato processing is a good example. Formerly 300 to 1000 gallons of water were required to treat 1000 pounds of potatoes. The potatoes were first dipped in a concentrated solution of sodium hydroxide, which softened the skin and outer layers, then scrubbed in water; treated this way, they produced much starch plus the wastes from peeling and blanching. These products contributed to the high BOD in the waste stream. Today potatoes are dipped briefly into a dilute caustic soda solution, dried, then dry scrubbed and rinsed. Not only is a quarter of the former amount of caustic soda required, but water needs are reduced by 80 percent and the peel wastes mixed with trimmings can be used for animal feed.

Human waste disposal is not a recent problem, though it certainly has been made more difficult by the sharp population rise of the past century. The Old Testament met and solved, for its time, the question of human waste disposal: "and thou shalt have a paddle upon thy weapon; and it shall be when thou wilt ease thyself abroad, thou shalt dig therewith and shalt turn back and cover that which cometh from thee." [3] Millions of farmers in Asia still utilize a similar approach, fertilizing their fields and rice paddies with "night soil." The people of medieval towns and cities, unable to return waste to the soil, dumped it from their windows into the street, requiring wellbred gentlemen of the day to defend their sensibilities by carrying an orange stuck with cloves to mask the foulness of the streets.

It is perhaps our misfortune that we have removed ourselves from the problem by the simple expedient of flushing a toilet. With the whoosh of six gallons of water, the problem of waste disposal is of no further concern to most of us except when a toilet stops up; then we are very concerned indeed.

Disposal of the enormous quantities of human wastes that have accompanied urban population growth has overwhelmed the primitive technology of the toilet/sewer pipe/sewage treatment plant. First, using pure water to flush wastes is extremely wasteful of water—13,000 gallons per person per year to get rid of 165 gallons of body waste. Also, sewer lines are very expensive to install and replace, as millions of suburbanites are discovering now that septic tanks are slowly being replaced by regional systems. Treatment plants are approaching power plants in cost and complexity. And still we are left in most instances with water so full of unwanted nutrients that eutrophication is inevitable. The incentive of economy of scale, which has led to enormous treatment plants, has also generated enormous piles of processed sewage or sludge that nobody wants. New York City has traditionally dumped its sludge and other solid wastes many miles out to sea, but the wastes haven't stayed there. In 1976 miles of beaches on the south shore of Long Island were closed because the sludge had returned, cast up to join the crude oil one normally expects to find on the beach. Loath to discard an easy solution to the sludge problem, the city continues to barge its wastes out to sea as though they were being dumped off the edge of the world.

But sludge, repellent as it is on the beach, is basically an aesthetic problem. More serious is chlorination of water before and often after use. Over

[3] Deuteronomy xxiii:12–13.

10 million tons of chlorine are used every year in North America to purify water supplies; 3 percent of this amount ends up in natural waterways as organochlorines of great variety. A disturbing phenomenon was first noticed in the water supply of New Orleans, where a bladder cancer rate three times that of other southern cities puzzled epidemiologists. It was discovered that the chlorine from treated city water combined with the witches' brew of organic industrial pollutants in the lower Mississippi (the source of New Orleans' water). Of the 66 organic compounds isolated from the river, several were in the polynuclear aromatic hydrocarbon group, potentially dangerous carcinogens that are not effectively removed by standard activated carbon filtration techniques.

Chlorine has been used to purify water in the United States because it is generally effective against most pathogenic bacteria. Ozone, which has been used in Paris for over half a century, is another water disinfectant without many of chlorine's side effects. There is no residue; its potent oxidizing propensity can destroy sulfides, cyanides, and pesticides; and iron and manganese can be oxidized, hydrolyzed, and precipitated out of waste streams or water supplies. Also, ozone, unlike chlorine, is not affected by pH or nitrate concentration, and it leaves no taste in treated water. However, it cannot be stored, equipment changeover would be expensive, and water can be recontaminated after it leaves the treatment plant since ozone, unlike chlorine, is not dissolved in the water. So it is likely that the United States will use ozone more to treat sewage than water supply, despite the carcinogenic implications of chlorination.

As ubiquitous as the toilet has become, there are alternatives. Body wastes could be incinerated, although the energy costs are high; or they could be composted. A nine-foot fiber glass container in the basement might receive wastes from the toilet and garbage from the kitchen and slowly, odorlessly turn them into compost that could be recycled in the back yard or used to repot the philodendron. A biological apparatus popular enough to be stocked by Sears Roebuck turns the wastes into water with a weekly fix of enzymes and bacteria. The end product is a quart of odorless, pathogen-free liquid that could be used to water the philodendron. The most fascinating alternative is the use of low viscosity oil in a conventional toilet. The oil would carry wastes to a gravity separation tank, where the oil would be drawn off the top, filtered, and pumped back to the toilet. The wastes would be pumped out periodically and hauled off to a central composting plant.

But the human waste disposal problem is not limited to our houses. More and more people are spending their leisure hours aboard a great variety of pleasure craft, many with toilets but few with means to handle the waste properly. In most instances waste is dumped overboard with little or no treatment. In addition to the sanitary wastes there is litter (one pound of paper, cans, and bottles, and one-half pound of garbage per capita per day of boating); bilge water containing lubricating oil leakage; and in large ships, ballast. The average freighter carries 1000 tons of ballast (usually water taken from one polluted harbor and released in another), making ships pollution carriers par excellence. In 1964, of the 50,000 ships clearing United States customs, 16,000 released 16 million tons of polluted ballast water. Other sources of vessel waste include wash water from cleaning operations, usually containing high concentrations of detergents, and accidental cargo discharges through negligence, collision, grounding, or sinking.

The United States Navy until quite recently disposed of its shipboard wastes over the side, causing an enormous sewage problem in large ports when the fleet was in. Consider how much waste is generated in a single day by a nuclear aircraft carrier with five thousand men aboard!

Some possibilities for aboard-ship sewage disposal include holding tanks, incinerators, biological treatment systems (BTS), and maceration-disinfection. Holding tanks are adaptable to any size vessel and minimize mechanical failure, but they are large and heavy. They are also suitable only for human wastes, and require shore support facilities that are nonexistent even in some large ports. Incinerators are lightweight, but have a high power requirement. Like holding tanks, they are limited to human waste, and, in addition, can be a fire hazard. A BTS can handle all kinds of sewage, since it is a miniature secondary sewage treatment system, but it is quite large and heavy and requires trained personnel for proper operation. Maceration-disinfection is an easily installed, lightweight system, occupying little space, but it assures no reduction in BOD or mineral and organic content, its disinfectant efficiency is not always certain, and it is subject to failure. Perhaps the most promising approach is a variant of the recirculating flush toilet. The airline model can handle eighty to a hundred uses before servicing; larger models, capable of servicing fifty people for seven to ten days, have been developed for ships.

ANIMAL WASTES

Humans are not the only waste producers, of course. Kansas, which is not overpopulated, has such a water pollution problem that no stream or river in the state is safe for drinking or swimming. The cause is the more than 200 feedlots scattered across the state (Figure 16.2). The 5.5 million cattle and 1.3 million hogs daily excrete the sewage equivalent of 70 million people. Most of this goes directly into streams and rivers with little attempt at control. Because of this pollution load some towns have had to use ten times the usual level of chlorination to purify their drinking water.

In the nation 1.2 billion animals produce 20 billion pounds of nitro-

Fig. 16.2 The animal wastes from this midwestern surface drainage system without treatment. The waste from one cow equals the wastes of ten people. (USDA)

gen per year. Much has been said about the desirability of returning this manna to the billion acres of farm land in the United States. If the livestock were distributed 1.2 per acre the problem would be solved, but of course they are not. The energy costs of redistributing manure more than three miles beyond its point of origin become prohibitive. Even if the manure could be transported, twenty pounds per acre would not support most crops in the style to which they have become accustomed. So the problem remains. However, new regulations will require feedlots, which process millions of livestock a year, to treat their wastes before releasing the effluent. Even so, it will take five to ten years before pollution from this source can be reasonably controlled.

One form of livestock has not been included in these calculations, however: man's best friend, the urban dog. In the United States today there are 40 million dogs. Although that is only 0.1 dog per capita, 46 percent of all American homes have at least one dog. The 500,000 dogs in New York City produce 150,000 pounds of feces and 90,000 gallons of urine per day. Dogs being dogs, this waste is liberally spread on the sidewalks and streets. It is interesting to speculate on the sudden popularity of dogs, particularly in cities, the least appropriate place for them; it is less interesting to cope with their wastes. A few well-publicized arrests of prominent dog owners might attract attention to the problem. Since dogs instinctively prefer fire hydrants and trees, neither of which are designed for their use, an analogous system of stations might be positioned strategically along streets and dogs trained to use them. Until this comes about the very least urban dog owners can do is curb their dogs.

TREATMENT OF HUMAN AND ANIMAL WASTES

Once the organic materials in wastes are broken down into their components by sewage treatment, the minerals must be removed to avoid overfertilizing the environment. Precipitation removes only some of the minerals; those like nitrates, which are highly water soluble, are more difficult to deal with. A useful approach, first used by a large food processor in New Jersey and later developed and refined by a research team at The Pennsylvania State University, uses the soil and its plants and animals as a living filter. Effluent is piped from a sewage treatment plant and sprayed on a field, pasture, or forest at a rate that is commensurate with soil absorption (Figure 16.3). If effluent is applied at a rate of two inches a week, 129 acres could filter a million gallons a day. The plant roots and soil microorganisms are especially efficient in removing phosphates and nitrates, the two nutrients that cause the most problems in aquatic systems.

Gratifyingly, experimentally grown crops benefited from the fertilizing effect of effluents; hay yield increased 300 percent and the nitrogen content of wheat increased by 30 percent. But there are problems with this approach. It requires the lack of surface drainage, which would short-circuit the process, and deep soil to allow maximum filtration.

A recent extension of this technique has been its application to revegetation of strip mine spoil banks. Because of their dark surface and exposed position, spoil banks become excessively hot and dry in the summer, ex-

Fig. 16.3 Year-round spraying of treated sewage effluent onto forest and crop lands at Pennsylvania State University fertilizes the soil and filters the effluent, returning clean water to the water table. (Robert S. Beese)

383

ceeding even the broad tolerance of weeds. In addition the soil is usually both infertile and acid, which makes establishment of seedlings impossible.

Application of sewage effluent to these banks ameliorates all these problems. Moisture, which also cools the ground surface by evaporation, allows a broad range of plants to become established, and the mineral nutrients which abound in the effluent encourage rapid and luxuriant plant growth. Finally, the addition of two inches of water a week helps leach some of the acid into lower soil levels, allowing the establishment of species requiring less acid soil. Since transport of the effluent is expensive, the spoil banks and sewage disposal plants should be as close together as possible. The potential benefits of the scheme might even justify the location of sewage plants in the center of spoil areas. Once vegetation is established and the vicious cycle of excessive heat and inadequate moisture is broken, the pipes distributing the effluent could be shifted to another barren area. When the area surrounding the sewage plant is revegetated, the effluent could be used indefinitely to increase the productivity of the new forest.

The same technique, using semi-solid sewage sludge rather than liquid effluent, is being employed by Chicago. The sludge is shipped down the Illinois River to Liverpool, where it is pumped in slurry form ten miles to a holding basin, then spread on 11,500 acres of strip mined land at the cost of $10 per ton.

INDUSTRIAL WASTE TREATMENT

The waste water from some industrial plants—food processing, textiles, rubber and plastics, machinery, and transportation equipment—can usually be accommodated by the plant's own sewage treatment equipment or by nearby municipal facilities for a fee. Wastes from paper, chemicals, petroleum, coal, and primary metals are not so easily handled because of the acidity, toxicity, or resistance of the wastes to bacterial breakdown.

REUSE AND BY-PRODUCTS

Recycling and reuse of water in the plup and paper industry has increased tremendously since 1950 and will continue as water supplies and pollution standards tighten. Lignosulfonates, a by-product of paper manufacturing, have dispersal and sequestering characteristics that make them usable as additives to drilling mud in oil wells and as stabilizers of unpaved road surfaces in the summer. Even though 425 million pounds of lignosulfonates are used yearly, the supply is much greater.

There are other possible uses of pulp wastes. Over 40 percent of the domestic supply of vanillin (artificial vanilla flavoring) is synthesized from lignosulfonate, as are glacial acetic and formic acids. The sugar xylose, which is quite abundant in pulping liquor, is very sweet but has few calories, making it a potential substitute for cyclamates or saccharin. The complex sugars from hemicellulose can be converted to ethanol (grain alcohol), for which there is a steady industrial demand. Hemicellulose can also be eliminated from the effluent by culturing a yeast, *Torula*, which can be harvested as a valuable protein source. However, competition with established chemical industries already producing these materials is great, and these by-product activities are not as profitable as they may appear.

The economic elimination of the small processor and his replacement with much larger operations is already reducing pollution loads in industry. Food processing plants that are large and diverse enough to afford their own disposal plants can effectively reduce the organic content of their wastes and ultimately the BOD of the aquatic environment. This has been demonstrated with canning plants, meat packers, and diary product processors.

Most industrial problems, then, can be handled by recycling, reuse, by-product utilization, more efficient and effective equipment, and biological breakdown of organic wastes. For the problems that remain, more radical methods have been proposed.

DEEP INJECTION WELLS

When oil wells are drilled, large quantities of salt brine are brought to the surface with the oil. One way to dispose of the brine has been to pump it, under pressure, down dry wells or new wells drilled for this purpose. In the past forty years over 40,000 brine injection wells have been drilled or utilized. The chemical industry and others have followed this example, using deep injection wells for the disposal of highly toxic or difficult-to-handle wastes generated in various processes. By 1975 over three hundred permits for such wells had been issued. As surface disposal became more and more restricted, other industries will doubtless use this technique as the cheapest and most convenient way to get rid of wastes. But deep injection wells cannot be put down anywhere; there must be permeable sedimentary rock layers such as limestone or sandstone, capable of transmitting fluids and porous enough to hold large quantities of liquid in the spaces between the grains of rock. To contain this liquid properly the porous layer must be bounded above and below by impermeable layers. The desired stratum must also be below the water table to prevent contamination (Figure 16.4). Although these requirements seem rather specialized, over half the land area of the United States appears to be suitable for injection, especially the southeastern coastal plain and the interior lowland of the Midwest. Wastes put into deep injection wells

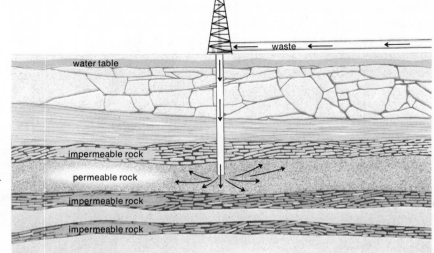

Fig. 16.4 A deep well injection must deposit the waste fluid in a permeable layer of rock bounded by impermeable layers. The water table lies much closer to the surface.

must have a low enough solid content to avoid filling the pores of the rock stratum, which would reduce its permeability. Potential dangers include the generation of heat by radioactive wastes, which may produce explosive steam, and the precipitation of salts or heavy metals, which may contaminate water supplies. In the last decade, well disposal has become more attractive as surface water standards have become more stringent. Hence wells are used by the petrochemical, chemical, steel, plastic, pulp, and photoprocessing industries. The effluents they dispose of include phenols, cyanides, phosphates, chlorides, nitrates, chromates, sulfates, alcohols, chlorinated hydrocarbons, acetates, and ketones. Although most of the wells are between 1000 and 6000 feet deep, some are shallower than 1000 feet, and others as deep as 12,000 feet.

One such deep injection well near Denver, Colorado has stirred up much controversy. This well was drilled through the flat strata into the crystalline bedrock 12,000 feet below. Fluids were both injected and deposited by gravity flow at rates varying from 2 to 6 million gallons a month, beginning in March 1962 and terminating in February 1966. Since a number of minor earthquakes were recorded in the Denver area during this period, it was thought that the deep injection well might have caused them. A comparison of earthquake frequency and waste injection (Figure 16.5) does indeed show an interesting correlation. The chances were calculated to be only one in 2.5 million that the earthquakes associated with the injection well in both time and space were solely due to coincidence. Apparently the fluid injected into the basement rock lubricated fracture lines, allowing tension built up over the years to be released through a series of slippages along these fault lines, which resulted in earthquakes. As the volume of fluid injected increased, either there was more slippage or a greater area was affected. The only solution beyond cessation of injection would be to remove some of the fluid already present, or, barring that, to wait for a natural decrease in the resistance to diffusion as the fluid percolates further and further from the well.

This example raises several questions about deep injection wells and liquid waste disposal in general. One wonders, in light of the Denver example, whether such wells should be used at all in areas of seismic activity. In addition, the qualifications outlined previously suggest that storage capacity is limited and perhaps should be reserved for wastes that are difficult to handle by conventional means. Injection wells certainly should not be used for mere convenience or economy. The presence of faults even in the most stable rock casts doubt on the ability of supposedly impermeable rock layers to contain wastes permanently and to prevent their introduction to the water table. Finally, we know little about confining the lateral spread of liquids in a stratum; this information would be of great significance should we wish to retrieve these wastes in the future. There are many instances of yesterday's garbage becoming today's food, and the time may come when it would be most useful to recover as resources the wastes we discard today.

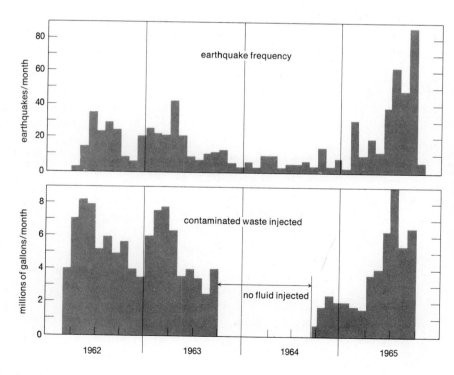

Fig. 16.5 When earthquake frequency is compared with the volume of fluid injected into a disposal well at the Rocky Mountain arsenal near Denver, Colorado, a cause and effect relationship is strongly suggested. (Modified from J. H. Healy et al., Science 161, 1968. Copyright 1968 by the American Association for the Advancement of Science)

The near future will doubtless see a sharp increase in by-product recovery and in the reuse and recycling of water. As this comes about, industy's role as a major polluter of water will steadily decrease.

EUTROPHICATION

In recent years a major controversy has arisen over the nature of the trigger factor responsible for eutrophication (see Chapter 2); some researchers support carbon, some phosphorus. The controversy about overproductive bodies of water seems to have been resolved by some experiments in a series of small lakes in northwestern Ontario which were oligotrophic and low in carbon. One dumbbell-shaped lake afforded a unique opportunity to treat one basin with carbon and nitrogen, and the other with carbon, nitrogen, and phosphorus. Two weeks after treatment the second lake produced a dense bloom of *Anabaena*, a blue-green alga characteristic of many eutrophic lakes (Figure 16.6). The first lake, despite the addition of carbon and nitrogen, remained oligotrophic. In following years, phosphorus-treated lakes quickly reverted to oligotrophy when phosphorus was withheld.

Other research seems to indicate that algal blooms are not necessarily induced but indigenous. Normally temperate lakes experience two blooms: a spring bloom of unicellular greens, cryptomonads, and diatoms that results from the spring overturn that recharges the surface water with nutrients from the lake bottom; and a summer bloom characterized by gelatinous-sheathed colonial greens that thrive despite the depletion of phosphorus and nitrogen by the spring bloom. Apparently the herbivorous zooplankton, which according to dogma are supposed to reduce the abundance of algae by grazing, actually stimulate the growth of the algae they feed upon. *Daphnia*, the chief grazer, feed on *Sphaerocystis*, a planktonic green alga enveloped in a polysaccharide sheath. But 90 percent of the algal cells not only pass intact through the gut of *Daphnia* but absorb vital nutrients from the remains of other edible algae and various *Daphnia* metabolites. Having procured their essential nutrients, they grow rapidly upon emergence from the digestive tract of the host grazer. As the grazers decline over the summer the phytoplankton shifts to slower-growing inedible blue-green algae, which can better survive on the less abundant nutrients, of the late summer and early fall.

Once again the environment is more complicated than we simplifiers and pigeonholers give it credit for being. Phosphorus is not exonerated by these research results, however, just put into perspective.

The major sources of phosphorus in our highly manipulated environments are domestic waste and agricultural runoff. The phosphorus content of domestic sewage is about evenly divided between human waste and household detergents.

Fig. 16.6 *Originally both basins of this lake in northwestern Ontario were oligotrophic. The upper basin was enriched with carbon, nitrogen, and phosphorus. The lower basin was enriched with just carbon and nitrogen. In two weeks the upper basin developed a massive algal bloom while the lower basin remained clear, which suggests that phosphorous acted as a trigger factor.* (D. W. Schindler, Fisheries and Marine Service, Freshwater Institute, Winnipeg, Manitoba, Canada)

DETERGENTS

The unusual cleaning powers of detergents (Figure 16.7) are not the result of a single magic molecule engineered by far-seeing chemists. There are many components, each tailored for a specific cleansing function, yet working together so that the result is greater than the potential of any

Fig. 16.7 *It is sobering to realize that this bewildering array of detergents will sooner or later end up in some environment, somewhere.*

389

single part. Typically, a detergent contains a surfactant, a builder, a silicate, and carboxymethylcellulose.

The surfactant or sudsing agent (30 to 50 percent of the total) is an organic agent that can penetrate between the soil particle and cloth or fabric. This is because the surfactant molecule is bipolar; one end is attracted to the dirt particle and the other is attracted to water. This bipolar action combined with machine agitation quite effectively removes dirt and, by lowering surface tension, grease as well.

Once in the wash water, dirt must be kept in suspension; this is one function of the builder. Another function is to soften water, eliminating the scummy precipitate soap produces in hard water, which contains a large amount of calcium and magnesium salts. While the quantity varies greatly from brand to brand, most detergents contain up to 50 percent builder. The remaining detergent ingredients, though present in small amounts, complement and complete the cleaning action of the surfactant and builder. Sodium silicate is added as a corrosion inhibitor and carboxymethylcellulose is an anti-redeposition agent that helps keep removed dirt in suspension until the wash water is flushed away.

At one time the surfactant caused problems because of its tendency to keep sudsing in the environment beyond the washing machine. A change in the structure of this component in 1965 alleviated this problem. But an even greater problem has since been recognized. The builder, which comprises up to half the packaged detergent, contains an impressive amount of phosphorus in the form of tripolyphosphate. Since this, like the other detergent ingredients, must be water soluble to perform its cleansing function, it is also available to microorganisms when it enters the environment in sewage effluent. Initially the potential fertilizing effect of tripolyphosphate was probably not considered important enough to worry about, but with the enthusiastic acceptance of detergents by the public, millions of pounds of phosphorus were soon being added to the environment each year. The result was algal blooms in increasing frequency across the country.

Since many bloom organisms are photosynthetic, the oxygen level in the water during the daylight hours is sharply augmented as oxygen is released in the photosynthetic process. But during the night, when there is no photosynthesis to balance respiration, which consumes oxygen, the oxygen content of the water may fall below the level necessary for respiration of higher forms of animal life; fish kills often result. This is a particular problem in the still water of lakes. In addition, windrows of algal mats washed up on lake shores decompose, producing hydrogen sulfide and other by-products, and often making bodies of water unsuitable for any use.

The connection between detergent builders and algal blooms was eventually recognized, and the industry is presently dealing with its second unanticipated problem. Unfortunately we cannot assume that once phosphates are somehow removed from detergents in manufacture or processed out of sewage effluent, algal blooms will quickly disappear, since detergents are only one source of the phosphorus we generate.

ALTERNATIVES TO DETERGENTS

But they are an unnecessary source, since we are not obliged to use detergents. Nearly 60 percent of the population of the United States lives in soft water areas, where sodium stearate or soap-based cleansers would work as well as detergents. For the hard water regions, lime soap dispersing agents (LSDA) are effective. These compounds—anionic fatty alcohols, fatty amides, fatty acid esters, and nonionic compounds based on tallow alcohols—disperse the lime soaps or scum normally precipitated in hard water. They are easily available from tallow, and are biodegradable and nontoxic. Since they have been used for years in bar soap, it would not take an industrial revolution to transfer the LSDAs to laundry use. But unfortunately for the environment, detergents are more profitable than soap for the industry to manufacture and sell. Caustic soda replacements for phosphates in some laundry products were supposedly dangerous, causing the EPA, the Food and Drug Administration, and the Council on Environmental Quality to change their minds about phasing out phosphates and urge the public to purchase phosphate-based detergents as the lesser evil. The government would evidently rather support removal of phosphates from the effluent than control their entrance in detergents.

AGRICULTURAL RUNOFF

Despite the enormous quantity of phosphorus being added to the environment in detergents, we are adding several times this quantity in the fertilization of farmlands. As the world's population continues to increase, the need for greater productivity in agriculture becomes critical, and increased fertilization is one of the chief means to this end. But when highly soluble fertilizer is used, 10 to 25 percent is leached away into the surface runoff before the plants can use it. This represents a loss to the farmer and a burden to the aquatic ecosystems, which are being grossly overfertilized. Another agricultural source of phosphorus is animal waste. Livestock, increasingly grouped in feedlots, contribute 70 million pounds of phosphorus per year, almost as much as detergents.

SOME SOLUTIONS

While the phosphorus problem will never be completely solved, there are several ways to control the various sources of man-generated phosphorus.

Where it exists at all, sewage treatment consists of one or two stages. Primary treatment simply removes suspended solids; after the filtering process, the remaining liquid is released into the environment. Secondary treatment goes a step further and utilizes bacteria to break down into inorganic compounds the sludge or organic wastes that were settled out in the primary process. The water is then filtered, chlorinated to remove the bacteria, and released. The BOD is greatly reduced because of the in-plant decomposition of organic material, but the effluent still contains large amounts of phosphates, nitrates, and most other nutrients known to promote plant and animal growth. Primary and secondary treatment of sewage is only partly effective. Some kind of tertiary treatment to remove nutrients *must be included* if artificial enrichment of surface water is to be controlled.

There are several possible tertiary treatments using existing technology. The effluent can be prebloomed—that is, held in shallow tanks or pools for a time to allow algal growth to remove nutrients. Algae can then be filtered out, leaving the water considerably reduced in its nutrient content. Problems with this approach are the space necessary for the holding ponds and the need to supply heat to keep algae growing at a high rate in the winter in most northern states. Perhaps heat generated from the activated sludge phase of secondary treatment or coolant water from a power plant could be used to heat the water to allow a longer season of algal growth. The algae filtered out of the final effluent could be processed and sold as a protein feed for livestock, generating some economic return. A more promising solution uses lime or alum to take phosphorus out in the form of insoluble precipitates that can then be treated to regenerate the precipitator and perhaps provide some form of phosphorus that has agricultural or industrial use.

Unfortunately nitrates in sewage are much more difficult to remove because, unlike phosphates, most nitrates and ammoniates are water soluble. One possibility involves the use of *Nitrosomonas* and *Nitrobacter* to nitrify the nitrates to ammonia. By adjusting the pH to 10 or 11 and aerating it, the ammonia can be stripped off as a gas.

URBAN RUNOFF

We have long assumed that once all point sources of pollution were eliminated water quality would quickly rebound, if not to primeval levels, at least to the point where most waterways would be safe for swimming, fishing, and other recreational uses. However, the pavement of cities collects vast amounts of pollutants, fallout from chimneys, and car exhausts which storm sewers direct into the nearest waterway after every heavy rainfall. Even a city of modest size can introduce 250,000 pounds of lead and as much as 30,000 pounds of mercury per year into adjacent surface water. Altogether urban rainwater runoff carries more heavy metals such as lead, mercury, copper, and zinc into waterways than does the discharge from most industries.

DEATH OF A GREAT LAKE?

Most problems of excessive aquatic productivity, however unpleasant, have been limited to streams, segments of rivers, and small lakes. But with the appropriate conditions, there is no limit on the size of over-productive waters: large lakes, seas, and ultimately even oceans can become overfertilized with catastrophic results.

Of all the world's overfertilized lakes, Lake Erie is one of the largest and best known. In fact, the western basin of this lake is so polluted that there is disagreement about whether this portion of the lake is merely dying or already dead. On the other hand, the eastern basin is relatively unpolluted.

Lake Erie, like the four other Great Lakes, is a glacially scoured lowland that was filled by the melting continental glacier around twelve thousand years ago. Although Lake Erie is not the smallest Great Lake, because of its shallowness (a mean depth of fifty-eight feet) it has the smallest volume. This shallowness is at the root of its problems.

Once clear and filled with valuable fish and game, western Lake Erie today embodies all that can go wrong in an aquatic system. The more desirable species of fish have disappeared; the once clear water is filled with excessive numbers of microorganisms; mats of filamentous algae at times cover whole square miles of lake surface; swimming is impossible in many places because of the quantity of untreated sewage in the water and the decaying vegetation blanketing the beaches; oil scums often cover harbors and coves, making boating and water sports unpleasant.

Of all the Great Lakes, Lake Erie is adjacent to the largest number of population centers; each has varied industries with effluents to be disposed of. Erie produces paper; Buffalo, flour and chemicals; Cleveland, petrochemicals and steel; Toledo, glass and steel; and Detroit, automobiles, steel, and paper (Figure 16.8). Naturally, large population centers contribute quantities of sewage, both treated and raw. And the agricultural land between the cities adds pesticides, herbicides, and fertilizers, giving the lake no respite. Bear in mind that this is (or was) a "great lake," 240 miles long and 50 miles wide, with a volume of 109 cubic miles!

FISH AND POLLUTION

The first symptom of lake-wide problems in Lake Erie occurred in the 1920s, when the fish crop—50 million pounds annually of cisco, whitefish,

Fig. 16.8 When Great Lakes cities with a population of 100,000 or more are spotted on a map, the clustering around Lake Erie helps to explain the critical nature of that lake's pollution problem.

pike, and sturgeon—began to fall. By 1965 the catch of these commercially valuable fish had fallen to just 1000 pounds. Lake Erie is certainly not devoid of fish, for about 50 million pounds of other types of fish are still caught every year; but the more valuable species have been replaced by catfish, carp, drum, and other less valuable types (called "rough" fish by commercial fishermen).

Why did this happen? During the warm season of the year all but the most shallow lakes stratify into three layers (Figure 16.9): a warm surface layer, epilimnion; a transition layer of rapidly changing temperature, thermocline; and a cold deep layer, hypolimnion. Under normal condi-

Fig. 16.9 In the summer deep lakes stratify into a cold hypolimnion, a zone of rapid temperature change or thermocline, and an upper layer of relatively warm water. The dark line describes this temperature profile.

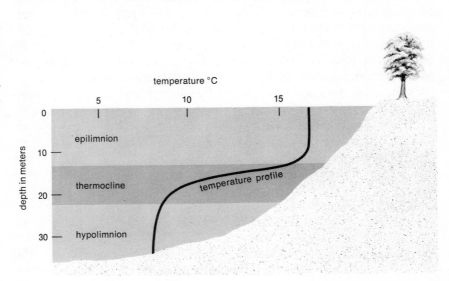

tions whitefish, cisco, and other cold-water fish move to the deeper, colder hypolimnion in summer, and return to the surface in fall when storms and colder weather mix the layers and the lake again becomes thermally homogeneous.

With increasing eutrophication, problems develop. Normally, a certain number of algae are found in the warm surface water during the summer. At the end of the growing season, they die and fall to the bottom, where they are broken down by bottom bacteria into inorganic nutrients held in the bottom mud. By the next summer, enough nutrients have leached from the watershed into the lake to support another population of algae. No more algae can grow than accumulated nutrients are able to support, and so a balance is maintained. When nutrients pour in from man-generated sources, the balance is upset. Great blooms of algae released from their dependence on natural nutrients fill the epilimnion during the summer, sinking to the bottom during fall and winter. When the lake stratifies the following summer, extra thick organic layers at the bottom so stimulate the growth of bacteria that the oxygen level of the hypolimnion begins to fall, often below the minimum requirements of fish. Because cold water can hold more oxygen than warm water, cold-water fish such as trout or cisco have developed, through evolution, higher oxygen requirements than warm-water fish such as carp or catfish. Hence, when the oxygen level of the cold deep water begins to fall, the valuable cisco, whitefish, and pike are eliminated.

THE FUTURE OF LAKE ERIE

The deoxygenation of the hypolimnion is far more serious than the loss of valuable fish. Under normal oligotrophic conditions, when the organic sediment load is light enough to allow reasonable oxygenation of the hypolimnion, the bottom mud is covered by a thin layer of iron in the insoluble or ferric oxidation state, usually ferric hydroxide. This compound not only absorbs much phosphorus from the water, but because of its insolubility seals the bottom mud, preventing exchange of nutrients in the mud with the water above.

When oxygen is exhausted, the iron changes to the soluble ferrous state. This not only puts phosphorus into solution as ferrous phosphate but exposes the bottom mud, allowing free entrance of nutrients into the lake water. The problem in Lake Erie, then, is both simple and overwhelming. Wherever pollution stimulates algal blooms, which later decompose and deoxygenate the bottom, nutrient-rich mud is exposed. Since the mud is capable of contributing its nutrients to the lake water, stimulating still more algal growth, deoxygenating more lake bottom, a vicious cycle is perpetuated. Even if all man-generated pollutants or nutrients were prevented from entering the lake, there might still be quite enough nutrients already in the lake to continue algal blooms and their problems far into the future.

Although the misuse of Lake Erie makes a rather depressing story, some smaller lakes have been snatched from the green slime of recreational death by active community concern and careful planning. Lake Washington, east of Seattle, is 24 miles long and 2 to 4 miles wide (Figure 16.10). Fifty years ago Seattle was far to the west and the lake's eastern shore was sprinkled with small towns, each with fewer than 10,000 inhabitants. The western shore was either parkland or large estates. Then in

Fig. 16.10 Considering its location, surrounded by Seattle and its suburbs, it is not surprising that Lake Washington became badly polluted as its eastern shore became urbanized. But when the people living in its drainage basin faced the problem squarely, effective measures were taken to restore the lake to the recreational uses enjoyed in the past. The body of water to the left is Puget Sound. (NASA)

1940 a floating bridge spanned the lake and population growth on the eastern shore began in earnest, rising from 33,000 in 1950 to over 120,000 in 1970. Although many of the larger communities built sewage treatment plants, the outfall of these and of the septic systems of communities without sewers flowed into the lake. By 1958 dissolved oxygen had disappeared from even the deepest part of the lake, driving out the salmon; water clarity had diminished to 2.5 feet, and algal growth made summer recreational use of the lake something less than pleasant. The problem wasn't really Seattle's, because most of its sewage was piped into Elliott Bay, an arm of Puget Sound. The difficulty lay in the typical hodge-podge of tax districts, townships, and cities that surrounded the lake. Clearly, the answer was a metropolitan system that would pull everything together.

The Metro concept was pioneered by a young lawyer, James Ellis, and a citizens' committee, which developed legislation supporting a metropolitan district that would handle sewage disposal, transportation, and land use planning. While the legislature passed the bill, a majority vote was required in both Seattle and the surrounding communities. In early 1958 voters in Seattle approved Metro, but the suburbs killed it. Since the entire Metro concept was apparently too progressive for 1958 it was cut down to sewage disposal only. After a long smelly summer, which must have changed the minds of many voters, the Metro package was resubmitted and passed in September 1958. By constructing interceptors all around the lake and building four large treatment plants on Puget Sound, all sewage discharges into Lake Washington were halted. Within a couple of years, even before the system was completed, the BOD in the lake dropped by 90 percent, fish returned to deep water, clarity increased to 15 feet, and phosphorus levels fell from 70 ppb to 22 ppb. The cost of the project was held to $2 per month per household.

The Lake Washington success story closely parallels that of San Diego Bay (see Chapter 17). The requirements are few but difficult to generate: a small group or an individual with time, drive, and vision to convert public apathy into concern; and a public willingness to spend money in perpetuity to achieve a desired goal. Given these two requirements any community, large or small, can come to terms with its environmental problems. Even as large a city as London can see results from its cleanup efforts. In 1958 there were no fish in the Thames River in metropolitan London. After two decades of persistent and systematic attention, pollution in the river was reduced to the point where over sixty species of fish including brown trout can either live in the river or pass through the polluted stretches into the cleaner headwaters.

THERMAL LOADING

With the rise of industry in the eighteenth century, water came to play an increasingly important role as a coolant in many manufacturing processes. With continued growth and diversification of industry, the demand for cooling water has soared. Today over 80 percent of the water used by industry in the United States is used for cooling. Of all industrial water users, the electric power industry is the largest, requiring 111 billion gallons per day. When limited, this loading of waste heat into a natural aquatic system caused few problems; but when industrial plants began to use almost the entire flow of a river for cooling purposes, environmental damage resulted.

HEAT AS A POLLUTANT

Why is addition of heat energy to an aquatic system even considered pollution? Although heat loading of a stream causes it to depart from its normal thermal character, which was our definition of pollution at the beginning of this chapter, there is a more specific reason to view thermal loading as a form of pollution. As the temperature of water increases, its ability to hold oxygen decreases. Since dissolved oxygen is the key to assimilation of organic wastes by microorganisms, any activity that might impair this assimilation can be labeled pollution.

The presence of dissolved oxygen is probably the single most important factor in the biology of aquatic systems, and a great variety of physical and biological interactions stem from it. Aeration or oxygenation is derived from two sources: exchange with the atmosphere and photosynthetic release by green plants. Depending upon the temperature differ-

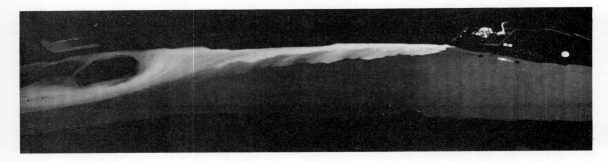

Fig. 16.11 An infrared aerial photo of hot coolant water from a coal-burning power plant being dumped into a river. Since infrared film is sensitive to heat, the lighter areas are those having the warmest surface. Note the slow rate of mixing of hot and cold water. (Environmental Analysis Department, HRB-Singer, Inc.)

ence between a heated effluent and the body of water into which it is being flushed, the heated discharge can either mix vertically and horizontally or stratify in a layer above the cooler, denser receiving water (Figure 16.11). If the temperature difference is small and the receiving water shallow, complete mixing usually takes place. If the temperature difference is great and the receiving water deep, stratification usually results: the colder water beneath is covered with a blanket of hot water, which not only carries less oxygen because of its higher temperature but is less likely to exchange with the cooler water beneath because of its different density. Biological reduction of the oxygen content of the atmospherically unreplenished water below might then produce anaerobic conditions.

With a given thermal load and assuming complete mixing, a stream or lake might have its temperature elevated by around 10°C, which could lead to a complete shift from cold- to warm-water forms of life. Such a change might cause little disruption to the productivity of a body of water once the adjustment had taken place. But in almost no instance would the production of heated effluent be constant for long enough periods to allow either adaptation or replacement to be effective. Shutdown of a power plant or factory for just one day in midwinter would have a disastrous effect on warm-water species introduced and maintained by the artificially high water temperature.

Much more unusual but occasionally observed is a cold effluent released into a warm river. The Fontana Dam, a unit of the Tennessee Valley Authority on the Little Tennessee River in North Carolina, releases cold bottom water from its reservoir downstream into the river, eliminating for many miles the warm-water fish usually characteristic of southern rivers. The Glen Canyon Dam has had the same effect on the Colorado River (see Chapter 4).

In the tropics, thermal loading can be much more of a problem because ambient water temperature is closer to the thermal maxima of aquatic life than in temperate systems. In Puerto Rico the thermal maximum of marine algae is only 4 to 6°C above the summer maximum while in France it is 10 to 13°C higher. Therefore a 3°C rise in ambient temperature could eliminate much of the biota of subtropical aquatic systems.

EFFECT OF TEMPERATURE CHANGE ON ORGANISMS

As temperature increases, dissolved oxygen content decreases, as we have seen, but respiration and oxidation rates double for every 10°C temperature increase. In order to meet the respiratory needs of warm-water fish, the dissolved oxygen content of water should be at least 5 ppm during sixteen of every twenty-four hours and should not fall below 3 ppm at any time (Figure 16.12). Even carp, which have an excep-

Fig. 16.12 Occasionally hot summer weather naturally heats shallow water to the point where it cannot hold enough oxygen to meet the needs of fish, causing them to suffocate. This is what killed these shad in the Anacostia River near Washington, D.C. (U.S. Department of the Interior, Fish and Wildlife Service)

399

tionally low oxygen requirement for fish, 0.5 ppm at 0.5°C, must have 1.5 ppm at 35°C.

But temperature interacts with other factors as well. At 1°C, carp can tolerate a carbon dioxide concentration of 120 ppm, but at 36°C a concentration of 55 to 60 ppm is lethal. Similar interactions are seen with pH, salinity, and toxicity. All organisms' survival ability is limited by temperature, but for most, acclimatization is possible to some extent if temperature change is gradual. Sudden change, either up or down, is most often lethal.

The life cycle of many aquatic organisms is closely and delicately geared to water temperature. Fish often are distributed, migrate, and spawn in response to temperature cues. When water temperature is artificially changed, the disruption of normal activities and patterns can be catastrophic. Some animals spawn as the temperature drops in the fall; others spawn as temperature rises in the spring. Shellfish, such as oysters, are so delicately attuned to temperature change that they spawn within a few hours after their environment reaches a critical temperature. Trout eggs take 165 days to hatch at 3°C, only 32 days at 12°C, and will not hatch at all above 15°C. Lifespan is also affected by water temperature; water fleas (*Daphnia*) live for 108 days at 8°C, but only 29 days at 28°C.

Even more subtle effects involve competition among various species, predation rates, incidence of parasitism, and spread of disease. Any one or a combination of these more covert factors can destroy a population as effectively as the more obvious thermal shock.

SIMPLIFYING THE ECOSYSTEM

Plainly, adding hot water to the environment is not the simple act of dilution it might appear to be. To put this subtle disturbance into perspective, we must view an organism in its ecosystem.

Natural ecosystems, whatever their size, are complex; the larger they are, the more complex. Our chief effect on ecosystems is to try, consciously or unconsciously, to simplify them. A potato field is a good example. To channel the productivity of a piece of land as directly as possible into a useful product—potatoes—we simplify the ecosystem by removing all plants or animals that might compete with the potato plants and thereby decrease the yield.

Cultivated plants were selected to survive the stresses (drought, direct sunlight, flooding, and wind) characteristic of human-affected environments. Most native plants have requirements too specialized to tolerate such stress conditions. However, one group of plants, weeds, can not only tolerate stress but can outcompete our plants and become superabundant.

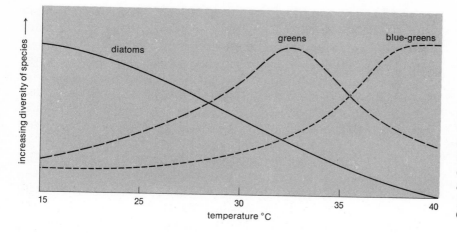

Fig. 16.13 The three most important groups of common freshwater algae, (a) diatoms, (b) greens, and (c) blue-greens, have radically different temperature tolerances. (Modifed from J. Cairns, Jr., Scientist and Citizen 10, 1956)

The appearance of weeds in a field is the first step in the successional process that reduces stress and ultimately leads to the return of a complex ecosystem capable of sustaining itself.

A typical nonpolluted stream may support as many as two dozen species of fish. After pollution, although there may be only three "weed" species, such as carp, killifish, and shiners, the *numbers* of fish may remain the same. The simplifying stress of pollution has channeled the productivity, which in the normal stream was shared by small numbers of many species, into large numbers of a few species.

Even more basic are the effects of stress on food chains. Three major groups of freshwater algae are important to food chains: diatoms, greens, and blue-greens. While all types are eaten by some organisms, most prefer diatoms to greens or blue-greens. Few consumers eat blue-green algae, which can be toxic to some aquatic and terrestrial organisms. These three algal groups differ in their temperature tolerances (Figure 16.13). As temperature rises the number of the more desirable diatom species decreases and the number of the greens and blue-greens increases. At a certain level the greens also decline, leaving the blue-greens most abundant at the higher temperatures. As the relative abundance of these primary producers shifts, the consumers depending upon them for food are affected. A water flea, for example, which might be able to tolerate the thermal extreme of 35°C, would probably starve to death if the diatoms on which it fed could not survive at that temperature. In turn, fish feeding on water fleas would be hard pressed to survive, however tolerant or adaptable they might be to the high water temperature.

Another factor affecting food chains involves the large volume of water used in cooling systems. A plant circulating 500,000 gallons a minute may intercept and enclose a considerable portion of the flow of a small river. Because microorganisms tend to grow in the pipes and reduce the flow, chlorine is used to control such growth. This affects organisms at the outfall, where the coolant is returned to the river, until the chlorine is diluted; it may also sterilize the water flowing through the cooling system. In some installations 95 percent of the organisms are killed during the cooling period. The thermal shock of a rapid 10°C rise is destructive to many species. If the cooling system's intake uses more than a small part of a river's flow, a considerable portion of its microfauna and microflora could be eliminated, with grave effects on the food chain downstream, even to the point of eliminating certain populations of fish.

A heated effluent, then, affects organisms directly and also influences the entire interaction of factors that make up the ecosystem. This makes it extremely difficult to predict the effects of thermal loading. With hydrologic models an engineer may be able to predict the degree of mixing of cooling water, its thickness, and the extent of its stratification, but assessing its total and often subtle biological consequences is far more difficult than determining the thermal death point of one or two fish.

COOLING THE COOLANT

There are several current approaches to removing heat from cooling water before it is reused or discarded.

WET TOWER

The most common practice is to run water in a thin sheet over baffles in huge hyperbola-shaped towers that use drafts of air entering at the base to remove heat by evaporation. A variant is to spray the hot water inside the tower in a fine mist. Cool air rising through the tower condenses the mist, releasing heat, which is carried out of the tow by the air column. In either case the cooled water is either discharged into the environment or recycled. Two problems associated with this wet tower technique are water loss (20,000 to 25,000 gallons per minute for a 1,000-megawatt plant) and fog formation on cold days. When the surface temperature is less than 0°C, the fog freezes on contact, forming hoar frost or rime ice, potentially damaging to vegetation and extremely dangerous on highways. The water loss not only vitiates somewhat the benefit of recycling but concentrates whatever pollutants the effluent contains.

An additional effect recently observed in Ohio and West Virginia is the production of a snowfall up to 2.5 cm deep as far as 43 km from the cooling tower. Apparently the supercooled water droplets changed to ice crystals and slowly fell downwind when weather conditions were conducive (Figure 16.14).

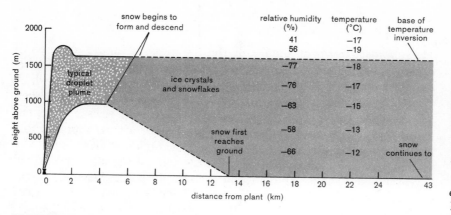

Fig. 16.14 Water droplets from this cooling tower rise to about 1500 meters or the base of the inversion layer, form ice crystals and snowflakes, and then fall out as far as 43 kilometers from the tower. (After M. L. Kramer et al., Meteorological Services, Inc., 1976. "Snowfall observations from natural-draft cooling tower plumes." Science 193; 1239-1241, figure 2. Copyright 1976 by the American Association for the Advancement of Science)

DRY TOWER

In a dry tower the heated effluent is contained in a system of pipes much like the radiator of an automobile. Air is passed over the pipes by a large fan, facilitating heat exchange by radiation and convection. Water loss and, to a lesser extent, fog are controlled by this method, but installation costs are much higher, perhaps two or three times the cost of a wet tower. Also, maintenance costs for one plant of 500-megawatt capacity were calculated at 3 percent of the power output or $500,000 a year to keep the blower fans operating. If large enough, the updraft of hot air could generate clouds.

Both types of tower are expensive to construct, and since they depend on pressure and temperature differentials across the tower base for maximum efficiency, they work best in cool climates. The hot American summers make cooling towers less efficient than in the cool summer climates in Europe, where these towers have become conspicuous features of the landscape (Figure 16.15).

Fig. 16.15 Those ghostly drumlike cooling towers are becoming more common in the United States as stricter effluent controls limit the amount of hot water that can be dumped into the surface water environment.

THE WASTE EXPLOSION

COOLING PONDS

This approach takes advantage of the few positive aspects of thermal loading. Warm-water outfalls in winter attract fish (and fishermen) because they extend the feeding period and forestall ice formation, which often prevents adequate oxygenation of the water beneath. By combining waste water from a power plant and effluent from a sewage treatment plant, the heat and nutrients, considered a nuisance in most environments, can be put to good use. If we supply heat-tolerant algae as primary producers and introduce warm-water fish to harvest the algae, water will have time to cool, its nutrient content sharply reduced, and its algae can be harvested as useful protein before being returned to the natural environment. One tropical species that might be used, milkfish (*Chanos*), is one of the few palatable fish that feeds on blue-green algae. This type of operation would probably have to be limited to northern latitudes, since heat tolerance of even tropical species would be exceeded in areas where heated effluents are released during long, hot summers.

There are, however, some pioneering attempts to make use of thermal discharges in the United States. Oysters are being cultivated year round in the thermal discharges of a power plant on Long Island (Figure 16.16). The intake water from the sea, which varies from 5 to 21°C during the year, is warmed by 10 to 12°C by mixing with a thermal discharge of 150,000 gallons per minute in a seven-acre lagoon. The young

Fig. 16.16 (a) By placing small oysters in the heated effluent of a power plant, growth can be greatly accelerated. The frames between the piers hold the oysters. (b) Every week the frames are removed from the water so the oysters may be checked and screened for uniform size. After eight to ten weeks the oysters are transplanted to cooler, deeper water, where they mature. (Long Island Oyster Farms)

Fig. 16.17 (a) When catfish fry are suspended in cages in the warm-water effluent from the power plant in the background, the fish grow more rapidly than in unheated water. (b) The fish are fed through the hole in the top of the cage. (Texas Electric)

oysters are constantly produced in nearby hatcheries and are placed on racks in the discharge canal for four to six months and then transplanted into cold water for two years to mature. Although this seems a long time to wait for an oyster, the normal maturation period is five years.

A Texas power company raises catfish in cages exposed to an effluent of 22 to 24°C in winter (Figure 16.17). With intensive feeding the experiment has yielded 100 tons per acre per year. However, all power plants have shutdown periods, sometimes at unpredictable times, which could

405

be very destructive if alternate means of supplying heated water were not available; thermal effluents often contain toxic quantities of heavy metals, rust inhibitors, biocides, or low-level radioactive wastes; and the wastes of the food crop must be treated before discharge back into the stream or estuary to avoid eutrophication of natural environments.

In terrestrial ecosystems, heated water could also be put to good use by applying it to crops. Preliminary evidence indicates that growth of some crops is accelerated by irrigation with warm water, suggesting the possibility of double cropping in areas of mild climate. Frost protection can also be achieved by spraying fruit trees with warm water. There are difficulties, however: frost is a problem in most orchards on only a few days each year, and irrigation is necessary for only a few months in the summer. A large power plant must cool 500,000 gallons per minute every day of the year. Also, the cooling effluent from nuclear powered plants contains slight amounts of radioactive minerals, which might be concentrated in crop plants irrigated with such an effluent.

These are problems that can be worked out; it is becoming increasingly evident that we cannot continue to inject our waste heat either into the water or into the air without causing serious environmental problems. As these examples indicate, there is a tremendous potential for ingenious uses of this heat energy—uses that must be exploited if the natural ecosystems are to survive until more efficient power sources are found.

FURTHER READING

Daniels, S. L., and D. G. Parker, 1973. "Removing phosphorus from waste water." *Env. Sci. & Tech.* **7**(8), pp. 690–694. The current choices.

Farnworth, E. G., and F. B. Golley, 1974. *Fragile ecosystems: evaluation of research and application in the neotropics.* Springer-Verlag, New York. Helps point out the ways in which tropical ecosystems differ from temperate systems in their response to trauma.

Josephson, J., 1975. "Green system for waste water treatmenent." *Env. Sci. & Tech.* **9**(5), pp. 408–409. Another kind of living filter.

Leich, H. H., 1975. "The sewerless society." *Bull. Atomic Scient.* November, pp. 38–44. Presents a survey of alternatives to the universal toilet.

Malin, H. M., Jr., 1973. "Processes cut canning pollution." *Env. Sci. & Tech.* **7**(10), pp. 900–901. Fine tuning of technical processes can make impressive inroads into the waste train.

Porter, K. G., 1976. "Enhancement of algal growth and productivity by grazing zooplankton." *Science* **192**, pp. 1332–1333. Research suggests that zooplankton grazers may actually increase the abundance of their food, which puts eutrophication and algal blooms in a new light.

Schindler, D. W., 1974. "Eutrophication and recovery in experimental lakes: implications for lake management." *Science* **184**, pp. 897–898. More fuel for the carbon/phosphorus eutrophication controversy.

Schuval, H. I., and N. Gruener, 1973. "Health considerations in renovating waste water for domestic use." *Env. Sci. & Tech.* **7**(7), pp. 600–604. Complete recycling, while desirable and ultimately necessary, is not without its problems.

CHAPTER SEVENTEEN

THE SUMP IN
THE SEA

Not so very long ago, eutrophication was thought to be limited to small bodies of fresh water or streams; if it occurred in the ocean, it only affected protected bays or harbors. While the eutrophication of Lake Erie should have prepared us, it still comes as a shock to learn that the Baltic, Mediterranean, and North Seas are in serious environmental trouble. With a flushing cycle of three to thirty years, wastes may pile up for decades before they are diluted by the open Atlantic. But by the time they get there, the Atlantic may not provide much dilution—Thor Heyerdahl, that inveterate drifter, reported seeing oil slicks almost all the way from Morocco to the West Indies from his papyrus raft. Moreover, marine pollution problems are complex, involving coastal features as well as the open sea.

About 20,000 years ago, extensive continental glaciers had tied up tremendous quantities of water, exposing the continental shelves as broad coastal plains. As the ice slowly melted, the ocean level began to rise, first flooding the incised lower channels of large rivers, forming estuaries. These estuaries were covered as the sea advanced over the flat coastal plain, and a series of barrier islands formed, separated from the mainland by broad, shallow lagoons. Ultimately, when all the coastal plain is flooded and its uplands are encroached upon by the sea, another set of estuaries will be formed. But because there has been some crustal movement as well as sea rise, the effect in eastern North America is uneven. To the north the entire coastal plain is flooded; Maine and the Maritime Provinces of Canada have coastlines indented with fjords, the result of the sea flooding the coastal headlands. Further south, parts of whole river systems have been flooded, forming Delaware and Chesapeake Bays. From Norfolk, Virginia south to Yucatán, Mexico, the sea has advanced only part way across the coastal plain; hence the characteristic barrier-island–lagoon dominates. Should the sea rise another hundred feet or so, the character of the southern coastline would change, with the flooding of its flat coastal plain, from the barrier-island–lagoon to the estuarine type. Since the sea is continuing to rise at the rate of less than three feet per thousand years, we have about fifty thousand years to make plans.

If the sea level were rising very much faster than it is, all coastal cities would be in imminent danger (see Figure 12.2). Why have so many great cities been built on or near estuaries? Since estuaries are usually drowned river mouths, they form natural harbors, protected from the oceans yet connecting the ocean and a river-drained hinterland. Because of this vital connection, estuaries serve as a focus of transportation. In addition, estuaries, combining characteristics of both fresh and salt water, are extremely productive.

USING ESTUARINE PRODUCTIVITY

This great productivity (see Chapter 2) has long been overlooked and underused because, unlike land areas, estuaries rarely have production and harvest in the same spot. These processes are constantly being moved here and there by the tide, and are separated not only in space but in time. There are two approaches to better use of estuarine production. We could overcome our narrow prejudices and eat more of the elements of the food web than we consider edible today. Or we could simplify the ecosystem somewhat by channeling more of the production into harvestable units or by introducing species more efficient at harvesting producers than those now naturally available. Ecosystem simplification, however, has its dangers. Although formidable, they are not insurmountable.

The point is that tidelands, however their productivity is used, are extremely valuable as producers of food and as spawning grounds for many economically valuable species. This is seen in the productivity values of the continental shelf (1.3 tons per acre per year) and the open ocean (0.5 tons per acre per year), compared to the 10 tons per acre per year of the estuaries. Too often a fisherman catching a striped bass thinks the fish exists in a biological vacuum, not remembering that fish must spawn to reproduce, that eggs must have the proper environment to hatch, and that the fry must have the right food sources to develop into catchable fish. Very often, too, he ignores the fact that these early stages in the life cycle of many ocean organisms may require radically different temperatures, salinity, mineral nutrient levels, and food supplies than are found in the open ocean—conditions that are unique to estuarine areas.

Unfortunately, the productivity and usefulness of estuaries are not as immediately obvious as those of good farmland or a stand of prime timber. So the estuarine complex remains wasteland to most people, to be tolerated until it can be developed. To overcome this negative attitude, Dr. Eugene Odum, a world authority on the ecology of salt marshes, put prices on aspects of marshes that we have considered intangible if we considered them at all: commercial sport fishery, $100 per acre; aquicultural potential, $630 per acre; tertiary waste treatment, $2500 per acre; life support values (absorption of CO_2, production of O_2, support of wildlife, and storm protection), $4100 per acre. The total per acre came to $7330. Mention this figure whenever anyone casually suggests using a local wetland as a sanitary landfill because it is wasteland anyway.

MISUSE OF THE ESTUARIES

Because of tidal flushing, estuarine areas can usually handle a level of mineral cycling that would turn a lake into a pea soup of eutrophication. But unfortunately the same factors that make an estuary productive make it vulnerable to pollution. The clay particles that concentrate nutrients gather hydrocarbons, biocides, isotopes, and heavy metals, and animals that filter out their food do the same. The ions of heavy metals, sinking rapidly into more saline water, may be carried back into an estuary rather than out to sea.

Because we assume that the tides will see to regular removal of wastes, we either make no effort to control pollutants or start so late that recovery is extremely expensive. As a result, the future of estuaries and their adjoining wetlands as a continuing resource is uncertain. Large tracts of marsh on the west coast of Florida have been dredged and urbanized, and the process continues, though more slowly. If this type of development proceeds around the perimeter of the Gulf of Mexico without a sustained effort to preserve some marshes for wildlife "nurseries," the harvest of various types of seafood in the Gulf, particularly shrimp, is bound to decline sharply.

ABUSE OF A BAY

Great South Bay, like Lake Erie, stands preeminent as a well-polluted body of water. In this instance, however, a sea edge is being affected, showing clearly that in time the open ocean itself could be similarly polluted. Great South Bay, on the south shore of Long Island, New York, is a lagoon some twenty-four miles long and up to three miles wide, with

an average depth of four feet, protected from the open Atlantic by the barrier of Fire Island (Figure 17.1). Just a few years ago most of Fire Island was incorporated into Fire Island National Seashore to assure the survival of a wild and relatively untrammeled stretch of sand dunes less than fifty miles from New York City. The bay, however, has been less fortunate.

Because of its small area and porous soils, Long Island has few streams of any size. What streams there are flow from the Ronkonkoma moraine, a line of rubble marking the southernmost extent of glaciation, across an almost flat plain, and then into various bays, including Great South Bay, as a series of small estuaries. The combination of fresh water and tidal flushing makes these streams ideal for raising ducks.

THE LONG ISLAND DUCK

Although ducks have been raised on Long Island since its settlement, large-scale duck farming did not develop until the 1920s and 1930s. In 1965, thirty-two farms in the Great South Bay area produced over 3 million ducks, 60 percent of the production in the United States, making Long Island duck a household word (Figure 17.2).

At first, ducks were penned on the rivers entering the bay and all duck wastes either entered the water directly or were flushed by rain from the stream banks. Later, small ponds or lagoons were constructed to settle out some of the solid wastes, but the soluble materials still drained into the streams and then into the bay.

The raw wastes of 100 ducks per day produce a total of 5.7 pounds of nitrogen (in the form of uric acid, which bacteria convert into ammonia), 7.6 pounds of phosphate compounds, and 3.6 pounds of soluble phosphate. To get rid of these wastes, 14–120 gallons of water a

411

Fig. 17.2 Duck farms lining the shores of Great South Bay have seriously polluted the water. Because Great South Bay is closely bounded by Fire Island and the mainland, there is little flushing of the bay by clean ocean water and wastes accumulate. (Michael Capizzi)

day per duck are required. Larger farms use 2–3 million gallons of water a day. Altogether, each day the duck industry on the bay produces 3300 pounds of nitrogen, 5600 pounds of phosphorus, and 55,600 pounds of suspended solids in a total effluent of 133 million gallons.

The solid materials turn the stream water gray and turbid and the heavier materials settle out in ten feet deep sludge deposits in some places, suffocating almost all the bottom life and greatly reducing the dissolved oxygen in the water. With oxygen in short supply, anaerobic conditions encourage sulfide bacteria to produce hydrogen sulfide. This gas then bubbles to the surface, buoying solids with it, forming lumps or rafts that drift about. Finer material is precipitated by contact with saline water in the river mouths. Soluble nitrates and phosphates, of course, are distributed widely in the bay.

A EUTROPHIC BAY

If Great South Bay behaved like a typical estuary, even this large quantity of mineral nutrients could be flushed into the sea by tidal action and diluted, sparing the bay the effects of overfertilization. But Great South Bay has only two inlets for entrance of sea water, Fire Island Inlet at one end and Moriches Inlet at the other. Flushing time is four to ten days and circulation is weak. Prevailing winds and currents from the southwest tend to confine the waste-enriched water to the east end of the bay farthest from the source of clean sea water. For these reasons, Great South Bay cannot assimilate large quantities of waste from any source.

Once in the bay, the wastes contribute nitrogen and phosphorus, which stimulate the growth of a very small green alga, *Nannochloris* (2–4 *millionths* of a centimeter in diameter), previously so rare that plankton surveys in the early years of this century failed to notice it at all. Normally oysters feed on diatoms, particularly *Nitzschia*, which has quite different ecological requirements than *Nannochloris*. *Nitzschia*, for example, requires a salinity of at least 15 parts per thousand, grows best at 10 to 20°C, and is unaffected by changes in the nitrogen-phosphorus ratio. *Nannochloris*, on the other hand, grows well in a variety of salinities, prefers temperatures in the range of 10 to 26°C, and doubles its growth rate when the water is enriched with ammonia-nitrogen, which suggests that nitrogen rather than phosphorus is a limiting factor. Apparently phosphorus regenerates more rapidly from decomposing organic matter than ammonia.

Because of poor circulation, bay waters have lower salinity, higher temperature, and higher nitrogen and phosphorus content than ocean water. Each of these factors selects for *Nannochloris* against *Nitzschia*. At times *Nannochloris* becomes so abundant that there may be 3–10 million cells per milliliter of bay water, reducing visibility through the water to less than one foot.

OYSTERS VERSUS CLAMS

Oysters feed by straining water through their gills and directing the food to their mouth, where it is ingested. But oysters feed efficiently only if the water is relatively clear. As the quantity of suspended particles increases, the feeding rate decreases. In plankton-rich water, the gills become covered with the tiny algal cells of *Nannochloris*, which interfere both with normal feeding and with respiration, leading to starvation or suffocation. As a direct result of eutrophication, oyster production declined sharply between 1940 and 1960, from 600,000 bushels a year to zero bushels in some years.

Although the duck farm wastes have had a very deleterious effect on the oyster industry, production of hard clams (*Mercenaria*) has soared, for this species can feed upon the pollution-induced *Nannochloris*, while the oyster cannot. If the problem were simply shifting productivity from oyster to clam, we might simply dig for clams instead of diving for oysters. But the problem is not that simple. Besides their nutrient content, duck wastes contain a variety of bacteria similar to those found in man. They are collectively called coliform bacteria, and are used as an index of pollution by the Bureau of Public Health. One of these bacteria, *Salmonella*, often found in clams growing in polluted water, causes an intestinal infection so violent that the victim may be cured of eating raw clams for life. As a result of such bacterial contamination, 40 percent of

413

Fig. 17.3 Windrows of eel-grass washed up from Great South Bay. When these masses of dead plants decompose, hydrogen sulfide is produced in such quantities that the beach is unusable. (Dan Jacobs)

the clam beds in Great South Bay have been closed. When you consider that this closed area can produce 300,000 bushels of clams a year, worth over $2 million, the economic result of bay pollution comes into focus.

POLLUTION FROM PEOPLE

Although we have emphasized duck farms, population growth in Suffolk County has also contributed to bay pollution. Most of the housing disposes of its wastes through cesspools or septic tanks, which percolate wastes, rich in mineral nutrients and bacteria, through the very porous Long Island soil into the water table that drains into the bay. In all probability, if the duck farms were to disappear tomorrow, the unsewered wastes of central Long Island could easily keep Great South Bay oversupplied with both mineral nutrients and bacteria. Further organic pollution is contributed by the increasing number of pleasure craft being used in the bay (see Chapter 16).

Nannochloris is not the only alga to be stimulated by overfertilization. A filamentous green alga (*Cladophora*) forms great floating mats, at times almost thick enough to stand on. When these finally sink during the fall and winter they accumulate in the holes left in the bay bottom from sand dredged for beach stabilization. Anaerobic conditions lead to production of hydrogen sulfide, which then bubbles to the surface the following summer, often in such quantity that it blackens housepaint on shorefront homes. A third plant, eelgrass (*Zostera*), is also affected. Normally eelgrass is found in small clumps scattered over the bay floor. It not only stabilizes the sandy bottom but shelters the highly prized bay scallop. But with overfertilization, eelgrass spreads rapidly, covering the bay bottom for miles. Storms and the changes of season loosen the blade-

414

like leaves of this plant, which then wash up on shore to decay anaerobically because of their sheer volume; again hydrogen sulfide is produced, and the beaches are covered with a slippery organic slime (Figure 17.3).

THE SOLUTION OF THE BAY PROBLEM

Great South Bay could be rid of the pollution caused by the ducks if they were grown like chickens or turkeys in pens or houses without access to stream water, and if the wastes were removed mechanically and treated or disposed of. But ducks do not feather well unless they are allowed to swim, and since the sale of duck feathers often represents the difference between profit and loss, the duck grower feels he cannot separate his ducks from the outside environment. With such a narrow profit margin, farm sewage treatment plants are probably not economically feasible. However, it is only a matter of time before the rolling lawns of suburbia supplant the duck farms of Suffolk County as they have the potato farms of Nassau County; so the problem of duck farms is perhaps only of passing concern.

Increased flushing of the bay has been suggested as a solution, but present inlets must be carefully studied from all ecological angles before being supplemented by manmade inlets. New inlets should not be constructed at the expense of organisms that cannot tolerate the salinity that full-strength ocean water would supply. The duck wastes deposited as shoals of sludge in rivers and at their mouths must be dredged so that their mineral nutrient content is permanently taken out of circulation. Finally, onshore facilities must be developed at marinas, yacht clubs, and town docks to handle wastes generated and stored in holding tanks aboard the ever-growing fleet of leisure craft. Great South Bay and other estuaries with similar problems can be cleaned up, not easily or cheaply, but there is no inherent ecological reason why oysters, ducks, and people cannot coexist in an ecosystem satisfactory to all.

SAN DIEGO BAY

Encouraging evidence that once polluted bays can be cleaned up is provided by San Diego Bay (Figure 17.4). Today the bay is clean and sparkling; in 1963, it was in the typically brownish-red advanced stage of eutrophication. The change was accomplished by bonds costing $1.50 a month per household, a price the people of San Diego were obviously willing to pay. San Diego Bay, like Great South Bay, is tailor-made for problems—fifteen miles long and up to two miles wide, it has a single outlet to the sea and is the home port for one fourth of the Navy as well as 100 tuna boats. The eutrophication was caused by more than 60 million gallons of sewage, mostly untreated, dumped into the bay per day. Effluent from tuna canneries and kelp processing plants and wastes from the large number of ships in the harbor also contributed to the pollution. Water clarity was less than six feet and the coliform bacteria count was ten times the permissible level, forcing the closing of many beaches. After a couple of false starts a $40 million bond issue was approved by the voters in 1960 and construction began on interceptor lines around the bay leading to a new treatment plant on the ocean with outfalls two miles out to sea. The completed system serves seven

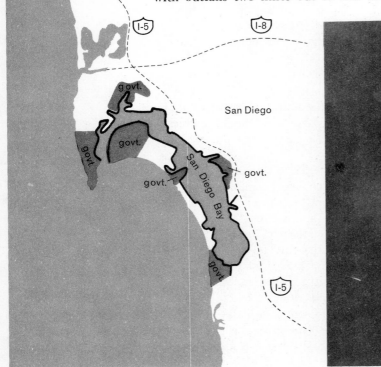
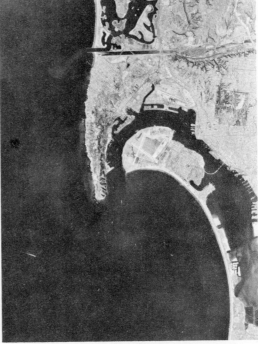

Fig. 17.4   San Diego Bay, virtually surrounded by the city of San Diego and a chain of federal installations, was rapidly becoming a sewer in the early 1960s when a strenuous effort was made to construct sewage treatment plants with outfalls well offshore. Today the bay is again the recreational focus of San Diego, as it should be. (NASA)

cities in the region and all the naval shore installations. The improvements after completion of the system in 1964 were surprisingly quick: fish began returning to the bay, clarity ranged up to thirty feet, the bacteria count fell enough to reopen beaches, and dissolved oxygen rose again to a safe range. What happened in San Diego Bay can happen in any similarly polluted body of water if public concern can be channeled into willingness to be taxed or assessed to make the improvements.

The greatest threat to one of the country's most famous bays has been not pollution—that battle was fought and won several years ago—but filling. San Francisco Bay has been shrinking steadily since 1850, when the discovery of gold in the Sierran foothills began a deluge of sediments from hydraulic mining that lasted until 1884. By then, over 1000 billion cubic yards of silt had been deposited in the bay. Deeper areas became shoals, mudflats became tidal marsh, and marshes dry land. In addition, cities in the bay area, hemmed in by hills and rough ground, looked eagerly to the bay for cheap new land for expansion. As recently as 1960, developers planned to fill in 23 square miles of bay (about half the area of San Francisco), using as fill San Bruno Mountain, that wild ridge that protects San Francisco from the barbarians to the south (Figure 17.5).

By the middle 1960s, everyone had plans for filling in the bay. Sixty percent of the original marshland had already been developed. Encouraged by the now shallow bay, the ample supply of fill from parallel developments in the hills, and apathy as broad as the bay itself, developers almost succeeded in filling up the rest of the bay and creating in its place another smog-filled basin indistinguishable from San Jose or Los Angeles.

Fig. 17.5 *San Francisco Bay like Caesar's Gaul is divided into three parts: San Francisco Bay to the southwest, San Pablo Bay to the northeast, and Suisun Bay to the southeast. Note the extensive mudflats and salt marshes at the lower end of San Francisco Bay, and the eastern edge of San Pablo and Suisun Bays. San Bruno Mountain cuts across the San Francisco Peninsula just north of the X-shaped airport on the eastern edge of San Francisco Bay.* (NASA)

Fortunately a groundswell of environmental awareness emerged just in time. A number of local groups such as the Save San Francisco Bay Association were organized and began to ask difficult questions. "Save the Bay" stickers appeared on car bumpers all over the Bay Area, and in 1965 the McAteer-Petris Act set up the San Francisco Bay Conservation and Development Commission (affectionately known to area residents as BCDC) to review development schemes for bayfront property. While certain bay lands such as the diked salt ponds so strikingly visible on flights into San Francisco Airport are not included under BCDC jurisdiction, wholesale filling in of the bay has been halted.

OIL ON THE WATER

Oil pollution of the ocean is not entirely a by-product of human sloppiness. At least 600,000 tonnes of crude oil seep into the ocean from natural sources every year; 40 percent of this "leak" takes place in the Pacific. But we have been able to best that minute dribble by a considerable amount—at least 3 million, perhaps as much as 10 million tonnes of oil are released into the sea each year by ships, 10 percent accidentally, the rest by intent.

The discovery of huge reserves of oil in the Near East and in South America stimulated a tremendous increase in the quantities of crude oil shipped to North America and Northern Europe for refining. A typical tanker carrying crude oil during World War II held 16,000 tons of oil. By 1965, average capacity had almost doubled. New tankers today carry 326,000 tons, and some tankers are on order that will hold 720,000 tons. There is talk of a ship with a one-million-ton capacity; each such tanker would hold almost the entire daily production of crude oil in the United States.

Very large crude carriers (VLCCs), are purely creatures of economics. Since 80 percent of their bulk lies below the surface like an iceberg, they are sometimes called oilbergs. In fact, their bulkiness causes them to lie so low in the water that most ports are closed to them and shipping lanes customarily used by smaller draft ships are no longer usable. Severely limited in maneuverability, VLCCs need far more sea room than most ships and cannot respond quickly to the captain's or pilot's judgment—it takes 3 miles or 22 minutes to stop a 250,000-ton VLCC operating at 16 knots. At less than 4 knots almost all maneuverability is lost. Because of the relentless drive for economy of scale, equipment is highly automated; this allows the ships to sail unmanned for long periods. Frequent breakdowns have been the result. Several VLCCs have exploded and sunk in mid-ocean, presumably a result of unobserved malfunctions. Despite these problems, VLCCs have indeed been profitable.

Cheaply built by Japanese shipyards that could guarantee a fixed cost and delivery date, a tanker that cost $10 million could often pay for itself in a few voyages. Small wonder that hundreds of VLCCs were on order when the bubble broke. A combination of recession, oil embargo, and higher prices suddenly gave the world an enormous surplus of tankers. The VLCC is profitable only when it is full of oil heading for a market; tied up in port it is very expensive to maintain. The million-ton tanker may be a long time coming.

TANKERS AND POLLUTION

With their huge cargoes of oil and inherent clumsiness and structural weaknesses, the VLCCs were destined for trouble. Trouble first came on March 18, 1967. The Torrey Canyon, a 970-foot tanker carrying 117,000 tons of Kuwait crude oil from the Persian Gulf to Milford Haven, England, ran aground fifteen miles west of Land's End in Cornwall, seven miles northeast of the Isles of Scilly. The oil was contained in eighteen storage tanks each holding 6500 tons. As a result of the grounding, six of these tanks were ruptured; by March 26 some 30,000 to 40,000 tons of crude oil had been released into the western end of the English Channel. Initially there was hope of refloating the Torrey Canyon and of salvaging both ship and cargo, but heavy seas soon broke the back of the vessel, dooming any hopes of recovering either. For the next six weeks, until drained and able to sink, the Torrey Canyon continued to spill the remaining 75,000 tons of oil she contained. For several days the oil slick was kept well offshore by storm winds, but with a change of the weather the oil began to pile up on the coasts of England and France, causing great consternation to governments and holiday-seekers alike.

But the Torrey Canyon episode was only a reminder that oily wastes are constantly being discharged into the sea from a great variety of sources, which together pose a sizable problem. Some pollution is produced by all ships large or small, whatever their cargo. Slop water from routine ship maintenance, which picks up oil from machinery lubrication, bilge water, oily wastes from engine rooms—all find their way into the ocean. But the tanker is the big problem. Let us look at a typical modern tanker carrying 300,000 barrels of oil—a barrel is forty-two gallons—in thirty-three tanks in three rows of eleven tanks each. After emptying her cargo the ship still contains 1700 barrels of oil, 500 in the pipelines and 1200 coating the insides of the tanks. Oil in the pipes is drained into one tank and pumped ashore. When the ship turns around to pick up another load of crude oil, ballast water is pumped from the sea into several central tanks to stabilize the otherwise empty ship for the return run. The mixture of oil and water in the ballast tanks soon separates; the water below is pumped into the sea and the oil above pumped into a collection tank. While this is going on, the other tanks are cleaned with steam. This mixture is also pumped into the collection tank. By the time the ship has traveled a few thousand miles her tanks are cleaned and filled with sea water, and the 1200 barrels of waste oil from the previous trip are in the collection tank to be pumped ashore at the next stop.

This is what modern tankers are supposed to do, and most large oil company tankers are probably reasonably careful and conscientious. But 60 percent of the tanker fleet is independently owned or chartered and there is little doubt that regulations are not scrupulously adhered to. Far too many of these ships simply dump the 1200 barrels of crude waste overboard at the first opportunity. The ocean is large, the nights are dark, and detection is difficult. Prosecution under existing anti-pollution laws is hampered by the need to prove willful negligence, a provision that is almost impossible to enforce.

OFFSHORE WELLS

A third source of waste is rapidly becoming a major problem. At one time most oil wells were located on land or in very shallow bays or estuaries. But with improvement of deep drilling techniques over water, offshore wells are being drilled on continental shelves all over the world. The North Sea, the Gulf of Mexico, the Arctic Ocean, and the Pacific Coast of the United States have suddenly been opened up to oil exploration and exploitation.

On January 28, 1969, workmen removing a drilling bit from a 3500-foot well in the Santa Barbara Channel off the coast of Santa Barbara, California, were greeted with a gush of oil indicating a "blown" well. Normally, well holes are cased with pipe, which allows the well to be capped should any accident threaten uncontrolled flow of oil from the well. In this instance the well casing extended only thirty-nine feet below the 200-foot channel bottom. Apparently under great pressure, the oil penetrated a nearby fault in the rock below the casing level, thus bypassing the pipe that was supposed to contain it and flowing to the surface without restriction. While no one was sure how much oil was actually flowing from the well, flow rates of nearby wells suggested about 21,000 gallons per day. Despite frantic efforts to cap the well by pouring 8000 barrels of drilling mud and 900 sacks of cement down the well, the flow continued unabated for eleven days. The oil slick covered 800 square miles at its greatest extent and probably produced an even greater uproar in southern California than the Torrey Canyon wreck produced in Europe.

Before we examine the effects of marine discharges of oil on oceanic plants and animals and the techniques used to cope with the problems, we must look more carefully at what happens to oil when it is released into the oceanic environment.

Oil does not float around unchanged until it is washed ashore. All oils, regardless of type, contain some volatiles that evaporate readily. Hence up to 25 percent of the volume of spilled oil is lost through evaporation during the first few days. Then photooxidation as well as bacterial decomposition work on the remaining mass. By the end of three months at sea, only 15 percent of the original volume remains—a dense asphaltic substance. These are the black, tarry lumps that most frequently wash up on beaches and stick to one's feet and clothing. With massive discharges close to shore, however, there is not enough time for much decrease in volume to take place, and a thick layer of sticky oil is deposited on anything solid in its path. This happened in both the Torrey Canyon and Santa Barbara spills.

Several approaches were followed in trying to clean up the aftermath of the Torrey Canyon. At sea, the slicks were bombed in an attempt to ignite the oil and burn it off. Because the volatiles that would carry a fire had evaporated, aviation fuel was dumped on the slicks to try to ignite them, but without much success. The French used a different technique: they dumped quantities of ground chalk on the slicks in a generally successful effort to absorb, then sink the oil and so prevent its being cast up onshore. The technique used on the largest scale, mostly by the British, was to disperse the slick with detergents and emulsify it into small droplets that could be more readily attacked and decomposed by bacteria. Detergents have no effect whatever on oil other than dispersing it. Over 2.5 million gallons of detergents were used in a dispersion attempt both at sea and ashore. Despite the quantity used, the results were disappointing; not only did the detergent fail to disperse the slicks, but it had a more negative effect on the flora and fauna than the oil might have had.

Until quite recently it was thought that once the aromatics evaporated, oil was not particularly harmful to marine organisms. But a relatively small spill, 700 tons of #2 fuel oil (oil burner fuel) into Buzzards Bay off Cape Cod in 1969, has forced us to revaluate that comforting notion. For the first time the modern techniques of gas-liquid chromatography were used by a research team headed by Max Blumer from the Woods Hole Oceanographic Institution, fortuitously located nearby. Their study of this pollution episode showed that oil emulsified by sea water and weighed down by mineral particles quickly contaminated the bottom sediments. Because the oil reduced the cohesion of bottom sediments, the spread of contaminated sediments over the sea floor was accelerated. Through gas-liquid chromatography, the individual hydrocarbons that comprise the fuel oil could be identified and followed over time, much as a fingerprint can be traced on the objects a person handles.

Right after the spill, 95 percent of the animals characteristic of the bottom community were killed; the same occurred in the salt marshes and tidal creeks contaminated by the oil. But after a few days most of the oil had evaporated and some measure of recovery had begun. At this point most previous studies of oil spills proclaimed that the worst was over. But when the hydrocarbons involved were traced with chromatographic techniques, it was found that after eight months unaltered oil could still be recovered from sediment near the point of spillage. One year later bacterial degradation of the oil components had only begun, but the least toxic hydrocarbons disappeared first.

Once on the bottom, the oil entered the fat and flesh of marine organisms. When contaminated oysters were placed in clean water they lost their oily taste, but when they were checked with gas-liquid chromatograph techniques fuel oil was found in the same concentration and composition as at the beginning of the period of flushing. The evidence suggested that the hydrocarbons were not only *not* flushed out but may remain intact throughout the oyster's lifetime. Obviously, taste cannot be trusted as a criterion of contamination.

Other research has indicated that low levels of hydrocarbons found in oil may affect the behavior as well as the physiology of marine organisms. If the oil either blocks or mimics natural stimuli, sex attraction, food finding, homing, and escape from predators may be affected. Oil may also concentrate various fat-soluble compounds such as DDT or PCBs (see Chapters 5 and 6) into the surface film of the water.

Tropical reefs, which contain many species of algae as well as the more photogenic corals, are just being recognized as important sources of both nitrogen and detritus for the small, brightly colored fish so characteristic

Fig. 17.6 The Great Barrier Reef off the northeastern coast of Australia can be seen as the L-shaped chain of islands extending southeast from the top of the photo. The white specks over the Coral Sea are cloud trains characteristic of tropical oceans; the cape is Bustard Headland between Bundaberg and Rockhampton, Queensland. (NASA)

of this setting. Nitrogen is contributed by fish which graze on the algae and release sizable amounts of nitrogen in their feces; turbulence on the reef front breaks off small pieces of algae which are fed upon by reef herbivores and detritivores; and the reef algae directly release peptides and free amino acids. The coral polyps secrete mucus, which acts as a cleansing agent; but because it is sticky it traps and concentrates zoo-plankton. Therefore the mucus is eaten by small reef fish. Mucus is also rich in triglycerides and wax esters, which some fish can metabolize as a form of energy.

Crude oil and its components can affect many of these reef functions. For example, oil is easily absorbed by the coral mucus and transferred into the fish that eat it. Since many of the world's most splendid coral reefs (Figure 17.6) are near shipping lanes (Australia's Great Barrier Reef in particular), increasing oil pollution of tropical oceans may have long-term consequences in these ecosystems.

THE INTERFACE PROBLEM

At any given moment 3 to 4 percent of the sea is covered with white-caps, which generate 100,000 breaking bubbles per second per square meter. When the bubbles rise to the surface they break and shoot a tiny volume of water into the air at 110 miles per hour. It has been calculated that this seemingly inconsequential mechanism injects 300 billion tons of sea water into the atmosphere per year. When the water evaporates, the salt particles, with whatever organic materials were found in the surface film that the bubble broke through, travel on the wind, (Figure 17.7), form condensation nuclei for raindrops, and return to earth usually

Fig. 17.7 Coastlines with heavy surf generate a salt-water aerosol which is swept inland by prevailing winds. The local vegetation can handle the salt, but not the pollutants that are becoming more prevalent in sea water.

quite far from the place of origin. A specific example of this phenomenon was discovered south of Genoa, Italy, where pine trees were found dying because the needles were covered by a film of oil blown in from a slick offshore. Plainly, air and water pollution are not discrete problems!

ENVIRONMENTAL REPERCUSSIONS

The murre (*Uria*), a strange little bird weighing about two pounds and vaguely resembling a penguin, is the most abundant sea bird in the Northern Hemisphere (Figure 17.8). Altogether, there are probably 50 million murres in the world eating 50 million pounds of fish per week. During the summer they have what may be a critical effect on mineral cycling, and hence productivity, in the Arctic. Murres feed on bottom fish and their excretions release to the surface water mineral nutrients such as nitrate and phosphate that ordinarily would sink to the bottom of the sea with the death of these bottom fish or their predators. This is extremely important in maintaining the fertility of surface Arctic waters. The situation is especially critical off the southeast coast of Newfoundland, where many tankers find it convenient to flush their wastes into the sea. The resulting slicks kill at least 1000 birds a day in this region and perhaps as many as a million a year. Once again we are interfering with a biogeochemical cycle without knowledge of the ultimate effects of our actions.

The effect of detergents used in enormous quantities, however, is obvious to anyone. Although detergent used far away from the shore affects organisms only in the immediate surface layers, treatment of polluted shores has killed large numbers of organisms of varying kinds, as well as producing secondary effects on species not directly affected. Unfortunately, the detergents used in the Torrey Canyon cleanup, unlike those used in household products today, were of the hard or nonbiodegradable type. As with the oil, it is the volatile fraction of the detergent that is most toxic. For this reason, on the open sea, detergent toxicity to organisms declines sharply after a few days.

In addition to barnacles, crabs, and snails, the chief victim of detergent toxicity on rocky coasts is quite ironically the limpet—one of the few organisms observed to remove in its feeding activities the very oil film that generated concern. Another unexpected effect of the Torrey Canyon cleanup was the great increase in the green alga, sea lettuce or *Enteromorpha*, which grew out of control following the death of the snails that normally keep it in check. This recalled the similar recovery of heavily grazed pastures when the rabbit population of Great Britain was sharply reduced by disease several years ago (see Chapter 8).

Fig. 17.8 Northern murres are one of the most abundant sea birds in the northern hemisphere. (Courtesy of the American Museum of Natural History)

NOBODY'S OCEAN

Oil spills and tanker accidents raise some basic questions about our use of the oceans. All accidents cannot be prevented; tankers are inherently dangerous and every oil well has a certain probability of polluting sometime in some way. The circle of potential damage is greatly increased, however, when the oil well is perched on the continental shelf surrounded by very pollutable water.

But the problems of the ocean in the last two decades of this century go far beyond mere pollution. We are now coming to realize that the ocean and the continental shelves that surround it contain as much or more mineral resources than the continents themselves. As we begin to run out of certain essential metals such as copper or even iron, exploration of the ocean becomes more and more imminent. Already hundreds of millions of dollars are being poured into nodule recovery. Discovered around 1900 in the Pacific by the famous Albatross oceanographic expedition, nodules have since been found in other oceans too. Around 5 cm in diameter, the potato-like nodules are soft, porous, and crumbly. But they contain manganese, nickel, copper, cobalt, molybdenum, aluminum, and iron. Some estimates suggest that the Pacific may contain as much as 1700 billion tons of nodules. This would translate into tremendous quantities of vital minerals (Table 17.1), enough to last for thousands of years.

But as we pause on the edge of the exploitation of this vast bonanza three major questions loom up.

Table 17.1
Comparison of the Supply of Selected Elements from Terrestrial and Oceanic Nodule Sources *

ELEMENT	TIME UNTIL TERRESTRIAL RESOURCE EXHAUSTED (YEARS) †	ESTIMATE FROM PACIFIC OCEAN NODULES (BILLION TONS)	TIME UNTIL NODULE RESOURCE EXHAUSTED (YRS)
Manganese	100	358	400,000
Aluminum	100	43	20,000
Nickel	100	14.7	150,000
Copper	40	7.9	6,000
Cobalt	40	5.2	200,000

* Based upon data in Luard, Evan, 1974. *The control of the sea bed: A new international issue.* Taplinger, New York.

† Based on 1960 rate of consumption.

1. What happens to the economy of a country like Zambia, which now relies heavily on copper for its foreign exchange, if offshore supplies of copper lower the world price and make copper mining unprofitable in Zambia?
2. Who is responsible for whatever ocean pollution or ecosystem disturbances result from the nodule exploitation?
3. And perhaps most importantly, who owns the resource? The basic flaw in our relationship to the world ocean is that unlike San Francisco Bay or Lake Erie, it belongs to no one. Beyond the continental shelf, where most nations exert some proprietary interest and perhaps even concern, the ocean is up for grabs. The traditional doctrine of "firstest with the mostest" would deliver the spoils to those nations best equipped to exploit the resource—the United States, Germany, Japan, and the USSR—leaving landlocked and poor coastal nations with the proverbial short-end of the stick.

But the United Nations has become vitally concerned with the future of the world ocean and its resources and is making a concerted effort to set up some ground rules. For if the ocean belongs to no one it also belongs to everyone. Once full-scale exploitation begins it will be too late to share either the resources or the responsibility for their orderly and environmentally sound harvesting.

FURTHER READING

Blanchard, D. C., 1972. "The borderland of burning bubbles." *Sat. Rev.,* 1 Jan. pp. 60–63. Describes some very interesting research with some startling implications.

Blumer, M., et al., 1971. "A small oil spill." *Env.* **13**(2), pp. 2–12. A pivotal paper on the long-term effects of oil on marine organisms.

Heald, E. J., 1971. "The production of organic detritus in a South Florida estuary." *University of Miami Sea Grant Tech. Bull.* No. 6. A beautifully executed study.

Luard, D. E. T., 1974. *The control of the sea bed: a new international issue.* Taplinger, New York. Fine discussion of a very complex resource and problem.

Mostert, N., 1975. "The age of the oilberg." *Audubon* **77**(3), pp. 18–43. A brief history of the supertanker.

Pestrong, R., 1974. "Unnatural shoreline." *Env.* **16**(9), pp. 27–35. An account of the shrinkage of San Francisco Bay since settlement.

Wiebe, W. J., R. E. Johannes, and K. L. Webb, 1975. "Nitrogen fixation in a coral reef community." *Science* **188**, pp. 257–259. Still another reason to protect coral reefs carefully.

CHAPTER
EIGHTEEN

THE AIR AROUND
AND IN US

LEST WE THINK air pollution a contemporary phenomenon, John Evelyn in January 1684 wrote: "London, by reason of the excessive coldness of the air hindering the ascent of the smoke, was so filled with the fuliginous steam of the sea coal, that one could hardly see across the streets, and this filling the lungs with its gross particles, exceedingly obstructed the breast so as one could hardly breathe." [1] Edward I (1307–1327) ordered a subject put to torture for burning coal and fouling the air, an act sure to be recalled with some relish when one is trapped next to a table of smokers in a restaurant.

Is it possible to go far enough back in time to encounter a halcyon period when the air was pure? If we think of pure air as we think of pure water, probably not. Air is always a mixture of many things. In addition to the three gases, nitrogen, oxygen, and carbon dioxide, air also includes varying amounts of water vapor, dust, and every conceivable element and compound that wind or our activities distribute.

Long before our debut, however, dust storms, fires, volcanoes, and ocean storms polluted the air with vast quantities of particles and impurities of various sorts. The pollution continues: in 1883, a volcanic explosion pulverized the island of Krakatoa in the East Indies and threw very fine dust high into the atmosphere to circle the earth for several years before finally settling out. There is some suspicion that this dust,

---

[1] Wise, W., 1968. *Killer smog: the world's worst air pollution disaster*. Rand McNally, Chicago.

by reflecting solar energy back into space, may have contributed to a depression in the earth's mean temperature that occurred in the succeeding decades. It also produced a long series of lovely sunsets through the reflection and diffraction of the sun's rays by the many dust particles.

SULFUR OXIDE SMOG

For thousands of years wood, or perhaps dried dung or peat, was the only fuel used, but at some point it was discovered that the black, shiny, strangely lightweight stone we now call coal could make a very hot flame that lasted longer than a wood fire. Apparently coal was used, if sparingly, for some time in the Far East prior to its "discovery" by Marco Polo. Supposedly, Polo introduced coal, or at least the concept of its combustibility, into Europe. Considering the decimation of forests around population centers and the growing scarcity and expense of wood and charcoal, one would think the idea of using coal would have been welcomed. But this was a Europe where the Church considered almost any new idea heretical.

When coal is burned, sulfur compounds, especially sulfur dioxide, are released in the smoke. While this was unpleasant enough in itself, perhaps the fumes suggested to the medieval mind the sulfur and brimstone associated with Lucifer. Whatever the reason, coal replaced wood with surprising slowness. But the gradual enlightenment of the medieval mind and perhaps the greater effect of the soaring price of wood finally brought coal into common usage throughout Europe; with that, of course, came the sulfur dioxide fumes. John Evelyn, in 1661, recognized the problem and proposed a reasonable solution for his time: banish the offending industry, although the individual coal hearth pushing its sulfur-laden smoke through thousands of chimneys all over London was equally to blame. Evelyn's suggestions were ignored and for almost 300 years nothing was done about the problem. Once accepted and even romanticized by nineteenth-century novelists, the beloved British hearth was not to be easily given up.

But all Englishmen did not ignore the problem. In 1905 a London physician, Dr. Harold Des Voeux, described the combination of smoke and fog as "smog." However, it was not until years later that the word was again used—and misused at that.

THE EFFECTS OF SULFUR OXIDE SMOG

The Meuse Valley in Belgium is heavily industrialized; there are coke ovens, blast furnaces, power plants, glass factories, and steel mills. During the first week of December 1930 the valley was covered with a stagnant air mass that entrapped a smothering blanket of smog. Over a thousand people became ill and sixty died, ten times the normal death rate. In late October 1948, Donora, a small mill town on the Monongahela River in Pennsylvania, similarly surrounded by low hills and containing a steel mill and a zinc reducing plant, reported seventeen deaths after three days of similar conditions. An additional 42 percent of the population became ill. The normal daily death rate was two; hence the increase could only be attributed to the smog. The symptoms in both the Meuse Valley and Donora were throat irritation, hoarseness, cough, shortness of breath, nausea, and feeling of chest constriction.

The major cause of each of these disasters was the sulfur oxides. These compounds are found in greatest concentration in the air surrounding the major industrial cities of the world. This does not mean, however, that the amounts were lethal. Rather, as the concentration rose the sulfur oxides, in addition to many other pollutants, produced lethal results.

Sulfur dioxide, for example, is not an especially toxic gas, but in a humid atmosphere it is converted into sulfates or sulfuric acid, catalyzed in part by soot particles, and adsorbed onto the fine particles or fly ash that also result from combustion. Most of the human body is protected from the environment by thick skin, and much of that in turn is protected by clothing. The major point of vulnerability thus lies in the delicate membrane lining the eyes, nose, and respiratory tract, which is far more sensitive to injury than the skin and much more absorbent. Aerosols or fine particles carrying damaging compounds are inhaled into the lungs. The smaller the particle, the more deeply it penetrates the lungs.

Particulate matter is usually eliminated by the cells lining the walls of the respiratory system. Each cell has a hairlike cilium, which beats twelve times per second. Beating in waves, these cilia work dust and other foreign material into the mouth, where it can either be expelled or swallowed. A polluted atmosphere containing sulfur dioxide, ozone, or nitric oxide can inhibit cilia action, allowing particles to remain in the respiratory system and cause damage.

Particles 5 μm or more in diameter are removed by the cilia from the nose and bronchial tree. Smaller particles are deposited in the alveoli (tiny air sacs in the lungs), and particles less than $\frac{1}{2}$ μm usually behave like gases, settling in alveolar air spaces. Unfortunately it is these smallest particles that serve as deposition nuclei for a wide array of toxic substances—lead, antimony, selenium, arsenic, nickel chromium, and silicon.

The four major types of respiratory damage from air pollutants are bronchitis, broncial asthma, emphysema, and lung cancer.

Chronic bronchitis is characterized by permanent damage to the bronchial tubes, resulting in reduction or failure of ciliary action and overpro-

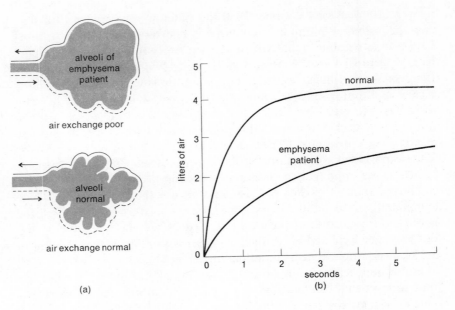

Fig. 18.1   The lung alveoli are tiny air sacs providing surface area which facilitates uptake of oxygen by the bloodstream. The graph shows that the amount of air held in the lungs of an emphysema patient is far less than that inhaled by a normal person. (Courtesy of the Oregon Tuberculosis and Health Association)

duction of mucus by gland cells. Because ciliary action cannot dislodge the extra mucus, a chronic cough develops. The mucus also constricts the opening of the bronchial system, causing shortness of breath.

Bronchial asthma is usually the result of the allergic reaction of the bronchial membranes to foreign protein or other materials. The membranes swell and make it difficult to expel air from the lungs. This explains the characteristic symptoms of wheezing and shortness of breath.

Emphysema follows the constriction of the finer branches of the bronchial tubes, the bronchioles (Figure 18.1). When air is exhaled, more air remains in the alveoli than should; when new air is inhaled, the overinflated sacs balloon larger and larger until they explode. This causes two adjacent sacs to unite. The gradual reduction in the number of air sacs destroys the capillaries through which oxygen is taken up by the red blood cells and slowly pushes out the chest, giving a characteristic "pigeon-chested" appearance. The loss of oxygen exchange capacity of the lungs leads to slow oxygen starvation of the entire body and chronic shortness of breath.

Lung cancer is stimulated by various substances called carcinogens: one, benzpyrene, is characteristic of coal smoke; others, like cigarette tars, are inhaled deeply by millions of smokers. It has been calculated that a reduction of benzpyrene from 6 μg to 2 μg per 1000 cubic meters could reduce the incidence of lung cancer in urban areas by 20 percent. Both tars and benzpyrene remain in the lungs in part because of the inhibition of the cilia, which might otherwise remove them.

When you consider that over a lifetime, the average person breathes 580 million times, sampling 8 million cubic feet of air, it is not surprising that when air contains pollutant particles various chronic lung conditions may develop. In Great Britain, where a large proportion of the population lives in very smoggy cities, fully 21 percent of men from forty to fifty-nine years old have chronic bronchitis. This condition causes 10 percent of all deaths in Great Britain.

The connection between asthma and air pollution was clearly demonstrated after World War II among servicemen stationed near Yokohama, Japan. Individuals with no previous history of asthma developed the classic symptoms of wheezing, coughing, shortness of breath, and sleeplessness. Even transfer to Tokyo did not improve the condition. Once out of the Kanto Plain, where both Tokyo and Yokohama are located, most cases rapidly cleared up. In one case a soldier, racked by asthma in Yokohama, spent six asthma-free years in the United States only to have a recurrence of asthma on a later visit to Yokohama. Even the common cold and other upper respiratory tract diseases are more frequent in cities, showing a distinct correlation with increase of pollution level in the late fall and winter, abetted quite probably by the extreme dryness of most houses and apartments during the winter season (see Chapter 11). By suppressing antibody production, air pollutants may lower the body's resistance to infection and increase allergen sensitization.

Despite the strong circumstantial evidence linking air pollution to chronic disease, many are not convinced. A vice-president of a large oil company recently wrote:

> This complex and troubled world we live in is so full of significant, pressing, and perplexing problems that we can ill afford the luxury of wasting effort on imaginary problems or trying to discover problems where none exist. Because human health is of such vital personal concern to each of us that we are naturally inclined to get emotional about it, we should be particularly cautious in ascribing or assuming a cause-and-effect relationship between air pollution and health until scientifically reliable supporting evidence is available.[2]

This somewhat cautious view was not shared by the Surgeon-General of the United States.

> . . . much of the speculation and controversy about whether or not air pollution causes disease is irrelevant to the significance of air pollution as a public health hazard. We are accustomed to thinking that a disease state is brought about by a single cause—a carryover from a period in public health history when virtually total emphasis was placed on the

[2] *Scientist and Citizen* **7** (3), p. 3.

bacterial or viral agent which had to be present before a communicable disease could be recognized and dealt with. . . .

New criteria must be employed in assessing the damage of air pollution —criteria which include statistical evidence that a disease condition exists in a population, epidemiological evidence of the association between the disease and the environmental factor of air pollution, reinforced by laboratory demonstration that the air pollutants can produce similar diseases in experimental subjects. . . . But the qualitative message at hand conveys a clear message. There is no longer any doubt that air pollution is a hazard to health.[3]

Sulfur dioxide affects plants as well as people. In the form of sulfite, at concentrations of less than 0.4 ppm, it kills leaf cells, causing large red or brown blotches on leaves between the veins. Since sulfur often accompanies ores of silver, copper, and zinc, smelters which roast these ores to recover the metal have until recently poured huge quantities of sulfur dioxide into the atmosphere with disastrous effects on the surrounding vegetation.

Materials do not escape the effect of sulfur oxides either. A combination of fly ash and sulfur dioxide in a humid atmosphere greatly accelerates the rusting and corroding of metals. The agent of this increased level of corrosion is rainfall, which has become increasingly acid over the past 20 years. Rainfall is usually slightly acid because of the carbon dioxide that dissolves in the raindrops as they fall, forming a very dilute carbonic acid solution (see Chapter 1). But in Europe and parts of the northeastern United States the pH of rainfall has dropped from around 5.7 to 3, a result of rising levels of sulfur dioxide, which absorbs moisture to form a sulfuric acid aerosol that is washed out of the air by rainfall. The effects of such acid rainfall on building materials are obvious and ubiquitous (Figure 18.2). Less obvious but far more serious are the effects on natural ecosystems: changes in leaching rates of nutrients from foliage or soils, and small but important changes in the acidity of rivers and lakes. Since removal processes normally take several days, sulfur-contaminated air can be moved downwind hundreds or even thousands of miles during that time.

The problem will increase in importance as our contribution to the sulfur cycle increases. At present, we release about one half the amount of sulfur naturally generated. By 1999 industrial sulfur will increase to equal and in some places in the Northern Hemisphere, surpass that produced by natural processes. To understand the magnitude of this increase we will have to clarify the rate at which sulfur dioxide is converted to sulfates in both polluted and unpolluted air, the efficiency of precipitation in scrubbing these compounds out of polluted air, and the amount of sulfur

Fig. 18.2 This monster started out as a princely figure three hundred years ago at Oxford University. The soft Portland sandstone was no match for the acid fog produced over the intervening years by coal-burning hearths. While much of England is converting to gas from the North Sea fields, the damage remains.

[3]Ibid.

compounds generated by biological systems (the biogenic factor). Recent research in Salt Lake City, Utah indicates that at certain seasons biogenic sulfur equals that produced by industrial sources. Until these unknowns are clarified we cannot be sure of the importance of our role in the sulfur biogeochemical cycle. All the more reason to control sulfur oxide emissions wherever possible.

THE CONTROL OF SULFUR OXIDE SMOG

Efforts to control air pollution are usually concerned with the visible smoke, comprised of small particles of fly ash that can be easily controlled. Electrostatic precipitators installed in factory or power plant chimneys can remove up to 99 percent of the fly ash usually scattered into the environment (see Chapter 19). High voltage wires charge the ash particles, attracting them in groups to a set of vertical plates. When these are tapped or vibrated, the ash falls into hoppers below and is removed. Although the market has not been fully exploited, by using fly ash to make concrete, bricks, and paving material, a power plant producing large quantities of fly ash should at least be able to return the installation and operating cost of the precipitators, since it costs at least $2 a ton just to dispose of the fly ash. In the United States, which produces over 30 million tons of fly ash a year, only 18 percent is recovered.

The shift from coal to oil in many homes and industries has resulted in a particulate pollution decline in most cities in the United States. But few people realize that a smokeless chimney can be just as serious a polluter as one belching clouds of black smoke. Many poisonous substances are colorless—sulfur dioxide, for example. At the moment there is no one economical method for removing sulfur dioxide, especially in small quantities, from effluent gases. If the sulfur dioxide content is large enough, wet scrubbers such as a sodium carbonate solution can be used to remove sulfur dioxide. Installation costs for scrubbing equipment at one power plant were $10 per kilowatt capacity; subsequent maintenance cost $1.17 per ton of coal used. The system removed up to 91 percent of the sulfur dioxide from the flue gases. If powdered limestone with small amounts of iron oxide as a catalyst is injected into the flame region of power plant boilers, a plant burning 5,000 tons of coal containing 3 percent sulfur per day can reclaim 300 tons of sulfur dioxide a day at the cost of 465 tons of powdered limestone.

Another approach, adopted by New York and Chicago, is to limit the sulfur content of the fuels, rather than try to trap the sulfur dioxide as it leaves the chimney. Pretreatment of both coal and oil, although expensive, is certainly practicable. The fluidized bed technique is another possibility (see Chapter 15).

One hydrothermal process recently developed by the Battelle Memo-

433

rial Institute of Columbus, Ohio grinds the coal into a powder, which is then made into a slurry by adding an aqueous solution of sodium and calcium hydroxides. The slurry is pressurized for thirty minutes at 350 to 2500 pounds per square inch and 225 to 350°C (the pressure and temperature depend on the type of coal being treated). The leaching fluid is then drained off, regenerated, and recycled in a way that makes recovery of the sulfur and metals possible. The coal is washed, dried, and burned. This process removes almost all the pyritic sulfur, half the organic sulfur, part of the ash, some of the toxic metals, and about 5 percent of the coal.

Utility companies are often reluctant to go into the chemical business, but if you produce 300 tons of sulfur dioxide a day, you *are*, like it or not, in the chemical business. Another problem is that many plants are too small to accomodate a complex sulfur recovery system that may be larger than the original plant itself. In addition, the variable nature of power plant operations, with units starting and stopping in response to power demands, makes it difficult to send a steady supply of by-product chemicals to a market.

In European cities, where the sulfur oxide problem is aggravated by home fires, a possible solution is conversion to natural gas or oil. From the point of view of sulfur dioxide reduction, electricity would be the ideal solution, but most people cannot afford this type of heating. Natural gas would be the next best choice, and low sulfur fuel oil after that. Until this is done air pollution control can only be partially achieved. The recent discovery of large natural gas deposits in the North Sea has certainly helped; because of this nearby source of gas, London heating systems have been almost entirely converted from coal to natural gas. The result has been an amazing decrease in the density and frequency of late fall and early winter smog episodes, and a substantial increase in the frequency of sunny days. However, natural fuels are in short supply and the need for a cheaper and more abundant source of fuel is acute.

PHOTOCHEMICAL SMOG

In 1859 Colonel Drake drilled the first oil well near Titusville, Pennsylvania. With the increasing pace of technological development it was only a few decades more before the internal ("infernal" as pessimists would have it) combustion engine was developed, and soon after that the automobile.

A NEW KIND OF SMOG

Because of the relatively late appearance of the automobile, most older cities had to fit it somehow into the scheme of pre-existing roads, urban centers, and suburbs. But Los Angeles grew up with the automobile, which delayed, perhaps forever, effective mass transit systems and made the city dependent upon the automobile. To accommodate this crush of traffic a freeway system was developed, attracting still more cars which required still more freeways in a transportational illustration of Parkinson's second law—expenses rise to meet income. At the height of this activity a haze, at first light and occasional, began to spread over the city. People started to complain of eye irritation and shortness of breath, and certain crops were blighted, particularly leafy vegetables and flowers, whose value depended upon their unblemished leaves and petals. Somehow people picked up Des Voeux's descriptive word, smog, to describe the phenomenon. However, the phenomenon in Los Angeles involved neither smoke nor fog.

Believing otherwise, the city cracked down on incinerators and industrial smoke producers. The smog remained. Next the oil refineries were put under a strict emission control; the smog got worse. Finally Haagen-Smit, a chemist from California Institute of Technology, identified the problem—automobile exhausts in combination with the unique geography of the Los Angeles Basin.

Los Angeles is a beautifully situated city, facing the Pacific in a broad fertile basin, surrounded by mountains up to 10,000 feet high (Figure 18.3), and favored with a warm, dry climate. In the early years, people were attracted by the prospect of warm, sun-filled days, groves of orange trees, lovely vistas of soaring mountains. Today the sun is often obscured by a yellowish-brown haze, the orange groves are either subdivided or killed by smog, and clear vistas are limited to occasional days in winter.

Fig. 18.3 What is so rare as a day in Los Angeles when the San Gabriel Mountains seem close enough to touch. A few years ago Los Angeles had no definite downtown marked by high-rise buildings because of the threat of earthquakes. Today, engineering advances have allowed the construction of the typically bland towers that characterize and homogenize most American cities. (Southern California Visitors Council)

435

Apparently the very factors which at one time made the city so attractive
have set it up for one of the worst pollution problems in the country.

The city is surrounded on three sides by mountains, the Santa Moni-
cas to the northwest, the San Gabriels to the northeast, and the Santa
Anas to the southeast. Although these mountains effectively shield Los
Angeles from the hot, dry winds of the Mohave Desert to the east, they
also prevent circulation of air. In addition, the weather of most of southern California during most of the late spring, summer, and early fall is
dominated by a large high-pressure area capping the basin with dry,
warm air. Because of the stagnant high pressure and the encircling mountains, the only air movement is a gentle sea breeze from the cold Pacific
Ocean.

THE ROLE OF TEMPERATURE INVERSION

If we were to attach a thermometer to a balloon and have it radio back
the temperature as it ascended, we would see a rather unusual profile
(Figure 18.4). Generally, the air temperature decreases at a constant rate
from the earth's surface well up into the upper atmosphere. But this
is not always the case. Sometimes the temperature decreases steadily as
the balloon rise only for the first 1500–3000 feet, then it *increases* for a
few thousand feet, and finally it resumes a steady decrease. This reversal
of the usual temperature profile is called a temperature inversion. The
initial decrease in temperature is a result of the cool ocean breeze flowing
in at a very low altitude over the basin. The next layer is the warm, dry

*Fig. 18.4   On a clear day in
Los Angeles, the temperature
decreases with increasing altitude. When the area is
capped by a mass of warm
stable air, the temperature
increases with altitude for
several thousand feet, preventing the dissipation of
pollutants generated from
below. This increase is shown
by the curve at the left of the
graph.*

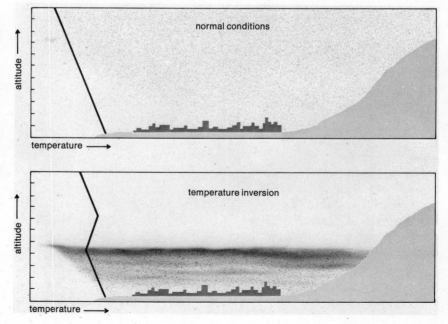

air of the stationary high, which is several thousand feet thick; above this layer, the temperature again declines with altitude. The effect of the warm, dry air of the high-pressure mass is to act as a lid covering the entire basin. Pollutants generated in the basin rise in the cool surface air until they meet the warmer air above at about 1000–1500 feet. Since they cannot penetrate this inversion layer, they spread out laterally and accumulate in the surface of the basin. The only escape is a very gradual drift southeast where, under the influence of sea breezes, the polluted air flows over some of the mountain passes into the Mohave Desert and has been traced as far east as Arizona. Between June and October there is a temperature inversion 80 to 90 percent of the time over Los Angeles.

There is a third factor. Because the inversion layer is warm and dry, it remains cloudless most of the time. This allows the energy in sunlight to interact with the pollutants generated from below, producing a second generation of new pollutants. For this reason the Los Angeles smog is principally photochemical, not a mixture of smoke and fog as it is in London. There are other differences between the two types of smog as well. Smog in London occurs mostly in late fall or winter in the early morning with temperatures in the –1 to 4°C range; the humidity is high and fog is usually present. The major effect on people is lung irritation. In Los Angeles, smog reaches its peak during the summer at midday with the temperature ranging from 24 to 32°C; humidity is low and the sky cloudless. The effect on people is eye and nose irritation.

Photochemical smog is found in any city that generates a quantity of internal combustion engine exhaust and has a high incidence of sunny days (Figure 18.5).

Fig. 18.5 Tears are now joining the millions of hearts left in San Francisco as smog completes the illusion of Manhattan West.

437

THE AUTOMOBILE AS A POLLUTION SOURCE

The internal combustion engine was developed with the goals of reliable performance, smooth operation, and low cost, without any regard for the waste products of the combustion process. In the early years of the automobile it mattered little, because the concentration of cars in proportion to the area of cities was insignificant. But as the number of cities grew their collective combustible wastes grew as well, until pollution became critically important. So today we are burdened with a highly sophisticated, powerful engine spewing out considerable quantities of pollutants which, once released into the air, are beyond our control.

Most of the combustion products are vented to the atmosphere through the tailpipe. Although gasoline burns most efficiently at a 15:1 air-fuel ratio, a high-compression engine requires a rich mixture of fuel with air: 13 or 12:1. This means that the hydrocarbons in the fuel are not completely burned. A high-compression engine also requires high octane gasoline, that is, gas with higher proportions of aromatics or volatile components that are also incompletely burned in rich mixtures.

THE COMPOSITION OF GASOLINE

If gasoline were a single compound and burned completely, the end products would be carbon dioxide and water, and there would be no emission problem; but gasoline is not a single compound, nor is it burned completely. A typical gasoline contains three kinds of hydrocarbons: paraffins and olefins, which burn well at low speeds; and aromatics, which work well at high speeds. But paraffins often explode spontaneously before ignition, causing engine knock and wasted power. To combat this, tetraethyl lead was added. Lead oxide then formed on the plugs and valves, so ethylene dichloride and dibromide were added to clean up the lead deposits. In addition antioxidants, metal deactivators, antirust and anti-icing compounds, detergents, and lubricants have been added. Small wonder that when this incredible mess is burned the combustion products are more than just carbon dioxide and water!

When fuel mixed with air (containing 78 percent nitrogen) is combusted, nitrogen dioxide is formed. As luck would have it, the ideal conditions for nitrogen dioxide generation are high temperature followed by rapid cooling, precisely the conditions provided by an internal combustion engine.

Evaporation contributes volatile hydrocarbons of great variety; combustion adds carbon dioxide, carbon monoxide, and nitrogen dioxide, and of course a large amount of incompletely burned hydrocarbons. These materials, together with sulfur dioxide produced by industry, enter the atmosphere and interact not only with each other, but, more importantly, with sunlight.

SUNLIGHT AS A REACTANT

Although we are most sensitive to the visible or light portion of the electromagnetic spectrum, it is the shorter wavelengths, or ultraviolet, which have more energy than the longer infrared radiation. It is this ultraviolet radiation that reacts with pollutants to form the secondary products that may cause more problems than the primary ones. Nitrogen dioxide, for example, is split by ultraviolet radiation into nitric oxide and atomic oxygen. Some of this atomic oxygen reacts with the nitric oxide, forming nitrogen dioxide again. This is called an autocatalytic reaction because nitrogen dioxide, once formed as a combustion product, can continue to regenerate itself in the atmosphere. In another important reaction, atomic oxygen combines with oxygen to form ozone. Ozone has great oxidative potential and is quite reactive; it attacks rubber, causing it to crack and ultimately to decompose. In fact, one of the clues suggesting the photochemical nature of ozone production in the atmosphere was the observation that rubber cracked only during the day.

The physical form of smog is an aerosol, that is, a fine dispersion of either particles or droplets that are less than twenty-five thousandths of an inch in diameter. At least one source of these droplets is the ultraviolet energized reaction of sulfur dioxide and various hydrocarbons, especially the olefins. Other secondary pollutants are the irritants formaldehyde, acrolein, and peroxyacetylnitrate (PAN) derived from further reactions of nitrogen dioxide and nitric oxide.

A typical photochemical smog, then, contains the primary pollutants carbon monoxide, sulfur dioxide, nitrogen oxides, hydrocarbon fragments from incompletely combusted fuel, volatile hydrocarbons evaporated from gasoline, and finally materials released from combusted additives such as lead, boron, bromine, and so on. Many of these primary smog components react with each other and with sunlight to produce secondary and even tertiary pollutants: nitric oxide, PAN, ozone, acrolein, and formaldehyde, to name just a few. How do these materials affect the environment?

EFFECTS OF PHOTOCHEMICAL SMOG

The gross effects of photochemical smog result from its dispersion in the atmosphere as an aerosol. Experiments using aerosols produced from various combinations of pollutants reduced visibility in the atmosphere from 26 to 6.5 miles. If the particles had been allowed to grow to a point of equilibrium, further reduction of visibility would have ensued. This reduction of visibility is not only aesthetically unpleasant but reduces sunlight received at the earth's surface, makes driving and flying more hazardous, and may act together with other pollutants to produce various adverse physiological effects in humans.

But photochemical smog has its greatest impact in the differing effects of its major components on plants and on us.

CARBON MONOXIDE

Carbon monoxide is one of the least reactive of the pollutants in photochemical smog, and is tolerated by the body in concentrations up to 10 ppm without noticeable effect. It is potentially quite dangerous because it is odorless, tasteless, and colorless, unlike many other pollutants. In the body it has a special affinity for hemoglobin, the substance in the red blood cells that normally combines with oxygen to distribute it throughout the body. As the level of carbon monoxide increases in the body, less oxyhemoglobin and more carboxyhemoglobin is formed. Since carboxyhemoglobin does not provide oxygen for the respiratory needs of the body cells, increasing concentrations of this compound endanger survival. A moderate smoker exposes himself to around 30 ppm of carbon monoxide, resulting in a 5 percent level of carboxyhemoglobin. When a heavy smoker is placed in an urban environment where carbon monoxide concentration in the air may average 20 to 30 ppm, the additive effect may approach the danger level of 100 ppm. Probably 20 to 30 ppm total should be the maximum allowed, for the physical effects—decline in sensitivity to environmental stimuli and lack of energy and endurance—begin to be felt above this level. Although at a busy intersection in a large city one may breathe 20 ppm of carbon monoxide, it is possible to get much higher doses, for example 370 ppm behind a car stopped for a red light. Pregnant women who smoke heavily increase the levels of carboxyhemoglobin both in their bodies and in the fetus they are carrying; this can reduce the amount of oxygen delivered to developing fetal tissues. Some estimates suggest that smoking mothers have twice the incidence of stillbirths and death of newborns as nonsmokers.

In addition to its direct effects, carbon monoxide reacts with the hydroxyl radicals in air to produce nitrogen dioxide, which enhances the conversion of sulfur dioxide into sulfuric acid and is involved in the photooxidation of oxygen into ozone.

For all the carbon monoxide we produce—270 million tons per year—natural sources produce half that found in the atmosphere, more than 3.5 billion tons in the Northern Hemisphere alone. Since the residence time is only a month or so, there are obviously important sinks that effectively reduce the ambient level of carbon monoxide in the atmosphere;

soil fungi and bacteria have been suggested as possibilities, and there must certainly be others. The fears of world-wide build-up of carbon monoxide now appear groundless. A few years ago similar fears were expressed that oxygen would be used up if combustion continued to increase, more forests were cleared, and more fields paved. Some calculations by a geochemist, W. S. Broecker, have laid that fear to rest. Broecker estimated that if all known fossil fuels were oxidized, less than 3 percent of the earth's oxygen supply would be used up; that if all photosynthesis stopped, less than 1 percent of the world's oxygen supply would be required to decompose this enormous biomass completely. Apparently our pollutants will become limiting long before our oxygen supply.

THE ORGANIC COMPOSITION

The hydrocarbons and nitrogen oxide products such as acrolein, PAN, and formaldehyde irritate the eyes and nose and even attack nylon stockings. Any student who has dissected a frog recalls the tearful fumes of formaldehyde. Typical concentrations of PAN in smog range from 0.05 to 0.6 ppm. PAN enters the leaves of plants through the stomates and causes the spongy mesophyll cells to collapse (Figure 18.6). The resulting air space gives leaves a silvered or bronze appearance, ruining their sale as leaf vegetables.

Orange trees, although more resistant than leafy vegetables, are also affected by high concentrations of PAN. The twigs are killed, giving the tree a moth-eaten appearance, and the number of food-producing leaves is so reduced that the crop of oranges is severely diminished. Because of smog damage, commercial orange production has shifted from the Los Angeles basin to the Sierran foothills on the edge of the San Joaquin Valley. While 50 percent of the reactive hydrocarbons such as PAN are generated by motor vehicles, 40 percent come from industrial sources, the chief being solvent evaporation.

OZONE

Ozone is also an irritant, but it can impair vision and depress body temperature as well. Its threshold for direct action is around 1 ppm. While the natural concentration of ozone is about 0.02 ppm, it may range as high as 0.5 ppm or more in severe photochemical smog. Ozone attacks the palisade layer in plant leaves (Figure 18.6), causing brown flecks to appear, especially in tobacco leaves, which are very sensitive to ozone. The flecking considerably reduces the value of the leaves, particularly those used as cigar wrappers. Natural vegetation is affected by ozone as well; there has been pronounced dieback of ponderosa pine in the San Bernardino Mountains southeast of Los Angeles. These mountains, which form

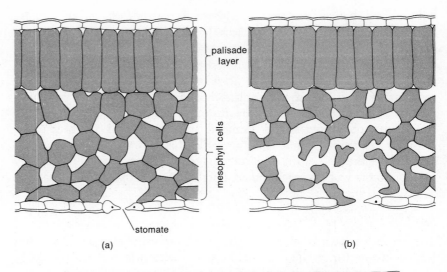

palisade
layer

mesophyll cells

stomate

(a)

(b)

Fig. 18.6 (a) Cross section
of a normal leaf; (b) cross section of a leaf whose spongy
mesophyll cells have been
damaged by smog entering
the leaf through the stomates;
(c) cross section of a leaf
whose palisade layer has been
damaged, causing small
flecks to appear on the leaf
surface.

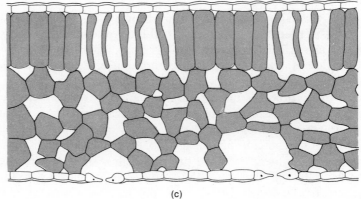

(c)

one rim of the basin, are subject to heavy concentrations of smog drifting
out of the Los Angeles area. White pine in the eastern United States
develops a similar browning of its needles from ozone. This effect has
been noticed in the Cumberland Mountains of Tennessee near Oak
Ridge and along parkways in suburban areas such as the Merritt Parkway
in Connecticut.

CONTROL OF PHOTOCHEMICAL SMOG

Control the automobile exhaust and you control photochemical smog
(Figure 18.7). Like all simple solutions to involved problems, there are
hidden complications. As we have seen, the automobile was developed

without any particular interest in emission control. Suddenly after eighty years the hue and cry goes up to control emissions.

In 1970 Congress passed the Clean Air Act, which calls for a 90 percent reduction of hydrocarbon and carbon monoxide levels, using a 1970 model car as a standard, and a 90 percent reduction in nitrogen oxide emission, using a 1971 model car as a benchmark. By 1975, cars would be limited to 0.41 g per mile of hydrocarbons, 3.4 g per mile of carbon monoxide, and 3 g per mile of nitrogen oxides. In 1976 permissible nitrogen oxide emissions would be reduced to 0.4 g per mile. However, a combination of the 1973–1974 oil embargo and difficulties experienced by the auto industry in cleaning up emissions have led to several extensions of emission reduction schedules. The major problem, tailpipe emission, is by far the most difficult to control. Of the several possibilities, catalytic converters have been adopted by most American manufacturers. Catalytic converting works well when new, but becomes less effective as fuel additives coat the catalyst. In addition, the catalytic converter causes reductions in gas mileage although air conditioners, automatic transmissions, and greater car weight have a collectively greater impact on gas mileage. After twelve thousand miles the catalyst must be replaced. For this reason the major auto manufacturers in the United States are lowering the compression ratio of their engines to eliminate the need for leaded gasoline. But even without lead additives in the gasoline, catalyst lifetimes beyond twenty-five thousand miles are unlikely. Then too, a second catalyst must be present to take care of the nitrogen oxides. Finally, the catalytic converter, which was snatched out of Detroit laboratories and

Oliphant in The Denver Post

" . . . Then, when the bag is full of hydrocarbons and noxious gases, you simply take if off and throw it away!"

Fig. 18.7 Editorial cartoon by Pat Oliphant. (Copyright by the Denver Post; reprinted with permission of the Los Angeles Times Syndicate.)

443

rushed into production in a desperate effort to avoid costly engine modification, was found to be 30 percent efficient as a producer of sulfuric acid mist. The catalytic converter seems to be a blind alley.

A more likely development is much more use of stratified charge and Wankel engines. Developed initially in foreign imports, these engines could be used in future American cars. In one version of the stratified charge engine, a rich air-fuel mixture is pre-ignited; the flame front then invades the main part of the cylinder, igniting a much leaner mixture of fuel and air, which drives the pistons. The leaner the fuel-air mixture, the lower the emission level. The Wankel, a rotary engine, is "dirty," producing twice the hydrocarbons, about the same carbon monoxide, and 20 to 60 percent lower nitrogen oxides than a standard engine; but because of its small size and high-temperature exhaust gases, a thermal reactor can be easily used to complete combustion of the hydrocarbons and carbon monoxide. Unfortunately the Wankel's gasoline consumption is 30 percent higher than a normal piston engine's.

ALTERNATIVE ENGINES

The most reasonable alternatives to internal combustion engines are the Stirling-cycle engine, the turbine, the steam or Rankine engine, and electricity.

The Stirling engine works on the principle of constant burning of fuel, which makes it a closed-cycle external combustion engine. With large amounts of excess air involved in the combustion process, hydrocarbons and carbon monoxide levels are well below the Clean Air Act Standards. With an exhaust gas recirculation system, nitrogen oxides could be kept below the 0.4 g per mile limitation.

A gas turbine consists basically of a compressor and a turbine wheel on a common shaft. The combustion chamber lies in the air-flow path between them. Since the turbine operates at very high air-fuel ratios, the emission of unburned hydrocarbons and carbon monoxide is quite low, but the production of nitrogen oxides is relatively great because of the high operating temperature of the engine. Reduction in the output of nitrogen oxides would require a catalyst active at less than 1093°C; such a catalyst has not yet been found. The turbine has the advantages of quick starting, no warmup, and low vibration and noise level; but fuel consumption at low speeds is excessive, acceleration poor, and the engine cannot be used in braking. These problems are not insuperable, however. Once a major manufacturer tools up, turbine cars could be mass produced at approximately the same cost as present cars.

Steam engines are undergoing a renewal of interest. With modern technology and new materials, compact and low-maintenance reciprocating steam engines are quite feasible both in performance and in emission control. The transmission system required is relatively simple and the long-standing problem of warmup time can be licked by modern boiler technology. Even if steam automobiles are not developed, fleet vehicles such as trucks, buses, and taxis could be converted to steam.

Electric automobiles use energy stored in batteries. Regardless of type, batteries work on the principle of a reversible chemical action between unlike electrodes placed in a conducting solution or electrolyte. The problem with battery-driven cars remains their limited range. The still unattained solution is a battery of long life and high power. In present batteries, as the power increases the energy level falls off, reducing the range. New battery systems such as sodium-sulfur and lithium-chlorine show promise of combining both power and range.

The ideal battery for use in an electric automobile would deliver 220 watt-hours of power per kilogram, last five years, and cost around $20 per kwh. The lithium-chlorine battery, which has a theoretical output of 2600 wh/kg, is plagued with electrode problems and has produced only 155 wh/kg in laboratory tests so far. The sodium-sulfur battery has had problems with its beta alumina electrode, which cracks with repeated charge-discharge cycles. Neither battery is likely to see widespread use before 1985.

The most logical solution to the automobile emission problem, short of abandoning cars for mass transport (Chapter 13), would be to replace the standard internal combustion engine. Since this will take at least a decade to accomplish, transitional types such as the stratified charge and Wankel engines would buy time to develop such alternatives to internal combustion as the Stirling or Rankine engines. For the first time in many years it looks as though the next decade could see a marked reduction in the frequency and density of photochemical smog in our cities. If the alarums about impending shortages of gasoline (see Chapter 15) are taken literally and the price of gasoline continues to increase substantially, alternate fuels may become economically attractive. One such possibility is hydrogen. Not suitable as a primary source of power because of the high energy cost involved in its production, hydrogen may be quite useful as an energy carrier, since it is efficient and, unlike electricity, easy to store. When burned, hydrogen produces water and levels of nitrogen oxides lower than other fuels. This makes it an attractive energy source for transportation. However, it is bulky and presently very expensive to produce by electrolysis. But the problems are economic rather than technical and the economics of fuel supply are clearly entering an era of rapid change.

AIR POLLUTION AND THE FOREST ECOSYSTEM

Forests respond to air pollution in three ways, depending on the severity of the pollution: they act as a sink; their growth and processes are depressed; or they are simplified. During the growing season, vegetation filters out or absorbs ammonia, hydrogen fluoride, sulfur dioxide, chlorides, nitrates, ozone, and PAN. Because of their high surface-to-volume ratio, trees are particularly efficient scrubbers of dirty air. Ozone and PAN can be detoxified without much damage to the system if the initial concentrations are low. Sulfate and nitrogen compounds are converted into useful nutrients and enter the ecosystem's mineral cycling process. Heavy metals may be passed on to primary consumers. But the forest's relationship with air pollutants isn't one-way. Carbon monoxide, hydrogen sulfide, ammonia, and nitrogen oxides are produced by vegetation at six times the rate produced by our activities. In addition, 70 percent of the forest tree species in the United States produce volatile hydrocarbons, some of which may be related to the production of ozone. The Smoky Mountains of Tennessee and North Carolina are not smoky because of automobile emissions (although we're working on that) but from the production of natural terpenes and other volatile hydrocarbons.

If incoming pollutant concentrations continue to increase, the sink function of the forest ecosystem is overwhelmed. Consistent deposition of heavy metals on leaves leads to a build-up of these materials in the litter on the forest floor. Since many of these heavy metals are toxic to fungi, the decomposition cycle may be slowed or altered, yielding fewer and lower-quality nutrients for vegetative growth. As the pH of rainfall drops, the increasingly acid rain leaches calcium and other important nutrients out of the forest soil. As increasing concentrations of ozone begin to suppress photosynthesis, growth and production slow down.

Reproduction may also be hampered: PAN reduces the yields of citrus; ozone reduces pollen germination in some species; and sulfur dioxide decreases the yield of pine seed. Limestone dust seems to interfere with the reproduction of black and scarlet oak and basswood. And pollinating insects may be adversely affected by excess fluorine emissions.

With still higher levels of air pollution, trees may simply not be able to live. Smog from Los Angeles flowing over the San Bernardino Mountains affects ponderosa pine by reducing exudation pressure. This decreases the rate of oleoresin flow, lowering the moisture content of the wood and making the trees more vulnerable to the invasion of western pine and mountain pine beetles, which have seriously damaged the ponderosa pine forests of southern California. Similarly in the Rocky Mountains an increase in fluorine levels in lodgepole pine needles has contributed to a build-up of populations of pine needle scale, pitch mass borer, and needle miner. Sulfur dioxide increases the stomatal aperture in leaves, facilitating the entrance of microorganisms while increasing moisture stress. Of course the pathogens may be adversely affected by air pollutants too, especially ozone. But unfortunately, they are less sensitive than the host vegetation.

The final stage is loss, first of sensitive species, then of the tree canopy itself. The loss of ponderosa pine in the San Bernardinos seems to be accompanied by an increase in the number of the more resistant sugar pine, white fir, and incense cedar. The more exposed ridges, however, are becoming covered with chaparral. Total loss of canopy is depressingly visible in the heart of the Appalachians. In the early 1900s Ducktown, Tennessee, located near a copper deposit, released forty tons of sulfur dioxide a day into the air of a southern Appalachian valley. Not only were seven thousand acres of the vegetation killed and another seventeen thousand reduced to sparse grass, but most of the topsoil, exposed to rain without the protection of vegetation, washed away, leaving a desert in the midst of one of the lushest forests in North America (Figure 18.8). When controls were finally instituted and the sulfur dioxide converted to the useful by-product sulfuric acid, the return on the once-wasted sulfur dioxide proved, ironically, greater than on the copper. The desert remains.

Fig. 18.8 When the vegetation of this once lush hillside was destroyed by SO_2 fumes from a copper smelter, erosion removed the topsoil, making revegetation of the area extremely difficult and slow.

CARBON DIOXIDE AND CLIMATE

Because of its natural presence in the atmosphere and its basic role in photosynthesis and respiration, carbon dioxide is not commonly regarded as an air pollutant. But since the beginning of the Industrial Revolution the use of fossil fuels for combustion has released enormous quantities of carbon dioxide into the atmosphere. At present, the atmosphere contains around 2.3×10^{12} tons of carbon dioxide (0.03 percent) and the ocean another 1.3×10^{14} tons. Exchange between the atmosphere and the ocean amounts to about 200×10^9 tons per year, so the ocean acts as a reservoir or buffer of carbon dioxide in equilibrium with the carbon dioxide content of the air. If amounts of atmospheric carbon dioxide decrease, more is released from the ocean; conversely, if the carbon dioxide content of the air increases, the ocean tends to absorb more. The rate of change, however, is slow. It takes at least 1000 years for 50 percent of the change, up or down, to be accommodated by the ocean.

THE GREENHOUSE EFFECT

In the atmosphere, carbon dioxide does not affect shortwave radiation. Upon striking the earth, however, shortwave radiation is transformed into, and reradiated as, longwave radiation or heat. This heat is absorbed by the carbon dioxide molecules and transferred to the atmosphere. It is this heat transfer that is ultimately responsible for long-term climate and short-term weather. Because of the balance of incoming light and outgoing heat the mean temperature of the earth remains at about 14°C. This phenomenon of carbon dioxide absorption of heat is called the greenhouse effect. Shortwave radiation or light also passes easily through glass, and is converted to longwave radiation or heat in a greenhouse. Because of the lack of convection and the inability of the heat to pass out through the glass, the greenhouse stays warm. The same thing happens in a closed car on a hot day.

It has been theorized for a number of years that as combustion pours more and more carbon dioxide into the atmosphere it will accumulate faster than the sea can absorb it. More carbon dioxide in the atmosphere will absorb more outgoing longwave radiation and the earth's mean temperature will begin to rise. Since a rise of only a few degrees would melt the earth's icecaps and raise the sea level by 400 feet, the problem is not merely academic (see Chapter 17).

Before 1900 the average carbon dioxide concentration in the Northern Hemisphere was approximately 290 ppm. Today it is 330 ppm, an increase proportional to the rate of fossil fuel combustion during this time. But at the same time we are dramatically increasing the quantity

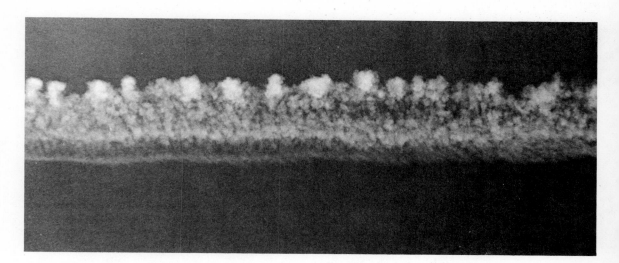

of dust particles in the atmosphere. This tends to reflect shortwave radiation back into space, thereby cooling the earth. No one is at all sure which of these processes is in the ascendancy or whether there is a balance.

Another experiment has been initiated by high flying jets. The condensation trails or contrails of jets are quite conspicuous in the sky (Figure 18.9). Usually they disperse quite rapidly; but sometimes they persist and occasionally they bleed together and cover an otherwise clear sky with a blurry cirrus overcast. This cools the earth below by as much as 15°C, which has been shown to prevent the formation of thunderstorms—a development that presents us with advantages and disadvantages.

Because of concern over the unknown environmental effects of the supersonic transport, flying at 50–70,000 feet, and because of economic considerations, development of an American SST was halted in 1971. One problem that has been brought up since then is the possibility that nitrogen oxides from SST exhaust could act as a catalyst, destroying the ozone layer that presently shields earth from dangerously high levels of ultraviolet radiation. A decrease of only 5 percent in the ozone concentration would elicit a 10 percent increase in the UV intensity.

Despite its critical importance in the upper atmosphere, ozone is rather variable in concentration making it hard to trace our additions to or subtractions from the ozone layer. The eleven-year sunspot cycle seems to be responsible for the peaks recorded in 1941 and 1952. In 1963 atmospheric testing of thermonuclear weapons seems to have generated enough nitrogen oxides to reduce the ozone concentration temporarily. After the test ban treaty, ozone returned to normal levels. The three major agents for ozone destruction are oxygen, which accounts for 18 percent of the ozone lost; the hydroxyl radical, 11 percent; and nitric oxide, 50 to 70

Fig. 18.9 Carbon particles from jet exhausts form condensation nuclei for moisture in the stratosphere. Sometimes the droplets disappear as fast as they form, and sometimes they spread slowly until the whole sky is covered with a thin, light-absorbing film of human-induced cirrus clouds.

449

percent. In 1974 a great flap arose about the halocarbon propellants in aerosol cans, which were alleged to be a fourth ozone destroyer. Halocarbons are generally quite stable and inert. But as they float into the stratosphere UV radiation breaks them up into highly reactive chlorine radicals, which interact with ozone.

A recent report by the National Research Council Committee on Impact of Stratospheric Change suggested that if halocarbons continued to be released at the 1973 rates stratospheric ozone might be reduced by 7 percent. By increasing the flux of ultraviolet light (see Table 14.1) at the ground surface, this would increase the incidence of skin cancer. Over a longer term the halocarbons would absorb infrared in the 8 to 13 micrometer range where the atmosphere is relatively transparent to outgoing radiation. Any reduction of this escape for outgoing radiation would increase the mean temperature of the atmosphere in addition to whatever temperature increase is caused by the slow rise of CO_2 in the atmosphere. Although the effect may only be 0.5°C over a period of fifty years, major effects on climate result from as little as 1°C changes in the earth's mean temperature.

In consequence, the committee recommended that halocarbon aerosols be banned by 1978, and that halocarbon refrigerants be restricted in automobile air conditioners and in industrial refrigeration units. However, the United States is responsible for only one half of the halocarbons released to the atmosphere.

NOISE

While we are unsure of the ultimate effect of some forms of air pollution, there is no doubt about the effect of one of our activities in the first few hundred feet of the atmosphere—noise. Without question, noise can damage hearing; there is no threshold for ear damage (Figure 18.10). Claims for insurance compensation for loss of hearing have climbed to over a billion dollars a year in the United States alone, prompting industry to take noise reduction programs seriously. But more subtly, noise increases tensions already heightened by the other stresses of urban life. Noise can affect blood pressure and ultimately the heart. Unfortunately we have no earlids to shut out noise at night, so we can be victimized at all hours.

The obvious solution is to identify the sources of noise and then work towards reducing the level of sound from these sources. Unlike some other environmental problems, the technology for noise abatement has been available for some time. A good example is provided by construction equipment. In 1969 a major manufacturer of air compressors brought out a new model that reduced the noise level from 110 decibels to 82 decibels. Because the quiet compressor cost 40 percent more than the older, noisier models, the construction industry was uninterested. Today, however, the cost differential has been reduced to 10 percent, the public is losing some of its apathy, and cities are beginning to consider ordinances that offer scientific standards for regulation and contain punitive "teeth" to bring compliance. In 1971, for example, New York proposed a noise control code that would set specific noise-level standards in decibels for garbage trucks, air conditioners, public-address systems, emergency sirens, and construction equipment. Unfortunately subways, railroads, aircraft, and motor vehicles cannot be included in a city ordinance because of conflicting federal and state regulations. But the proposed code represents a great leap forward from the typical "nuisance" codes that were virtually unenforceable.

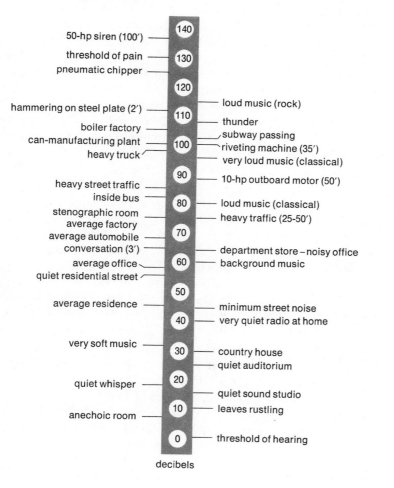

Fig. 18.10 Noise is measured in dynes/cm², watts/cm², or, most commonly, decibels. Some common environmental sounds are listed here in ascending decibel values. (Modified from C. Stark, *Stereo Review* 23, 1969)

Subway noises have been sharply reduced by rubber-tired cars in some of the newer subway systems of the world. But even existing obsolete systems, such as those in Boston, New York, and Philadelphia, could be greatly improved with welded rails, aluminum-centered steel wheels, polyurethane foam between the ties, insulation pads under the tracks, and sound-deadening materials on car underbodies and station walls. The only such obstacle to such improvements is public apathy.

Much of the problem of urban noise lies in our inability to get away from it. New office buildings and apartment houses not only are notoriously transparent to outside sounds but also generate a complete range of noises of their own—elevator doors, air conditioning, light fixture hum, knocking radiator pipes, echoic halls and lobbies. Building code changes or stronger enforcement of existing codes could be very helpful in reducing the noise levels in new construction. Even more important is some form of land use planning (see Chapter 20) that would isolate the noisier components of our urban society, such as airports, or control development near such facilities. One crude but simple method for estimating the potential noise that can be anticipated at a building site has been worked out by the Federal Department of Housing and Urban Development. One member of a two-person team reads aloud while the other moves away with a tape measure until only a few words can be heard in a 10-second period. If the distance measured is 7 feet or less, the site is unacceptable; 7 to 25 feet precludes housing without extensive acoustic insulation; 26 to 70 feet is typical for residential sites; over 70 feet is ideal.

One of the greatest sound generators is the jet airplane. Not that noise from piston aircraft was insignificant, but in the 1940s and 1950s before jets were introduced, airports were relatively small and flight volume moderate. Since the introduction of jets at O'Hare International Airport in Chicago in 1958, traffic there has grown to 1200 flights a day; at peak hours jets come and go every forty seconds, moving 23.5 million people through O'Hare every year. In 1960, sixteen airports were served by jets; in 1967, 150; in 1970, 350; and in 1975, 500. The safest way for a jet aircraft to approach a runway is to follow a long, low trajectory. Unfortunately, this is also the noisiest way. Even more unfortunately, areas right up to the edges of large new jetports were allowed to be subdivided and are jammed with residential housing today.

Because of this lack of land use planning, the city of Los Angeles was required by landowner suits in 1971 to spend $200 million to buy up 400 acres of residential development on the edge of Los Angeles International Airport. The lesson was well learned, apparently, for strict land use controls are planned for the new airport under construction at Palmdale, California.

LIGHT POLLUTION

In many areas of the United States, and not just in the downtowns of large cities, the night sky has brightened to the point where only the brightest stars are visible. Even in the country, farm lights and the glow from distant cities wash out the spectacle of a lustrous Milky Way, the hazy patches of nebulae and star clusters, and the icy sparkle of Sirius, Vega, Betelgeuse, and other once bright stars. But these are aesthetic considerations. The major observatories, particularly those constructed before the rampant suburban sprawl of the past thirty years, have been troubled not only with broad band washing out of faint light from distant objects such as quasars, but with narrow band spectral interference from mercury and sodium vapor street lamps.

Fig. 18.11 Although it would seem that the Kitt Peak Observatory is located in the middle of nowhere, Tucson is close by and growing fast enough to be fogging the photographic plates of the telescopes from scattered waste light at night. (Kitt Peak National Observatory)

As we have seen (Chapter 15), buildings and parking lots are grossly overlit; in many instances, streets and highways are too. Often little effort is made to focus the light on the road surface, where it is needed— much of the light bleeds away uselessly into the night. When the light sources are relatively limited in number and municipal jurisdictions are not complex, measures can be taken. This is being done in Tucson to accommodate the nearby Kitt Peak Observatory (Figure 18.11). Lamps with shields to control back scattering of light and filter glass to control the blue end of the spectrum are beginning to afford some relief.

The sky and the sea have long borne the brunt of our misuse, partly because their very immensity seemed to preclude any long-term effect of our efforts, and partly because both belong to no one. But while it is possible to avoid a polluted sea by living inland, polluted air is in everyone's lungs. Slowly we are coming to realize the subtle cause-and-effect relationship between polluted environments and the increasing incidence of asthma, bronchitis, emphysema, hypertension, and heart deterioration—a relationship so long ignored because these debilities are not glamorous diseases, but the result of the body's inability to cope indefinitely with a broad spectrum of specific stresses.

The significance of all types of air pollution has begun to dawn upon us and the options are clear, perhaps for the first time in our history. Continued inaction in dealing with these problems is unconscionable for our generation, and suicidal for the next.

FURTHER READING

Bodkin, L. D., 1974. "Carbon monoxide and smog." *Env.* **16**(4), pp. 34–41. Explores the possibilities of a synergistic relationship between carbon monoxide and smog.

Hammond, A. L., and T. H. Maugh, II, 1974. "Stratospheric pollution: multiple threats to earth's ozone." *Science* **186,** pp. 335–338.

Josephson, J., 1974. "Cleaning coal by solvent refining." *Env. Sci. & Tech.* **8**(6), pp. 510–511. Another approach to cleaning up coal.

Longo, L. D., 1976. "Carbon monoxide effects on oxygenation of the fetus in utero." *Science* **194,** pp. 523–525. Smoking may be hazardous not only to you but to your children—and not because of lung cancer.

Maugh, T. H., II, 1976. "The ozone layer: the threat from aerosol cans is real." *Science* **194,** pp. 170–172. Apparently halocarbon aerosols are on the way out.

Robinson, A. L., 1976. "Advanced storage batteries: progress but not electrifying." *Science* **192,** pp. 541–543. Update on the prospects for a really useful storage battery.

Slack, A. V., 1973. "Removing SO_2 from stack gases." *Env. Sci. & Tech.* **7**(2), pp. 110–119. A review of alternative processes.

Smith, W. H., 1974. "Air pollution effects on the structure and function of the temperate forest ecosystem." *Env. Poll.* **6,** pp. 111–129. Thorough review.

CHAPTER NINETEEN

SOLID WASTES: MIDDENHEAP INTO MOUNTAIN

OUR FIRST COMMUNAL living areas were probably caves, well sheltered from the weather and potential enemies. Solid wastes—excrement, bones, old tools, charcoal, and ashes—were quite literally thrown away, over the shoulder. When the resulting piles or middenheaps got a bit lumpy underfoot, or became too offensive, it was a simple matter to cover up the mess and start all over. After a few hundred years a small cave would fill up, forcing the occupants to find new quarters, but some of the larger caves accommodated thousands of years of continuous occupation and hundreds of feet of wastes.

The cities, though they came much later in our history, were hardly more subtle in their handling of solid wastes. Discarded materials were freely scattered just outside the city wall or around the dwellings. When destroyed by fire or war, ancient cities were often rebuilt upon their solid wastes and rubble. Over hundreds or thousands of years, the once-level sites of cities slowly became mounds, often abandoned and covered with sand or soil, but occasionally still inhabited by a few hundred people perched above the surrounding countryside on their huge waste heap (Figure 19.1).

An astonishingly complete historical record of daily life in caves and cities can be pieced together by careful archeological digging. But exploration of past cultures by examination of their waste is by no means limited to prehistoric times. Williamsburg, Virginia was restored after very careful archeological scrutiny uncovered the nature of building materials,

techniques, and tools, deduced from the scraps and wastes associated with the construction of every building. Excavations in the older parts of eastern seaboard cities often bring to light old bricks, pieces of bottles, and crockery that tell much about the past. New York's Central Park, once a shanty town of squatters' huts, has pieces of glass and crockery scattered throughout, some dating from the 1840s and 1850s.

TODAY'S WASTE

In many ways, however, the solid wastes with which we are faced today are quite different from those of even the recent past. There is, for example, a much greater variety of more stable wastes. A simple glass bottle can at least be broken to take up less space, and a steel can will rust away in a few years; but a plastic bottle or an aluminum beer can lasts indefinitely. Even more serious is the rate at which solid wastes are accumulating. The average person throws away five pounds of wastes per day, or 1800 pounds a year.

Of the 125 million tons of commercial/household waste produced each year, one third is discarded packaging. We have come a long way from a plain brown bag or newspaper-wrapped fish; today and increasingly in the future, items will be packaged "for the convenience of the consumer." Take for example the plastic bubble packs hung on hooks by the thousands in all stores (Figure 19.2). The merchandise, a few nails or an electric socket, is plainly in view, but the package usually serves as advertising space for the manufacturer; it is less handy to carry, is difficult to open, and its contents surely cost the consumer more than the same item bought unpackaged. The so-called convenience foods with their aluminum foil covers and pans, pressurized cans of just about every liquid—all add immeasurably to the trash load to be disposed of and to the cost of the material sold. Those tiny picnic-sized containers of salt, for example, inflate the price of the product to eight times the price of salt bought by the pound.

THE KINDS OF WASTES

Of course, discarded packages are not the sole ingredient of household wastes, any more than household wastes represent all wastes produced by contemporary society. Before we look at disposal techniques we should have some idea of which wastes are causing the biggest problems and why. Since industrial wastes have already been considered (see Chapter 16), our prime focus here will be on consumer- rather than producer-generated wastes.

What is the nature of household solid wastes? One revealing analysis done by archeologist William Rathje and his students in Tucson showed that almost $100 worth of food is wasted per household per year. About 8 percent by weight of the total food that went into these households was wasted—things like whole loaves of unopened bread, unwrapped steaks, fruit, vegetables, and other apparently edible food products. Since the study was based on analysis of garbage routinely collected from a sample

Fig. 19.2 One of the greatest challenges of modern life is to open one of these ubiquitous bubble packs without tears.

457

of middle-class homes, it does not include food wastes eliminated in sink disposal units or liquids simply poured down the drain.

Another more general breakdown is shown in Table 19.1. Notice that the largest category, miscellaneous paper, accurately reflects a part of the packaging revolution.

Table 19.1
Breakdown of Household Wastes in the United States*

WASTE	WEIGHT PERCENT	WASTE	WEIGHT PERCENT
Cardboard	7	Leather, rubber,	
Newspaper	14	molded plastic	2
Misc. paper	25	Garbage	12
Plastic film	2	Grass clippings, dirt	10
Wood	7	Textiles	3
Glass, ceramics, stone	10	Metal	8

* Subcommittee on Environmental Improvement, 1969. "Cleaning our environment, the chemical basis for action." American Chemical Society, Washington, D.C.

PAPER

At one time waste paper, particularly newspaper, was carefully saved by most households to be sold to the rag man for small but welcome change. Later it was given away to neighborhood charity collection drives, and now it is thrown away with the trash because no one will cart it away. What has happened? The paper industry's demand for waste paper has certainly declined: in 1945, 35 percent of the waste paper generated was reused; by 1966 this figure had fallen to 21 percent, and by 1980 less than 18 percent is likely to be reused.

The slackening demand has probably been due to the increased efficiency and lower cost of harvesting virgin pulp. Other causes include the small margin of profit in handling waste paper, resistance to change on the part of large paper users who are potential users of recycled paper, and the financial interests large newspapers have in virgin pulping operations. These factors have been matched by a sharp increase in the cost of handling the collection, transport, and processing of waste paper. The packaging revolution has contributed mightily to the pileup of waste paper because of the huge increase in volume and the contamination of paper with aluminum and plastic coats. Furthermore, special inks and treatments, because of their variety, can be extremely expensive and difficult to separate from the useful paper pulp. Some success has been achieved in efficient and inexpensive de-inking of waste newsprint, but fancy paper wrappings and containers frequently are not worth the trouble. To make matters worse, special coatings, however attractive to the consumer, retard the natural decomposition of waste paper in landfill dumps and lead to delays in reuse of the land.

alternative to paper waste disposal.

One way around the sluggish waste paper market might be to head in a new direction. Instead of trying to remake paper from paper, the cellulose could be treated with cellulase, an enzyme from a special strain of the fungus *Trichoderma viride*, to produce glucose, which when fermented can produce ethyl alcohol. Preliminary cost analyses suggest that alcohol might be produced for a quarter of the current industrial price. Since most ethyl alcohol in use today is derived from ethylene, a petroleum distillate, a switch to cellulose-based alcohol might result in a considerable saving of crude oil. The alcohol could be used as a nonpolluting fuel without the problems more exotic new fuels might cause (see Chapter 15).

CANS

The tin can, which has been a mainstay of the food industry for over 100 years, is made not of tin but steel, covered with as thin a layer of tin as technology will allow the manufacturer to apply. Tin does not react with the contents of the can and has a pleasing shiny surface which, unlike the underlying steel, does not rust quickly. Although tin cans have been around for many years, their life in the natural environment is relatively short. The thin tin coat weathers away in the open, exposing the underlying steel to fairly rapid rusting. In humid climates most tin cans will rust away in a few decades—sometimes much sooner. Campers have long made it a habit to throw their tin cans into the campfire before burying them because this helps remove the tinned layer and exposes the cans to rusting more rapidly.

Ironically, tin coating, which allows rustable steel to be used and so predisposes the can to environmental decay, makes the cans virtually worthless as iron scrap because of the contamination with tin, which is incompatible especially with the newer basic oxygen steel-making furnace. For this reason cans are thrown away rather than salvaged.

However, there is one growing use for scrap cans. With ever stricter controls over smelting effluents and the decreasing quality of copper ores in the United States, the copper industry is shifting from smelting the copper by roasting the ore to dissolving the copper from its ore. This is done with sulfuric acid passed over shredded tin cans. The iron in the cans, which is more chemically active than the copper, replaces copper in solution. The copper is precipitated out on the cans, collected, and refined. The remaining iron is still waste, of course, so the process can hardly be called recycling. But at least some use has been made of an item

459

THE WASTE
EXPLOSION

Fig. 19.3 *Have you seen these artifacts before? Convenient to use, easily disposed of, virtually impossible to recycle, at least they're buried in the natural litter after a few years. "Out of sight, out of mind" is the name of the game.*

presently regarded as useless. Over 100,000 tons of cans per year are used in this process, mostly in the Southwest. However, this use absorbs only 2 to 3 percent of the available waste can supply, and at best in the future will only take care of a sixth of the cans discarded each year.

But the tin can now seems to be on the way out because chrome- and resin-coated steel has become cheaper than tinned steel and is more acceptable as scrap to the steel mills. Aluminum has also made great strides in the container market. Like the new steel cans, aluminum cans can be reused as scrap, but they are so readily discarded that their collection is unlikely. Once thrown away piecemeal, their retrieval expense is as much as thirty cents a can. While the new steel cans will corrode if the tough chromium or resin coats are broken, the aluminum can is practically indestructible when dumped into the environment (Figure 19.3). At present 25 percent of the aluminum produced in the United States each year winds up as trash.

BOTTLES

Whatever the change in metal cans, glass as a packaging material will endure. Since 75 percent of glass is silica sand, the most abundant substance in the earth's crust, cost of raw material is low and likely to remain so. At the present rate of bottle production, sand reserves are calculated to last around 3 billion years. However, some glass companies have expressed concern that, should bottle production increase significantly in the future, the sand supply might become dangerously depleted a little over a billion years from now.

Glass bottles are reasonably destructible. Despite the danger from broken glass, breaking at least reduces the bulk of a glass bottle or jar.

460

But volume is less a problem than number. Once, most glass bottles were stoutly built to be used many times. It was later realized, however, that bottle return is a nuisance to the consumer, the middleman, and the bottler, who must at times clean some incredibly dirty bottles.

A few years ago some merchandising genius discovered that for every returnable bottle, used twenty times on the average, twenty nonreturnable bottles could be sold; this discovery resulted in the "disposable" bottle. In the next few years far greater quantities of bottles will probably be added to the disposal problem. But if the total energy requirements for returnable and nonreturnable bottles are examined, disposable bottles are not nearly as cheap as has been supposed (Table 19.2).

Table 19.2
Energy Expended (in Btu) for One Gallon of Soft Drink
in 16-ounce Returnable or Throwaway Bottles*

OPERATION	RETURNABLE (8 fills)	THROWAWAY
Raw material acquisition	990	5,195
Transportation of raw materials	124	650
Manufacture of container	7,738	40,624
Manufacture of cap (crown)	1,935	1,935
Transportation to bottler	361	1,895
Bottling	6,100	6,100
Transportation to retailer	1,880	1,235
Retailer and consumer	——	——
Waste collection	89	468
Separation, sorting, return for processing, 30 percent recycle	1,102	5,782
TOTAL ENERGY EXPENDED IN BTU PER GALLON		
Recycled	19,970	62,035
Not recycled	19,220	58,100

*From Hannon, Bruce M., 1972. "Bottles, cans, energy." *Environment* **14**(2), pp. 16–17. Copyright © 1972 Scientists' Institute for Public Information.

Responding to the problem of roadside litter (66 percent of roadside trash is bottles and cans), Oregon passed a law in 1972 prohibiting the use of nonreturnable cans and bottles in the state. Bottles now carry a two- or five-cent deposit, and pull-tab cans were outlawed altogether. As a result of this legislation, 350 jobs were lost in container-producing facilities but there was a gain of 140 jobs in trucking, 575 jobs in warehousing and handling, plus other job gains in glassblowing and related areas. Litter, essentially bottles and cans, decreased by as much as 81 percent according to some estimates. Despite fierce opposition by manufacturers and brewers, similar legislation has been passed by Vermont, Maine,

461

and Michigan, and is being considered in many other states and by Congress as well.

Fortunately the glass industry is not oblivious to the problem it is generating. Several kinds of self-destructing bottles are being tested by industry-sponsored research. One is a bottle that can withstand normal droppage but when struck hard fractures, like auto safety glass, into harmless granules that are much more easily disposed of than the bulky bottle. Broken glass of any sort is a good landfill material because it is dense, less subject to settling, and insoluble. A second approach to disposable bottle-making is the production of water-soluble glass, covered inside and out with a waterproof layer to last out the shelf life. When the layer is broken the glass quickly dissolves. Perhaps we shall end up flushing soda bottles down the sink; if so, the problem will not really have been solved. Instead of getting rid of a pound of solid glass bottle, we will be asking a sewage plant to get rid of a pound of synthetic material dissolved in the sewage effluent.

One enterprising use of waste glass has been in the production of glass-phalt, a paving material that uses ground glass as the aggregate. This has the advantage of availability in large quantities in urban areas where other forms of aggregates are scarce and expensive, and usefulness for cold-weather paving when asphalt is difficult to work.

AUTOMOBILES

Throwing away tin cans or bottles is one thing; throwing away a junked car is quite another (Figure 19.4). As recently as 1960 one could get $40

Fig. 19.4 Abandoned cars are bulky and difficult to store before being recycled.

or $50 for an old car for a wrecker could make his profit by stripping off useful parts and valuable scrap, since a typical car contains sixty-six pounds of aluminum, thirty-seven pounds of copper, thirty-five pounds of zinc, and twenty pounds of lead; then he could squash the remainder into a small bale worth about $40. The steel industry at the time used a 50:50 mixture of scrap steel and iron ore to make new steel and consumed over 40 million tons of scrap in the process. But the steel industry's conversion to the more efficient oxygen furnace changed the bright picture for scrap steel. Not only did the new furnace use only one half as much scrap steel as the old one, but the scrap had to be much cleaner, with a much lower content of metals other than iron, especially copper.

For a time in the 1960s there was a glut of abandoned cars; in 1965 190,000 cars were abandoned, close to 50,000 in New York City alone. But a rising market for scrap—junkers are currently worth $25 to $35—and improved technology are beginning to reduce the inventory. Several impressive car-eating machines capable of dealing with the backlog have been developed by large scrap firms. One such machine can chew 1400 cars a day into small pieces which can be efficiently sorted into steel and nonsteel piles by magnets. This scrapyard separation produces a grade of scrap that is much more salable than the customary bales of mixed metals.

Regardless of the handling techniques, two problems remain: the cost of transporting junked cars to modern regional processing yards; and air pollution from burning the cars, which has been thought necessary to eliminate plastic, rubber, and upholstery materials. The first problem might be handled by small hydraulic crushers that can flatten a standard sized car to a thickness of one foot and thus make it possible to ship large numbers of cars by flatbed truck or rail to regional collection centers. One alternative has been the development of portable car eaters which work their way around a region, junkyard by junkyard, eating as they go. Air pollution from burning out cars has been eliminated by reducing cars to small pieces of scrap in a powerful hammermill, leaving the nonmetals to be recycled, used as landfill, or incinerated. This approach would tend to concentrate this phase of the business in regional centers where business volume would support the necessary antipollution equipment.

TIRES

Usually by the time a car is scrapped the tires have been removed for salvage. But most cars run through at least three or four sets of tires in their lifetime and these too create disposal problems: altogether, 100 million tires are discarded every year (Figure 19.5). Because many states have minimum tread requirements enforced by yearly inspection, tires with a worn tread are often thrown away even though over 80 percent of the rubber in the tire remains. Some are recapped, but more and more

Fig. 19.5 *If these old tires were suddenly given a value of even five cents,
how long would they continue to
molder in this salt marsh?*

people who have experienced poorly recapped tires prefer new tires. In
contrast to the 10 percent of tires recapped in the United States, 80 percent of all tires are recapped in less affluent foreign countries. In addition,
reclaimed rubber processing for various purposes in the United States has
fallen from 30 percent in 1945 to 10 percent or less today and continues
to decline.

Most old tires end up in landfill, for which they are poorly suited. Occasionally they are burned to protect citrus orchards from frost or to burn
green timber in right of way clearance. But burning rubber in the open
air causes about the thickest, blackest smoke of any combustible and is
outlawed in many places.

One promising solution to the pileup of discarded tires is being developed by Firestone Rubber and the United States Bureau of Mines.
Shredded tires are placed in a closed vessel and heated without air to
500°C. At this temperature the rubber yields 140 gallons of liquid oils
per ton of scrap; these oils are similar to and as useful as those from
coal. Also, 1500 cubic feet of gas with a heating value equivalent to that
of natural gas is produced. The residue solids have a very high carbon
content that might be useful as a basis for other products.

Another approach would add ground-up tires to asphalt for use in road
surfaces. "Rubber" roads would flow less in summer, be more resilient in
winter, and reduce skidding. As little as 2 percent rubber added to road-
surfacing asphalt would utilize 60 percent of the waste tires currently being put to no good use.

PLASTICS

For thirty years polymer chemists have been hard at work developing virtually indestructible plastics. They have done their work well, for we now buy a pound of very biodegradable hamburger in a styrofoam tray and polyethylene wrap that will last far longer than the hamburger. Despite their ubiquity, plastic packages comprise no more than 6 percent of roadside litter—but their bright colors, familiar shapes, and resistance to decay cause them to remain an eyesore long after paper products have returned to nature (Figure 19.6).

So today polymer chemists are being called upon to produce biodegradable plastics. Most plastics resist soil bacteria and fungi because of their high molecular weight and low surface area, which present few loose molecule ends for the microorganisms to attack. Consequently one approach to biodegradability is to incorporate in the micromolecular chain a sensitizer that would absorb UV radiation and cause the chain to break. Since the strength of plastic depends on the length of its component polymer chains, the plastic object would slowly break up on exposure to UV in the natural environment. The small pieces would be broken down more slowly into carbon dioxide and water, but the litter problem would be solved. Polyvinyl chloride plastics would probably have to be handled

Fig. 19.6 *(a) The plastic bottle sometimes seems to last forever. But notice the hole in the side of this one. Years of exposure to sunlight causes many plastics to become brittle and slowly crumble away. (b) Next to plastic bottles, plastic coffee cups are most commonly seen in salt marshes, where they flow in on the tide.*

in another way since the intermediate breakdown products would be chlorinated hydrocarbons, of which the environment has quite enough already.

YESTERDAY'S DISPOSAL TECHNIQUES

Despite some progress in handling a few of the major waste categories, techniques for disposal of the overwhelming mass of solid wastes have hardly been improved since Roman times. Open dumps still receive 69 percent of solid wastes; sanitary landfill, 22 percent; incineration, 8 percent; and resource recovery, 1 percent.

LANDFILL

One step beyond the open dump is the so-called sanitary landfill. Of the 12,000 landfill sites around the country, less than 6 percent qualify for the term sanitary; the rest are little more than open dumps. To carry out sanitation efficiently, it is necessary for a bulldozer to compact each truckload as it is dumped, then for a dragline operator to cover it quickly with earth, and then for another bulldozer to compress and smooth the site to make room for another load of waste.

The advantage of a properly maintained sanitary landfill is the prompt burial of garbage and trash before it has a chance to catch fire, blow away, or attract vermin. A good site can accommodate a great deal of trash and can be situated on old strip mines, sand and gravel pits, or abandoned quarries, which are forms of presently wasted land found in almost every state. When the site is filled to capacity, a two- to three-foot layer of earth is laid over the last trash layer, and a park or recreational area can be created.

Since only 6 percent of landfill sites qualify as sanitary, obviously the ideal conditions described are not often achieved. Too often trash is not covered immediately, but once a day or every other day. Much paper and light trash gets blown about and the site along with surrounding properties frequently becomes an eyesore. Most sites that are selected do not need the improvement of sanitary landfill. Salt marshes, for example, are favorite landfill sites along the coasts. Though they are valuable ecologically and aesthetically, they are in danger of complete elimination, simply because they are handy and "empty." Further, the anaerobic decay of the buried trash causes low and erratic settling, making construction of buildings unwise for many years after the site has been filled. When a landfill site is unsuitable, the water table may be contaminated with obnoxious seepage from the buried trash, endangering nearby wells.

Some large landfill sites that have been receiving wastes for many years are being tapped for methane. One landfill in the Los Angeles area is producing 1 million cubic feet of methane per day with the potential for 6 million cubic feet per day. Deep wells draw off the gas, which is filtered, purified, deodorized, then fed into the local gas supply.

Despite some problems, sanitary landfill can be a useful disposal technique, especially for small towns, if well sited on true wasteland and scrupulously tended—conditions much more easily promised than realized.

INCINERATION

Another ancient disposal technique is to burn waste. In its primitive form, incineration swaps one problem, solid waste disposal, for two, air pollution and solid waste disposal. When anything burns, particularly a heterogeneous mass such as trash, smoke is produced in great quantity; after the combustibles are consumed the noncombustible glass and metals remain to be carted away, usually to a landfill site or out to sea.

The poor design and operation make most incinerators, whether backyard, apartment house, or municipal, simply roofed burning dumps. When the new air pollution standards were set up, cities were forced to close down incinerators because such equipment could not meet their own standards. Apartment house and office building incinerators, although handy for occupants and welcomed by city sanitation workers, pour large quantities of soot, fly ash, and smoke into the atmosphere.

Another pollutant being generated in increasing quantities by incineration is exceedingly corrosive hydrogen chloride, which is released when polyvinyl chloride (PVC), a component of plastic, is burned. Over 1 million tons of PVC are produced annually in such diverse forms as garden hose, rainwear, shoe soles, floor coverings, and so on. Since 50 percent of the PVC is chlorine, the potential combustion of this plastic in the future makes emission control of incinerator stacks imperative.

Properly designed and operated incinerators can, however, cope with large amounts of combustible trash. Many European cities have been able to combine trash disposal with heat generation, and have put to use the thermal energy that in United States incinerators goes up the chimney as waste. One reason that American cities have lagged behind Europe in incinerator technology has been the availability of cheap fuel in the United States compared with its shortage in Europe. In Munich, a ton of coal may cost four times its price in the United States, which inspires more creative efforts to use alternate sources of heat. But as air pollution regulations become more strict and fuel becomes scarce, more and more attention will be given to designs that both eliminate smoke release and use the heat produced to subsidize the cost of antipollution devices. One

467

useful proposal is to build small incinerators capable of handling the solid wastes of about 150,000 people, locating these strategically to cut transportation costs. The steam could be used to generate electricity, easing peak period power loads, or perhaps in a desalinization scheme for a city in a dry climate.

One of the most ambitious plans for utilizing the caloric value of solid waste has been put forward by the St. Louis Union Electric Company. Its proposed incinerators would use 3 million tons of waste from the St. Louis metropolitan area to generate 6 percent of the regions power supply. The state of Connecticut has begun a program to construct ten regional plants to convert by combustion 84 percent of the state's solid waste into 10 percent of the state's electric power needs.

The 20 million tons of fly ash that are potentially precipitable from incinerator chimneys make extremely fine bricks and concrete, but because building supply firms seem unaware of this raw material and incinerator operators seem to have little ability to promote a resource, most fly ash either goes up the chimney or, if precipitated out, is dumped as fill along with the noncombustible solids.

One tin can or piece of copper wire is worth very little; but the 125 million tons of incinerator ash produced each year contain 9 million tons of metal worth $400 million! The metal in some ash piles has been valued at $12 a ton, making ash piles a more valuable source of metal than many ore deposits. But this metal continues to be dumped as trash since its recovery is presently uneconomic. Perhaps in a few decades city trash heaps will be eagerly mined for their valuable supplies of metals.

COMPOSTING

Another old method used widely in Europe but much less frequently in the United States is composting. Compost is the rich, dark remains of organic garbage which has been aerobically decayed, losing its odor in the process, and thus turning materials previously buried in landfill projects into a valuable soil conditioner.

Despite their obvious advantage in making use of an otherwise wasted resource, composting plants have some drawbacks. Often poorly designed, like incinerators, they can produce odors that make them unpopular neighbors. To be properly run they need reasonably pure organic garbage, which means that such garbage must be isolated in the homes of the district served and picked up separately from paper and solid trash. Tests show that less than 10 percent of households involved in such a program seem able to keep their garbage uncontaminated. This means that the garbage must be sorted before composting or screened afterward, which adds considerably to the processing expense. In addition, most people have a misconception about the nature of compost. Like vermiculite and perlite, it is a good soil conditioner; it loosens the texture of heavy soil and increases the absorptive capacity of sandy soil. It is, however, rather low in nutrients and cannot be considered a fertilizer. Often composting plants have trouble locating a steady market for their product even if it is dried and bagged; this has led to abandonment of the process by many cities.

RESPONSIBILITIES OF SOLID WASTE DISPOSAL

When we look at the performance of industry in squeezing the last bit of iron from low-grade taconite deposits or the last hydrocarbons from crude oil, we are impressed with the level of technological skill coupled with economy of operation. Until recently this expertise ended with the marketing of the product. Of course some firms have always stood by their products with warranties, or double-your-money-back guarantees, but in no instance did the concern of the manufacturer extend beyond the reasonable life span of the product. Today, however, population growth and the packaging revolution have begun to overwhelm our antiquated system of waste collection and disposal. Many manufacturers and industrial organizations are coming to the conclusion that they bear some responsibility for the design of their products beyond the point of successful marketing. But a great part of any changing attitude is due to the realization that if manufacturers do not volunteer changes that will help the nation cope with the rising tide of waste, they will soon be *required* to make changes. The detergent industry, which switched in 1965 from nonbiodegradable to biodegradable surfactants, did so because of the threat of state laws banning the older type of detergent. It is no coincidence that the glass industry has begun to explore the possibilities of self-destructing bottles at a time when dozens of state legislatures have considered banning, limiting, or taxing no-deposit-no-return bottles. But industry is no more to blame than a federal government that was willing to spend $300 million a year on chemical and biological warfare research of questionable usefulness, while it was spending only $15 million on the study of solid waste disposal systems, which we need desperately.

AN ARCHAIC DISPOSAL SYSTEM

Although industry's nascent efforts to make more disposable disposables are commendable, the waste handling system is badly flawed at both ends: initial collection and ultimate disposal. Most of the expense of waste disposal lies in the cumbersome, noisy, and ineffective method of carting by trucks. Many years ago human wastes were deposited in outhouses, which were cleaned out periodically by a man with a horse and wagon. Today in cities, human wastes are deposited in receptacles connected by sewers to central disposal plants. Can you imagine emptying your chamber pot at the curb on the way to work in the morning? Yet our beer cans and soft drink bottles go into a trash can that is emptied into a truck and hauled away to some dump or landfill.

NEW APPROACHES

From this point of view, our whole system of waste collection is badly out of date. Buying a fleet of shiny new trucks that make less noise and hold more trash is no more an improvement than replacing a horse and wagon with a truck. Plainly what is needed is a solid waste pipeline analogous to the sewage waste disposal system now accepted as a basic element of urban life. One pilot system worked out in Sundeberg, a suburb of Stockholm, Sweden, uses a vacuum-sealed pipeline that collects the solid wastes from 5000 apartments. Since the pipe openings are twenty to twenty-four inches wide, most household wastes are easily accommodated. The air stream in the pipe pushes materials thrown into the system along at fifty feet per second to an incinerator over a mile and a half away. The incinerator then supplies heat to the apartments in winter. The ability of the system to move heavy materials was convincingly demonstrated recently when an automobile battery was found in the incinerator. The great advantage of the Swedish system is the elimination of presizing; virtually everything can go down a two-foot-wide pipe. The drawback is the difficulty of moving solids by vacuum tube over distances much greater than a mile or two.

A research team at the University of Pennsylvania has overcome this distance difficulty by using a water slurry system to carry wastes. It uses a much smaller pipe than in the Swedish system, and wastes are pulped and shredded before being transported. Solid wastes would be fed into a combination pulper and shredder, which would chew paper, cans, bottles, bones, and other wastes into small fragments that could then be flushed through an independent system to a plant where the waste could either be incinerated or dried and economically shipped by rail to outlying landfill sites.

More attention is being given to the reclamation of fibers from such slurries. Paper fibers a few thousandths of an inch in diameter are often one sixteenth to one eighth of an inch long. Because of these unique qualities these fibers can profitably be reclaimed from other contaminants by fine screens and reused in making paper. As soon as the technology can be worked out, fiber recovery will have much promise in reducing solid waste volume.

But even when the transportation problem is solved we are still faced with the problem of what to do with the wastes, for all we have really done is to collect them and reduce their volume somewhat. The key to the whole problem of solid, liquid, or gaseous waste disposal is not disposal at all, but recycling. We still have the old caveman mentality about wastes; we think that all we have to do when the local environment fills up with wastes is to throw them a little farther. So we build our smoke-stacks higher, carry our nerve gas canisters farther out to sea, and truck our garbage to the next town. Now the signs are everywhere that our total environment is beginning to fill up. By the end of this century, a slim twenty years from now, there may be no more landfill sites and the sea may be too polluted to receive any more trash. Then what can we do?

The soundest approach is to develop systems capable of handling the entire waste stream. One partial recovery system being developed by the Bureau of Mines first incinerates the wastes, reducing the volume significantly. The residues are then screened to remove ash and dirt. Then ferrous metals are removed by magnets and the remainder of the residue is pulverized by a hammermill and screened to remove glass. Aluminum is separated from the other metals by suspension in a liquid flotation apparatus. The glass isolate can be sorted by a high intensity magnetic field, which responds to the ferric impurities in glass, or by a photocell coupled to small air jets. Systems such as this have much promise in handling a continuous flow of the diverse waste materials generated in urban centers.

But the central difficulty with recycling has always been that wastes by definition are worthless, certainly not worth spending any money to reclaim. This view is in part the result of our current level of affluence and the apparent inexhaustibility of sources of raw materials. Ultimately, of course, certain raw materials will become scarce and today's waste will be tomorrow's resource. Can the natural environment survive that often postponed date? The evidence now apparent to us all indicates that it cannot. We cannot wait for the valueless to become valuable, as in time it must; we must deliberately *place* value upon the valueless, by whatever means, bearing in mind that the environment has until now borne the brunt of our disregard. Virtue is never easily inculcated, and recycling materials in our urban environments will not come easily either.

Numbers of concerned citizens have struggled valiantly to spur the recycling of wastes by laboriously collecting bottles, paper, and aluminum cans; then sorting, baling, or crushing the materials, and attempting to find firms that will take them. As commendable as these efforts are,

471

Fig. 19.7 Thousands of scavengers prowl roadsides all over the country picking up aluminum cans, which can be recycled for about ten cents per pound. It is hard work for very little return, but human effort for some profit is the ultimate answer to the solid waste problem.

they are doomed to failure because the effort is applied to the wrong end of the problem. Government must be made aware of the role it must play in making the whole concept of recycling economically viable. Once this is done, entrepreneurs will quickly spring up to turn a buck by recycling materials (Figure 19.7). Also, business must adopt a new design ethic that will include not only the economics of manufacture and aesthetics of the finished product, but the ease with which the product can be recycled. Automobiles could be much more easily recycled if recycling were considered in the original design.

One approach government might follow could be a special tax on virgin materials, which would heighten interest in raw materials currently regarded as waste. This would both conserve the virgin materials and reduce the waste burden. Another approach might be to set up tax incentives for industries that find new ways to use wastes associated with either the manufacture or ultimate disposal of their products. Still another would be to eliminate the inequity in transport costs between scrap and virgin materials.

Railroad rates for hauling scrap iron are 2.5 times those for hauling ore, even though the railroads make 30 percent more profit carrying the scrap than they do on ore. Iron miners are allowed a 15 percent depletion allowance as a profit tax deduction; this benefit is not extended to scrap recyclers. However, the basic reason for the lack of interest in recycling lies in the structure of the steel industry. Four companies, U.S. Steel,

Bethlehem, Armco, and Republic, control 60 percent of the steel market; this situation suggests restricted competition, higher prices, and inefficient technology. Because of the vertical integration of these companies—they also mine ore and coal, transport their own goods, and even erect their own steel, but do not deal extensively with scrap steel—it's easy to see that increasing the use of scrap iron isn't likely to fit conveniently into their corporate structures. So 25 percent of the steel scrap collected in the United States is exported.

Recycling is hardly new. Even today 60 percent of the lead and 40 percent of the copper in use comes from scrap. As population levels off, as inevitably it must, 90 to 100 percent of most currently used materials will have to be recycled, just as living organisms have recycled water, oxygen, and carbon dioxide for the past billion years. In following suit with our refuse, we will finally be returning to that steady-state environmental balance known to all other organisms on our planet.

FURTHER READING

Cutler, H., and G. S. Goldman, 1973. "Transportation bugaboo of scrap iron recycling." *Env. Sci. & Tech.* **7**(5), pp. 408–411.

Forester, W. S., 1973. "Plastics resource recovery dilemma." *Env. Sci. & Tech.* **7**(10), pp. 894–895.

Goddard, H. C., 1975. *Managing solid wastes: economics, technology, and institutions.* Praeger, New York. A good overall picture of the solid waste problem.

Guillet, J. E. (ed.), 1973. *Polymers and ecological problems.* Plenum Press, New York. Both Forester and Guillet present some background on the complicated problem of what to do with plastic after it has served its purpose.

Josephson, J., 1974. "Making sugar and protein from trash." *Env. Sci. & Tech.* **8**(9), pp. 784–785. Utilization of cellulose as a raw material for products other than paper.

Kakela, P., 1975. "Railroading scrap." *Env.* **17**(2), pp. 27–33. Shows, as does the Cutler and Goldman paper, that the problem of recycling is not one of technology but of economics.

Lewicke, C. K., 1973. "Scrap tires can yield marketable products." *Env. Sci. & Tech.* **7**(3), pp. 188–190. Imaginative proposals for recycling rubber that will never come about as long as virgin rubber is cheaper than used.

Packard, V., 1960. *The waste makers.* McKay, New York. Planned obsolescence and the economics of throw-away from a time when it was all just getting started.

PART SEVEN

WE THE PEOPLE: PROBLEM AND SOLUTION

Despite the long and harrowing list of problems cited in the foregoing chapters, our situation is not hopeless. Although we must assume full responsibility for the results of our manipulations, we have the resources and knowledge to correct many of our mistakes: what we have lacked has been motivation. But there are signs that environmental awareness is slowly rising among the technocrats and bureaucrats to whom we have delegated decision-making power. Land-use planning is finally beginning to be seriously considered not only by crowded cities, but by underpopulated and underdeveloped rural communities as well. The concept of restoring or rehabilitating environments once regarded as hopeless wasteland is becoming regarded as a viable option. Serious analyses of the productive resources of earth are suggesting that population growth be limited as soon as possible, and despite rapidly growing populations in some underdeveloped countries there are indications that the worldwide rate of growth may be slowing down for the first time in many years. Finally, more and more people are looking seriously at simpler life styles and the tacit assumption that ever-increasing economic growth and development are the only means of achieving human happiness.

CHAPTER TWENTY

LAND USE PLANNING

"THAT SOLE AND despotic dominion which one man claims and exercises over external things of the world in total exclusion of the right of any other individual in the universe"—thus did Sir William Blackstone define property from the security of eighteenth-century London. Despite all that has happened in the ensuing two hundred years, many would still agree with Sir William. But the belief that land is property and therefore a commodity to be bought and sold, developed and exploited, conveying privileges but not obligations, is by no means universal.

LAND AS A COMMODITY

In the early 1800s Tecumseh, chief of the Shawnee in what is now Ohio, was approached by land-hungry settlers from the poor hill farms of New England. When offered money for land, Tecumseh was amazed: "Why not sell the air, the clouds, the Great Sea?" In Mexico, Indian elders administered the tribal lands, which the tribesmen had the right to use. The Spanish conquest and the relentless flood of new Americans pouring west put an early end to such naïve notions. The rush was on. By 1853 the United States government had inherited, bought, or conquered its share of North America and settled down to the enormous task of getting rid of its vast holdings. The colonial experience of crown lands owned by the king was still too close to make the idea of permanent federal ownership of the new lands acceptable. The prime agricultural lands and forests of the Midwest and East were the first to be dispersed. Then in order to stimulate the linking of the East and West Coasts by

477

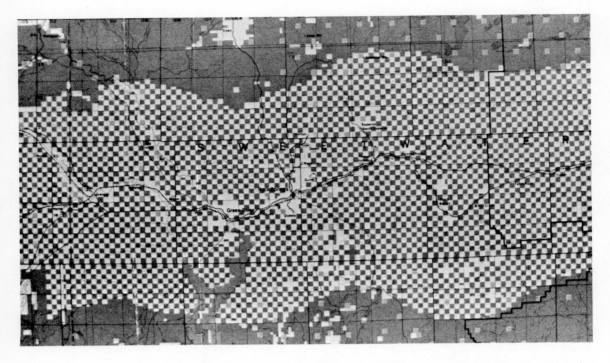

Fig. 20.1 To encourage its extension to the Pacific, the Union Pacific Railroad was given public land in a strip 20 miles wide on both sides of the right-of-way (here in southwestern Wyoming). The land was ceded in alternate sections, hence the checkerboard. The dark gray tone is public land, mostly Bureau of Land Management; the light gray blocks are state lands; and the white areas are in private hands, including those of the Union Pacific Railroad.

rail, the government gave 150 million acres to various railroads as an incentive (Figure 20.1). The Illinois Central was given a six-mile strip on either side of its right of way; the Union Pacific, a twenty-mile strip, and the Northern Pacific, a forty-mile strip. States were given 84 million acres to support schools and colleges and 65 million more acres as compensation for constructing wagon roads, canals, railroads, and river improvements. By the time the Homestead Act was passed in 1862 much of the most fertile land was already privately owned, but 250 million acres were allotted to settlers nevertheless.

By 1900 only dry, rough, or mountainous pieces of the public domain were left—Nevada, Arizona, Utah, and the like. The party was over. In a few more years the tide turned and the federal government began buying back some private land in the eastern states for military bases, national forests, parks, and wildlife refuges. But the bulk of the public domain was now the private domain. For many years it didn't matter very much—timber was removed where profitable, crops were harvested, and life went on. After World War II, however, when the economic stagnation of the 1930s had passed, a new-found affluence generated by war-fed industries enabled a much larger percentage of the population to own land—and buy they did. The rise of suburbia, which was discussed in Chapter 12, began to inundate the level croplands, small farms, and wooded land adjacent to major cities.

Much fertile and valuable farmland has already disappeared beneath the suburbs—for example, Nassau County in New York, Orange County in the Los Angeles Basin, and the Santa Clara Valley southeast of San Jose. In the latter instance, 70 percent of the farmland in Santa Clara County was classified as prime agricultural land in 1949. But as the city of San Jose grew, the rich valley in which it is situated became desirable to developers. The same characteristics that make land desirable to a farmer (flatness, depth of soil, accessibility, lack of large rocks or ledges) also make it attractive to the developer, who must keep in mind the expense of land preparation before construction is possible.

In 1950, when Sunnyvale, California had a population of 4000, a man bought a fourteen-acre strawberry patch for $1800 per acre and paid $73 in taxes on the plot. In 1976, taxes had increased to $14,000 and the owner reluctantly sold his property for $60,000 per acre. This pattern was repeated many times in the Santa Clara Valley; soon bulldozers removed the orchards and subdivision housing began to spring up. In this way, 15 to 20 percent of California's best agricultural land has already been lost. Nationally, only 72 million of the total 465 million acres of arable land are considered prime, and one half of this cropland has already been urbanized.

The problem, then, is not the total number of acres either in open space or in urban use but the quality and distribution of the land that is being converted from one use to the other. The thousands of unused square miles still available in Wyoming or Nevada offer little for either the farmer or the urbanite. While it is not likely that the urban sprawl will soon be stopped, it can be regulated with provision for more balanced land use.

LEAPFROGGING

Another problem that can be avoided by comprehensive planning is leapfrogging. As land close to the city rises in price the developer looks for cheaper land farther out on which he can still make a high profit. He leapfrogs the undeveloped but expensive land nearer the city and builds farther out. This results in a chaotic mosaic of developed and undeveloped land that is extremely difficult and expensive to service with rapid transit, sewers, water, fire and police protection, and garbage collection.

Nevertheless, the new residents demand these services; to supply them the local government raises property taxes on the surrounding farmland. Since the farmer's income is rather fixed, after a few years of rapidly climbing tax assessments he is forced to sell his land to a speculator, who sells it to a developer, who builds new houses that require more services. And so the sprawl goes until no open space is left. On a smaller scale, a farmer pressed for cash may slowly sell lots fronting along a road,

479

thereby isolating his remaining land and decreasing both its value and its accessibility to future development. Even more important, this practice puts great pressure on a rural road system incapable of handling the traffic thrust upon it.

Concerned with this vicious cycle, a number of communities have tried various ways to keep valuable productive farmland and vital open spaces from being gobbled up by development.

1. Preferential assessment. Land is assessed on its value as cropland, not its potential as shopping centers or housing sites.
2. Tax deferrals. Should a farmer sell his property for development, he pays the difference in taxes between its value as agricultural land and its market value as developed land for a retroactive number of years.
3. Conservation districts. The farmer agrees not to sell out to a developer for a specified number of years. But farmers are often surrounded by new neighbors who object to the noise of farm machinery and the danger of farm pesticide sprays.
4. Linking of taxes to income. Since many small farmers are poor and elderly and operate on a very small profit margin, some communities have tied tax assessment to the farmer's income. In return, if the farmer sells a large capital gains tax, as high as 60 percent, is usually levied.
5. Development rights. In this offshoot of the scenic easement idea that was quite popular ten years ago, a landowner sells the right to develop his property to the government, which will not develop, in return for lower taxes. The price paid for the development rights is usually linked to the going rate for developed land.
6. Land bank. The local government or some municipal or state agency purchases land and leases it out at 5 percent of the purchase price per year, usually with an option to buy if the land is kept in agriculture. The city of Stockholm has purchased large tracts of land on its outskirts. The object is not to prevent growth but to control it, to the benefit of the city, which has to supply services to the new residents, rather than a developer whose only responsibility is his profit.

Development is not, of course, limited to agricultural lands. As more and more families buy suburban housing and continue to increase their buying power, many purchase land for second or vacation houses. These are often far removed from urban centers. Coastlines are especially attractive and vulnerable from this standpoint (Figure 20.2). Consequently over 93 percent of the Atlantic and Gulf coasts is privately owned. In Maine the coastline contains 36 percent of the state's population, but less than 2 percent is in public ownership. Without public ownership access to the beach is usually denied, putting unbearable pressure on the few public points of access. Many coastal communities whose town beaches and parks have been overwhelmed by out-of-town and out-of-state users have resorted to resident-only permits and stiff parking fees to deal with the problem. The basic question is whether one has to buy a piece of the coast (assuming any is available) to have access to the beach or whether this access is the right of every citizen. Increased public ownership is not without problems, however. The more people are attracted to the coast by greater public ownership and access, the more parking lots, highway improvements, motels, bars, restaurants, and shopping centers spring up unless they are tightly controlled by some master plan. The alternative to comprehensive planning is as much ugly sprawl as might have occurred with haphazard private development.

Access is only one problem associated with coastal land use. Construction of roads and buildings in an unstable environment gives the landowner an inevitable erosion problem. The extremely expensive answer has been to restabilize breached dunes, close inlets, and build groins or stone piers to prevent sand from being washed away, defying the inevitable like King Canute. On publicly owned barrier islands, the best solution would be to remove existing roads and prohibit new ones. Once the sea is free to wash over the barrier island, equilibrium will be restored. Transportation can be supplied by mainland-based ferries and by small buses that can run along the hard sand of the beach leaving nothing but tread marks that are smoothed by the next tide.

A simple but revolutionary solution would be to put all beaches and barrier islands under public ownership, and allow only the most temporary and replaceable recreational facilities to be built. Then we could

Fig. 20.2 Second homes on the rolling Marin highlands are more interesting than most, but still mar the beautiful curves of the hills. If such development is carried to its logical conclusion, then the cherished view from all houses can only be that of other houses.

let these ephemeral features come and go as they please. Those who fear that all beaches would soon slip away into the sea can be reminded that there will always be sand beaches for recreation somewhere because sand eroded from one beach is not usually dumped into the middle of the ocean, but is piled up on another beach (see Chapter 10).

If such a prescribed dose of public ownership is unpalatable, then some form of land use control should be established. This could be administered as a zoning regulation, which would prohibit the construction of houses on the most unstable sities. The ultimate alternative to such measures is, of course, complete freedom to build a house wherever one wishes—on top of a sand dune, at the high tide line, or even a quarter mile out to sea. But in exchange for this right the builder should not expect public subsidy when his investment is threatened by shifting sand or storm-whipped waves.

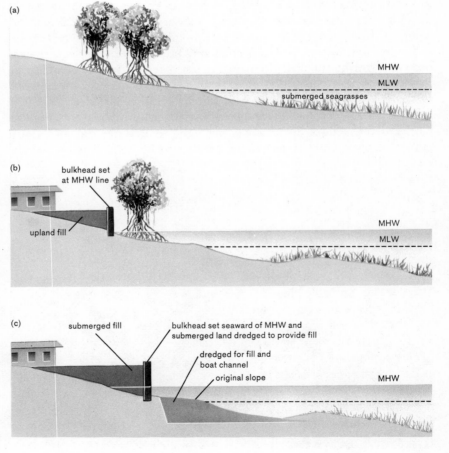

Fig. 20.3 (a) A natural shoreline along a tropical mangrove coast. (b) In an ideal development scheme which avoids dredging, the bulkhead is placed to protect existing mangroves and seagrasses. (c) The worst possible development (most often practiced) destroys seagrasses and shallow water by dredging to obtain fill which in turn destroys the mangroves, totally eliminating the original habitat. (Redrawn after Voss, from J. M. Carlton, 1969. "Land building and stabilization." Environmental Conservation 1 (4):285–294, figure 7)

On the west coast of Florida the problem of coastal development is not so much erosion as destruction of estuarine productivity (see Chapter 17). Usually bulkheads are constructed below the mean highwater line and backfilled with sediments dredged from boat channels (Figure 20.3). While this allows the property owner to dock his boat literally in his front yard, the environmental costs are high. The network of boat channels in such a development often becomes stagnant and eutrophic from septic tank drainage. Moreover, the productivity of the mangrove fringe, the dredged shallows, and the turtlegrass beds, either dredged or silted, is lost.

In response to these problems Congresss passed the Coastal Zone Management Act of 1972, which provides developmental guidelines for the coastal states but allows decisions on development to be made locally. In return, the act requires the states to set up a system of land classification that identifies those sites most suitable both for development and for protection and supports the states, supervision of particularly fragile areas.

BACK TO THE LAND

Our heightened awareness of environmental problems, the continued decrease of urban amenity, and the growing disaffection of many for an increasingly mechanized life have brought about a revival of the romantic back-to-nature movement that sweeps the country every few decades. The ideal is to get away from the dominance of a manmade environment and become an integral part of nature. This may still be possible on some Pacific atoll, but not in Alaska, British Columbia, or the rugged mountains of the American West. First, when we are cut off from contact with other people for very long we become dulled to our surroundings and the excitement of new experiences. This is particularly true of urbanites who settle in remote country. To lead a life in complete harmony with the natural environment requires a tradition of skills, knowledge, and even attitudes more complex than learning how to repair a TV or perhaps even becoming a nuclear physicist; the necessary mental attitudes are probably beyond the abilities of most urbanites. Most dreams of escape to a simpler life hinge on settling down somewhere, but the very act of settling soon overwhelms the meager resources of many environments. The most successful hunting and gathering cultures live in shifting camps, not permanent settlements. A cabin in the woods quickly exhausts easily accessible fuel and game.

Any potential escapee depends on manmade articles—guns, tools, clothing, medical supplies; and because wilderness life is harsh, with a higher than usual accident rate, the dependence on these goods is all the greater. Finally, there is an almost innate human tendency to make life easier by substituting an outboard motor for a canoe, a chainsaw for a crosscut saw, a propane gas stove for a wood burner. Soon the back-to-nature purist has been converted to a pioneer and his wilderness cabin becomes a beachhead for civilization in the natural environment. We have all dreamed of being part of a Swiss Family Robinson or a Natty Bumppo paddling across a glimmerglass somewhere, but we should be able to distinguish between romantic visions and environmental realities before we head for a natural paradise.

ZONING

Despite the strong Western European tradition of bias toward private ownership of land and its degradation to a mere commodity, which is reflected in the defense of private property in the United States constitution, the United States since 1900 has slowly retreated from Blackstone's absolutist position, quoted at the beginning of this chapter. Early in this century swarms of immigrants living in slums that make today's ghettos seem like luxury housing began to trouble the conscience of civic leaders and led to the first restrictions affecting public health and sanitation, light and air in private property. A few years later Washington, D.C., Baltimore, and Los Angeles passed laws that first restricted certain facilities to specific zones and then limited the height of buildings.

By 1916 New York City extended the concept of zoning to the entire city, dividing it into comprehensive zones for various uses. The phenomenon of zoning grew rapidly from this modest and halting start. Zoning was adopted by many cities, especially after the Supreme Court recognized zoning as a proper exercise of police power in the Euclid Village versus Ambler Realty Company case of 1926. This was heady business in 1926, for the basic principle of zoning is to regulate land use without reimbursing the landowner for restrictions on the use of his property.

Euclid Village sought to set up three zones, industrial, commercial, and residential. With the approval of the court this was done; and the pattern was so frequently imitated by other cities that it came to be known as Euclidian zoning. Today urban zoning regulations are much more complex, with dozens of subcategories for each of the Euclidian divisions; but the principle remains the same. Other forms of zoning soon followed the Euclid decision; now almost all cities have very complex zoning regulations designed to control population density, parking, building bulk, and size of lots. The pervasiveness of zoning can be seen in one not very extreme example in Glassboro, New Jersey, where an ordinance requires each unit in an apartment complex to have central air conditioning, a garbage disposal, a central TV antenna, an automatic washer/dryer for every eight bedrooms, eight square feet of swimming pool or tennis court per

*Fig. 20.4 Setbacks evolved
as a curious compromise between the builder's desire to
get every possible square foot
out of a building site, and the
town planner's concern with
limiting the mass of huge
boxes.*

hundred square feet of living space, and two offstreet parking places per unit even though there can only be 1.35 bedrooms per unit.

Concerned over the rapid conversion of Wall Street and midtown into dark gloomy canyons, New York City in the 1920s required new buildings to be constructed with a regular series of setbacks to allow sunlight to reach the streets. This gave buildings of that period a strange resemblance to ziggurats (Figure 20.4). More recently the regulation was changed to encourage ground level setbacks that provide arcades and public plazas in exchange for extra floor space. Unfortunately many plazas that have resulted from the regulation are neither useful nor pleasant (Figure 20.5).

In recent years zoning regulations have come under attack, especially in the suburbs, for both environmental and social reasons. Minimum lot size rules are very wasteful of space; instead of controlling the pace of development they may accelerate it to the point where no open land is left. An alternative is cluster housing.

This plan allows houses to be built closer together in a tract, and frees the remainder of the land from development. The concept embodied in cluster zoning is quite old. Farmhouses in parts of French-speaking Quebec, for example, are grouped in small villages, allowing all of the surrounding land to be farmed intensively rather than tying up several acres per family with houses and outbuildings.

The open space saved from housing can be used for recreation and to preserve some of the values people seek when they move from the city center to the suburbs in the first place—a semblance of a natural environment, free from parking lots, houses, and utility poles. For cluster

Fig. 20.5 (a) On a sunny day this plaza is thronged with office workers eating their lunches, listening to street musicians, and just enjoying the sun. (b) In contrast, this north-facing plaza, a cool and windswept expanse, is something to hurry across despite the monumental planters filled with flowers.

housing to work, continuing provisions must be made to preserve the open land. Occasionally the whole concept is vitiated by later owners who decide to sell the commons to free themselves of maintenance costs.

Cluster zoning (Figure 20.6) is only one way to reserve open land in urban areas. Easements, which involve the purchase of development rights rather than the purchase of the land itself, can be used to preserve wooded or scenic land. Claiming more land than required for a building project and then placing the excess in an open space program is another approach. Gifts from large landholders or exchanges of land parcels are still other ways to obtain open space.

But regardless of the physical arrangement of houses on a subdivision tract, zoning interferes with and is often intended to prevent the construction of low or moderate cost housing such as mobile homes. This prohibition effectively keeps minorities and the poor from leaving their ghettos and joining middle America in the lily-white suburbs. The major criticism of zoning is that it is piecemeal and reflects the jurisdictional jungle typical of our metropolitan areas—there are 100 jurisdictions in the San Francisco Bay area, 61 in Cleveland, 200 in Philadelphia, and 500 in New York. It is also easily influenced, unduly complex, and so rigid that innovations such as cluster housing are often smothered in red tape.

One of the most pressing concerns facing any small town near or in a metropolitan area has been controlling growth to preserve small-town values. Ramapo, New Jersey, was suddenly faced with this problem when the Tappan Zee Bridge opened, making the town an easy twenty-five-mile commuting trip from New York City. In 1966 the town developed a policy to preserve its semirural, suburban character. It was decided that 72,000 people in 20,000 residences would satisfy this aim if the new housing were located in and around the existing urban core and no multiple-family dwellings were permitted. A schedule of eighteen years was allowed for the sequential construction of services—parks, schools, roads, sewers, and so forth—and building permits were to be based on the proximity of the proposed site to these services. Points were granted on a sliding scale with a maximum of five points per facility. Construction could begin only when fifteen points had accumulated. Because all projected services would be completed eighteen years no building permit had to be denied, only delayed. Other towns like Petaluma, California

Fig. 20.6 By clustering the housing and using forms sympathetic to the environment, much of the natural beauty of the seacoast at Sea Ranch, California is preserved. (Aero Photographers)

have obtained court support for limiting growth by restricting the number of building permits issued.

The question that often arises in suburban or rural areas is whether to develop land suitable for housing at all. The town of Closter, New Jersey, when faced with a controversy over its attempt to acquire eighty acres for an open space program, made some calculations and drew the following conclusions: eighty acres would allow the construction of 160 houses, which would bring at least 200 new children into the local school system. Estimating that it would cost the town $720 per year to educate each child ($144,000), $4000 to collect the additional garbage, $6000 for police protection, and $2000 for extra fire hydrants and miscellaneous services, the total expense to the community if this land were developed would be $156,000. Calculated land tax revenues would amount to $100,000 a year. Thus the development of the eighty acres would have *cost* the town $56,000 a year. In the enthusiasm for growth of urban housing, so often encouraged by merchant's associations eager for new business, the ultimate costs of "growth and progress" are rarely spelled out. If they were, the desire for development might be tempered and effective plans made to control it (Figure 20.7).

Fig. 20.7 Attracting industry has traditionally been the goal of most small towns wishing to "grow up." The environmental and social costs of this growth are rarely considered.

LAND USE CONTROL LAWS

For all the conflict over zoning there has been a noticeable change in land use concepts, a movement away from the static view of land as a commodity, and a grudging recognition that natural systems do not follow jurisdictional boundaries. So San Francisco Bay, Lake Tahoe, and the Hackensack Meadows are finally being treated as totalities. Frustration over the multiplicity of zoning commissions has given impetus to the formation of regional or state bodies with a voice in developments affecting land use.

1. Hawaii. One of the first states to respond to the threat of uncontrolled urban growth was Hawaii, which set up a Land Use Commission in 1961. The island of Oahu was divided into four districts; conservation, agricultural, rural, and urban. The first district is administered by the state Department of Land and Natural Resources, the second and third by the Land Use Commission, and the last by the Honolulu Zoning Commission. Since agricultural land in Hawaii is concentrated in the hands of corporate farming interests sympathetic (at least in 1961) to limiting development of agricultural land, the enabling legislation passed without undue difficulty. Since then, despite some developers' complaints about the high cost of undeveloped land close to Honolulu, the plan seems to have been effective in controlling and directing normal residential and tourist-oriented growth. However, constantly rising labor costs are phasing out pineapple farming, which is not very easily mechanized. Probably by 1980 most land now producing pineapple will either have been converted to sugar cane or made available for development. This may pose a problem for the LUC, which was set up to protect the agricultural sanctity of these fields.

2. Vermont. The Land Use and Development Act of 1970 set up an Environmental Board and eight district commissions. Permits are required for subdivisions with lots smaller than ten acres, all subdivisions with more than ten lots, and all subdivisions at altitudes above 2500 feet. But permits are not always applied for and punishment of violations is weak.

3. Minnesota. In 1967 the state legislature approved the Twin Cities Metropolitan Council to coordinate planning and development in the metropolitan area of Minneapolis–St. Paul, to prepare a comprehensive plan for the area, and then to implement that plan. Legislatures are notoriously unwilling to create challenges to their authority, but somehow the TCMC was given the authority to reverse the plans of various state agencies, including the power to rule on private land use around a proposed new regional airport. Many in the legislature now fear that they have created a Frankenstein, while members of the TCMC are concerned because the transit and airport commissions maintain their independence. Both concerns are legitimate and nicely illustrate the problems of controlling growth. Everyone—including land use commissions —favors some kind of control over growth, as long as the control is of someone else's growth.

4. New York. The country's largest park is located not in Wyoming but in New York State. Adirondack Park contains 6 million acres, making it three times the size of Yellowstone. But only 38 percent is state-owned. The rest is in private hands; much of this private land is in forest, but

some is in agriculture, tourist facilities, and housing (92 towns shelter 125,000 permanent and 90,000 seasonal residents). Concerned with the prospect that uncontrolled development on the private land might make a shambles of the park, the legislature in 1971 set up an Adirondack Park Agency with the authority to draw up a land use plan for the private lands within the park boundary. As soon as the individual towns prepared their own land use plans, the APA would return some of the responsibility for regulation to the local level. To no one's surprise the APA became a scapegoat for ills more fairly ascribed to the recession of the early 1970s. But the APA, proceeding as though it had never heard of public relations, seemed to go out of its way to become the heavy in the drama. Its attitude illustrates a frequent problem of land use management: flexing the muscle of bureaucratic righteousness when the situation demands the suppleness of a gymnast.

5. California. In 1976 the California legislature finally passed a comprehensive plan for preserving the coast. This occurred four years after a temporary coastal commission had been established to draw up a permanent plan and to exercise interim control over coastal development. The state commission and six local commissions have the power to control development in a 1000-yard strip from Oregon to Mexico, a coastline of 1072 miles.

Like all innovations, present land use laws suffer because they are pioneering in an area where attitudes change slowly. Every term, Congress dutifully considers national land use legislation, which often passes one house but somehow is never enacted. This failure may reflect the fears of down-home constituents that such legislation is just another of big brother's efforts to usurp local control over life and property. The real lack is not bureaucratic machinery, but a grassroots realization that land is not a renewable commodity. Land is the productive base of what we call civilization, and the supply is running out.

Aldo Leopold, author of *A Sand County Almanac*, felt that we had of necessity developed ethics that differentiated social from antisocial conduct by means of a golden rule that integrates the individual to society, and democracy, which relates social organization to the individual. But he feared that the third ethic, which would relate both individual and society to the environment, was lacking. Leopold defined such an ecological ethic as a limitation on freedom of action in the struggle for existence. Or, more simply, less is more.

Part of the problem is that we are outgrowing the land. Suburbanites, who are increasingly affluent enough to buy themselves a piece of what was once our common heritage, often view that cottage at the lake, beach, or desert as another toy like a stereo, sports car, or sailboat. We are more and more remote from that level of primary production that

sustains us all, elephant, emu, and Eskimo. Produce now comes home in a neat plastic shroud, as bugless and spotless as though it had been made in a factory (Figure 20.8). This is not an entirely unsuitable symbol. As farming becomes more and more capital intensive, its factory-like aspects grow more striking.

Fig. 20.8 In the produce department of this super-market, every item has been shrouded in plastic wrap.

We were originally a nation of small farmers with some sense of land stewardship—if not for the sake of the environment, then at least for our children and grandchildren. But we have moved toward consolidation of land into corporate farms based on the premise that exploitation is much more profitable than conservation. Already huge corporate farms control 31 percent of the farmland in Florida, 28 percent in Utah, and 19 percent in California. Ironically, the incentive for this development is not the greater efficiency of better management the corporate approach might bring to farming, but the opportunities afforded by the tax system, market structure, and farm price support policies to increase profits at the expense of the environment. Further, a concomitant of urbanization has been the degradation of land ownership into a mere cover for extracting profit from urbanization.

For all their defects, zoning and land use laws have arisen because we are more and more concerned about the problem of land tenure and use. As more people make greater demands on less land, the concept of total private control over land will probably change even more. There are alternatives to exclusive private ownership on the one hand and public ownership on the other.

491

One approach being tried in Minnesota and Georgia is a form of land trust. Land is held in perpetuity by the trust, which means that it cannot be bought or sold by the individuals living on it. Uses to which the land can be put are specified and the land cannot be sublet. Should the tenant leave, he is reimbursed for capital improvements made during his tenacy. Such arrangements should aim for life stewardship of property if the land is properly cared for. This would provide the motivation to invest time and money for the financial or personal satisfaction of the investment. But the trust could be cashed in at any time, avoiding any suggestion of being chained to the land like a serf or tenant farmer.

Such plans of course assume an ecologically sound land use classification of available land. These classifications are already in the works in many states, which are in the throes of determining which land is best suited for conservation, agriculture, and development. Since these decisions will affect the lives and fortunes of present landowners, they are extremely difficult to make and easily influenced by those with the most to gain or lose. But the only alternative seems to be business as usual until the last acre of forest has its A-frame or mobile home and the last quarter section of farmland has been divided for housing. In many metropolitan areas this has already taken place. We can no longer afford to insist naïvely that it can't happen in *our* neighborhood.

FURTHER READING

Carter, L. J., 1974. *The Florida experience: land and water policy in a growth state.* Johns Hopkins University Press, Baltimore. Comprehensive report on land and water misuse in Florida over the years.

Ducsik, D. W., 1974. *Shorelines for the public: a handbook of social, economic, and legal considerations regarding public recreational use of the nation's coastal shoreline.* MIT Press, Cambridge. Overview of the status of public access to our shoreline.

Graham, F. J., 1976. "Rebellion in the mountains over Adirondack Park plan." *Audubon* **78**(2), pp. 116–118. The problems of centralized land use control.

Haskell, E. H., and V. S. Price, 1973. *State environmental management: case studies of nine states.* Praeger, New York. Different approaches to the problem of how best to utilize land.

Leopold, A., 1949. *A Sand County almanac.* Oxford University Press, New York. A classic statement of our patterns of land use.

Listokin, D. (ed.), 1974. *Land use controls: present problem and future reform.* Center for Urban Policy Research, Rutgers University, New Brunswick, New Jersey. The ins and outs of zoning.

McClellan, G. S. (ed.), 1971. *Land use in the United States: exploitation or conservation.* Wilson, New York.

Pilkey, O. H. Jr., O. H. Pilkey, Sr., and P. Turner, 1975. *How to live with an island; a handbook to Bogue Banks, North Carolina*. North Carolina Department of Natural and Economic Resources, Raleigh. Common sense guidelines on how to live in an unstable environment.

Raup, P. M., 1973. "Changes in rural America." *Earth Journal* **3**(4), pp. 9–13. Documents the passing of the small farm and the impact of corporate farming.

Reitze, A. W., Jr., 1974. *Environmental planning: law of land and resources*. North American International, Washington, D.C. Excellent sourcebook on the legal aspects of land use.

CHAPTER TWENTY-ONE

ENVIRONMENTAL RESTORATION

IF CULTURAL PROGRESS over the last million years of evolution were graphically portrayed the result would probably be a straight line, but its slope would depend upon the bias of the observer. An optimist would see the line sloping upward, a realist would see a horizontal line, and a pessimist, a line sloping downward. Any perturbations in the line, and there have been many, would be smoothed over by the great time span. But if we look at just a small time segment we see many peaks and lows, representing the best and worst of our cultural capabilities. A particularly striking recent example was the intense but short-lived flowering of the arts and sciences in Germany between World Wars I and II. The relaxation of international tension, the sense of a new era that major wars often elicit, the throwing off of an authoritarian government for a more permissive democratic regime—all were part of the reason for it. The sense of that age is beautifully captured in the art of George Grosz and Paul Klee, the music of Alban Berg, Kurt Weill, and Paul Hindemith, the writing of Thomas Mann and Hermann Hesse, and the scientific vision of Albert Einstein and Lise Meitner.

One small but extremely interesting facet of this cultural bubbling up was an idea generated by the brothers Heck. Lutz Heck was director of the Berlin Zoo and his brother Heinz headed the Tierpark Hellabrun, a world-famous zoo in Munich. Perhaps encouraged by being the first to breed the African elephant successfully in captivity, Heinz Heck in 1921 began to assemble in his zoo a diverse collection of strange, half-wild cattle: the Hungarian, Podolian steppe, Scottish highland, gray and brown Alpine, Corsican, and piebald Friesian. Heck's goal was to syn-

494

thesize the long-extinct wild ancestor of his motley herd, the aurochs. While the last aurochs had died hundreds of years before, artifacts remained in the form of bones, skulls, horns, skins, and many pictures. With these fragments as his only guide, Heck began a breeding program to try to pull together the bits and pieces of the aurochs that existed in the genes of the semiwild stock he had collected from all over Europe. Lutz Heck expressed this plan succinctly:

> No creature is extinct if the elements of its heritable constitution are still to be found in living descendants. All that needs to be done is to apply the experience of the breeder to the assembling of the inherited elements scattered among these descendants. To this end a sure eye is needed to detect the primitive qualities of the various races of cattle: the nearest approach to the horn of the aurochs, or its combativeness, or its long legs, or the colour of its hide, or the small udder of the wild animal. The next step is to devise a well-considered plan of breeding, various races being crossed in order to combine all the qualities similar to those of the aurochs, and so its heritable constitution, in a single animal. If this is successfully done, the aurochs of ancient times must eventually reappear from its tame descendants.[1]

Fig. 21.1 A small herd of aurochs bred by Lutz Heck at the Munich Zoo from many breeds of cattle. Although these animals breed true they can only be considered a facsimile of the original aurochs, which became extinct long ago. (Photo by Lothar Schlawe, courtesy Munich Tierpark Hellabrunn)

Much to the surprise of everyone (except perhaps the Heck brothers) the experiment succeeded. An animal whose young closely resembled the parents *was* put together from all the genetic races that resembled strongly the aurochs (Figure 21.1). The result was, of course, not a recreation of the original aurochs, but rather a facsimile much like an artist's

[1] Street, P., 1964. "Recreating the aurochs and tarpan." *Animals* **5**, London, pp. 250–254.

conception of a brontosaurus or pterodactyl. The "experience of the breeder" and "a sure eye" are rather different selecting mechanisms than the ability of an individual to survive an unusually cold winter, or a herd to protect itself from a pack of wolves.

But despite these qualifications, the Hecks had accomplished something unique—scattered genes had been rounded up and linked together into a self-reproducing form. If this could be done with an organism it could be done with an ecosystem. If enough pieces of any natural system still exist to provide some concept of what the original system looked like, there is a reasonable chance that by combining the pieces a self-reproducing system can be established. Like Heck's aurochs, such a reassembled system might differ in subtle but important ways from the original, but given time and a free hand, natural selection could work to bring both organism and system in line with the reality of a natural environment. Heinz Heck was lucky that in 1921 there were still a number of rather primitive cattle stocks available as raw material. As we continue to improve our breeding lines of cattle, corn, and cantaloupe by reducing their variability, the older varieties, not to mention the original natives, tend to be lost. The corn blight in the early 1970s dramatically demonstrated how small the genetic pool of most of our staple foods has become through this process. Unfortunately circumstances are similar in natural systems. We have deeply disturbed most natural systems, particularly in Europe and parts of Asia. The fragments are either widely scattered or, in some cases, lost; so we have no idea how the original ecosystem functioned or even what it looked like. In the remaining fragments, invasion by alien plants and animals has diluted the existing natural elements to the extent of obscuring their original relationships.

At this point we must distinguish between restoration and rehabilitation of environments. Restoration suggests an attempt to return the landscape to the closest possible approximation of the original flora, fauna, and species diversity. Rehabilitation, on the other hand, implies returning some form of productive vegetal cover to derelict land even if this requires the use of exotics. If restoration is to be a viable possibility, we must develop techniques to pull together the scattered pieces of natural systems before further destruction and dilution make restoration an impossible goal. Restoration is valuable not for sentimental reasons or as an ecological tour de force, but to preserve from irretrievable loss genetic information that will become invaluable in the next several decades. Fortunately, the importance of environmental restoration has been recognized and work is underway in a variety of systems. What we learn from these pioneering projects can then be applied to other endangered systems.

THE HISTORICAL ROOTS

For a very long time we have been managing the environment, or at least the aspects within the grasp of our technology (see Chapter 3), not attempting to imitate nature, but rather to reorder it. Consider the typical farm. It requires a constant input of energy to deter natural processes such as succession, which would increase species diversity of the fields beyond the reduction to the absurd that a farm, after all, is. The same working against natural processes can be seen in the history of gardens. For thousands of years gardens were formal, artificial affairs with an emphasis upon utility, containing fruit trees and often beds of herbs and flowers laid out in intricate geometric patterns (Figure 21.2). This tradition of rigid layouts stretched without a break from the atrium garden of a Roman villa through the medieval gardens of the monastery cloister, reaching its culmination in the geometric (though hardly utilitarian) excesses of seventeenth-century Versailles. The right angle and straight edge reigned supreme.

But in the late eighteenth century the rise of the romantic movement in arts and letters had a strange reverberation in England. Lancelot "Capability" Brown, a gardener and minor architect, almost singlehandedly created the art of landscape gardening and began a revolution in the way

497

people perceived their environment. Capability Brown's genius was to create with great care the illusion of being in a natural environment, breaking completely with the ancient gardening tradition of creating an environment totally artificial in its rigid geometry. Sometimes starting with nothing but barren fields, sometimes with an old-fashioned formal garden, Brown would evoke a scene of pastoral beauty, vistas through the forest, a pond nestled in the hills, mounds of greenery swirling in graceful curves, all persuading the viewer that the scene had always been part of the natural landscape (Figure 21.3). It was, of course, an extensive and expensive manipulation involving the damming of streams to form lakes, the construction or leveling of villages, the planting or cutting of trees, and the construction or removal of low hills—all to achieve a desired aesthetic effect. Despite the massive manipulation, the result was intended to appear natural rather than manmade like the formal gardens of the past.

Compared with a formal garden, Brown's landscapes did indeed look natural; but they were not modeled on any natural environment that existed at the time, for even in 1750 truly natural environments had disappeared from much of England. Brown's landscapes were modeled on the highly modified environments that characterized most of Europe then as now; the interplay of natural and unnatural that the work of Dutch and English landscape painters has made a standard of "natural" beauty for many. Since the aesthetic effect he created was at best only a highly romanticized evocation of nature, Brown had little compunction

Fig. 21.3 This typically English landscape was designed and planted by the landscape architect Capability Brown in the eighteenth century.

498

about using whatever exotic plants were available to fit the needs of his designs.

A Capability Brown landscape, for all its "natural" appearance, is not, nor was it intended to be, a restored environment. But Brown did play a very important role in changing people's view of what remained of their natural environments. From the classical-medieval concept of nature as disorder ultimately to be ordered by our work, a new view was beginning to emerge: that nature had its own intricate order and values, which were often aesthetically pleasing and instructive as well.

On the basis of this promising beginning it might be supposed that the British would sooner or later be moved to go several steps further and try to recreate one of the natural environments that played such an important role in English history, the oak wood, for example. But thousands of years of management had taken their due and there was little real evidence of what Sherwood Forest looked like to Robin Hood, the New Forest to the Norman kings who hunted there, or what Julius Caesar saw when he stepped ashore in 55 B.C. Some of the pieces probably remain, but as with Humpty Dumpty there are few clues to how they all fit together. But today the Queen's men are trying with increasing success to manage the pieces available to them.

ENVIRONMENTAL RESTORATION IN BRITAIN

A classic example of the problems facing restoration of former environments can be found in the Scottish Highlands. Originally, perhaps 2000 years ago, the higher elevations were covered with some kind of pine forest grading through birch and ash to some kind of oak forest below. Today we know most of the species involved, but not very much about how they were organized into communities. Demands over the centuries, first for ship timber, then charcoal, then cropland, gradually reduced the original vegetation to small scraps that may have been cut or replanted, sometimes with alien species; in general the remnants were profoundly affected. But the final destruction of this forest came with the formation of the United Kingdom in 1707, which put an end to the warring between Scots clans and brought social changes culminating in the introduction of sheep in large numbers. Grazing by sheep converted most of the Highlands into an enormous pasture characterized by grasses, heather, and mosses. The rabbit, which had been introduced into Britain by the Normans in the twelfth century, reached the Highlands in the nineteenth century and added to the problem.

This constant grazing pressure, plus the gradual growth of mosses over the mineral soil most tree seeds need to germinate gradually eliminated any chance for reproduction of the original vegetation; and so the moors

Fig. 21.4 Moorland is characteristic of Scotland and the Appenine Mountains of northern England—this example is Howgill Fells in North Yorkshire, England. If covered with their original forest vegetation, these hills would strongly resemble the Smoky Mountains of North Carolina. (Peter Stuttard)

came into being (Figure 21.4). Since all this happened hundreds of years ago, the Scot has come to regard moors as the natural vegetation of the Highlands rather than a strange result of overgrazing by rabbits and sheep. Much the same process took place in the southwestern United States, although in this case within memory of living inhabitants. The original vegetation over much of west Texas and eastern New Mexico was a desert grassland with occasional shrubs. But overgrazing combined with the elimination of fire allowed a tremendous population explosion of mesquite and juniper, which invaded the grassland. Today the dense clumps of mesquite and juniper seem always to have been there, like the moors of Scotland.

When, after World War II, the British Forestry Commission announced a program of reforestation in the Scottish Highlands, there was quite a public outcry. Since the moor vegetation had come to be regarded as natural, the plan to restore a forest environment was viewed with the concern Americans might express if the Forest Service decided to cut all the windbreaks in Nebraska and replace them with the native prairie grasses. With no emulation whatever of the sensitivity with which Capability Brown placed thousands of trees in his landscapes, the Forestry Commission established plantations of single species in blocks scattered across the rugged Highland landscape like a crazy quilt (Figure 21.5). Since then, the lesson has been learned and reforestation is proceeding in a more aesthetically pleasing manner (Figure 21.6). But the problems are many. Large herds of red deer, maintained for hunting, relish the tender buds and twigs of the young trees; this means the plantations must be fenced. Then the dense accumulation of acid, soggy

Fig. 21.5   Early efforts to reforest the moorlands of Scotland met with much criticism because of the lack of aesthetic considerations in the planting schemes. Crazy-quilt bands and zigzags persist until the trees are harvested.

Fig. 21.6   In contrast to Fig. 21.5, these slopes have been reforested in sympathy with the roll of the land.

Fig. 21.7 To convert moorland turf to forestland, the heavy sod of mosses and grasses must be broken and fertilized before the tree seedlings are set out.

Fig. 21.8 These young spruce trees are making thrifty growth in former moorland in Scotland.

502

organic material—peat—has to be scored by heavy machinery (Figure 21.7) and fertilized to get the seedlings planted and off to a good start (Figure 21.8).

This reforestation project must be considered a type of environmental rehabilitation, since the Forestry Commission is not attempting to restore the original species (about which not enough is known for accurate restoration anyway). But at least an effort is being made to return the Highlands to what is probably their most ecologically sound use, the production of timber and wood products. Scots pine, the original Highland pine, is being planted; but other fast-growing species of economic value, native or foreign, are being used in whatever environments seem suited to their needs.

More characteristic of British environmental restoration projects are the attempts to maintain representative examples of the chalk grasslands and the coppice-with-standard forest. This forest type is composed of planted shrub species—hazel, sweet chestnut, hornbeam, or even oak—which are cut or coppiced for poles on a regular basis every eight to twenty-five years. The standards are also planted species, usually oak, grown traditionally for ships' timbers but more recently for lumber (Figure 21.9). Both these types are human-maintained artifacts that have existed for so long that they have gained natural status. Unfortunately, both are highly unstable and revert to other vegetation types without continuing management. Since the tradition of allowing unused land to revert to the self-reproducing or climax vegetation of the region has been

Fig. 21.9 This young coppice-with-standard woodland in England consists of clumps or coppices of hornbeam interspersed among the thicker boles of the standard species, oak. In the springtime the forest floor is covered with anemones.

lost along with that climax vegetation, some European restóration efforts try to maintain examples of the human-dominated systems. But efforts are also being made to restore some beech woodland on what was recently chalk grassland, and English oak in the coppice-with-standard woodland.

The chalk downs are rolling hills in the south of England, which, because of their well-drained and relatively light soil, were cleared of their ash and beech forests and farmed or grazed in Neolithic times (Figure 21.10). With the foundation of medieval monasteries, which maintained large flocks of sheep, most of the chalk ridges, with their thin soil, became pastures. For nearly five hundred years and in some places far longer, the grazing pressure of generation after generation of sheep had a selective

Fig. 21.10 This chalk grassland in southern England is being maintained by grazing. The fine lines along the contours of the hillside on the left are trails left by grazing sheep.

effect on the flora of the chalk grasslands, producing a group of species resistant to grazing pressures and forming a community of plants found nowhere else.

Moors, once formed, tend to persist even if they are not grazed, partly because of the remoteness of appropriate tree or shrub seeds and the unlikelihood of their becoming established in the thick layer of peat even if planted. But the chalk grasslands are quite susceptible to invasion by thorny shrubs once grazing pressure is removed. And that is precisely the problem today over most of the chalk grasslands of southern England. Sheep have been withdrawn from many of the chalk downs for economic reasons, and thousands of acres of downs have either been plowed or invaded by shrubs. The problem has been aggravated by myxomatosis (Chapter 8), which severely reduced the rabbit population that maintained the grassland in the absence of sheep. Why be concerned with the loss of grasslands that aren't natural anyway? Because aesthetically they are a more pleasing landscape than the shrubs that replace them, and because they contain a rich variety of plants and animals that disappear when the shrubs invade.

The heir to this and other problems of vegetation management is the Nature Conservancy (not to be confused with the private American organization of the same name). Set up by the government in 1949, its functions are "to provide scientific advice on the conservation and control of the natural flora and fauna of Great Britain; to establish, maintain, and manage nature reserves in Great Britain, including the maintenance of physical features of scientific interest; and to develop the scientific services related thereto." [2] The Nature Conservancy has been quite active in the campaign to restore and manage representative samples of man-dominated systems, as well as to restore native beech and oak woodland. It maintains an active research program to support its efforts toward these ends.

The most obvious restorative technique for declining chalk grasslands would be to restore the grazers that normally maintained the vegetation. But if this is done in the summer the flower crop, especially orchids, is reduced; if grazing takes place in the winter the livestock refuse to eat the coarse grasses and thorny shrubs that tend to invade and replace the desirable plants. If supplemental feed is offered, the hay introduces exotic weeds. In the old days the flocks grazed in spring and summer, but since they were constantly on the move, grazing damage to flowering plants was light. The solution seems to be a short, intense feeding period in May and June, which encourages the eating of coarse grass while it is still green, and the thorny shrubs before the thorns harden. Flowering plants that have been grazed often recover and flower again. But it is not always feasible to run livestock on the relatively small reserves; and so mowing, burning, and local application of herbicides have been used to control the invasion of undesirable species. If managed to preserve rare insects, the grassland should be grazed much less frequently, say every third year. Vegetation management is neither simple nor obvious.

The coppice-with-standard artifact was once quite common in Kent, Sussex, and Hampshire, but is now becoming rather rare. The extremely slow growth of the oaks coupled with lack of demand for the poles has led to a wholesale replacement of coppice-with-standard woodlands by more productive and valuable species, often exotic conifers. Because conditions during the first seven years after coppicing are quite favorable to many interesting and rare species of insects, the Nature Conservancy has

[2] Blackmore, M. (ed.), *The Nature Conservancy Handbook 1968*, p. 5. Her Majesty's Stationery Office, London.

Fig. 21.11 When the coppice species are freshly cut the coppice-with-standard woodland is quite open and parklike. This allows development of a succession of insect and plant species quite characteristic of this vegetation type.

continued to coppice its coppice-with-standard woodlands despite unfavorable economic conditions (Figure 21.11).

True environmental restoration—an attempt to recreate the original vegetation—is being attempted on the Scottish island of Rhum, an island eight by eight miles in size, originally forested with pine, birch, elm, rowan, and oak, which has been virtually treeless for several hundred years. Small areas are being fenced and planted with a mixture of native tree species grown locally from seed obtained from the few remaining trees. Much more of the island will be replanted as soon as the herd of red deer is reduced to a sustained-yield level. In another example, Yarner Wood in Devon, a mixed oak and pine forest with some birch, beech, and ash, is being allowed to develop naturally without further intervention. But in England that is far more difficult than it might seem. Many woodlands have been grazed or used for winter shelter for livestock or deer and consequently have no understory saplings to replace the trees in the canopy. If the woods are fenced to exclude the larger animals, the ground vegetation becomes so luxuriant that small mammals multiply enough to replace the larger animals as destroyers of seeds and tree seedlings. The situation is exacerbated when gamekeepers eliminate most of the large carnivores and birds of prey that normally keep small mammal populations within bounds. Finally, exotic species such as rhododendron or sycamore (sycamore maple in American usage) may compete with the native species; should they be allowed to remain or be eliminated?

The British experience, then, while quite different from our own in its attempts to maintain systems that would be regarded in the United States as in need of restoration rather than maintenance, does include some experiments designed to allow as close a return as possible to the systems originally present.

THE AMERICAN EXPERIENCE

Since our continent was so recently settled, compared with Britain, virtually no natural system of any size in the United States has disappeared without a trace. Many systems have been destroyed, but the elements of these systems still exist in large enough associations to allow the possibility of reassembly. However, this will not always be so; hence the urgency in getting research started in as many diverse systems as possible. A major start toward this end has been made by the International Biological Programme, which, although oriented toward productivity of systems and the development of system models, has nevertheless generated a great deal of rather basic information about the major North American ecosystems.

Probably one of the first attempts to recreate a natural environment in the United States was undertaken in New York's Central Park over 120 years ago. Around 1850 the area now occupied by the park was covered with squatters' huts and shacks, and was on the outskirts of New York City. Period drawings and woodcuts show almost no trees or shrubs. In fact, there was little vegetation of any kind (Figure 21.12). The designer of the park, Frederick Law Olmsted, had to start from scratch. Even knowing that the original site was treeless, it is difficult to realize that almost every tree and shrub was planted by hand (Figure 21.13) in the fashion of Capability Brown. For the park as a whole, Olmsted had no intention of restoring the land to its original appearance. Like Brown, his "professional grandfather," Olmsted wanted to create an informal, aesthetically pleasing landscape; and a great deal of digging, filling, damming, and pumping was required to achieve this end. But in the midst of all of the "natural" artificiality, Olmsted intentionally created a small area he called the Ramble, which was to be as natural a wood as he could design. So he planted native species that he supposed

Fig. 21.14 *Planned as a natural area by Olmsted, who used mostly native species, Central Park's Ramble today appears like a bit of forest that has wandered in from Westchester County.*

might have been there originally: trees, shrubs, and herbs. Today, 120 years later, the trees have matured and probably reproduced several times, filling in the spaces, creating their own patterns. Walking through the Ramble early in the morning when the park is deserted, the effect is quite magical—that of being out in the country miles away, surrounded by a very natural-looking landscape (Figure 21.14), yet knowing that the sound of white water (or is it surf?) in the distance is really rush-hour traffic on Fifth Avenue and Central Park West.

If some sort of natural system can be created in the very navel of megalopolis, then why not recreate prairies, forests, or marshes where they have been badly misused or destroyed? The thought has occurred to many. In 1963 A. S. Leopold (son of Aldo Leopold), a rather perceptive zoologist at Berkeley, put together a four-step procedure for reconstructing ecosystems:

1. Historical research to determine what the area looked like before we began to alter things.
2. Ecological research to find out how the plants and animals are related to each other and to the ecosystem, and which environmental factors are most important in maintaining the area as we wish to see it.

509

3. Pilot experiments, based on the information gained from ecological research, to establish the feasibility of proposals.
4. Full-scale management of large ecosystems based on the more workable of the pilot studies.

TALL GRASS PRAIRIE

The first three of these steps had already been carried out on the tall grass prairie system by several groups in the Midwest several years before Leopold published his paper. The first such project was undertaken by H. C. Greene, a botanist on the staff of the University of Wisconsin. In 1945, Greene realized that the tall grass prairie, which had played such an important role in the history of the Midwest, had virtually disappeared as a system, plowed into cornfields over the preceding hundred years. All that remained, at least in Wisconsin, were a few small remnants scattered along railroad right of ways, in old cemeteries, and around abandoned schoolhouses. Even these odd scraps were disappearing one by one. Consequently Greene took over the management of thirty-five acres of a former sand priairie with small groves of bur oak at the University of Wisconsin Arboretum in Madison and began his restoration program. Many approaches were used at first since there were few precedents to follow: sowing seed of various prairie grasses and herbs, planting seedlings grown in the greenhouse, setting out blocks of sod taken from nearby prairie fragments, and transplanting mature prairie plants from remnants about to be developed. This introduction phase lasted for several years, proceeding as fast as time, funds, and the supply of plant materials allowed. By 1952, 214 species characteristic of the prairie in Wisconsin had been reintroduced. Except for some very persistent introduced grasses such as Kentucky blue grass, the prairie species had become sixteen times more abundant than in 1945 and the introduced weeds, which had formerly dominated the plot, had declined by the same factor.

In 1964 the Morton Arboretum in Lisle, Illinois, twenty-five miles southwest of Chicago, having just lost a small piece of prairie remnant to utility company construction, decided to replace a twenty-five-acre weedy meadow with a tall grass prairie. Since earlier restoration projects had been criticized for using commercial seed from remote sources and transplants that potentially introduced soil organisms foreign to the local area, it was decided to use only mixtures of seed gathered from local sources.

At one time the prairie stretched from horizon to horizon, Saskatchewan to Texas and Colorado to Illinois. While there was ample opportunity for slow genetic exchange among populations over this vast territory, there was also a tendency for local adaptations to day length, soil factors, and temperature extremes. So virtually all widely distributed species differentiated into local adaptation units or ecotypes. The Morton Arboretum wanted to be sure that those ecotypes well adapted to conditions in northern Illinois were used in stocking its prairie. Introduced commercial strains of former components of the prairie such as switch grass can often be so successful that the nongrasses or forbs such as shooting star, sunflower, and compass plant, which are as important a part of the tall grass prairie as the grasses, are crowded out. Within ten years the synthesized prairie at the Morton Arboretum had accommodated 125 prairie species in six acres, and the acreage is being increased as materials become available.

All the prairie restorations attempted so far have been pilot experiments designed to explore the best techniques for restoring grassland systems. These techniques may become extremely important if and when a prairie national park is established. Over forty years ago, at a time when many splendid sites were still available, Victor Shellford, an ecologist at the University of Illinois, recommended that national parks should preserve not only scenic wonders, but viably large tracts of representative biomes. Many of these ecosystems have been preserved: the eastern deciduous forest in Great Smoky Mountains National Park; tropical forests in the hammocks of Everglades National Park; the coastal and lake dunes in several national seashore or lakeshore areas; the redwoods and big trees in Redwood and Sequoia National Parks; the superb conifer rain forests in Olympic National Park; and many desert systems in several parks and national monuments. But the gorgeous sea of tall grasses that so impressed the early settlers in the Midwest is totally unrepresented. Ideally, such a park should include up to 1 million acres and be fenced to allow introduction of bison, antelope, elk, and their predators, wolves and coyotes. While the ideal is perhaps unlikely because of the numbers of cattle that 1 million acres of good grassland could support, a much smaller tract of 57,000 acres in the Flint Hills of eastern Kansas has been proposed but bitterly opposed by ranchers, who see any withdrawal of range land as a threat to the entire cattle industry. Even if such a modest prairie lands national park is finally established, restoration work will be needed to bring the whole tract back to its former productivity, for overgrazing is rife in the grasslands of most of North America.

However, the goal of environmental restoration needn't be regarded merely as the establishment of some kind of open-air museum. It is possible to apply ecological principles to the rehabilitation of working ranchland with the aim of producing superior beef. An excellent example is provided by the Lasiter Ranch.

After World War II, rising land prices in south Texas obliged Tom Lasiter to relocate to Colorado, where he purchased 25,000 rather battered acres of shortgrass prairie rangeland near Matheson. Departing sharply from contemporary ranching methods, Lasiter began by stocking his ranch lightly to allow recovery of the long-overgrazed grassland. The results were so gratifying—tripling of the yield of forage per acre— that Lastiter determined to keep his stocking rate low. By carefully rotating the stock on his pastures, he prevented overgrazing, weakening of the grass cover, and soil erosion. A no-poisoning, -trapping, or -shooting policy has resulted in a balanced population of native range species; the natural buildup of coyotes and other predators was accompanied by a corresponding decline in jackrabbit and cottontail populations. Poisonous weeds and plants have been controlled by the light stocking rate, which, by maintining a good cover of grasses and forbs, eliminates the weeds that characteristically invade overgrazed lands. Since the pastures are large the stock have more freedom to choose their food and thus behave more like the original grazers in the system, the bison. In short, Lasiter has required that his cattle adjust to a natural environment complete with the native species of coyotes, gophers, rabbits, and hawks; a natural environment that he has supported by maintaining intact that complex of vegetation on a stabilized soil. A simple application of basic ecological principles perhaps, but these principles are so rarely applied that Lasiter's experiment appears like an oasis in a desert of misuse.

WETLANDS

One of the most endangered ecosystems in North America is the coastal wetland type characterized by cordgrass, *Spartina alterniflora* (see Chapter 17). Once this habitat was extremely abundant along the Altanic coast from New Hampshire to northern Florida. But years of sanitary landfilling and dredging for marinas and seashore developments have gobbled up vast acreages. While there are still huge tracts remaining along the more remote stretches of coast, such as the eastern shore of Virginia and the Georgia coast, the more heavily populated states like Connecticut have about run through their wetland capital.

Because wetlands were long regarded as wasteland—property that could not be conveniently drained for farming, did not provide particularly good grazing, flooded every spring tide, and produced hordes of mosquitoes—their development was viewed as a public benefit. With the pioneering research of Eugene Odum and his students at the University of Georgia we have finally begun to understand how important coastal wetlands really are as primary producers in the food web that reaches offshore into the estuaries and shallow continental shelf (see Chapter 17). Still another important function of coastal wetlands has been discovered recently: their ability to take up phosphates and nitrates from estuarine water and release oxygen. By so doing, wetlands have a significant effect in reducing the nutrient and BOD burden of coastal water. This latter function makes wetlands extremely valuable as natural purification systems in areas of high population density, where increasing quantities of pollutants are finding their way into coastal waters. Unfortunately, this discovery came at a time when most wetlands in the vicinity of urban complexes had long been filled with the city's wastes. After a marsh has been filled with thirty feet of trash there is little chance for restoration. But if new marshes—even if they are simplified compared with the original vegetation—can be established in approrpriate sites, then the trend of wetland destruction can be at least slowed or even reversed. Considering the importance of wetlands in the productivity of estuaries and coastal waters and their role in pollution control, it might well repay a coastal state to subsidize establishment of new marshes wherever feasible. Should that enlightenment come to pass, the know-how will be available. At least three groups have successfully established tidal marshes: one, headed by Ernest Seneca of North Carolina State University; a private research group, Environmental Concern, Inc., at St. Michaels, Maryland; and a Corps of Engineers project in San Francisco Bay.

Several years ago Seneca and his associates planted a sand flat near Oregon Inlet on North Carolina's Outer Banks with plugs of cordgrass. Using hand labor at first, only a few acres were planted. The second season a tobacco planter was adapted to accept the cordgrass plants and a larger area was planted. Although snow geese attracted to the new planting the first winter caused much damage, the plants recovered and the marsh flourished.

The plan of Environmental Concern was somewhat more ambitious. An island in Chesapeake Bay that was being eroded into fragments (Figure 21.15) was purchased by the Nature Conservancy (this time the

Fig. 21.15 Hambleton Island in Chesapeake Bay before marsh restoration was begun was rapidly being eroded into a string of islets. (Environmental Concern, Inc.)

Fig. 21.16 Six months after cordgrass was planted, the young marsh was apparently well on its way to establishment. (Environmental Concern, Inc.)

private American group), with which the project was initially associated. Bank sand was barged out to the gap between two of the fragments and dumped to provide the proper elevation for cordgrass establishment. In the spring of 1972 workers began planting cordgrass plus several other species of plants capable of tolerating the brackish bay water. Instead of using vegetative shoots dug from existing marshes, researchers grew plants from seed and peat pots of the seedlings were then placed in a two- to three-foot grid on the flat. Growth was quite vigorous the first summer and many plants flowered (Figure 21.16). During the first winter Canada geese fed heavily on the plants but enough plants survived, together with a plentiful germination of seeds produced the preceding summer, to assure stabilization of the flat surface with a complete cover of plants likely by the end of the second or third year. While the costs of constructing artificial flats preclude their widespread use, many natural sand or mud flats exist, particularly near harbors or channels that must be dredged periodically. These natural flats could easily be planted and stabilized with marsh plants using the techniques developed by Seneca and Environmental Concern. While what would be created is not the same marsh that took 3000 years to evolve, a productive beginning of the process would have been made.

The Corps of Engineers, constructing a flood control channel near the mouth of Alameda Creek, used a 110-acre evaporation pond to receive dredging spoils. Under the direction of Paul Knutson the spoils were graded, allowing their partial flooding at high tide. Some twenty acres were planted with various combinations of pickleweed and cordgrass cuttings, seed, and seedlings; in the higher areas, brass button, curly dock, and salt grass were used. The remaining ninety acres will be allowed to revegetate naturally.

The usual approach to dredging spoil disposal has been to dump the wastes on a diked tidal marsh, but since this is rarely allowed now that states are beginning to protect their wetlands, the spoils could be dumped in shallow water and planted promptly with reasonable assurance of stabilizing the spoils with marsh vegetation and at the same time increasing the potential productivity of the harbor or estuary. Of course, spoils heavily contaminated with hydrocarbons, heavy metals, or biocides pose special problems, as does the question of how the area to be covered with spoil compares in productivity with the marsh that will be established. These complications aside, tidal marsh synthesis or, in the broader sense, restoration, is a concept whose time has come.

Despite our growing awareness of the importance of intact natural systems of all kinds as sources of primary production, reservoirs of genetic information, buffers against the rising tide of pollution, and certainly not least their aesthetic and recreational appeal, we are running short of areas that can be saved. By the year 2000 all currently available land will either have been saved or developed. With rising demands for more recreational space from a larger public with far more leisure time, the additional land will have to come from areas currently regarded as wasteland whose environments will have to be restored, if not to their pristine glory, at least to aesthetically pleasing natural systems capable of reproducing themselves. Strip mined land, quarries, slag heaps, eroded farmland, true wasteland of all types will have to be pressed into service to satisfy the demand. While much work has been done in Britain and Germany, two countries that have already run out of land, few of these techniques have yet been applied to analogous situations in the United States. We can be ready with the expertise and tools if the projects described and others like them are recognized as the hope of the future that they are and are fully supported with both public and private funds.

FURTHER READING

Bolling, A., 1971. "Tallgrass prairie park." *Nat'l Parks and Conser. Mag.* March, pp. 6–10. A capsule history of the attempts to establish a prairie-land national park.

Cairns, J., Jr., K. L. Dickson, and E. E. Herricks (eds.), 1977. *Recovery and restoration of damaged ecosystems.* University of Virginia Press, Charlottesville. Provides some guidelines to restoring ecosystems.

Colbert, F. T., 1971. "The Lasiter ranch: applied range ecology." *Nat'l Parks and Conserv. Mag.* March, pp. 18–20. Application of ecological principles to a rancher's problems can be both practical and profitable.

515

WE THE PEOPLE:
PROBLEM AND
SOLUTION

Green, B. H., 1972. "The relevance of seral eutrophication and plant competition to the management of successional communities." *Biol. Conser.* **4**(5), pp. 378–384. Increased fertility may not always be the goal in managing plant communities.

Hutnik, R., and G. Davis (eds.), 1973. *Ecology and reclamation of devastated lands.* Gordon & Breech, New York. Two volumes of papers from a symposium. Much information here.

Ovington, J. D., 1964. "The ecological basis of the management of woodland nature reserves in Great Britain." *J. Ecol.* **52,** pp. 29–37 (Suppl.) Covers the types of environmental management and reconstruction being explored in England.

Schramm, P. (ed.), 1970. *Proceedings of a symposium on prairie and prairie restoration.* Knox College Biol. Field Station, Special Publ. No. 3.

CHAPTER TWENTY-TWO

SUPPORTING EARTH'S POPULATION

CONSIDERING THE THIN line between feast and famine for many of today's 4 billion people, how many people can the earth support? While natural resources in the form of timber, ores, oil, and such are important considerations in determining the supportive capacity of earth, demands for these commodities could be sharply reduced by intensive recycling of these materials, or even by lowering our standard of living. This is not possible with food. Therefore, a broad discussion of natural resources has been intentionally omitted to allow fuller treatment of the food problem. (Energy resources, however, are discussed in Chapter 15.)

FOOD RESOURCES AND PEOPLE

As a general rule one acre of fertile land per capita is required for a nation to be self-sufficient in food production. France, Sweden, and Denmark, with about one acre per capita, all achieve this self-sufficiency. India and Pakistan, on the other hand, lie very close to the boundary between self-sufficiency and dependency with 0.3 hectares (ha) per capita. China with 0.2 ha is a chronic food importer, while England with 0.16 ha per capita must import significant amounts despite high yields and intensive farming. In contrast the United States has 1.1 ha, Australia 1.6 ha, and Canada 2.6 ha per capita, enabling all three countries to export large quantities of food. Despite this margin of food production, at least two thirds of the world's people suffer from undernourishment or malnutrition.

517

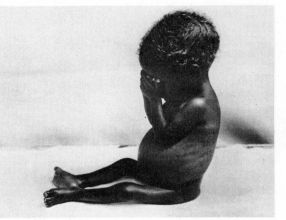

Fig. 22.1   Kwashiorkor is the African name for a disease of young children whose food contains too little protein. The spindly legs and swollen belly are characteristic symptoms of this condition. (FAO)

There is a distinct difference between undernourishment and malnutrition. Undernourishment is quantitative—an insufficient intake of calories leading to simple hunger; malnutrition is qualitative—the number of calories may quash hunger pains, but there is not enough protein in the diet to avoid chronic debilities or secondary infections and diseases. Children up to the age of six have an especially great need for protein. When this is not available a protein deficiency syndrome, kwashiorkor, develops; it is characterized by digestive tract disturbances, skin sores particularly on the legs, swelling of some parts of the body, wasting of others, and a reddening of the hair (Figure 22.1). Some years ago during the Nigeria-Biafra civil war, magazines were filled with the haunting pictures of Biafran children suffering and dying from malnutrition. But older children and adults suffer from malnutrition too, and the susceptibility to illness, lethargy, and apathy it induces place a steady drain on the human resources of developing countries.

However, protein supplements must be given with some care lest the cure be worse than the problem. In northeast Brazil some children suffering from malnutrition who were given a dried skim milk supplement developed blindness as a result. The reason? Without vitamin A, which is necessary in the production of lubricating fluids in the eye, the cornea becomes ulcerated, then softened and finally opaque. Since vitamin A is fat-soluble, skim milk is low in this vitamin; so when the milk protein stimulated growth without providing the necessary amount of vitamin A to support that growth, the children's bodies mobilized their remaining supplies of vitamin A and the eye disorder followed. Another even more bizarre instance was seen in Colombia, where a population was found with a 40 percent infestation of *Entamoeba histolytica*, a protozoan that generally burrows into the intestinal wall, causing a serious condition called amoebiasis. However, despite the high level of *Entamoeba* infestation, the incidence of amoebiasis was negligible. The answer to this puzzle was found in the high-starch diet of the people. Because of the low protein intake, production of starch-digesting enzymes was reduced, allowing a much higher level of starch to persist in the intestine. The protozoans were found to be feeding on this starch rather than attacking the intestinal wall. If this population had been given protein supplements without concurrent efforts to control the *Entamoeba* infestation, the incidence of amoebiasis would probably have soared, causing more problems than the lack of protein.

Whatever the effect of inadequate diet, only part of the blame can be laid to economic inequities. Other more peripheral problems prevent full realization of a nation's agricultural productivity. Religious attitudes, such as those that protect cows and monkeys in India, have been very difficult to resolve. These animals consume huge quantities of food that could contribute directly to agricultural production. Nationalism, understandably important to nations that have only recently emerged from the shadow of colonialism, has led to irrational attitudes and goals that have absorbed much scarce capital that underdeveloped countries could put to much better purposes.

Faced with the problem of widespread hunger in the world today, we must use presently available technology to increase productivity of less developed countries (LDCs) until they either become self-sufficient in food production or sufficiently industrialized so that they have enough foreign exchange to purchase food on the world market. But the gap between the haves and the have nots is wide. The United States has 160 million ha in crops, or 0.77 ha per capita. Deducting the 20 percent of our crops that are exported leaves 0.62 ha per capita. The rest of the world can crop 1.5 billion ha; this area, divided among the world's 4 billion people, gives 0.38 ha per capita.

If we consider energy as well as arable land, the disparity becomes even more bleak. To feed the world in the style the average United States citizen now takes for granted would require 5000 billion liters of fuel per year. Such a consumption of energy would exhaust known resources of crude oil in thirteen years.

PRESENT TECHNOLOGY

Only North America has maintained an average annual 2 percent growth rate in agricultural production over a long enough period (thirty years) to assume that this rate will continue. As a result, of the 90 million tons of grain in world trade, 70 million tons is produced by the United States. Today food production is increasing at 2.3 percent a year in the United States, but at less than half that rate in Latin America and Africa.

In the Middle East, rates in many instances are substantially below the rates of population increase. There are several possibilities for improvement.

PLANT BREEDING

Of the 700,000 species of plants in the world nearly 80,000 are edible, but only 3000 are normally considered crop plants. Three hundred species are in abundant use, but only twelve species or genera provide 90 percent of all edible crops. The leading food plants in order of their importance are rice, wheat, corn (two thirds of the annual crop is eaten by livestock), potatoes, soybeans, sorghum, barley, rye, millet, cassava, sweet potato, coconut, bananas, and plantains. Obviously, an incredible number of potential food plants growing in all conceivable environments is unexploited. More will be said about developing new crop plants, but in the short term much can and is being done to imrpove the major crop plants already in worldwide use.

For example, the International Rice Research Institute at Los Baños in the Philippines developed a variety of rice over a five-year period that has increased production of rice in one instance in the Philippines from 710 to 10,000 pounds per acre where intensively cultivated (Figure 22.2). This strain, IR-8, has been introduced to other Asian countries as well and has increased average rice yields from two to four times. In the few years since its development IR-8 has been planted on 20 million acres in Turkey, India, Pakistan, and the Philippines. With the introduc-

Fig. 22.2 Although IR-8 rice yields heavily, it does so only when fertilized. The rice on the right has been fertilized; that on the left is unfertilized. (FAO)

*Fig. 22.3   Triticale, a new grain result-
ing from a cross between wheat (Triti-
cum) and rye (Secale) is widely adaptable to different climates. The grain on the
left was grown in Mexico, the grain in the
center in Manitoba, and the grain on the
right is ordinary wheat.* (University of
Manitoba, Department of Plant Science)

tion of IR-8, Pakistan became self-sufficient in rice production for the
first time in many years.

In a parallel development Mexico gathered together a "germ bank" of
over a thousand different varieties of corn, and was able to develop several
high-yielding new varieties adapted to high elevations, low soil moisture,
and other special environments. This improvement in corn yield, together
with irrigation where feasible, greater use of fertilizer, and better transport facilities, has enabled Mexico to raise its agricultural productivity by
4 percent per year in recent years. Unfortunately, this gain has been
mitigated somewhat by a population growth rate of over 3 percent per
year.

These developments have been particularly important because, until
recently, most of the world's agricultural expertise was derived from temperate zone climates, soils, and crops, which had limited application to
crop cultivation in the tropics.

Another improvement in a basic cereal crop has been accomplished by
crossing wheat and rye to form a new species called *Triticale* (Figure
22.3). Perfected in Canada, this new grain is highly resistant to lodging
(the tendency of grain plants to be blown flat by wind, making them un-
harvestable), has a higher protein content than most other cereals, is
a good livestock feed, has a greater yield than either of its parents, and
combines vigor with wide adaptability to climate.

Other recent plant breeding developments include a wheat with an
increased yield of 30 percent; a leguminous (a member of the pea
family) livestock feed well adapted to the tropics; a new variety of corn,
opaque-2, with a much augmented supply of a very valuable amino acid,
lysine; and the discovery in Ethiopia of two strains of sorghum with

521

three times the lysine content of regular sorghum, a finding of great importance to the 300 million people who subsist on sorghum.

This last discovery underlines the need to locate and keep in reserve the thousands of varieties of the world's major food plants. When a high-yielding plant variety is developed, we tend to discard the traditional varieties, which are soon lost. Already many valuable and locally adapted strains of food plants have become extinct; as this green revolution spreads, hundreds more are likely to be lost. This is just one of the problems associated with the green revolution. Many of the "miracle grains" are susceptible to disease and insects. What resistance exists is limited to a few genes, making the grains quite vulnerable to a new strain of pathogen. This happened to the potato in Ireland in the 1840s, to corn in the United States in 1970, and to IR-8, which succumbed to a virus carried by green leafhopper that almost totally destroyed the Philippine rice crop in 1972. The opaque-2 corn that raised such hopes proved to be unacceptable to the consumer; the soft kernels made too fine a flour, affecting the quality of cornbread. Consequently opaque-2 corn, where grown at all, is used to feed hogs.

High yields are obtained only with intensive use of biocides, fertilizers, and irrigation—all requiring enormous amounts of capital to produce and supply, and exacting an increasingly apparent environmental toll. Paul Ehrlich, an ecologist especially concerned with population growth, estimates that for India to fertilize at the intensive level used by the Dutch, almost half the fertilizer produced in the world would be required.

THE GREEN REVOLUTION

In most tropical agricultural systems, the small farmer has low yields but, more important, low risk. He grows many varieties of different crops, so that regardless of pests and the weather he can harvest something every season. The point of the green revolution is to increase the yield of one crop, usually one strain. To make the maximum profit requires the maximum risk; the farmer faces an all or nothing situation. This might be acceptable for a large landowner, but it can mean disaster for a peasant with a few acres.

Economically, the green revolution can only take place if heavily subsidized by a government. This causes increased production but increased internal prices as well. On the international market the grains are usually sold at a loss because the world price is less than the government price paid to stimulate farmers to grow the new grains. There is also a philosophical problem. The theory of Malthus quoted in Chapter 23 is sometimes called the dismal theorem. In 1956 the economist Kenneth

Boulding described an "utterly dismal theorem"—any technological improvement ultimately increases the sum of human misery by allowing a larger proportion of people to live at the same level of misery and starvation. An example to ponder: in the Ireland of 1600, 2 million people lived in wretched poverty. With the introduction of the potato (a green revolution?) in the 1700s, Ireland's population rose to 8 million by 1835. As a result of the potato blight in the 1840s, 2 million people starved to death, 2 million emigrated, and 4 million remained in wretched poverty!

INTENSIVE AGRICULTURE

New high-yield plant varieties cannot even be grown, however, without improved cultivation. The land must be properly prepared by tractors capable of breaking the soil more quickly and effectively than water buffalo or oxen; it must be fertilized with the right formulation applied in the proper concentration at the best time; and the crop must be quickly and efficiently harvested, processed, and stored. Finally, if the increased yield is to be passed on to the people, distribution routes and new transport techniques and systems must be developed; otherwise isolated people may be reduced to starvation simply because there is no effective way to get food to them.

Presenting peasants with improved seed, then, is clearly only the beginning. The orchestration of the necessary accompanying technology requires time and usually outside help and money. Once begun, however, it can generate its own continued momentum. In the meantime, people continue to go hungry. While the diet of LDCs is roughly comparable with that of developed countries in the caloric intake per day, there is a critical lack of protein in the former.

PROTEIN SUPPLEMENTS

At least three protein concentrates have been developed: incaparina, laubina, and fish protein concentrate (FPC). Incaparina is a mixture of cottonseed flour, whole corn cooked and ground, yeast, calcium carbonate, and vitamin A. The resulting powder contains 25 percent protein and can be mixed with water and drunk like dried milk or added as a supplement to food. Laubina is made of wheat, chick peas, bone ash, sucrose, and vitamins A and D. Like incaparina, it is compounded of materials whose taste is known and recognized by the people it is intended to serve, and this goes a long way to ensure its acceptance, for people are exceedingly conservative about the food they eat. Rice-eating people would often rather starve than eat wheat or barley, which are unknown to them. Americans are no exception. When was the last time *you* ate roasted grasshoppers, lizard, or rattlesnake meat? Many confirmed beef eaters will not touch even the liver, much less heart, kidneys, tripe, or brain.

Fish protein concentrate has the advantage of being produced from just about any kind of fish, especially trash fish not normally eaten. When the fish is ground up and the oil and water removed, the end result is a fine, free-flowing powder. Odorless, tasteless, and containing 80 percent protein, FPC can be produced for about 25 cents a pound. As a powder it can be added to a great variety of baked and cooked foods to supplement the diet with protein. Just about any country with a fishing industry, fresh or salt water, should be able to generate this superb source of animal protein cheaply enough to raise protein consumption at least to minimal levels, buying time until the slower techniques of increasing agricultural production are implemented.

Fig. 22.4 Although idealized by this museum diorama, the species diversity of East African ungulates and their adaptation to a savanna environment still exists despite the pressures of development and population growth. (Courtesy of the American Museum of Natural History)

GAME RANCHING

Another underexploited source of protein is wild game. One of the symbols of progress in an LDC is the establishment of a livestock industry to supply protein for internal consumption or for export income. Where no suitable stock exists, as was true in New Zealand, domesticated grazing animals may be profitably introduced. But New Zealand is an exception; most other grasslands of the world have numbers of native grazers well adapted to the environment and the available forage (Figure 22.4). Until recently the value of wild game as a protein source, equal to or surpassing any stock that might be introduced, was ignored.

Then some pioneering work in East Africa by Pearsall and Dasmann disclosed that wild game is more efficient at grazing and even more productive of protein than introduced stock. The difference lies in the food habits, water requirements, and mobility of game. Cows are quite fussy, eating only certain grasses and leaving the rest. If the number of cows is increased, overgrazing takes place, leaving stock and range in very poor condition. Since cows are not very mobile they tend to overgraze and they require sizable water supplies.

Game, on the other hand, is beautifully adapted to the many niches in the environment: elephants eat the bark and roots of trees; giraffes feed on the higher branches of trees; eland, a species of large African antelope, feed on the lower branches, and so on. Because of this diversity, a much broader range of vegetation is utilized by game than domesticated cattle, and thereby becomes potentially available to man. Wild animals are much more mobile than stock, and when the browse becomes thin, they are capable of traveling miles in search of better range; therefore, overgrazing in the natural environment is rare. Finally, most of the wild grazers in East Africa have low water requirements; for example, the gemsbok and oryx take no water at all and the zebra can go from one to three days without water. One of the major drawbacks to the introduction of stock in many parts of Africa is its susceptibility to disease spread by the tsetse fly. Wild animals that evolved with the fly are immune.

Recognizing these advantages, Dasmann made a cost analysis study comparing stock and native grazers on a large ranch in Rhodesia. He found that while a cow was supported by one acre in England and was ready for market in a year, in Rhodesia the comparable figures were thirty acres and four years. Although native grazers supplied only a pound more of meat per acre per year, there was a major difference in production cost: the profit margin on the beef was $1416 per year while the profit on the game amounted to $8960 per year. This differential was due to the greater cost of maintaining species introduced into an alien environment. Harvesting of large native game that is abundant and in no danger of extinction is clearly desirable both from an ecological and economic point of view, for any habitat can only support so many animals. Any surplus causes starvation or increases stress on the other species.

Suggestions have been made from time to time that appropriate browsers be introduced to the rangelands of the American Southwest. Up to some 10,000 years ago there were a number of native browsers feeding on various desert shrubs as well as grass. The Shasta ground sloth, for example, ate yucca, creosote bush, and agave. But the sloth and most of its fellows seem to have been eliminated by superpredation (see Chapter 9) 10,000 years ago and their niches have remained unoccupied. The only major replacement, the cow, can utilize only a small fraction of the total biomass available. The desert shrub community that covers 1 million square miles in the Southwest regularly produces 1200 pounds of dry matter per acre per year, twice that produced by most grasslands. If the range were stocked with an exotic browser that could utilize this production, the range could support as many as 15 to 30 million new browsers. If the new species were carefully selected, there need be no competition with the cattle that now stock the range, or with the native bison, antelope, elk, sheep, and deer. A sustained-yield harvest based on a herd of 30 million eland (one possibility) would provide an enormous quantity of protein from forage that is presently unused. In view of the problems of mammalian introduction in other countries, red deer in New Zealand particularly, great care would have to be taken before such an experiment were allowed.

Another time-buying factor is the continuing surplus of food produced by the United States, Canada, Australia, and New Zealand. Until recently, up to 60 percent of the United States wheat crop was distributed abroad under Public Law 480, the Food for Peace Program. The USDA estimates that by 1984 demands for this surplus by hungry nations will exceed the supply. If in the remaining five years the recipient countries cannot increase their food production at least to the self-sufficiency level or control their population growth, there seems no alternative to the mass famine Malthus predicted in 1798.

FUTURE TECHNOLOGY

With great application and perhaps a bit of luck, the world can avoid the famine predicted for it in the next two or three decades. But what of 1999 and beyond? What hope does technology provide for the accommodation of two, three, or four times the present population of the world or even a more slowly growing population over a long period of time?

INCREASE OF CULTIVATED LAND

Only about 40 percent of the earth's total land area is capable of productive use, at least in the direct sense of cropland, grazing, or timber production. The other 60 percent is tied up in ice and snow, mountains, and desert. Of the potentially arable land only 25 percent could reasonably be brought under cultivation and only one third of this land is in Asia, where the demand is most critical: six out of every ten humans live in Asia.

For a better idea of why it is so difficult to bring new land under cultivation despite its apparent suitability, let us look at a commonly

Fig. 22.5 As lush as this rain forest appears, the soil beneath it is relatively unfertile, for most of the nutrients are already incorporated into the vegetation and are quickly recycled. (Photo by Eli Morowitz, U.S. Forest Service)

cited example. The terra firma soils which occupy most of Amazonia bear a luxuriant rain forest (Figure 22.5). But as we saw in the discussion of soil (Chapter 1), the forest, once established, accumulates and then recycles most of its mineral nutrients, using the rather infertile soil mostly as a means of absorbing moisture. When the forest is removed, the action of sunlight, temperature extremes, and alternation of wet and dry conditions causes rapid erosion and a swift decline in fertility.

Amazonia has for generations been heralded as the future breadbasket of Brazil, if not the world. But despite the influx of millions of settlers from arid northwestern Brazil, the results have not been the integration of expanded agriculture into Brazil's national economy but rather the extension of subsistence farming into a new region. Nearly 2 million people have settled along the 930-mile Belem-Brasilia highway, but most depend on food produced elsewhere.

Athough the plinthite soils that form laterite are not as abundant in the tropics as was once believed, (they total 5 percent in Amazonia and 11 percent in tropical Africa) clearing of tropical forests often leads into a downward spiral of productivity. The cropland that replaces most tropi-

527

cal forests is usually abandoned after a few years and replaced by a successional forest. But before this can in turn be replaced by the original rain forest, cutting for firewood and timber destroys vegetation and opens the land to a second round of cultivation. With increasing loss of fertility, succession leads to a savanna of nonnutritious grasses, bamboo, and ferns, which is swept by frequent brush fires, further delaying the reestablishment of the rain forest.

Fertilization is not as easily accomplished as in temperate areas because nitrogen tends to vaporize in direct sunlight and high soil temperatures, and phosphorus reacts with iron to form insoluble compounds. Frequent downpours cause more consistent leaching of nutrients too.

While year-round warmth and abundant moisture might seem to make tropical agriculture extremely productive, anyone with a greenhouse knows that these conditions allow pests and diseases to breed and thrive freely. In general, tropical agriculture is based on short-term exploitation rather than long-term sustained yield. But to obtain a consistent high yield in tropical systems an enormous input of energy must be made, either as hand labor or as fuel energy. Many tropical regions have neither.

Far from being the economic mainstay of the Brazilian economy, Amazonia contributes only 1 percent of the gross national product while requiring 3 percent for its maintenance. It is extremely unlikely that the Amazon basin will ever be successfully used for conventional crop farming.

One other example of attempting to bring new land under cultivation was the great East African groundnut scheme. Much of East Africa is a savanna of scattered shrubs and low trees mixed with grass. In 1947 the British, then administrators of the territory, decided to open over 3 million acres of the countryside to the cultivation of groundnuts, or peanuts, as they are known in the United States. Research was done to assure that peanuts would grow satisfactorily in the climate and soil of East Africa. Then 30,000 acres were bulldozed and plowed, with great difficulty as it turned out, for the roots of trees and shrubs in areas of low rainfall are long and ropy and exceedingly difficult to remove. This accomplished, it was found that the stones in the soil, which were extremely hard and sharp-edged, damaged farm implements, compacted under the tread of tractors, and made the soil almost impervious. In addition, alternation of heavy rain and drought scuttled crop after crop. In 1951, after investing over $100 million, the British admitted failure.

As a general rule, any area of the world not already grazing cattle, growing trees, or producing crops is not capable of doing so using current technology. With much research and development, some of these marginal areas may yet be made productive, perhaps in ways beyond our present imagination. But we cannot tacitly assume that presently unproductive land is simply waiting for our touch to be brought into production.

IRRIGATION

There are large tracts of desert around the world that are neither too sandy, too mountainous, nor too cold to be farmed, if water could be supplied. The problem is not water supply per se, for in the next few decades desalinization with probably reduce the cost of fresh "manufactured" water from its present $1.00 per 1000 gallons to the point where economics will allow its use in irrigation (25 cents or less per 1000 gallons). However, once desalinated, water must be moved against gravity, over mountain ranges, and up high plateaus, for few deserts are located at sea level, even if they are adjacent to the seacoast. All of the long-distance water supply systems of large cities—New York's from the Delaware River and the Catskills, Los Angeles' from the Sierra and Owens Valley—operate on a gravity flow system. The billion-dollar California water scheme, which is bringing water from northern California to southern California (see Chapter 4), can compete with local desalinization only because the transport of this water is partially free due to gravity. If some way is developed to overcome the cost of moving desalinated water up from sea level, it may well be possible to bring water to the desert, but that is only a part of the problem.

Unless water is drained as well as applied to irrigated land, the water table rises close to the surface and waterlogs the surface soil, which then acts like a wick that becomes steadily more salty. If the soil is not properly drained to remove these salts, they accumulate, making agriculture progressively more difficult. Today excess salinity has made infertile 20 to 30 percent of Iraq's potentially irrigable land, 20 percent of the Indus Plain in Pakistan, 15 percent of India's irrigated land, a third of Peru's coastal soils, and 25 percent of agricultural land in the Patagonian region of Argentina. The problem is increasing in northwestern Mexico and the Imperial and Coachella Valleys in the United States also. Tube wells can be drilled to lower the water table, drainage tiles can be laid, and desalinization plants can lower the salinity of the irrigation water; but these solutions are expensive, prohibitively so in many LDCs. Other possibilities include drip irrigation and the breeding of salt-resistant plants.

Originally developed in Israel, drip irrigation applies a small but steady supply of water to the individual plant. Results include large savings of water, lessened evaporation, and a more favorable root zone environment, which increases yield. In the conventional furrow method half the

529

water applied goes unutilized—it is either lost to deep percolation or evaporates from the surface before plants can absorb it. During this time it becomes polluted with silt, salts, fertilizers, and biocides.

Because level terrain is not a requisite, as it is for the furrow method, orchards using the drip method can be planted on steep hillsides, fertilizers can be applied only to the desired plant roots, and weed growth is much more easily controlled. Because of the saving in water alone, the high capital costs of drip equipment can often be amortized in a few years. However, the method is more suited to fruit crops than to row crops and the lines are easily clogged with silt or iron salts. Although drip irrigation is not the entire solution to a complex problem, it certainly can be of some use in irrigated zones over most of the world.

NEW CROP VARIETIES

Another possible approach is the development of salt-tolerant crops. In 1976 a new strain of barley was grown in soil watered with sea water. To obtain this strain, however, some 6200 different types of barley were examined and crossed to select for this salt-resistant characteristic. Thus, while the lead time for such selection is likely to be rather long, it may well be possible to breed salt resistance into other crops as well.

Assuming marginal lands and deserts could ultimately be cultivated, what crops would be planted? We have seen how few of the edible plants have been exploited; most plants, particularly those which have been intensively bred, are native to and grow best in the temperate zones of the world. But any new land being brought under cultivation is likely to be in the tropics. We need an extensive research program that will screen the thousands of potentially edible tropical plants, isolating those that seem to offer the best possibilities: suitability to soils characteristic of the new lands, high protein content, resistance to drought and pests, and acceptability to the people in need of these foods. These initial efforts must be followed by an intensive selection and breeding program to combine the most useful features into new crop plants. Since the development time is long in plant breeding and selection programs, present efforts must be greatly accelerated if suitable crops are to be ready to take care of any sudden technological advances in marginal land use.

Nitrogen, one of the nutrients whose lack limits crop yields most severely, has quadrupled in price in the past few years because of the large quantity of fuel energy required to produce it, hence nitrogen-fixing plants are again being regarded as a way around this economic impasse. Therefore the discovery in Brazil of some strains of maize that contain a nitrogen-fixing bacterium (*Spirillum lipoferum*) in their roots was reported with some excitement. If we could develop corn or wheat varieties that produce their own nitrogen as do legumes such as soybeans, crop yields could be boosted and costs greatly reduced. However, *Spirillum lipoferum* is not an effective nitrogen fixer below 25°C, which would rule it out in most temperate areas. Nonetheless, the principle is quite promising.

THE OCEAN

What kind of harvest can we expect of the world ocean? Altogether, the ocean fixes around 18 billion tons of carbon each year in the process of photosynthesis. The open sea, about 90 percent of the total ocean area, produces fifty grams of carbon per square meter per year. Shallow coastal waters and estuaries produce about twice this, and local upwellings (areas where nutrient-rich deep water comes to the surface, causing a sharp increase in productivity) may produce up to six times as much as the open sea.

A good example is the anchovy fishery off the coast of Peru. Here the Humboldt Current moves west offshore, causing an upwelling of cool, nutrient-rich water. The bloom of plankton that results provides the productive base for the anchovy, a small sardine, which in turn supports millions of sea birds. Throughout the nineteenth and part of the twentieth centuries the droppings or guano of these birds, collected from the rocky islands on which the birds nested, provided a major source of the world's fertilizer. In the last decade, however, the anchovy itself has been harvested, not as fertilizer, nor as a source of protein for undernourished people, but as a protein supplement for the poultry industry in the world's developed countries. The chicken you barbecued last weekend grew to its bland three-month maturity on fish meal from Peru.

Because of the high profits from the anchovy fishery the harvest rapidly rose to a peak of 12 million tonnes in 1970 and then crashed in 1972, when the fish disappeared. Part of the reason for the rapid dispersal of the anchovy was El Niño, a periodic penetration of warm currents from the north which suppresses the upwelling on which the productivity of the system is based. But part of the blame must rest on rapacious overfishing of the resource. Recognizing this abuse, the Peruvian government responded by nationalizing the fishing industry, halting fishing for almost two years, reducing the number of fishing boats by 50 percent, and limiting the catch to 6 million tonnes per year, a harvest that fishery experts feel will provide a sustained yield. As a result of these policies and a weakening of the El Niño effect, the catch rose to 3.6 million tonnes in 1974 and returned to the maximum permitted by 1977.

With our present technology we are harvesting in most instances only the fish at the end of the food chain (Figure 22.6). In the open ocean

531

Fig. 22.6 This etching by Brueghel embroiders a bit on the "big fish eat little fish" aspect of the aquatic food chain.

food chains may have five links between the algae producers and the fish that are harvested. Coastal waters usually have three links, and the areas of upwelling only two. Because energy is lost between each link, the shorter the food chain, the greater the amount of energy that can be harvested.

When the yields of the three types of oceanic water are compared, the open ocean appears to be a biological desert, producing only a small fraction of the fish harvested and with little likelihood of any increase. In contrast, the upwellings that form only 1 percent of the ocean surface produce *one half* of the world's harvest of fish.

Annual production of fish is about 240 million tons, but not all of it can be harvested. Some fish must remain to breed and, since man is not the only fish predator, others are taken by sea birds and mammals. Perhaps 100 million tons are available to man on a sustained yield basis. In 1967 the fish catch was 60 million tons. At the current rate of increase, 8 percent per annum, the ocean will be yielding as many fish as it can *within a few years*. Indeed, some parts of the ocean are already overexploited: the area between the Hudson Canyon and the Nova Scotia shelf produced 1 million tons of fish in the early 1960s but the catch has been falling off ever since.

Quite irrationally, at least one half of the fish caught commercially is thrown away because of finicky public attitudes about which fish are edible and which are not. Since fish contain all the amino acids necessary for us to manufacture protein, a huge amount of valuable protein is being wasted. An efficient system of trawlers working from a mother-ship base could easily deliver all the fish caught to the factory ship, which could clean and freeze the most desirable fish, then process the trash fish into fish protein concentrate. The Russians are exploring this possibility; indeed it seems too efficient and profitable to ignore.

MARICULTURE

Another promising possibility is raising some types of seafood under controlled or semi-controlled conditions, opening the way for more convenient and efficient harvesting and processing than is possible today with wild populations of fish and shellfish.

Of all the thousands of edible species of plants and animals in the sea, surprisingly few are eaten and even fewer (50 out of 20,000) are systematically cultivated. A few species of seaweed are grown in Japanese estuaries and surely far more could be grown in other countries. But seaweed is not to everyone's taste, although we all eat considerable quantities as alginate, a stabilizer that is finding its way into more and more processed foods (see Chapter 6). Oysters have been raised for centuries and have proved to be a valuable and nourishing food capable of yielding 6000 pounds per acre. But increasing pollution of estuaries is destroying more beds than are currently being developed. Mussels, a favorite shellfish in the Mediterranean countries, are almost totally ignored as a food supply in North America. With their superb flavor, far superior to most clams, and their extreme abundance along rocky coasts (Figure 22.7),

Fig. 22.7 For many years mussels were not considered fit for human consumption in the United States. As the realization slowly dawned that they are indeed delicious, we found that the most accessible beds were polluted by sewage outfalls. Perhaps this will provide an incentive to take care of the waste problem.

mussels are one of many unexploited food sources in North America. Some forms of shrimp, milkfish, and mullet are raised in ponds with considerable success, particularly in Asia. Conch, abalone, lobster, blue crab, and other species of shellfish could be raised in tank farms or salt water ponds. Some recent work done in Massachusetts has reduced the time required for lobsters to reach sexual maturity from eight years to eighteen months, suggesting that lobster farming may soon become a practical operation. Research is also progressing on the utilization of thermal effluent for rearing food species (see Chapter 16).

HARVESTING ALGAE

While the annual production of fish and shellfish may seem enormous, most of the true production of the ocean lies, like the greatest mass of an iceberg, out of sight. When we catch fish, we are harvesting only a tiny portion of the food chain energy represented by that fish. Behind every ounce and a half of tuna that we eat, there is one pound of mackerel, ten pounds of herring, 100 pounds of zooplankton, and 500 pounds of phytoplankton. Phytoplankton consists of the unicellular algae that begin the whole food chain by fixing carbon into food by photosynthesis. Rather than accepting all the loss of energy involved in long food chains, it would make far more sense to harvest algae directly. On an average the algae in one acre of sea surface could yield about three tons dry weight, compared with the average yield of twenty pounds of fish per acre of ocean.

The problem is that harvesting algae is not easily done: getting those three tons of algae out of the water is one major problem, converting them into palatable protein is another, and persuading people to eat this protein in preference to fish is yet another. It would be more convenient to grow algae in tanks under optimum conditions than to try straining them out of huge quantities of water, but pilot operations of this type have never been as productive as expected. Apparently much more research is necessary before algae can either be harvested or raised directly as a major source of protein.

The potential yield resulting from shortened food chains applies to the land as well as the sea. Beef as a harvester of energy is incredibly inefficient; the yield of protein is forty-three pounds per acre per year. If the protein is in the form of milk, the yield is increased slightly to seventy-seven pounds per acre per year. Soybeans can yield 450 pounds of protein per acre per year and processed alfalfa, 600 pounds. When the demand for protein becomes great enough, eating beef as a major source will become an increasing luxury, and then disappear altogether. Two thirds of the earth's population has already, of necessity, made the shift.

Even within the spectrum of plants already utilized, we can do much better than the 4.5 million calories per acre per year provided by wheat; potatoes give 8 and sugar beets 13 million calories per acre per year. The difference is due to the small fraction of the wheat plant we actually eat, less than 30 percent. In contrast, 50 to 65 percent of the sugar beet or potato plant is directly edible. When the pinch becomes sharp enough we may have to shift to crops that are more completely edible, or we may breed new varieties of grain that have edible stems as well as heads.

DIRECT SYNTHESIS

The short-circuiting of food chains is but one way to eliminate as much waste as possible by going to the primary producer. The next logical step would be direct synthesis from an abundant organic source. Three approaches have already been worked out on a pilot basis. Roughage waste from cereal crops, corn cobs, and straw, when treated with a hot acid, forms a molasses-like substance that can be fermented to produce yeast protein. Although it would be ten times as expensive as molasses from sugar cane or sugar beets, it could be done. Conversion of most of the woody residues from today's crops could lead to a doubling of our present food supply.

Another approach treats soybeans with a mild alkali that aids in the extraction of the soybean protein. This extract can be processed like synthetic fabric fibers; when extruded in a suitable bath, the extract coagulates into fibers ranging from one- to thirty-thousandths of an inch in diameter. These can be oriented in parallel lines or at right angles, forming a mat (Figure 22.8a). The resulting material is tasteless but can be flavored and colored to resemble in taste and texture the familiar forms of meat: chicken, beef, sausage, and luncheon meats (Figure 22.8b). Although at present more expensive than the real thing, like every pilot project, it probably tastes as good as many meats currently available and could serve the valuable function of weaning the meat-eating public to an acceptable substitute when the real thing becomes too expensive and scarce a source of protein.

The most revolutionary approach to direct synthesis of food involves crude oil. Anyone who has spent time in the tropics realizes that there are microorganisms that will attack anything, no matter how indigestible or poisonous it may seem to us. A few years ago a French research group found some microorganisms that could use petroleum as a food source and thus be harvested as a substantial yield of protein. One enthusiastic estimate suggests that the equivalent of all animal protein needed by the world today could be produced from but 3 percent of the annual crude oil production of the world; however, tooling up from a test tube to the scale necessary to supersede beef as a protein source presents extensive techni-

Fig. 22.8 (a) Soybean protein can be processed like synthetic fabric fibers. (Ralston Purina Co.) (b) When oriented at right angles to form a mat and artificially flavored and colored, a wide variety of animal-protein foods can be simulated. (Worthington Foods)

cal problems. In the meantime, the world's oil supply is being rapidly depleted. Direct chemical synthesis of food, though feasible, is still some years, perhaps decades away.

Where does the world stand then when present and future technology is turned to the task of producing food? If the rate of world population growth could be reduced to 2 percent and at the same time the rate of food production everywhere could be raised by the same amount, the population of the earth could double by the year 2000 without mass starvation.

Balancing serendipitous technological developments against natural disasters, we are still left with a big if. While many countries have made great strides toward balancing their population growth and food production rates by decreasing the birth rate, increasing food production, or both, many more have made no progress in either.

As late as it is, we still have before us the choice of voluntarily limiting our population and our consumption of raw materials. Before long, however, limited availability of food and natural resources will remove that choice forever.

FURTHER READING

Bardach, J. E., J. H. Ryther, and W. O. McLarney, 1972. *Aquaculture: the farming and husbandry of freshwater and marine organisms.* Wiley, New York. Complete review of the state of the art.

Borgstrom, G., 1973. *Focal points: a global food strategy.* Macmillan, New York. Some interesting case studies.

Eckholm, E. P., 1976. *Losing ground, environmental stress and world food prospects.* W. W. Norton, New York. Another assessment of the world's future food supply.

Ehrlich, P. R., and A. H. Ehrlich, 1970. *Population, resources, environment.* W. H. Freeman, San Francisco. An excellent resource book.

Jahoda, J. C., and D. L. O'Hearn, 1975. "The reluctant Amazon Basin." *Env.* **17**(7), pp. 16–20, 25–30. The myth of an Amazonian breadbasket dies hard.

Janzen, D. H., 1973. "Tropical agroecosystems." *Science* **182**, pp. 1212–1219. A look at the pluses and minuses of tropical agriculture.

Miller, J., 1973. "Genetic erosion: crop plants threatened by government neglect." *Science* **182**, pp. 1231–1233. Discusses the loss of local plant varieties as glamorous super breeds become more widely used.

Moromarco, S., 1974. "Growing plants with salt water." *Science News* **105**, pp. 406–407. A novel and portentous approach.

Pimental, D. W. et al., 1975. "Energy and land constraints in food protein production." *Science* **190**, pp. 754–761. The energetics of producing food.

CHAPTER
TWENTY-THREE

POPULATION CONTROL

OF ALL THE PROBLEMS discussed in this book, overpopulation is the one problem the entire world must share. But we have become so concerned about the quantitative aspects of the billions of people we fatalistically anticipate in the next few decades that we forget the critical importance of the *quality* of life on earth. For hundreds of millions living in under-developed countries, life is so impoverished that quality, in our affluent terms, is unknown.

There are signs posted all over downtown Edinburgh, Scotland, that read "The amenity of our streets is commended to your care." The Scots sign is thought-provoking far beyond its literal intent, for the amenity of future life on earth *is* in our care. Amenity is being able to show your children skunk cabbages pushing up through the corn snow of March, going swimming and being able to see your toes, visiting a national park rather than a national parking lot. It is very easy to pick some point in time past and say, "Those were the days," regretting the subsequent loss of amenity, for the passage of time never seems to add to the quality of life, only the quantity. Like the realtor who advises buying land now, for it will never be cheaper, we must make a stand now, for the quality of life will only lessen in the future.

But an even more important aspect of amenity is personal freedom. The Wild West of the frontier days was wild because of the freedom, not simply opportunity, to lead your life as you wished. As populations grew, the freedoms began to wither away. For a while one could always follow a frontier north, south, east, or west; but there are no more frontiers in our country. Backpack into the most remote wilderness and you will surely run into another family doing the same. As the number of people increases, the number of problems arising from interactions increases, more laws are passed, more freedoms are limited. If you feel hemmed in now, sharing North America with 300 million other North Americans, think of the restrictions necessary to allow 600 million or a billion North Americans to live peaceably together.

The only way to preserve what amenity and personal freedom remain is by population control. This is possible with the means at hand, but first we must overcome our superstitions, religious objections, political barriers, and just plain ignorance. Not until *all* the people of the world fully understand the consequences of unrestricted growth can present solutions be applied, and better ones developed.

In 1798 Thomas Malthus published *An Essay on the Principle of Population . . .* in which he wrote:

> The power of population is indefinitely greater than the power in the earth to produce subsistence for man.
>
> Population, when unchecked, increases in a geometrical ratio. Subsistence increases only in an arithmetical ratio. A slight acquaintance with numbers will show the immensity of the first power in comparison with the second.
>
> This implies a strong and constantly operating check on population from the difficulty of subsistence. This difficulty must fall some where and must necessarily be severely felt by a large portion of mankind.[1]

Malthus was concerned about overpopulation in England. Unfortunately for the plausibility of his theory, disaster did not overtake England; population did increase, but so did subsistence—spectacularly so. Yet Malthus was correct in his basic analysis of the problem.

HUMAN POPULATION GROWTH

Unlike animals, which breed until limited by predation, starvation, or disease, we have the unique ability to limit both our death rate and our birth rate. Even so, it took from the beginning of our evolution until 1850 for our population to reach a billion.

In the hunting and gathering stage, each of us required about two square miles to survive. At this cultural stage, the accessibility of food stabilized our population, until the agricultural revolution removed that limitation. But the earth's resources are not uniformly distributed,

[1] Hardin, G. 1969. *Population, evolution, and birth control.* W. H. Freeman, San Francisco.

and while agriculture flourished in some areas, other areas were nonproductive. This led to population increases in countries with adequate resources, but limitation by starvation in others. By the eighteenth century, when Malthus made his observations, land and food shortages in many European countries had led to some desperate social conditions.

But by several quite fortuitous developments Europe was saved and Malthus' theory was temporarily discredited. First, the discovery of North and South America, then Australia and New Zealand, provided outlets for surplus population. These new empires generated capital that permitted the Industrial Revolution to sweep Europe more quickly than it might otherwise have done. In addition, these colonies provided a market for goods produced by the mother country. Then efficient agriculture, stimulated by the Industrial Revolution, allowed not only a population increase but a slow rise in prosperity. Advances in medicine lowered the death rate, but the birth rate fell also, for the newly industrialized population desired to limit its families in order to feed and educate them better.

Convinced of the desirability of constant population growth, governments had always encouraged people to have large families to run the machinery in factories, and when necessary to man the guns that served the national interest. While it was certainly useful to governments and industry to have a large labor pool, it was not long before one of the laborers, the Englishman Francis Place, came to the conclusion that it was in the best interest of laborers to limit their numbers and thereby increase their value and power. From this humble background arose the concept of family planning. While the acceptance of family planning increased gradually and steadily through the first half of the twentieth century, the catalyst for its rapid expansion came with the surge in population growth after World War II. It became obvious then that concentrated study and action were necessary to control a world population beginning to strain world resources seriously.

THE DEMOGRAPHIC TRANSITION

If we review the ebb and flow of the population of western European countries we can see a pattern of demographic transition from one stage to another that is being repeated throughout the world. The first stage was a population with high but fluctuating birth and death rates. No matter how many children were born, few survived the hazards of childhood or disease to become reproducing adults, so the population was either stable or slow in growing. In the second stage, because of improved medicine and health care, the death rate began to fall much more rapidly than the birth rate. The decrease was not regular; in fact, in some modern instances, the drop was precipitous. This was seen when malaria was controlled in Sri Lanka after World War II; the death rate fell from over twenty per thousand in 1946 to ten per thousand in 1954, although the birth rate remained high. In the third stage, both birth and death rates were low and the population was again slow-growing or stable.

England passed through just such a demographic transition between 1650 and 1900; at the beginning of this period, both birth and death rates hovered around thirty-five per thousand per annum. By 1750 the death rate had fallen to twenty-one per thousand while the birth rate remained at thirty-four per thousand. By 1880 the birth rate had fallen to sixteen per thousand, nearly matching the death rate of twelve per thousand.

How can we explain this demographic transition? When people are poor in an agrarian setting and the death rate is high, children are an economic asset in the struggle to wrest a living from the soil and parents are dependent upon them for security in their old age. Since many children die before reaching a productive age, many must be born to close the gap. When the death rate falls rapidly, as it has in most countries in recent years, rural women, long used to almost annual pregnancy throughout their childbearing years, quickly find themselves with larger families than they had anticipated. Thus, the burgeoning birth rate and annual growth rate in many underdeveloped countries do not necessarily represent a *desire* to have large families; rather, more children are surviving than previously.

As farms are mechanized, fewer hands are needed, so rural people flock into the cities for greater opportunity than farm life provides. Now numerous children become an economic liability, expensive to feed, clothe, and educate; hence fewer are desired and fewer are born. Since farm mechanization and movement to cities reflect increased prosperity and industrialization, the process of development tends to reduce the birth rate.

But the principle of the demographic transition was developed empirically from the western European experience. Since the present situation in the LDCs is not strictly comparable, can the demographic transition principle be used to draw reasonably sound conclusions about the future population of these countries and, collectively, the world? The contrasts between LDCs and the western European developed countries are many.

1. In western Europe mortality declined gradually over two hundred years; in the LDCs the mortality rate has dropped drastically in the thirty years since World War II and today is much lower than it was in the early stages of the Industrial Revolution in Europe.

2. The birth rate of pre-industrial Europe was rarely higher than thirty-five per thousand; in Afghanistan it is greater than fifty per thousand, and in Tanzania and Iran, greater than forty-five per thousand.

3. Throughout the entire demographic transition, European population growth was eased by the departure of millions of emigrants; today emigration is not a possibility for most LDCs.

4. Even at the peak of their population growth western European countries rarely had a population doubling time of less than fifty years; Algeria, the Dominican Republic, and Colombia, which are growing at a rate close to the biological maximum, will double their populations in fifty years.

Counterbalancing these dissimilarities are the more rapid development in the LDCs; modern methods of birth control; government planning; international assistance; and a more rapid rate of fertility decline once measures are taken. All these complicating factors suggest that the demographic transition principle has limited predictive use. A more important factor than the degree of development or urbanization is the social status of the breeding population. If a large proportion of the population of an LDC has access to social and economic amenities such as health service, education, employment, and some form of credit, family planning is much more easily introduced. Countries where social status has been given prime attention—Sri Lanka, Uruguay, Taiwan, South Korea, Cuba, and China—have made the greatest progress in steadily reducing their birth rate.

Even when the birth rate has been significantly reduced by war, disease, or starvation—the "natural" limits—it is still subject to unpredictable fluctuations and even to fashion. By the mid-1930s Germany, France, and England became concerned at the close approach of birth to death rates, and governments, fearing underpopulation for the first time since the Great Plague of the mid-fourteenth century, started to subsidize large families directly and indirectly. At that time one or two children were considered fashionable, and anyone with four or five was often hard pressed to support them and subject to a subtle disapproval by friends and relatives. After World War II the return of social stability led to a jump in the birth rates of most western countries, and families of three or four children again became acceptable. But after a few years the birth rate of most developed countries began to fall again. The United States was the exception for quite a while. As late as 1957 its birth rate was around twenty-five per thousand. With a death rate of nine per thousand, the annual rate of growth [2] was 1.6 percent, greater than that of Italy,

[2] Annual rate of growth = (birth rate − death rate) 10.

Japan, or India at that time. Had the growth rate continued at this level for only 150 years, the population of the United States would have climbed from 150 million to over 3 billion. But fortunately in 1958 the birth rate began to fall (no one is quite sure why), dropping to 14.8 per thousand in 1975. However, it would have to stay at this level for seventy years to result in zero population growth. This is because the number of births depends on both the fertility rates and the number of women in their childbearing years. Since a large number of females have already been born, the population base will continue to grow until this group of females stops having children.

Not until all countries achieve and sustain this low fertility level can world population be stabilized. Unfortunately, at present two thirds of the world is in stages one and two of the demographic transition. Latin America is now the fastest growing region, not because of its higher birth rate but because of its lower death rate (see Table 23.1).

Table 23.1

Some Population Statistics of Selected Countries and Regions (1974)

AREA	POPULATION * (HUNDREDS OF MILLIONS)	RATE OF GROWTH † (PERCENT)	DOUBLING TIME (YEARS)
Europe	410	0.6	116
U.S.A.	210	0.9	77
USSR	250	1.0	70
Asia	2316	2.6	27
Africa	401	2.7	26
Latin America	329	3.0	24

* Data from the National Geographic Society.
† Data from the *United Nations Demographic Yearbook*, 1974.

While the overall growth rate of the world is about 2 percent, there is a great disparity between the developed and relatively stable nations of Europe and the rapidly growing LDCs of South America, Africa, and Asia. At 2 percent growth, 180,000 babies are born every day, adding 65 million to the world's population every year. Projections of the present growth rate beyond the next few years are extremely difficult because of the many factors, almost unmeasurable let alone predictable, that affect the number of children born in any given year.

MOTIVATION AND POPULATION CONTROL

However desirable they may be as national goals, neither population growth nor population decrease can be imposed. People respond not to external coercion but to internal motivation; the most remote goals can be achieved if people are properly motivated. Conversely, government policies can be effectively undermined if motivation is lacking, as Prohibition conclusively demonstrated in the United States two generations ago. Thus, family planning has no hope of success unless people are motivated by moral, economic, legal, or social means.

Family planning is not synonymous with birth control, for birth control is specifically designed to limit the number of births. Since the purpose of family planning is to plan for the size of a family, help is also given to couples who have problems conceiving children. But far more people are desirous of controlling births than eliciting them, and family planning is commonly used as a euphemism for birth control. When questioned, most women express the desire to control the size of their families and not simply to give birth to child after child throughout their childbearing years. To help such women, many underdeveloped countries—India, Pakistan, Turkey, Colombia, Morocco, Kenya, and Jamaica, to name just a few—have set up birth control programs and clinics.

Since the family planning movement dispenses birth control information as well as information to help overcome sterility, there has been much opposition to family planning activities in Roman Catholic countries. While the Catholic Church is still unrelenting, in 1961 the National Council of Churches sanctioned the practice of birth control, removing some of the religious deterrents to a realistic program of population control. Attitudes on birth control are sometimes further complicated by nationalist or political groups who feel that birth control is being applied toward a political or even racist end; some black groups in the United States and Hindus in India have made this charge. But as long as birth control information and devices are made available without coercion to everyone who wants them, such a charge is unwarranted.

Plainly, the social and moral attitudes within our society and throughout the world will have to undergo considerable modification before birth control becomes a way of life for the entire population. At present, young single women are under considerable social pressure to marry and raise a family, despite education or challenging career possibilities. While greater economic and social opportunities have become available to women quite recently, through the activities the women's liberation movement, much more will have to be done in this area if population growth is to be effectively checked. It is no coincidence that in a seventeen-nation sample, the higher the position of women in society, the lower the birth rate.

It has been popularly supposed that in primitive societies, and by implication in our hunting-gathering past, the rigors of the harsh environment and limited food supply necessitated a very high level of fertility merely to break even. However, recent studies of the nearest analog we have to those long-gone times, the !Kung bushmen of southwestern Africa, suggest that the fertility level of our ancestors may have been much lower than is found in most LDCs today. The tasks required of women would not allow them to be unduly incapacitated by caring for many children. Family planning may have been accomplished by nursing children until they were at least five. Since nursing women produce hormones that inhibit ovulation and the life expectancy was around thirty years, there wasn't much time for childbearing.

POPULATION POLICIES

Governments have directly attempted to encourage population growth for years. Governments could, however, discourage population growth by the same means. This might be accomplished by rewarding childless individuals with at least equal, if not lower, tax burdens than parents, hence removing the attractive tax deduction reward for having children. Other proposed schemes involve setting up an inverted tax scale, increasing the tax with every child. Delayed marriage, already beginning to take place as a result of increased educational opportunities and requirements, might be further encouraged by government subsidy. The government of India recently passed a law that raised the minimum marriageable age from 18 to 27 in males and from 15 to 18 in females.

Social pressure, which usually tends to push people into marriage and then into raising families, may at times have a negative effect on population growth. During the Depression the birth rate fell dramatically in most countries and the one- or two-child family became the norm.

Finally, those parents who can financially and emotionally support more than two children should be encouraged to increase the size of their families not by further natural births, but by adoption. Circumstance and accident will always result in parentless children who need love and protection as much as one's own. At the moment the family is the only institution capable of fulfilling the needs of *all* of society's children.

In Europe birth control has varying degrees of official recognition. In the Scandinavian countries and Great Britain it is legal; in France, Belgium, and the Netherlands it is considered semi-legal, that is, a couple may practice birth control for medical reasons. However, in Italy, Portugal, Spain, and Ireland, still predominantly Catholic countries, birth control remains illegal. Neither the United States nor Canada has a national policy on family planning, nor are such plans likely to be developed in the near future. Sweden and Great Britain officially encourage family planning, but most other Western European countries have no defined population policy. France is an exception; it has an active government-sponsored program providing subsidies for larger families, with increasing benefits as the number of children increases. The dissemination of appropriate propaganda also helps the French government to express its approval of larger families. Ironically, France has been plagued by periods of population decline over much of the twentieth century.

Japan presents another type of government policy on family planning. Japan's 110 million people are jammed into a land area about the size of Montana but much more mountainous. As a result there has been societal as well as governmental pressure for a reduced birth rate. This has by and large been accomplished over the last couple of decades. Legalized abortion and widespread use of contraceptives have reduced the birth rate from 34.3 in 1947 to 18.6 in 1974. For years now, small families have been the socially accepted practice in Japan. However, with increasing industrial output the country is experiencing a labor shortage—rather, a shortage of cheap labor, for more and more young people are going on to school and postponing their entry into the labor market. When they do, it isn't as cheap factory labor. As a result, a subtle change in government policy is taking place. Instead of removing the heavy subsidy on rice farming and retraining the farmers released for industrial jobs, a return to larger families has been suggested as the easiest solution to the problem.

This last example is interesting because it illustrates the major problem with population control today. Countries have no coordination of their political and economic policies. When one country experiences a decline in population it does not draw on the population resources of another country; instead, it chooses to view people as a natural resource and to seek to increase the size of this resource. But people are not a natural resource; rather, people consume natural resources. If we have overpopulation in any one country, that country must tap the resources of the countries which are still underpopulated to meet its consumer needs. If we are to have realistic population control we must change the view that population is related to specific political economies.

Most countries drift along until traumatized by some event or sudden realization of where they are headed. Then they begin to involve themselves with some kind of population control program. In Egypt the catalyst seemed to be the realization that during the time it took to build the Aswan High Dam population growth wiped out the expected gains in food production from newly irrigated lands. In Mexico the stimulus was the rapid consumption by population growth of the wheat surplus produced by the green revolution.

In Pakistan, thousands of teams have been dispatched into the countryside to contact all eligible fertile couples and provide encouragement and training in the use of birth control methods. At the same time the countryside is being flooded with cheap contraceptives.

This pattern is becoming more and more common. Nearly two thirds of the world's population lives in countries where some kind of birth control program is underway. In response, the world birth rate is finally falling faster than the death rate, from 34 births per 1000 in 1965 to 30 per 1000 in 1974. This decrease is reflected in the slowing of the world's population growth to 1.6 percent in 1975.

BIRTH CONTROL METHODS

Once the economic and social motivations for smaller families are established, the means of achieving the goal of fewer births can be implemented. Ideally, people should have children only when they want them. This is the essence of family planning. Too many families have children who are unwanted, and often resented as well. The unwanted child often matures into an unwanted adult, maladjusted and a burden to society.

STERILIZATION

The means of avoiding childbirth are many, running the gamut from celibacy to abortion, but the most reliable method is sterilization. The term has an ominous ring to it because of the implied permanence of the operation. Often confused with castration by the uneducated, sterilization of the male simply prevents the release of sperm. This is accomplished in a minor operation, vasectomy, that severs the sperm ducts and can be performed in a few minutes with a local anesthetic. Females can also be sterilized in a simple operation called a laparoscopic tubal ligation, which takes thirty minutes and leaves two small scars that quickly disappear. Sterilization is rapidly becoming one of the most popular forms of contraception in the United States. By 1975 over 8 million men and women had been sterilized.

Sterilization has *no* physiological effect on the sex drive, although if the significance of the operation is not clearly understood, there may indeed be psychological effects on the libido. Studies of Japanese couples in which the male was sterilized showed that in only 3.5 percent of the couples was the frequency of sex reduced; in contrast, 28.5 percent reported an increase, probably due to the release from anxiety over possible conception. The major drawback of sterilization is its implied permanence and the hesitation of many doctors in the United States to sterilize because of the everpresent threat of lawsuits from patients who have changed their minds.

A way around this problem that has already been used is the deposition of a supply of sperm in a sperm bank by a husband before steriliza-

547

tion. Then, should conception be desired at some time in the future, the sperm can be withdrawn from the deep freeze and used to inseminate the wife artificially, unless of course she has already been sterilized. In this case adoption would be in order.

In India, sterilization is encouraged by cash incentives, and over 4 million people, mostly males, have been sterilized in the past ten years. With the possibility of new techniques for temporary sterilization, such as blocking rather than severing the fallopian tubes or sperm ducts, this contraceptive technique may become as accepted in developed countries as it is in some underdeveloped ones.

Of all the modern contraceptive techniques available, the rhythm method, although widely practiced, is the least effective. This is most unfortunate since it is one of the few contraceptive techniques endorsed by religious bodies otherwise opposed to contraception, notably the Catholic Church.

In theory, if a woman knows when she has ovulated and does not have intercourse until the egg has left her body, conception can be avoided. Unfortunately most women are not aware of when they ovulate, although by monitoring of vaginal temperature and glucose levels the time can sometimes, but not always, be pinpointed. To make things worse, at least one sixth of all women in their reproductive years have irregular periods that make calendar watching useless. Then too, the rhythm of a period can be upset by tension, anxiety, and illness. Finally, expecting an uneducated and unsophisticated person to avoid conception by using the rhythm method is not so much ingenuous as it is cynical.

MECHANICAL METHODS

There are many mechanical contraceptive devices available, for example, the condom, the diaphragm, and the IUD (intrauterine device). IUDs are made of stainless steel or nonreactive plastic and may be just about any shape (Figure 23.1).

When an IUD is inserted into the uterus it serves as a mild irritant which interferes with the implantation of a fertilized egg into the uterine wall that is necessary to begin embryonic development. While this irritation is tolerated by most women, some 30 percent are made uncomfortable or bleed, necessitating removal of the IUD. Another 10 percent eject them spontaneously. A second generation IUD, T-shaped and copper, has reduced side effects to less than 1 percent. IUDs made of copper seem to be the most effective. Apparently some of the copper dissolves, is absorbed, and serves to attract leucocytes or white blood cells, which in some way interfere with survival or development of the freshly fertilized egg. The great value of this device for those women who are receptive to it is that once inserted by a physician it can protect

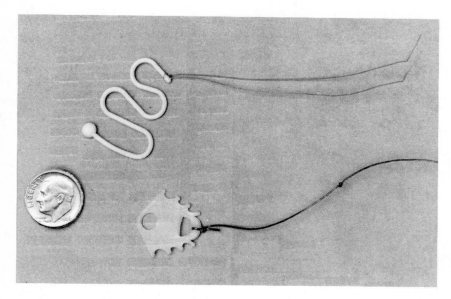

Fig. 23.1 These are a few of the great variety of intrauterine devices that have been used.

against conception indefinitely. Generally after two years, 55 to 60 percent of the women fitted with IUDs are still successfully wearing the device. The remainder must use alternative methods. Because of problems with expulsion, pain, and bleeding, IUDs have not been very successful in most LDCs.

CHEMICAL METHODS

The first contraceptive pill, marketed in 1959, contained two hormones, a progesterone and an estrogen, which prevented ovulation. However, the estrogen mimicked some of the effects of pregnancy: nausea, bleeding, weight gain, and nervousness, and more seriously, the tendency of the blood of pregnant women to form blood clots. The incidence of deaths from this side effect is low—3 per 100,000 users—much lower than the death rate from normal pregnancies.

Unfortunately the possibility of side effects was not thoroughly explored at the time the pill was introduced. So when Senate hearings in late 1969 publicized some of the problems of contraceptive pills, many women gave up the pill in panic, without being made aware of the odds, which as far as side effects are concerned, favor the pill over normal pregnancy. Still, millions of American women are taking the pill with close to 100 percent effectiveness when the sequence is closely followed. The real problem with the pill is its cost, which, unless subsidized, makes it available only to the higher income groups. Another problem interfering with its use in underdeveloped countries is the irregular pattern of intake that is required.

549

A second generation of chemical contraceptives is being researched and will probably be available in a few years. By enclosing a prescribed dose of progesterone in a permeable plastic ring which can be inserted in the vagina much like a diaphragm, a small but steady dose of hormone can be absorbed. Progesterone alone seems to have an effect on the sperm, making it unable to fertilize the egg. Further, progesterone, unlike estrogen, does not prevent ovulation. The ring lasts for three weeks and is replaced after menstruation if contraception is to be continued. Another approach is to impregnate with progesterone a small piece of plastic, perhaps the size of a pencil lead, then insert it just under the skin. Theoretically such an insert could regularly meter out the prescribed dose of progesterone over a year or perhaps even the reproductive life span of a woman. If pregnancy were desired, the implant could be easily removed and conception could take place on the next cycle.

Another group of compounds, the prostaglandins, have some promise of providing agents that can produce labor, induce abortion, and cause contraception after fertilization, the long sought "morning after" pill. Prostaglandins, normally found in very small quantities in cells throughout the body, seem to act as enhancers or suppressors of hormones. However, they are not themselves hormones.

A somewhat more distant prospect of drug control over contraception is provided by a hormone awkwardly called luteinizing hormone-releasing hormone/follicle-stimulating hormone-releasing hormone (LH-RH/FSH-RH). Its function is fortunately simpler than its name: it controls the synthesis and release of luteinizing and follicle-stimulating hormones produced by the pituitary gland. These two hormones then cause the ovaries and testes to secrete their respective sex hormones. LH-RH/FSH-RH could be used to disrupt the normal menstrual cycle and prevent ovulation; the pituitary gland might be prevented from releasing LH and FSH, thus preventing ovulation; if LH-RH/FSH-RH can be neutralized then it might be possible to immunize women for several months; ovulation might be induced in the middle of the menstrual cycle, allowing for intercourse without danger of pregnancy during the rest of the cycle.

Lest women feel that they are forever to bear the brunt of contraceptive application and potential side effects, the possibility of male contraceptives is becoming more feasible. Apparently antigens exist in sperm and testes that can cause antibodies to form in the female, interfering with reproductive processes. An enzyme, lactate dehydrogenase (LDH-X), has been isolated that might be injected into a male whose body would produce antibodies to the enzyme, thereby interfering with sperm production. Another possibility is the ability of 5-thio-D-glucose to interfere with the glucose metabolism that enables the testes to produce sperm. While male contraceptives are clearly possible, it may well be at least a decade before any one of these possibilities is worked out.

While new oral or implanted chemical contraceptives look promising, an eight-year testing period is required by the FDA to anticipate possible side effects. This is done to protect the public, as is the FDA's charge, but every drug, including aspirin, has side effects. Considering that during an eight- to ten-year development-testing program some underdeveloped countries are well on the way to doubling their population, this is a long time to wait. Many women are far better off taking the pill than running the risk of complications in pregnancy, or worse yet, being unable to sustain the life they have created.

The effectiveness of four of the major contraceptive techniques is listed in Table 23.2, which will allow you to take your own measure of the risk of pregnancy..

Table 23.2

Comparative Effectiveness of Various Contraceptives*

METHOD	PREGNANCIES PER MILLION USERS
pill	5,000
IUD	30,000
diaphragm	120,000
rhythm	240,000

* Djerassi, C., 1969. "Prognosis for the development of new chemical birth control methods." *Science* 166:468–473.

THE ABORTION QUESTION

Abortion has been practiced for centuries, despite censure on religious, moral, and legal grounds. The widespread practice of abortion to terminate unwanted pregnancies has recently been brought more forcefully to the attention of governments, since abortion rates are particularly high in those countries where birth control is illegal. In Italy, for example, there is probably one abortion for every live birth and in Santiago, Chile, 40 percent of all hospital admissions involve abortion attempts. Where contraceptives fail, abortion should be considered as a method of birth control, but its legitimacy or acceptance is a far more complicated question.

Biologically, egg and sperm cells are neither more nor less "human" than any other cell in our bodies. Hence it makes little biological difference whether an egg and sperm are killed by their failure to be united or shortly after their union by removal from the body naturally or artificially. The question arises then, at what point does this fertilized egg become human? Medically and legally, humanity is recognized after five months. Should an embryo die before this point it is regarded merely as tissue and disposed of like an excised gall bladder or tonsil. After five months the embryo becomes a fetus, and under common law it has a legal identity. Should a natural abortion or stillbirth take place after this point the body is buried and the woman is regarded as having given birth.

Since most induced abortions are performed within the first three months of pregnancy, a good two months before the law formally recognizes civil identity, there should be no legal interest in such abortions. This has not been the case, however, and the reason is historical. In the last century, when most anti-abortion statutes were written, abortions performed at any time by anyone were dangerous. This was a time when surgery was quite risky because of the almost total lack of sanitation in the operating room. Abortions were regarded as fifteen times more dangerous than natural childbirth. To protect women from this risk, abortions were declared illegal with almost no exceptions.

Today an abortion performed by a physician during the first trimester (pregnany is usually divided into three periods of three months) is quite safe, involving only one eighth of the danger of complications associated with live birth, with no risk of subsequent sterility.

In recognition of this change in the medical status of abortion, anti-abortion laws have been under attack in the courts on the basis that the right to choose abortion should reside with the woman who, after all, must bear the responsibility for her actions. Medically and legally, there is no reason why a woman should not have an abortion in her first trimester of pregnancy if she so desires.

In response to this pressure the United States Supreme Court in 1973 handed down a decision that makes unconstitutional state laws forbidding abortion during the first trimester. As a result of this decision, abortion laws are presently in a state of flux in the United States. Most of the countries of western and southern Europe and South America still have restrictive abortion laws. India is considering the legalization of abortion as Japan did just after World War II. Apparently shocked by the huge increase in abortions that followed liberalization, the Japanese government subsequently embarked on a massive program to encourage the use of contraceptives and is even considering reinstating controls on abortion. Similar public reactions are seen in other areas after abortion laws have been relaxed. But much of the increase in abortion simply reflects the shift from furtive, unreported abortions often resulting in in-

jury or death, to hospital- or doctor-supervised abortions that are reported as a routine statistic along with chicken pox or measles. In the
United States, for example, there used to be at least 1 million illegal
abortions per year. Now that abortion has been legalized nationally, these
formerly illegal abortions will doubtless be viewed by outraged moralists
as a "rising tide of immorality." Forgotten will be the millions of abortions which have always taken place, legally or illegally.

The chief opponents of legalized abortion through the years have
been religious bodies, particularly the Roman Catholic Church. The
Church has maintained, not as dogma but as current teaching, that
the soul is present from the moment of conception and that any unnatural interference with its progression through to birth is a sin. This concept is called immediate animation. But the Church's view on the matter
has not always been so; no less an authority than St. Thomas Aquinas
held that the soul developed gradually as the embryo slowly became
human, a view congruent with contemporary legal opinion. But after the
death of St. Thomas this mediate animation concept fell out of favor, although it has never been eliminated as an option. It is quite possible
that in future years the Church may again alter its position in view of the
seriousness of overpopulation and its threat to *all* of our institutions.

What then of the role of abortion as a form of birth control? Despite
its present ease and increasing legality, no one would seriously recommend abortion in place of one of the contraceptives previously discussed.
It is far more desirable to prevent a conception than to terminate one.
Yet an unwanted pregnancy is often a traumatic experience even if resolved by abortion. Abortions can perform a valuable service to society by
allowing those women who are least fit physically, emotionally, and financially to avoid the birth of an unwanted child. The ultimate social and
moral cost to a society that tolerates the production of unwanted children is surely far greater than any circumstances surrounding an abortion.

FUTURE POPULATION

If the world makes no effort to control population there will be 6 billion people in the year 2000. Two billion more people can probably be
accommodated on earth, but adding 4 billion more staggers the imagination, for the earth is barely able to support its present population; indeed most people live at a subsistence level far below the embarrassing
affluence of western Europe and North America. When you consider
that Americans, who account for 6 percent of the world's population,
are absorbing a disproportionate amount of the world's raw materials to
maintain their affluent standard of living, it is not surprising that the
LDCs have thought it hypocritical for us to urge them to control their

populations while developed nations continue to grow, albeit more slowly, and use still more of the world's resources. Our insistence upon pollution control is also misinterpreted by nations just beginning to industrialize. LDCs should not be denied the benefits of technology simply because of the problems it has generated. Just as developed nations have shared their medical and food production expertise, they can also share the birth and pollution control technology they have gained through the hard experience of overpopulation and badly polluted environments. LDCs could then, be spared the ill effects of development by careful planning while enjoying the benefits of the rising standard of living that development allows.

If the population of the world were frozen at its present level there might be some hope that technology could in the next several decades begin to feed and house the world's population adequately and perhaps even begin to close the yawning gap between the few who have and the many who do not. But any increase in population beyond present numbers, 1 or even 2 percent, so widens the affluence gap as to make it virtually impossible for the average Asian or African *ever* to have the good life which we as Americans now consider our inalienable right. A reduction in the growth rate is not enough. Population growth must cease altogether, not just for India, China, Egypt, or Jamaica, but for the United States, the U.S.S.R., New Zealand, and Denmark. For it is not the Indian, Chinese, or Egyptian peasant who is making unprecedented demands on world resources, generating sonic booms, or releasing radioactive wastes; it is the middle class of the world. Caught up in a cycle of more-demanding-more, *they* must bear the responsibility for much of the world's pollution and share the responsibility for the population control that must come.

Short of mass starvation, is there any hope of halting the population explosion? Lester Brown of the Overseas Development Council presents a scenario he feels is possible. Four developed countries have already achieved population stability: West Germany, East Germany, Austria, and Luxembourg. In fact the population of the two Germanies declined by over 100,000 in 1975. Other countries—Belgium, the United Kingdom, Sweden, Finland, Hungary, and the United States—have such low and still declining birth rates that population stability could be achieved by 1980. A number of LDCs have managed to sustain a decline in birth rate of 1 birth per 1000 per year—Barbados, Taiwan, Mauritius, Hong Kong, Tunisia, Singapore, Costa Rica, Egypt, Chile, and South Korea. Brown proposes a goal of 25 births per 1000 for all LDCs by 1985. From 1985 to 2005 this rate would remain stable until the bulge of people in their childbearing years had had their children. Then the rate would drop rapidly until by 2015 the earth's population could be stabilized at about 6 billion. Naïve dream or realizable hope? Much depends on the success of the LDCs in reducing their birth rates to at least 25 per 1000 in the next decade.

FURTHER READING

Black, F. L., 1975. "Infectious disease in primitive societies." *Science* **187,** pp. 515–518. Infectious disease may be one of the results of civilization.

Blake, J., 1971. "Reproductive motivation and population policy." *BioSci.* **21**(5), pp. 215–220. Explores some of the problems of achieving zero population growth.

Brown, L. R., 1974. *In the human interest.* W. W. Norton, New York. A broad view of the population problem.

Callahan, D., 1972. "Ethics and population limitation." *Science* **175,** pp. 487–494. A far-ranging discussion of the ethics involved in population control.

Dumond, D. E., 1975. "The limitation of human population: a natural history." *Science* **187,** pp. 713–721. The impact of urbanization on population growth.

Maugh, T. H., II, 1974. "5-Thio-D-Glucose: a unique male contraceptive." *Science* **186,** p. 431. A new *male* contraceptive in the works?

Nortman, D., 1974. "Quantity vs. quality of life." *Bull. Atomic Scient.* June, pp. 13–16.

CHAPTER
TWENTY-FOUR

ALTERNATIVES

ALL THE ENVIRONMENTAL PROBLEMS we have discussed are rooted in the growth of a human population that steadily demands more raw materials and produces more wastes. We have now reached the point where the ability of natural environments to provide the former and absorb the latter is beginning to break down. It is tempting to theorize that checking or even reducing the rate of population growth will automatically solve our environmental problems. However it is not simply the numbers of people that degrade the environment; their attitudes, affluence, and rates of consumption are of critical importance too.

Compare, for example, an American town of 10,000 with a Chinese village of the same population. The village, relatively self-sufficient, has its maximum environmental impact in the immediate vicinity, polluting the local water- and airsheds perhaps, eroding its farm lands, and deforesting the local hills. The American town, on the other hand, with its enormous demands for energy, transportation, and material goods, affects environments all over a world which daily provides for its needs—for instance, iron ore from western Australia, aluminum ore from Guyana, tropical hardwoods from Malaysia, fuel oil from Kuwait. Some of the resources are renewable, more are not, but the recovery of them all has a negative effect on the environment.

Until recently economic growth has been regarded as synonymous with progress and has been eagerly solicited. Not so long ago growth advocates in Rhode Island (whose state mascot is the plucky Rhode Island Red hen) proudly called themselves "rooster boosters." In many parts of the country however, the booster's crow is being challenged by the worried clucking of environmentalists and economists, who are beginning to question the assumed relationship between all-out growth and prosperity. Although the concept of zero population growth has gained considerable acceptance, the idea of zero economic growth has generated an international brouhaha.

Economic growth is usually defined by economists as a per capita rise in the real net national product; that is, the sum, adjusted for price changes, of all consumer, business, and government expenditures on goods and services including investment in new capital ventures. Shorn of its jargon, economic growth simply means *more*. More people to buy more cars that need more roads whose construction requires more workers who need more houses, more schools, more services—and so *ad infinitum*. With every link 'in this chain there is an opportunity to sell either goods or services and thereby increase income, status, or both. Most of the great fortunes made in the United States in the last 200 years arose from the application of hard work to an opportunity afforded by economic growth. Many believe the opportunity still exists.

Traditionally, economic growth has depended on population growth to provide its new consumers. Obviously if zero population growth is vigorously pursued, those new consumers will no longer be produced and some economic adjustment will have to be made. The ultimate adjustment is no-growth. This means that the production of goods and services would have to be controlled so that both over- and underproduction would be discouraged. Prices and incomes would be stabilized and "opportunities" would become more limited. In short, the doctrine of *more* would be replaced by *no more*.

Although a thorough discussion of economic growth and no-growth is far beyond the scope of this book, the basic arguments for growth and nongrowth can be briefly summarized before looking at alternatives.

THE CASE FOR ECONOMIC GROWTH

Many economists believe that, as a practical matter, only continued economic growth can bring about a redistribution of wealth, higher living standards, increased employment, and an expansion of government-supplied social services, while maintaining a relatively open and free market. Let's examine each of these growth benefits more closely.

REDISTRIBUTION OF WEALTH

Although this has gone slowly, proponents of growth maintain that redistribution of wealth can only come about by adding more wealth to the entire system so that both poor and rich as well benefit. This is possible only in a growth economy; in a no-growth society the poor could gain wealth only at the expense of the rich, who are not likely to yield their wealth gracefully.

HIGHER LIVING STANDARDS

In 1960 the median family income was $5260. By 1970 it had almost doubled to $9820. Income among blacks has soared from $7.9 billion in 1948 to $46 billion in 1971. Clearly the period of rapid economic growth which characterized the late 1950s and early 1960s had much to do with this impressive increase in the American standard of living. In 1975 the official poverty line was $5500 a year for an urban family consisting of a working man of 38, his nonworking wife, their fifteen-year-old son, and eight-year-old daughter. This income represents a 73 percent increase since 1950. At this rate another twenty years of growth would raise the annual income of this family to almost $8712 without government subsidy.

INCREASED EMPLOYMENT

The only chance for a last-hired, first-fired ghetto black or an Arkansas farmboy just off the bus in Chicago to pull down the brass ring of the middle class is to get a job. Jobs are already scarce for college graduates let alone high school dropouts. Continued or even stimulated economic growth is the only way employment can be provided for all these people.

EXPANSION OF SOCIAL SERVICES

Presently much of the cost of environmental protection and the vast state and federal welfare programs comes from the annual increase in taxes generated by a growing economy. Since a no-growth economy would mean a constant tax base, new government programs would have to compete with established programs for funding.

FREE MARKET

The major beneficiary of a relatively free market for goods and services is the consumer who has at times an almost bewildering variety of choices. Close supervision of the economy to limit over- and underproduction would fix the composition of the goods and services market and inevitably lead to a deterioration in their quality and a sharp reduction in the spectrum of choices now available.

The classic economists from Adam Smith to John Stuart Mill, while espousing economic growth as at least a palliative for the ills of human-kind, theorized that economic growth and decline were but phases preceding an ultimate steady-state or no-growth economy. However, the no-growth steady state seems rather elusive since the theory makes no provision for technological change. Thus the 200 years of increasing pollution and environmental destruction that have accompanied economic growth have led some economists to suggest that we cannot wait for ultimate states, we must take the bull by the horns and create a no-growth economy in the here and now.

Without question, pollution has been the handmaiden of growth; it is what economists call an external diseconomy, a cost that is imposed on the general public but is not charged for. Besides pollution of water and air, other external diseconomies include noise, congestion, increased stress through crowding. The automobile, whose production has become a mainstay of our economy, is a prime example of a product whose external diseconomies are borne by everyone.

But the indictment of growth involves more than a growing distaste for pollution and the pressures of development. The quality of life itself has been seriously eroded, values such as privacy, serenity, concern for others have been damaged and even lost. Many of these disturbing aspects of contemporary life have been associated with growth, just as the ills of previous generations have been associated with big government, big business, or the Church.

We are the only species that is out of balance with our environment. The relationship of all other species to their environments is dynamic, but over the long run, steady state. Obviously no species, ours included, can indefinitely postpone the ultimate crunch when our needs can no longer be provided by earth's environment. The longer we postpone putting our house [1] in order the sooner and more devestating the final collapse.

While many people believe that the increase in pollution and decrease in the quality of life, assuming they can be directly tied to growth, are worth enduring for the benefits of growth discussed above, no-growth proponents feel that growth as a solver of social and political problems has been overrated and oversold. Let's review the list of supposed benefits provided by growth—redistribution of wealth, higher living standards, increased employment, expansion of social services, and a free market—from the point of view of the no-growth advocate.

[1] The root of the term *ecology* comes from the Greek *oikos* meaning house.

REDISTRIBUTION OF WEALTH

Since the eighteenth century, economic growth has been touted as the natural course of capitalism and the source of profit to all those fortunate enough to have a finger in the pie. While the pie contains far more fingers today than it did 200 years ago (in 1774 only 10 percent of the taxpayers owned 89 percent of Philadelphia's taxable property), most Americans still do not profit directly from growth. Less than 2 percent of the population owns 82 percent of all stocks, 38 percent of all federal bonds, and 29 percent of all cash. And in spite of greatly increased federal interference with the traditions of a *laissez-faire* economy and what the property-owning minority regards as confiscatory taxation, the 10 percent of the population who in 1910 received a third of all income continues to do so today. To be sure, income in the United States doubled between 1930 and 1970 but so did prices, the magnitude of social problems, and the cost of our attempts to solve them. If wealth is to be redistributed it will be by a higher tax on capital gains, limits on charitable deductions, and an increase in inheritance taxes.

HIGHER LIVING STANDARDS

While the median family income did indeed rise from $5260 in 1960 to $9820 in 1970, the proportion of families earning half of this median dropped only 1 percent, from 20 percent to 19 percent. Indeed some economists project that by 1990, although the number of families living in poverty will fall from 5 to 2.5 million, the number of unrelated individuals living in poverty will stay at 5 million. At the same time income among blacks rose from $7.9 to $46 billion, the income among whites soared from $146.2 to $649 billion increasing the income disparity from $138.3 billion in 1948 to $603 billion in 1971. In more personal terms, the gap between white and black median family income in the same period doubled from $2174 in 1947 to $4270 in 1971.

More general and pervasive because they effect everyone, are the hidden costs of growth. While the environmental price of growth is becoming obvious, its social and economic costs are rarely so clear. As a town grows, its growing population's need for housing increases land values. Single-family houses are divided into small apartments; these are torn down to make way for multiunit buildings; and these are replaced in turn by high-rise apartment buildings (Figure 24.1). As population density increases, store rents increase, raising prices of food and merchandise. Congestion and pollution increase, the pulse of life quickens, and stress is compounded. To escape the high costs in the urban centers many flee to the suburbs, trading off the cost of commuting for the lower population density that means lower rents. And the cycle begins anew.

Fig. 24.1 *(a) The inevitable cycle of urban growth begins with fine old single-family homes often built in another century. (b) These are subdivided into many small apartments. (c) Small apartment buildings are the next step. (d) Finally high-rise apartments cover whole blocks.*

A study of standard metropolitan statistical areas (SMSAs) estimates that wages increase by 9 percent per order of population magnitude (a city of 10 million has on the average 9 percent higher wages than a city of 1 million), taxes increase still faster, and the cost of living grows by 4.5 percent per order of magnitude. The tax expenditure per capita for governing New York City is $892; for SMSAs down to 250,000 it ranges down to $353 per capita; 100,000 to 250,000, $275; 50,000 to 100,000, $246; and 25,000 to 50,000, $233. The cost of services in relation to population is even more disparate.

Statistics such as these lead to questions about the economic and social advantages of growth. Cities like Petaluma and Ramapo (see Chapter 12) are wondering how much growth they can afford. States have seen the dangers too. Oregon is no longer heralding the wonderful life in the Northwest lest too many newcomers make life less wonderful. Even Florida is debating how many winter-weary sunbathers it wants to welcome.

INCREASED EMPLOYMENT

A development effort in Puerto Rico following World War II suggests that economic growth and employment do not necessarily go hand in hand. Operation Bootstrap was planned to transform a poor, agrarian, overpopulated, and underdeveloped tropical island into a modern, industrial society whose development would offer an alternative to trading rural poverty in Puerto Rico for urban poverty in Miami or New York. With the inducements of tax exemption, cheap and abundant, if unskilled, labor, and free access to United States markets, labor-intensive industry—textiles and electronics especially—established plants in Puerto Rico. By 1955 the net income from manufacturing had surpassed that from agriculture for the first time.

That same year the first refinery opened using the then-cheap oil from Venezuela to provide a relatively inexpensive energy source for the island. In the succeeding years petrochemical and other energy-intensive industries began to replace labor-intensive industries in Puerto Rico. Today the oil industry employs only 1 percent of the total Puerto Rican labor force and provides only 5 percent of the total island income, but it consumes 35 percent of the island's available energy and massively pollutes the air, the water table, and the rather fragile tropical marine ecosystem that characterizes Puerto Rico's south coast. Even worse, 95 percent of the raw materials generated by the petrochemical plants are exported to the mainland, where they are processed into various products. Thus 21 percent of the energy consumed in Puerto Rico contributes to the growth somewhere else of the labor-intensive industries the island desperately needs,

562

while environmental costs are locally borne. Proponents of zero economic growth claim that the Puerto Rican example is not unique.

The relationship between growth and employment is complicated even more by a fluctuating birth rate. In 1915 the birth rate in the United States reached an all-time high and then began to decline. Twenty years later this population bulge entered the labor market in the middle of what might have been just another periodic economic fluctuation. But the presence of an extra few million unemployed exacerbated the situation and prolonged the Great Depression until World War II came to the rescue. The pattern is being repeated now that the postwar population boom that peaked in 1957 is beginning to deliver job seekers into a goods-saturated market. The economy must provide 1.4 million new jobs a year just to keep unemployment at 6 percent; if unemployment is to be reduced to 4 percent, then 2.6 million new jobs plus the annual increment of 1.4 million must be found. Traditional heavy industry is not apt to absorb many of these unemployed since only three-fourths of present industrial capacity is being used. Furthermore, since labor accounts for 75 percent of the cost of most products, many industries are automating as rapidly as technology will allow. Between 1950 and 1968 the oil industry doubled its production with 10 percent fewer workers. In sum, growth cannot be relied on to solve the unemployment problem.

EXPANSION OF SOCIAL SERVICES

Taxes on growth-related enterprises and increased personal income are not the only sources of more tax revenues in our economy. If the costs to the government of federal subsidies to business, tax loopholes for corporations, and overcharges by monopolies, for instance, were eliminated there would be more than enough saved (at least $300 billion per year according to some estimates) to address pollution abatement and federal poverty programs.

FREE MARKET

A free market basket filled with a plethora of goods for everyone has another aspect glossed over by growth enthusiasts. The market today tends to be saturated with goods or services of questionable social need while more basic needs go unanswered. One symptom of market saturation is the underused industrial capacity of the United States; another is the stampede of business firms to conglomerate and thereby avoid overdependence on a single, glutted market.

The aircraft industry perhaps best illustrates some of the complex interactions between private enterprise, government, a saturated market,

WE THE PEOPLE:
PROBLEM AND
SOLUTION

and growth. Until the mid-1960s, 700,000 workers were directly employed in the aircraft industry; another 400,000 worked in related areas—for airlines, in airports, for travel services. For some years sale of United-States-produced aircraft constituted 5 percent of all United States trade abroad. Buoyed by an apparently steady 10 percent annual growth in the demand for travel, airplane capacity was expanded enthusiastically; Boeing's 707 was rushed into obsolescence by the enormous 747. But as plane occupancy began to slide below the break-even level of 47 percent, the profits of United States airlines ($428 million in 1966) became a loss of $175 million in 1970. How can an airline make a profit with less than half the seats filled? The answer is, in part, the noncash depreciation expense which enables airlines to continue to survive or even thrive (while showing losses.) Furthermore, the Civil Aeronautics Board set fares on main trunk routes at artificially high levels. Its rules allowed many airlines to compete for these highly profitable routes but until very recently didn't allow them to price their services competitively. So airlines competed by offering bigger, new planes that wasted both fuel and material and carried few people.

Despite the weak economic picture in the early 1970s, cities continued (and some still continue) to expand their airports on the basis of the optomistic projection of 10 percent growth per year (Figure 24.2). Sacramento was quite interested in 1973 in enlarging its airport capacity 38 times to allow 500,000 takeoffs and landings a year rather than the 13,000

Fig. 24.2 Despite the rather meager demand for seats and overcapacity provided by huge new jets, airports continue to expand.

the airport routinely handled. In this same period of decreasing loads and rising airline deficits, New York was desperately looking for a site for a fourth jetport and Miami was hoped to develop a giant airfield in the middle of the Everglades. The Dallas-Fort Worth area has found itself saddled with a huge new airfield that has failed to meet initial expectations of its ability to lure new business to the area.

The problems of decreasing loads were shared by the airplane manufacturers. Research and development of new aircraft is extremely expensive and the finished product even more so. Consequently a large number, usually several hundred, must be sold just to break even. In 1971, Lockheed found itself unable to cover its expenses and asked the government to back loans to it to avoid bankruptcy. The government acceded to prevent losing a prime defense contractor, to preserve many thousands of jobs in the industry, and to stem related loss of jobs in associated industries.

THE DILEMMA

After examining the arguments for and against growth, a number of thought-provoking questions remain. Before we decide that the dilemma of whether to grow or not to grow is insoluble, we need to examine the space between the two camps.

1. Is unemployment an unfortunate by-product of growth that will one day be eliminated or is it woven into the socioeconomic fabric of our ever-changing society by labor unions that are unwilling to make acquisition of the credentials of skilled labor available to all, and by businessmen unable or unwilling to employ minorities? We should keep in mind that since the cost of labor is already high in the United States a large pool of unemployed serves industry by acting as a brake on rising labor costs. If laborers were in short supply and industries had to compete for them, labor costs would soar. On the other hand, union-supported increases in minimum wage rates act to protect high-priced union workers from the competition of the low-skilled unemployed and allow unions to seek constantly higher wage rates for their members. In either case, while pro-growth defenders publicly bemoan the spiraling cost of social welfare—especially payments to the unemployed, some no-growth supporters cynically view welfare costs as a pacifier to inhibit the organization of the presently impotent unemployed into a potent political force. As such, present welfare costs would be a bargain.
2. Do supporters of no-growth adequately consider the needs of the minorities and their employment? As it happens, the industries that

565

would be first hit by stringent controls on growth—automobile, chemical, primary metal production and fabrication, and nonelectrical machinery—are those which offer minorities, particularly blacks, their greatest employment opportunities.

3. Are the Cassandras in the no-growth camp overstating their case? *The Limits to Growth*,[2] a study sponsored by the Club of Rome, concluded that "if the present growth trends in world population, industrialization, pollution, food production, and resource depletion continue unchanged, the limits to growth on this planet will be reached sometime within the next one hundred years." But every model, simple or complex, requires a series of assumptions. The Doomsday Models, as they are called, assume a fixed supply of resources and no technological change, assumptions that contradict past experience. If anything has characterized the spectacular growth of the gross national product in the United States during the past 50 years it has been constant and innovative technological change. Of course, until very recently many changes had unforeseen and unfortunate environmental consequences, but we cannot blame technology for these mistakes.

   The no-growth school's assumption of a fixed and constantly diminishing supply of raw materials ignores the possible discovery of new supplies, more efficient use of existing materials through better technology, the substitution of more available materials through better technology, and the substitution of more readily available materials for scarce ones (e.g., aluminum wire for copper wire). Perhaps most important, the no-growth view overlooks the tendency of sharply increased prices for rare materials to stimulate location of more supplies, more economical use, or the search for substitutes.

4. Is there a basic incompatibility between the concern for the quality of life preferred by no-growth advocates and the massive intervention of government into our lives that checking growth would entail? A no-growth economy would have to be even more carefully planned and controlled than those in Eastern Europe. Government intervention has already made running a business onerous enough with endless paperwork without more red tape that further control would elicit.

5. Although there have been many projections of the consequences of continued growth (*The Limits to Growth* is only one example) have the ultimate consequences of no-growth been as carefully considered? If, for example, we back off from the high technology of synthetic fibers which are very consumptive of energy and petrochemicals, what happens? The production of the alternative natural fibers—cotton and wool—is not without its own set of problems. Cotton is a nutrient-demanding plant which, under today's cultural techniques, also re-

[2] D. Meadows et al. 1972. *The limits to growth.* Universe Books, New York.

quires vast quantities of biocides to deliver its fiber (see Chapter 5).
Sheep, as traditionally raised, have by overgrazing caused extensive
erosion or even ruin of large areas of grassland all over the world (see
Chapter 3).

6. Are economists, many of whom are professionally committed to the
furtherance of economic growth, the best arbiters of whether it is ad-
visable or not? Human society is only one of many interlocking systems
which contribute to the total environment of our planet. Perhaps ecologists with a broader perspective of the role that the increase in human
welfare plays in the total environment can better judge the impact
and worth of economic growth.

ALTERNATIVES

Fortunately we are not faced with an absolute choice between business
as usual or a wrenching change in our society. Redirection of economic
growth is certainly a viable alternative. The EPA estimates that for every
billion dollars spent to clean up water pollution, 25,000 jobs will be created. New York State, which passed a $2.7 billion environmental public
works program to clean up the state's waterways, figured that at least
150,000 jobs lasting six months or more would be created as a result.
Similarly, given the incentive, Detroit could concentrate on producing
mass transit equipment instead of trying to sell a million more cars than
last year, thereby contributing to the problem instead of the solution.

Unemployment and production could be eased by lowering the work
week from 40 to 30 hours, giving more people the opportunity to work
less. However, if workers are not to take a pay cut, then employers must
pass on the costs of extra employment by increasing prices. (Is it better,
socially, to pay more for products and thereby reduce unemployment, or
to pay more taxes to support more unemployed?)

SERVICE INDUSTRIES

We might also shift employment from the production of goods to the
development of services. Maybe we have enough electric can openers and
transistor radios and not nearly enough child-care centers; medical, social,
and educational paraprofessionals; social programs for adolescents; retraining centers for dropouts and unskilled unemployed; facilities for the
aged. How can we pay for these programs? The late Indochinese involvement cost the United States several hundred billion dollars over a ten-year
period without significant benefit to the American taxpayer, yet we are
not starving in the streets as a result. Closer to home are the billions now
being spent on welfare programs. Most of this money has produced only

taxpayer resentment and loss of self-respect among welfare recipients, who cannot find jobs.

Suppose instead that some of the welfare money were used to train those presently receiving aid to staff these badly needed service programs. For example, welfare mothers in ghetto neighborhoods might be trained and given financial assistance to set up day-care centers; or they might be trained to assist in the public schools as paraprofessional teachers. Long after their children had grown up they would have marketable skills.

JOB INVOLVEMENT

It is often claimed that no one on welfare is going to work if he doesn't have to. There is evidence, however, that the problem may be the kind of work available. Welfare recipients do not prefer unemployment to employment; they may prefer unemployment to the mindless, dehumanizing work available to them.

In 1972 workers on one of the most highly automated production lines in the automobile industry went out on strike—not for higher wages, but for a more interesting approach to their work, the so-called Swedish method. This technique makes a team responsible for an entire vehicle; the workers follow it down the line, endlessly varying their tasks rather than endlessly repeating them. In England several years ago the tasks of two tobacco workers were simply alternated. One woman weighed and cut tobacco while another wrapped. When the jobs were switched twice during the shift, productivity went up almost 14 percent and the workers were pleased with even this modest relief from the tedium of the job. But employers, perhaps conditioned by fifty years of demands for more pay, often refuse to recognize this need; to them, all workers want is more money.

De-emphasizing jobs that consist of routine mechanical procedures easily converted to automation in favor of jobs in the service area would put some pride and pleasure back into work. Of course the service sector can only employ so many people. A retreat from the huge economy-of-scale industries in which workers perform as anonymous automatons might be another answer. In all these approaches, the basic need is to give workers some independence, responsibility, and dignity. E. F. Schumacher, formerly a staff economist on the British Coal Board, has some suggestions for the less developed countries of the third world that apply as well to the urban and rural unemployed of the United States:

1. Realize that it is far more important for everyone to produce *something* than for a few to produce much.
2. Consequently, locate workplaces where people live.
3. The workplace must be cheap.

4. The production tools and methods must be simple.
5. The products must be produced from local materials and designed for local use. Schumacher describes a bad example: an African textile mill which was highly automated because the local workers were unskilled, whose equipment was so sophisticated that it had to be imported along with management and maintenance staff, and which had to import its raw material because the local cotton fibers were too short. Another triumph of development or a slip backward into neocolonialism?

INTERMEDIATE TECHNOLOGY

In response to the needs of local people everywhere the concept of intermediate technology has sprung up. Schumacher's Intermediate Technology Development Group in Britain, and Volunteers in Technological Assistance in the United States act as clearinghouses for information, putting villagers in Nigeria or Bangladesh, or poor farmers in Georgia, in touch with technology experts who can help them find simple, inexpensive solutions to their technical problems.

The New Alchemy Institute on Cape Cod has taken a more experimental approach in its design of what it calls the ark—a three-tiered arrangement of tanks enclosed as a greenhouse. In the lower tank are fast-growing fish—tilapia or carp. Nutrient-rich water from this tank is pumped by a windmill to the upper tank, heated by solar energy, and purified by bacteria in a bed of crushed shells. The nutrients are taken up by algae, which flow into the middle tank filled with *Daphnia*, a small invertebrate that feeds the fish in the lower tank. In three months fish can be harvested from the system, and vegetables can be grown in containers above the ponds. While this type of system is difficult to scale up to an industry-sized operation, modular replication can be applied to adapt the ark to local uses. The major advantage of such a system is the freedom it offers from the sophisticated and expensive technology of other food production schemes. Even more important, local people are brought close to the source of their sustenance and given an important role in the management of their own lives.

NEW WINE FOR OLD BOTTLES

Although it is a viable alternative, thinking small would be extremely difficult after centuries of doing the opposite. Just how difficult can be seen in the federal solar energy project. Unlike competing sources of energy, sunlight is available to everyone; and, unlike fusion power, it can be put to use by small groups of people or even individuals. But the federal government, conditioned by years of working with traditional energy sources, apparently can think only in terms of huge, centralized installations involving massive engineering, developed by aerospace companies for the existing utility industry. Consequently, the potential of solar energy is skeptically regarded by government energy officials and derided by the energy industry. However, the general public is enthusiastic about solar energy because it is becoming aware of the possibility that decentralization of energy supply offers—to get out from under the thumb of the giant utilities. Imagine the deep satisfaction after years of high energy bills of being able to tell the local power company that their services are no longer required!

Another progressive tack would be to reorient the goals of existing agencies rather than attempt to eliminate them altogether. For example, the Army Corps of Engineers, which for decades has responded to floods by building dams—if floods recurred there weren't enough dams—could just as well use its appropriations to help relocate industry and housing out of chronically inundated floodplains and convert the land back to farming, grazing, or recreational use. The Soil Conservation Service could stop channelizing streams (see Chapter 4) to drain wetlands and begin reconstructing wetlands to increase wildlife habitat and accommodate flood waters.

There are many such ways to stop spending money on environmentally misguided uses and apply these funds to better uses of the environment and our human resources. Investment in small local industries along the lines outlined by Schumacher could help keep the unemployed from flooding city ghettos and buy some time to begin the gigantic project of scaling down our megalopolises until they again become attractive and healthful environments.

REORIENTING OUR PRIORITIES

If we take the view that progress has a qualitative as well as a quantitative aspect, then unrestrained growth is clearly inimical to progress. The same population growth which traditionally has provided new markets, more profits, and greater consumer affluence has eroded our personal freedoms and steadily debased our environment. Once we realize that our definition of progress must be broadened to include quality, we can begin to plan our economy to accommodate this change. This may mean a no-growth economy; much more likely, it may mean a highly modified and reoriented economy devoted to growth of quality rather than mere quantity. But it certainly will not involve life as we have known it.

Even with a stable population, the world's industry should be fully occupied for decades just satisfying the minimum demands of the world's people for decent housing with the electricity, pure water, and sanitary facilities that most Americans now take for granted. This is an enormous market which has barely begun to develop, but when it is satisfied, diversification to meet the increasing leisure needs of the earth's then stable population should assure continuing profits for industry and a better life in both quantitative and qualitative terms for us all.

The usual moral drawn from the fable of the tortoise and the hare is that steady efforts to solve problems will ultimately win out. But if we let the hare symbolize our yearning for a good life and the tortoise represent steady population growth, another moral can be drawn: despite the slow pace of the tortoise there is a point beyond which the late-starting hare cannot possibly catch up, no matter how hard and fast he runs. We are probably within a few decades of a time when the sheer mass of people on the earth will make continuing degradation of the environment irreversible for the affluent and the deprived. While the cost of "catching up" is already staggering, it is not yet beyond our reach. But if we should falter now, not only will the universal goal of peace and happiness for humankind slip from our grasp, but our very humanity will become extinguished in a struggle for mere survival.

FURTHER READING

Callenbach, E., 1975. *Ecotopia*. Banyan Tree Books, Berkeley, California. Pleasant fantasy about life in a seccessionist Pacific Coast, post-1980.

Daly, H. E. (ed.), 1973. *Toward a steady-state economy*. W. H. Freeman, San Francisco. Good collection of papers questioning growth as a national and social objective.

Darrow, K. and R. Pam, 1976. *Appropriate technology sourcebook*. A Volunteers in Asia Publication. Box 4543, Stanford, California. Some concrete examples of what appropriate technology is all about.

Firestone, S. 1971. *The dialectic of sex*. Rev. Ed. Bantam Books, New York. One of the most thought-provoking books written in the last decade. If carried out, Firestone's social revolution would have far more impact on the economy and probably the environment than any of the changes suggested in this chapter.

Hammond, A. L., 1974. "Zero energy growth: Ford study says it's feasible." *Science* **184**, p. 142.

Hines, L. G., 1973. *Environmental issues: population, pollution, and economics*. W. W. Norton, New York. Critique of growth in quantity but not quality.

Olson, M. and H. H. Landsberg (eds.), 1973. *The no-growth society*. W. W. Norton, New York. Interesting variety of opinions. See especially Willard Johnson's paper, easily the most carefully documented and thought out of the lot.

Ophuls, W., 1977. *Ecology and the politics of scarcity*. W. H. Freeman, San Francisco. Explores the political implications of a steady-state society.

Passmore, J. A., 1974. *Man's responsibility for nature: ecological problems and western traditions*. Charles Scribner's Sons, New York. Philosophical background.

Quigg, P. W., 1976. "The new technologists." *Audubon* **78**(1), pp. 122–128. Technology wrought small and human in scale.

Sanchez-Cardona, V., T. Morales-Cardona, and P. L. Caldari, 1975. "The struggle for Puerto Rico." *Env.* **17**(4), pp. 34–40. Case study of the pitfalls of economic growth.

Schumacher, E. F., 1973. *Small is beautiful: economics as if people mattered*. Harper & Row, New York. Revolutionary ideas from an economist.

Terkel, S., 1974. *Working: people talk about what they do all day and how they feel about what they're doing*. Pantheon, New York. Moving firsthand accounts of why work has become a dirty four-letter word.

Watt, K. E. F., 1974. *The titanic effect: planning for the unthinkable*. Dutton, New York. Closely reasoned exploration of why growth is not always the best choice.

APPENDIX 1

KEEPING INFORMED on the current developments in our interactions with the environment requires more than reading an occasional newspaper. Many periodicals, wholly or in part, deal with our place in the environment. The following list is by no means complete; but it does include serveral points of view. Many of these publications can be found in local libraries, most in college or university libraries. The asterisk indicates organizations whose main thrust is toward active participation in preserving the landscape or improving the quality of our environment.

Professional Journals Often Containing Articles of Interest to Everyone

AMERICAN FORESTS
The American Forestry Association
1319 18th Street, N.W.
Washington, D.C. 20036
monthly

BIOLOGICAL CONSERVATION
Elsevier Publishing Co., Ltd.
Ripple Road, Barking
Essex, England
quarterly

BIOSCIENCE
American Institute of Biological
  Sciences
1401 Wilson Boulevard
Arlington, Virginia 22209
to members of AIBS only, bimonthly

ENVIRONMENTAL POLLUTION
Elsevier Publishing Co., Ltd.
Ripple Road, Barking
Essex, England
quarterly

ENVIRONMENTAL SCIENCE &
  TECHNOLOGY
American Chemical Society
  Publications
1155 Sixteenth Street, N.W.
Washington, D.C. 20036
monthly

JOURNAL OF RANGE MANAGEMENT
Society for Range Management
2120 Birch Street
Denver, Colorado 80222

JOURNAL OF SOIL AND WATER
  CONSERVATION
The Soil Conservation Society of
  America
7515 Northeast Ankeny Road
Ankeny, Iowa 50021
bimonthly

JOURNAL OF WILDLIFE
  MANAGEMENT
The Wildlife Society
Suite 611
7101 Wisconsin Avenue, N.W.
Washington, D.C. 20014
quarterly

NATURE
Subscription Department

Macmillan (Journals) Ltd.
Brunel Road, Basingstoke
Hampshire, England
weekly

POLLUTION ABSTRACTS
Dept. Y–5
P.O. Box 2369
La Jolla, California 92037
bimonthly

SCIENCE
American Association for the
  Advancement of Science
1515 Massachusetts Avenue, N.W.
Washington, D.C. 20005
weekly

→»» «««←

Periodicals Intended Primarily for Nonspecialists

AUDUBON
* National Audubon Society
950 Fifth Avenue
New York, New York 10022
bimonthly
beautifully illustrated

THE CANADIAN FIELD-NATURALIST
The Ottawa Field-Naturalists' Club
Box 3264, Postal Station "C"
Ottawa 3, Canada
quarterly

ENVIRONMENT
Scientists' Institute for Public
  Information
P.O. Box 755
Bridgeton, Missouri 63044
10 issues
*probably the broadest coverage of all
these magazines*

THE FUTURIST
World Future Society
P.O. Box 19285, Twentieth Street
  Station

Washington, D.C. 20036
bimonthly
*exceedingly interesting speculations
about the future*

THE LIVING WILDERNESS
* The Wilderness Society
1901 Pennsylvania Avenue, N.W.
Washington, D.C. 20006
quarterly

NATIONAL PARKS MAGAZINE
* National Parks Association
1701 Eighteenth Street, N.W.
Washington, D:C. 20009
monthly

NATIONAL WILDLIFE
* The National Wildlife Federation
1412 16th Street, N.W.
Washington, D.C. 20036
bimonthly
*also publishes an annual Conserva-
tion Directory listing organizations,
officers, phone numbers, and publications; a very useful compendium*

NATURAL HISTORY
The American Museum of Natural
    History
Central Park West at 79th Street
New York, New York 10024
10 issues

NEW SCIENTIST
New Science Publications
128 Long Acre
London, WC2E 9QH
England
weekly

OCEANS
Oceans Publishers, Inc.
7075A Mission Gorge Road
San Diego, California 92120
monthly

SCIENCE AND PUBLIC AFFAIRS
Bulletin of the Atomic Scientists
935 E. 60th Street
Chicago, Illinois 60637
10 issues
primarily concerned with atomic en-
ergy and disarmament but increas-
ingly oriented to broader environ-
mental issues

SCIENCE NEWS
Science Service, Inc.
1719 N. Street, N.W.
Washington, D.C. 20036
weekly

SIERRA CLUB BULLETIN
* Sierra Club
  530 Bush Street
  San Francisco, California 94108
  monthly

APPENDIX 2

THE FOLLOWING ORGANIZATIONS and those marked with an asterisk in Appendix 1 are representative of the many environmentally concerned groups which seek to improve our deteriorating relationship with our environment. For details of their programs, write to the organization directly.

Air Pollution Control Association
4400 Fifth Avenue
Pittsburgh, Pennsylvania 15213
educational group involved with the art and science of air pollution control

American Institute of Architects
1785 Massachusetts Avenue, N.W.
Washington, D.C. 20036
professional organization that promotes excellence in urban design, community planning, and preservation of historic architecture

American Shore and Beach
    Preservation Association
P.O. Box 1246
Rockville, Maryland 20850

Appalachian Trail Conference
Box 236

Harpers Ferry, West Virginia 25425
manages the volunteer maintenance of the Appalachian Trail, and can provide guidance to groups that wish to establish and maintain trail systems

Conservation Foundation
1717 Massachusetts Avenue, N.W.
Washington, D.C. 20036

Defenders of Wildlife
1244 19th Street, N.W.
Washington, D.C. 20036
mostly concerned with humane treatment of wildlife and elimination of unnecessarily cruel methods of trapping and capturing

Ducks Unlimited
P.O. Box 66300
Chicago, Illinois 60666

Environmental Defense Fund
162 Old Town Road
East Setauket, New York 11733
an organization of lawyers and scientists which undertakes legal action to bring about amelioration of environmental abuses

The Environmental Law Institute
Suite 620
1346 Connecticut Avenue, N.W.
Washington, D.C. 20036
conducts a program of research in environmental law and provides a document service to lawyers and scholars

Friends of the Earth
529 Commercial Street
San Francisco, California 94111
lobbies for ecologically sound land use, restoration, and preservation

Izaak Walton League of America
1800 North Kent Street, Suite 806
Arlington, Virginia 22209

League of Conservation Voters
317 Pennsylvania Avenue, S.E.
Washington, D.C. 20003
nonpartisan group promotes election of ecologically aware politicians whose actions are monitored by analysis of roll-call votes on environmental issues

National Trust for Historic
  Preservation
740 Jackson Place, N.W.
Washington, D.C. 20006
will provide advice and technical assistance to groups wishing to restore and preserve sites or buildings of historic significance

Nature Conservancy
1800 North Kent Street
Arlington, Virginia 22209
main interest is preserving examples of various environments, grasslands, forests and deserts, for educational purposes

Scientists' Institute for Public
  Information
49 East 53rd Street
New York, New York 10022
coordinates the utilization of scientists in public information programs

Trout Unlimited
4260 E. Evans Avenue
Denver, Colorado 80222

Water Pollution Control Federation
2626 Pennsylvania Avenue, N.W.
Washington, D.C. 20037
concerned with the application of the best engineering principles known to the design, construction, and operation of waste water collection and treatment systems

World Wildlife Fund
1319 18th Street, N.W.
Suite 728
Washington, D.C. 20036
seeks to preserve endangered species throughout the world

Zero Population Growth
1346 Connecticut Avenue, N.W.
Washington, D.C. 20036

Many of the regional offices of the Environmental Protection Agency have compiled lists of the environmental organizations within their areas. To obtain such a list contact the Public Affairs Director in your district.

REGIONAL OFFICE	AREAS SERVED
Boston, Massachusetts 02203 (617) 223-7210	Connecticut, Maine, Massachusetts, New Hampshire, Rhode Island, Vermont
New York, New York 10007 (212) 264-2525	New Jersey, New York, Puerto Rico, Virgin Islands
Philadelphia, Pennsylvania 19106 (215) 597-9815	Delaware, District of Columbia, Maryland, Pennsylvania, Virginia, West Virginia
Atlanta, Georgia 30309 (404) 526-3727	Alabama, Florida, Georgia, Kentucky, Mississippi, North Carolina, South Carolina, Tennessee
Chicago, Illinois 60606 (312) 353-5250	Illinois, Indiana, Michigan, Minnesota, Ohio, Wisconsin
Dallas, Texas 75201 (214) 749-1962	Arkansas, Louisiana, New Mexico, Oklahoma, Texas
Kansas City, Missouri 69108 (816) 374-5459	Iowa, Kansas, Missouri, Nebraska
Denver, Colorado 80203 (303) 837-3895	Colorado, Montana, North Dakota, South Dakota, Utah, Wyoming
San Francisco, California 94111 (415) 556-2320	Arizona, California, Hawaii, Nevada, American Samoa, Guam, Trust Territories of the Pacific, Wake Island
Seattle, Washington 98101 (206) 442-1220	Alaska, Idaho, Oregon, Washington

INDEX

NOTE: Major or defining discussions are identified in *italics*, illustrations in **boldface.** Illustrations appearing during the course of a discussion are not indicated specially.

abortion, 322, *551–553*
acetylcholine, 90
Achillea, **28**
acid wastes, 339, *376–377*
acidity of soil, *15*, 60
acids, as food contaminants, *129*
acrolein, 439, 441
Adams, Henry, 284
adaptation, *34–35*
additives, food, *116–121*
  testing of, 134
Adelie penguins, 100–101
Adirondack Park, 489–490
Adirondack Park Agency (APA), 490
adobe, *242–243*
adoption, 545
aerobic bacteria, 48, 378
aerosol cans, 450
aerosols, 429, *439–440*
  in air, 4
  generated at home, 255
  from ocean surf, **423**
affluence, and environmental harm, 556
Afghanistan, **244**
Africa
  extinction in, 185
  food production in, 519
  population statistics, 543
  savanna environment of, **524–525**
  western, *43*
African leopard, 193
African Plate, **11**
African rhino, 195
age ratio, 31
agene, 132
Agent Blue, 91. *See also* herbicides
Agent Orange, *91–94. See also* 2,4-D; 2,4,5-T

Agent White, 91. *See also* 2,4-D; pilcoram
Ageratum, 180
agricultural runoff, 391
agriculture
  and deforestation, 62–63
  energy use for, 362–363
  environmental effects of, *46–56*, 497
  future developments of, *526–531*
  intensive, 523
  see also crops; cultivated land
Ailanthus tree, 236
air, *4–6*, 13
air conditioners, 253, 256, 258, 366
air cushion vehicles, 296–297
air pollution
  and atmospheric temperature, **436**
  and cities, 264
  and coal combustion, 341
  from domestic heating, 252
  and forest ecosystem, *446–447*
  from geothermal power, 358
  historic description of, 427–429
  from incineration and wastes, 467–468
  natural sources of, 427–428
  from water pollution, **423**
  see also smog
air transport, 298–299, 363–364. *See also* jet transport
aircraft industry, *563–565. See also* air transport; jet transport
airport expansion, 298–299, **564–565**
Alameda Creek, 514
Alaska, North Slope, 301

Alaska pipeline, *301–302*
albatross, 101
albedo, *46*
aldrin, 90, 104, 107, 111. *See also* organochlorines
alfalfa caterpillar, 178
alfalfa protein, 534
algae
  blue-green, 19, 388, **401**
  and DDT, **92**
  filamentous, *27*
  freshwater, **401**
  green, 413–414, 424
  harvesting of, 534–535
  and Nile fertility, 76
  and organochlorines, 101–102
  in soil, 14
  and temperature variation, 401–402
  in tidal environments, 22
  in tropical reefs, 422–423
algal bloom, *26–27*
  and forestry practice, 61
  and lake pollution, 395–396
  and phosphorus levels, 388–391
alginate, 129
all-terrain vehicles, 296–297
Allegheny River Basin, 83
allergies, 431
alpha radiation, *315*
  naturally occurring, 334
  and sickness from, 320–321
Altamaha River, 23
aluminum, 460, 463, **472**
aluminum industry, 361, 365
alveoli, *429–430*
Amazon Basin
  animal collection in, 198
  development of, 59, 292–293
  fertility of, 61, 527–528
ambergris, 191

amenity, 538
American chestnut, 174
American elm, **97**
Ames, Bruce, 134
amino acids, 18. *See also* protein
ammonia
  in animal waste, 411–413
  and nitrogen cycling, 19
  and vegetation, 446
Ammonium (NH_4^+), 18
amoebiasis, 518–519
Amtrak, 364
Anabaena, 388
Anacostia River, **399**
anaerobic bacteria, 48, 378
Anagrus wasp, 113
anchovy, 107
Andes Mountains, *58–59*
angiosarcoma, 126
animal tests
  of additives, 119
  monkeys for, 197–198
animal waste, *381–382*, 391
  and biological oxygen demand, 378
  treatment of, 383–384
Animas River, 331
Antarctic Plate, **11**
Antarctica, **4**
antelope, 184, 196
anthracite coal, 339
antibiotics, *122–123*
antioxidants, *128–129*
Apalachicola River, 84
aphids, **105**
Appalachia, 339
Appalachian Trail, 234
apples, **109**
aquatic systems, 26, *397–402.*
  See also bays; estuarine environment; oceans; rivers; salt marshes

579

aqueducts, 54–**55**
Aquinas, St. Thomas, 553
Aransas Wildlife Refuge, 199
architecture
  and energy conservation,
    364–366
  function and environment of,
    241–248
  and internal environment,
    251–257
  and outer environment,
    248–251
Arctic environment
  housing in, 242–243
  radioactivity in, 319
Argentina, 529
argon, 4
armadillo, **161**
aromatics, 438
arsenic, 340
arsenic trioxide, persistence of,
  105
arsenicals, 90
artificial flavor, *130–131*
artificial insemination, 212
asbestos bodies, **152**
asbestos disease, *151–154*
ascorbic acid, 128
Asia, **161**, 543
*Assessment of Accident Risks in
  United States Commercial
  Nuclear Power Plants, An*,
  325–326
asthma, bronchial, *430–431*
Aswan High Dam, 49, 76–79
asymptomatic lead poisoning,
  143–144
Atchafalaya Basin, 81
Athabasca oil deposit, 343
atherosclerosis, 334
Athos Mountain, **52**
Atlantic Ocean, 86, 408. *See also*
  oceans
atmosphere, 3–7
  beryllium in, 150
  energy in, **6**
  lead in, 145–148
  particles in, 449
  radioisotopes in, 328
  temperature of, **5**, 436–437
atmospheric testing, 320
atomic bomb, 317–**318**
  homemade, 352
  isotopes from, 315
atomic fallout. *See* fallout
atomic fission, 315–318
atomic fusion, 318–319, 352
atomic oxygen. *See* ozone
atomic pile, 317
Auburn Dam, **350**
Audubon Society, 204
auk, 209
aurochs, **495–496**
Austen, Jane, 216
Austin, Thomas, 172
Australia
  extinctions in, 185
  fertile land in, 517
  Great Barrier Reef, **422**
  prickly pear in, 178
  rabbits in, 164, 172–**173**, 178
Australian koala, 206
Australian Plate, **11**
autobahns, 287
autocatalytic reaction, *439*

automobile
  and atmospheric lead, 145–147
  and cities, 294–296
  energy use by, 363–364
  and highway development, 284
  and oil needs, 343
  pollution control in, 442–445
  as pollution source, 437–439
  production of, 568
  and smog, 434–435
  social costs of, 559
  as waste, **462**–463, 472
  see also internal combustion
    engine
auxins, 91
azodrin, 95–96
Aztecs, 163

Bacillus thuringensis, 178
bacon, 127–128
bacteria
  and acid wastes, 376
  anaerobic, 48, 378
  biological control with,
    178–179
  and carbon monoxide, 441
  coliform, 413, 416
  control of, 181
  nitrogen fixing, 530–531
  and organic waste, 377–378
  and plastic wastes, 465
  as pollution indicators, 413
  and sewage treatment, 392
  in soil, 14, 19, 48
bald eagle, 98–**99**
Baltic Sea, 408
Baltimore, Maryland, 484
Bambi, 221
bamboo, 92
Bangladesh, **246**
barium, 316
barrier island, **226–229**
  and coastal productivity,
    408–409
  development of, 481–482
Barro Colorado, 230
bass, 169
basswood, 446
bats, **101**
Battelle Memorial Institute,
  433–434
battery power, 445
Bay Area Rapid Transit (BART),
  279
bays
  abuse of, 410–418
  productivity of, *21–25*
  see also Great South Bay; San
    Diego Bay; San Francisco
    Bay
Beach, A River of Sand (film), 227
beaches
  development of, 480–483
  erosion cycles of, 226–227
beaver dams, 29
Becquerel, Henri, 314
beech woodland, 504–506
beef, 123–124. *See also* cattle;
  grazing
bees
  herbicides and, **109**
  killer-, 167
Belgium, 545
benzoic acid, 127
benzpyrene, 430
Berg, Alban, 494

Bering land bridge, 159–161
Bering Straits, 184
beryllium, *149–151*
  in coal, 340
  in fission reactions, 317
  random effect of, 154
beta radiation, *315*
  and nuclear power generation,
    328
  sickness from, 320–321
Big Ditch Project, 84
Bikini Atoll atom test, **318**
bio-magnification, 96–*104*
biocides
  accumulation of, 96–104
  and agribusiness, 181–182, 368
  delayed effects of, 103–108
  dependency on, 111–113
  development of, 94
  in estuaries, 410
  and FDA, 117
  in humans, 102–104
  and natural controls, 179
  nonselectivity of, 95–96,
    108–111
  in oceans, 100–102
  persistence of, 104–108, 116
  resistance to, 94–96, 113
biogeochemical cycles, 15–19
biological control, 111, *175–178*
biological islands, 230
biological oxygen demand
  (BOD), 377–378
  and food processing wastes, 385
  and sewage effluent, 381, 392
biological treatment system
  (BTS), 381
biorational agents, *179–180*
biosphere, *20–36*
birds
  biocide accumulation by,
    96–100
  as introduced species, *170–172*
  mercury poisoning of, 140–141
birds of paradise, 193
birds of prey, 98–100. *See also*
  predators
birth control, 544–545
  effectiveness of, 542
  and government policy,
    545–547
  methods, 547–553
birth defects
  and herbicides, 93
  and PCBs, 124–125
  from radiation, 322
  see also abortion; mutation
birth rates
  current world trends, 554
  and employment, 563
  limiting of, 542
  and species populations, 31
  transitional, 540–543
bis-chlormethyl-ether (BCME),
  126
bison, **189**
bituminous coal, **339**
black death, 274
Black Hills bighorn sheep, 207,
  209
black oak, 446
blackouts, 336
Blackstone, William, 477, 484
Blackwater River, 80–82
bleached flour, 132–133
blister pack, **457**

blood cells and radiation, 322
blood fluke, 78–**79**
blue buck, 196
blue-green algae, 19, 388, **401**
Blue Ridge Parkway, 234
blue whale, 192
Blumer, Max, 421
boats and pollution, 380–381. *See
  also* tankers
Bodega Head atomic power plant,
  327
body burden
  of biocides, 102–104, 107
  of cadmium, 148–149
  of lead, 147–148
  of mercury, 139
  of PBCs, 125
boiling water reactor (BWR), 328,
  348
bone disease, 148
bone marrow, 322
bontebok, 196
Boone Club, 213
Bormann, F. H., 61
Borneo, 62
Boston, Massachusetts
  airport, 298
  Commonwealth Avenue, 286
  harbor, 266
  North End, 273
  waste cycling in, 366
botanicals, 90
bottles, 460–462, 469
botulism, 127–128
Boulding, Kenneth, 522–523
bowhead whale, 191–192
Brahmaputra River, **57**
braided rivers, **52**
Brasilia, Brazil, **277**
Brazil, 345, 527. *See also*
  Amazon Basin
bread, *131–133*
breeder reactors, 349, **351**–352
breeding, animal, 209–212
breeding sites, 207
Breughel, P., **532**
brine injection, 385
broad spectrum biocides, 95
Broecker, W. S., 441
Broley, Charles, 98
bronchial asthma, *429–430*
bronchioles, 430
bronchitis, chronic, *429–430*
Brookhaven National Laboratory,
  324
Brown, Lancelot (Capability),
  497–499, 507
Brown, Lester, 554
brown pelican, 107
browsers, 525–526
Bryce Canyon, 221
bubble pack, **457**
bubonic plague, 274
buffalo, 163–164, *189*
builder (detergent), 390
building permits, 487–488
buildings and energy, 364–366.
  See also architecture
bunch grass prairie, 46–47, **202**
Burchell's zebra, 196
Burle-Marx, Roberto, 292
burning, controlled, 41–42, 55,
  205, 210, 220–**223**. *See also*
  fire
bus transport, 300

butylated hydroxyanisole (BHA), 128–129
butylated hydroxytoluene (BHT), 128–129
Buzzard's Bay, 421–423
by-products
  from food processing, 378
  heat as, 467–468
  from industrial wastes, (384–385)
  methane as, 467
  from waste paper, 459
  see also recycling

cabbage maggot, 95
cabbage worm, 178
Cactoblastis moth, 179
Cade, Thomas, 211
cadmium, 148–149
  in atomic piles, 317
  dose effect of, 154
cadmium sulfide, 360
calcium
  and cadmium poisoning, 148
  cycling of, 60
  metabolism and DDT, 98–100
calcium chloride, 374
calcium hydroxide, 131
California
  coastline of, 490
  geothermal power in, 357
  highway design in, **291**
  land use planning in, 490
  salt marshes of, **23**
  water scheme, 68–69, 529
California condor, **203**–205, 210
California grape leafhopper, 113
California spotted alfalfa aphid, 113
California State Water Project, 69, 529
Calvert Cliffs decision, 350
camels, **161**, 184
Canada, 517
canals
  and irrigation, 48–50
  and species introductions, 83–87
  and U.S. transport, 282–283
Canberra, Australia, 277
cancer
  and asbestos, 151
  and food additives, *119–121*, 129
  and hormones, 124
  isotopes and therapy for, 325
  of liver, 126
  of lungs, 331, 430–431
  radiation induced, 334–335
  in urban areas, 127–128
Canete Valley, 112
cans as waste, 361, 459–460
Cape Hatteras National Seashore, 227
cape lion, 196
Cape Lookout National Seashore, **228**
cape mountain zebra, 196
carbamates, 90
carbon, cycle, **16**–*17*
  and eutrophication, 26
  in fission reactions, 317
  and oceanic productivity, 531
carbon dioxide
  and algal blooms, 26–27

atmospheric cycling of, **4**, **6**–8, 16
  and climate, 448–450
  generation in home, 255
  and smog formation, 438–439
  and soil formation, 11–13
carbon-14, 315, 325
carbon monoxide
  generation in home, 255–256
  and smog formation, *438–441*, 443–444
carbonate ions, 15
carbonates, 12
carbonic acid, 11–13
carboxymethylcellulose, 390
carcinogens
  biocides as, 111, 127
  BCME as, 126
  benzpyrenes as, 430
  chlorinated hydrocarbons as, 126–127
  food additives as, *119–121*, 127–131
  generation in home, 255
  mutagens as, 134
  vinyl chloride as, 126
  in water supply, 380
carcinomas, 153
  cardinal, 161
caribou, 205, 319
Carlsbad Caverns, **101**
carnivores, **23**, 25
  and DDT, 98–100
  see also predators
Carolina parakeet, 172, 196
carp, 399–400
Carroll, Lewis, 136–137
carrying capacity, 31, 70
Carson, Rachel, 114
Cartier, Jacques, 189–190
catalytic converters, **443**
catfish
  cultivation of, **405**–406
  "walking," 170
Catholic church
  and abortion, 553
  and birth control, 544–545
cats, 108, 201
cattle, 42–46, 525–526. *See also* grazing
cattle egrets, 161
Central Arizona Project, 71
Central Park, 261, 266
  atmospheric effects of, 267–**268**
  creation of, 216
  as environmental restoration, 507–**509**
  excavations of, 456
  population pressures in, 233
Central Valley Project, 68–69
cercariae, 78–**79**
cesium-137, 315, 319
chain reaction, *316–318*, 348
chalk grasslands restoration, 503–505
channelization, 70, *80–81*
Chanos, 404
Chanute, Kansas, 72
chaparral, 53, 203
Chapman, H. H., 219–220
Chattahoochee River, 84
Chelators, 144
chemical industry, 385–386
chemical weathering, *11–12*
chemotaxis, 102

Chesapeake Bay, 513
chestnut blight, 174
Chicago, Illinois
  fuel standards in, 433
  industrial development in, 274
  and Lake Michigan, 299
chicken, 122, 123
children
  hyperactivity in, 131
  and lead poisoning, *142–148*
Chironomus, 377
chloralkali plants, 140
chlordane, 90, 104, 107. *See also* organochlorines
chlorides, 446
chlorinated dibenzofurans, 125
chlorinated hydrocarbons, 90
  broadscale use of, 110–111
  control of, 107
  disposal of, 386
  and eggshell thickness, **99**
  in public water supply, *126–127*
chlorination, 127, 379–381
chlorine, 402
chlorine dioxide, 132
cholinesterase, 90
Chow, T. J., 145
chromium-51, 328
chromosomes, 322, 375
chronic bronchitis, 431
chronic lead poisoning, 143–144
Cichla ocellaris, 169
cigarette smoking
  and benzpyrene, 430
  and cadmium, 148–149
  and carbon dioxide, 440
  and lead consumption, 146
  and radiation, **332**–334
cilia, 429–430
Cincinnati, Ohio, 145–146
cirrhosis, 129
cities
  antisocial activity in, 270–271
  automobiles in, 294–296
  development of, 273–275, **561**
  expressways in, 293–296
  future of, 278–279
  housing in, **561**
  lead generation in, 145–147
  location and forms, 259–261
  mass transit in, 300
  mental health in, 264–265
  microclimate of, 261–264
  nature in, 236–237
  noise in, 450–452
  open spaces in, 233, 264–273
  plants in, **236**
  powerlines in, **306**
  renewal programs in, 268–271, 293–294
  runoff from, 392–393
  see also urbanization
citric acid, 128, 129
citrus thrip, 110
Cladophora, 414
clams, 319, 413–414
Clark, William, 163
clay-humus particles, *14–15*, 60
clays, 13, 21
Clean Air Act, 443–444
Cleveland, Ohio
  and airport transportation, 298
  greenbelt, 266
  zoning in, 487
climate
  alteration of, 159

and architecture, 241–243
  and carbon dioxide, 448–450
  and housing design, 248–251
  and soil formation, 11–13
  and water supply, 9, 74
climax community, 30
  European, 503–504
Clockwork Orange, A, 271
Closter, New Jersey, 488
Clostridium, 48
clouds, 6–7
cluster housing, 485, **487**
coal, 338–342
  and acid waste, 376–377
  and air pollution, **432**
  industrial consumption of, 361
  introduction of, 428
  lead in, 145–148
  and mercury contamination, 142
  mining of, 63–66
  and natural gas, 346
  power generation from, **398**
  processing of, 17, 433–434
  U.S. sources of, **339**
  see also air pollution
coal gasification, *340–341*
Coal River, 66
coal tar dye, 130–131
coastal upwelling, 532
coastal water
  food chains in, 532
  restoration, 512–515
Coastal Zone Management Act of 1972, 483
coastline
  of California, 490
  destruction of, 226–229
  development of, 480–483
Cobalt-60, 320, 325
coccinellids, 105
cogeneration, 366
cogon grass, 92
cold fronts, **4**
coliform bacteria, 413, 416
Colorado, 70
  oil shale deposits in, **344**
Colorado potato beetle, 54, 167, **168**, 180
Colorado River, 68–69, 75–76
  basin, 331
Columbus, Christoforo, 164
commensalism, 32
Committee on the Biological Effects of Ionizing Radiation, 335
commons, 216
community, 28–31
composting
  of human waste, 380
  of solid waste, 468–469
concrete, 364–365
condensation trails, **449**
Conestoga wagon, *281–283*
Connecticut
  Merritt Parkway, 286
  salt marshes, **22**
  solid waste disposal in, 468
Connecticut River, 234
conservation districts, 480
contaminants, 116
  in food, *121–127*
  in water, 333
  weeds as, 54
continental drift, 10–**11**, 159

continental shelf ·
  productivity of, 409
  resources in, 425
contraceptives, 547
  chemical methods, *549–551*
  comparative effectiveness of, 551
  mechanical methods, *548–549*
  and pest control, 172
contrails, **449**
controlled harvesting, 209
cooling ponds, *404–406*
cooling towers, 402–**403**
copper, 463, 468
copper acetoarsenite, 89
coppice-with-standard forest, **503–507**
cordgrass, **22**, 512–515
core banks, **228**
Coriolis' force, 9
cormorants, 101
corn, 521–522
corn leaf aphid, and herbicides, 105
corona discharge, 304
cosmetic pests, 110
cosmic rays, 312, 323
cotton crop, 95–96, 109, 112–113
cottony-cushion scale, **179**
Council on Environmental Quality, 391
Coxsackie virus, 104
coyotes, 196–197
creatinine-5-oxime, 128
Critias (Plato), 51–53
critical mass, *317*, 348
Crockett Club, 213
crops
  environment of, 400–401
  heated effluent and, 406
  introduction of, 46–47
  leading, 520
  new varieties of, 530–531
  see also agriculture
cross-fostering, 200
Crow, James, 323
cryptococcal meningitis, 171
cryptomonads, 388
cultivated land
  and evolution, 517
  increase of, 526–530
  intensive processing of, 523
  see also agriculture
cultivated plants, 400–401. *See also* crops
Cumbernauld, Scotland, 276–277
curie, 321
Curie, Irene, 315
Curie, Marie, 314
Curie, Pierre, 314
cyclamates, 130
cyclodiene, 95
cytochrome, 143

dams
  environmental effects of, 75–79
  and floodplain development, 82–83
  for power generation, **350**, 354–356
  and solid waste disposal, 374
  and water supply, 70
Daphnia, 388, 400, 569
"Dark Ages," 54

Dasmann, Raymond, 525
dawn redwood, 210–**211**
DCA (3,4-dichloroaniline), 106
DDE, 101, 107. *See also* dichloro-diphenyl-trichloro-ethane (DDT)
death rates, 31
  transitional, 540–543
decibel chart, **451**
deciduous forest preserve, 511. *See also* forest ecosystem
deep injection wells, 385–387
Deep Throat, 271
deer, **161**
defoliants, 92. *See also* herbicides
deforestation
  of ancient world, 50–56
  of tropical forests, 61–63
  see also forest ecosystem; forestry
Delaney Amendment, 117, 128, 141
Delaware River basin, 83
demographic transition, 540–543
Denmark, 517
density-dependent population control, 32
density-independent population control, 32
Denver, Colorado, 386–**387**
Des Voeux, Harold, 428, 435
desalinization, 73–**74**
  and food supply, 529
  and sea thermal power, 361
desert environment
  housing in, **244**
  irrigation in, 529
detergents
  and eutrophication, **389**–391
  and oil spills, 421, 424
  regulation of, 469
detritus
  in estuarine food webs, **22**, 25, 93
  in tropical reefs, 422–423
Detroit, Michigan, 274
deuterium, 315, 352–354
development
  costs of, 488
  and land use, 478–480
  and population, 542
  in Third World, 554
  and watershed problem, 82
development rights, 480
Devonian shale, 346
diatoms
  and estuarine productivity, 23–24
  in Great South Bay, 413
  in lake environments, 388
  and radiation, 319
  and temperature variation, 401–402
dichloro-diphenyl-trichloro-ethane, **401**-402
dichloro-diphenyl-trichloro-ethane (DDT), 88-**90**
  accumulation of, 96–98
  ban of, 106–108
  and birds of prey, 99–100, 211
  body burden of, 104, 107
  as food contaminant, 123
  and gypsy moth, 166
  and oceanic pollution, 422
  and PCBs, 124–125
  persistence of, 104–105

resistance to, 94–95
  structure of, **89**
dieldrin, 104, 107, 109–111. *See also* organochlorines
dielectric constant, 8
diet, and disease, 518–519
diethylstilbestrol (DES), 123–124. *See also* hormones
dinoflagellates, 23–24
dioxin, 93–94
dire wolf, 184
disease
  and agriculture, 54
  and air pollution, 429–432
  and diet, 518–519
  introduction of, 162–164
  see also asbestos; beryllium; cadmium; cancer; lead; mercury; radiation
dismal theorem, 522
Disney, Walt, 221
disparlure, 180
DMF (juvenile hormone analog), 180
DNA, 34
dodo, **185**, 209
dogs, 201, 382
Dogwood, 60
Donora, Pennsylvania, 429
doomsday models, 566
dose-effect, **119**, 154
Douglas fir forest, 221
Douglas fir tussock moth, **107**, 167
Drake, E. L., 434
dredging of rivers, 80–81
drip irrigation, 529–530
drought, 44–46
dry tower, 349, **403**
duck farming, 411–**412**, 415
Ducktown, Tennessee, 447
dune stabilization, **229**, 481
Durand, A. B., 217
dust, in air, 4, **6**, 7
Dutch elm disease, 96, **97**
dyox, 132

earth, **4**
  environment of, *3–19*
  mean temperature of, **262**, 448
earthquakes, 10
  and deep well injection, 386–**387**
  from geothermal power, 358
earthworms, and DDT, 98
ecological ethic, 490
economic growth, 556
  case against, 559–567
  case for, 557–558
  see also growth
ecosystems
  communities within, 28–29
  construction of, 509–510
  energy in, 20–21
  limiting factors of, 25–28
  productivity of, 21–22
  simplification of, 400–402, 409
  smog in, 432
  species diversity in, 208
  stability of, 165
  see also environmental restoration
ecotones, **30–31**, 41–42
ecotypes, **28**

Edward I, 427
Eel River, 68–69
eelgrass, **414**
egg cells, 34–34, 322
eggs, mercury content of, 140–141
eggshell thickness and biocides, 98–100, 107
Egler, Frank, 302
egret, 193
Egypt, 49
Ehrlich, Paul, 522
Einstein, Albert, 494
Ekrafane Ranch, 45
El Niño effect, 531
electric automobiles, 445
electric power
  and building industry, 364–366
  cost of, 368
  industrial consumption of, 361
  from solid waste incineration, 468
  see also energy
electromagnetic spectrum, **312**
electronic smog, 311–314
electrostatic precipitators, 433
Eleocharis acicularis, 376
elephant foot waste basket, **194**
Ellis, James, 397
embryo, 552
  and radiation, 322
emphysema, **430**
employment
  and growth, 558
  and pollution control, 567
  steady-state approach to, 562–563
  see also unemployment
"empty" calories, 519
emulsifiers, as contaminants, 120, **129**
encephalitis, 171
endangered species
  through habital destruction, 198–205
  hunting of, 193–197
  plants as, 200–201
  with specialized breeding sites, 205–207
  in U.S., 186
  whales as, 190–193
  see also predator control
endrin, 90. *See also* organochlorines
energy
  in agricultural system, 48
  atmospheric effect on, **6**
  and bottling revolution, 461
  conservation of, *361–366*
  crisis, 367
  economics of, 367–369
  flow of, 25, 30, 337
  and food supply, 519
  needs, 337–338
  see also coal; electric power; gas; nuclear power plants; oil
England. *See* United Kingdom
Engelmann spruce beetle, 110
English sparrow, 170–171
Enrico Fermi fast breeder reactor, 326–327, **351**
Entamoeba histolytica, 518–519
Enteromorpha, 374, 424. *See also* algae
environment
  housing in, 242–243

manipulation of, 215–229
see also ecosystems;
   environmental restoration
Environmental Concern, Inc.,
   513–514
Environmental Impact Statement
   (EIS), 287, 350, 356
environmental restoration
   in United Kingdom, 499–507
   in United States, 507–515
epilimnion, **394–395**
epithelium, 322
eradication, 175
Erie Canal, 282
erosion
   of coastal features, 226–229
   and grazing, **42**, 43, 50, 53
   of Himalayas, 57
   and lake productivity, 27
   of Levant, 51
   logging and, 61
   of Nile Delta, 77–78
   by ORVs, 296–297
   of river systems, 81
   and SO₂ fumes, **447**
   from strip mining, 63–66
Erythronium americanum,
   208–209
Escherichia coli, 102, 122
Eskimos, 241, 246, 319
*Essay on the Principle of
   Population, An* (Malthus),
   539–540
Esthwaite Water, England, 28
estrogen-simulating hormones, in
   food, 123–124
estrogens, and birth control, 549.
   See also hormones
estuarine environment, 408–410
   DDT contamination of, **97**
   organisms of, 93
   and PCB, 125
   pollution of, 533
   productivity of, *21–25*,
      409–410, 483
   restoration of, 512–515
   see also salt marshes
ethanol, 385
Ethioipia, **58**
ethyl alcohol, 345, 459
ethylene cycle, 48
ethylene dibromide, 145
ethylene dichloride, 145
eucalyptus, 58
Euclid Village v. *Ambler Realty
   Company*, 484
Euphrates River, 49–50
Eurasian Plate, **11**
Europe
   acid waste in, 377
   birth control in, 545
   deforestation of, 53–55
   population statistics, 543
European corn borer, 105
eutrophication, 26–28, 388–397
   of bays, 410–418
   of coastal waters, 483
   see also water pollution
evaporation, and rainfall, 10
evapotranspiration, *10*
Evelyn, John, 427, 428
Everglades kite, 206
Everglades National Park, 511
evolution
   and land formation, 159

and mutation, 35
of weeds, 54
expressways, 286–296. *See also*
   highways
extinction, *184–186*
   through competition, 196–197
   cost of, 207–209
   by direct assault, 186–193
   by habitat destruction,
      198–205
   in island habitats, 207
   and live animal trade, 197–198
   novel uses lead to, 193–195
   resynthesis and, 495–496
   and superstition, 194–195
   susceptibility to, 205–207
   and trophy hunting, 195
   see also endangered species
eye, and radiation, 322

factory ships, **191**
fallout, 315
   in food chains, 319–320
   genetic effects of, 322–323
   naturally occurring, 323–324
family planning, 540, 544–545
famine, 44–46
farming industry, 491
farmlands, and suburbanization,
   479–480. *See also*
   agriculture; cultivated land
Farsta, Sweden, 277
faults, 10. *See also* earthquakes
favela, **258**
feedlots, **382**
feldspar, 12
fenitrothion/DDT mixture, 104
fertilization
   and green revolution, **520**
   by sewage effluent, **383**
   in tropical soils, 528
   and water table, 391
   see also nitrates, phosphates
fetus, 552
fiber glass, 153
fibers, inhalation of, 153
filamentous algae, **27**
fin whale, 192
fire
   elimination of, 223–225
   and forest management,
      218–223
   and hunting, 185
   niches maintained by, 203–205
   see also burning, controlled
fire ant, 110–111, 175
Fire Island, **228**, **411**
Fire Island National Seashore,
   411
Firestone Rubber Corporation,
   464
fish
   cultivation of, 404
   an introduced species, **169**–170
   nutrition of, 25
   oxygen need, 377
   and pollution, 393–395,
      401–402
   and river dredging, 80–81
   and thermal loading, 399–402
fish kills, **399**
fish protein concentrate (FPC),
   523–524, 533
fishing industry
   and Aswan Dam, 77
   and canal building, 86

and damming, 79
limits to, 531–532
and mercury, 140
and oceanic contamination,
   102
and PCBs, 125
fission power plants. *See* nuclear
   power plants
fission products. *See* radioactive
   wastes
5-thio-D-glucose, 550–551
flood control, 81–83
floodplain development, *80–83*
Florida, 483
Florida alligator, 193
Florida Barge Canal, 84
Florida Everglades, 206, 511
flour processing, 132
flowing systems. *See* rivers
fluidized bed process, *341*
fluorescent lamps, 365–366
   beryllium in, 149–150
fluorine, 340
fly ash, 433, 468
Folsom Dam, **350**, 351
Fontana Dam, 399
food
   biocides in, 103
   chemical synthesis of, 536
   and future technology,
      526–536
   leading crops, 520
   and population, 517–519
   and present technology,
      519–526
   processing wastes from, 378,
      383, 385, **491**
   surplus producers of, 526
food chains
   biocides in, 96–104
   in coastal waters, 532
   defoliants, and, 93
   energy in, 337
   estuarine, 22–25, **97**
   mercury in, 138, 140
   oceanic, 102, 531–532, 534
   radio contamination in,
      319–320, 331
   shortening of, **169**, 534–535
   and species populations, 31
   stress effects on, 401–402
food dyes, *130–131*
Food for Peace Program, 526
food webs. *See* food chains
forest and grasslands ecotone,
   41–42
forest ecosystem, 59–63
   air pollution in, 446–447
   management of, 238
   radioactivity in, *324*
   stored carbon in, 16–17
   see also environmental
      restoration; forestry; rain
      forest; tropical forest
forestry
   burning practices, 218–221
   and herbicides, 91
   in temperate climates, 62–63
   tropical, 61–63
   see also environmental
      restoration; forest ecosystem;
      rain forest
formaldehyde, 439, 441
fossil-fueled plants, 338–339
   radioisotopes from, 320
Four Corners Area, 65

fox, 108, **161**
France, 320, 517, 545–546
Franklin, Benjamin, 213
free market, 558, 563–565
free radicals, 305, 321
fresh water shark, 207
Fresno, California, pedestrian
   mall in, **295**
frost free refrigerators, 366
fuel, cost of, 368. *See also* coal;
   energy; gas; oil
Fuller, Buckminster, 246
Fulton, Robert, 283
fungi
   and plastic waste, 465
   in soil, 14
fungicides, 181
   cadmium in, 148
   mercury in, 140–141
fusion, and power production,
   352–354

gallinules, 109
gallium arsenite, 360
game
   mercury in, 141
   ranching, **524–526**
gamma radiation, 312, *315*, 321,
   324
Ganges River, **57**
gardens
   English, **498**
   formal, **278**
   as managed environments,
      497–499
   planting of, 53–54
   Renaissance, **497**
   see also landscaping
garrigue, 53
Gary, Indiana, 263
gas
   and Alaska pipeline, 301
   from coal, 340
   industrial consumption of, 361
   radioactive wastes as, 328
   recycled, 366
   solubility of, 8
   see also methane; natural gas
gas-cooled breeders, 352
gas diffusion plants, 349
gas turbine, **444**
gasoline, 363–364
   alternatives to, 345
   composition and smog,
      438–439
   demand for, 343, 363–364
   lead in, 145–148
   shortage of, 367–369
Gatun Lake, **169**, 230
gazelle, 196
Generally Regarded As Safe
   (GRAS), 128
genetic defects, 322. *See also*
   mutations
genetic pool
   and endangered species,
      205–206
   and resynthesis of species,
      495–496
geologic eras, **160**
geologic features, 221–222
geological cycles. *See*
   biogeochemical cycles
geopressured beds, 346
Georgia land trust, 492
geothermal power, 356–358

Gerard, R. D., 73, **74**
"germ bank," 521
Germany, 286–287
geysers, 357
ghetto
 highway in, 293–294
 lead poisoning in, 143–144
 life in, 265
giant beaver, 184
giant buffalo, 184
giant kangaroo, 185
Gilpin, Joshua, 376
gingko, 210–211
giraffe, 35–**36**
glaciation, 184–185
Glacier National Park, 232
glass, as waste, 460–462
glass industry, 469
Glassboro, New Jersey, 484–485
glassphalt, 462
Glen Canyon Dam, **75**–76, 399
glycerides, 129
goats, 42–43, 201
Gofman, John, 334–335
gold-198, 325
golden eagle, **99**
Golden Gate Park, **189, 211, 233,
 266**
golden trout, 169
goldfish, 170
gonads, and radiation, 322
gossyplure, 180–181
Gottmann, Jean, 275
governments
 and abortion, 551–553
 and energy conservation, 369
 and population, 545–547
 and recycling, 472
 and solid waste standards, 469
 see also U.S.
grain, 140–142
Grand Banks, Newfoundland,
 190
Grand Canyon, 221
Grand Canyon City, 232
Grand Canyon National Park, 76
Grand Canyon Village, 231
granite, 11–13, **29**
grape phylloxera, 167
grasslands, 41–43
grasslands, chalk, 503–505. See
 also prairies
gray whales, 191–192
grazing, 41–47
 in ancient greece, 53
 efficiency of wild animals,
 524–526
 in English forests, 506
 and environmental restoration,
 505, 511–512
 and erosion, **42**, 50
 and grassland environment,
 202, **504**, 511–512
 by introduced animals, 162
 and moors, 499–500
greak auk, **189–190**
Great Barrier Reef, **422**
Great Bitter Lake, **78**, 85
great horned owl, **99**
Great Lakes
 lamprey invasion of, **84**
 and PCBs, 125
 population and pollution of,
 394
 see also Lake Erie

Great Plains
 buffalo in, 189
 coal deposits in, **339**
 horse introduction into,
 163–164
Great Smoky Mountains National
 Park, 511
Great South Bay, **410–415**
Great Valley, California, **202**
great white heron, 32, 206
Greece, agriculture in, 51–53
green algae, **401–402**, 413–414,
 424
Green Bay, Wisconsin, 96
green plants, as producers, 21
Green Revolution, 522–523
Green River Basin of Wyoming,
 344
Green River formation, 343–344
green sunfish, 169
greenbelts, 266
Greene, H. C., 510
greenhouse effect, 255, 358,
 448–450
grizzly bears, 230
Grosz, George, 494
ground sloth, 184
growth
 and carrying capacity, 70
 in cities, 268
 costs of, 488
 and land planning, 480
 limits to, 566
 of population, 554
 and progress, 556
 redirection of, 567
 role of, 69
 see also economic growth
Guatemala, herbicides in, 109
Guinea, 43–46
Gulf of Mexico, 410
gypsy moth, 105, 165, **166**, 180

Haagen-Smit, A. J., 435
habitat, 33–34
 destruction of, 198–205
 manipulation of, 203–204, 210
 see also niche
Hahn, Otto, 316
half-life
 of biocides, 104
 of isotopes, 315
halocarbons, 450
hardwoods, and herbicides, 91
hares, 108. See also rabbits
Hartford, Connecticut, 295–296
Hawaii Land Use Commission,
 489
Hawaiian goose, 211–212
heart disease
 and cadmium, 148
 and radiation, 334
heat
 in aquatic environments,
 397–402
 in admosphere, 6
 conservation in building,
 252–253
 and energy transfer, 21
 of ocean, 8–9
 as a pollutant, 398–402
 as waste disposal byproduct,
 467–468
 see also temperature
heat of fusion, 8
heat of vaporization, 7–8

heating, 365–366. See also air
 conditioners
heavy water, 348
Heck, Heinz, 494–496
Heck, Lutz, 494–496
heliograph, 249
hemoglobin, 129, 143, 440
heptachlor, 90, 104, 107, 110, 111.
 See also organochlorines
herbicides, 90–94
 alternatives to, 113
 and environmental restoration,
 505
 residues of, 105
 and right-of-way management,
 302–303
herbivores, **23**
Heronemus, William, 360
Herpes simplex virus, 104
Hesse, Hermann, 494
Heyerdahl, Thor, 408
Highway Trust Fund, 294–295
highways
 in the city, 293–296
 design of, 287–**290**
 and environment, 288–293
 growth of, 284–287
 and housing construction, **256**
 landscaping of, 290–292
 litter on, 461–462
 ozone pollution near, 442
 rights of way, 360
 saline pollution from, 374–376
 scenic, 234
Himalayas, **57**
Hindemith, Paul, 494
Hiroshima, 318
histoplasmosis, 171
Homer, 51
Homestead Act, 478
Homo sapiens, 3
hoof and mouth disease, 175
hormones
 for biological control, 180
 as contaminants, *123–124*
horses, **161**–164, 171, 184–185,
 235
hot dogs, 127–128
hot springs, 357
house design
 form and function of, *241–248*
 and humidity, 253–254
 light in, 254–255
 and outer environment,
 248–251
 and temperature, 252–253
 and ventilation, 255–257
House of Seven Gables, **245**
house sparrow, 170–171
household waste, 457–458
housing rehabilitation, 272–273
Howard, Ebenezer, 276, 278
Hubbard Brooks Experimental
 Forest, New Hampshire, 208
Hudson River, 234–**235**
human waste, 378–*381*
 treatment of, 383–384
 and phosphorus pollution, 388
humidity, 253–254
humpback whale, 192
humus, *14*, 60
hunting and gathering societies,
 539, 544–545
hydrocarbons
 in auto exhaust, 443–444
 in estuaries, 410

natural production of, 446
 in smog, 441
hydroelectric power, 354–356
hydrogen
 as fuel source, 445
 and soil acidity, 60
hydrogen bomb, 102, *318–319*,
 352
hydrogen chloride, in solid waste,
 467
hydrogen fluoride, 446
hydrogen ions, 15
hydrogen sulfide, 350
hydrologic cycle, *10*
 and pollution, 423–424
hydrosphere, 7–10
hyperactivity, 131
hypertension, and cadmium, 148
hypolimnion, **394–395**

ibex, 194
ice caps, melting of, **262**
igloo, 241–**242**, 246
Illuminating Engineering Society,
 365
incandescent lamps, 366
incaparina, 523
Incas, 59, 163
incense cedar and fire exclusion,
 225
incineration, 467
India, 517, 522, 548
Indian rhino, 195
Indian subcontinent, **57**
Indian tiger, 193
Indus River, **57**
Industrial Revolution
 climatic changes from, 263,
 448
 coal and, 338
 and population, 540–541
industry
 energy use by, 362
 and urban development, **488**
 wastes from, 378, 384,
 441–442
infant mortality, 440
influenza B, 104
infrared heat, 312
inorganic chemicals, 136. See also
 asbestos; beryllium;
 cadmium; lead; mercury
insecticides. See biocides
insects
 and air pollution, 446
 as biological controls, 179
 exports of, 167–168
 as introduced species, *165–168*
insulation, 365–366
Insulation Workers Union of New
 York, 151
integrated control, *113–114*. See
 also biological control
intensive agriculture, 523
intermediate technology, 569
Intermediate Technology
 Development Group, 567
internal combustion engine
 alternatives to 444–445
 and pollution, 437–439
 and smog, 434
International Biological
 Programme, 507
International Commission on
 Radiological Protection, 334

International Rice Research Institute, 520
International Union for the Conservation of Nature and Natural Resources Red Books, 193
International Whaling Commission, 191
interstate highway system, **286**, 287–296
intrauterine devices (IUDs), **548–549**。
introduced species
  birds as, 170–172
  and canal building, 85–86
  control of, 174–182
  and extinction, 201–202
  fish as, 169–170
  insects as, 165–168
  mammals as, 172–173
  naturally occurring, *159–161*
  plants as, 174
  see also agriculture
inversion layer, **403, 436–437**
invertebrates, oxygen need of, 377–378
iodine-131, 315
ionization, 320–321
ions, *13*
  from nuclear power plants, 328
  and radiation, 321
  in soil, *14–15*
IR-8 rice, **520–522**
Ireland, birth control in, 545
iron, 395
iron-59, 328
irrigation, 70
  in ancient world, 48–50
  and future food supply, 529–530
  of highways, 291
  radiation in, 331
isotopes, 315, 325, 328, 351, 410.
  See also radioisotopes
Isthmus of Panama, 159–161
itai-itai, 148
Italy, birth control in, 545
ivory-billed woodpecker, **206–207**
ivory trade, 193–194
Izaak Walton League, 213

jack pine, **204**
jackals, 108
Japan, 191–192, 546, 552
Javan rhino, 195
jet transport, **564**
  and air pollution, **449**
  and noise pollution, 452
  supersonic, 449
job involvement, 568, 569
Joliot, Frederic, 315
Jungle, The (Sinclair), 116
juniper, grassland invasion by, 500
juvenile hormone analog, 180
juvenile hormones, 180

Kaibab Plateau, 210
Kansas, 284–**285,** 381
Kanto Plain, Japan, 431
kaolinite, 21
Kariba Dam, 79
kelong, *244*
Kenai Peninsula, Alaska, 205
Kennedy Airport, 298
kepone, 111

kerogen, 343–344
Khmer civilization, 61
killer bees, 167
King's Canyon, 225
Kirtland's warbler, **204**–205, 207
Kitt Peak Observatory, **453**
Klamath River, 68–69
Klee, Paul, 494
Knipling, E. F., 177
Krakatoa, 427
krypton, 4, 316
krypton-85, 328
!Kung bushmen, 545
kwashiorkor, **518**
Kyoto, Japan, 263

lactate dehydrogenase (LDH-X), 550
ladybird beetle, **105**
lagoons, *408–411*
LaGuardia Airport, 298
Lahontan cutthroat, 169
Lake Atitlan, 170
Lake Burullus, 78
Lake Erie, 393–397
Lake George, 105
Lake Idku, 77–**78**
Lake Lodoga, 207
Lake Manzala, 78
Lake Mead, 75–76, 330–332
Lake Michigan, 125
Lake Nasser, 76–79
Lake Nicaragua, 207
Lake Powell, 75–76, 330–332
lake trout, 105
Lake Washington, **396**–397
lakes
  eutrophication of, **389**
  food chain simplification in, **169**
  history of, 27–28
lamb, 123–124
lampreys, 83–**84**
land
  attitudes toward, 477, 490–491
  control law, 488–492
  return to, 483–484
  see also agriculture; cultivated land; soil
land bank, 480
land bridges, **161**
land trust, 492
land use law, 491
land use planning, 452, *477–492. See also* zoning
landfill, *466–467*
  paper in, 459
  tires in, 464
  vinyl chloride in, 126
  of wetlands, 512–513
landforms, interpretation of, 10.
  See also topography
landscaping
  by Capability Brown, **498**
  of highways, 290–292
  and housing design, **250–251**
  see also gardens
laparoscopic tubal ligation, 547

LaPorte, Indiana, 263
lapse rate, *5*
largemouth bass, 170
lasers, 353–354
Lasiter, Tom, 511–512
Lasiter Ranch, 511–512
Lassen National Park, 225

laterite soil, 61, 527
Latin America. *See* South America
laubina, 523
lead, *142–148*
  atmospheric, 145–147
  in coal, 340
  dose effect of, 154
  in gasoline, 438, 443
  recycling of, 463
  from urban runoff, 392–393
lead arsenate, 146
lead chromate, 146
lead poisoning, *142–148*
lead-210, 333
League of American Wheelmen, 284
leapfrogging, 479
lecithin, 129
Lee, Robert E., 80
Leopold, Aldo S., 490, 509
less developed countries (LDCs), 519
  demographic transition in, 541
  and population control, 549, 553–555
  see also Third World
Letchworth, England, 276
lethal dose (LD-50), 322
Levant, 51
Lewis, Merriweather, 163
lichens, **29, 33,** 319
Liebig's Law of the Minimum, 25
light
  in housing design, 254–255, 365
  pollution by, 453–454
  scattering of, 7
  spectrum of, **312**
light water nuclear reactor (LWR), 348–351
lignite, 66, **339–340.** *See also* coal
lignosulfonates, 384–385
Likens, G. E., 61
lime soap dispensing agents (LSDA), 391
limiting factors, 25–28, 30
Limits to Growth, The, 566
lindane, 90, 104. *See also* organochlorines
Linsley Pond, Connecticut, 28
liquid-metal-cooled fast breeder reactor (LMFBR), 351–352
liquid waste disposal, 385–387
  radioactive, 328
lithium, 315, 316
lithosphere, *10–19*
liver
  and radiation, 320–322
  and vinyl chloride, 126
living standards
  and environmental harm, 556
  and growth, 558
  steady-state approach to, 560–562
lizard fish, 85
llama, **161**
lodgepole pine, **446–447**
lodgepole pine scale, 110
London, England, 266–267, 397
Long Beach, California, 260–261
Long Island Duck, 411–**412,** 415
Long Island Expressway, 291
long wave radiation, *7. See also* heat; temperature

Longgood, William, 121
longleaf pine, 218–221
Los Angeles
  airport development in, 452
  automobiles in, 145, 435–437
  highway landscaping in, 291
  PCB contaminants in, 125
  suburbanization of, 479
  water supply of, 68–69
  zoning laws in, 484
Los Angeles International Airport, 452
Los Padres National Forest, Sespe Wild Area of, 203
low pressure areas, **4**
lung conditions, 331, 430–431
luteinizing hormone-releasing hormone/follicle-stimulating hormone-releasing hormone (LH-RH/FSH-RH), 550
lygus bug, **95–96**
lymph nodes, 322, 334
lynx, 31

McAdam, J. L., 282
macadam pavement, 282
maceration-disinfection, 381
McHarg, Ian, 266
MacLeod, Norman, 44
macronutrients, 25
Madagascar, 149
magnetic fields, 305
magnetohydrodynamics (MHD), 342, 359
Maine, 461
malaria, 53, 54, 78, 89, 108
malathion, 90, 109, 110. *See also* organophosphates
Malaysia, 62
male contraceptives, 550
malic acid, 129
malnutrition, *518*
Malthus, Thomas, 522, 539–540
mammals
  extinction of, *184–186*
  as introduced species, *172–173*
mammoth, **161**
manganese-54, 328
mangrove islands, 230
mangrove marches, **24–25, 482–485**
  and herbicides, 91, 93
Manhattan Island, 261
  atmospheric sulfur dioxide in, **268**
  see also New York City
Mann, Thomas, 494
manure, recycling of, 382
manzanita and fire, **224**
maquis, 53
maraschino cherries, 131
mariculture, 533–535
Marin, County, California, 481
marriage trends, 544
Marshall Islands, 318, 320
marshes. *See* salt marshes
"Martha," 188
mass transit, 294–296
  and airports, 298–299
  energy use by, 363–364
  future forms of, 299–300
  and steam power, 445
  and suburban development, 277
mastodons, 184

585

Mauritius, 185
Mayan civilization, 61
Mediterranean fruit fly, 175
Mediterranean region, 51–53
Mediterranean Sea, **78**, 85, 408
megalopolis, 274–275
Meitner, Lise, 316, 494
Memphis, Tennessee, 293
mental health, 264
Mercenaria, 413–414
mercuric chloride, 137–138
mercury, 136–137
  alkyl salths of, 138
  aryl salths of, 138
  in coal, 340
  dose-effect of, 154
  in the environment, 139–142
  inorganic compounds of, 137–138
  organic compounds, 138–139
  and saline waste, 375
  from urban runoff, 392–393
Merritt Parkway, 442
Mesa Verde, 346
mesophyll cells, **441–442**
Mesopotamia, agriculture in, 49–**50**
mesosphere, 6
mesotheliomas, 151–153
mesquite, 500
metabolism,
  of food, 129
  of food additives, 120–121
  of lead ions, 143
Metasequoia, 210–**211**
methane,
  in air, 4
  and coal mining, 346
  from landfill, 467
  and water pollution, 378
methanol, 345
methoprene, 180
methoxychlor, 90
methoxyethyl mercury, 140
methyl mercury, 138–141
metro concept, 397
metroliner, 299
Meuse Valley, Belgium, 428–429
Mexican free-tailed bats, 100
Mexico, 529
Mexico City, 260
Miami, Florida, 299
mica, 12
Michigan, 462
microclimates, *261–264*. *See also* orographic effect
microcuries, *321*
micromicrocuries, *321*
micronutrients, 25
microorganisms,
  in aquatic system, 22, 26
  and nitrogen fixation, 19
  in soil, 14–15
microwave oven, **314**
microwave towers, **313**
microwaves, *311–314*
middenheaps, 455
Middle East, 520
Midtown Manhattan Study, 264–265
migrating species, 210
milkfish, 404
milkweed bug, 180
milky disease, 111, 178–179
Mill, John Stuart, 559
Miller, Arthur, 185

millicuries, *321*
Minamata disease, 137–138
mine tailings, radioactive, 330–334
minerals,
  in aquatic environment, 24, 424–425
  cycling of, 59–63
  in soil, **14**–15, 446
minipark, **267**
minke whale, 192
Minneapolis-St. Paul, Minnesota, 489
Minnesota, 489–492
minorities, employment, 565–566
miracidia, 78–**79**
mirex, 110–111
Misfits, The (Miller), 185
Mississippi River, 80–81, 83–127
Missouri River, **355**
moa, 185
Mobile, Alabama, 84
mobile homes, 366, 487
mockingbird, 161
Modoc sucker, 169
modular housing, 278
molybdenum-99, 328
mongoose, 108, 201–202
monk parakeet, **172**
monkey, as test animals, 197–198
monoculture, 182, 208
Monsanto Chemical, 125
Mont St. Michel, **273**
montmorillonite, 21
moors, **500–502**, 504
Moriches Inlet, **228**
Morris, T. M., 376
Morristown National Historical Park, Jockey Hollow Area, 167
Morton Arboretum, 510–511
Mount Rainier, 218
mountain environments, 51–53, 56–59
mountain lion, 196–197, 210
mountains, building of, 10, 159
mud algae, 23
mule deer, 210
Muller, Hermann, 323
Muller, Paul, 89
multi-use practices, 63
multichannel river, **52**
multinational corporations, 63
murre, **424**
muskrat, 173
mussels, 23–24, **533**
mutagen, 34, 134
mutations, 34–35, 322
mutualism, 32
mycorrhizae, 32
myxomatosis, 178, 504

nagana, 46
Nagasaki, Japan, 318
Nannochloris, 413–414
Nassau County, 479
National Academy of Sciences, 335
National Audubon Society, 213
National Council of Churches, 544
National Environmental Policy Act (NEPA), 287
national forests, 107–108
National Moose Range, 205

National Park Service, 167, 218, 232
national parks
  development in, **231–233**
  and ecosystems preservation, 511
  founding of, 217–218
national power grid, 368
National Research Council Committee on Impact of Stratospheric Change, 450
National Seashore Areas, 226
Native Americans, 162–164
natural areas, hierarchy of, 232–233
natural gas, 338
  and air pollution, 434
  economics of, 367–369
  as energy source, 344–347
  see also gas; methane
natural selection, 34–35
Nature Conservancy (U.K.), 505
Nature Conservancy (U.S.), 236, 513–514
nature preserves, 235–236
Nazca Plate, **11**
needlerush, 376
neighborhood effect, 149–153
nene, 212
Neosho River, 72
Nepal, 57
net national product, 557
Netherlands, birth control in, 545
neutrons, 316–317
Nevada, 318
New Alchemy Institute, 569
New England housing, **245**
New Haven, Wooster Square, Connecticut, 272
New Orleans, Louisiana, 127, 273, 380
New River, Virginia, 734
New Town, 276–278
New World
  climate and housing in, 243–248
  extinctions in, 184–185
  introduction from, 164
  see also North America
New York City
  abandoned automobiles in, 463
  airports in, 298–299
  animal waste in, 381
  blackouts in, 368
  Bronx River Parkway, 286
  Chelsea area, 273
  fuel standards in, 433
  Greenwich Village, 272–273
  noise pollution control, 451
  population density in, 274
  Prospect Park in, 266–267
  radiation levels in, 324
  suburbanization of, 479
  topography and building in, 261
  transportation in, 282–283
  Upper West Side, 272
  waste disposed by, 379
  zoning laws in, 484–485
  see also Central Park
New York State, 489–490
New Zealand, 164, 185, 524
Newark Airport, 298
Nicaragua, 109
niches, 33–34
  and extinctions, 185

fire maintained, 203–205
Nigeria-Biafra war, 518
"night soil," 379
Nile River, **49**, 76–79
Nile River Delta, **78**
nitrates,
  from animal wastes, 383
  and biocides, 105
  disposal of, 386
  as fertilizer, 77
  in food, 129
  and logging, 61
  oceanic cycling of, 424
  in sewage effluent, 392
  and vegetation, 446
  see also nitrogen
nitric oxide, 429
Nitrobacter, 19, 392
nitrogen
  in air, 4
  in animal wastes, 411–413
  cycle, **18**–*19*
  fixation of, 18
  and new food supply, 530–531
  oxidation states of, 18–19
  as pollutant, 381–382
  in smog formation, 438–439
  solubility of, 7–8
  in tropical reefs, 422–423
  see also nitrates
nitrogen dioxide, 127–128, 438–439
nitrogen oxide, 441, 443–444
nitrogen trichloride, 132
Nitrosomonas, 19, 392
nitrosopyrrolidine, 128
Nitzschia, 413
no-growth economy. *See* steady-state economy
nodules (mineral), 425
noise pollution, 450–452
  by ORVs, 296
nonreturnable cans and bottles, 461
North Africa, 54
North America
  animal migrations, **161**
  deforestation of, 55–56
  horse introduction into, 163–164
  natural introduction in, 161
  see also New World
North American Plate, **11**
North American Water and Power Alliance (NAWAPA), 69–**70**, 74
North Sea, 408
Northern Hemisphere
  lead in, 145
  radioactive fallout in, 319
Norway rat, 170–171
nuclear explosives
  and canal building, 85–86
  and oil deposits, 344
nuclear power plants
  accident scenarios for, 325–327
  construction of, **326–327**
  coolant systems, **349**
  and desalinization, 73
  fuel elements, 348
  and radioactive waste, 325–335
  radioisotopes from, 320
  rise of, 347–352
Nuclear Regulatory Commission (NRC), 326, 335, 350
nutria, 173

nutrient exchange capacity, 15
nutrients
  and ecosystem productivity, 21
  in processed foods, 132–134
  from sea water, 74
  see also food; minerals; protein

oak leaf roller, 167
Oak Ridge, Tennessee, 349
oak woods, **29**
oceans
  biocides in, 100–102
  and carbon dioxide levels, 17, 448
  currents, 9
  and desalinization, 73–74
  farming of, 533–535
  formation of, 159
  and future food supply, 531–533
  lead in, 147
  pollution of, 408–409, 418–424
  and precipitation, 10
  productivity of, 409
  radioactive waste in, 319–320, 329
  responsibility for, 425–426
  surf aerosols from, **423**
  temperature of, 9
  thermal power from, 361
  and water supply, 8–10
octane rating, 145
Odum, Eugene, 410, 512
off-road vehicles (ORVs), **296–297**
offshore wells, 420
O'Hare International Airport, 452
Ohio River, 84
oil
  adoption as fuel, 338
  and air pollution, 433–434
  economics of, 367–369
  as energy source, 342–345
  industrial consumption of, 361
  pipelines for, 301–302
  as pollutant, 418–424
  production of, 17
  as protein source, 535–536
  and transportation needs, 363–364
  see also automobiles; photochemical smog
oil sands, 343–346
oil shale, 343–345
Old Testament, 379
olefins, 438
oligotrophy, 26–28, 395
Oliphant, Pat, **443**
Olmsted, Frederick Law, 216, 507
Olympic National Park, 511
omnivores, **23**
opaque-2 corn, 522
open space
  and development costs, 488
  zoning for, 485–487
Operation Bootstrap, 562
Operation Cat Drop, 108
Orange County, 479
orangutan, 197
Oregon, 70, 461
organic compounds, as food additives, 119–121
organic wastes, 26, 377–378
organochlorines, 90

environmental effects of, 100–102
  persistance of, 105
  from water treatment, 380
organophosphates **90**
  control of, 107
  poisoning by, 106
  resistance to, 113
Orgyia pseudotsugata, 107
ornithosis, 171, 198
orographic effect, 263
  and cooling towers, 402–**403**
oryx, **195**
osprey, 98–**99**, 107
ostrich, 193
overbreeding, *133–134*
overgrazing, 42, 46–47. *See also* grazing
overpopulation, 538–543
  and crowding, 270
  see also national parks
Overton Park, Memphis, Tennessee, 293
Owens pupfish, 169
Owens Valley, 68–69
oxygen
  in air, 4, 6, 7
  in aquatic environment, 390–391, 398
  in bloodstream, **430**
  cycle, **16**–18
  demand for, 377–378
  origin of, 17
  and ozone destruction, 449
  pollution by, 398
  in soil, 13
  in water, 8, 399–400
  world supply of, 441
  see also ozone
oxygen-18, 325
oysters
  cadmium in, 149
  cultivation of, **404**–405, 533
  in Great South Bay, 413–414
  radiation and, 319
ozone
  atmospheric formation of, 6–7, 439
  and cilial action, 429
  in forest communities, 446
  level in cities, 264
  from power lines, 305
  in smog, 441–442
  as water purifier, 127, 380
ozone layer
  and atmospheric energy, **6**
  and jet transport, 449–450
  origin of, 17

Pacific Ocean, 86, 125. *See also* oceans
Pacific Plate, **11**
packaging, 469
  plastic in, 465
  as waste, 456–458
paints, lead in, 142–144
Pakistan, 517, 529
Palace of Fine Arts, Mexico City, **260**
Paleo-Indians, 184–185
Palestine vipers, 108
palisade layer, 441–**442**
Panama Canal, 85–86, 230
Pangaea, 159
paper
  manufacturing of, 140, 384–385

as waste, 458–459
paraffins, 438
parasite-host bonds, 32
  and biological control, 175–176
parasites
  and agriculture, 54
  and biocides, 110
  and integrated control, 114
  and introduced species, 165
parathion, 90, 109. *See also* organophosphates
Paris green, 89
parks, 215–218
  in cities, 266–268, 293
  concepts of, 498–499
  local, 232–233
  and people, 230–232
  problems in, 221–225
  state, 232
  see also national parks
parkways, 234. *See also* highways
parrot fever, 171, 198
parrots, 196, 198
Pasamaquoddy Bay, 356
passenger pigeon, *186–188*
pathogens, 114
Peace River, 332
peacock bass, **169**
Peale's falcon, 211
Pearsall, New Hampshire, 525
peccary, **161**
pedestrian malls, **295**
Peking's Imperial Garden, 211
pelagic birds, 101
pelican, **99**
Peneios River, **52**
penguins, 101
penicillin, as contaminant, 122
Pennsylvania, 284–**285**
Pennsylvania Turnpike, 286
People's Republic of China, 320, 517
Pere David's deer, 211
peregrine falcon, 98–**99**, 107, 211
permafrost, 301
peroxyacetylnitrate (PAN), 439, 441, 446
personal freedom, 538–539
Peru, 529
pesticides. *See* biocides
pests, *171*
  and agriculture, 54
  biological control of, 176
Petaluma, California, 487
pH, *15*. *See also* acidity
pheromones, **107**, *180–181*
Philadelphia, Pennsylvania
  Fairmont Park, 266
  lead concentration, 146
  Society Hill, 272
  zoning in, 487
Philippines, 62
phosphate bonds (ATP), 21
phosphate fertilizer, 332
phosphates
  in animal waste, 411–413
  cycling, 22–23
  in estuarine ecosystem, 26–33
  oceanic recycling of, 424
  plant roots and, 383
phosphoric acid, 128–129
phosphorus, in water environment, 26, 388–392. *See also* phosphates
phosphorus-32, 325

photochemical smog, *434–437*
  control of, 442–445
  effects of, 439–442
photosynthesis, *10*
  and air pollution, 446
  in aquatic environment, 23–24, 390–391, 531
  energy utilization by, 337
  and organochlorines, 101–102
  and oxygen supply, 17
  terrestrial, 21
photovoltaic cells, 359–360
phylloxera, 167
physical weathering, *11–12*
phytodexins, *180–181*
phytoplankton, 22, 24, **97**, 388, 534
pica, 143
picloram, 91, 106. *See also* herbicides
picocuries, *321*
pigeons, 170–172
pigs, 42–43, 201
pill, the 549
  morning after, 550
pilot lights, 366
pine bark beetle, 167
pine forests
  controlled burning of, **222**, **223**
  fire exclusion and, **225**
  and mineral cycling, 60
pink cotton bollworm, 180–181
pipelines
  for oil and gas, 345–346, 363–364
  rights of way, 301–302
  for solid waste, 470
Place, Francis, 540
plague, 89
Plains Indian, and horses, **163**
plankton, 21, 531
plant breeding, and food supply, 520
plants
  endangered, 200–201
  as introduced species, *174*
  radiation and, 324–325
  roots of, 13–14
  see also vegetation
plastic wastes, **465**
plate tectonics, 10
Plato, 51–53
plazas, **486**
Pleistocene, **161**, 184–185
plinthite soils, *13*, 293, 527
plutonium, 317
plutonium-239, 351–352
podzol, *13*
polar ice, 8
pollarding, **269**
pollution
  and growth, 559
  index of, 413
  light as, 453–454
  noise as, 450–452
  oxygen as, 398
  radioactive, 327–328
  see also air pollution; estuarine environment; eutrophication; water pollution
polonium-210, 333
polychlorinated biphenols (PCBs), 90, **124**–**125**, 422
polymers, as food dyes, 131
polyoxyethylene, 129

...C), 126,

...1

...+41
an... 446–447
Pont-du...ard, 55
population
  fluctuations in, 542–543
  and food supply, 517–519,
    520–521
  future trends in, 553–555
  and government policy,
    545–547
  and growth, 539–543
  motivation for control of,
    543–547
  and pollution, 58, **394**,
    414–415
populations (species), 31–32
porcupine, **161**
porpoise, 192, 207
Portugal, 545
possum, **161**
post roads, 282–283
potato, 164, 522
potato beetle, 89
Potomac River, 233–234
Powell, John Wesley, 46
power lines
  aesthetics of, 304–307
  rights of way, 302–**303**
  underground, 305–307
power
  cost of, 368
  U.S. sources of, **337**
  see also coal; electric power;
    energy; gas; geothermal
    power; nuclear power plants;
    oil; solar energy
prairie dog, 46–47
Prairie du Chien, Wisconsin, 83
prairies, 46–47, 189
  restoration of, 510–512
precipitation
  in cities, 263–264
  control of, 10
  and soil formation, 11–13
  and vegetation cover, 46
  see also orographic effect
predator-prey relationship, 31–32
  and biocides, 95
  and biological control,
    175–176
  and environmental restoration,
    507
predators, and biocides, 98–100,
    105, 108
  control of, 46–47, 196, 210,
    223
  destruction by ORVs, 297
  and food chain contaminants,
    319
  and hormone controls, 180
  and integrated control, 114
  introduced, 207
  and introduced species, 165
preferential assessment, 480
Prescott, James, 270
preservatives, *127–129*
pressurized water reactor (PWR),
    326, 328, 348
prickly pear, 179
Pride and Prejudice (Austen), 216
primary consumers, 25

primary producers, **23**, 25
primary succession, 29–30, 32
primates, endangered, 199
producer-consumer bonds,
    175–176
producers, **23**, 25
progesterone, 550
Project Gas Buggy, 344
propanil, 106
propellants, and ozone layer, 450
prostaglandins, 550
protein
  deficiency disease, **518**
  in detritus, 25
  formation of, 18
  and nitrogen cycling, **18–19**
  novel sources of, 534–**536**
  supplements, 519, 523–524
protoplasm, 25
Pryor Mountains, Montana, 185
pseudofeces, 23
Pseudomonas, 19
psittacosis, 171, 198
public transport, 294–296. *See
    also* mass transit
Puerto Rico, 562
Puget Sound, **396**
pulp waste, 140, 384–385

quagga, 196
quarantine, 175
quartz, 12

rabbits, 164, 172–**173**, 178,
    504–505
rad, *321*
radar, 311–312
radiation
  and biological control, 177
  dose measurement of, *321*–322
  and heredity, 322–324
  levels, 334
  nature of, *314*–315
  and plants, 324–325
  solar, 5
  and vegetation, **324**
radiation sickness, 320–322
radiation spectrum, *311*–312
radioactive wastes, 327–328, 347
  disposal of, 329–335, 386
radioisotopes, carbon-14, 315,
    325
  cesium-137, 315, 319
  chromium-51, 328
  cobalt-60, 320, 325
  deuterium, 315, 352–354
  gold-198, 325
  iodine-131, 315
  iron-59, 395
  krypton-85, 328
  lead-210, 333
  manganese-54, 328
  oxygen-18, 325
  phosphorus-32, 325
  plutonium-239, 351–352
  polonium-210, 333
  radium-226, 330–333
  radon-222, **332–333**
  strontium-90, 315, 320
  thorium-232, 351
  tritium, 352–354
  uranium-234, 316
  uranium-235, 316, 348, 351
  uranium-238, 316, 349, 351
  zinc-65, 319
  see also isotopes

radium, 314–315
radium poisoning, 103
radium-226, 330–333
radon, 315, 331–332
radon-222, **332–333**
ragwort, 2,4-D in, 105
railroads, 283–284
  and energy needs, 363–364
  highspeed, 299
  and land use, 477–478
  rights of way, **478**
rain forest
  African, **43**
  and agriculture, 527
  conifer type, 511
  nutrient cycling in, **527**
  see also Amazon Basin; tropical
    forests
rainbow trout, 169
rainfall. *See* precipitation
Ramapo, New Jersey, 487
rapid transit. *See* mass transit
Rasmussen, Norman, 325–326
Rasmussen Report, 325–326, 350
rats, 176–177, 201
recreation
  in cities, 266–268
  and water power generation,
    356
  see also off-road vehicles; parks
recycling
  of aluminum cans, **472**
  of animal waste, 382
  of automobiles, 463
  of domestic water, 71–74
  of fiber, 470
  of fly ash, 433, 468
  of industrial energy, 361
  of industrial wastes, 384–385
  of metals, 468
  of paper, 458–459
  of radioactive waste, 332–333
  of solid waste, 471–473
  of tires, 464
red crayfish, and biocides,
    108–109
red deer, 164
Red Number 40, 131
Red Number 2, 130–131
Red Rock Lakes, Montana,
    212–213
Red Sea, 77, **78**, 85
red spider mite, 109–110
red trout, 169
redlining, 270
redtailed hawk, **99**
Redwood National Park, 511
reforestation, 55–56
  in Britain, 500–504
rehabilitation (environmental),
    496
  of strip mined areas, 65–66
  see also environmental
    restoration
reindeer, and Arctic fallout, 319
reintroduction, 209, 212–213
religious attitudes
  and birth control, 544
  and food supply, 519
  see also superstition
rem, *321*
Renaissance, 54–55
reproductive cells, 34–35
resistance
  to antibiotics, 122
  to biocides, 94–96

resource supply, 566
respiration (by plants), 13
respiratory system
  beryllium and, 149
  cadmium and, 148
  smog and, 429
restoration (environmental). *See*
  environmental restoration
resynthesis of lost species, 209,
    494–496
reuse, 384–385, 459–460. *See
    also* recycling
Reyes syndrome, 104
rhinoceros, 195
Rhodesia, 79
Rhum Island, Scotland, 506
rhythm method, 548
rice
  asbestos contamination of, 154
  and biocides, 108–109
  IR-8 type, **520**
rice stinkbug, 109
right whale, 191–192
rights of way, 300–307
  of railroads, **478**
Riley, C. V., 179
riverboats, 282–283
rivers
  and agriculture, 48–50
  and recreation, 234
  scenic, **235**
  and water supply, 72
  see also estuarine environment
roach fish, 169
roads. *See* highways
robins, 31, 96–98
Rochdale, England, 263
rock dove, 170–172
Rocky Mountain Arsenal, **387**
Rocky Mountain Basin, **339**
Rocky Mountain Fort Union, 346
Rocky Mountain National Park,
    232
rodenticides, 90
roentgen, *321*
Roentgen, Wilhelm, 314
Rome, Italy
  agriculture in, 54–55
  lead poisoning in, 147
Roosevelt, Theodore, 116
root-fungi associations, 32
Rubinoff, Ira, 86
Ruhr Valley, 274
Russian antelope, 212

saber-toothed tiger, 184
saccharin, 130
Sacramento, California, **350**
Sacramento Delta, 68–69
sagebrush ecotone, **30**
Sahara Desert, **4**, **43**
Sahel, 43–46
saiga, 212
St. Louis Union Electric
    Company, 468
St. Michaels, Maryland, 513–514
saline wastes, 374–376
salinity and irrigation, 529
salmon, 125, 207
Salmonella, 102, 122, 413
Salmonella typhimurium, 134
salt and highways, **375**. *See also*
    saline wastes
salt marshes
  of California, **23**, **417**
  DDT in, **97**

food webs in, **22**
formation of, **228**
as landfill areas, 466
restoration of, 512–515
valuation of, 410
see also estuarine environment
San Andreas Fault, 327
San Bruno Mountain, **304, 417**
San Diego Bay, 415–**416**
San Francisco, California
  airport construction in, 299
  Golden Gate Park, **189, 211, 233, 266**
  highway landscaping in, 291
  rapid transit in, **279**
  smog in, **437**
  urban renewal in, **269, 272**
San Francisco Bay, 69, **417**–418, 487, 514–515
San Francisco Bay Conservation and Development Commission (BCDC), 418
San Jose, 479
San Pablo Bay, **417**
Sand County Almanac, A (Leopold), 490
Santa Barbara oil spill, 367, 420–421
Santa Clara valley, 479
sardine industry, 77
satellite town, 277
savanna, 43
  cultivation of, 528
  game grazing on, **524**–525
scallops, 319
scarlet oak, 446
scavengers, 100
scenic easement, 233–234
Schistosoma masoni, **79**
schistosomiasis, 78
Schmitt Music Center, Minneapolis, **265**
Schumacher, E. F., 568–569
Scottish Highlands, 499–503
screw worm, 177
sea lettuce, 424
sea otter, 193
Seattle, Washington, **396**–397
seaweed as food, 533
secondary succession, 29–30
sei whales, 192
selenium, 340
Seneca, Ernest, 513–514
Sequoia National Park, 218, 225, 511
Serengeti National Park, 34, 210
services industries, 567
sesquioxides, *12*, 13, 61
setbacks, **485**
settlements, 48, 54
sevin, 166
sewage wastes, 379–382
  as fertilizer, **383**
  modern treatment methods, 383–384, 392
  primitive treatment of, 373–374
sex attractants, *180–181*
shales. *See* oil shales
Shaw, J. P., 220
sheep and erosion, **42**–43, 499–500, **504**–505
Shellford, Victor, 511
ships, sewage disposal by, 380–381. *See also* tankers
shopping malls, 294–**295**

shortwave radiation, 6, 7, 312
shrews, 100, **161**
silicon, 360
silicon dioxide, 12
siltation
  of Mediterranean, **52**, 53
  and Nile fertility, **49**, 76
  and strip mining, 65
  and Tigris-Euphrates region, 49–50
  and watershed management, 61
Sinclair, Upton, 116
skua, 101
Slama, Karel, 179–180
slash and burn cultivation, 62
sleeping sickness, 46, 196
slums, **258**, 268–271
  and highway construction, 293–294
Smith, Adam, 559
Smith, R. Blackwell, Jr., 120
Smithsonian Institution, 201
smog
  control of, 433–434
  effects of, 439–442
  photochemical, *434–437*
Smokey, the bear, 220–221
snowmobiles, 296–297
snowshoe hare, 31
social services, and growth, 558, 563, 565
sodium benzoate, 127, 131
sodium chloride, 374. *See also* saline wastes; salt
sodium cyanide, 197
sodium dimethyl arsenate, 91
sodium fluoroacetate, 108
sodium nitrate, 127–129
sodium silicate, 390
soil
  acidity of, 15
  and agriculture, 48
  composting of, 468–469
  ethylene in, 48
  fertility of, 14–15
  and fertilizers, 528
  formation of, *11–13*
  fungi in, 441
  and irrigation, 529
  organic component of, *14–15*
  and plastic wastes, 465
  and saline pollution, 374–376, 529
  structure of, *13*
  as waste filter, 383–384
solar energy
  in atmosphere, 5–8
  fixing of, 21
  and power generation, 358–360, 569–570
  and world oceans, 8–9
solid waste
  early disposal of, 455–**456**, 466–470
  kinds of, 456–466
  new approaches to disposal, 469–473
  from oil shales, 344–345
  radioactive, 327–328
  and salt marsh reclamation, 515
sorbatin, 129
sorbic acid, 127
sorghum, 521, 522
sound measurement, **451**
South Africa, 196

South America
  animal migrations in, **161**
  food production in, 519
  natural introductions in, 161
  population statistics, 543
South American Plate, **11**
Southern corn leaf blight, 105
Southern Hemisphere, **4**, 145
soybeans, 534–**536**
"spaceship earth," 3
Spain, 545
Sparrow, A. H., 325
Spartina alterniflora, **22**, 512–515
speciation, 159
species, 33–36
  tolerance range and distribution of, 28
species diversity, *30–31*
  and agriculture, 48
  in ecosystems, 208
sperm bank, 547–548
sperm cells, 34–35, 322
sperm whale, 191–192
spermaceti, 191
Sphaerocystis, 388
Spirillum lipoferum, 530–531
spleen, 322, 334
spongy mesophyll cells, 441–**442**
sporocysts, 79
spray schedules, *21*, 24, 25
spruce budworm, 167
spruce sawfly, 178
Sri Lanka, 541
Standard Metropolitan Statistical Areas (SMSAs), 562
standing crop, *21*, 24, 25
standing systems, 8. *See also* lakes
starling, 171
steady-state economy
  case for, 559–565
  criticisms of, 565–567
steam engines, 444–445
steamboat, 282–283
steel recycling, 463, 473
Stein, Gertrude, 259
Steller's sea cow, 209
sterilization
  of pests, *176–177*
  and populaton control, 547–548
  temporary, 548
Stevens, John, 283
Stevens, Thomas, 284
stillbirths
  and contaminants, 126
  from lead poisoning, 147
  and smoking, 440
Stirling engine, 444–445
Stockholm, Sweden, 478–480
stone walls, **56**
Strassman, F., 316
stratified charge engine, 444
stratosphere, 5–6, 319
Straw Dogs, The, 271
strip mining, 63–*66*
  and landfill, 466
  and sewage disposal, 383–384
  see also acid wastes
strokes, 334
strontium-90, 315, 320
sub-bituminous coal, **339**–340
subsidence, 358. *See also* earthquakes
suburbs
  intentional, 277

land use in, 478–480
rise of, 273–276
and urban space, 264
see also urbanization; satellite towns
succession, 29–30, 401
Sudan, 43
Suez Canal, **78**, 85
Suisun Bay, 417
sulfate aerosols, 328
sulfates, 432–433
sulfur
  in coal, 339–340
  cycling of, 432–433
  in oil, 343
sulfur dioxide
  in air, 4, 429
  from coal combustion, 339–340
  corrosive effects of, **432**
  in foods, 127, 131
  and smog formation, 432–434, 438–440
  and vegetation, 267–**268**, 432, 446–**447**
sulfur oxide
  from coal combustion, 341
  from geothermal power, 358
  smog, 428–434
sulfuric acid
  in auto emissions, 444
  as byproduct, 341
  and carbon monoxide, 440
  from mining, 376–377
  and vegetation, 432
Sumatran rhino, 195
sump, 337
sun, energy of, 21, 337. *See also* solar energy; sunlight
Sundeberg, Sweden, 470
sunlight
  and housing design, 249–250
  and plastic wastes, **465**
  and pollution, 437, 439
  see also solar energy; sun
superovulation, 212
supersonic transport (SST), 449
superstition, and extinction, 194–195
surfactant, 390
Susquehanna River, 83
sustained yield, 63
Sweden, 140–141, 470, 517, 545
swordfish, 139
synthetic fuels, 343
syphilis, 164

tall grass prairie, 510–512. *See also* prairies
talus slope, 11–**12**
Tamplin, Arthur, 334–335
tankers, 418–421
Tapiola, Finland, 277
tapir, **161**, 184
tartaric acid, 129
tax deferrals, 479–480
TCAB, 106
technology
  desertion of, 566–567
  and domestic architecture, 257
  and food supply, 519–526
  and future food supply, 526–536
  and future transport, 299–300
  and growth, 559
  and human misery, 523

36-87

, 62. *See also* ...system; rain forest; ... forests
te... latitudes, 10
temperature
  and air pollution, **436**
  and algal growth, **401**
  of atmosphere, 4-7
  changes of and organisms, 399-400
  in cities, 261-263
  and house design, 252-253
"1080" (sodium fluoroacetate), 108
Tennessee River, 84, **355**
Tennessee Valley Authority, 350, 399
teratogenic compound, 93
terrestrial systems, *21-25*
Tertiary period, 159, **160, 161**
test ban treaty, 318-320
tetraethyl lead, 146, 438-439
Thailand, **243, 244**
Thames River, 397
Themeda-Pennisetum grasslands, 34
thermal breeders, 352
thermal loading, 397-402
  and mariculture, **404, 405,** 534
  and nuclear power generation, **349**
  treatment methods, 402-406
thermocline, **394-395**
thermodynamics, laws of, 20-22
Third World
  biocides in, 104, 107
  demographic transition in, 541-543
  environmental stresses in, 56
  forestry in, 62-63
  and population control, 553-555
  productivity of, 519
  protein supply in, 523-525
  see also less developed countries
Thompson's gazelle, 34
thorium, 314
thorium-232, 351
3,4-dichloroaniline, 106
3,4-dichloroproprionanilide, 106
thymus, 322
tidal power, 356
tidelands, 409. *See also* estuarine environment; salt marshes
Tigris-Euphrates Rivers system, **50**
Tilden, John, 165
tin recycling, 468
tires, as waste, 463-**464**
tobacco contamination, **332-334**. *See also* cigarette smoking
toilet designs, 380-381
Tokaido Express, 297
tomato, 164
Tombigbee River, 84
toothed sperm whale, 191
top carnivore, **23,** 25
  and radiation, 319-320
  see also predators
topography
  of cities, 259-261

and highway design, **285,** 287-290
and smog, 435-437
and soil formation, 11-13
Torrey Canyon disaster, 419, 421, 424
Torrey pine, **200**
Torula, 385
total energy system, 366
town square, **216**
toxaphene, 100, 104, 109. *See also* organochlorines
Toxic Substances Control Act of 1976, 125, 134
trace elements, 4
trachoma, 78
tract housing, **249, 251**
trail bikes, 296-297
trails, *234-235*
Trans-Amazon Highway, 292-293
transpiration, 10, 13, 61
transport
  energy requirements for, 363-364
  future forms of, 299-300
  jet, 449, 452, **564**
  urban, 279
  see also automobiles; highways; mass transit; railroads
tree ducks, 109
trees, 268. *See also* forest ecosystem
Trichoderma viride, 459
trichomes, **333**
tripolyphosphate, 390
Triticale, **521**
tritium, 352-354
trophic structure, 25
trophy hunting, 195
tropical environment and housing, **243, 244**
tropical forests
  clearing of, 527-528
  herbicides in, 91-93
  mineral cycling in, 60-61, **527**
  preserved, 511
  see also Amazon Basin; forest ecosystem; rain forests
tropical reefs, 422-423
troposphere, **5**
trout, 169
trout lily, **208**
Trouvelot, Leopold, 165
truck transport, 363-364
  and garbage disposal, 469-470
  and highway construction, 286
trumpeter swan, 212-213
trypanosome, 46, 196
tsetse fly, 46, 196
tubal ligation, 547
Tubifex, 377
Tucson, Arizona, 453
tuna, 102, 139
  and radiation, 319-320
tundra falcon, 211
Twin Cities Metropolitan Council, 489
2,4-D, 91-94, 105-106
2,4,5-T, 91-94, 106
2-naphthylamine dye, 120
typhus, 89

Uinta Basin, 344
ultraviolet radiation, *312*
  glass and, 255

and oxygen formation, 17
and ozone layer, 6-7, 449-450
and plastic wastes, 465
and smog formation, 264, 439
undernourishment, 518
unemployment, 565-566. *See also* employment; work
Union Pacific Railroad, **478**
Union of Soviet Socialist Republics, 191-192, 543
United Arab Republic, 76-79
United Kingdom
  birth control in, 545
  demographic transition in, 549
  environmental restoration in, 499-507
  fertile land in, 517
  Forestry Commission, 500-502
  Office of Coal Research, 347
United Nations, 426
United States of America
  abortion in, 552-553
  agricultural production in, 519
  biocides in, 106
  climate and housing in, 243-248
  coal deposits in, **339**
  endangered species in, 186
  energy supply and needs of, 337-338
  environmental restoration in, 507-515
  fertile land in, 517
  land use policy in, 477-478, 490
  mine drainage in, 376-377
  oil reserves in, 342-**344**
  population statistics of, 543
  power sources in, **337**
  quarantine laws of, 175
  transport in, 281-284
  water power capacity of, 354
  water supply of, 67-71
U.S. Army Corps of Engineers, 66, 70, 80, 82, 83, 368, 514, 570
U.S. Atomic Energy Commission, 325-326, 335, 347, 352
U.S. Bureau of Land Management, 185
U.S. Bureau of Mines, 347, 464, 471
U.S. Bureau of Reclamation, 70
U.S. Civil Aeronautics Board, 564
U.S. Constitution, 484
U.S. Court of Appeals, 124
U.S. Department of Agriculture, 80, 110, 141, 179, 526
U.S. Department of Housing and Urban Development, 452
U.S. Department of the Interior, 80
U.S. Energy Research and Development Agency, 326
U.S. Environmental Protection Agency, 107, 126, 181, 339, 391, 567
U.S. Federal Power Commission, 367
U.S. Food and Drug Administraiton, 103, 116-117, 123, 125, 130-131, 134, 141, 181, 391, 551

U.S. Forest Service, 107, 218-221, 232
U.S. Navy, 381
U.S. Public Health Service, 149, 198
U.S. Soil Conservation Service, 70, 570
U.S. Supreme Court, 293, 484, 552
U.S. Surgeon General, 431-432
University of Chicago, 317
unsaturated fatty acids, **128**
uranium
  as fuel element, **348**
  isotopes of, 316-317, 349, 351
  and nuclear fission reaction, 314-317
  production of, 331, 349-350
  tailings from, 330-332
uranium-234, 316
uranium-235, 316, 348, 351
uranium-238, 316, 349, 351
urban renewal, 268-271, 293-294
urban runoff, 392-393
urban sprawl, 479-480
urbanization, 273-275, 338
  and growth, 560-562
  and population, 541
  see also cities, suburbs
Uria, 424
Utah, **344**
utility companies, 434
utility poles, 307. *See also* power lines
utility wires, 306. *See also* power lines
"utterly dismal theorem," 523

Vällingby, Sweden, 277
vanillin, 384-385
varves, *102*
vasectomy, 547
vedalia beetles, **179**
vegetation
  and air pollution, 432, 441-**442,** 446-**447**
  destruction by ORVs, 296
  and highway salting, **375**
  and house design, **250**
  and radiation, 324-325
  see also forest ecosystem; landscaping
vegetation management, 505. *See also* environmental restoration
Venice, Italy, 260
ventilation, 255-257
Vermont, 461, 487
Vermont Land Use and Development Act, 489
very large crude carriers (VLCC), *418-420*
vest pocket parks, 233, **267**
vibram soles, *234-235*
Victorian housing, **247, 272**
Vienna, Austria, 266
Vietnam, 62-63, 91-94
village greens, 216
vinyl chloride, *126,* 138. *See also* polyvinyl chloride
viruses
  as biological controls, 178
  nuclear polyhedrosis group, 178
  in recycled water, 72-73

590

visible light, 312. *See also* sunlight
vitamin A, 518
vitamin D, 148, 255, 264
Volunteers in Technological
    Assistance, 569

wagon roads, *281–283*
"walking" catfish, 170
walrus, 193–194
Wankel engine, 444–445
Washington, D.C., 266, 484
waste disposal. *See* sewage wastes;
    solid wastes; water pollution
water
    and atmospheric energy, **6**
    for cooling, 347–349
    cultural uses of, 68
    cycle, **16**
    distribution of, 8–10
    domestic recycling of, **72**
    and growth, 69–70
    metabolic need for, 67–68
    and oxygen cycling, 17–18
    public supply of, 68–81
    qualities of, 7–8
    recycling of, 71–74
    in soil, 13
    and strip mining, 65
    transport of, 529
    world supply of, 67
    see also bays; estuarine
        environment; oceans; rivers;
        salt marshes
water pollution
    and air pollution, **423**
    categories of, 374–382
    by oil, 418–424
    thermal, 397–402
    treatment methods, 391–393,
        402–406
    see also eutrophication
water power, 354–356
water table, 13
    and deep well injection, **386**
    herbicides in, 106
    and irrigation, 529
    and landfill, 466
water vapor, 4–9
watershed, 82
    of lakes, 27–28
wealth, and growth, 557–558
    steady-state critique of, 560
weathering, 11–13, **29**
weeds, 53–54, 171, 400–401
Weill, Kurt, 494
welfare programs, 567–568
Welland Canal, 83–84
wells, for waste disposal, 385–387
West Africa, **43**
West Germany, 66, 109
West Virginia, **64,** 284–**285**
Western Hemisphere, 162
wet scrubbers, 433
wet tower, 402
wetlands. *See* estuarine
    environment; salt marshes
whalebone, 191
whales, *190–193*
whaling, **190, 191**
wheat, **521**
white blood cells, 322, 334
white tailed gnu, 196
whooping crane, **199,** 205
wild cat, 108
wild mountain goat, 194
wild turkey, 213

wildebeest, 34
wilderness areas, 229–232
wildlife, 296–297. *See also*
    endangered species; game
wildlife management, 209–210
Wiley, Harvey W., 116–117
William Floyd Parkway, 292
Williams, Carroll, 179
Williamsburg, Virginia, 455–456
Wilson, Alexander, 187
wind, 264
wind power, *360–361*
Wisconsin, 510
wood duck, 207
Woodwell, G. M., 324
work, attitudes toward, 568–569
World Health Organization
    (WHO), 140
World War II, 89
World Wildlife Fund, 213
Worzel, J. L., 73–**74**
Wyoming, **344**

X-rays, 312, 314–315, **323**
xenon, 4
xylose, 385

Yarner Wood, Devon, England,
    506
yarrow plants, **28**
yeast protein, 535
yellow fever, 89
Yellowstone National Park, 212,
    218, 230–232
Yosemite National Park, 218,
    224, 225, 230–231
yushi disease, 124–125

Zambesi River, 79
zebra, 196
Zeidlar, Othmar, 89
zero economic growth, 557
zero population growth, 557
zero tolerance rule, 141
ziggerats, **485**
zinc beryllium nitrate, 149
zinc recycling, 463
zinc-65, 319
Zion Canyon, 221
zoning, 482, *484–488,* 491
zoo animals, 197–198
zooplankton, 534
Zostera, **414**